SECOND EDITION

INTRODUCTION TO LAW

JOANNE BANKER HAMES
DeAnza Community College

YVONNE EKERN
West Valley College

Upper Saddle River, New Jersey

Library of Congress Cataloging-in-Publication Data
Hames, Joanne Banker.
Introduction to law / Joanne Banker Hames, Yvonne Ekern.
p. cm.—(Prentice Hall paralegal series)
Includes index.
ISBN 0-13-013829-0
1. Legal assistants—United States. 2. Law—United States. I. Ekern, Yvonne. II. Title.
KF320.L4 H35 2002
349.73—dc21 2001036486

Publisher: Steve Helba
Executive Editor: Elizabeth Sugg
Editorial Assistant: Anita Rhodes
Managing Editor: Mary Carnis
Production Management: WordCrafters Editorial Services, Inc.
Production Editor: Linda Zuk
Production Liaison: Brian Hyland
Director of Manufacturing and Production: Bruce Johnson
Manufacturing Manager: Cathleen Petersen
Design Director: Cheryl Asherman
Senior Design Coordinator: Miguel Ortiz
Composition: Publishers' Design and Production Services
Printer/Binder: Courier-Westford
Cover Design: Amy Rosen
Cover Printer: Coral Graphics

Prentice-Hall International (UK) Limited, *London*
Prentice-Hall of Australia Pty. Limited, *Sydney*
Prentice-Hall Canada Inc., *Toronto*
Prentice-Hall Hispanoamericana, S.A., *Mexico*
Prentice-Hall of India Private Limited, *New Delhi*
Prentice-Hall of Japan, Inc., *Tokyo*
Prentice-Hall Singapore Pte. Ltd.
Editora Prentice-Hall do Brasil, Ltda., *Rio de Janeiro*

10 9 8 7 6 5 4 3 2 1
ISBN 0-13-013829-0

CONTENTS

Chapter 11 BUSINESS PRACTICE: THE LAW OF BUSINESS ORGANIZATIONS AND BANKRUPTCY 233

Chapter 12 CRIMINAL PRACTICE: CRIMINAL LAW AND JUVENILE LAW 256

Chapter 13 CIVIL PROCEDURE BEFORE TRIAL 279

Preface

The study of law attracts students for a variety of reasons. Many see the law as a career choice, as a lawyer, a paralegal, or some other related professional. Some are interested because of personal dealings with the legal system, while others are interested simply because it is a fascinating subject. Whatever reasons motivate the student, an introductory class in law must accomplish certain basic objectives. Students must develop an understanding of the organization of the legal system. They must comprehend some basic legal concepts related to procedural and substantive law. Students should also be introduced to cases, statutes, and the Constitution, the sources of all of our laws. While students in an Introduction to Law class should not be forced to learn about the law entirely through reading cases, some experience in reading cases is essential to learning about the law.

Our years of teaching paralegal students have convinced us that any introductory law course must begin with and emphasize the development of a strong legal vocabulary. Also important is the opportunity to use and develop the analytic skills so important to any legal professional. Our goal, therefore, in writing this text is to help instructors by providing beginning students with a book that keeps their interest while providing an overview of the organization and operation of the legal system, as well as an introduction to some of the basic concepts of the substantive and procedural law. More important, however, we have included several features that give students the opportunity to develop a strong legal vocabulary and to build their analytic skills.

The Second Edition of *Introduction to Law*

Feedback from instructors and students who use this text convinces us that the basic organization and features of this textbook are successful. Students have especially appreciated the extensive vocabulary definitions in the margin, the interesting cases, and the wide use of common hypothetical cases to explain the application of legal principles. These features remain in the text. However, the law has never been, nor will it ever be, a static entity. Any useful textbook dealing with the law must reflect these changes. As a result, where applicable, the law has been updated. Other changes reflect the changing face of the legal system, as well as our desire to provide students with more practice building analytic skills and more exposure to the area of legal ethics.

In the last few years, the most important changes in the legal system have come about because of the developments in technology, including the Internet. We have endeavored to reflect those changes in the second edition of *Introduction to Law*. Each chapter now contains two new features: Technology Corner, listing the Web addresses and names of Internet sites applicable to the chapter material; and Featured Web Site, an overview of a helpful Internet site along with exercises requiring the student to "go online." Developments in technology resulted in our completely revising two chapters appearing in the first edition—"Law Practice: Day to Day Procedures" and "Law and Technology." Clearly, these are no longer separate subjects and are therefore combined in a new chapter, "Technology and Law Practice: A Paralegal Perspective." The relevance of technology to the different aspects of substantive and procedural law are now incorporated into the chapters dealing with the topics rather than appearing in a separate chapter.

Although technology is important, any student of the law must develop keen analytic skills. In this second edition we provide more opportunity for this to occur. We expanded the coverage of legal research, analysis, and writing from one chapter to two. We also added "Questions for Analysis" at the end of each chapter and continue to provide questions for analysis at the end of each case.

Our treatment of legal ethics has also been expanded in Chapter 1. The textbook still contains several hypothetical situations for analysis ("Ethical Concerns"), along with an appendix with the ethical rules from NALA and NFPA. Furthermore, the availability of information on the Internet has allowed us to include exercises leading the students to the ethical rules of their own states.

Instructional and Learning Features of *Introduction to Law*

The many features of *Introduction to Law* make it an excellent choice for both the student and the instructor. Students will find an easy-to-read text with a built-in dictionary, realistic factual situations, and high-interest cases. Instructors will find an organized text containing questions to help students review text material, hypothetical situations for class analysis and discussion, and assignments in each chapter. In addition, an *Instructor's Manual* provides the instructor with chapter outlines, answers to review questions, a test bank and transparency masters. The supplemental material is especially helpful to adjunct faculty. More specifically, *Introduction to Law* contains the following features:

- **Legal Vocabulary** is identified in **boldface** type. The key terms are defined in the margins of the text where the terms appear, and are also listed at the end of each chapter for review.
- A **Case File** containing a hypothetical factual situation opens each chapter. This case file serves as an introduction to the subject matter, encouraging the student to think about the subject matter in a law office or everyday setting, rather than simply as more textual reading.
- Carefully selected and edited **case law** appears in each chapter. The case law introduces students to reading the law and assists with the development of critical-thinking skills. The cases are interesting and even familiar. Most cases have been edited, in an effort to shorten them and to give beginning students the opportunity to ascertain the important concepts of the case without being confused. (In editing the cases we have taken some liberties with normal rules of editing.) To assist the student we have also provided a brief introduction to each case, as well as questions for **Case Analysis** following the case.

- A **Technology Corner** box in each chapter provides a list of Internet sites that are relevant to the material in the chapter. A **Featured Web Site** box in each chapter provides an overview of one important Web site, along with student assignments using the site.
- **Ethical Concerns** boxes in each chapter contain hypothetical situations presenting ethical questions suitable for class discussion. Students are given the opportunity to apply the various ethical rules to real-life situations.
- A **Chapter Summary** is included in every chapter. The summaries are short overviews of the major concepts covered in the chapter.
- Basic **Questions for Review** follow each Chapter Summary. These questions are designed to assist the student in focusing on the most important concepts in the chapter.
- **Questions for Analysis** at the end of each chapter require the student to apply the concepts covered in the chapter.
- An **Assignments and Projects** section, which follows the Questions for Analysis, contains hands-on activities to help the student build necessary skills.
- Most chapters include a feature we call **A Point to Remember**. This practical information helps students focus on the skills and concepts that will help them in their legal studies.
- A complete **Glossary** at the end of the text contains definitions for all highlighted vocabulary used in the text.
- A **Mock Trial** is in Appendix III and a **Basic Citation Reference Guide** is included as Appendix IV. The mock trial could be used at the end of Chapter 17 ("The Trial"). We have found that a mock trial is fun and memorable for the students. We have provided the basic fact pattern and the legal issues. The trial is a good opportunity for students to apply the materials presented in the preceding chapters.
- Appendix VII, **Recent United States Supreme Court Decisions**, contains summaries of important recent cases. In the various chapters, students are asked to do factual analysis based on the cases.
- A complete ***Instructor's Manual*** is available. The instructor's manual contains suggested course syllabi, chapter outlines, answers to questions for review, and suggestions for additional teaching materials. It also includes a test bank with answers and transparency masters.

ACKNOWLEDGMENTS

No textbook can be produced through the sole effort of its authors. The second edition of *Introduction to Law* is no exception.

These efforts include the knowledge of valued professionals, such as: Mercedes Prieto Alsonso-Knapp, Florida International University, FL; Alan Katz, Cape Fear Commuunity College, NC; Laura Barnard, Lakeland Community College, OH; Linda Cabral Marrero, Mercy College, NY; Jacalyn J. Royal, Lake Mary, FL; as well as professionals from Fresno City College, Mildred Elley Business School, George Washington University, Hofstra University, and others.

We would like to thank several individuals whose recommendations, assistance, and encouragement have made this work possible and enjoyable. Daily contributions came, first and foremost, from our husbands, Bill Ekern and Mark Hames: they have each contributed their special talents and knowledge to improving this text. More importantly, they have been a constant source of encouragement and support. Special thanks are also extended to Delene Waltrip and Hope Allen, paralegals extraordinaire; and to administrators at our respective colleges, Terry Ellis, Lawrence Burke, Dave Fishbaugh, and Ginny Aragon, who have been a constant source of support. Our appreciation is also extended to Elizabeth Sugg of Prentice-Hall and Linda Zuk of WordCrafters Editorial Services, who have given us valuable assistance in the completion of the second edition of this text.

About the Authors

Joanne Banker Hames is an attorney who has been actively involved in paralegal education since 1977 and is now a full-time instructor and the coordinator for the ABA-approved paralegal program at DeAnza Community College located in the heart of Silicon Valley. She earned her J.D. from Santa Clara University Law School and has been an active member of the California Bar since 1972. Prior to her involvement in paralegal education, she practiced law in a firm specializing in personal injury litigation. She is also the co-author of *Civil Litigation* and *Legal Research, Analysis, and Writing: An Integrated Approach.*

Yvonne Ekern is the chairperson of an ABA-approved Paralegal Program and Division Chair of the Applied Arts and Sciences Division of West Valley Community College. Prior to completing law school, she taught high school English and Math in California and Missouri. She graduated from the University of Idaho School of Law in 1985. While working in criminal and family law offices, she taught part-time in several Silicon Valley paralegal programs and is now the full-time chairperson of the West Valley College Paralegal Program, located in Saratoga, California. She is also an instructor in that program. She is the co-author of *Legal Research, Analysis, and Writing: An Integrated Approach.* She has over twenty years of teaching experience.

CHAPTER 1

THE LEGAL COMMUNITY AND PROFESSIONAL RESPONSIBILITY

The Technology Corner boxes provide starting points to finding legal information using the Internet. Look at each site. Bookmark the addresses you find most helpful.

Web Address	Name of Site
www.abanet.org/	American Bar Association
www.nala.org/	National Association of Legal Assistants
www.paralegals.org/	National Federation of Paralegal Associations
www.abanet.org/cpr/home.html	ABA Center for Professional Responsibility
www.paralegals.org/Development/modelcode.html	NFPA—Model Code of Ethics
guide.lp.findlaw.com/01topics/14ethics/cases.html	Selected U.S. Supreme Court Decisions about Attorneys

Caution: Web addresses may change and some may disappear. If you experience difficulty loading a Web page, try to delete the information to the right of the last slash mark (/). You may need to work all the way back to the ".com" or ".edu" or ".gov" or ".org" and so forth.

CASE FILE: *PEOPLE V. TERRY JACOBS*

Terry Jacobs has always been fascinated by the law. Terry's spare time is spent watching television shows about lawyers and police or reading legal thrillers written by authors such as Grisham and Turow. At one time Terry even considered becoming a lawyer, but the thought of seven years of college and the corresponding cost made Terry put aside the thought of law school. Instead, Terry went to the Internet site for amazon.com and purchased several books on the law written for paralegals. After reading the books, Terry started a paralegal business called Jacobs Paralegal Services. As part of this business Terry often helped people obtain divorces. Unfortunately, the local bar association claims that Terry is engaged in the unauthorized practice of law. After investigating the matter, the local prosecutor filed criminal charges against Terry.

Advertisement

JACOBS PARALEGAL SERVICES

Quality Legal Assistance With:

- **Divorces**
- **Bankruptcies**
- **Other Legal Matters**

SEC. 1–1 INTRODUCTION

For thirty-six days following the 2000 presidential election, citizens throughout the United States were glued to their televisions and radios, waiting to see who would prevail in the election. It seemed that each day some new legal maneuvering took place. Lawsuits were filed in several courts. Appeals inevitably followed. Eventually, the case reached the U.S. Supreme Court—not once, but twice. As the time for the selection of electoral candidates grew near, the public anxiously awaited the final decision from the Supreme Court. Through it all, newscasters brought us the latest developments and interviewed countless "constitutional experts" to tell us what it all meant.

This was not the first time in recent history that the public has been fascinated by legal proceedings. A few years earlier, when O. J. Simpson was tried for murder, millions of viewers were also glued to their television sets to see what surprises the prosecutors and the "Dream Team" would present to the judge and jury. A camera in the courtroom brought the trial into American living rooms. In addition, radio and television stations brought in legal experts to explain and comment on the trial. Years after the trial was over, several books on the trial reached the best seller lists. Not unexpectedly, a television movie was made chronicling the events.

Clearly, the law can be a fascinating topic. More than that, however, it affects all aspects of our lives, from the selection of our president to the way we drive our automobiles. At times the law is simple and straightforward. At other times it can be complex and involved, requiring experts to explain and interpret it.

Whether your goal is to eventually work in the law or whether you are just interested in law, you should know certain basic concepts about the American legal system. This text is intended to introduce you to some of the basics of the legal system in the United States. You will not learn everything there is to learn about the law, because that is an impossible task. However, as you go through the various chapters you will see how the legal system is organized and how it functions. You will read about some important areas of law and see how legal disputes are handled both in and out of court.

The starting point in learning about the law is to become familiar with the participants who make up the legal community. This first chapter introduces you to the various members of the legal community. It also introduces some of the important ethical rules that guide these professions.

SEC. 1–2 THE LEGAL PROFESSION

LAWYERS

lawyer
An individual who is authorized by a state to practice law.

attorney
Another term for *lawyer*.

bar examination
An examination administered by a state that tests an individual's knowledge of the law and is a prerequisite to being allowed to practice law.

A **lawyer**, who is also called an **attorney**, is an individual licensed by a state to practice law. States generally require that individuals take and pass a special examination, a **bar examination**, before they can be licensed to practice law. The license is valid only within the state that issues it. If an individual wishes to practice law in a state on a regular basis, that individual must be licensed within that state. Prior to taking a bar examination, most individuals have completed a four-year bachelor's degree program followed by a three-year law school program. On completion of law school, most graduates receive a *Juris Doctor* ("doctor of law") degree. Because of the ever-changing nature of the law, some states now require licensed attorneys to regularly complete a certain number of hours of continuing education in order to maintain their license to practice law.

THE PRACTICE OF LAW

Lawyers practice their profession in different ways. Many lawyers work in privately owned law firms. The lawyers may be the employees or owners of the law firm, either individually, in *partnership* with other lawyers, or in an *association* with other lawyers. The law firm may even be incorporated. A law *partnership* operates under the same partnership laws as any business. The partners share profits and each is responsible for all of the liabilities of the business. However, because of certain ethical rules, only licensed attorneys can be partners. An *association* is a type of business organization where lawyers may share office and support-staff expenses, but do not share in the profits of the law practice itself. In some cases the law practice is incorporated. In such an event, the state laws regulating corporations apply to the organization. *Shareholders*, or owners of the corporation, are generally limited to attorneys.

Not all lawyers work in private law firms. Many work for local, state, or federal government organizations such as prosecutors' offices (sometimes known as district attorneys), public defenders' offices, state attorneys' offices, or the U.S. Attorney's office. Other attorneys work in legal departments of corporations or insurance companies. In these instances, the attorneys are usually salaried employees, although the heads of some of these organizations may be elected or appointed officials.

The nature of the day-to-day work done by attorneys depends on where the attorney works or the area of expertise or specialty of that attorney. However, what constitutes the practice of law is somewhat consistent among all legal practitioners.

Although there is no exact definition of the practice of law, generally the practice of law includes such activities as appearing in court, giving legal advice, and preparing legal documents to meet specific client needs.

SEC. 1–3 THE PARALEGAL PROFESSION

paralegal
An individual whose training and education enables him or her to assist lawyers by performing certain legal tasks that have traditionally been done by lawyers.

legal assistant
Another term for *paralegal*.

Because of the complexities of the law, most people rely on the work and efforts of professionally trained individuals whenever they have a legal problem. Traditionally, these trained individuals have been attorneys. But in recent years, with the emergence of the paralegal profession, this has begun to change. **Paralegals**, also known as **legal assistants**, are individuals whose training and education enable them to assist lawyers by performing various legal tasks. Although they cannot give legal advice or appear in court, paralegals, under the supervision of a lawyer, can do much of the legal work that has traditionally been done by lawyers. If a paralegal has been properly trained and is properly supervised, clients receive the same level of legal work as they would from attorneys working alone, and they receive it at a more affordable cost.

In the O. J. Simpson murder trial, the defendant was represented by several attorneys who were labeled "the Dream Team." Even though most parties could not even begin to afford the type of legal services provided in this case, more and more parties do find that legal services are being provided by a "team" consisting of lawyers, paralegals, and other support staff. By properly utilizing a support staff, especially paralegals, today's attorneys have found that their time can be most efficiently and economically spent doing the things that require the expertise they gained in law school. Conversely, clients have found that when paralegals, rather than attorneys, perform certain legal tasks, the cost of the legal services is greatly reduced. The value of paralegals to the legal community is so great that labor experts predict that the paralegal profession will continue to be one of the fastest-growing professions in the United States for years to come.

PARALEGALS IN THE LEGAL ENVIRONMENT

Most paralegals work under the supervision of attorneys either in private law offices, government law offices (such as prosecutors' offices), or in the legal departments of corporations or other businesses. A paralegal who works in a firm that handles automobile accident cases might interview clients and witnesses, draft documents that are filed in court, or summarize medical records. On the other hand, a paralegal who works for a probate attorney might be involved in gathering and organizing financial data or preparing inheritance tax returns.

The day-to-day tasks that paralegals perform are as varied as the types of law that are practiced. However, certain knowledge and skills are commonly required of all paralegals who work in any legal environment. Paralegals need to have a basic knowledge of the legal system, substantive laws, and legal procedures. Subsequent chapters in this book will cover these areas. Legal assistants should also have some knowledge of the substantive and procedural laws of the state in which they work. This is the focus of most formal paralegal education. In addition, every paralegal should know and understand the ethical obligations that bind legal professionals. Those obligations are discussed later in this chapter.

A POINT TO REMEMBER

Paralegals cannot engage in the unauthorized practice of law. They cannot appear in court or give legal advice. However, under the supervision of an attorney, they can perform many tasks often done by lawyers, such as interviewing clients, drafting legal documents, and doing legal research.

In addition to the specific legal knowledge required of a paralegal, legal assistants must also possess certain basic skills. These include the following:

Oral and Written Communication Skills

Paralegals commonly interview clients and witnesses, and then summarize in writing the content of such interviews. Paralegals frequently communicate orally and in writing with the courts, attorneys, other paralegals, and clients. Additionally, paralegals might draft all types of legal documents.

Research Skills

Some paralegals do extensive legal research and writing for attorneys, while others do very little. However, all paralegals must have basic legal research skills, if only for their own benefit. Furthermore, all paralegals should have general research skills. For example, as a paralegal you might be asked to locate the address of a distant court; in a medical malpractice case, you might be asked to research certain medical conditions.

Critical Thinking/Analytical Skills

Critical-thinking skills are essential for anyone working as a true legal assistant and are required for most if not all of the legal work done by paralegals. For example, the ability to analyze and synthesize facts is required for legal research and preparing legal documents. It is also needed for reviewing legal documents and reviewing and evaluating evidence.

Organizational Skills

Most case files in a legal office contain numerous documents. In some major lawsuits the number of documents may be in the thousands. Paralegals may be responsible for indexing and organizing all of them. If a case is in litigation, many time deadlines are also critical. Certain papers may have to be filed in court or served on other parties to the lawsuit, or court appearances by the attorney might be set. Someone must keep track of everything; often that someone is a paralegal.

General Office/Computer Skills

If you work as a paralegal in a law office you will be expected to possess general office skills. Today that means you must be computer literate. Word processing skills are a must. Most law firms use the word processing software Microsoft Word, although some may use WordPerfect. Ability to use the Internet is also essential. Legal and factual research uses the Internet. Most courts are now online. And, of course, no office operates without e-mail. In addition, you should be familiar with general filing and billing procedures, possess proper telephone etiquette, and know how to handle general business communication.

Independent Paralegals

Not all paralegals work in law offices. Some, like Terry Jacobs, prefer the benefits of self-employment. In some instances they work as independent contractors, offering their services to different attorneys for specific legal projects. For example, they might do a legal research project, handle a probate, or summarize documents in a specific case. Paralegals who work like this are sometimes referred to as *independent* or *freelance paralegals*; they do much the same type of work as traditional paralegals.

Contrasted with paralegals who work independently for attorneys are those who offer their services directly to the public. This type of work presents serious ethical and legal questions because, absent specific legislation to the contrary, only attorneys can give legal advice, appear in court, or otherwise engage in the practice of law. In recent years many state legislatures have considered the issue of trained nonattorneys providing limited legal services to the public. The term **legal technician** rather than *paralegal* is sometimes used to designate these individuals. Advocates of legal technicians stress the need for affordable legal services, while opponents stress the dangers of allowing nonattorneys to practice law, even to a limited extent.

legal technician
A term used to describe a nonattorney who is authorized to engage in a limited practice of law.

Regulation of Paralegals

Unlike attorneys, paralegals are not generally licensed by any government agency. In fact, in most states anyone can be called a paralegal. However, a number of states have considered or are considering some type of regulation of paralegals. See the box titled "Regulation of Paralegals" for an example of recent legislation passed in California related to paralegals. Aside from governmental regulation, the paralegal profession itself has adopted some forms of self-regulation. Two major professional organizations have established professional standards and voluntary certification for paralegals: the National Association of Legal Assistants (NALA) and the National Federation of Paralegal Associations (NFPA). NALA administers a national examination that tests paralegal competency. Paralegals who pass the examinations are referred to as **Certified Legal Assistants (CLAs)**. CLAs are required to take several hours of continuing education regularly to maintain their status. NALA also administers certain specialty examinations to paralegals who have passed the basic CLA examination. NFPA has also decided to administer a competency examination. This exam is known as PACE (Paralegal Advanced Competency Exam).

Certified Legal Assistant (CLA)
A paralegal or legal assistant who has passed a special examination given by the National Association of Legal Assistants.

Both NALA and NFPA have sought to enhance the paralegal profession by adopting codes of ethical standards for paralegals. These rules are found in Appendix II. Neither organization, however, has authority to punish or discipline anyone who violates these standards.

Although the paralegal profession has been largely unregulated, changes are beginning. For example, California recently enacted legislation limiting the use of the term *paralegal* to those who work for attorneys and who have certain paralegal educational or experience. Continuing legal education is also required. California also regulates independent paralegals who provide services to the public. These individuals, who are often referred to as *licensed document assistants*, must meet educational or experience requirements. They must be licensed and bonded. Unlike attorneys, however, they do not need to take an examination to be licensed.

Regulation of Paralegals

California Business and Profession Code § 6450

(a) "Paralegal" means a person who either contracts with or is employed by an attorney, law firm, corporation, governmental agency, or other entity and who performs substantial legal work under the direction and supervision of an active member of the State Bar of California, as defined in Section 6060, or an attorney practicing law in the federal courts of this state, that has been specifically delegated by the attorney to him or her. Tasks performed by a paralegal include, but are not limited to, case planning, development, and management; legal research; interviewing clients; fact gathering and retrieving information; drafting and analyzing legal documents; collecting, compiling, and utilizing technical information to make an independent decision and recommendation to the supervising attorney; and representing clients before a state or federal administrative agency if that representation is permitted by statute, court rule, or administrative rule or regulation.

(b) Notwithstanding subdivision (a), a paralegal shall not do any of the following:

(1) Provide legal advice.

(2) Represent a client in court.

(3) Select, explain, draft, or recommend the use of any legal document to or for any person other than the attorney who directs and supervises the paralegal.

(4) Act as a runner or capper, as defined in Sections 6151 and 6152.

(5) Engage in conduct that constitutes the unlawful practice of law.

(6) Contract with, or be employed by, a natural person other than an attorney to perform paralegal services.

(7) In connection with providing paralegal services, induce a person to make an investment, purchase a financial product or service, or enter a transaction from which income or profit, or both, purportedly may be derived.

(8) Establish the fees to charge a client for the services the paralegal performs, which shall be established by the attorney who supervises the paralegal's work. This paragraph does not apply to fees charged by a paralegal in a contract to provide paralegal services to an attorney, law firm, corporation, governmental agency, or other entity as provided in subdivision (a).

(c) A paralegal shall possess at least one of the following:

(1) A certificate of completion of a paralegal program approved by the American Bar Association.

(2) A certificate of completion of a paralegal program at, or a degree from, a postsecondary institution that requires the successful completion of a minimum of 24 semester, or equivalent, units in law-related courses and that has been accredited by a national or regional accrediting organization or approved by the Bureau for Private Postsecondary and Vocational Education.

(continued)

Regulation of Paralegals (continued)

(3) A baccalaureate degree or an advanced degree in any subject, a minimum of one year of law-related experience under the supervision of an attorney who has been an active member of the State Bar of California for at least the preceding three years or who has practiced in the federal courts of this state for at least the preceding three years, and a written declaration from this attorney stating that the person is qualified to perform paralegal tasks.

(4) A high school diploma or general equivalency diploma, a minimum of three years of law-related experience under the supervision of an attorney who has been an active member of the State Bar of California for at least the preceding three years or who has practiced in the federal courts of this state for at least the preceding three years, and a written declaration from this attorney stating that the person is qualified to perform paralegal tasks. This experience and training shall be completed no later than December 31, 2003.

(d) All paralegals shall be required to certify completion every three years of four hours of mandatory continuing legal education in legal ethics. All continuing legal education courses shall meet the requirements of Section 6070. Every two years, all paralegals shall be required to certify completion of four hours of mandatory continuing education in either general law or in a specialized area of law. Certification of these continuing education requirements shall be made with the paralegal's supervising attorney. The paralegal shall be responsible for keeping a record of the paralegal's certifications.

(e) A paralegal does not include a nonlawyer who provides legal services directly to members of the public or a legal document assistant or unlawful detainer assistant as defined in Section 6400.

(f) If a legal document assistant, as defined in subdivision (c) of Section 6400, has registered, on or before January 1, 2001, as required by law, a business name that includes the word "paralegal," that person may continue to use that business name until he or she is required to renew registration.

ETHICAL CHOICES

You have just completed your first year of your paralegal education. Your neighbor and good friend was just in an automobile accident. She tells you how the accident happened and asks if she has a good case. What should you tell her?

Paralegal Education

The traditional definition of a paralegal includes the fact that paralegals have special training and education. In the early days of the paralegal profession, in the 1960s and 1970s, few formal paralegal programs existed. Instead, many law firms hired intelligent and educated individuals and trained them to be paralegals. As the paralegal profession has grown and developed, formal paralegal education has become a prerequisite for many if not most paralegal jobs. Formal paralegal programs are offered by numerous educational institutions, both public and private, and can vary in length and depth of material covered. To provide some standard, in the 1970s the American Bar Association (ABA) established certain guidelines for paralegal education and undertook to approve programs that met those guidelines and requested approval. These requirements for approval relate to curriculum, faculty, and support services of the educational institution. The ABA works closely with an organization known as the American Association for Paralegal Education (AAfPE). Paralegal programs can join AAfPE even if they are not approved by the ABA.

PARALEGALS AS PROFESSIONALS

In a 1989 case, *Missouri v. Jenkins*, the U.S. Supreme Court discussed the role of paralegals in the practice of law. *Missouri v. Jenkins* was an aftermath of a major school desegregation case filed in Kansas City, Missouri. After a lengthy court battle, the plaintiffs in the case won. According to Section (abbreviated §) 1988 of the United States Code, the attorneys for the prevailing party were entitled to collect reasonable attorney fees from the losing party. In this case, the attorneys for the prevailing party used paralegals extensively and wanted reimbursement for their time at a rate of $35 to $40 per hour, which was the common rate at which paralegal time was billed to clients. The paralegals themselves were actually paid in the range of $15 per hour. The trial court awarded fees for the paralegal time at the rate of $35 to $40 per hour; the other side appealed and requested a hearing in the U.S. Supreme Court. In writing this decision, the Court made frequent reference to the United States Code (abbreviated U.S.C. in the decision).

Missouri v. Jenkins

391 U.S. 274 (1989)

ABOUT CASE LAW IN GENERAL

Before you read the excerpt from Missouri v. Jenkins, *you should know what case decisions are. Published case decisions (or case law) are decisions of cases written by judges. Most often, these are decisions from judges who heard appeals in cases. They all involve real people or organizations who had real disputes. When you read the case itself, you are reading what the judges said about those people and their dispute. The decision was intended primarily to resolve their dispute. Because of the concept of* ***precedent*** *or* ***stare decisis****, this decision can have a far-reaching effect in the legal system. Precedent or* stare decisis *means that once a specific factual dispute has been resolved in a particular way, if the same factual dispute arises again, it should be resolved in the same way. When judges write an opinion, they usually include a brief history of the factual dispute between the parties. They also discuss the reasons for their decision. In discussing the reasons for their decision, judges frequently refer to other cases or statutory law they considered. When they do this they also give a* **citation** *for that law. A citation is a standard reference that tells readers where they can find the law. The case name for this case,* Missouri v. Jenkins, *is followed by a citation. This is a reference to a book in which this case is published. In this citation, the book is abbreviated as* U.S. (United States Reports). *The abbreviation is preceded by a volume number and followed by a page number. Case law and citations are explained in more detail in Chapters 3, 4, and 5.*

precedent
The example set by the decision of an earlier court for similar cases, or similar legal questions that arise in later cases.

stare decisis
"It stands decided"; another term for *precedent*.

citation
A standard abbreviated way of explaining where law is found.

OPINION

Missouri's contention is that the District Court erred in compensating the work of law clerks and paralegals (hereinafter collectively "paralegals") at the market rates for their services, rather than at their cost to the attorney. While Missouri agrees that compensation for the cost of these personnel should be included in the fee award, it suggests that an hourly rate of $15—which it argued below corresponded to their salaries, benefits, and overhead—would be appropriate, rather than the market rates of $35 to $50. According to Missouri, § 1988 does not authorize billing paralegals' hours at market rates, and doing so produces a "windfall" for the attorney.

We begin with the statutory language, which provides simply for "a reasonable attorney's fee as part of the costs." 42 U.S.C. § 1988. Clearly, a "reasonable attorney's fee" cannot have been meant to compensate only work performed personally by members of the bar. Rather, the term must refer to a reasonable fee for the work product of an attorney. Thus, the fee must take into account the work not only of attorneys, but also of secretaries, messengers, librarians, janitors, and others whose labor contributes to the work product for which an attorney bills her client; and it must also take account of other expenses and profit. The parties have suggested no reason why the work of paralegals should not be similarly compensated, nor can we think of any. We thus take as our starting point the self-evident proposition that the "reasonable attorney's fee" provided for by statute should compensate the work of paralegals, as well as that of attorneys. The more difficult question is how the work of paralegals is to be valuated in calculating the overall attorney's fee.

The statute specifies a "reasonable" fee for the attorney's work product. In determining how other elements of the attorney's fee are to be calculated, we have consistently looked to the marketplace as our guide to what is "reasonable." A reasonable attorney's fee under § 1988 is one calculated on the basis of rates and practices prevailing in the relevant market, *i.e.*, "in line with those [rates] prevailing in the community for similar services by lawyers of reasonably comparable skill, experience, and reputation," and one that grants the successful civil rights plaintiff a "fully compensatory fee," comparable to what "is traditional with attorneys compensated by a fee-paying client."

If an attorney's fee awarded under § 1988 is to yield the same level of compensation that would be available from the market, the "increasingly widespread custom of separately billing for the services of paralegals and law students who serve as clerks" must be taken into account. All else being equal, the hourly fee charged by an attorney whose rates include paralegal work in her hourly fee, or who bills separately for the work of paralegals at cost, will be higher than the hourly fee charged by an attorney competing in the same market who bills separately for the work of paralegals at "market rates." In other words, the prevailing "market rate" for attorney time is not independent of the manner in which paralegal time is accounted for. Thus, if the prevailing practice in a given community were to bill paralegal time separately at market rates, fees awarded the attorney at market rates for attorney time would not be fully compensatory if the court refused to compensate hours billed by paralegals or did so only at "cost." Similarly, the fee awarded would be too high if the court accepted separate billing for paralegal hours in a market where that was not the custom.

We reject the argument that compensation for paralegals at rates above "cost" would yield a "windfall" for the prevailing attorney. Neither petitioners nor anyone else, to our knowledge, has ever suggested that the hourly rate applied to the work of an associate attorney in a law firm creates a windfall for the firm's partners or is otherwise improper under § 1988, merely because it exceeds the cost of the attorney's services. If the fees are consistent with market rates and practices, the "windfall" argument has no more force with regard to paralegals than it does for associates. And it would hardly accord with Congress' intent to provide a "fully compensatory fee" if the prevailing plaintiff's attorney in a civil rights lawsuit were not permitted to bill separately for paralegals, while the defense attorney in the same litigation was able to take advantage of the prevailing practice and obtain market rates for such work. Yet that is precisely the result sought in this case by the State of Missouri, which appears to have paid its own outside counsel for the work of paralegals at the hourly rate of $35.

Nothing in § 1988 requires that the work of paralegals invariably be billed separately. If it is the practice in the relevant market not to do so, or to bill the work of paralegals only at cost, that is all that § 1988 requires. Where, however, the prevailing practice is to bill paralegal work at market rates, treating civil rights lawyers' fee requests in the same way is not only permitted by § 1988, but also makes economic sense. By encouraging the use of lower-cost paralegals rather than attorneys wherever possible, permitting market-rate billing of paralegal hours "encourages cost-effective delivery of legal services and, by reducing the spiraling cost of civil rights litigation, furthers the policies underlying civil rights statutes."* Such separate billing appears to be the prac-

*It has frequently been recognized in the lower courts that paralegals are capable of carrying out many tasks, under the supervision of an attorney, that might otherwise be performed by a lawyer and billed at a higher rate. Such work might include, for example, factual investigation, including locating and interviewing witnesses; assistance with depositions, interrogatories, and document production; compilation of statistical and financial data; checking legal citations; and drafting correspondence. Much such work lies in a gray area of tasks that might appropriately be performed either by an attorney or a paralegal. . . .

tice in most communities today. In the present case, Missouri concedes that "the local market typically bills separately for paralegal services," and the District Court found that the requested hourly rates of $35 for law clerks, $40 for paralegals, and $50 for recent law graduates were the prevailing rates for such services in the Kansas City area. Under these circumstances, the court's decision to award separate compensation at these rates was fully in accord with § 1988.

CASE ANALYSIS

1. The parties to a case are the people or organizations who have brought their dispute to court. Who are the parties in this case? Which party petitioned the Supreme Court for review? Can you tell which party won the case at the trial level?
2. Describe the nature of the dispute between the parties in this case. How did the Court resolve the dispute?
3. What does the Court say about the nature of work done by paralegals? Do you think this has any impact on how judges and lawyers view the paralegal profession?
4. Is the Court treating paralegals more like secretaries or more like attorneys? Explain.

SEC. 1–4 LEGAL SUPPORT STAFF

LEGAL SECRETARIES

Another important member of the legal team is the legal secretary. As with other legal professionals, the work done by legal secretaries in law offices varies depending on the education and experience of the legal secretaries and the area of specialty of the firm employing them. Their jobs may be primarily secretarial in nature, but in some cases are much more involved. Before the advent of the paralegal profession, many legal secretaries not only did traditional secretarial work, but also performed many of the tasks now assigned to paralegals. In fact, in the early days of the paralegal profession, many new paralegals had been legal secretaries.

Most legal secretarial jobs include such activities as word processing, scheduling appointments, notifying clients of court dates, and calendaring court appearances. Although such tasks are primarily secretarial, a limited knowledge of the law and the legal process is necessary. Legal secretaries frequently deal with the courts; furthermore, they must know the proper format for preparing various types of legal documents as well as be familiar with court rules regarding the filing of any court documents. In some cases, the work of legal secretaries extends beyond secretarial functions and into the realm of paralegal work. Some legal secretaries draft legal documents, interview clients, and summarize records. Often legal secretaries, like the lawyers for whom they work, become experts in certain areas of the law. They may be known as *litigation secretaries, patent secretaries,* or *corporate secretaries.*

In larger law firms, marked distinctions exist between the paralegal job and the legal secretary position. Each has very definite assigned tasks. In smaller firms, however, the differences between a legal secretary and a paralegal are sometimes hard to determine. Generally, however, paralegals have more formal legal education and are expected to work more independently than legal secretaries. Attorneys who operate small law firms may not need both a legal secretary and a paralegal. They will therefore often seek a "legal secretary/paralegal" for their support staff. That is, they want someone who can perform the job of both the legal secretary and the paralegal.

Law Clerks

law clerk
A term used to refer to a law student interning or working in a law firm while attending school.

legal memorandum
An informal interoffice document written to communicate the results of legal research and the resulting legal analysis.

The term **law clerk** is most commonly used to refer to law students interning or working in the law firm while attending school. In most cases their jobs in law firms involve considerable legal research and preparation of **legal memoranda**, which are written explanations and analyses of factual and legal problems.

Other Support Staff

Depending on the size of the law firm and the nature of its work, several other legal support positions may exist in a law firm. These include case assistants, case clerks, document coders, and calendar clerks. Although their actual job descriptions may vary from firm to firm, in general case, assistants and case clerks assist paralegals. Document coders usually read and extract information from documentary evidence in a case and enter that information into a computerized database. Calendar clerks maintain the office calendar, which may include court appearances, client appointments, and filing dates. Many paralegals begin their careers in one of these support positions.

A POINT TO REMEMBER

If you work in a law firm, you will be a member of a team. You must be willing and able to work harmoniously with all other members of that team, including attorneys and support staff.

A Question of Overtime Pay

Under federal labor rules found in the Code of Federal Regulations (C.F.R.) employees who work overtime must be compensated for that time unless they are "exempt." One category of exemption exists for an employee "who customarily and regularly exercises discretionary powers . . ." [29 C.F.R. 541.1(d)]. Furthermore this requirement is met "by the employee who normally and recurrently is called upon to exercise and does exercise discretionary powers in the day-to-day performance of his duties" (29 C.F.R. 541.107).

Questions

1. Do you think paralegals are entitled to overtime pay according to this law?
2. What factors are important in making this determination?
3. What about other law office support staff?
4. What about attorneys?

SEC. 1–5 COURT PERSONNEL

The legal community consists not only of attorneys, paralegals, and support staff, but also of the personnel of the various courts in which attorneys appear. Litigation attorneys and their support staff, including paralegals, are in regular contact with judges, court clerks, court reporters, and bailiffs.

JUDGES

judge
An individual who presides over an American court.

Judges preside over American courts and are decision makers within the court system. The exact role of any judge depends on the specific court and whether a jury is also involved. A more detailed discussion of the role of judges in the court system is found in Chapter 17. Judges normally have a legal background; in fact, some courts require that judicial candidates have a minimum number of years of experience before they qualify for the position. The selection process of judges depends on the law of the jurisdiction in which the judge serves. In federal courts, all judges (for trial courts, appellate courts, and the Supreme Court) are nominated by the president and confirmed by the Senate. Each state has its own process of judicial selection, which may include public election and/or executive appointment. In addition to regular judges, today many trial courts use the services of individuals known as *magistrates, commissioners,* and *referees,* sometimes referred to as **quasi-judicial officers**. Quasi-judicial officers usually have limited judicial functions and often hear only certain types of matters—for example, traffic cases or pretrial motions. They are selected by the judges they assist.

quasi-judicial officers
Individuals who are not judges but who fulfill limited judicial functions; they include magistrates, commissioners, and referees.

COURT CLERKS

court clerk
A court employee who assists the court and the judge by filing documents, marking and safeguarding evidence, reviewing documents that are submitted to the judge, and other similar tasks.

Court clerks are court employees who assist in the smooth operation of the court. They perform a variety of functions, including filing documents, marking and safeguarding evidence during a trial, and reviewing written orders submitted by attorneys for the judge's signature. While no special educational requirements for this position exist, court clerks are generally required to have some knowledge of court procedures.

COURT REPORTERS

court reporter
A person who records (electronically or stenographically) the testimony that takes place during the open court proceedings; the court reporter will produce a transcript.

Court reporters are specially trained individuals who record verbatim the oral proceedings that take place in court. Their training usually consists of learning to be proficient on the stenographic machine used in court, as well as learning about the legal system with an emphasis on terminology. In many states, court reporters are licensed by the state only after passing an arduous examination.

BAILIFFS

bailiff
An individual who is responsible for the safety of the judge and for order within the courtroom; sometimes known as a *court deputy* or *court attendant*.

Bailiffs, sometimes called *court deputies* or *court attendants*, provide safety and order within the courtroom. In the federal courts this position is sometimes filled by a deputy U.S. marshal. In state courts the bailiff may be a peace officer, although this is not always the case.

A POINT TO REMEMBER

Maintaining a good relationship with all court personnel is essential for every law firm. Always be polite and considerate when dealing with anyone working in the court.

SEC. 1–6 AGENCY PERSONNEL

The legal community is not limited to those who work in law offices or in the courts. Government agencies and offices often play an important role in many types of law practice. Not all types of law practice require attorneys to deal with the courts. The practice may, however, require members of the firm to deal with any number of government agencies, either because documents must be filed with the agency or information must be obtained from it. For example, a lawyer who incorporates businesses must file articles of incorporation with the secretary of state's office in the state in which the business is to be incorporated. If corporate securities (such as stock) are to be offered on a national exchange, then the Securities and Exchange Commission regulates that activity. Other agencies include state departments of motor vehicles, state boards that regulate workers' compensation cases (cases of employees who been have injured on the job), state departments of real estate, and state consumer agencies. Many other federal, state, and local agencies exist.

A large body of law regulates the rights and powers of many of these agencies. One of the important aspects of this law relates to disputes that arise concerning the actions of the agency. In a dispute over some action taken by an agency, the disputing parties must often try to resolve that dispute within the agency itself rather than immediately filing a lawsuit in a court. This process usually involves a formal hearing known as an **administrative hearing**.

administrative hearing
A hearing before an administrative agency regarding a dispute between an individual and the agency.

SEC. 1–7 PROFESSIONAL ORGANIZATIONS

An examination of the legal community would not be complete without including a list of some common professional organizations for the various members of the legal community.

AMERICAN BAR ASSOCIATION (ABA)

The ABA is a national organization that strives to promote high professional standards within the American legal community and to safeguard the administration of justice to the public. Membership in this organization is voluntary and is open to all attorneys. Paralegals may also join. More information can be found on the ABA Web site at www.abanet.org/.

State Bar Associations

In order for attorneys to be authorized to practice law in any state, they must belong to the state bar association of that state. State bar associations traditionally monitor the ethical conduct of attorneys practicing within the state and impose sanctions on lawyers found to have violated the ethical standards of the profession. These organizations speak for the legal community to legislators, often endorsing or opposing proposed legislation that affects the legal system.

Local Bar Associations

Local bar associations are generally local (county or city) organizations that attorneys voluntarily join. They often provide continuing legal education for lawyers and sometimes try to resolve disputes with clients, especially those involving fees. They may also provide special legal services to the needy.

American Trial Lawyers Association (ATLA)

ATLA is a national professional group consisting primarily of trial or litigation lawyers. It also allows paralegal membership. This organization provides continuing education for members, and is often vocal in connection with any proposed legislation that affects the rights of individuals to litigate their disputes. To read more about ATLA, go to its Web site at www.atlanet.org/.

National Association of Legal Assistants (NALA)

NALA is a professional organization for paralegals or legal assistants that strives to promote high professional standards for the paralegal profession. As described earlier, it has adopted a code of ethics for paralegals and also administers a national examination that paralegals may choose to take if they meet the prerequisites. This organization confers the title of CLA on paralegals who pass the organization's examination. Membership in NALA is voluntary and is open to all paralegals. To read more about NALA and the CLA exam, go the NALA Web site at www.nala.org/.

National Federation of Paralegal Associations (NFPA)

NFPA is primarily a national organization consisting of local paralegal associations, although individuals may join. Like NALA, it strives to promote high professional standards for the paralegal profession. It has adopted a code of ethics for paralegals and is implementing a national examination that qualified paralegals may take. NFPA maintains a Web site at www.paralegals.org/.

American Association for Paralegal Education (AAfPE)

AAfPE is a national organization of paralegal schools and educators. It sets standards for paralegal education and works with the ABA in approving paralegal schools. Read more about this organization at www.aafpe.org/.

Local Paralegal Associations

Many local communities have their own professional organizations for paralegals and paralegal students. Usually they strive to promote the professional standards of the paralegal position by sponsoring educational seminars for the members and by closely watching proposed legislation regarding paralegals.

Sec. 1–8 ETHICAL RESPONSIBILITIES

fiduciary relationship
A special relationship of trust and confidence; it forms the basis of the attorney-client relationship.

disbarment
The action of denying an attorney the right to practice law in the state.

All members of the legal profession are bound by ethical standards. This includes not only attorneys but also paralegals and other support staff. When a lawyer agrees to represent a client, a special relationship is created between the lawyer and the client. This **fiduciary relationship** means that the attorney must exercise the highest degree of trust and care with that client. The relationship carries with it various duties or obligations for the attorney in handling the case. These duties are more than moral obligations. State bar associations require attorneys to adhere to a certain standard of conduct; failure of an attorney to do so will result in sanctions against the attorney, including reprimands, suspension, and disbarment. **Disbarment** results in an attorney being denied the right to practice law in the state. Specific rules of conduct, sometimes referred to as *canons of ethics* or *rules of professional conduct*, vary slightly from state to state. However, in general they are patterned after suggested standards published by the American Bar Association. The ABA has numerous publications regarding legal ethics, including *The Annotated Model Rules of Professional Conduct*. Remember that the ABA does not have the power to dictate any rules to attorneys because it is a voluntary association and has no regulatory power over attorneys. Attorneys are regulated by the state bar association of the state in which they practice. Many states, however, have patterned their rules after the ABA *Annotated Model Rules of Professional Conduct*. The ethical rules for individual states can be located on the Internet. Many of these rules are linked to the site maintained by NALA, www.nala.org/. They can also be accessed under "Legal Subjects," subtopic "Ethics and Professional Responsibility," on the Findlaw Web site at www.findlaw.com.

Since most paralegals are not regulated or licensed by any state, states generally do not have the power to impose mandatory rules of conduct. However, two paralegal associations, NALA and NFPA, have adopted recommended canons of ethics for paralegals. These rules are found in Appendix II. If you work as a paralegal you should read these rules carefully. Furthermore, a paralegal working under the supervision of a lawyer must also follow the ethical rules that govern attorneys. Because paralegals are not licensed, they are not subject to any disciplinary action by a state bar. If a paralegal violates any of the standards, however, other penalties might result. Because the attorney is responsible for his or her staff, any violation by a member of the staff reflects on the attorney and may subject the attorney to disciplinary proceedings. Any violation of the ethical standards is also a breach of the fiduciary duty to the client; the client may have a basis for a lawsuit against both the attorney and the member of the staff who violated the rules. While paralegals may be immune from punishment by a state bar, they are not immune from a civil lawsuit for money damages.

Some of the more common rules found in the ABA *Model Rules of Professional Conduct* and repeated in the canons of ethics suggested by NALA and NFPA deal with issues of confidentiality, conflict of interest, trust accounts, diligence, communication with opposing parties, and unauthorized practice of law.

Confidentiality

Most information that a client gives an attorney is confidential and privileged. The attorney is obligated not to voluntarily reveal the content of any communications that are intended to be private. Furthermore, the attorney cannot be forced to reveal any confidential information. However, the duty to preserve confidential information is not absolute. If a client tells an attorney that he or she intends to commit a crime in the future, the attorney is obligated to reveal this to proper authorities. If you work as a paralegal in a law firm, you must always follow the rule of confidentiality. You should not repeat any information you hear in the course of your work, not even to your spouse. This includes information about the identity of clients. While not all information you learn at work is confidential, the best practice is not to talk about anything. This ethical rule also influences other law office activities; that is, you should do nothing that would inadvertently result in a breach of this duty. For example, a telephone conversation with one client should not be conducted in front of other clients. Files should not be left where clients can see names or documents. Computer screens should not be visible to members of the public. Extra care should be taken when using fax machines or e-mail. An innocent mistake may still result in an ethical violation. Use of cell phones should also be carefully monitored because these conversations can be easily intercepted. Finally, while it is usually proper for you to discuss cases with other members of your firm, you should do so only in places where your conversations cannot be overheard.

If you work as a freelance paralegal, offering your services directly to the public, the rule of confidentiality may be different. You may still be in a fiduciary relationship with a client and thus owe your client your confidentiality. However, the law does not recognize this as a legal privilege. That is, if your client tells you something in confidence and you are later questioned about it by proper authorities, you probably do not have the privilege or right not to repeat what you have heard.

Competency

Another important ethical rule that governs attorneys and their staff is the requirement that they accept only cases that they are competent to handle and that they actually handle the cases competently. Competency certainly requires that attorneys have the requisite legal knowledge to handle a case. In an era when specialization is the norm, it may also require that an attorney associate with a specialist for a particular case. Competency requires that attorneys have sufficient time to devote to a case. Use of support staff such as paralegals can help with this. To remain competent, attorneys and paralegals should constantly participate in continuing legal education.

Conflict of Interest

Attorneys are not generally allowed to represent parties if that representation would result in a conflict of interest. A *conflict of interest* means that the attorney cannot give all of his or her loyalty to the client because of some personal or financial relationship that exists. As a paralegal you might find yourself in a conflict of interest. Conflicts can exist in the following situations:

1. You or a law firm for which you work or worked represents a party that you wish to sue. For example, suppose the law firm of Smith and Jones represented Brian Maloney in a divorce case. One month after the divorce was final, Maloney was involved in an automobile accident with Bridget Boyle. The accident was Maloney's fault. Boyle asks the law firm of Smith and Jones to represent her in a lawsuit against Maloney. The law firm cannot handle this case because their prior representation of Maloney causes a conflict of interest.
2. You have a personal relationship with someone who works in a law firm on an opposing side in a lawsuit (or potential lawsuit). For example, suppose that Michael Vu works as a prosecuting attorney and has filed criminal charges against Alan Green. Green goes to the law firm of Arias and Calla. Attorney Calla is married to Michael Vu. The law firm of Arias and Calla should not represent Green.
3. You have a financial or business relationship with a client or with someone who may be an opposing party in an action. For example, suppose attorney Marks is asked to represent Jennings in a lawsuit against ABC Corporation. Marks owns substantial shares of stock in ABC Corporation. This could create a conflict of interest.

The existence of a conflict of interest does not always mean that a law firm cannot handle a case. If a client knows about a potential conflict, the client can agree to allow the firm to continue the representation. In such a case, the member of the law firm who has the actual conflict is usually isolated from the case. This is sometimes referred to as an "ethical wall" or "Chinese wall." For an example of the type of problem that can arise with conflict of interest, read the case of *Phoenix Founders, Inc. v. McClellan* later in this chapter.

Attorney Fees and Trust Accounts

Various ethical rules affect attorney fees. In most cases attorneys can charge clients any fee, as long as the fee is not "unconscionable." Unfortunately the term *unconscionable* is not easily defined. However, it is clearly not the same as *reasonable*. For the most part, fees are regulated by the market, that is, what clients are willing to pay. There are, of course, some exceptions. For example, in a probate matter an attorney may be limited to an amount set by law. Although there may be no restriction on the fee charged, some states do require that the attorney have a written agreement setting out the fee.

Another rule governing fees concerns fee sharing. Attorneys are not allowed to share a fee with a nonattorney, including a paralegal. Nor are they allowed to pay a "finder's fee" to a nonattorney who refers cases to them.

The most stringent ethical rules concerning money relate to how attorneys handle funds that belong to a client or a third party.

In the course of handling any case, lawyers may be asked to handle funds that belong to their client or to a third party. For example, when an attorney settles an automobile accident case for a client who was injured, the insurance company representing the other motorist will send a settlement check to the attorney. The check will include all amounts due to the injured party and will normally be made payable to both the client and the attorney. From the proceeds of this check, the injured party will be expected to cover attorney fees and other costs. When the attorney receives this type of settlement, a certain percentage of the funds belongs to the client; another percentage belongs to the attorney as a fee. When an attorney receives funds that belong to others, those funds must be deposited into a special bank account called a **trust account**. Any law office that handles money belonging to clients or others is required to maintain such a trust account; the account is governed by rules of ethics. Usually attorneys keep one trust account into which all client funds are deposited. Accurate records must be kept for each client. Attorneys must exercise extreme care in managing this account. They cannot mix a trust account with their personal or business accounts (called **commingling**) and they cannot borrow from this account. Even an inadvertent misuse of trust funds can result in serious problems for an attorney.

trust account
A special bank account maintained by an attorney into which funds belonging to clients are kept.

commingling
Mixing client funds with the attorney's business or personal funds.

Diligence

Attorneys and paralegals are supposed to use due diligence in handling any case they accept. In other words, they must do the job they were hired to do. Lawyers should not accept a case unless they have the ability to handle the matter. This means they must be knowledgeable in the area of law controlling the case. It also means that they must have enough time to devote to the case.

Communication with Opposing Parties

Once a party to a case hires a lawyer, an attorney or paralegal for the opposing party must direct all communication through the other attorney. A member of the law firm that represents one party should not communicate directly with an opposing party, if that opposing party has his or her own attorney.

Unauthorized Practice of Law

Lawyers have an ethical responsibility not to do anything to assist another in the unauthorized practice of law. Paralegals must take care that they do nothing that constitutes the unauthorized practice of law. The definition of the practice of law, unfortunately, is not a clear one. Usually, however, it includes giving legal advice and appearing in court on behalf of another. As you read the remaining chapters in this book you will see various situations that can present problems for paralegals in this area. The unauthorized practice of law is more than breaching an ethical standard. It is also a crime. If you engage in such activities, you can be prosecuted and punished.

Phoenix Founders, Inc. v. McClellan

887 S.W.2d 831, 38 Tex. Sup. J. 12 (1994)

Phoenix Founders sued Beneke. Phoenix was represented by the law firm of Thompson & Knight. The firm of David & Goodman represented the Benekes. A paralegal who originally worked for Thompson & Knight left and went to work for David & Goodman for three weeks and then returned to Thompson & Knight. While at David & Goodman, the paralegal had some minor involvement in the case against Beneke. When she returned to Thompson & Knight, Beneke made a motion to disqualify the firm on the basis that they were now privy to confidential information. In the meantime, the paralegal had resigned from Thompson & Knight (the alternative being termination). The trial court disqualified the firm. They appealed. In the following opinion the appellate court discusses whether the firm should have been disqualified. The court concluded that the paralegal did obtain confidential information. However, the court could not say that any confidential information obtained by a paralegal was absolutely imputed to the law firm. The firm would not have to be disqualified if proper steps were taken to insulate the paralegal. The case was remanded to determine whether Thompson & Knight had in fact taken such steps.

OPINION

In this original proceeding, we consider whether a law firm must be disqualified from ongoing litigation because it rehired a legal assistant who had worked for opposing counsel for three weeks. We hold that disqualification is not required if the rehiring firm is able to establish that it has effectively screened the paralegal from any contact with the underlying suit.

The present dispute arises from a suit brought by Phoenix Founders, Inc., and others ("Phoenix") to collect a federal court judgment against Ronald and Jane Beneke and others. The law firm of Thompson & Knight represented Phoenix in the original federal court suit, which began in 1990 and ended in 1991, and has also represented them in the collection suit since its commencement in 1992. The Benekes have been represented in the latter suit by the firm of David & Goodman.

In July of 1993, Denise Hargrove, a legal assistant at Thompson & Knight, left her position at that firm to begin working for David & Goodman as a paralegal. While at David & Goodman, Hargrove billed six-tenths of an hour on the collection suit for locating a pleading. She also discussed the case generally with Mark Goodman, the Benekes' lead counsel.

After three weeks at David & Goodman, Hargrove returned to Thompson & Knight to resume work as a paralegal. At the time of the rehiring, Thompson & Knight made no effort to question Hargrove in regard to potential conflicts of interest resulting from her employment at David & Goodman.

Three weeks after Hargrove had returned, counsel for the Benekes wrote to Thompson & Knight asserting that its renewed employment of Hargrove created a conflict of interest. The letter demanded that the firm withdraw from its representation of Phoenix.

Hargrove resigned from Thompson & Knight the next week, after having been given the option of either resigning with severance pay or being terminated. The firm itself, however, refused to withdraw from the case. The Benekes then filed a motion to disqualify.

The trial court granted the Benekes' motion and disqualified Thompson & Knight from further representation of Phoenix. The disqualification order states that Hargrove possesses confidential information relating to the Benekes, and that all such confidential information was imputed to the firm of Thompson & Knight at the time she was rehired.

This Court has not previously addressed the standards governing a disqualification motion based on the hiring of a nonlawyer employee. With respect to lawyers, however, this Court has adopted a standard requiring disqualification whenever counsel undertakes representation of an interest that is adverse to that of a former client, as long as the matters embraced in the pending suit are "substantially related" to the factual matters involved in the previous suit. *NCNB Texas Nat'l Bank v. Coker*, 765 S.W.2d 398, 399–400 (Tex. 1989). This strict rule is based on a conclusive presumption that confidences and secrets were imparted to the attorney during the prior representation. *Coker*, 765 S.W.2d at 400.

The Benekes argue that the standards applied to the hiring of lawyers should also apply to the hiring of paralegals. Thus, the Benekes urge that the entire firm of Thompson & Knight must be automatically disqualified because of the confidences Hargrove obtained while working at David & Goodman.

We agree that a paralegal who has actually worked on a case must be subject to the presumption set out in *Coker*; that is, a conclusive presumption that confidences and secrets were imparted during the course of the paralegal's work on the case. This presumption serves to prevent the moving party from being forced to reveal the very confidences sought to be protected. Moreover, virtually any information relating to a case should be considered confidential: The Disciplinary Rules define "confidential information" to encompass even unprivileged client information.

We disagree, however, with the argument that paralegals should be conclusively presumed to share confidential information with members of their firms. The Disciplinary Rules require a lawyer having direct supervisory authority over a nonlawyer to make reasonable efforts to ensure that the nonlawyer's conduct is compatible with the professional obligations of the lawyer. If the supervising lawyer orders, encourages, or even permits a nonlawyer to engage in conduct that would be subject to discipline if engaged in by a lawyer, the lawyer will be subject to discipline. The Texas Committee on Professional Ethics has concluded that the Rules do not require disqualification of the new law firm, provided that the supervising lawyer at that firm complies with the Rules so as to ensure that the nonlawyer's conduct is compatible with the professional obligations of a lawyer.

This view is consistent with the weight of authority in other jurisdictions. The American Bar Association's Committee on Professional Ethics has considered whether a law firm that hires a paralegal may continue representing clients whose interests conflict with interests of the former employer's clients on whose matter the paralegal has worked. After surveying case law and ethics opinions from a number of jurisdictions, the Committee concluded that the new firm need not be disqualified as long as the firm and the paralegal strictly adhere to the screening process set forth in the opinion, and as long as the paralegal does not reveal any information relating to the former employer's clients to any person in the employing firm.

Underlying these decisions is a concern regarding the mobility of paralegals and other nonlawyers. A potential employer might well be reluctant to hire a particular nonlawyer if doing so would automatically disqualify the entire firm from ongoing litigation. This problem would be especially acute in the context of massive firms and extensive, complex litigation. Recognizing this danger, the ABA concluded that "any restrictions on the nonlawyer's employment should be held to the minimum necessary to protect confidentiality of client information."

We share the concerns expressed by the ABA, and agree that client confidences may be adequately safeguarded if a firm hiring a paralegal from another firm takes appropriate steps in compliance with the Disciplinary Rules. Specifically, the newly hired paralegal should be cautioned not to disclose any information relating to the representation of a client of the former employer. The paralegal should also be instructed not to work on any matter on which the paralegal worked during the prior employment or regarding which the paralegal has information relating to the former employer's representation. Additionally, the firm should take other reasonable steps to ensure that the paralegal does no work in connection with matters on which the paralegal worked during the prior employment, absent client consent after consultation.

Absent consent of the former employer's client, disqualification will always be required under some circumstances, such as (1) when information relating to the representation of an adverse client has in fact been disclosed, or (2) when screening would be ineffective or the nonlawyer necessarily would be required to work on the other side of a matter that is the same as or substantially related to a matter on which the nonlawyer has previously worked. Ordinarily, however, disqualification is not required as long as "the practical effect of formal screening has been achieved."

In reconsidering the disqualification motion, the trial court should examine the circumstances of Hargrove's employment at Thompson & Knight to determine whether the practical effect of formal screening has been achieved. The factors bearing on such a determination will generally include the substantiality of the relationship between the former and current matters; the time elapsing between the matters; the size of the firm; the number of individuals presumed to have confidential information; the nature of their involvement in the formal matter; and the timing and features of any measures taken to reduce the danger of disclosure. The fact that the present case involves representation of adverse parties in the same proceeding, rather than two separate proceedings, increases the danger that some improper disclosure may have occurred.

The ultimate question in weighing these facts is whether Thompson & Knight has taken measures sufficient to reduce the potential for misuse of confidences to an acceptable level.

The trial court is to reconsider the disqualification motion in light of today's opinion.

CASE ANALYSIS

1. Who brought this action in court and why?
2. Why did the firm of Thompson & Knight ask the paralegal, Denise Hargrove, to leave or be fired?
3. The court talks a great deal about formal screening (which is sometimes referred to as the "Chinese wall"). What types of things could be done in a law firm to achieve this?

Featured Web Site: www.nala.org/

The NALA Web site has extensive information about the paralegal profession.

Go Online

1. Briefly summarize the type of information available.
2. Determine whether the ethical rules for your state are accessible. If so, read them and summarize the rules, if any, on unauthorized practice of law, confidentiality, and conflict of interest. If your state's rules are not available, select those of a neighboring state.

Chapter Summary

The legal community includes several groups. Attorneys or lawyers are licensed by the state to practice law. However, most lawyers work with a team rather than alone. One important member of that team is the paralegal. Paralegals, or legal assistants, who work in law offices assist attorneys in performing legal tasks such as drafting documents, doing legal research, and interviewing clients. Other paralegals work independently, either for attorneys or sometimes for members of the public. No paralegal is allowed to appear in court, give legal advice, or otherwise engage in the unauthorized practice of law. Paralegals often receive formal education for their profession, but they are not obligated to do so. They are not licensed by the state. Support staff in law offices may also include legal secretaries, law clerks, case assistants, case clerks, and document coders. Working together, all of these individuals form a team for the rendering of legal services.

The legal community also includes individuals who work for the courts. These consist of judges, magistrates, commissioners, referees, court clerks, court reporters, and bailiffs or court deputies. Many government agencies are also part of the legal community.

Members of the legal community are all bound by various ethical standards. They must maintain confidentiality, act competently, follow rules concerning attorney fees, keep client funds in a trust account, avoid conflicts of interest, communicate through attorneys, and act diligently in representing clients.

Terms to Remember

lawyer
attorney
bar examination
paralegal
legal assistant
legal technician
Certified Legal Assistant
precedent
stare decisis
citation
law clerk
legal memoranda
judge
quasi-judicial officers
court clerk
court reporter
bailiff
administrative hearing
fiduciary relationship
disbarment
trust account
commingling

Questions for Review

1. Describe the paralegal profession.
2. What skills does a paralegal need?
3. What kinds of tasks can a paralegal not do?
4. Compare and contrast a paralegal and an attorney.

5. Describe the different personnel found in law offices.
6. Describe the various professionals who work in the courts.
7. List the professional organizations for attorneys and paralegals.
8. What are the advantages or disadvantages to individual paralegals and to the paralegal profession in general in allowing paralegals to join professional organizations of attorneys, such as the ABA and ATLA?
9. Describe the ethical rules that govern attorneys.
10. Describe the ethical rules that govern paralegals.

Questions for Analysis

1. Review the classified section of your local newspaper for job advertisements for attorneys, paralegals, and legal secretaries. Compare and contrast the job requirements and skills.
2. Review the Ethical Choices box in this chapter. Which NALA and/or NFPA rules or guidelines apply to the situation? Review your state's ethical rules. (*Hint*: Go to www.nala.org/ and find a link.) Which of those rules apply?

Assignments and Projects

1. Is there a local paralegal association for your area? If so, contact it and obtain information about that organization.
2. Interview a paralegal. What type of work does that person do? What skills are required for his or her job?
3. Read the case *Bush v. Gore* in Appendix VII. Summarize the court's opinion.

CHAPTER 2

THE AMERICAN LEGAL SYSTEM

Technology Corner

Web Address	Name of Site
www.supremecourtus.gov	U.S. Supreme Court
www.senate.gov/	U.S. Senate
www.house.gov/	U.S. House of Representatives
lcweb.loc.gov/global/explore.html	Library of Congress Internet Resource Page
www.gpo.gov	U.S. Government Printing Office
www.findlaw.com	FindLaw
www.lawlinks.com	LawLinks.com
www.alllaw.com/law/federal_law/	All Law.com—Federal Law
www.ncsconline.org/	National Center for State Courts
www.courts.net	Courts.Net
www.lib.lsu.edu/gov/fedgov.html	Louisiana State University—U.S. Federal Government Agencies Directory

CASE FILE: THE EBERHARDT MATTERS

Rory Eberhardt had a promising career as a software engineer in Silicon Valley. Recently, however, his life began to fall apart. Eberhardt had a substantial portion of his assets in technology stocks. Unfortunately, the market took a downturn and Eberhardt found himself in financial troubles. Creditors were hounding him and his home was near foreclosure. During this time, Eberhardt was approached by an individual who wanted Eberhardt to sell him certain "trade secret" information belonging to Eberhardt's employers. Because of his financial difficulties, Eberhardt succumbed to temptation and sold information. Eberhardt's employers discovered what he had done. As a result, they have sued him for damages. They have also reported him to the local police department, which is recommending that theft charges be filed against him. Additionally, the material that Eberhardt sold was classified information used in connection with a government contract. Eberhardt is afraid that treason charges might also be filed. To compound Eberhardt's problems, his wife has filed for divorce. Eberhardt contacted a law firm to represent him, but he could not afford their retainer. At this point he has decided to represent himself. He knows he must file documents in court in connection with the civil cases against him. He also hopes to be able to discuss the criminal cases with the prosecutor and try to plea bargain.

SEC. 2-1 INTRODUCTION

Rory Eberhardt knew that one of the first things he had to do was to obtain the phone number and addresses of the court and the prosecutor. He decided to start with the telephone book. The telephone book, however, listed multiple courts, all at different addresses. There were county municipal courts, county superior courts, county traffic courts, U.S. district courts, and state district courts of appeal. Eberhardt had no idea what happens at any of these courts. Which courts heard cases such as the one filed by his employer? Which courts heard divorce cases? Where did criminal cases take place? Eberhardt was even confused about the prosecutor's office. The telephone book listed addresses for a county prosecutor and for a federal prosecutor. Whom should he contact? The only thing that Eberhardt could tell about the courts and the prosecutors was that they all seemed to be part of some government. Some were county, some were state, and some appeared to be federal.

Although he might have been confused, Rory Eberhardt did make an important observation about our legal system. The operation of a legal system in America is primarily the function of government. Any legal system must have a mechanism for making laws, enforcing laws, and interpreting and applying laws to real-life factual situations. In the American legal system, these functions are performed primarily by different branches of our government. This process is complicated in the United States because of the way government is structured. In the United States, citizens are regulated primarily by two separate governments, federal and state, each maintaining separate and largely independent legal systems. Local governments also play a role, but most often local and state governments work together in the operation of one combined legal system. In this chapter you will see how the various branches of our federal government act to create a legal system. You will also see how the various branches of state and local governments act to create a different legal system.

SEC. 2–2 FEDERALISM—THE RELATIONSHIP BETWEEN FEDERAL AND STATE GOVERNMENT

federalism
A system of government in which the people are regulated by both federal and state governments.

In the United States, government operates under a principle called **federalism**. Federalism means that citizens are regulated by two separate governments, federal and state. The federal government has *limited* power over all fifty states. State governments have power only within their state boundaries. These powers are also limited in the sense that states cannot make laws that conflict with the laws of the federal government.

POWERS OF THE FEDERAL GOVERNMENT

The power of the federal government to regulate and make laws is not unlimited. It has only that power given to it in the U.S. Constitution. In particular, express powers are granted to the U.S. Congress in Article I, Section 8 of the Constitution, which gives Congress the right to regulate such matters as the coining of money, the post office, and the military. See the following box for a more complete list of these powers. Along with the express powers given in this section, the federal government is also given the power to make all laws that are necessary and proper for executing any of the stated powers. See Appendix I for a copy of the U.S. Constitution.

While Article I, Section 8 grants powers to the federal government, those powers are limited by the Tenth Amendment to the Constitution, which provides: "The powers not delegated to the United States by the Constitution, nor prohib-

Powers Granted to the U.S. Congress (Article 1, Section 8 of the United States Constitution)

1. Collect taxes; pay debts; provide for the common defense and welfare of the United States
2. Borrow money
3. Regulate commerce with foreign nations and between states
4. Establish rules for naturalization and bankruptcy
5. Coin and regulate money
6. Punish counterfeiting
7. Establish post offices
8. Establish copyright and patents
9. Establish inferior courts
10. Define and punish piracies and felonies on the high seas
11. Declare war
12. Raise and support armies
13. Maintain a navy
14. Regulate land and naval forces
15. Call forth a militia
16. Organize, arm, and train a militia
17. Govern the area to become the seat of federal government
18. Make all laws necessary to carry out the foregoing powers

ited by it to the States, are reserved to the States respectively, or to the people." As a practical matter, however, the power of the federal government to pass laws and to regulate is extensive. This is partly due to the Supreme Court's broad interpretation of the power to regulate interstate commerce, which is not limited to laws dealing with trade between the states. Congress has used this section to justify numerous laws, including civil rights legislation, where almost any connection with interstate activity exists. The case of *Katzenbach v. McClung* illustrates this.

Katzenbach, Acting Attorney General, v. McClung

379 U.S. 294 (1964)

Ollie's Barbeque, a restaurant, discriminated against African Americans. The U.S. Attorney General sued it under the Federal Civil Rights Act of 1964. Eventually the case reached the U.S. Supreme Court. The Civil Rights Act, which formed the basis of this case, applied only to businesses involved in interstate commerce. Ollie's was a small family-run restaurant. The record showed that part of the supplies bought by the restaurant were transported in interstate commerce, even though the restaurant operated solely within a state. The Supreme Court had to decide whether it should apply the Civil Rights Act to Ollie's. To do this, the Court had to decide whether Ollie's Barbeque was involved in interstate commerce. The following is an excerpt from this case. The U.S. Attorney General was seeking an injunction against the owner, ordering him to stop violating provisions of the Civil Rights Act of 1964. The Civil Rights Act is referred to as "the Act" by the Court. In this case, the Court makes numerous references to other cases it had decided. One case, Heart of Atlanta Motel v. United States, *was decided at the same time as this case. Other cases were decided much earlier.*

OPINION

THE FACTS

Ollie's Barbecue is a family-owned restaurant in Birmingham, Alabama, specializing in barbecued meats and homemade pies, with a seating capacity of 220 customers. It is located on a state highway 11 blocks from Interstate 1 and a somewhat greater distance from railroad and bus stations. The restaurant caters to a family and white-collar trade with a take-out service for Negroes. It employs 36 persons, two-thirds of whom are Negroes.

In the 12 months preceding the passage of the Act [Title II of the Civil Rights Act of 1964], the restaurant purchased locally approximately $150,000 worth of food, $69,683 or 46% of which was meat that it bought from a local supplier who had procured it from outside the State. The District Court expressly found that a substantial portion of the food served in the restaurant had moved in interstate commerce. The restaurant has refused to serve Negroes in its dining accommodations since its original opening in 1927 and since July 2, 1964, it has been operating in violation of the Act. The court below concluded that if it were required to serve Negroes it would lose a substantial amount of business.

The basic holding in *Heart of Atlanta Motel* answers many of the contentions made by the appellees. There we outlined the overall purpose and operational plan of Title II and found it a valid exercise of the power to regulate interstate commerce insofar as it requires hotels and motels to serve transients without regard to their race or color. In this case we consider its application to restaurants which serve food, a substantial portion of which has moved in commerce.

THE ACT AS APPLIED

Section 201(a) of Title II commands that all persons shall be entitled to the full and equal enjoyment of the goods and services of any place of public accommodation without discrimination or segregation on the ground of race, color, religion, or national origin; and § 201(b) defines establishments as places of public accommodation if their operations affect commerce or segregation by them is supported by state action. Sections 201(b)(2) and (c) place any "restaurant . . . principally engaged in selling food for consumption on the premises" under the Act "if . . . it serves or offers to serve interstate travelers or a substantial portion of the food which it serves . . . has moved in commerce."

Ollie's Barbecue admits that it is covered by these provisions of the Act. The Government makes no contention that the discrimination at the restaurant was supported by the State of Alabama. There is no claim that interstate travelers frequented the restaurant. The sole question, therefore, narrows down to whether Title II, as applied to a restaurant annually receiving about $70,000 worth of food which has moved in commerce, is a valid exercise of the power of Congress. The Government has contended that Congress had ample basis upon which to find that racial discrimination at restaurants which receive from out of state a substantial portion of the food served does, in fact, impose commercial burdens of national magnitude upon interstate commerce. The appellees' major argument is direct to this premise. They urge that no such basis existed. It is to that question that we now turn.

The Power of Congress to Regulate Local Activities

Article I, § 8, cl. 3, confers upon Congress the power "to regulate Commerce . . . among the several States" and clause 18 of the same Article grants it the power "to make all Laws which shall be necessary and proper for carrying into Execution the foregoing Powers . . ." This grant, as we have pointed out in *Heart of Atlanta Motel*, "extends to those activities intrastate which so affect interstate commerce, or the exertion of the power of Congress over it, as to make regulation of them appropriate means to the attainment of a legitimate end, the effective execution of the granted power to regulate interstate commerce." *United States v. Wrightwood Dairy Co.*, 315 U.S. 110, 119 (1942). Much is said about a restaurant business being local but "even if appellee's activity be local and though it may not be regarded as commerce, it may still, whatever its nature, be reached by Congress if it exerts a substantial economic effect on interstate commerce. . . ." *Wickard v. Filburn*, 317 U.S. 111, 125 (1942). The activities that are beyond the reach of Congress are "those which are completely within a particular State, which do not affect other States, and with which it is not necessary to interfere, for the purpose of executing some of the general powers of the government." *Gibbons v. Ogden*, 9 Wheat. 1, 195 (1824). This rule is as good today as it was when Chief Justice Marshall laid it down almost a century and a half ago.

This Court had held time and again that this power extends to activities of retail establishments, including restaurants, which directly or indirectly burden or obstruct interstate commerce.

Confronted as we are with the facts laid before Congress, we must conclude that it had a rational basis for finding that racial discrimination in restaurants had a direct and adverse effect on the free flow of interstate commerce. Insofar as the sections of the Act here relevant are concerned, §§ 201(b)(2) and (c), Congress prohibited discrimination only in those establishments having a close tie to interstate commerce, *i.e.*, those, like McClungs, serving food that has come from out of the State. We think in so doing that Congress acted well within its power to protect and foster commerce in extending the coverage of Title II only to those restaurants offering to serve interstate travelers or serving food, a substantial portion of which has moved in interstate commerce.

The power of Congress in this field is broad and sweeping; where it keeps within its sphere and violates no express constitutional limitation it has been the rule of this Court, going back almost to the founding days of the Republic, not to interfere. The Civil Rights Act of 1964, as here applied, we find to be plainly appropriate in the resolution of what the Congress found to be a national commercial problem of the first magnitude. We find it in no violation of any express limitations of the Constitution and we therefore declare it valid.

The judgment is therefore reversed.

CASE ANALYSIS

1. This case deals with the validity of Title II of the Civil Rights Act of 1964. Why is the Court discussing the interstate commerce clause of the U.S. Constitution?
2. Does a small family-owned business really have a substantial impact on interstate commerce? Why or why not?
3. Do you think that, under the interstate commerce clause, Congress would have the power to make a law that makes it a crime for a person to possess a gun in areas around schools? See *United States v. Lopez*, 514 U.S. 549, 115 S.Ct. 1624, 131 L.Ed. 2d 626 (1995). The court's syllabus is reprinted in Appendix VII.
4. Could Congress make it a federal crime for any business to discriminate because of race, sex, national origin, or age? Why or why not?

Powers of the State Government

preemption
A doctrine referring to the right of the federal government to be the exclusive lawmaker in certain areas.

States have very broad powers to make laws that apply within the state boundaries. They cannot, however, make laws that conflict with federal laws in areas that are **preempted** by the federal government. *Preempted* means that the federal government has the exclusive right to regulate a particular subject area. Some subject areas that cannot be regulated by states are set out in Article I, Section 10 of the Constitution, and include such activities as entering into treaties, coining money, and passing ***ex post facto*** laws. *Ex post facto* laws make a person criminally responsible for an act that was committed before the act was made a crime. Areas that are commonly regulated by states include criminal conduct, contractual relationships, civil tort liability, and forms of business such as partnerships and corporations.

ex post facto
"After the fact"; refers to laws that impose criminal responsibility for acts that were not crimes at the time the acts occurred.

Exclusive and Concurrent Powers of Federal and State Governments

The power of government to regulate is sometimes called **jurisdiction**. When the power to regulate a certain area belongs solely or exclusively to either the federal or state government, we say that the government has **exclusive jurisdiction**. For example, only the federal government has the power to regulate the coining of money. States cannot have their own currency. However, some areas can be regulated by both the federal and state government. A clear example of this is income tax. The federal government has the power to impose an individual income tax on its citizens. But states also have that power. When both state and federal governments have the right to regulate an area, those governments have **concurrent jurisdiction**. Another example of concurrent jurisdiction involves some of our criminal laws. For example, all states have laws making kidnapping a crime. If the victim is taken across a state line, the act is also a federal crime. The state government has the general right to make and enforce criminal laws, such as those against kidnapping. While the federal government does not have general power to make criminal laws, it does have the power to make all laws necessary to enforce its express powers. Making laws against kidnapping and taking the victim across state lines is considered to be within the power of the federal government under its express power to regulate interstate commerce. (The U.S. Supreme Court has given a broad interpretation to the term *commerce*, not limiting it to normal commercial transactions.) Thus, both state and federal governments have the power to make such laws.

jurisdiction
The power or authority to act in a certain situation; the power of a court to hear cases and render judgments.

exclusive jurisdiction
The sole power or authority to act in a certain situation.

concurrent jurisdiction
A term that describes situations where more than one entity has the power to regulate or act.

Conflicts between Federal and State Law—The Supremacy Clause

Because there are areas of concurrent jurisdiction, conflicts often exist between laws made by the federal government and laws made by states. Where a conflict exists, then federal law controls. This is because of the **supremacy clause** of the Constitution (Article VI): "This Constitution, and the Laws of the United States which shall be made in Pursuance thereof . . . shall be the supreme Law of the Land; and the Judges in every State shall be bound thereby, any Thing in the Constitution or Laws of any State to the Contrary notwithstanding." When a state passes a law that conflicts with the Constitution, the U.S. Supreme Court has the power to declare that state law unconstitutional and unenforceable.

supremacy clause
The clause in the U.S. Constitution making the Constitution and the laws of the United States the supreme law of the land.

However, the fact that both state and federal governments regulate an area does not necessarily create a conflict. For example, if a defendant kidnaps a victim and takes the victim across state lines, both federal and state laws are violated and the defendant could be tried in either the state or federal court (or both!) for the crime. Furthermore, in this situation the federal court has no priority over the state court.

Texas v. Johnson

491 U.S. 397 (1989)

In this case, defendant Johnson was found guilty in a Texas trial court for violating a state law making it a crime to burn the American flag. He did this at the Republican national convention held in Texas. Johnson appealed and eventually the U.S. Supreme Court granted certiorari. When the court grants certiorari, it is agreeing to hear the case. The question was whether burning the flag was protected under the First Amendment right to free speech. The Supreme Court held that it was. The following is an excerpt from the Supreme Court decision.

OPINION

After publicly burning an American flag as a means of political protest, Gregory Lee Johnson was convicted of desecrating a flag in violation of Texas law. This case presents the question whether his conviction is consistent with the First Amendment. We hold that it is not.

While the Republican National Convention was taking place in Dallas in 1984, respondent Johnson participated in a political demonstration dubbed the "Republican War Chest Tour." As explained in literature distributed by the demonstrators and in speeches made by them, the purpose of this event was to protest the policies of the Reagan administration and of certain Dallas-based corporations. The demonstrators marched through the Dallas streets, chanting political slogans and stopping at several corporate locations to stage "die-ins" intended to dramatize the consequences of nuclear war. On several occasions they spray-painted the walls of buildings and overturned potted plants, but Johnson himself took no part in such activities. He did, however, accept an American flag handed to him by a fellow protestor who had taken it from a flagpole outside one of the targeted buildings.

Of the approximately 100 demonstrators, Johnson alone was charged with a crime. The only criminal offense with which he was charged was the desecration of a venerated object in violation of Tex. Penal Code Ann. § 42.09(a)(3) (1959).[1] After trial, he was convicted, sentenced to one year in prison, and fined $2,000. The Court of Appeals for the Fifth District of Texas at Dallas affirmed Johnson's conviction, 706 S.W.2d 120 (1986), but the Texas Court of Criminal Appeals reversed, 755 S.W.2d 92 (1988), holding that the State could not, consistent with the First Amendment, punish Johnson for burning the flag in these circumstances.

Johnson was convicted of flag desecration for burning the flag rather than for uttering insulting words. This fact somewhat complicates our consideration of his conviction under the First Amendment. We must first determine whether Johnson's burning of the flag constituted expressive conduct, permitting him to invoke the First Amendment in challenging his conviction . . . .

The First Amendment literally forbids the abridgment only of "speech," but we have long recognized that its protection does not end at the spoken or written word. While we have rejected the "view that an apparently limitless variety of conduct can be labeled 'speech' whenever the person engaging in the conduct intends thereby to express an idea," *United States v. O'Brien*, 391 U.S. 367 (1968) at 376, we have acknowledged that conduct may be "sufficiently imbued with elements of communication to fall within the scope of the First and Fourteenth Amendments," *Spence v. Washington*, 418 U.S. 405 (1974) at 409.

The State of Texas conceded for the purposes of its oral argument in this case that Johnson's conduct was expressive conduct and this concession seems to us as prudent. Johnson burned an American flag as part—indeed, as the culmination—of a political demonstration that coincided with the convening of the Republican Party and its renomination of Ronald Reagan for President. The expressive, overtly political nature of this conduct was both intentional and overwhelmingly apparent. At his trial, Johnson explained his reasons for burning the flag as follows: "The American flag was burned as Ronald Reagan was being renominated as President. And a more powerful statement of symbolic speech, whether you agree with it or not, couldn't have been made at that time." In these circumstances, Johnson's burning of the flag was conduct sufficiently imbued with elements of communication to implicate the First Amendment.

[1]Texas Penal Code Ann. § 42.09 (1989) provides in full:
"§ 42.0. Desecration of Venerated Object
(a) A person commits an offense if he intentionally or knowingly desecrates:
(1) a public monument;
(2) a place of worship or burial; or
(3) a state or national flag.
(b) For purposes of this section, 'desecrate' means deface, damage, or otherwise physically mistreat in a way that the actor knows will seriously offend one or more persons likely to observe or discover his action.
(c) An offense under this section is a Class A misdemeanor."

If there is a bedrock principle underlying the First Amendment, it is that the government may not prohibit the expression of an idea simply because society finds the idea itself offensive or disagreeable.

In short, nothing in our precedents suggests that a State may foster its own view of the flag by prohibiting expressive conduct relating to it.

Johnson was convicted for engaging in expressive conduct. The State's interest in preventing breaches of the peace does not support his conviction because Johnson's conduct did not threaten to disturb the peace. Nor does the State's interest in preserving the flag as a symbol of nationhood and national unity justify his criminal conviction for engaging in political expression. The judgment of the Texas Court of Criminal Appeals is therefore affirmed.

CASE ANALYSIS

1. What gave the U.S. Supreme Court, a federal court, the right to review a Texas state law?
2. Suppose that Johnson had burned a Texas state flag instead of the U.S. flag.
   a. Would the U.S. Supreme Court have jurisdiction to hear the case?
   b. If the Supreme Court did hear the case, do you think the decision would have been any different?
3. In which court was Johnson first tried? List all of the courts that heard this case in the order in which they heard it.

In determining whether a conflict between state and federal law exists, a particular problem arises in the area of criminal procedure. If an individual is arrested for a state crime, such as murder, that individual is tried in the state court; the states are allowed to formulate their own procedural rules for this process. Furthermore, each state has a state constitution, which, like the federal Constitution, affords certain rights to individuals within that state. On the other hand, the U.S. Constitution affords criminal defendants certain basic rights not only in federal cases but also in state cases. In federal cases, those rights are specifically spelled out in the Bill of Rights (specifically the Fourth, Fifth, Sixth, and Eighth Amendments). These specific amendments were intended to apply only in federal cases. In state criminal cases, each state is bound to follow the Fourteenth Amendment to the Constitution, which provides in part: "nor shall any State deprive any person of life, liberty, or property, without due process of law, . . ." The U.S. Constitution does not set out specific rights that states must follow. Rather, it sets out a minimum standard that all states must follow, *i.e.*, due process. What this minimum standard means in specific instances has been decided by the Supreme Court. But remember that it is a *minimum* standard. States can grant more rights to criminal defendants and not be in conflict with federal law, because the federal government has not preempted this area of law. On the other hand, once the Supreme Court sets forth a specific minimum standard, states cannot take away a right. States are allowed to make laws in this area as long as those laws do not violate due process. Just because the state and federal rules *differ* does not automatically mean a conflict exists.

A POINT TO REMEMBER

When conflicts exist between federal and state laws, the federal law controls. However, not all differences result in a conflict. Do not assume that federal laws will always control. In determining whether a difference results in a conflict, first determine whether the federal law has preempted the area of law. If it has, then the federal law controls. If the federal law has not preempted the area, then you must read the federal law carefully to determine its meaning. You must understand the federal law to determine whether a conflict exists in the state law.

Blanton v. North Las Vegas

489 U.S. 538 (1989)

The following Supreme Court case and state statute deal with the issue of the right to jury trials for misdemeanors that carry a sentence of less than six months in jail. Read them both and see if any conflict exists.

OPINION

The issue in this case is whether there is a constitutional right to a trial by jury for persons charged under Nevada law with driving under the influence of alcohol (DUI). Nev. Rev. Stat. § 484.3792(1) (1987). We hold that there is not.

DUI is punishable by a minimum term of two days' imprisonment and a maximum term of six months' imprisonment. § 484.3792(1)(a)(2). Alternatively, a trial court may order the defendant "to perform 48 hours of work for the community while dressed in distinctive garb which identifies him as [a DUI offender]." The defendant also must pay a fine ranging from $200 to $1,000. § 484.3792(1)(a)(3). In addition, the defendant automatically loses his driver's license for 90 days, § 483.460(1)(c), and he must attend, at his own expense, an alcohol abuse education course. § 484.3792(1)(a)(1). Repeat DUI offenders are subject to increased penalties.

Petitioners Melvin R. Blanton and Mark D. Fraley were charged with DUI in separate incidents. Neither petitioner had a prior DUI conviction. The North Las Vegas, Nevada, Municipal Court denied their respective pretrial demands for a jury trial. On appeal, the Eighth Judicial District Court denied Blanton's request for a jury trial but, a month later, granted Fraley's. Blanton then appealed to the Supreme Court of Nevada, as did respondent city of North Las Vegas with respect to Fraley. After consolidating the two cases along with several others raising the same issue, the Supreme Court concluded that the federal Constitution does not guarantee a right to a jury trial for a DUI offense because the maximum term of incarceration is only six months and the maximum possible fine is $1,000. 103 Nev. 623, 748 P.2d 494 (1987). We granted certiorari to consider whether petitioners were entitled to a jury trial, and now affirm.

It has long been settled that "there is a category of petty crimes or offenses which is not subject to the Sixth Amendment jury trial provision." *Duncan v. Louisiana,* 391 U.S. 145, 159 (1968); *see also District of Columbia v. Clawans,* 300 U.S. 617, 624 (1937); *Callan v. Wilson,* 127 U.S. 540, 557 (1888).[2]

[A] defendant is entitled to a jury trial whenever the offense for which he is charged carries a maximum authorized prison term of greater than six months. . . . The possibility of a sentence exceeding six months, we determined, is "sufficiently severe by itself" to require the opportunity for a jury trial. As for a prison term of six months or less, we recognized that it will seldom be viewed by the defendant as "trivial or 'petty.'" But we found that the disadvantages of such a sentence, "onerous though they may be, may be outweighed by the benefits that result from speedy and inexpensive nonjury adjudications."

Applying these principles here, it is apparent that petitioners are not entitled to a jury trial.

[2]The Sixth Amendment right to a jury trial applies to the states through the Fourteenth Amendment (*Duncan v. Louisiana,* 391 U.S. 145 [1968]).

Now consider the following two statutes from another state, California.

"Except as authorized by law, every person who possesses not more than one avoirdupois ounce of marijuana, other than concentrated cannabis, is guilty of a misdemeanor and shall be punished by a fine of not more than one hundred dollars ($100)." (Calif. Health & Safety Code § 11357[b])

"No person can be convicted of a public offense unless by verdict of a jury, accepted and recorded by the court, by a finding of the court in a case where a jury has been waived, or by a plea of guilty." (Calif. Penal Code § 689)

CASE ANALYSIS

1. Is there a conflict between California Penal Code § 689 and the rule stated by the Supreme Court that jury trials are not required where the penalty is less than six months' incarceration?
2. Suppose that Jensen is charged with violating California Health and Safety Code § 11357 for possessing less than one ounce of marijuana. Assuming that this is a public offense and assuming that the maximum sentence is a fine of $100, is Jensen entitled to a jury trial to determine guilt? Why or why not?

Read the following case excerpt and see if you were right.

Tracy v. Municipal Court

22 Cal. 3d 760, 150 Cal. Rptr. 785, 587 P.2d 227 (1978)

OPINION

In these consolidated appeals we must decide whether indigent defendants charged with possession of less than an ounce of marijuana (Health & Safe. Code, § 11357, sub d.[B] are entitled to the assistance of appointed counsel and to trial by jury. In separate mandate proceedings the superior court held that such defendants are entitled to those rights on the ground that the offense is a misdemeanor and not an infraction. It entered judgments accordingly. The municipal courts and the People appeal. Despite the fact that the offense is punishable only by a fine of $100, we conclude that the Legislature meant precisely what it said when it designated the offense a misdemeanor and therefore the judgments must be affirmed.

A person charged with a misdemeanor is entitled to the assistance of court-appointed counsel (Pen. Code § 686) and to a trial by jury (Pen. Code § 689). Since these rights are afforded by statute we express no opinion on the constitutional issues raised by the parties. The judgments are affirmed.

SEC. 2–3 THE FEDERAL GOVERNMENT AND THE LEGAL SYSTEM

The federal government consists of three branches—executive, legislative, and judicial, each branch playing a distinct role in our legal system.

EXECUTIVE BRANCH

The executive branch of the federal government consists of the president and the president's cabinet. It also consists of the various law enforcement or police agencies. The primary responsibility of this branch is the execution and enforcement of the laws. You can read more about the executive branch on the White House Web site at www.whitehouse.gov.

LEGISLATIVE BRANCH

The legislative branch of our government consists of the House of Representatives (whose members are called *representatives* or *congressmen* and *congresswomen*) and the Senate (whose members are called *senators*). Representatives and senators are elected by citizens of the district and state which they represent and serve two- and six-year terms, respectively. The primary responsibility of this branch within our legal system is to make laws. The laws that it makes are called *statutes* or *codes*. You can read more about the legislative branch of the federal government at the House Web site, www.house.gov/, and the Senate Web site, www.senate.gov/.

Judicial Branch

The judicial branch of the federal government consists of the various federal courts. Briefly, the role of the judicial branch is to apply or interpret the laws in relationship to actual cases. Because the judicial branch is the heart of legal practice, the structure and operation of our federal courts is examined in more detail later.

Sec. 2–4 STATE GOVERNMENTS AND THE LEGAL SYSTEM

bicameral
A term that describes a legislature consisting of two houses.

Each state has the power to determine the type of government that exists within its boundaries. State governments are not a part of the federal government. Each state has its own separate and largely independent government. However, for the most part, state governments are patterned after the federal government. All states have an executive branch, normally headed by a governor; all states have a legislative branch, normally consisting of a **bicameral**, or two-house, structure; and all states have a judicial branch, consisting of various courts. The role of each branch of the state government in its legal system also parallels that of the federal government.

Although we are also subject to control by local governments, they do not operate completely independent legal systems. Rather, local and state governments usually combine to form one integrated state system. For example, a state may pass a law making drunk driving a crime. A drunk driver might be apprehended by a city police officer, who is enforcing the state law. The drunk driver might then be tried in a state court but be prosecuted by a county prosecutor. All these agents of local and state governments are working together. Each state government maintains a Web site. To find the site for your state, try the following address: www.state.[insert your state's postal abbreviation]us/ (for example, www.state.ny.us/ for New York).

The case of *Heath v. Alabama*, which follows, discusses the relationship of the states to one another and to the federal government.

Heath v. Alabama

474 U.S. 82 (1985)

In the following case, the petitioner, Larry Gene Heath, hired two individuals to kidnap and murder his wife. She was kidnapped in Alabama, taken across state lines, and murdered in Georgia. Heath pleaded guilty to a noncapital murder charge in Georgia. He was later charged with capital murder in Alabama. Heath claimed that the double jeopardy clause of the Fifth Amendment prohibited the action in Alabama. The Supreme Court had to decide whether double jeopardy applied or whether Heath could be prosecuted in two states for the same act. The Court held that since the two states were separate sovereigns and each has its own laws and own interests, each could prosecute the criminal case without any violation of double jeopardy. The following is an excerpt from that opinion.

OPINION

The question before the Court is whether the Double Jeopardy Clause of the Fifth Amendment bars Alabama from trying petitioner for the capital offense of murder during a kidnapping after Georgia has convicted him of murder based on the same homicide. In particular, this case presents the issue of the applicability of the dual sovereignty doctrine to successive prosecutions by two States.

In August 1981, petitioner, Larry Gene Heath, hired Charles Owens and Gregory Lumpkin to kill his wife, Rebecca Heath, who was then nine months pregnant, for a sum of $2,000. On the morning of August 31, 1981, petitioner left the Heath residence in Russell County, Alabama, to meet with Owens and Lumpkin in Georgia, just over the Alabama border from the Heath home. Petitioner led them back to the Heath residence, gave them the keys to the Heaths' car and house, and left the premises in his girlfriend's truck. Owens and Lumpkin then kidnapped Rebecca Heath from her home. The Heath car, with Rebecca Heath's body inside, was later found on the side of a road in Troup County, Georgia. The cause of death was a gunshot wound in the head. The estimated time of death and the distance from the Heath residence to the spot where Rebecca Heath's body was found are consistent with the theory that the murder took place in Georgia, and respondent does not contend otherwise.

Georgia and Alabama authorities pursued dual investigations in which they cooperated to some extent. On September 4, 1981, petitioner was arrested by Georgia authorities. Petitioner waived his *Miranda* rights and gave a full confession admitting that he had arranged his wife's kidnapping and murder. In November 1981, the grand jury of Troup County, Georgia, indicted petitioner for the offense of "malice" murder under Ga. Code Ann. § 16-5-1 (1984). Georgia then served petitioner with notice of its intention to seek the death penalty, citing as the aggravating circumstance the fact that the murder was "caused and directed" by petitioner. On February 10, 1982, petitioner pleaded guilty to the Georgia murder charge in exchange for a sentence of life imprisonment, which he understood could involve his serving as few as seven years in prison.

On May 5, 1982, the grand jury of Russell County, Alabama, returned an indictment against petitioner for the capital offense of murder during a kidnapping. Before trial on this indictment, petitioner entered a plea of former jeopardy under the Alabama and United States Constitutions, arguing that his conviction and sentence in Georgia barred his prosecution in Alabama for the same conduct.

After a hearing, the trial court rejected petitioner's double jeopardy claims. It assumed, *arguendo*, that the two prosecutions could not have been brought in succession by one State but held that double jeopardy did not bar successive prosecutions by two different States for the same act.

On January 12, 1983, the Alabama jury convicted petitioner of murder during a kidnapping in the first degree. After a sentencing hearing, the jury recommended the death penalty. Pursuant to Alabama law, a second sentencing hearing was held before the trial judge. The judge accepted the jury's recommendation, finding that the sole aggravating factor, [which was] that the capital offense was "committed while the defendant was engaged in the commission of a kidnapping," outweighed the sole mitigating factor, that the "defendant was convicted of the murder of Rebecca Heath in the Superior Court of Troup County, Georgia, . . . and received a sentence of life imprisonment in that court." *See* Ala. Code §§ 13A-5-49(4), 13A-5-50 (1982).

On appeal, the Alabama Court of Criminal Appeals rejected petitioner's plea of former jeopardy under the Alabama and United States Constitutions and affirmed his conviction. Petitioner then filed a petition for writ of certiorari with the Alabama Supreme Court, stating the sole issue to be "whether or not the prosecution in the State of Alabama constituted double jeopardy in violation of the 5th Amendment of the United States Constitution." The court granted his petition, and unanimously affirmed his conviction.

The Alabama Supreme Court noted that "[prosecutions] under the laws of separate sovereigns do not improperly subject an accused twice to prosecutions for the same offense," citing this Court's cases applying the dual sovereignty doctrine. The court acknowledged that this Court has not considered the applicability of the dual sovereignty doctrine to successive prosecutions by different States. It reasoned, however, that "[if] for double jeopardy purposes, Alabama is considered to be a sovereign entity *vis-à-vis* the federal government then surely it is a sovereign entity *vis-à-vis* the State of Georgia."

Petitioner sought a writ of certiorari from this Court, raising double jeopardy claims. No due process objections were asserted. We granted certiorari limited to the question whether petitioner's Alabama conviction was barred by this Court's decision in *Brown v. Ohio*, 432 U.S. 161 (1977), and requested the parties to address the question of the applicability of the dual sovereignty doctrine to successive prosecutions by two States. For the reasons explained below, we affirm the judgment of the Alabama Supreme Court.

Successive prosecutions are barred by the Fifth Amendment only if the two offenses for which the defendant is prosecuted are the "same" for double jeopardy purposes. Respondent does not contravene petitioner's contention that the offenses of "murder during a kidnapping" and "malice murder," as construed by the courts of Alabama and Georgia respectively, may be considered greater and lesser offenses and, thus, the "same" offense under *Brown v. Ohio, supra,* absent operation of the dual sovereignty principle. We therefore assume, *arguendo*, that, had these offenses arisen under the laws of one State and had petitioner been separately prosecuted for both offenses in that State, the second conviction would have been barred by the Double Jeopardy Clause.

The sole remaining question upon which we granted certiorari is whether the dual sovereignty doctrine permits successive prosecutions under the laws of different States which otherwise would be held to "subject [the defendant] for the same offence to be twice put in jeopardy." U.S. Const., amend. V. Although we have not previously so held, we believe the answer to this query is inescapable. The dual sovereignty doctrine, as originally articulated and consistently applied by this Court, compels the conclusion that successive prosecutions by two States for the same conduct are not barred by the Double Jeopardy Clause.

The dual sovereignty doctrine is founded on the common-law conception of crime as an offense against the sovereignty of the government. When a defendant in a single act violates the "peace and dignity" of two sovereigns by breaking the laws of each, he has committed two distinct "offences." *United States v. Lanza,* 260 U.S. 377, 382 (1922). As the Court explained in *Moore v. Illinois,* 14 How. 13, 19 (1852), "[an] offence, in its legal signification, means the transgression of a law." Consequently, when the same act transgresses the laws of two sovereigns, "it cannot be truly averred that the offender has been twice punished for the same offence; but only that by one act he has committed two offences, for each of which he is justly punishable."

In applying the dual sovereignty doctrine, then, the crucial determination is whether the two entities that seek successively to prosecute a defendant for the same course of conduct can be termed separate sovereigns. This determination turns on whether the two entities draw their authority to punish the offender from distinct sources of power. Thus, the Court has uniformly held that the States are separate sovereigns with respect to the Federal Government because each State's power to prosecute is derived from its own "inherent sovereignty," not from the Federal Government.

The States are no less sovereign with respect to each other than they are with respect to the Federal Government. Their powers to undertake criminal prosecutions derive from separate and independent sources of power and authority originally belonging to them before admission to the Union and preserved to them by the Tenth Amendment. The States are equal to each other "in power, dignity and authority, each competent to exert that residuum of sovereignty not delegated to the United States by the Constitution itself." *Coyle v. Oklahoma,* 221 U.S. 559, 567 (1911). Thus, "[each] has the power, inherent in any sovereign, independently to determine what shall be an offense against its authority and to punish such offenses, and in doing so each 'is exercising its own sovereignty, not that of the other.'" *United States v. Wheeler,* 435 U.S. 313, 320.

In those instances where the Court has found the dual sovereignty doctrine inapplicable, it has done so because the two prosecuting entities did not derive their powers to prosecute from independent sources of authority. Thus, the Court has held that successive prosecutions by federal and territorial courts are barred because such courts are creations emanating from the same sovereignty. Similarly, municipalities that derive their power to try a defendant from the same organic law that empowers the State to prosecute are not separate sovereigns with respect to the State. These cases confirm that it is the presence of independent sovereign authority to prosecute, not the relation between States and the Federal Government in our federalist system, that constitutes the basis for the dual sovereignty doctrine.

It is axiomatic that "[in] America, the powers of sovereignty are divided between the government of the Union, and those of the States. They are each sovereign, with respect to the objects committed to it, and neither sovereign with respect to the objects committed to the other." *McCulloch v. Maryland,* 4 Wheat. 316, 410 (1819). It is as well established that the States, "as political communities, [are] distinct and sovereign, and consequently foreign to each other." *Bank of United States v. Daniel,* 12 Pet. 32, 54 (1838). *See also Skiriotes v. Florida,* 313 U.S. at 77; *Coyle v. Oklahoma,* 221 U.S. at 567. The Constitution leaves in the possession of each State "certain exclusive and very important portions of sovereign power." *The Federalist* No. 9, p. 55 (J. Cooke ed., 1961). Foremost among the prerogatives of sovereignty is the power to create and enforce a criminal code. To deny a State its power to enforce its criminal laws because another State has won the race to the courthouse would be a shocking and untoward deprivation of the historic right and obligation of the States to maintain peace and order within their confines. Such a deprivation of a State's sovereign powers cannot be justified by the assertion that under "interest analysis" the State's legitimate penal interests will be satisfied through a prosecution conducted by another State. A State's interest in vindicating its sovereign authority through enforcement of its laws by definition can never be satisfied by another State's enforcement of its own laws. Just as the Federal Government has the right to decide that a state prosecution has not vindicated a violation of the "peace and dignity" of the Federal Government, a State must be entitled to decide that a prosecution by another State has not satisfied its legitimate sovereign interest. In recognition of this fact, the Court consistently has endorsed the principle that a single act constitutes an "offence" against each sovereign whose laws are violated by that act. The Court has always understood the words of the Double Jeopardy Clause to reflect this fundamental principle, and we see no reason why we should reconsider that understanding today.

The judgment of the Supreme Court of Alabama is affirmed.

It is so ordered.

CASE ANALYSIS

1. What is meant by dual sovereignty?
2. Where do states obtain their power to prosecute individuals for crimes?
3. Is there dual sovereignty between a city and the state in which it is located? Explain.

SEC. 2–5 THE COURTS AND THEIR ROLES

The everyday practice of law often revolves around the courts. As mentioned previously, different court systems exist for the federal government and for each state. Although state court systems are separate from the federal courts, most states pattern their court system after the federal system. All legal professionals should be familiar with both the federal court system and their own state court system.

THE FEDERAL COURT SYSTEM

The U.S. Constitution provides for the establishment of a Supreme Court and such inferior courts as Congress may establish. Today the federal court structure consists of trial courts (primarily the U.S. district courts, but also various specialized courts), appellate courts (U.S. courts of appeals), and one Supreme Court, as shown in Figure 2–1. The courts are arranged much like a pyramid, with the Supreme Court at the top, the courts of appeals in the middle, and the district courts at the bottom.

FEDERAL DISTRICT COURTS

Structure

In exercising its power to establish lower courts, Congress divided the United States into more than ninety separate districts and established federal district courts for each of the districts. These districts obviously do not parallel state lines, and many states have more than one district located within their boundaries. In addition, district courts exist for the District of Columbia, Guam, Puerto Rico, the Virgin Islands, and the Northern Mariana Islands. The number of judges assigned to each district depends on the needs of the individual courts and is influenced by the population of the district as well as by the federal budget. The U.S. district courts are referred to by the geographical region they serve—for example, the U.S. District Court for the Northern District of California.

Function

original jurisdiction
The power to first hear a case; court of original jurisdiction is where trial takes place.

trial
The open-court process where all parties present evidence, question witnesses, and generally put their case before the court.

District courts are courts of **original jurisdiction**, or more simply, trial courts. Original jurisdiction means the power to hear and determine the case first. Most federal cases begin in a district court. If you work in a law office, you will probably deal with the district court (or its state equivalent) more than the higher courts. If the case is in a federal court, this is the court where you will file papers in connection with lawsuits and where trials will take place. The role of a trial court, such as the federal district court, is to resolve disputes between parties. The process of resolving a dispute often involves a proceeding called a **trial**. At a trial, the parties present evidence supporting their position. Presiding over the trial is a judge who rules on all legal issues that arise during the trial. Depending on the kind of case, a jury may also be involved in the trial process. A jury is responsible for resolving questions or disputes regarding factual matters. If there is no jury, then the judge determines these issues.

Resolving disputes in a trial court involves two separate steps. First, the court must determine the facts of the dispute, then it must apply the appropriate law to those facts. For example, consider a criminal case in which the defendant, Davidson,

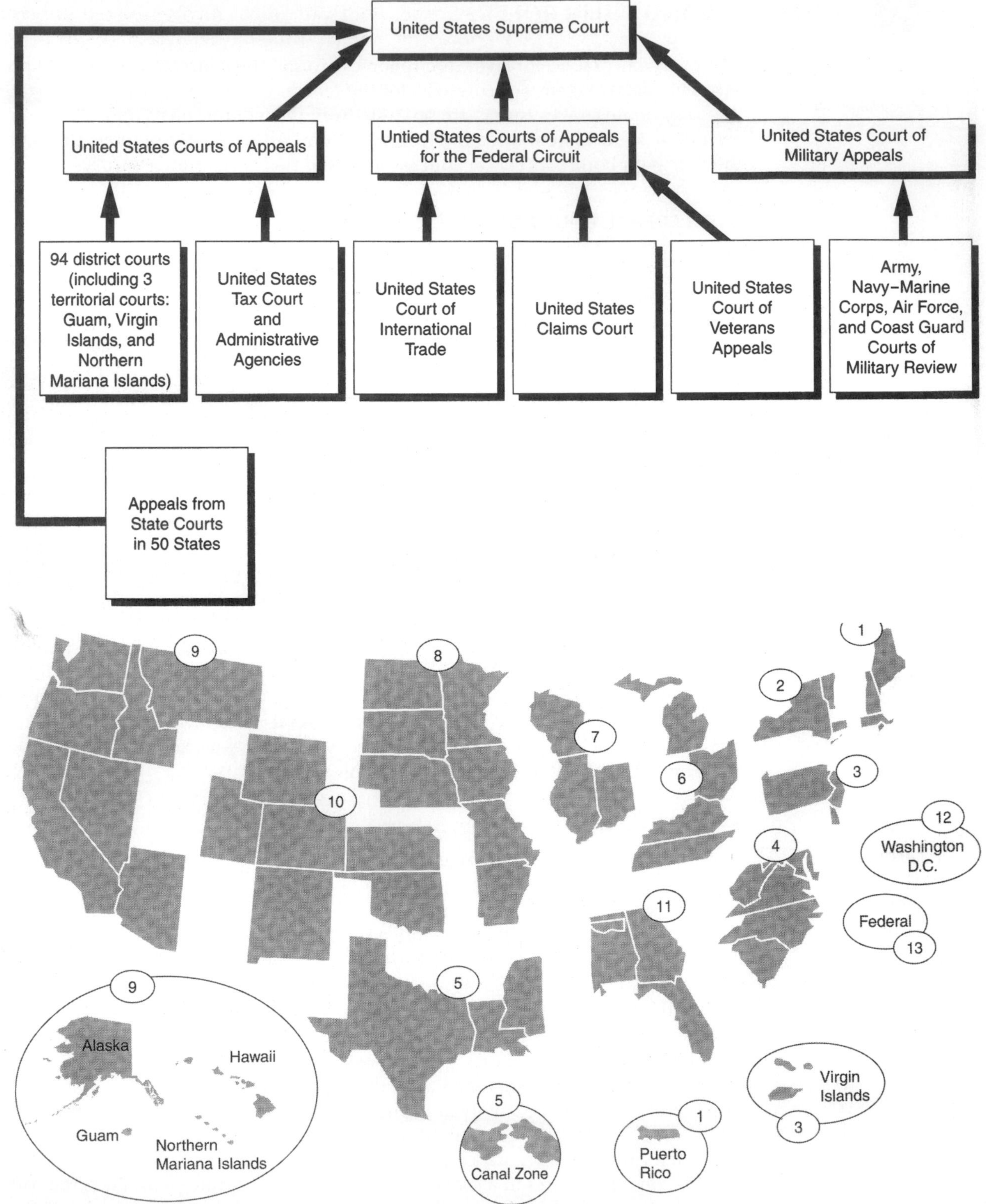

FIGURE 2–1 The federal court systems and the U.S. Supreme Court.

is accused of kidnapping. The prosecutor's case might revolve around the testimony of an eyewitness, Walters, who positively identifies Davidson as the perpetrator. But Davidson claims he is innocent and that at the time of the crime he was with his girlfriend The girlfriend **corroborates**, or supports, Davidson's claim. The trial court must to determine the true facts. Is Walters mistaken or lying? Or are Davidson and his girlfriend lying? These factual questions are determined by the **trier of fact**—the jury or, if there is no jury, the judge.

corroborate
To support the statements of another.

trier of fact
In a trial, the one who determines the true facts; either a jury or, if a case is tried without a jury, the judge.

Once a factual dispute is resolved, the trial court must apply the proper law to the facts. These laws are found in codes and cases decided by higher courts. For example, if the trial court finds that Walters was telling the truth, then it looks to the federal law regarding kidnapping.

Since the U.S. district courts are *federal* courts, they are allowed to hear cases only where **federal jurisdiction** exists. In criminal cases, federal jurisdiction exists when the crime is a violation of federal law. In civil cases, federal jurisdiction usually occurs when the dispute revolves around the U.S. Constitution or some federal law. Federal jurisdiction also exists when the United States is a party to the action or when the action is between residents of different states and the amount in dispute exceeds $75,000. This is known as **diversity of citizenship**. The concept of jurisdiction in civil actions is discussed more fully in Chapter 13.

federal jurisdiction
The power of the federal courts to hear a case.

diversity of citizenship
A basis for federal court jurisdiction where the plaintiff and defendant are residents of different states and the amount in controversy exceeds $75,000.

> **ETHICAL CHOICES**
>
> Assume that you work as a paralegal in a law office that has seven attorneys. While you are having dinner with your spouse in a restaurant, you see an attorney from your law firm having an intimate dinner with a local judge. The judge has been assigned to hear a case that your supervising attorney is handling. The attorney in question has had nothing to do with this case. What do you do?

Special Trial Courts

Certain kinds of federal cases are heard not in the district courts but rather in specialized trial courts, which include the following:

- Bankruptcy courts—Courts handling bankruptcy proceedings
- U.S. Court of International Trade—A court that handles cases involving international trade and custom duties
- U.S. Claims Court—A court that hears suits against the federal government for money damages in numerous civil matters
- U.S. Tax Court—A court that handles controversies between taxpayers and the Internal Revenue Service (IRS) involving underpayment of federal taxes.

Federal Appellate Courts

Structure

Thirteen federal jurisdictions make up the intermediate appellate level of the federal court system. The United States is divided into twelve separate geographical appellate areas, called *circuits*. In addition, one appellate court has national jurisdiction to hear appeals in patent, copyright, and trademark cases and all appeals from the U.S. Claims Court and the U.S. Court of International Trade. Cases heard in a court of appeals are normally heard by a three-judge panel that decides the case by a majority vote. Occasionally a case is heard by the entire panel of justices assigned to the particular circuit court. When this happens, the court is said to be sitting ***en banc***. The total number of justices assigned to each court of appeals differs from court to court and depends on caseload and budgetary constraints. A U.S. court of appeals is referred to by number, for example, the U.S. Court of Appeals for the Sixth Circuit (or sometimes the Sixth Circuit Court of Appeals).

en banc
A term that describes the entire panel of judges on a court hearing a case.

Function

appellate jurisdiction
The power of a court to review what happened in a lower court.

As the name suggests, a U.S. court of appeals is primarily a court of **appellate jurisdiction**, that is, a court of review. In our legal system, parties in most cases have the right to have an appellate court review what happened at the trial court. The one major exception to this occurs in criminal trials, where the prosecutor cannot appeal a *not guilty* verdict because of the constitutional right against double jeopardy. The purpose of appellate review is to guarantee that parties receive a fair trial. The appellate judges do not review the case to see if they agree with the outcome at the trial court. They review what happened at the trial court to make sure that the trial was fair.

In Chapter 1 you learned about two types of personnel who work in the trial courts—court clerks and court reporters. These individuals keep records that are important to the appeals process. The court clerk keeps copies of all documents filed in the case, as well as keeping original pieces of evidence introduced at trial. The court reporter keeps a verbatim report of the oral proceedings at court. When a case is appealed, each of these individuals prepares a transcript. A **clerk's transcript** contains copies of documents filed in the case. The **reporter's transcript** is a verbatim report of what everyone said in court. These transcripts are sent to the appellate court so that the judges can review what happened in the trial court. The attorneys in the case also submit written **appellate briefs**, documents that explain the factual and legal basis for and against the appeal.

clerk's transcript
A record containing copies of documents filed in connection with a court proceeding; prepared by a court clerk.

reporter's transcript
A verbatim record of the oral proceedings in court; prepared by the court reporter.

appellate brief
A written document containing factual and legal contentions; prepared by attorneys dealing with an appeal in a case.

jury instructions
The directions read to the jury by the judge; they simplify the law applicable to the case.

In exercising its appellate jurisdiction, the court examines the record to determine whether any *substantial* legal errors have been committed that denied the appealing party (the *appellant*) a fair trial. *Legal errors* consist of a number of different things, including erroneously admitted or excluded evidence and improper jury instructions. **Jury instructions** are statements of law read to the jury at the end of the trial. These statements of law must relate to the evidence that has been admitted at trial. If the court of appeals determines that the trial judge made an error in interpreting or applying the law, the court of appeals would be justified in reversing the decision if it found that the error was significant. Obviously, not every legal error results in a miscarriage of justice, and, therefore, not every legal error results in a reversal of a case. Suppose that in a murder trial there are ten eyewitnesses to a murder. After having nine of the witnesses recount their version of the homicide, a tired prosecutor asks the question, "Now isn't it true, Mr. Witness, that on the date in question you saw the defendant shoot and kill the victim?" If defense counsel objects to the question as leading, and her objection is overruled by an even more tired and bored judge, a legal error would be committed. Does that mean, however, that even though nine witnesses correctly and legally identified a certain defendant as the perpetrator, that the case should be reversed because a legal error had been committed? Such a result would not make sense and would probably be a miscarriage of justice in itself. Only when a legal error results in justice not being served will the appellate court reverse a decision.

affirm
To uphold; used in connection with an appeal to uphold the lower court's decision.

reverse
To change.

remand
To send back.

In reviewing a case, the appellate court can do a number of different things. Obviously, it can **affirm** or uphold the trial court's decision (which, incidentally, is what happens in most cases). Just as obviously, it can **reverse**, or change, the trial court's decision. It can also reverse and **remand**, that is, send the case back to the trial court for a retrial with instructions regarding procedure to be followed. For example, suppose Phillips has been found guilty of murder. At the trial, evidence against him consisted of, among other things, an eyewitness and a signed confession. If the appellate court were to find that the confession was illegally obtained in violation of *Miranda* rights, it would probably reverse the conviction. The appellate court would not have to free the defendant, however, where other admissible evidence remained. The appellate court could send the case back to the trial court (*remand* it) with instructions that the illegally obtained confession could not be used in a retrial against the defendant.

A POINT TO REMEMBER

Cases are not retried in the appellate courts. The appellate courts only review what happened at the trial courts to make sure that the parties received a fair trial. Courts of appeals reverse cases only where a substantial error has occurred.

ETHICAL CHOICES

Assume that you work as a paralegal or legal secretary for an attorney who represents your small city. Work for the city constitutes about 50 percent of the practice of your attorney. One of the responsibilities of your office is to draft proposed local ordinances at the request of the city council. You receive a telephone call from the mayor of the city, who tells you that the council is meeting that evening and he wants a draft of a proposed law that would ban all picketing within 200 feet of City Hall. You explain to the mayor that the attorney is out of town for three days. The mayor tells you that he knows that you do all the real work in the law firm and orders you to draft the proposal, adding that if this firm cannot get the job done, the city will have to look for another firm to represent it. You know the proposal would be illegal. What do you do?

THE U.S. SUPREME COURT

Structure

The U.S. Supreme Court, located in Washington, D.C., consists of nine justices, one of whom serves as the chief justice. Usually, when the Court hears cases, all nine of the justices participate in the case, each one having an equal vote in the decision.

Function

The Supreme Court is primarily a court of review that exercises appellate jurisdiction. It hears cases from the lower federal courts. It can also hear cases that originated in the state courts if the case involves a constitutional issue or a question of federal law. If the issues in the case relate only to state law, then the Supreme Court has no authority to hear the case. In most instances, the Supreme Court has discretionary power to review cases. It often exercises that power in cases of major importance or in cases where the lower courts are in disagreement regarding the law to be applied.

petition for writ of certiorari
A document filed with the Supreme Court requesting a hearing.

The Supreme Court cannot hear every case brought to it. Parties desiring a hearing before the Supreme Court usually file a document known as a **petition for writ of certiorari**. In this petition, the parties set out their reasons for requesting a hearing. The Court then votes on whether to grant the hearing. At least four of the justices must vote to hear the case or grant the petition for writ of certiorari. If the Court does grant certiorari, then it considers the merits of the case itself. A majority vote determines the outcome of the case. If the Court does not grant certiorari, the lower court's decision stands. If the Court agrees to hear a case on its merits, its decision is binding on all lower courts in the United States.

While the Supreme Court, like the appellate courts, is primarily a court of review, it has original jurisdiction in certain types of cases. Article III, Section 2, of the U.S. Constitution provides:

> In all cases affecting ambassadors, other public ministers and consuls, and those in which a state shall be a party, the Supreme Court shall have original jurisdiction. In all other cases before mentioned [Art. III Section 2.1] the Supreme Court shall have appellate jurisdiction, both as to law and fact, with such exception, and under such regulations as the Congress shall make.

The Courts and Technology

Like most organizations, the federal courts are affected by technology, especially the Internet. A survey of federal judges in 1997 revealed that more than 80 percent of those who responded used some sort of technology. Telephone conferencing was the most common, but the use of computers in the courtroom during trial was becoming more popular. Today, most courts now have a Web site where the public and attorneys can obtain general information, access court rules and calendars, and, in some instances, download forms. The U.S. Supreme Court Web site can be found at www.supremecourtus.gov/. All other federal courts can be accessed through the Web site of the Federal Judiciary at www.uscourts.gov/.

One important advance in the courts due to technology is the implementation of the Public Access to Court Electronic Records (PACER) system, which allows users to obtain at any time case and docket information from federal appellate, district, and bankruptcy courts. For a small fee, the PACER system offers electronic access to case dockets to retrieve information such as the following:

A listing of all parties and participants, including judges, attorneys, and trustees

A compilation of case-related information such as cause of action, nature of suit, and dollar demand

A chronology of dates of case events entered in the case record

A claims registry

A listing of new cases each day in the bankruptcy court

Appellate court opinions

Judgments or case status

Types of documents filed for certain cases

A POINT TO REMEMBER

The U.S. Supreme Court is the highest court in the nation. When it renders a decision, whether in the exercise of appellate jurisdiction or original jurisdiction, that decision is the final decision in the case.

FEDERAL JUDGES

All federal court judges or justices are appointed by the president, subject to approval by the Senate. The Senate conducts hearings on all individuals nominated by the president in order to assure that only qualified individuals take the bench. Once a person takes the bench as a federal judge, that person serves for life, or until he or she retires from the bench. However, a federal judge can be removed involuntarily through the impeachment process if the judge's misconduct warrants it. The selection process of federal judges was instituted to keep judges free from political influence in rendering their decisions. It does not, however, eliminate the political influence of the selection process. Obviously, presidents are very careful in selecting judges, and in particular Supreme Court justices, who tend to reflect their own moral and philosophical beliefs. In so doing, presidents can leave their mark on the country long after they leave office.

In addition to federal judges, some functions of the district courts are now performed by **magistrates**. Magistrates are appointed by the judges of the district court and must possess the qualifications to serve as a judge. They do such things as issue warrants and hear pretrial motions. Where the parties agree, a magistrate can also serve as the judge for a trial.

magistrate
A judicial officer; federal magistrates are appointed by judges of federal district courts; magistrates have some of the powers of a judge.

STATE COURT SYSTEMS

State court systems are established and organized according to state law. The various state systems resemble the federal system. All states have trial courts and courts of review. Some states, like the federal system, have three tiers of courts: trial courts, intermediate appellate courts, and a court of last review. Other states maintain a two-tiered system of courts: trial courts and one level of appellate courts. The function of trial courts and appellate courts is similar to that of their federal counterparts, although the names of the various courts are often different. For example, trial courts are sometimes called superior courts, municipal courts, circuit courts, city courts, surrogate courts, and even supreme courts. Furthermore, some states have more than one level of trial court.

State Court Judges

The selection of judges in states differs not only from the federal method but also from state to state. The selection processes include partisan elections, nonpartisan elections, and gubernatorial appointments. The selection process might also involve input from special nominating commissions or approval of the state senate.

Featured Web Site: www.uscourts.gov/

This Web site contains extensive information about the federal court system.

Go Online

1. Using the link feature, find out the following:
   a. Which U.S. district court governs your area?
   b. What is the Internet address for that court?
   c. Which appellate circuit court governs your area?
   d. What is the Internet address for that court?
2. Summarize the information on this site about the district courts.

Chapter Summary

The American legal system is operated by and through our government. Just as there are distinct federal and state governments, so also are there different federal and state legal systems. The core of our legal structure is the court systems, which exist for both the federal and state legal systems. The federal courts, and normally also the state courts, consist of a three-tier system: trial courts, appellate courts, and a Supreme Court. The role of the trial courts is to resolve factual disputes and then apply the appropriate law. The role of the appellate courts is to ensure that the parties have a fair hearing at the trial level. The role of the Supreme Court is to resolve disputes among the various appellate courts and to rule on issues of particular importance.

Terms to Remember

federalism
preemption
ex post facto
jurisdiction
exclusive jurisdiction
concurrent jurisdiction
supremacy clause
bicameral
original jurisdiction
trial
corroborate
trier of fact
federal jurisdiction
diversity of citizenship
en banc
appellate jurisdiction
clerk's transcript
reporter's transcript
appellate brief
jury instructions
affirm
reverse
remand
petition for writ of certiorari
magistrate

Questions for Review

1. Explain federalism.
2. Describe the power of the federal government to regulate.
3. Explain the difference between concurrent and exclusive jurisdiction.
4. What is the relevance of the supremacy clause?

5. Describe the federal court system.
6. What is original jurisdiction?
7. What is appellate jurisdiction?

Questions for Analysis

1. Review the box titled "Powers Granted to the U.S. Congress" and consider the following:
   a. Would you expect the lawsuit by Eberhardt's employer to be in state court or federal court?
   b. Would you expect the Eberhardt divorce case to be in state court or federal court?
   c. Would a federal or county prosecutor be handling the Eberhardt theft charges?
   d. Would a federal or county prosecutor be handling a treason case against Eberhardt?
2. Read the hypothetical case in the mock trial in Appendix III. If this happened in your city, which court would have jurisdiction?
3. Review the Ethical Choices boxes in this chapter. Which NALA and/or NFPA rules or guidelines apply to the situations? Review your state's ethical rules. (*Hint*: Go to www.nala.org/ and find a link.) Which of those rules apply?
4. In 1994 a federal law was enacted giving victims of gender-motivated violence (i.e., sexual assault) the right to sue for civil damages. Do you think such a law is constitutional? See the case summary of *U.S. v. Morrison* in Appendix VII.
5. A conflict between state and federal criminal law arose in the case of *United States v. Oakland Cannabis Buyers Cooperative*, found in Appendix VII. Explain how the court resolves the problem.

Assignments and Projects

1. Find the addresses of the nearest U.S. district court and U.S. court of appeals. Which district are you in? Which circuit are you in?
2. Review the *Katzenbach* case. Explain the role of each branch of government in this case.
3. Visit one of your local courts. Write a brief report on what you observed.

CHAPTER 3

LAWS

THEIR SOURCES

3–1 Introduction
3–2 Constitutional Law
3–3 Case Law
3–4 Statutory Law
3–5 Administrative Regulations

Technology Corner

Web Address	Name of Site
www.law.cornell.edu/uscode/	United States Code
http://uscode.house.gov/	United States Code
www.law.cornell.edu/constitution/constitution.overview.html	U.S. Constitution
www.gpo.ucop.edu/search/fedfld.html	Federal Register
www.law.cornell.edu/rules/frcp/	Federal Rules of Civil Procedure
www.findlaw.com/casecode/	FindLaw: Cases and Codes
www.lawsource.com/also/	American Law Sources Online
www.access.gpo.gov/nara/cfr/index.html	Code of Federal Regulations
www.courts.net/	Courts.Net

CASE FILE: *PEOPLE V. HARDTACK*

Officer Harry Hardtack has been a police officer with the Centerville City Police Department for seven years. Recently he was accused of using excessive force in making two separate arrests. In one case he was accused of punching a man who was handcuffed. In another incident he was accused of unnecessarily grabbing a suspect by the throat. As a result, both the county prosecutor and the U.S. Attorney are considering filing criminal charges against Hardtack. He has also been suspended without pay from the police force. He retained Mitchell Bates, an attorney, to represent him.

SEC. 3–1 INTRODUCTION

Michael Bates, the attorney handling the Hardtack matter, must consider a number of different questions, including the following:

1. Did Hardtack use excessive force in making the arrests in question?
2. What are the specific criminal charges facing Hardtack and what type of behavior constitutes a violation of these charges?
3. Under what circumstances can a police department suspend an officer without pay pending an investigation?

These questions can be answered only after the appropriate laws are reviewed.

Laws are categorized according to their source as either constitutional law, case law, statutory law, or administrative rules and regulations. The answers to Bates's questions will not be found in only one source. Bates must review all of these sources to find the laws or rules that apply to Hardtack. Since Hardtack's problems result from an arrest, the laws of arrest must be reviewed. These laws are found in the U.S. Constitution, state constitutions, state and federal cases, and state and federal codes. The criminal charges facing Hardtack can be found in both state and federal codes. State and federal cases, however, interpret these code sections and give us situations where the codes have been applied. Finally, administrative regulations govern Hardtack's relationship with his employer.

In Chapter 2 you saw that separate legal systems exist for federal and state governments and that each branch of government plays a specific role in the legal system. In this chapter you will see that different sources of laws are found in these different legal systems. You will also review the different types of laws generated by the legislative and judicial branches of government.

sources of law
Places where laws are found: constitutions, cases, statutes, and administrative regulations.

Most disputes are controlled by *either* federal or state law. However, in some cases, like that of Hardtack, both federal and state laws must be consulted. Although the substance of state and federal laws differs extensively, the **sources of law** are similar: constitutions, cases, statutes, and administrative regulations.

SEC. 3–2 CONSTITUTIONAL LAW

constitution
A document whose primary purpose is to establish a government and define its powers.

The federal government and each state have **constitutions**—documents whose primary purpose is to establish the government and define its functions and obligations in relationship to the people. The U.S. Constitution establishes and defines the role of the federal government and its relationship to the people of the United

States. Furthermore, the U.S. Constitution applies only to the federal government, unless expressly made applicable to the individual states. Each state constitution establishes and defines the role of state government and its relationship to citizens of that state.

THE FEDERAL CONSTITUTION

The U.S. Constitution was drafted in 1787 and fully ratified by 1790. It established and defined the various departments of our federal government (Articles I, II, and III), as well as describing the role of the federal government *vis-à-vis* that of the states (Article IV). Today the U.S. Constitution contains the original seven basic articles in addition to 27 amendments, which have been adopted over the years. A copy of the U.S. Constitution is found in Appendix I.

The U.S. Constitution serves two functions with respect to our laws. First, as explained in the previous chapter, it establishes the power and limits of the federal government to make other laws (which usually appear in the form of statutory law). Second, the Constitution itself contains various rules or "laws." Many of these are found in the various amendments to the Constitution, including the **Bill of Rights**, the first ten amendments to the U.S. Constitution. Several of these amendments deal with rights that criminal defendants have in our legal system. For example, the Fourth Amendment to the Constitution prohibits the federal government from conducting unreasonable searches and seizures (that is, the law of search and seizure). The Sixth Amendment, among other things, guarantees the right to counsel in criminal cases. Since Hardtack is facing various criminal charges, these amendments have some application to the Hardtack case.

Bill of Rights
The first ten amendments to the Constitution.

The U.S. Constitution is the supreme law of the land. However, if any term in the Constitution is unclear when applied to a factual situation, then it is the job of the U.S. Supreme Court to interpret that term. That interpretation is binding on all lower courts.

STATE CONSTITUTIONS

Each state has its own constitution, which is similar in function to the federal Constitution. Furthermore, state constitutions are often patterned after the federal Constitution and incorporate similar provisions. They are the supreme law for the state whenever a question of state law is in issue.

A POINT TO REMEMBER

The U.S. Constitution as interpreted by the U.S. Supreme Court is the supreme law of the land whenever a federal question is involved. If the question is one of state law, then the state constitution as interpreted by the highest court of the state controls.

SEC. 3-3 CASE LAW

COMMON LAW

common law
A body of law developed through the courts.

precedent
The example set by the decision of an earlier court for similar cases or similar legal questions which arise in later cases.

stare decisis
"It stands decided"; another term for *precedent*.

American law is based primarily on English **common law**, a system in which laws were developed through the courts and through case decisions. The common law was based on the concept of **precedent** or ***stare decisis***. It was *not* based on a set of written laws or rules enacted by the government. In fact, until a factual dispute arose and was resolved in the courts, there was no rule or law that controlled. When parties had a legal problem, their dispute was presented to a judge, who decided the case. The decision then becomes precedent. That is, if the same factual dispute were later presented to another court, the judge would decide it the same way the first judge did. Precedent is also referred to as *stare decisis*, which means "it stands decided." This refers to the fact that a particular factual dispute has been decided in one way by the court, and if the same factual dispute arises again, it must be resolved the same way. Over centuries, the common law developed into an extensive body of law.

CASE LAW—INTERPRETATION OF CONSTITUTIONAL AND STATUTORY LAW

In America, many common-law principles have been written and adopted by state and federal legislatures, and have thus become statutory law. In fact, in our legal system, laws are supposed to be made by the legislature. However, our courts and their decisions still play a vital role in our legal system, and the concept of precedent or *stare decisis* is still applied. One of the court's roles is to interpret and apply laws to factual situations. For an example of how the court does this, read the case of *Koon v. United States*, which follows.

Koon v. United States
Powell v. United States

518 U.S. 81 (1996)

This case concerns the criminal action brought against the police officers in the Rodney King beating. The officers were convicted of criminal charges under the federal civil rights statute. The trial judge then imposed sentence. Under federal law, sentencing must follow certain guidelines established by a special commission created by Congress. These guidelines provide sentencing standards. The trial judge is allowed to depart from these standards only under certain circumstances. In the Koon *case, the trial judge considered various factors and reduced the sentence, departing from the standard sentence. In particular, the trial court considered the effect of the conviction on the officers' employment, the fact that this was a first offense, and the hardship to the officers because of the dual prosecution by both state and federal authorities. The government appealed. The following is the decision of the U.S. Supreme Court regarding the issue. In this opinion, the Court held that the first two factors could not be considered by the trial court in sentencing, because they were already reflected in the sentencing guidelines. The hardship caused by double prosecution could be considered, however. The Supreme Court remanded the case for reevaluation.*

(continued)

OPINION

The petitioners' guilt has been established, and we are concerned here only with the sentencing determinations made by the District Court and Court of Appeals. A sentencing court's decisions are based on the facts of the case, however, so we must set forth the details of the crime at some length.

On the evening of March 2, 1991, Rodney King and two of his friends sat in King's wife's car in Altadena, California, a city in Los Angeles County, and drank malt liquor for a number of hours. Then, with King driving, they left Altadena via a major freeway. King was intoxicated. California Highway Patrol officers observed King's car traveling at a speed they estimated to be in excess of 100 m.p.h. The officers followed King with red lights and sirens activated and ordered him by loudspeaker to pull over, but he continued to drive. The Highway Patrol officers called on the radio for help. Units of the Los Angeles Police Department joined in the pursuit, one of them manned by petitioner Laurence Powell and his trainee, Timothy Wind.

King left the freeway, and after a chase of about eight miles, stopped at an entrance to a recreation area. The officers ordered King and his two passengers to exit the car and to assume a felony prone position—that is, to lie on their stomachs with legs spread and arms behind their backs. King's two friends complied. King, too, got out of the car but did not lie down. Petitioner Stacey Koon arrived, at once followed by Ted Briseno and Roland Solano. All were officers of the Los Angeles Police Department, and as sergeant, Koon took charge. The officers again ordered King to assume the felony prone position. King got on his hands and knees but did not lie down. Officers Powell, Wind, Briseno, and Solano tried to force King down, but King resisted and became combative, so the officers retreated. Koon then fired taser darts (designed to stun a combative suspect) into King.

The events that occurred next were captured on videotape by a bystander. As the videotape begins, it shows that King rose from the ground and charged toward Officer Powell. Powell took a step and used his baton to strike King on the side of his head. King fell to the ground. From the 18th to the 30th second on the videotape, King attempted to rise, but Powell and Wind each struck him with their batons to prevent him from doing so. From the 35th to the 51st second, Powell administered repeated blows to King's lower extremities; one of the blows fractured King's leg. At the 55th second, Powell struck King on the chest, and King rolled over and lay prone. At that point, the officers stepped back and observed King for about 10 seconds. Powell began to reach for his handcuffs. (At the sentencing phase, the District Court found that Powell no longer perceived King to be a threat at this point.)

At one minute, five seconds (1:05) on the videotape, Briseno, in the District Court's words, "stomped" on King's upper back or neck. King's body writhed in response. At 1:07, Powell and Wind again began to strike King with a series of baton blows, and Wind kicked him in the upper thoracic or cervical area six times until 1:26. At about 1:29, King put his hands behind his back and was handcuffed. Where the baton blows fell and the intentions of King and the officers at various points were contested at trial, but, as noted, petitioners' guilt has been established. Powell radioed for an ambulance. He sent two messages over a communications network to the other officers that said "ooops" and "I havent [sic] beaten anyone this bad in a long time." Koon sent a message to the police station that said "Unit just had a big time use of force. . . . Tased and beat the suspect of CHP pursuit big time." King was taken to a hospital where he was treated for a fractured leg, multiple facial fractures, and numerous bruises and contusions. Learning that King worked at Dodger Stadium, Powell said to King: "We played a little ball tonight, didn't we Rodney? . . . You know, we played a little ball, we played a little hardball tonight, we hit quite a few home runs. . . . Yes, we played a little ball and you lost and we won."

Koon, Powell, Briseno, and Wind were tried in state court on charges of assault with a deadly weapon and excessive use of force by a police officer. The officers were acquitted of all charges, with the exception of one assault charge against Powell that resulted in a hung jury. The verdicts touched off widespread rioting in Los Angeles. More than 40 people were killed in the riots, more than 2,000 were injured, and nearly $1 billion in property was destroyed. On August 4, 1992, a federal grand jury indicted the four officers under 18 U.S.C. § 242, charging them with violating King's constitutional rights under color of law. Powell, Briseno, and Wind were charged with willful use of unreasonable force in arresting King. Koon was charged with willfully permitting the other officers to use unreasonable force during the arrest. After a trial in United States District Court for the Central District of California, the jury convicted Koon and Powell but acquitted Wind and Briseno.

The Court of Appeals affirmed petitioners' convictions, but it reversed the District Court's [sentence]. Only the last ruling is before us.

The Sentencing Reform Act of 1984, as amended, 18 U.S.C. § 3551 *et seq.*, 28 U.S.C. §§ 991–998, made far-reaching changes in federal sentencing. Before the Act, sentencing judges enjoyed broad discretion in determining whether and how long an offender should be incarcerated. *Mistretta v. United States*, 488 U.S. 361, 363, 102 L. Ed. 2d 714, 109 S. Ct. 647 (1989). The discretion led to perceptions that "federal judges mete out an unjustifiably wide range of sentences to offenders with similar histories, convicted of similar crimes, committed under similar circumstances." S. Rep. No. 98–225, p. 38 (1983). In response, Congress created the United States Sentencing Commission and charged it with developing a comprehensive set of sentencing guidelines,

28 U.S.C. § 994. The Commission promulgated the United States Sentencing Guidelines, which "specify an appropriate [sentencing range] for each class of convicted persons" based on various factors related to the offense and the offender. United States Sentencing Commission, Guidelines Manual ch. 1, pt. A (Nov. 1995) (1995 USSG). A district judge now must impose on a defendant a sentence falling within the range of the applicable Guideline, if the case is an ordinary one. The Act did not eliminate all of the district court's discretion, however. Acknowledging the wisdom, even the necessity, of sentencing procedures that take into account individual circumstances, Congress allows district courts to depart from the applicable Guideline range if "the court finds that there exists an aggravating or mitigating circumstance of a kind, or to a degree, not adequately taken into consideration by the Sentencing Commission in formulating the guidelines that should result in a sentence different from that described." 18 U.S.C. § 3553(b). To determine whether a circumstance was adequately taken into consideration by the Commission, Congress instructed courts to "consider only the sentencing guidelines, policy statements, and official commentary of the Sentencing Commission." Turning our attention, as instructed, to the Guidelines Manual, we learn that the Commission did not adequately take into account cases that are, for one reason or another, "unusual." 1995 USSG ch. 1, pt. A, intro. comment 4(b). The Introduction to the Guidelines explains: "The Commission intends the sentencing courts to treat each guideline as carving out a 'heartland,' a set of typical cases embodying the conduct that each guideline describes. When a court finds an atypical case, one to which a particular guideline linguistically applies but where conduct significantly differs from the norm, the court may consider whether a departure is warranted." The Commission lists certain factors which never can be bases for departure (race, sex, national origin, creed, religion, socio-economic status, 1995 USSG § 5H1.10; lack of guidance as a youth, § 5H1.12; drug or alcohol dependence, § 5H1.4; and economic hardship, § 5K2.12), but then states that with the exception of those listed factors, it "does not intend to limit the kinds of factors, whether or not mentioned anywhere else in the guidelines, that could constitute grounds for departure in an unusual case." 1995 USSG ch. 1, pt. A., intro. comment 4(b).

The first question is whether the District Court abused its discretion in relying on the collateral employment consequences petitioners would face as a result of their convictions. The District Court stated: "Defendants Koon and Powell will be subjected to a multiplicity of adversarial proceedings. The LAPD Board of Rights will charge Koon and Powell with a felony conviction and, in a quasi-judicial proceeding, will strip them of their positions and tenure. Koon and Powell will be disqualified from other law enforcement careers. In combination, the additional proceedings, the loss of employment and tenure, prospective disqualification from the field of law enforcement, and the anguish and disgrace these deprivations entail, will constitute substantial punishment in addition to any court-imposed sentence. In short, because Koon and Powell are police officers, certain unique burdens flow from their convictions."

We conclude that the District Court abused its discretion by considering petitioners' career loss because the factor, as it exists in these circumstances, cannot take the case out of the heartland of 1992 USSG § 2H1.4. As noted above, 18 U.S.C. § 242 offenses may take a variety of forms, but they must involve willful violations of rights under color of law. Although cognizant of the deference owed to the district court, we must conclude it is not unusual for a public official who is convicted of using his governmental authority to violate a person's rights to lose his or her job and to be barred from future work in that field. Indeed, many public employees are subject to termination and are prevented from obtaining future government employment following conviction of a serious crime, whether or not the crime relates to their employment. Public officials convicted of violating § 242 have done more than engage in serious criminal conduct; they have done so under color of the law they have sworn to uphold. It is to be expected that a government official would be subject to the career-related consequences petitioners faced after violating § 242, so we conclude these consequences were adequately considered by the Commission in formulating § 2H1.4.

We further agree with the Court of Appeals that the low likelihood of petitioners' recidivism was not an appropriate basis for departure. Petitioners were first-time offenders and so were classified in Criminal History Category I. The lower limit of the range for Criminal History Category I is set for a first offender with the lowest risk of recidivism. Therefore, a departure below the lower limit of the guideline range for Criminal History Category I on the basis of the adequacy of criminal history cannot be appropriate. 1992 USSG § 4A1.3. The District Court abused its discretion by considering appellants' low likelihood of recidivism. The Commission took that factor into account in formulating the criminal history category.

The two remaining factors are susceptibility to abuse in prison and successive prosecutions. The District Court did not abuse its discretion in considering these factors. The Court of Appeals did not dispute, and neither do we, the District Court's finding that "the extraordinary notoriety and national media coverage of this case, coupled with the defendants' status as police officers, make Koon and Powell unusually susceptible to prison abuse." Petitioners' crimes, however brutal, were by definition the same for purposes of sentencing law as those of any other police officers convicted

(continued)

under 18 U.S.C. § 242 of using unreasonable force in arresting a suspect, sentenced under § 2H1.4, and receiving the upward adjustments petitioners received. Had the crimes been still more severe, petitioners would have been assigned a different base offense level or received additional upward adjustments. Yet, due in large part to the existence of the videotape and all the events that ensued, "widespread publicity and emotional outrage . . . have surrounded this case from the outset," which led the District Court to find petitioners "particularly likely to be targets of abuse during their incarceration." The District Court's conclusion that this factor made the case unusual is just the sort of determination that must be accorded deference by the appellate courts.

As for petitioners' successive prosecutions, it is true that consideration of this factor could be incongruous with the dual responsibilities of citizenship in our federal system in some instances. Successive state and federal prosecutions do not violate the Double Jeopardy Clause. *Heath v. Alabama*, 474 U.S. 82, 88 L. Ed. 2d 387, 106 S. Ct. 433 (1985). Nonetheless, the District Court did not abuse its discretion in determining that a "federal conviction following a state acquittal based on the same underlying conduct . . . significantly burdened the defendants." The state trial was lengthy, and the toll it took is not beyond the cognizance of the District Court.

The goal of the Sentencing Guidelines is, of course, to reduce unjustified disparities and so reach towards the evenhandedness and neutrality that are the distinguishing marks of any principled system of justice. In this respect, the Guidelines provide uniformity, predictability, and a degree of detachment lacking in our earlier system. This too must be remembered, however. It has been uniform and constant in the federal judicial tradition for the sentencing judge to consider every convicted person as an individual and every case as a unique study in the human failings that sometimes mitigate, sometimes magnify, the crime and the punishment to ensue. We do not understand it to have been the congressional purpose to withdraw all sentencing discretion from the United States District Judge. Discretion is reserved within the Sentencing Guidelines, and reflected by the standard of appellate review we adopt.

The Court of Appeals erred in finding that victim misconduct did not justify the departure and that susceptibility to prison abuse and the burdens of successive prosecutions could not be relied upon. Those sentencing determinations were well within the sound discretion of the District Court. The District Court did abuse its discretion in relying on the other two factors: career loss and low recidivism risk. When a reviewing court concludes that a district court based a departure on both valid and invalid factors, a remand is required unless it determines the district court would have imposed the same sentence absent reliance on the invalid factors. As the District Court here stated that none of the four factors standing alone would justify the three-level departure, it is not evident that the court would have imposed the same sentence if it had relied only on susceptibility to abuse in prison and the hardship of successive prosecutions. The Court of Appeals should therefore remand the case to the District Court. The judgment of the Court of Appeals is affirmed in part and reversed in part, and the case is remanded for further proceedings consistent with this opinion.

It is so ordered.

CASE ANALYSIS

1. What law is the court interpreting here? Be specific.
2. What was the factual controversy in this case?
3. Would this case have any applicability in determining whether Hardtack used excessive force? Explain.

Case Law—The Power to Invalidate Statutory Law

Because the federal Constitution is the supreme law of the land, neither the federal legislature nor state legislatures can enact any legislation that contradicts the provisions of the U.S. Constitution. One of the fundamental questions related to the court's ability to interpret laws is the authority of the courts to examine the validity or constitutionality of various laws passed by federal and state legislatures. The Supreme Court decided very early that it had the power to strike down laws that conflicted with the Constitution. To this date, this is one of the important roles played by our courts. To see how the Court considers the constitutionality of a statute, read the Supreme Court case of *Tennessee v. Garner*, which follows.

Tennessee v. Garner

471 U.S. 1 (1985)

This case arose after a young burglary suspect was shot and killed by a police officer while attempting to flee the scene of the crime. He was not armed. The father of the victim filed a civil lawsuit against the police officer and the state of Tennessee. The officer was acting in accordance with a state law that authorized the use of deadly force under this circumstance. At trial, the court found in favor of all defendants. The Court of Appeals reversed, stating that the use of force in this case violated the U.S. Constitution because it was unreasonable. The state of Tennessee petitioned the U.S. Supreme Court for a review.

The following is the opinion of the Supreme Court, in which the Court agreed with the Court of Appeals, stating that the use of force in making an arrest must be reasonable. The use of deadly force is generally limited to situations in which the perpetrator posed an immediate and serious threat to those around him. In reaching its decision the Court explores the history of this area of law, commenting on the common-law rule that one could shoot a fleeing felon and explaining why the rule is no longer appropriate.

OPINION

This case requires us to determine the constitutionality of the use of deadly force to prevent the escape of an apparently unarmed suspected felon. We conclude that such force may not be used unless it is necessary to prevent the escape, and the officer has probable cause to believe that the suspect poses a significant threat of death or serious physical injury to the officer or others.

I

At about 10:45 P.M. on October 3, 1974, Memphis Police Officers Elton Hymon and Leslie Wright were dispatched to answer a "prowler inside call." Upon arriving at the scene they saw a woman standing on her porch and gesturing toward the adjacent house. She told them she had heard glass breaking and that "they" or "someone" was breaking in next door. While Wright radioed the dispatcher to say that they were on the scene, Hymon went behind the house. He heard a door slam and saw someone run across the backyard. The fleeing suspect, who was appellee-respondent's decedent, Edward Garner, stopped at a 6-foot-high chain link fence at the edge of the yard. With the aid of a flashlight, Hymon was able to see Garner's face and hands. He saw no sign of a weapon, and, though not certain, was "reasonably sure" and "figured" that Garner was unarmed. He thought Garner was 17 or 18 years old and about 5'5" or 5'7" tall. While Garner was crouched at the base of the fence, Hymon called out "police, halt" and took a few steps toward him. Garner then began to climb over the fence. Convinced that if Garner made it over the fence he would elude capture, Hymon shot him. The bullet hit Garner in the back of the head. Garner was taken by ambulance to a hospital, where he died on the operating table. Ten dollars and a purse taken from the house were found on his body.

In using deadly force to prevent the escape, Hymon was acting under the authority of a Tennessee statute. The statute provides that "[if], after notice of the intention to arrest the defendant, he either flees or forcibly resists, the officer may use all the necessary means to effect the arrest." Tenn. Code Ann. § 40-7-108 (1982).

The incident was reviewed by the Memphis Police Firearms Review Board and presented to a grand jury. Neither took any action.

Garner's father then brought this action in the Federal District Court for the Western District of Tennessee, seeking damages under 42 U.S.C. § 1983 for asserted violations of Garner's constitutional rights. The complaint alleged that the shooting violated the Fourth, Fifth, Sixth, Eighth, and Fourteenth Amendments of the United States Constitution. It named as defendants Officer Hymon, the Police Department, its Director, and the Mayor and city of Memphis. After a 3-day bench trial, the District Court entered judgment for all defendants. It dismissed the claims against the Mayor and the Director for lack of evidence. It then concluded that Hymon's actions were authorized by the Tennessee statute, which in turn was constitutional. Hymon had employed the only reasonable and practicable means of preventing Garner's escape.

The Court of Appeals for the Sixth Circuit affirmed with regard to Hymon, finding that he had acted in good-faith reliance on the Tennessee statute and was therefore within the scope of his qualified immunity. It remanded for reconsideration of the possible liability of the city, however, in light of *Monell v. New York City Dept. of Social Services*, 436 U.S. 658 (1978), which had come down after the District

(continued)

Court's decision. The District Court was directed to consider whether the use of deadly force and hollow point bullets in these circumstances was constitutional.

The District Court concluded that *Monell* did not affect its decision. It found that the statute, and Hymon's actions, were constitutional.

The Court of Appeals reversed and remanded. It reasoned that the killing of a fleeing suspect is a "seizure" under the Fourth Amendment, and is therefore constitutional only if "reasonable." The Tennessee statute failed as applied to this case because it did not adequately limit the use of deadly force by distinguishing between felonies of different magnitudes—"the facts, as found, did not justify the use of deadly force under the Fourth Amendment." Officers cannot resort to deadly force unless they "have probable cause . . . to believe that the suspect [has committed a felony and] poses a threat to the safety of the officers or a danger to the community if left at large."

The State of Tennessee, which had intervened to defend the statute, appealed to this Court. The city filed a petition for certiorari. We noted probable jurisdiction in the appeal and granted the petition.

. . . II

Whenever an officer restrains the freedom of a person to walk away, he has seized that person. *United States v. Brignoni-Ponce*, 422 U.S. 873, 878 (1975). While it is not always clear just when minimal police interference becomes a seizure, there can be no question that apprehension by the use of deadly force is a seizure subject to the reasonableness requirement of the Fourth Amendment.

A

A police officer may arrest a person if he has probable cause to believe that person committed a crime. *United States v. Watson*, 423 U.S. 411 (1976). Petitioners and appellant argue that if this requirement is satisfied the Fourth Amendment has nothing to say about how that seizure is made. This submission ignores the many cases in which this Court, by balancing the extent of the intrusion against the need for it, has examined the reasonableness of the manner in which a search or seizure is conducted. It is plain that reasonableness depends on not only when a seizure is made, but also how it is carried out. *United States v. Ortiz*, 422 U.S. 891, 895 (1975); *Terry v. Ohio*, 392 U.S. 1, 28–29 (1968).

B

The balancing process demonstrates that, notwithstanding probable cause to seize a suspect, an officer may not always do so by killing him. The intrusiveness of a seizure by means of deadly force is unmatched. The suspect's fundamental interest in his own life need not be elaborated upon. The use of deadly force also frustrates the interest of the individual, and of society, in judicial determination of guilt and punishment. Against these interests are ranged governmental interests in effective law enforcement. It is argued that overall violence will be reduced by encouraging the peaceful submission of suspects who know that they may be shot if they flee. Effectiveness in making arrests requires the resort to deadly force, or at least the meaningful threat thereof. "Being able to arrest such individuals is a condition precedent to the state's entire system of law enforcement." Brief for Petitioners 14.

Without in any way disparaging the importance of these goals, we are not convinced that the use of deadly force is a sufficiently productive means of accomplishing them to justify the killing of nonviolent suspects. The use of deadly force is a self-defeating way of apprehending a suspect and so setting the criminal justice mechanism in motion. If successful, it guarantees that that mechanism will not be set in motion.

The use of deadly force to prevent the escape of all felony suspects, whatever the circumstances, is constitutionally unreasonable. It is not better that all felony suspects die than that they escape. Where the suspect poses no immediate threat to the officer and no threat to others, the harm resulting from failing to apprehend him does not justify the use of deadly force to do so. It is no doubt unfortunate when a suspect who is in sight escapes, but the fact that the police arrive a little late or are a little slower afoot does not always justify killing the suspect. A police officer may not seize an unarmed, nondangerous suspect by shooting him dead. The Tennessee statute is unconstitutional insofar as it authorizes the use of deadly force against such fleeing suspects.

It is not, however, unconstitutional on its face. Where the officer has probable cause to believe that the suspect poses a threat of serious physical harm, either to the officer or to others, it is not constitutionally unreasonable to prevent escape by using deadly force. Thus, if the suspect threatens the officer with a weapon or there is probable cause to believe that he has committed a crime involving the infliction or threatened infliction of serious physical harm, deadly force may be used if necessary to prevent escape, and if, where feasible, some warning has been given. As applied in such circumstances, the Tennessee statute would pass constitutional muster.

III

A

It is insisted that the Fourth Amendment must be construed in light of the common-law rule, which allowed the use of whatever force was necessary to effect the arrest of a fleeing felon, though not a misdemeanant.

Most American jurisdictions also imposed a flat prohibition against the use of deadly force to stop a fleeing misdemeanant, coupled with a general privilege to use such force to stop a fleeing felon.

The State and city argue that because this was the prevailing rule at the time of the adoption of the Fourth Amendment and for some time thereafter, and is still in force in some States, use of deadly force against a fleeing felon must be "reasonable." It is true that this Court has often looked to the common law in evaluating the reasonableness, for Fourth Amendment purposes, of police activity. On the other hand, it "has not simply frozen into constitutional law those law enforcement practices that existed at the time of the Fourth Amendment's passage." *Payton v. New York*, 445 U.S. 573, 591 (1980). Because of sweeping change in the legal and technological context, reliance on the common-law rule in this case would be a mistaken literalism that ignores the purposes of a historical inquiry.

B

It has been pointed out many times that the common-law rule is best understood in light of the fact that it arose at a time when virtually all felonies were punishable by death. "Though effected without the protections and formalities of an orderly trial and conviction, the killing of a resisting or fleeing felon resulted in no greater consequences than those authorized for punishment of the felony of which the individual was charged or suspected." American Law Institute, Model Penal Code § 3.07, Comment 3, p. 56 (Tentative Draft No. 8, 1958) (hereinafter Model Penal Code Comment). Courts have also justified the common-law rule by emphasizing the relative dangerousness of felons.

Neither of these justifications makes sense today. Almost all crimes formerly punishable by death no longer are or can be. And while in earlier times the gulf between the felonies and the minor offenses was broad and deep, today the distinction is minor and often arbitrary. Many crimes classified as misdemeanors, or nonexistent, at common law are now felonies. These changes have undermined the concept, which was questionable to begin with, that use of deadly force against a fleeing felon is merely a speedier execution of someone who has already forfeited his life. They have also made the assumption that a "felon" is more dangerous than a misdemeanant untenable. Indeed, numerous misdemeanors involve conduct more dangerous than many felonies.

There is an additional reason why the common-law rule cannot be directly translated to the present day. The common-law rule developed at a time when weapons were rudimentary. Deadly force could be inflicted almost solely in a hand-to-hand struggle during which, necessarily, the safety of the arresting officer was at risk. Handguns were not carried by police officers until the latter half of the last century. *See* L. Kennett & J. Anderson, *The Gun in America*, 150–151 (1975). Only then did it become possible to use deadly force from a distance as a means of apprehension. As a practical matter, the use of deadly force under the standard articulation of the common-law rule has an altogether different meaning—the harsher consequences—now than in past centuries. *See* Wechsler & Michael, *A Rationale for the Law of Homicide*: I, 37 Colum. L. Rev. 701, 741 (1937).

One other aspect of the common-law rule bears emphasis. It forbids the use of deadly force to apprehend a misdemeanant, condemning such action as disproportionately severe. In short, though the common-law pedigree of Tennessee's rule is pure on its face, changes in the legal and technological context mean the rule is distorted almost beyond recognition when literally applied.

IV

The District Court concluded that Hymon was justified in shooting Garner because state law allows, and the Federal Constitution does not forbid, the use of deadly force to prevent the escape of a fleeing felony suspect if no alternative means of apprehension is available. This conclusion made a determination of Garner's apparent dangerousness unnecessary. The court did find, however, that Garner appeared to be unarmed, though Hymon could not be certain that was the case. Restated in Fourth Amendment terms, this means Hymon had no articulable basis to think Garner was armed.

In reversing, the Court of Appeals accepted the District Court's factual conclusions and held that "the facts, as found, did not justify the use of deadly force." We agree. Officer Hymon could not reasonably have believed that Garner—young, slight, and unarmed—posed any threat. Indeed, Hymon never attempted to justify his actions on any basis other than the need to prevent an escape. The District Court stated in passing that "[the] facts of this case did not indicate to Officer Hymon that Garner was 'non-dangerous.'" This conclusion is not explained, and seems to be based solely on the fact that Garner had broken into a house at night. However, the fact that Garner was a suspected burglar could not, without regard to the other circumstances, automatically justify the use of deadly force. Hymon did not have probable cause to believe that Garner, whom he correctly believed to be unarmed, posed any physical danger to himself or others.

The judgment of the Court of Appeals is affirmed, and the case is remanded for further proceedings consistent with this opinion.

So ordered.

CASE ANALYSIS

1. Which constitutional provisions apply to this case and how do they apply?
2. What statutory law is the Court interpreting here?
3. Did the Court strike down the Tennessee statute? Quote the language that applies.
4. What common-law rule was mentioned by the Court?
5. Why did the Court not follow the common-law rule?
6. In this case, the Court found that the use of deadly force in arresting an individual is a violation of the Fourth Amendment. Hardtack is accused of using excessive force (not deadly). Does this case apply to Hardtack? Why or why not? Quote language in the case that supports your position.

Case Law—The Factual Controversy

All case law originates with a controversy between two or more parties. The parties bring that controversy before a court, asking the court to resolve the dispute. The controversy must be a real, legitimate dispute, not one that is fabricated for the purpose of bringing it to court. It is not the function of the court, nor does the court have authority, to render advisory opinions to individuals.

Once a court is presented with a real, factual dispute, it then has the power to resolve that dispute by applying appropriate legal principles. The power of the court is, however, limited by the facts actually presented. For example, suppose Brady is arrested for drunk driving. After the arrest, police search the entire car, including the trunk, without Brady's permission and without a search warrant. In so doing, they find stolen contraband in the trunk of his car. If Brady should make a motion to prevent the prosecution from using the stolen goods in court, a judge would have to decide whether the search, under the facts presented, was unreasonable and violated the Fourth Amendment. The court could not, however, make a decision regarding facts not part of the actual dispute. In Brady's case, the court could declare that the trunk search was legal under the circumstances, but it could not go on and say that police have the right to search trunks anytime a minor traffic stop has been made. The court could not do that because Brady was not stopped for a minor traffic offense. In other words, the power of the court to render legal decisions is limited by the facts that it is asked to resolve.

Because the law in each case is limited by the facts, the development of a thorough body of law through the case method is a slow process. Nevertheless, many important areas of law, both criminal and civil, have developed, and are continuing to develop in this manner. To see exactly how legal principles develop, a review of the history of the right to an attorney in state criminal cases provides a good example. The basic law involved is the Fourteenth Amendment, which provides that no state may deny an individual due process of law. The question for court interpretation involved the obligation of the state to provide lawyers, free of charge, for indigent defendants.

capital offense
A criminal offense that carries a death penalty.

The first case to be presented to the Supreme Court was the case of *Powell v. Alabama*, 287 U.S. 45 (1932). In this case, a group of young men were being tried for rape, which was at that time a **capital offense**, an offense punishable by death. The defendants were poor and could not afford their own attorney. The state refused to provide them with adequate legal representation for their trial. They were convicted and sentenced to die, then appealed their case to the U.S. Supreme Court. The Court decided that in capital cases, due process (the Fourteenth Amendment) required appointment of counsel by the state. The rule, however, was limited by the facts. The Supreme Court's holding was that in *capital* cases, the state must appoint counsel for indigent defendants. The decision did not apply to *noncapital* offenses. In 1963, more than thirty years later, in the case of *Gideon v. Wainwright*, 372 U.S. 335 (1963), the Court was asked the same question in respect to *felony* cases, that is, whether the state must pay for lawyers for indigent felony defendants. The Court said it did. But this case applied only to felony cases, not misdemeanors or minor infractions. In 1972, the Court was again asked the same question, but in respect to misdemeanor cases. The court decided that for some misdemeanors, the right to court appointed counsel existed. It took the court forty years to be presented with appropriate factual questions to allow it to render a complete analysis of the problem. An excerpt from the Court's decision in *Powell v. Alabama* follows.

Powell v. Alabama

287 U.S. 45 (1932)

OPINION

The petitioners, hereinafter referred to as defendants, are negroes charged with the crime of rape, committed upon the persons of two white girls. The crime is said to have been committed on March 25, 1931. The indictment was returned in a state court of first instance on March 31, and the record recites that on the same day the defendants were arraigned and entered pleas of not guilty. There is a further recital to the effect that upon the arraignment they were represented by counsel. But no counsel had been employed and aside from a statement made by the trial judge several days later during a colloquy immediately preceding the trial, the record does not disclose when, or under what circumstances, an appointment of counsel was made, or who was appointed. During the colloquy referred to, the trial judge, in response to a question, said that he had appointed all the members of the bar for the purpose of arraigning the defendants and then of course anticipated that the members of the bar would continue to help the defendants if no counsel appeared. Upon the argument here both sides accepted that as a correct statement of the facts concerning the matter.

Under Alabama statute the punishment for rape is to be fixed by the jury, and in its discretion may be from ten years imprisonment to death. The juries found defendants guilty and imposed the death penalty upon all. The trial court overruled motions for new trials and sentenced the defendants in accordance with the verdicts.

In this court the judgments are assailed upon the grounds that the defendants, and each of them, were denied due process of law and the equal protection of the laws, in contravention of the Fourteenth Amendment, specifically as follows: (1) they were not given a fair, impartial, and deliberate trial; (2) they were denied the right of counsel, with the accustomed incidents of consultation and opportunity of preparation for trial; and (3) they were tried before juries from which qualified members of their own race were systematically excluded. These questions were properly raised and saved in the courts below.

The only one of the assignments which we shall consider is the second, in respect of the denial of counsel; and it becomes unnecessary to discuss the facts of the case or the circumstances surrounding the prosecution except in so far as they reflect light upon that question.

However guilty defendants might prove to have been, they were, until convicted, presumed to be innocent. It was the duty of the court having their cases in charge to see that they were denied no necessary incident of a fair trial. With any error of the state court involving alleged contravention of the state statutes or constitution we, of course, have nothing to do. The sole inquiry which we are permitted to make is whether the federal Constitution was contravened; and as to that, we confine ourselves, as already suggested, to the inquiry whether the defendants were in substance denied the right of counsel, and if so, whether such denial infringes the due process clause of the Fourteenth Amendment.

It is hardly necessary to say that, the right to counsel being conceded, a defendant should be afforded a fair opportunity to secure counsel of his own choice. Not only was that not done here, but such designation of counsel as was attempted was either so indefinite or so close upon the trial as to amount to a denial of effective and substantial aid in that regard.

The constitution of Alabama provides that in all criminal prosecutions the accused shall enjoy the right to have the assistance of counsel; and a state statute requires the court in a capital case, where the defendant is unable to employ counsel, to appoint counsel for him. The state supreme court held that these provisions had not been infringed, and with that holding we are powerless to interfere. The question, however, which it is our duty, and within our power, to decide, is whether the denial of the assistance of counsel contravenes the due process clause of the Fourteenth Amendment to the federal Constitution.

In the light of the facts outlined—the ignorance and illiteracy of the defendants, their youth, the circumstances of public hostility, the imprisonment and the close surveillance of the defendants by the military forces, the fact that their friends and families were all in other states and communication with them necessarily difficult, and above all that they stood in deadly peril of their lives—we think the failure of the trial court to give them reasonable time and opportunity to secure counsel was a clear denial of due process.

But passing that, and assuming their inability, even if opportunity had been given, to employ counsel, as the trial court evidently did assume, we are of the opinion that,

(continued)

under the circumstances just stated, the necessity of counsel was so vital and imperative that the failure of the trial court to make an effective appointment of counsel was likewise a denial of due process with the meaning of the Fourteenth Amendment. Whether this would be so in other criminal prosecution, or under other circumstances, we need not determine. All that it is necessary now to decide, as we do decide, is that in a capital case, where the defendant is unable to employ counsel, and is incapable adequately of making his own defense because of ignorance, feeblemindedness, illiteracy, or the like, it is the duty of the court, whether requested or not, to assign counsel for him as a necessary requisite of due process of law; and that duty is not discharged by an assignment at such a time or under such circumstances as to preclude the giving of effective aid in the preparation and trial of the case. To hold otherwise would be to ignore the fundamental postulate, already adverted to, "that there are certain immutable principles of justice which inhere in the very idea of free government which no member of the Union may disregard." *Holden v. Hardy*, 169 U.S. 366. In a case such as this, whatever may be the rule in other cases, the right to have counsel appointed, when necessary, is a logical corollary from the constitutional right to be heard by counsel.

The judgments must be reversed and the causes remanded for further proceedings not inconsistent with this opinion.

CASE ANALYSIS

1. What law is this Court interpreting? Be specific.
2. Review the definition of the term *remand* from the previous chapter. Were the defendants in this case set free by the Court?
3. Does the decision in this case apply to all felony cases? Quote the language in the case that supports your answer.
4. This case started in the Alabama courts. Is it binding in your state? Explain.
5. What are the various sources of law relied upon by this Court in its decisions? Give examples from the case.
6. What did the Supreme Court say about possible violations of the Alabama state constitution? Explain.

Stare Decisis

To assure consistency in case law from court to court, the doctrine of *stare decisis* applies. Literally, *stare decisis* means "it stands decided." In our legal system today, *stare decisis* requires courts to follow decisions of higher courts when faced with similar factual disputes. Once the Supreme Court decides an issue, all lower courts must follow its decision. In other words, if a lower court is faced with the same set of facts as the Supreme Court, it must apply the same rule of law (that is, the factual dispute has been decided by the higher court).

The concept of *stare decisis* is limited, though, in two main ways. First, the concept applies only between higher and lower courts. Trial courts are bound by the decisions of courts of appeals. Trial courts and courts of appeals are bound by decisions of the Supreme Court. The doctrine does not apply to courts on the same level. A court of appeals in one judicial district, for example, is not bound by the decision of a court of appeals in another district, and one trial court is not bound by the decision from another trial court. Furthermore, only cases that are published become *stare decisis*. The various courts of appeals in all jurisdictions decide many cases that never become **binding case law** (case law that must be followed by lower courts). Appellate court cases are generally published only if they contain a new interpretation or clarification of law. The decision to publish a case is made by the justices deciding the case, although that decision is reviewable by the higher court. Cases decided by the Supreme Court are all published. Second, the concept applies only to decisions within the legal system from which they came. In other words, the trial court of one state is not bound by the appellate court of another state. On the other hand, if a federal question is involved, then the decisions of the federal courts of appeals and the U.S. Supreme Court are binding on state courts.

binding case law
Case law that must be followed by lower courts.

SEC. 3-4 STATUTORY LAW

statutory law
Law enacted by a legislature.

Statutes at Large
A chronological compilation of statutes.

code
A topical organization of statutes.

Statutory law plays an important role in the Hardtack case. The criminal charges he faces are found in state and federal codes. The potential civil liability is also based on **statutory law**. In general, statutory law is the set of laws or rules enacted through our legislative process (discussed in the following sections). As statutes are enacted, they are published in the order in which they are passed. This publication is known as ***Statutes at Large***. Unfortunately, because the order of publication is chronological and not topical, the *Statutes at Large* are not very "user friendly." In other words, it is almost impossible to find the complete law on any topic in this publication. Therefore, most statutory law is included in some form of **code**. A code is a topical organization of the statutes or laws passed by a legislature. In our federal system, statutory law adopted by Congress is normally included in the United States Code (abbreviated U.S.C.). The United States Code is broken down into various categories such as the Federal Penal Code, the Bankruptcy Law, and the Federal Rules of Civil Procedure. Most states also have state codes, which are again broken down into various subject matters. For example, your state may have such codes as the Penal Code, the Civil Code, the Code of Civil Procedure, the Corporation Code, and the Vehicle Code. Many local (city and county) governments also have their own rules, generally known as *local ordinances*. These usually include such rules as parking regulations, building requirements, licensing requirements, and leash laws. Since it is the function of our legislature to make laws, it naturally follows that most statutory law is adopted through the legislative process. However, state governments, unlike the federal government, allow the people to initiate and enact statutory law. The power of the people to regulate operates through the processes of *initiative* and *referendum*, which are discussed in a later section.

THE LEGISLATIVE PROCESS—THE FEDERAL GOVERNMENT

The enactment of statutory law is usually a lengthy process consisting of the following steps:

bill
Proposed legislation.

- **Legislation proposed**—Any written law or statute naturally begins with some sort of proposal. In our federal system, just as in any state system, proposed legislation can be drafted by a member of Congress or by any interested individual or group. When drafted, the proposal is known as a **bill**.
- **Bill introduced**—Before Congress will act on any proposed legislation, it must be introduced and sponsored by a member of Congress. Ordinarily, bills can be introduced either in the House of Representatives or in the Senate. The one major exception is a tax measure, which must originate in the House of Representatives. When the bill is introduced, it is given a number.
- **Bill referred to committee**—After a bill has been introduced, it is then referred to the appropriate committee for consideration. Both the House and the Senate have a number of standing committees that concentrate on certain matters. For example, the Judiciary Committee consists of lawyers and handles matters referring to our judicial system. Once the bill has been referred to the proper committee, the committee reviews and

discusses the proposal, often holding public hearings on the bill. If a committee looks favorably upon a bill, it prepares a committee report with its recommendations and analysis of the bill. If a committee looks upon a bill unfavorably, it could also issue a report so indicating. However, more often, if a committee feels the bill has no merit it simply fails to issue any report. When the committee does so, the bill never gets to the full house for a vote. It dies in committee.

- **Bill voted on by legislators**—Once a report is issued, the bill is considered by the whole house and voted upon. If it receives a majority vote of approval, it is passed and sent to the other house.
- **Action by other house**—When referred to the other house, the bill goes through the same process again. If the bill is amended or changed, a joint committee from both houses normally convenes and agrees on a single bill. The same bill must be approved by both houses before it can be submitted to the president. Once passed by both houses, the bill is sent to the president for approval.
- **Executive options**—The president has the power to sign or approve the bill or to veto the proposed legislation. If the president does nothing with the bill, it is deemed approved after ten days, unless Congress adjourns within that ten-day period. If Congress does adjourn within ten days of submitting a bill to the president, and the president does nothing with the bill, it is deemed vetoed (this is called a *pocket veto*). In order to override a presidential veto, a two-thirds majority of each house must vote to do so. If a bill is approved by the president or the veto is overridden, then the law is given a number and identified by that number and by the Congress, for example, "Law 100, 95th Congress." After that it is generally included with existing laws of a similar topic in a code. See the box titled "Statutory Law" for an example of federal statutory law.

The Legislative Process—States

initiative
An action by citizens to enact legislation through the voter process.

referendum
Approval of legislative action by the voters.

Since most state governments are patterned after the federal government, the legislative process in the states closely parallels the federal process. However, as mentioned earlier, state governments may provide for statutory law to be created through the voter process, *i.e.*, by **initiative**. An initiative, like any statutory law, starts with a proposal. The sponsors then take their proposal to the general public in the form of a *petition*. If the petition gathers a sufficient number of signatures, it is put on the ballot for general voter approval. Also, state governments occasionally provide that certain kinds of laws, even if initiated through the state legislature, need voter approval. This is known as a **referendum**. For an example of a state statute, see the box titled "Statutory Law."

Sec. 3–5 ADMINISTRATIVE REGULATIONS

In recent times our government has undertaken many functions through numerous boards, departments, commissions, and agencies. We have such agencies as the tax board and social security. Also, recall from the *Koon* case that Congress cre-

Statutory Law

Federal Statutory Law (United States Code)
18 U.S.C. § 242

Whoever, under color of any law, statute, ordinance, regulation, or custom, willfully subjects any person in any State, Territory, Commonwealth, Possession, or District to the deprivation of any rights, privileges, or immunities secured or protected by the Constitution or laws of the United States, or to different punishments, pains, or penalties, on account of such person being an alien, or by reason of his color, or race, than are prescribed for the punishment of citizens, shall be fined under this title or imprisoned not more than one year, or both; and if bodily injury results from the acts committed in violation of this section or if such acts include the use, attempted use, or threatened use of a dangerous weapon, explosives, or fire, shall be fined under this title or imprisoned not more than ten years, or both; and if death results from the acts committed in violation of this section or if such acts include kidnapping or an attempt to kidnap, aggravated sexual abuse, or an attempt to commit aggravated sexual abuse, or an attempt to kill, shall be fined under this title, or imprisoned for any term of years or for life, or both, or may be sentenced to death.

State Statutory Law (California Penal Code)

Battery defined (California Penal Code § 242)

A battery is any willful and unlawful use of force or violence upon the person of another.

Punishment for battery (California Penal Code § 243)

(a) A battery is punishable by a fine not exceeding two thousand dollars ($2,000), or by imprisonment in a county jail not exceeding six months, or by both that fine and imprisonment.

Questions

1. Review the facts in the Case File at the beginning of the chapter. Has Hardtack violated the federal statute? Explain.
2. Has Hardtack violated the state statute? Explain.
3. If Hardtack were charged with violating the federal statute, which court would hear the trial?

ated the United States Sentencing Commission and charged it with developing a comprehensive set of sentencing guidelines. These rules or guidelines controlled the way that the judge could sentence in that case. States also create special agencies or boards such as those that handle disputes regarding workers who are injured on the job. These agencies have been given the power and authority to enact rules and regulations that have the force and effect of law. They also have been given the power to set up methods of resolving disputes outside the courtroom forum. This promises to be an area of major importance in the use of paralegals.

ETHICAL CHOICES

Assume that you work for the prosecutor's office. You are organizing a file in preparation for trial and come across the name and telephone number of a witness who identified the perpetrator of the crime as someone other than the defendant named in the case. It does not appear from the file that the defense attorney has been advised of this fact. You bring this to the attention of the attorney handling the case, who tells you to forget about it. After all, it isn't the prosecutor's job to defend anyone accused of a crime. What do you do?

ETHICAL CHOICES

Assume that you work for the public defender's office. You are organizing a file in preparation for trial and come across the name and telephone number of a witness who positively identified the perpetrator of the crime as the defendant named in the case. It does not appear from the file that the prosecutor has been advised of this fact. You bring this to the attention of the attorney handling the case, who tells you to forget about it. After all, it isn't the defense attorney's job to worry about this. The defendant, your client, has been accused of child molestation. What do you do?

Featured Web Site: www.findlaw.com/casecode/

This Web site provides a gateway to extensive state and federal case law and statutory law.

Go Online

1. List the types of federal law that can be found on this site. Be specific.
2. Go to the U.S. State Laws for your state. List the types of state law that can be found on this site.
3. Try the following:
   a. Browse the U.S. Code by Popular Name and find the Civil Rights Act of 1964. What is the code section and code title of this act?
   b. Access the U.S. Supreme Court opinions. What is the citation for the *Amistad* case? Go to the opinion for this case and scroll to the end. Who wrote the dissenting opinion?

Chapter Summary

Separate laws exist for both the federal and state legal systems. In each system, however, the sources for these laws are similar. In the federal legal system, laws are found in the U.S. Constitution, federal cases, federal statutes, and administrative regulations. In state legal systems, laws come from similar sources: state constitutions, state cases, state statutes, and administrative regulations.

A constitution is a document that establishes the framework of the government, gives that government the right or power to make certain laws, and defines the obligations of that government to its people. Case law includes law found in decisions of certain appellate and supreme courts. The concept of *stare decisis,* which regulates case law, requires lower courts to follow the rules established by higher courts in prior court decisions. A statute is a law enacted by a legislature. Statutes are organized into codes. Administrative regulations are rules made by various administrative agencies acting under authority given to them by a legislature.

Terms to Remember

sources of law
constitution
Bill of Rights
common law
precedent
stare decisis
capital offense
binding case law
statutory law
Statutes at Large
code
bill
initiative
referendum

Questions for Review

1. What is the purpose of the U.S. Constitution?
2. What is the purpose of a state constitution?
3. What is common law?
4. How does case law work in the United States?
5. Describe how a bill becomes law in the federal system.
6. Explain the terms *initiative* and *referendum.*

Questions for Analysis

1. Review the Bill of Rights, found in Appendix I, and refer to the Case File at the beginning of the chapter. If Hardtack is accused of any crimes, what rights does he have? Does it matter whether he is charged with a federal crime or a state crime? Review the *Heath* case in Chapter 2 and the *Koon* case in this chapter. Based on these cases, could Hardtack be prosecuted for both state and federal crimes for his actions?
2. A group of concerned parents in the city of Elmwood wants to see a curfew imposed on anyone under age eighteen. How can they get such a law imposed (such as legislative action, court case)?
3. Peter, Paul, and Mary are sixteen-year-olds who live in Elmwood, a city with a 10 P.M. curfew for anyone under age eighteen. They think the law is unfair and violates their constitutional rights, and they want it changed. How can they go about doing this?
4. Review the Ethical Choices boxes in this chapter. Which NALA and/or NFPA rules or guidelines apply to the situations? Review your state's ethical rules. (*Hint*: Go to www.nala.org and find a link.) Which of those rules apply?
5. Discuss the relationship between case law and statutory law as illustrated in the case of *United States v. Playboy Entertainment Group, Inc.* found in Appendix VII.

Assignments and Projects

1. Obtain a copy of your state constitution. How does it compare to the U.S. Constitution?
2. Review the cases and statutes found in this chapter. Based on these, draft a set of questions to ask Hardtack during his initial interview.

CHAPTER 4

FINDING THE LAW

LEGAL RESEARCH

Technology Corner

Web Address	Name of Site
www.law.cornell.edu/	Legal Information Institute
www.law.indiana.edu/	Indiana University School of Law
www.washburnlaw.edu/	Washburn University School of Law

CASE FILE: THE WELCH FAMILY LAW MATTER

Ms. Jennifer Welch dissolved her marriage two years ago. She now realizes that her former spouse intentionally hid substantial assets from her. Ms. Welch discovered this information from her husband's business partner; the partner was unaware that she had no knowledge of certain assets. She wants to know whether she can go back to the court and request her share of the hidden assets. The couple initially discussed bifurcating the property issues, but at the time Mr. Welch insisted that all issues be resolved at one time. Additionally, she believes his income has increased significantly in the past year. She wants an increase in her child support award. The court reserved jurisdiction over the support issues. The dissolution proceedings were lengthy, bitter, and expensive. Ms. Welch feels that attorneys are a necessary evil. Her former husband is an attorney. Ms. Welch was married for eight years. The couple has three sons.

A law library need not be intimidating.

SEC. 4–1 INTRODUCTION

A law library can be an intimidating place. At first, it may seem overwhelming. The researcher must be prepared before going to the library. There are several things you can do before your first visit to a law library to increase your chances of finding answers in a reasonable amount of time, with as little frustration as possible. It is important to make every attempt to fully understand the issue(s) to be researched before opening any books. Understanding your case—that is, the client's legal problem and the significant facts—will greatly increase the likelihood of a successful research adventure. Prepare an outline of the sources you plan to use. Create a research plan before you begin the research. This will help you focus and will keep you on track once your research begins.

SEC. 4–2 BEFORE YOU BEGIN

primary sources
The resources that provide the actual law; laws are found in statutes, case law, and the Constitution.

secondary sources
Tools used to understand the law; one such tool is a legal encyclopedia, which explains the law.

Once the researcher realizes that the resources in the library fall into categories, the library is no longer a mystery. There are two basic types of sources in all legal collections: **primary sources** and **secondary sources**. Listed here are some of the resources that fall into the categories of primary and secondary sources.

Primary Sources	*Secondary Sources*
Constitutions	Dictionaries
Statutes	Encyclopedias
Rules, regulations, and ordinances	Form books
Case law	Periodicals
	Treatises
	Digests

This list is not all-inclusive, it merely provides an overview of the types of materials contained in a law library. The secondary sources explain the law and aid in finding the law; the primary sources *are* the law. Finding relevant primary law is the ultimate goal.

You almost always do legal research in connection with a case your office is handling. Therefore, before the process of legal research begins, you must thoroughly understand the facts of your client's case.

Know the Facts

The attorney who accepted the Welch case discussed in the Case File at the beginning of the chapter and conducted the initial interview with the client may send a memo asking a research assistant to conduct some initial research. Research is performed as a direct result of a set of facts. The facts come first. The law is applied to the facts. Assume in the Welch case that the proper jurisdiction for the case is California.

Analyze the Facts

Factual comparison usually takes place after the researcher has clarified the client facts and located case law that may apply to the client's legal situation. A process of comparison of relevant facts is a good starting place in the legal analysis process. The effective legal researcher works to locate case law that is as factually similar to the client facts as possible. Because our legal system is based on precedent, the sorting and comparison of facts are essential legal analysis skills.

Factual comparison may at first seem confusing and somewhat arbitrary. However, once you establish a process for factual comparison, the confusion dissolves. When you compare the client's facts with the facts of a reported case, look for the following:

	Client's Case	Published Case
Factual Similarities		
Factual Unknowns		
Factual Differences		

This chart enables you to easily compare and contrast the facts of your client's case with the facts of a reported case. A good number of similarities of relevant facts indicates that the case may apply in your client's situation. A good number of differences in the relevant facts indicates that the case may not apply. When there are significant gaps or unknown facts, the reported case will probably not apply to your client's case. As a legal researcher, you are searching for cases that are factually and legally very similar to the case you are researching.

Identify the Issues

issue
A question that must be decided by a court.

Ask yourself the following question as you begin each legal research assignment: "Do I understand the client's problem(s)?" If the answer is yes, you are ready to attempt to identify the **issues**, or the questions that must be decided by a court. Once the issues are clearly stated, it is time to focus on the facts. If you are unclear on the legal issues, ask for guidance.

In the Welch case, Ms. Welch has at least two legal questions. On a very basic level, she wants to know the following:

1. Whether, after final judgment, she can reopen her family law matter concerning property
2. Whether she can request an increase in child support

Use the Relevant Facts to Define the Issues

relevant
Relevant evidence relates directly to the issue; a relevant fact is a fact that is tied directly to the client's legal question.

Before you do any actual research, you must focus on the **relevant** facts. The identification of relevant facts may present a challenge. In the Welch example, even if you are unfamiliar with family law issues, it is possible to identify the relevant facts. The first issue might generally be restated as follows: Under what circumstances will the court review a family law final judgment? The second issue might be generally restated as follows: Under what circumstances will the court increase child support after final judgment?

Now that the issues have been clarified, it is time to begin identifying the facts. Facts fall into one of three categories: *relevant, explanatory*, and *unnecessary*.

Relevant facts—These are the key or significant facts.

Explanatory facts—These facts help the researcher understand what happened. They are not relevant, in a legal sense, to the issue.

Unnecessary facts—The factual information in this category is irrelevant to the legal issue.

Sort the Facts

In the Welch case the facts of the first issue might sort out this way:

Under what circumstances will the court review a family law final judgment?

Relevant

- significant hidden assets
- assets were intentionally not disclosed
- there is a final judgment on file with the court

Explanatory

- Ms. Welch came across this information from her former spouse's business partner
- the length of the marriage

Unnecessary

- the dissolution was bitter, expensive, and lengthy
- the former spouse is an attorney
- the client's opinion of attorneys

You have studied and categorized the facts and identified the legal issue concerning the hidden assets. You are now prepared to begin the research.

SEC. 4–3 WHERE TO BEGIN THE RESEARCH

Your choice of sources with which to begin your research will vary. If you have a general understanding of the area of law to be researched and a good grasp of the relevant legal vocabulary, proceed directly to the primary sources. Such sources might include the Constitution, statutes, and case law. If you are in an unfamiliar area of the law, it is most efficient to begin the research process with the secondary sources. They explain the law and provide an overview of the legal issues and vocabulary. Such sources include dictionaries, encyclopedias, form books, periodicals, treatises, and digests.

DICTIONARIES

All unfamiliar legal terms must be defined. You cannot understand the legal principles if you do not understand the legal vocabulary.

bifurcate
To sever from the trial; in family law, it means that the divorce or dissolution may be granted, but the parties will need to come back to court to adjudicate another issue—for example, their property issues.

The Welch case presents a term that may be unfamiliar or even new: **bifurcate**. Before you go any further, that term must be defined. A legal dictionary is a good starting place. In general, bifurcation involves separation, in this case the separation of issues.

ENCYCLOPEDIAS

legal encyclopedia
A collection of legal information; a secondary source of the law.

finding tools
The resources used to locate primary and secondary sources; for example, a digest.

annotation
A brief summary of a statute or a case.

Further research in secondary sources might include background material in a **legal encyclopedia**. This material is arranged alphabetically. In most instances there will be a table of contents for the specific section in which you are interested. Some secondary sources are called **finding tools** because they are heavily annotated. The **annotations** direct the reader to other sources, including primary sources. For example, a legal encyclopedia includes a section on family law, sometimes referred to as *domestic relations*. There will always be an index to the legal encyclopedia. After locating the topic of interest through the index or table of contents, you will gain background information and begin to develop the legal vocabulary necessary to understand and correctly state the legal issue presented by the client's factual situation. There may also be an index to the family law section. In addition to the state encyclopedias, there are *Corpus Juris Secundum* (C.J.S.) and *American Jurisprudence 2d* (Am. Jur. 2d). These two sets of books are very large national encyclopedias.

Let's look at the Welch problem in a legal encyclopedia. You might choose to look in the state encyclopedia, in this case *California Jurisprudence 3d* (Cal. Jur. 3d), the California state encyclopedia. The Family Law volumes have an index. Figure 4–1 shows a page from this index.

INDEX

FIGURE 4–1 Index of *California Jurisprudence 3d*. Reprinted with permission of Bancroft-Whitney, Law Publishers.

Notice that the general topic is Support of Persons, the subtopic is Child Support, and under the subtopic Child Support is "modification." After scanning the sections under "modification" we find that § 1139 (contained in the Family Law volumes of the encyclopedia) covers the topic of "change in circumstances necessary for modification." After we locate this reference, we need to find § 1139. Figure 4–2 shows two pages taken from Volume 33 of *California Jurisprudence 3d*. A summary is followed by the information in § 1139.

b. Grounds for Modification [§§ 1139–1143]

§ 1139. Necessity for change in circumstances
§ 1140. Exceptions to change of circumstances rule
§ 1141. Facts constituting change of circumstances
§ 1142. Parent's ability to pay; earning capacity
§ 1143. Modification of existing orders to conform with guideline

Summary

In order to justify a modification there must have been a substantial change in the material circumstances since the original order was made. However, in any proceeding involving the modification of child support, the court should always adopt a course that is for the child's best interests (§ 1139). A change of circumstances need not be shown where a stipulated child support order provides for child support below the guideline formula, where modification is sought pursuant to the simplified procedure for modification, or where there is an absence of findings in the order sought to be modified (§ 1140). The decision whether and to what extent modification should be allowed is within the court's discretion (§ 1141). The parent's increased earnings may be a sufficient change of circumstances justifying modification. And in certain circumstances, earning capacity of the supporting parent, rather than actual earnings, may be considered (§ 1142). Where the court is requested to modify a child support order in order to comply with the guideline, the court may, in certain circumstances, order a "phase-in" of the formula amount of support to provide the payor with time for transition to the full formula amount (§ 1143).

As to the effect of agreements between parents for child support generally, see § 1080.

68. Fam C § 3651(d).

Any proper modification of a decree relating to child support may, in consideration of the best interests and welfare of the children be ordered on application of the mother, despite her previous agreement limiting the father's obligation for support. *Singer v Singer (1970, 2nd Dist) 7 CA3d 807, 87 Cal Rptr 42.*

As to stipulated child support agreements, see § 1117.

As to modification of agreements between the parties generally, see §§ 559 et seq.

33 Cal Jur 3d (Rev) Part 1 647

FIGURE 4–2 Grounds for modification. Reprinted with the permission of Bancroft-Whitney, Law Publishers.

§ 1139 **FAMILY LAW**

§ 1139. Necessity for change in circumstances

The considerations on which the doctrine of res judicata is based, that the court should not be called on to adjudicate twice on the same set of facts and that an adversary should not be twice vexed for the same cause of action, if applied strictly, require the rule that an application to modify an order for the support of a child cannot be based on the same set of facts that existed when the original order was made. That is, in order to justify a modification it is held that there must have been a substantial change in the material circumstances since the original order was made.[69] And on a second application for a modification it must be shown that there has been a substantial change of circumstances since the order on the first application was made.[70] But in any proceeding involving the modification of child support, the court should always adopt a course that is for the child's best interests.[71]

Each application for modification must be determined on its own facts, and the exercise of the trial court's discretion in that regard will not be disturbed unless abuse of the power is shown.[72] Moreover, the evidence presented must be considered in the light favorable to supporting rather than to defeating the order determining the application for modification.[73]

69. *Evans v Evans (1960, 2nd Dist) 185 CA2d 566, 8 Cal Rptr 412; Crain v Crain (1960, 2nd Dist) 187 CA2d 825, 9 Cal Rptr 850; Burns v Burns (1961, 1st Dist) 190 CA2d 714, 12 Cal Rptr 68, 89 ALR2d 103; Philbin v Philbin (1971, 2nd Dist) 19 CA3d 115, 96 Cal Rptr 408; Petersen v Petersen (1972, 1st Dist) 24 CA3d 201, 100 Cal Rptr 822; In re Marriage of Catalano (1988, 1st Dist) 204 CA3d 543, 251 Cal Rptr 370.*

In passing on an application for a change in child support payments, the trial court has the right to require that there be circumstances different from those already passed on by the court in making the previous order for support payments. *De Lima v De Lima (1962, 1st Dist) 207 CA2d 74, 24 Cal Rptr 179.*

Annotations: Divorce: voluntary contributions to child's education expenses as factor justifying modification of spousal support award, 63 ALR4th 436; Change in financial condition or needs of parents or children as ground for modification of decree for child support payments, 89 ALR2d 7; Remarriage of parent as basis for modification of amount of child support provisions of divorce decree, 89 ALR2d 106.

70. *Evans v Evans (1960, 2nd Dist) 185 CA2d 566, 8 Cal Rptr 412.*

71. *Evans v Evans (1960, 2nd Dist) 185 CA2d 566, 8 Cal Rptr 412.*

72. *Petersen v Petersen (1972, 1st Dist) 24 CA3d 201, 100 Cal Rptr 822.*

73. *Petersen v Petersen (1972, 1st*

FIGURE 4–2 Continued

Notice that the section (§) numbers are located at the top of the page. The actual page numbers are found at the bottom of the page. This set is organized through the index, as are many legal materials, by section numbers rather than by page numbers. In other words, the index refers to sections instead of pages.

Form Books

form book
A legal resource filled with sample forms and explanations on how and when to use the forms; many are now available on disk or CD-ROM.

Form books are another practical resource. Examples of many types of legal documents are provided. Most states have one or more sets of forms manuals and resources. Form books also exist for federal practice. The forms provide the researcher with a sample to follow. For example, suppose the research assistant is asked to draft a power-of-attorney agreement. The researcher might choose to check the form books to locate an example from which to work; this saves time and money for the client. The researcher first checks the general index for the form books set. The "power of attorney" reference is easily located. The index directs researchers to the appropriate section, where there is a discussion of the power of attorney and one or more examples.

Legal Periodicals

The term *legal periodicals* covers a variety of publications. Many legal periodicals are monthly publications of bar journals or magazines. Most states have a bar journal; the American Bar Association publishes the *American Bar Association Journal*, and there are many other specialty journals. These periodicals address current legal issues. Also included under the broad topic of legal periodicals are the **law reviews**. Law reviews are usually published by law schools. Students research and write articles for their school's law review. Law review articles tend to provide in-depth coverage of a specific legal issue or an important case. Sometimes, judges and attorneys will contribute to law reviews. These sources are often helpful if you know very little about your research subject matter.

law review
A publication containing articles written by judges, professors, and attorneys; it also contains case summaries written by law school students. Most law schools publish one or more periodic law reviews each year.

Treatises

treatise
A book that reviews a special field of law; a summary of the law on a particular subject; often called a *hornbook*.

A **treatise** is a book or set of volumes dedicated to a single topic or area of law, from which a researcher may perform in-depth research on a specific or narrow topic. For example, suppose the research assistant is directed to perform research on the differences between comparative negligence and contributory negligence. The researcher could go to *Prosser on Torts*, which provides detailed information on most civil topics. After using the index and locating the necessary background information on comparative and contributory negligence, the researcher is now ready to proceed with the research project.

Digests

digest
An index to reported cases, arranged by subject; a short summary of the case is provided.

A **digest** is a set of books that indexes case law by topic. It is a secondary source that leads the researcher directly to the primary source, case law. There are digests available for most states, all regions, and all Supreme Court case law. Topics are arranged alphabetically. The researcher looks up the topic to be researched and is directed to specific cases addressing the topic. This research tool is addressed, in detail, in legal research courses.

SEC. 4–4 CASE LAW

case law
A collection of reported cases.

reporter
A set of published volumes of cases by courts.

LEXIS
A computer-assisted legal research service provided by Reed Elsevier.

Westlaw
A computer-assisted legal research service provided by West Publishing Company.

rules of law
Legal principles that are applied to the facts; generally derived from statutes, case law, and the Constitution.

holding
The legal principle to be taken from the court's decision.

precedent
The example set by the decision of an earlier court for similar cases or similar legal questions which arise in later cases.

Once you have reviewed secondary sources of law and have a basic understanding of the law, you can proceed to the primary sources, such as **case law**. Cases are collected in large sets of books known as **reporters**. These same cases are available on CD-ROM and in online databases such as **LEXIS** and **Westlaw**. Our focus in this chapter is on the printed versions of case law.

WHAT IS A CASE?

A reported case is an opinion written by a judge. After a dispute has been presented to the court, the judge writes an opinion explaining the reasoning of the court. This opinion contains an overview of the relevant facts of the case, the legal issues presented to the court for resolution, the **rules of law** that the court used in explaining its decision, and the court's **holding**.

The importance of case law becomes apparent when we recall that our legal system relies on **precedent**. A court looks to past decisions to aid it in its decision-making process. Therefore, researchers must look to previous decisions in an attempt to locate cases that are similar to the factual and legal situation being researched.

WHERE TO FIND CASE LAW

Cases are published by several publishers and are located in a number of resources. Each state publishes or arranges to have published its appellate and supreme court cases. New York, Texas, Florida, New Jersey, Washington, California, and other states publish their opinions in what are known as official publications of their case law. Other states such as North Dakota have arranged with the West Publishing Company to publish their case law in the appropriate regional reporters. A concise guide to the resources in which the various states publish their case law is found in *The Bluebook: A Uniform System of Citation*. In addition to the traditional paper publications, most state case law is available on various CD-ROM products and in the online legal databases of LEXIS and Westlaw. Increasing collections of state and federal case law are found at various sites on the Internet.

Case law reporters—Case law reporters are books filled with decisions. There are case law reporters for most states. There are also large sets of books known as regional reporters. A regional reporter publishes selected case law from a geographical region of the United States.

LEXIS/NEXIS and Westlaw—LEXIS/NEXIS and Westlaw are huge online legal databases. Use of these services is through contract with the publishers. Both services should be used only by people trained to search in large legal databases. Case law is only one of the many resources available through LEXIS/NEXIS and Westlaw.

CD-ROM products—Several publishers now offer case law on CD-ROM. These products often combine the ease of using books with the speed of using an online database.

Internet—There are Internet sites for case law retrieval. Because the Internet is growing and changing at a rapid rate, it is difficult to offer a reliable list of research sites. Some law schools continue to maintain reliable Web sites. Try the following Internet site for United States Supreme Court case law: http://www.law.cornell.edu.

FEDERAL CASE LAW

Cases decided by federal courts are published in the various federal reporters. For example, U.S. Supreme Court cases are available in written format from several publishers.

United States Reports—This is the *official* publication of Supreme Court cases. It is published by the federal government.

Supreme Court Reporter—This is an unofficial publication of all Supreme Court cases. It is published by West Publishing Co., the largest legal publisher in the United States. The cases are identical to the cases published in the *United States Reports*. The only differences are the format in which the cases are published and the editorial enhancements.

Lawyer's Edition—This, too, is an unofficial publication of all Supreme Court cases. It is published by LEXIS Law Publishing. The cases are identical to the cases in the *United States Reports* and the *Supreme Court Reporter*. Again, the differences involve format and editorial comments.

It is important to realize that there are several potential sources in which you may locate any Supreme Court case. The text of the opinion—that is, what the justices have written—will be identical in each source.

A Supreme Court case citation looks like this:

> *Meritor Savings Bank, FSB v. Vinson*,
> 477 U.S. 57, 106 S. Ct. 2399, 91 L.
> Ed. 2d 49 (1986).

The name of the case is placed first. The name must be underlined or italicized. The remainder of the citation, the parallel cites, explain where the case is located in each of the three sets of reporters containing U.S. Supreme Court cases. Appendix IV lists common citation formats for a variety of legal resources.

There are several reporters reporting federal case law. Most important to the beginning legal researcher are the *Federal Reporter 3d* and the *Federal Supplement*. The *Federal Reporter 3d* publishes U.S. court of appeals opinions. The *Federal Supplement* includes cases from the U.S. district courts and some special courts.

A POINT TO REMEMBER

All case citations are arranged in the following fashion: the volume number is first, the abbreviation for the name of the reporter is next, and the page on which the case begins follows the reporter abbreviation. The official reporter will always be listed first; the citations that follow are the unofficial publications. The year of the decision is usually placed at the end of the citation, or in some instances just after the name of the case, but always in parentheses.

State Case Law

regional reporter
A set of published volumes of cases by courts in specific regions of the United States; for example, the *Pacific Reporter* or the *Northeastern Reporter.*

State court cases are published in state and **regional reporters**. For example, in California, state cases are printed in the official reporters, *California Reports* and *California Appellate Reports,* and in the unofficial reporter, the *California Reporter*. In addition, selected cases are found in the regional reporter, the *Pacific Reporter*. The *Pacific Reporter* includes cases from a number of western states, including California. Therefore, in California, cases will be found in at least two reporters, and some will be found in a third reporter, the *Pacific Reporter*.

Figure 4–3 shows the first two pages of the *Marvin v. Marvin* case. Some of the important information is explained. The margin notes explain how to read this introductory material. Read the explanations carefully.

This version of the *Marvin* case is published in the *California Reporter,* which is published by West Publishing Co. West developed a "key number" system many years ago. The key numbers identify legal topics by a number and cross-reference the number and the information to other West publications. You will learn to use the key number system in your legal research and writing classes. Put simply, you may take a key number and its topic from a case and look it up in a digest (if it is published by West) and you will locate other cases that involve the same topic. This allows you to expand the search for additional cases.

The entire *Marvin* case (Figure 4–3) is set forth in Appendix V. Also included is the 1981 case that followed the original *Marvin v. Marvin* decision.

How to Read and Use Case Law

Most cases are compiled in a similar format. The format becomes familiar as one reads a good number of cases. Knowing what to expect and looking for the basic components of a case will help you to read a case *one* time, rather than over and over in a seemingly vain attempt to master the court's reasoning. Case law will contain each of the following components:

> **Facts**—The key facts are provided by the court. The facts are essential to the researcher. In legal research you will read case law in an attempt to locate cases that are similar, factually and legally, to your client's case. Without the facts, no effective comparisons may take place. Many judges provide the facts at the very beginning of the case.

"Official" citation for Marvin v. Marvin → 18 Cal.3d 660

MARVIN v. MARVIN ← *proper case name*

Cite as, Sup., 134 Cal.Rptr. 815

815 ← *page number in the California Reporter*

jury process. First, once aware that after sitting through a lengthy trial he himself may be placed on trial, only the most courageous prospective juror will not seek excuse from service. Secondly, if jury deliberations are subject to compulsory disclosure, independent thought and debate will surely be stifled. (*Clark v. United States* (1932) 289 U.S. 1, 13, 53 S.Ct. 465, 77 L.Ed. 993.)

We conclude that a motion for new trial on grounds enumerated in the first four subdivisions of section 657 must be presented solely by affidavit. Insofar as it is contrary, *Saltzman v. Sunset Tel., etc., Co.* (1899) 125 Cal. 501, 58 P. 169, is overruled.[2]

Having examined defendants' other contentions, we find them of insufficient merit to warrant discussion.

The judgment is affirmed.

WRIGHT, C. J., and McCOMB, TOBRINER, MOSK, SULLIVAN and RICHARDSON, JJ., concur.

end of case preceding Marvin v. Marvin

KEY NUMBER SYSTEM

This key indicates the break between cases

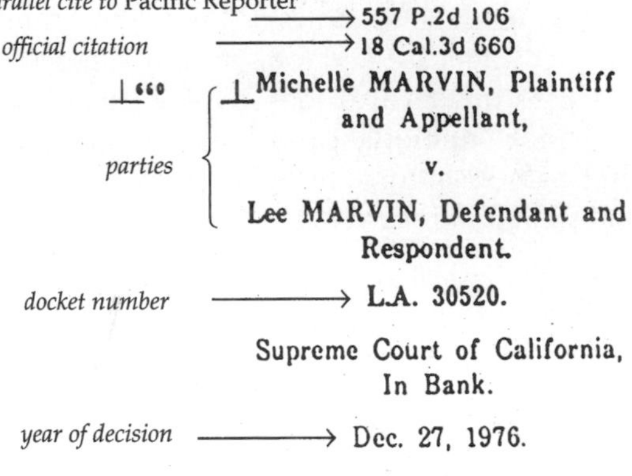

parallel cite to Pacific Reporter → 557 P.2d 106

official citation → 18 Cal.3d 660

parties

Michelle MARVIN, Plaintiff and Appellant,

v.

Lee MARVIN, Defendant and Respondent.

docket number → L.A. 30520.

Supreme Court of California, In Bank.

year of decision → Dec. 27, 1976.

summary of case → Woman who had lived with man for seven years without marriage brought suit to enforce alleged oral contract under which she was entitled to half the property which had been acquired during that period and taken in man's name, and to support payments. The Superior Court, Los Angeles County, William A. Munnell, J., granted the judgment on the pleadings for defendant, and plaintiff appealed. The Supreme Court, Tobriner, J., held that provisions of the Family Law Act do not govern the distribution of property acquired during a nonmarital relationship; that court should enforce express contracts between nonmarital partners except to the extent the contract is explicitly founded on the consideration of meretricious sexual services, despite contention that such contracts violate public policy; that in the absence of express contract, the court should inquire into the conduct of the parties to determine whether that conduct demonstrates implied contract, agreement of partnership or joint venture, or some other tacit understanding between the parties, and may also employ the doctrine of quantum meruit or equitable remedies such as constructive or resulting trust, when warranted by the facts of the case; that in the instant case plaintiff's complaint stated a cause of action for breach of an express contract and furnished suitable basis on which trial court could render declaratory relief; and that the complaint also could be amended to state a cause of action founded on theory of implied contract or equitable relief. *← end of summary*

Reversed and remanded. ← *decision of the court*

Clark, J., filed concurring and dissenting opinion.

Digest Topic ↓ *Digest Number* ↓

1. Appeal and Error ⟹916(1)

Where trial court rendered judgment for defendant on the pleadings, Supreme Court had to accept the allegations of the complaint as true, determining whether such allegations stated or could be amended to state a cause of action. } *headnote*

2. Defendants inaccurately contend *Bardessono v. Michels* (1970) 3 Cal.3d 780, 793–794, 91 Cal.Rptr. 760, 478 P.2d 480, holds that a litigant may call witnesses in support of motion for new trial. The *Bardessono* court merely noted the *Saltzman* holding, neither applying it nor relying upon it in the opinion.

FIGURE 4–3 First two pages of the *Marvin* case. Reprinted with the permission of West Publishing Co. (from the *California Reporter*).

816 134 CALIFORNIA REPORTER 18 Cal.3d 660

headnotes are written by editors to help the reader

2. Parties ⇐52
Pleading ⇐248(1)

No error was committed in denying plaintiff's motion, made on the opening day set for trial, seeking to file a proposed amended complaint which would have added two counts and a new defendant to the action.

3. Lewdness ⇐3

Where married man was living with unmarried woman, only the man could have been guilty of violating former statute prohibiting living in a state of cohabitation and adultery, and the unmarried partner could neither be convicted of adulterous cohabitation nor of aiding and abetting other partner's violations. West's Ann.Pen.Code, § 269a.

4. Contracts ⇐112

Contract between nonmarital partners is unenforceable only to the extent that it explicitly rests on the immoral and illicit consideration of meretricious sexual services, despite contention that enforcement of such a contract would violate public policy, and enforceability of such a contract is not precluded when one partner contributes only homemaking services.

5. Contracts ⇐61, 103

A promise to perform homemaking services is a lawful and adequate consideration for a contract.

to read more about this topic, the reader is directed to go to the topic contracts in the West Digest and look under "Key Number" 112

6. Contracts ⇐112

The fact that a man and woman live together without marriage and engage in a sexual relationship does not in itself invalidate agreements between them relating to their earnings, property or expenses, nor is such an agreement invalid merely because the parties may have contemplated the creation or continuation of a nonmarital relationship when they entered into it; such agreements fail only to the extent that they rest on a consideration of meretricious sexual services, and not on the ground that the agreement is "involved in" or made "in contemplation of" a nonmarital relationship; disapproving Heaps v. Toy, 54 Cal. App.2d 158, 128 P.2d 813. West's Ann.Civ. Code, §§ 1607, 1676.

7. Contracts ⇐112, 137(3)

Court will not enforce a contract for the pooling of property and earnings if it is explicitly and inseparably based upon services as a paramour, but even if sexual services are part of the contractual consideration, any severable portion of the contract supported by independent consideration will be enforced.

8. Husband and Wife ⇐267(7)

An improper transfer of community property is not void ab initio, but merely voidable at the instance of the aggrieved spouse. Civ.Code, § 172, St.1917, p. 829.

9. Contracts ⇐108(2)

Where wife had opportunity to assert her community property rights in divorce action and her interest was fixed and limited in interlocutory and final decrees in that action, enforcement of alleged contract between the former husband and another woman, with whom he lived during the period which began before the divorce was final, against property awarded to the former husband by the divorce decree would not impair any rights of the former wife, and contract was not on that account violative of public policy. Civ.Code, § 169.2, St. 1959, p. 3767; West's Ann.Civ.Code, §§ 169, 5118.

10. Contracts ⇐111

Where alleged contract between man and woman who lived together did not by its terms require the man to divorce his wife nor reward him for so doing, it was not invalid as an agreement to promote or encourage divorce, and such ground for invalidity of the contract would not apply in any event if the marriage in question was beyond redemption.

11. Frauds, Statute of ⇐4

"Marriage settlement," within statute providing that all contracts for such settlements must be in writing, is an agreement in contemplation of marriage in which each party agrees to release or modify property rights which would otherwise arise from the marriage, and thus alleged oral contract

FIGURE 4–3 Continued.

Judicial history—The judicial history explains the prior proceedings—in other words, what happened in the lower court(s). This component is usually included early in the case.

Issues—Issues are the legal questions before the reviewing court.

Rules—Rules are the primary law relied upon by the court in the analysis or reasoning component of the case.

Analysis—The analysis or reasoning component of most cases is the longest section. The analysis usually follows the facts, judicial history, and a basic statement of the issues. This component contains a discussion of the facts, issues, and appropriate rules or laws relied upon by the court.

Conclusion—The conclusion is the legal outcome of the case. The holding of the court is often referred to as the conclusion.

Many students of the law learn to read cases looking for issues, rules, analysis, and a conclusion. This is known as the *IRAC* method. This method of reading case law prepares the researcher to effectively summarize or brief the case. Add the relevant facts and the basic judicial history and you have a complete summary of the case.

Each paragraph of a case will include one or more of these six components. As you read a case, identify the components of every paragraph. This allows you to focus and sort out the case as you read it, rather than going back and rereading the case. Some paragraphs contain more than one element. For example, paragraphs of analysis may also contain rules/law and possibly some relevant facts.

It is not possible, nor is it prudent, to give only one label to each paragraph of a decision. But remember, each paragraph must contain at least one of the six components. Do not become frustrated if you find four elements in one paragraph. Rather, congratulate yourself on careful analysis.

stare decisis
"It stands decided"; another term for precedent.

Because of the doctrine of precedent or **stare decisis**, when you use case law you must show factual similarities between your case and the cases you found in your research. First, compare the facts of the cases you locate in your research with the facts of your client's situation. If the facts are similar, or easily analogous, the case may be considered precedent. The attorney who assigned the research project will want to review your work.

Second, contrast the facts of the cases you research with the facts of your client's situation. Significant factual differences will probably mean that the case should not be used in an attempt to support your client's position.

ETHICAL CHOICES

You have completed the initial research in a contract case. You found several cases that clearly indicate that your client will not recover the damages he believes he has incurred. What should you do?

A POINT TO REMEMBER

When performing legal research one must be conscious of the jurisdiction in which the *cause of action* (the client's legal problem) arose. In general, if your client lives in Florida and the cause of action arose in Florida, your research will take place in the Florida codes, cases, and practice guides. Similarly, if the cause of action involves a federal issue, research must be performed in federal research sources.

After comparing the facts, you must compare the legal issues. Ask yourself, "Are my client's problems the same as, or similar to, the problems in the case I have located?" If the answer is yes, the case *may* be considered precedent. Compare the facts in the Case File at the beginning of this chapter with the facts of the *Modnick* case. Try to identify the six case law components in the following case. Try to pencil in one or more elements in the margin next to each paragraph.

In re Marriage of Modnick

33 Cal. 3d 897 (1983)

Modnick *is a family law/domestic relations decision. The legal issue addressed is, "Does the failure of one spouse to disclose the existence of a community property asset constitute extrinsic fraud?" When the Modnicks dissolved their marriage, Mr. Modnick disclosed only one bank account in his name; that account had a seven-dollar balance. After an IRS investigation, Mrs. Modnick discovered that her former husband had willfully not disclosed other substantial bank accounts. She moved to set aside the final judgment. The trial court denied her motion. The appellate court reversed and vacated the interlocutory and final judgments of dissolution insofar as it related to the property settlement incorporated into the divorce decree and the spousal support award.*

OPINION

In a marital dissolution proceeding, does the failure of one spouse to disclose the existence of a community property asset constitute extrinsic fraud?

I

After 22 years of marriage, Marilyn and Zelig Modnick separated in September of 1974. The next month, Marilyn petitioned the superior court for a dissolution of the marriage, alleging irreconcilable differences between the parties.

A trial began on September 18, 1975, and, after several continuances, concluded on April 26, 1976. Zelig testified that he had no bank accounts other than one checking account with a $7 balance. His financial declaration also did not reveal the existence of any other accounts.

At the end of the trial, the court ordered the marriage dissolved, awarded Marilyn spousal support, and divided the community property in accordance with the stipulation of the parties. An interlocutory judgment of dissolution was filed in December of 1976. Both Marilyn and Zelig approved the form and content of the judgment.

In August of 1978, the Modnicks received notice that the Internal Revenue Service (IRS) was investigating their tax liability for the years 1974 through 1978. The IRS investigation concerned unreported income earned by Zelig and deposited in various bank accounts. These accounts, containing thousands of dollars, were not disclosed during the dissolution.

Marilyn alleges that at first she "did not know or understand the details about" the IRS investigation. Subsequently, through her counsel, she filed a motion to set aside

(continued)

the interlocutory judgment on the ground of fraud. The motion was heard by the trial court and denied "without prejudice to being set for hearing on after-discovered community property issues."

Following a hearing in November of 1980, the trial court denied Marilyn's motion to set aside the final judgment. She appeals from that order.

II

The principal question raised by this appeal concerns Zelig's concealment of a community property asset which should have been divided between the parties when their marriage was dissolved. Marilyn claims that the failure to disclose the existence of community property constitutes extrinsic fraud. Therefore, she maintains that the trial court erred in denying her motion to vacate the interlocutory and final judgments of dissolution.

The law is well settled that extrinsic fraud is a proper ground for setting aside an alimony award and a property settlement incorporated into a divorce decree. *Kulchar v. Kulchar*, 1 Cal. 3d 467, 470–471, 82 Cal. Rptr. 489, 462 P. 2d 17 (1969); *Jorgensen v. Jorgensen*, 32 Cal. 2d 13, 17–21, 193 P. 2d 728 (1948). Extrinsic fraud is a broad concept that "[tends] to encompass almost any set of extrinsic circumstances which deprive a party of a fair adversary hearing." It "usually arises when a party . . . has been deliberately kept in ignorance of the action or proceeding, or in some other way fraudulently prevented from presenting his claim or defense." [Citation omitted.]

No abstract formula exists for determining whether a particular case involves extrinsic, rather than intrinsic, fraud. "It is necessary to examine the facts in the light of the policy that a party who failed to assemble all his evidence at the trial should not be privileged to relitigate a case, as well as the policy permitting a party to seek relief from a judgment entered in a proceeding in which he was deprived of a fair opportunity fully to present his case." *Jorgensen v. Jorgensen*, 32 Cal. 2d at 19.

The cases have uniformly recognized that the failure of one spouse to disclose the existence of community property assets constitutes extrinsic fraud. *Boeseke v. Boeseke*, 10 Cal. 3d 844, 849–850, 112 Cal. Rptr. 401, 519 P. 2d 161 (1974).

The key principle underlying these cases is that each spouse has an obligation to inform the other spouse of the existence of community property assets. This duty stems in part from the confidential nature of the marital relationship. It also arises from the fiduciary relationship that exists between spouses with respect to the control of community property.

When one spouse manages a community asset, he or she exercises control over the property interests of the other spouse. Therefore, the controlling spouse has a duty to disclose the existence of that asset. This fiduciary relationship does not terminate with the separation of the spouses or the commencement of a dissolution proceeding. The duty of disclosure continues until the marriage has been dissolved and the community property divided by the court.

When a husband fails to reveal the existence of community property during the dissolution proceedings, he deprives [his] wife of an opportunity to protect her rights in the concealed assets. Thus, the non-disclosure constitutes extrinsic fraud and warrants equitable relief from a judgment dividing community property between the parties.

Applying these principles to the present case, it is clear that Zelig's conduct amounted to extrinsic fraud. Not only did he fail to disclose the community property to his wife and the court, but he took deliberate steps to conceal the asset. Zelig removed his name from the account in 1974 and transferred ownership of it to two of his relatives. In addition, he did not report the income deposited in the account to the IRS. Marilyn only discovered the existence of the account after the tax fraud investigation.

III

In the present case, Zelig deliberately concealed the existence of a community property asset which should have been distributed between the parties at the time the marriage was dissolved. This fraud deprived Marilyn of an opportunity to litigate her interest in the concealed property. As a result, the property provisions of the divorce decree must be set aside. To hold otherwise would serve to encourage spouses to engage in the objectionable practice of secreting community property assets.

The order of the trial court denying Marilyn's motion to vacate the interlocutory and final judgments of dissolution is reversed insofar as it relates to the property settlement incorporated into the divorce decree and the award of spousal support. In all other respects, the order is affirmed. The case is remanded to the trial court for further proceedings consistent with this opinion.

CASE ANALYSIS

1. Compare the facts of the *Modnick* case with the facts of the Welch case provided in the Case File at the beginning of this chapter. What do the two cases have in common? How do the cases differ?
2. Are there additional facts you need to know about the Welch case in order to do a complete comparison with the *Modnick* case? If so, what do you need to know?

SEC. 4–5 STATUTORY LAW

statute
A legislatively created law; a written enactment.

Statutes, or codes, are laws enacted by the legislature. They are grouped together by subject matter. Federal statutory law is found in the United States Code; state statutory law is found in individual state codes. The subject matter is arranged into titles or chapters and the titles are broken down into section numbers.

The following is a simple North Carolina statute.

Chapter 14: Criminal Law

Subchapter III: Offenses against the Person

Article 8: Assaults

N.C. Gen. Stat. Section 14–34.5: Assault with a Firearm on a Law Enforcement Officer

> Any person who commits an assault with a firearm upon a law enforcement officer in the performance of his or her duties is guilty of a Class E felony.

This is the law as it is printed in the code. The most useful codes are *annotated*. These annotations direct the researcher to cases using or explaining the code section. Case interpretations of statutes are important because of the doctrine of precedent; once a court has interpreted a code in a particular way, other courts may be bound by the interpretation. In this way the code sends the researcher to another primary source—case law.

pocket part
A removable supplement to a volume of statutory law; includes all changes or additions to the material contained in the hardbound volume.

Before you move on in your research, you must check the pocket part for this volume. The **pocket part** is a removable supplement to a volume of statutory law. The pocket part is located in the pocket in the back of the volume. This is how the codes (and other legal materials) are kept current. Pocket parts are replaced on a yearly, semiyearly, or sometimes even quarterly basis. Always look up the code section in the bound volume *and* the pocket part. Any changes to the code since publication of the bound volume are found in the pocket part.

USING STATUTORY LAW

Statutes, or codes, are primary law. We look to the statutes to provide concise statements of the law.

Statutes are sometimes difficult to understand. There is a method to evaluating statutes. Break the statute down into elements or steps. The preceding North Carolina statute may be more easily read and analyzed when it is pulled apart and rewritten into the following elements:

1. Any person
2. who commits an assault
3. with a firearm
4. upon a law enforcement officer
5. in the performance of his or her [the officer's] duties
6. is guilty of a Class E felony.

Once the elements of the statute are clear, you must decide whether the statute applies to your client's fact pattern. This is the first step in the factual analysis process.

Featured Web Site: www.lawguru.com

This Web site has an extensive array of legal materials.

Go Online

1. Locate the "Legal Research" tools.
2. Summarize the legal research tools available on this site.

Chapter Summary

Finding and understanding the law is an essential element of your legal education. A basic familiarity with the law library and key resources should be one of your primary goals as a researcher. Understanding the facts of your client's problem is the first step. The second step is articulation of a legal problem or issue. The third step involves locating relevant legal resources. Secondary sources and finding tools are used to locate and interpret primary law such as case law, statutes, and the Constitution.

Terms to Remember

primary sources	form book	rules of law
secondary sources	law review	holding
issue	treatise	precedent
relevant	digest	regional reporter
bifurcate	case law	stare decisis
legal encyclopedia	reporter	brief
finding tools	LEXIS	statute
annotation	Westlaw	pocket part

Questions for Review

1. Name two basic sources of the law. Include three examples of each type of source.
2. Name and explain the three types of facts.
3. What is a legal encyclopedia?
4. What is case law?
5. What is precedent?
6. Why are pocket parts important?

Questions for Analysis

1. Apply the North Carolina assault statute found in Section 4–5 to the following facts.
   a. Bobby is angry with his supervisor. He takes a gun to work, intending to scare his supervisor. He waves the gun around while yelling at the supervisor. The police are called. Officer Goodman approaches Bobby and asks for the weapon. Bobby accidentally fires the gun, injuring Officer Goodman in the hand. Did Bobby violate the assault statute? Explain your response.

b. Bobby is angry with his supervisor. He takes a gun to work, intending to scare his supervisor. He stops at a local saloon to fortify himself for the confrontation with his supervisor. While Bobby is having a beer, the bartender notices the gun in Bobby's coat. John Goodman, an off-duty security guard, is having coffee at a table. The bartender tells him about Bobby's gun. Goodman approaches Bobby and asks for the weapon. Bobby accidentally fires the gun, injuring Goodman. Did Bobby violate the assault statute? Explain your response.

2. Summarize the factual dispute in *Lorilland Tobacco Co. v. Reilly*. The case syllabus (summary) is found in Appendix VII.

Assignments and Projects

1. Read the *Modnick* case again. As you read the case, identify the facts, the issues, the rules or laws, the holding, and the conclusion. Notice how the court explains or analyzes in this decision. Refer back to the Welch case at the beginning of the chapter. Identify each fact that applies to each element of fraud.
2. Locate the following cases. For each, write the correct citation, including the year. You may use an online source such as Findlaw, or you may locate the cases in a print resource in the law library.
   491 U.S. 274
   372 U.S. 335
   367 U.S. 643
   384 U.S. 436
   474 U.S. 82

CHAPTER 5

USING THE LAW

ANALYSIS AND LEGAL WRITING

Technology Corner

Web Address	Name of Site
www.dictionary.com/	Dictionary.com
www.onelook.com/	OneLook Dictionaries
www.thesaurus.com/	Thesaurus.com
www.bartleby.com/141/	The Elements of Style
www.law.cornell.edu/citation/citation.table.html	Introduction to Basic Legal Citation
www2.law.cornell.edu/cgi-binfoliocgi.exe/citation?	Basic Legal Citation

CASE FILE: THE TRAN FAMILY LAW MATTER

In the Tran family law matter, the couple never married. However, they lived together for almost twenty years, most of their friends think they are married, and they own a good deal of real and personal property. Most of the property is held in some form of joint ownership. The supervising attorney seems to remember that in the mid-1970s there was a California case, *Marvin v. Marvin*, that addressed issues similar to the issues in the Tran matter.

SEC. 5-1 INTRODUCTION

legal analysis
The process of comparing and contrasting facts and legal issues.

Once you have completed your research, you must analyze your results and then communicate your findings to the appropriate person. Legal analysis often involves several steps. The process of comparing or aligning the facts of a client's case with the elements of a statute is one step of **legal analysis**. Similarly, comparing the facts and issues of a client's case with the facts and issues of a reported case is another step in the process of legal analysis. With practice, finding the law is not difficult. The question becomes, "What do I do with it, now that I have found it?" Locating relevant case law and statutes that apply to a client's situation is often the ultimate goal of the legal researcher.

When you begin serious research, you will be armed with the facts of your client's case, which will help you identify and articulate the legal issues involved. In Chapter 4 you learned to categorize facts as *relevant, explanatory,* or *unimportant.* Once you have done so, you are ready to compare and contrast the facts of reported decisions with the facts of your client's situation, as described in Chapter 4. This process is an essential analytical skill.

A researcher's job is not complete until the law is analyzed and communicated.

SEC. 5-2 APPROACHING A LEGAL RESEARCH ANALYSIS AND WRITING PROJECT

OVERVIEW

These questions or considerations are designed to help the legal writer focus on the project and recognize problem areas.

1. What exactly is the research project or what is your goal?
2. Who is the reading audience?
3. What legal issues does the research explore?
4. How will the reading audience benefit from the results of the research?
5. List the most important points you must get across to your audience.
6. List the legal authority that supports each point listed in question 5.

7. Which citation manual must be followed?

   [*Uniform System of Citation* (Bluebook), *Chicago Manual of Style*]
8. Is there a length restriction? If so, what is it?
9. How long is your current draft?
10. When must this project be completed?

These questions help the writer focus and provide structure to the process of research, analysis and writing.

Preparing a First Draft

1. Reread the directions. Ask yourself:

   Do I fully understand what I have been asked to do? If not, get clarification.

   Do I have a mental picture of the document I must create? If not, get an example.

   Do I have a deadline?

   Do I have special instructions?
2. Begin the project *only* after framing clear answers to the preceding questions.
3. Begin the project in a logical fashion.

   Using a word processor, create an outline of the material to be covered. Leave plenty of space between the sections.

   Fill in the outline with key words and phrases.

   Make a separate list of problem areas.

   Identify the easy parts of the project. Consider doing these portions first.

   Identify the difficult part of the project. Create a special approach for this part of the project.
4. Choose one section of the project and begin writing the first draft. Do not worry about spelling, grammar, consistency, or anything else at this point. Just get your ideas on paper. There will be plenty of time to edit your work.

A POINT TO REMEMBER

While drafting, try not to slow yourself down worrying about small writing errors. Get your ideas on the screen or page. You will have time to go back and edit your work. Sometimes valuable ideas are lost because we try to make our first draft absolutely perfect. Draft the document. Go back to edit.

5. Complete one section of the first draft before you move on to another section. Try to accomplish closure of small portions of the project. This will serve you well in the workplace. It is easy to show your supervisor small portions of a project; in this way the supervisor sees you are organized and proceeding in a logical fashion.

6. Consider this: Will placing material into a chronology help you? Will the chronology help the reader? If it helps you, do it, in an effort to get your ideas on paper. If a chronology will not be particularly helpful to the reader, do not use it in the final copy.

   A chronological list may help the writer sort out a large number of facts or events. This list probably does not belong in the final written product, but it is a good outlining tool during the drafting stage.

   As you look at a long, often very detailed list, you may begin to see where you can combine facts or events. Or you may begin to see a pattern emerge. For example, if you have a series of judicial events, think about lumping them into a time frame, or addressing the happenings at each court level, or saying "Petitioner's various motions to reopen the case were repeatedly denied" or "Defendant's motions were heard favorably in the appellate court, but the state supreme court was not so lenient. . . ."

   Remember, not all judicial events are equal in importance; even the number of hearings or trials may not be significant. In a summary the writer cannot possibly cover everything in the original document. The writer must make choices based on knowledge and analytical skill, learned through practice.

7. If you are summarizing a document, is it written in a specific format or order? If there *is* a specific format or order, adopt it if at all possible. Until you fully understand the document to be summarized, you will not be able to create an effective summary. Ask yourself the following questions:

   On what does the author of the document focus?

   On what does the author spend the most time?

   What seems most critical to the author of the document? (*not* What do *you* think is most important?)

   Follow the format of the original document.

8. Go back to the directions. Are you still focused? Have you done what you were asked to do? Is your document clear and concise? Is it in the appropriate format? When is the deadline?

9. At this point, put your draft away for twenty-four to forty-eight hours. Just let it sit, avoid even thinking about it. Then get out a brightly colored pen (felt pens are hard to miss); reread the directions (yes, again), and start reading at the beginning, marking as you go. Look for the following:

   Errors (spelling, grammar, etc.)

   Passive voice (use active voice, if possible)

   Long sentences (count the words!)

Topic sentences (make sure you have them)

Format consistency

Internal consistency

Vagueness

Redundancy

10. At this point, you should have marked all sorts of things. Make the necessary corrections and put the document aside. You are done. Going over and over and over a document is not realistic. Of course, we all strive for some degree of perfection, but the sheer reality of the working world often precludes perfection in all aspects of every project. Remember: Sometimes our changes are just changes, not improvements. You can overthink and overedit your work. Closure is a good thing!

Beginning the Writing Process

Initial Considerations

Before you begin to write, go back to your initial instructions. Have you followed them?

Did you answer the questions clearly and concisely?

Did you respond to all of the questions?

Can you honestly tell your supervisor that your research results are accurate and current and have been validated?

Have you been as thorough as possible?

If your response to each of these questions is yes, then you are ready to begin the actual writing process. After the research is complete, note taking and copying is replaced with analysis and writing.

The Thesis Paragraph

A professional analysis is focused and clear from the first word, laying a solid foundation for the reader. Before you begin to write, slow down and consider what your reader knows about the problem. You may have worked with the project for many hours and become extremely familiar with all aspects of the problem. However, the reader may have little or no knowledge.

A legal discussion or argument should begin with a thesis paragraph. In this paragraph, you will do the following:

1. Set forth the client's problem.
2. State the legal issue(s).
3. Briefly explain the legal rules governing the issues.
4. State the legal conclusion (the thesis).

The thesis paragraph thus provides a short overview of the internal organization of the argument section of a trial brief or the discussion section of a memorandum. Clearly, this important paragraph cannot be written until the research is complete and the final analysis is performed.

The following paragraphs are taken from the Argument section of the Brief for the United States as Amicus Curiae Supporting Petitioner in *Minnesota v. Dickerson,* 508 U.S. 366 (1993). Notice that each paragraph follows the format set out previously.

> I. The Minnesota Supreme Court erred in holding that the police officer who searched respondent exceeded the scope of the protective pat-down search authorized under *Terry v. Ohio. Terry* authorizes a "careful exploration" of a suspect's outer clothing for weapons. 392 U.S. at 16. Officer Rose's brief and limited touching of the pocket of respondent's jacket was an appropriate part of the "careful" examination permitted under *Terry.* Officer Rose did not engage in the sort of prolonged and intrusive manipulation of clothing about which the state supreme court expressed concern. Nor does the record support the suggestion of the state supreme court that Rose made a discrete, conscious decision to continue handling the object in respondent's pocket after concluding that the object was not a weapon. Instead, the officer's act of feeling the object was merely a continuation of a pat-down search indisputably justified at its inception. For that reason, the officer's actions are distinguishable from the conduct found to constitute a separate, unauthorized search in *Arizona v. Hicks,* 480 U.S. 321 (1987).
>
> II. The Minnesota Supreme Court also erred in holding that the sense of touch can never provide probable cause to believe that the object felt is contraband. This Court has recognized that probable cause can be acquired through senses other than the sense of sight. For example, in *United States v. Johns,* 469 U.S. 478 (1985), the Court held that the "distinct odor of marihuana" provided probable cause to believe that the vehicles from which the odor emanated contained contraband. Moreover, this Court's decision in *Terry* is premised on the ability of police officers to detect concealed firearms by touching the outside of a suspect's clothing. Many lower federal courts have held that the sense of touch may provide probable cause to believe that an item is contraband. In holding to the contrary, the court below mistakenly relied on the differences it perceived between the sense of sight and the sense of touch. Those differences do not warrant a categorical prohibition of the use of the sense of touch to acquire probable cause.

Sentences and Paragraphs

Sentences are groups of words that express a complete thought. A sentence must have a noun and a verb. In legal writing it is best to keep your sentences short and direct. A concise, well-thought-out sentence is easy to read and understand. Long, convoluted sentences are hard to follow and may actually present unwanted ambiguities.

An effective *paragraph* is a grouping of related sentences that flow logically and address one idea. It should be clear to the reader why a certain sentence is in a certain paragraph. Good paragraph construction takes time and patience. For each sentence, the writer must ultimately answer the question: Why is *this sentence* in *this paragraph*?

Consider the type of analysis to be used in the paragraph before drafting the body of the paragraph. A good paragraph does not assume too much knowledge on the reader's part; it is self-explanatory. Various analytical tools are available to the legal writer. A well-constructed paragraph may use a chronological narration of the facts, comparison and contrast, or cause and effect to present the information.

Most paragraphs begin with a special type of sentence; a *topic sentence*. A good topic sentence introduces issues or subissues and connects back to the thesis paragraph. An effective topic sentence creates unity in the paragraph by summarizing the point made in the entire paragraph. The topic sentence forces the writer to articulate the point of the paragraph. Sentences in a paragraph need to be more than just vaguely related to each other. The topic sentence sets forth the relationship at the very beginning of the paragraph.

A POINT TO REMEMBER

Topic sentences may be added after the paragraph has been drafted in rough format. If you find that writing good topic sentences slows you down or even stops the flow of your writing, add them during the editing process.

Avoid placing a citation in the topic sentence. Readers are distracted by citations, and may miss the actual emphasis of the sentence.

During the editing process, make an outline using only the first (topic) sentences of each paragraph. Review this outline. Does it flow? Can you easily follow the information? Topic sentences are a good way to check the internal organization of most legal documents.

These are the topic sentences from the two paragraphs taken from one of the briefs filed in the *Minnesota v. Dickerson* case.

Topic Sentence

> The Minnesota Supreme Court erred in holding that the police officer who searched respondent exceeded the scope of the protective pat-down search authorized under *Terry v. Ohio*.

Topic Sentence

> The Minnesota Supreme Court also erred in holding that the sense of touch can never provide probable cause to believe that the object felt is contraband.

Each sentence introduces the topic of the paragraph and is clear and concise.

The following paragraphs are from the *Minnesota v. Dickerson* decision. Notice the Court's use of detail and simple chronology. Each paragraph opens with a simple topic sentence. This topic sentence sets the scene for the information in the remainder of the paragraph.

> On the evening of November 9, 1989, two Minneapolis police officers were patrolling an area on the city's north side in a marked squad car. At about 8:15 P.M., one of the officers observed respondent leaving a 12-unit apartment building on Morgan Avenue North. The officer, having previously responded to complaints of drug sales in the building's hallways and having executed several search warrants on the premises, considered the building to be a notorious "crack house." According to testimony credited by the trial court, respondent began

walking toward the police but, upon spotting the squad car and making eye contact with one of the officers, abruptly halted and began walking in the opposite direction. His suspicion aroused, this officer watched as respondent turned and entered an alley on the other side of the apartment building. Based upon respondent's seemingly evasive actions and the fact that he had just left a building known for cocaine traffic, the officers decided to stop respondent and investigate further.

The officers pulled their squad car into the alley and ordered respondent to stop and submit to a patdown search. The search revealed no weapons, but the officer conducting the search did take an interest in a small lump in respondent's nylon jacket. The officer later testified: "As I pat-searched the front of his body, I felt a lump, a small lump, in the front pocket. I examined it with my fingers and it slid and it felt to be a lump of crack cocaine in cellophane." The officer then reached into respondent's pocket and retrieved a small plastic bag containing one fifth of one gram of crack cocaine. Respondent was arrested and charged in Hennepin County District Court with possession of a controlled substance.

Editing and Revision Process

1. Print the document. If time permits, let it sit for a day or two before you look at it again. Reread your instructions. Have you adequately responded to the initial questions?
2. Look over the document. Do not read it; just glance through it.
3. Is the organization of the document readily apparent, without actually reading it? If not, consider going back and working in appropriate point headings.
4. Check to see that each paragraph contains a topic sentence or a sentence that serves as a transition from the previous paragraph.
5. Does the discussion or argument section begin with a thesis paragraph? If not, insert a thesis paragraph now.
6. Make sure each paragraph contains facts or law to support your position.
7. Identify the verbs. Highlight the following: *was, were, is, are, has been, have been, had been, becomes, became, went, did,* and *came.* Where possible, replace these with active verbs. Active verbs create a mental picture of a specific sensation, activity, or sound in the reader's imagination.
8. Place transition words or phrases between sentences and paragraphs when appropriate.
9. Reread the opening of your document. Does it clearly and concisely introduce the topic of your writing? If not, edit or rewrite.
10. Reread the conclusion. Does it clearly and concisely conclude your document? If not, edit or rewrite. When you complete the conclusion, ask yourself whether you have created a tone of finality.

Finally, ask yourself the following questions: Did you understand the parameters of your project? Is your writing clear and concise? Is your research accurate, current and validated? Have you been thorough?

Keeping Legal Writing Simple

> **A POINT TO REMEMBER**
>
> Your legal writing is not meant to *entertain* the reader. It is usually designed to inform or convince the reader. Many of the tools that fiction writers use to entertain—for example, varying sentence length, creative use of adjectives, and unnecessary words—must be avoided in legal writing. You are writing with a very specific purpose. Stay focused on the purpose of the document and the audience who will ultimately read it.

Use Short Sentences

Keep your sentences short. Use twenty-five words or less as your benchmark of an easily readable sentence. Long sentences become hard to read or even unreadable. As you review your written work, look for sentences that are longer than three lines. Edit those sentences; in most cases they are too long for your reader to easily follow. Editing may involve cutting the sentence down in size or rewriting it as more than one sentence.

Use Active Voice

Use *active voice* whenever possible. Sentences written in active voice usually follow this pattern of construction: subject-verb-object. In other words, open with the actor, move to the action, and then go on to the object of the action. Active-voice sentences are very easy to read because they open with a specific actor who then does something to someone or some object.

- Active voice: She quickly regretted her actions.
- Passive voice: The actions were quickly regretted by her.

- Active voice: Victor kicked the ball.
- Passive voice: The ball was kicked by Victor.

- Active voice: Susan drove the vehicle.
- Passive voice: The vehicle was driven by Susan.

Notice that the active-voice sentences are shorter than the passive-voice sentences. Check for passive voice while you edit your writing. If you think about it while you are drafting, it will slow you down and you may even lose your thoughts.

Avoid Unnecessary Words

Keep your legal writing simple. Get to the point, rather than introduce the point. Over the years, somewhere in one of our English courses, we were told to introduce the topic. So we learned to open our sentences with a phrase that tells the reader what we are about to do. Edit those phrases and words out of your legal writing.

Use Specific, Concrete Terms

Use specific terminology in your legal writing. Ambiguity arises when vague words invade the legal writing. Be as specific as the facts of your situation allow. Use the most important facts to tell a clear story about people.

SEC. 5-3 THE CASE BRIEF

case brief
A short summary of a published case.

Before completing a legal analysis and writing project, you might find it helpful to brief the case law you have found. A **case brief** is one way to summarize a reported case. The brief helps you identify the key facts and issues; then you are prepared to compare the reported case with your client's situation.

THE COMPONENTS OF A CASE BRIEF

A judge, writing to inform the legal community, has certain goals in every reported case. It is important that the reader of any case understand the following:

Who are the parties?

If the case is an appeal, what happened in the lower court(s)?

What happened to bring these parties into court in the first place?

What is the legal question before *this* court?

What rules (primary law) did the court rely on in reaching its decision?

How did the court analyze the facts in light of the legal question and the rules?

How did the court resolve the dispute?

These questions lay the foundation for the components of a case brief. Most case briefs will contain at least the following elements:

Name and citation of the case—The name of the case, the citation, and the year are essential. Always provide the name and full citation of the case at the beginning of the case brief.

Miranda v. Arizona,	384 U.S. 436,	86 S. Ct. 1602, 16 L. Ed. 2d 694	(1966)
Name	Official Citation	Unofficial Sources	Year

Judicial history—The judicial history explains how the case traveled through the courts. The reader of the brief needs to know who sued whom and why. Let the reader know what happened in each of the lower courts.

Facts—Include only the facts that are relevant to the court's reasoning and decision.

question presented
A statement of the legal issue presented to the court for resolution.

adjudicate
To resolve; when the court adjudicates an issue, the issue is resolved. Adjudication is the process of exercising judicial power.

Issue(s)—The issue is the **question presented** to the court for resolution. The issue or question presented should be one sentence long and is best written as a question. Most of the cases you read are cases with judicial history. This means that lower courts have already **adjudicated** these issues. The case you are briefing is probably an appeal of what the lower court decided. Many times the issue is stated in the format of "Did the lower court err when it held . . . ?" This question presented, or issue, is simply asking, "Did the last court to hear this case make one or more mistakes in its resolution of the legal issues?"

Rule(s)—The rules section is usually a listing of the laws the court relied on in the analysis or reasoning. This might include statutes, case law, articles or amendments from the Constitution, or other primary sources of the law. This section does not include *every* source discussed by the court, just the relevant primary sources. Each statute, case, or constitutional reference should include a very brief statement explaining the topic of the statute, the relevance of the case law cited, or the title of the constitutional reference. There is no need to go into depth in this section, because all of this will be explained in the analysis section.

Analysis or reasoning—This is the lengthiest section of most case briefs. It is also the most important section. The analysis incorporates much of the information from the facts, issues, and rules into a focused discussion. If you are asked to read and brief a case for someone else, that person has not read the case. The reader must understand why the court resolved the issues as it did. This section never includes the writer's personal analysis or opinions. Think of the analysis as a summary of how the court analyzed the facts and issues. Notice the laws used or discussed by the court. All of this will provide the court's rationale or reasoning that supports the ultimate holding or conclusion made by the court.

Conclusion or holding—The conclusion or holding is the court's answer to the issue or question presented. Each issue will have a conclusion. It is easiest simply to list each issue with its answer. Keep this section short and to the point. This is not a discussion section.

A POINT TO REMEMBER

Whenever possible, make a copy of the case you plan to brief. In the margins, for each paragraph, note which element (or elements) are included in that paragraph. This technique helps you focus as you read and provides organization as you begin writing the brief.

Try the notes-in-the-margin technique with the following case. *Gideon v. Wainwright* is an important U.S. Supreme Court case that was decided in the early 1960s. The Court actually overrules one of its earlier decisions. Notice the Court's discussion of the *Betts v. Brady* case.

As you read the case, locate the following:

The name and the citation of the case—names of litigants and correct legal citation for this reported case.

The judicial history—What happened in the lower court(s)?

The facts—What happened to bring the parties before the court?

The issues— What is the legal question before *this* court?

The rules— What rules (primary law) did the court rely on in reaching its decision?

The analysis— How did the court analyze the facts in light of the legal question and the rules?

The conclusion— How did the court resolve the dispute?

Gideon v. Wainwright

372 U.S. 335, 83 S. Ct. 792, 9 L. Ed. 2d 799 (1963)

This 1963 case is a benchmark in criminal justice. Mr. Gideon successfully challenged the state of Florida in a battle over whether he was entitled to a court-appointed attorney. The issue here is whether the trial and conviction of Mr. Gideon violated his rights under the Fourteenth Amendment. Mr. Gideon requested a court–appointed attorney. The court denied his request. He defended himself on charges of breaking and entering a poolroom. A jury found him guilty. Mr. Gideon appealed based on the court's denial of his request for court-appointed counsel. The Florida State Supreme Court upheld the lower court's decision. The U.S. Supreme Court reversed the Florida Supreme Court and in the process overruled Betts v. Brady. *The Court followed* Powell v. Alabama *and held that the right to counsel is fundamental and essential to a fair trial.*

SYLLABUS

Charged in a Florida State Court with a noncapital felony, petitioner appeared without funds and without counsel and asked the Court to appoint counsel for him; but this was denied on the ground that the state law permitted appointment of counsel for indigent defendants in capital cases only. Petitioner conducted his own defense about as well as could be expected of a layman; but he was convicted and sentenced to imprisonment. Subsequently, he applied to the State Supreme Court for a writ of habeas corpus, on the ground that his conviction violated his rights under the Federal Constitution. The State Supreme Court denied all relief.

Held: The right of an indigent defendant in a criminal trial to have the assistance of counsel is a fundamental right essential to a fair trial, and petitioner's trial and conviction without the assistance of counsel violated the Fourteenth Amendment.

Betts v. Brady, 316 U.S. 455 (1942), [is] overruled.

OPINION

I

Petitioner was charged in a Florida state court with having broken and entered a poolroom with intent to commit a misdemeanor. This offense is a felony under Florida law. Appearing in court without funds and without a lawyer, petitioner asked the court to appoint counsel for him, whereupon the following colloquy took place:

"The COURT: Mr. Gideon, I am sorry, but I cannot appoint Counsel to represent you in this case. Under the laws of the State of Florida, the only time the Court can appoint Counsel to represent a Defendant is when that person is charged with a capital offense. I am sorry, but I will have to deny your request to appoint Counsel to defend you in this case.

The DEFENDANT: The United States Supreme Court says I am entitled to be represented by Counsel."

Put to trial before a jury, Gideon conducted his defense about as well as could be expected from a layman. He made an opening statement to the jury, cross-examined the State's witnesses, presented witnesses in his own defense, declined to testify himself, and made a short argument "emphasizing his innocence to the charge contained in the Information filed in this case." The jury returned a verdict of guilty, and petitioner was sentenced to serve five years in the state prison. Later, petitioner filed in the Florida Supreme Court this habeas corpus petition attacking his conviction and sentence on the ground that the trial court's refusal to appoint counsel for him denied him rights "guaranteed by the Constitution and the Bill of Rights by the United States Government." Treating the petition for habeas corpus as properly before it, the State Supreme Court, "upon consideration thereof" but without an opinion, denied all relief. Since 1942, when *Betts v. Brady*, 316 U.S. 455, was decided by a divided Court, the problem of a defendant's federal constitutional right to counsel in a state court has been a continuing source of controversy and litigation in both state and federal courts. To give this problem another review here, we granted certiorari. 370 U.S. 908. Since Gideon was proceeding in *forma pauperis*, we appointed counsel to represent him and requested both sides to discuss in their briefs and oral arguments the following: "Should this Court's holding in *Betts v. Brady*, 316 U.S. 455, be reconsidered?"

The facts upon which Betts claimed that he had been unconstitutionally denied the right to have counsel appointed to assist him are strikingly like the facts upon which Gideon here bases his federal constitutional claim. Betts was indicted for robbery in a Maryland state court. On arraignment, he told the trial judge of his lack of funds to hire a lawyer and asked the court to appoint one for him. Betts was advised that it was not the practice in that county to appoint counsel for indigent defendants except in murder and rape cases. He then pleaded not guilty, had witnesses summoned, cross-examined the State's witnesses, examined his own, and chose not to testify himself. He was found guilty by the judge, sitting without a jury, and sentenced to eight years in prison. Like Gideon, Betts sought release by habeas corpus, alleging that he had been denied the right to assistance of counsel in violation of the Fourteenth Amendment. Betts was denied any relief, and on review this Court affirmed. It was held that a refusal to appoint counsel for an indigent defendant charged with a felony did not necessarily violate the Due Process Clause of the Fourteenth Amendment, which for reasons given the Court deemed to be the only applicable federal constitutional provision. The Court said:

> "Asserted denial [of due process] is to be tested by an appraisal of the totality of facts in a given case. That which may, in one setting, constitute a denial of fundamental fairness, shocking to the universal sense of justice, may, in other circumstances, and in the light of other considerations, fall short of such denial." 316 U.S. at 462.

Treating due process as "a concept less rigid and more fluid than those envisaged in other specific and particular provisions of the Bill of Rights," the Court held that refusal to appoint counsel under the particular facts and circumstances in the Betts case was not so "offensive to the common and fundamental ideas of fairness" as to amount to a denial of due process. Since the facts and circumstances of the two cases are so nearly indistinguishable, we think the *Betts v. Brady* holding if left standing would require us to reject Gideon's claim that the Constitution guarantees him the assistance of counsel. Upon full reconsideration we conclude that *Betts v. Brady* should be overruled.

II

The Sixth Amendment provides, "In all criminal prosecutions, the accused shall enjoy the right . . . to have the Assistance of Counsel for his defense." We have construed this to mean that in federal courts counsel must be provided for defendants unable to employ counsel unless the right is competently and intelligently waived. Betts argued that this right is extended to indigent defendants in state courts by the Fourteenth Amendment. In response the Court stated that, while the Sixth Amendment laid down "no rule for the conduct of the States, the question recurs whether the constraint laid by the Amendment upon the national courts expresses a rule so fundamental and essential to a fair trial, and so, to due process of law, that it is made obligatory upon the States by the Fourteenth Amendment." 316 U.S. at 465. In order to decide whether the Sixth Amendment's guarantee of counsel is of this fundamental nature, the Court in *Betts* set out and considered "relevant data on the subject . . . afforded by constitutional and statutory provisions subsisting in the colonies and the States prior to the inclusion of the Bill of Rights in the national Constitution, and in the constitutional, legislative, and judicial history of the States to the present date." 316 U.S. at 465. On the basis of this historical data the Court concluded that "appointment of counsel is not a fundamental right, essential to a fair trial." 316 U.S. at 471. It was for this reason [that] the *Betts* Court refused to accept the contention that the Sixth Amendment's guarantee of counsel for indigent federal defendants was extended to or, in the words of that Court, "made obligatory upon the States by the Fourteenth Amendment." Plainly, had the Court concluded that appointment of counsel for an indigent criminal defendant was "a fundamental right, essential to a fair trial," it would have held that the Fourteenth Amendment requires appointment of counsel in a state court, just as the Sixth Amendment requires in a federal court.

We think the Court in *Betts* had ample precedent for acknowledging that those guarantees of the Bill of Rights which are fundamental safeguards of liberty immune from federal abridgment are equally protected against state invasion by the Due Process Clause of the Fourteenth Amendment. In many cases . . . this Court has looked to the fundamental nature of original Bill of Rights guarantees to decide whether the Fourteenth Amendment makes them obligatory on the States. Explicitly recognized to be of this "fundamental nature" and therefore made immune from state invasion by the Fourteenth, or some part of it, are the First Amendment's freedoms of speech, press, religion, assembly, association, and petition for redress of grievances . . .

We accept *Betts v. Brady's* assumption, based as it was on our prior cases, that a provision of the Bill of Rights which is "fundamental and essential to a fair trial" is made obligatory upon the States by the Fourteenth Amendment. We think the Court in *Betts* was wrong, however, in concluding that the Sixth Amendment's guarantee of counsel is not one of these fundamental rights. Ten years before *Betts v. Brady,* this Court, after full consideration of all the historical data examined in *Betts,* had unequivocally declared that "the right to the aid of counsel is of this fundamental character." *Powell v. Alabama,* 287 U.S. 45, 68 (1932). While the Court at the close of its *Powell* opinion did by its language, as this Court frequently does, limit its holding to the particular facts and circumstances of that case, its conclusions about the fundamental nature of the right to counsel are unmistakable. . . .

In light of this and many other prior decisions of this Court, it is not surprising that the *Betts* Court, when faced with the contention that "one charged with crime, who is unable to obtain counsel, must be furnished counsel by the State," conceded that "expressions in the opinions of this court lend color to the argument. . . ." 316 U.S. at 462–463. The fact is that in deciding as it did—that "appointment of counsel is not a fundamental right, essential to a fair trial"—the Court in *Betts v. Brady* made an abrupt break with its own well-considered precedents. In returning to these old precedents, sounder we believe than the new, we but restore constitutional principles established to achieve a fair system of justice. Not only these precedents but also reason and reflection require us to recognize that in our adversary system of criminal justice, any person hauled into court, who is too poor to hire a lawyer, cannot be assured a fair trial unless counsel is provided for him. This seems to us to be an obvious truth. Governments, both state and federal, quite properly spend vast sums of money to establish machinery to try defendants accused of crime. Lawyers to prosecute are everywhere deemed essential to protect the public's interest in an orderly society. Similarly, there are few defendants charged with crime, few indeed, who fail to hire the best lawyers they can get to prepare and present their defenses. That government hires lawyers to prosecute and defendants who have the money hire lawyers to defend are the strongest indications of the widespread belief that lawyers in criminal courts are necessities, not luxuries. The right of one charged with crime to counsel may not be deemed fundamental and essential to fair trials in some countries, but it is in ours. From the very beginning, our state and national constitutions and laws have laid great emphasis on procedural and substantive safeguards designed to assure fair trials before impartial tribunals in which every defendant stands equal before the law. This noble ideal cannot be realized if the poor man charged with crime has to face his accusers without a lawyer to assist him. A defendant's need for a lawyer is nowhere better stated than in the moving words of Mr. Justice Sutherland in *Powell v. Alabama*:

> "The right to be heard would be, in many cases, of little avail if it did not comprehend the right to be heard by counsel. Even the intelligent and educated layman has small and sometimes no skill in the science of law. If charged with crime, he is incapable, generally, of determining for himself whether the indictment is good or bad. He is unfamiliar with the rules of evidence. Left without the aid of counsel he may be put on trial without a proper charge, and convicted upon incompetent evidence, or evidence irrelevant to the issue or otherwise inadmissible. He lacks both the skill and knowledge adequately to prepare his defense, even though he may have a perfect one. He requires the guiding hand of counsel at every step in the proceedings against him. Without it, though he be not guilty, he faces the danger of conviction because he does not know how to establish his innocence." 287 U.S. at 68–69.

The Court in *Betts v. Brady* departed from the sound wisdom upon which the Court's holding in *Powell v. Alabama* rested. Florida, supported by two other States, has asked that *Betts v. Brady* be left intact. Twenty-two States, as friends of the Court, argue that Betts was "an anachronism when handed down" and that it should now be overruled. We agree.

The judgment is reversed and the cause is remanded to the Supreme Court of Florida for further action not inconsistent with this opinion.

CASE ANALYSIS

1. Why didn't the original trial court appoint a lawyer for Mr. Gideon?
2. Why was the *Betts* case overruled?

How to Write a Case Brief

Each of the six elements should be set forth as a separate section of the brief. Paragraphs explaining the element follow each section title. The Analysis, or reasoning, section will combine or synthesize much of what is included in the Facts, Issues, and Rules sections.

If a research assistant were asked to read and summarize the *Gideon* case, the brief might look like the following case brief. Remember, each person who reads a case will view it somewhat differently. This is just one way to write a case brief.

Gideon v. Wainwright

372 U.S. 335, 83 S. Ct. 792, 9 L. Ed. 2d 799 (1963)

Judicial History: Gideon was convicted of a noncapital felony and sentenced to imprisonment in the state of Florida. His application for a writ of habeas corpus was denied by the Florida State Supreme Court. Gideon appealed to the U.S. Supreme Court.

Facts: Gideon was charged with breaking and entering a poolroom. When the trial court denied his request for counsel, he conducted his own defense. The jury found him guilty.

Issues: (1) Did Gideon's trial and conviction violate his rights under the Fourteenth Amendment?

(2) Should *Betts v. Brady* be overruled? (This issue was raised by the Court. Both sides were asked to discuss the issue.)

Rules: Fourteenth Amendment—due process clause

Sixth Amendment—"In all criminal prosecutions, the accused shall enjoy the right . . . to have the Assistance of Counsel for his defense."

Betts v. Brady, 316 U.S. 455 (1942)—stated that "appointment of counsel is not a fundamental right, essential to a fair trial. . . ." (*Betts* is reconsidered in *Gideon* and overruled.)

Powell v. Alabama, 287 U.S. 45 (1932)—the right to counsel is fundamental and essential to a fair trial. (Followed in *Gideon*.)

Analysis: The facts of the *Gideon* case are very similar to the facts of the *Betts v. Brady* case. The *Betts* case held that "a refusal to appoint counsel for an indigent defendant charged with a felony did not necessarily violate the due process clause of the Fourteenth Amendment." The Court overruled *Betts v. Brady*. Relying on the Sixth Amendment, the Court found that "counsel must be provided for defendants unable to employ counsel unless the right is competently and intelligently waived." The fundamental safeguards of liberty are protected by the due process clause of the Fourteenth Amendment. The Sixth Amendment guarantee of counsel is one of these fundamental safeguards. The Court cites the sound wisdom upon which the *Powell v. Alabama* case was decided. In *Powell*, the Court explained that a criminal defendant needs the "guiding hand of counsel at every step in the proceedings against him."

Conclusion: The judgment of the Florida State Supreme Court was reversed. The cause was remanded to that court for further action not inconsistent with this opinion. *Betts v. Brady* was overruled.

concurring opinion
A separate opinion written by one or more justices in a case; this opinion agrees with the ultimate decision of the majority of the court, but with a reasoning that differs from the reasoning of the majority of the court.

dissenting opinion
A separate opinion written by one or more justices in a case; this opinion disagrees with the decision of the majority of the court.

This is only one approach to briefing the *Gideon* case. No two people will write the exact same brief. The format for the brief may differ, but the information contained will generally fall into the six categories set forth in the sample case brief.

A POINT TO REMEMBER

Some cases include **concurring opinions** and/or **dissenting opinions**. You need to include a section explaining the concurrence or dissent if there is something important that your reader needs to know.

SEC. 5-4 THE LEGAL MEMORANDUM

legal memorandum
An informal interoffice document written to communicate the results of legal research and the resulting legal analysis.

A case brief is the first step in preparing a formal written legal analysis, often called a **legal memorandum**. Unlike a case brief, a legal memorandum compares your client's facts and issues with those found in reported cases. It also analyzes the statutory law that is appropriate to the facts of your case. A legal memorandum is prepared for various purposes. It can be an objective analysis that discusses pros and cons of the client's case. This type of analysis is usually for in-house use and is sometimes called an *interoffice legal memorandum* or a *memo of law*. On the other hand, a legal analysis could be used to support your client's position in court. As such, it is adversarial and not objective. Depending on the type of court process involved, the analysis could be a *memorandum of points and authorities*, a *trial brief*, or an *appellate brief*. Although the format for each of these may be different, the basic approach is the same.

WRITING A LEGAL MEMORANDUM

The following sections describe the components of a memorandum of law. Pay close attention to the type of information that is included in each section. The headings for the sections are called *point headings*, they guide the reader through the memorandum.

Statement of Facts

The statement of facts should be a concise statement of all relevant and explanatory facts. The information for this statement comes from your supervising attorney, your client, or documents found in the client file. Obviously you had to identify key facts before you started your research. However, what is or is not a key fact is often affected by the results of your research. Therefore, you should not write the statement of facts for a memorandum until your research is completed.

Facts are generally presented in one of the following ways:

1. *Chronologically*—A common and easy way of organizing facts in a memorandum of law is chronologically. State the facts in the order in which they occurred.
2. *By party*—Another way of organizing the facts is by party. Where multiple parties exist, they all may have their own version of the facts. Separately state each version.
3. *According to the elements of a cause of action*—When your memorandum concerns whether a cause of action exists, the facts can be presented in the same order in which you plan to discuss the elements of the cause of action.

Issue Statement

The issue statement is the question you are asked to research. The attorney requesting the research usually provides the issue statement. Sometimes you are given a very general research question, and after researching the question you determine that other questions or issues must also be addressed. Many research problems have more than one issue. These questions should also be included in the issue statement of your memorandum. The issue statement of your memorandum should be phrased as a question or questions. Review Chapter 4 for a more thorough discussion of identifying and stating the issues.

Discussion/Analysis

The discussion section in a memorandum is the section in which you explain the results of your research, answer the question or questions in the issue statement, and give the reasons for your answers. This section of the memorandum will include some of the information from the previous sections. It is not uncommon for very important information to be included in several sections of the memo.

Within the memorandum you should use *point headings* to separate the discussion of different issues. Point headings, which are required in more formal argumentative writing, are similar to chapter titles or titles of various sections within a chapter. Headings help the reader stay focused to your ideas. They can also help the writer stay focused.

Conclusion

Every memorandum should have either a conclusion or a brief answer section. Some have both. This should be a short summary of your findings. Often it contains a short and concise answer to the question raised in your issue statement.

Citing Authorities

Format

Citation of legal authorities in any type of legal writing should be in acceptable format. Often this means complying with the rules set out in *A Uniform System of Cita-*

tion ("the Bluebook"). However, your state may have its own style manual. If so, you should follow those rules. An attorney may use your memorandum as the basis for the more formal memorandum of points and authorities or trial or appellate brief. If you follow the *Bluebook* rules or your own state's style manual, you may find that when you cite a case, it is only necessary to give the official cite. Parallel cites (unofficial cites) are not needed. However, your decision to use parallel cites in a legal memorandum should also be based on some practical considerations—specifically, the type of legal authority found in your office. If your law firm has an unofficial case reporter, you must cite it in any memorandum.

A POINT TO REMEMBER

If you have photocopied important cases or statutes for your research, you might want to attach them to your memorandum. The attorney will probably want to read important legal authority. Attaching it to your memorandum will save time.

Using *Id.* and *supra*

In writing any type of legal memorandum, you will also occasionally use a shorthand or abbreviated way of citing cases. Once a case has been fully cited within the memorandum, it is not necessary to use a complete citation each time you refer to the case. If the case was the immediately preceding citation, the term *Id.* is substituted for the case name and citation. Thus, the case *United States v. Tarpley*, 945 F.2d 806 (1991), becomes *Id.* If the citation is used to support a quotation, it then becomes *Id.* at 806. *Id.* is used only when the citation is the immediately preceding citation. If citations to any legal authorities (not just cases) intervene, you cannot use *Id.* The following are accepted shorthand ways of abbreviating this case:

Tarpley, 945 F.2d 806

Tarpley, 945 F.2d at 807

945 F.2d at 807

Normally when using a shorthand abbreviation you use the first name of the parties rather than the second name. Thus, in abbreviating the case name *Smith v. Jones*, you would use *Smith*. However, where the first name is a common one such as *People* or *U.S.*, you must use the second name to avoid confusion.

Supra is used for authorities other than cases and statutes. (Although it is not approved by the *Bluebook*, you will see *supra* used with cases by attorneys and judges.)

Using Quotations

Using quotations to emphasize your point can be an effective writing tool. Overusing quotations, on the other hand, will distract the reader. You should keep quotations to a minimum. If your quotation is longer than three or four lines, reread it to see if you really need all of it. Also remember that quotations of less than three lines or less than fifty words are incorporated into the text with quotation marks. Longer quotations are indented on both right and left margins and are single-spaced. In any case, all quotations must give the citation, including the page number.

The following is a short memorandum.

FACTS

Our client, police officer Randy Rambeaux, made a traffic stop of an automobile because the driver failed to signal when making a right hand turn. The occupants of the vehicle were two young Latino males. According to one of the occupants and an independent witness the following events occurred. Rambeaux approached the car and ordered the two out of the car. When the occupants did not respond, Rambeaux opened the driver's door, grabbed the driver and pulled him out of the car. After the driver exited the vehicle, Rambeaux struck him on the head with his baton and said, "Why don't you guys go back where you belong. This country is for Americans." Rambeaux disputes that version of the facts. He states that as he was approaching the suspects' vehicle he noticed several passengers in the vehicle. Because of the location of the passengers he was unable to watch the driver and passengers at all times. Fearing for his safety, he requested that the driver and passengers exit the vehicle. Since they refused to follow his request, Rambeaux opened the driver's door and signalled for the driver to exit. As the driver exited the vehicle, he slipped and fell, hitting his head on the sidewalk. Rambeaux denies hitting anyone with the baton. He also denies making the statement. At the time of the incident, Rambeaux was off duty and was driving his own motorcycle. Since he had just gone off duty, he was still in uniform.

ISSUE

Assuming that the prosecutor can prove the allegations against Rambeaux, does Rambeaux face potential criminal liability under federal law?

DISCUSSION

I. INTRODUCTION

Assuming that the suspects' version of the facts can be proven, Title 18 §242 of the United States Code may create criminal liability for Rambeaux. This section makes it a federal crime for anyone acting under color of authority to deprive any inhabitant of any state of any Constitutional rights or subject that person to different punishments or penalties because of that person's race or color:

> Whoever, under color of any law, statute, ordinance, regulation, or custom, willfully subjects any inhabitant of any state, Territory or District to the deprivation of any rights, privileges, or immunities secured or protected by the Constitution or laws of the United States or to different punishments, pains or penalties on account of such inhabitant being an alien, or by reason of his color, or race . . . shall be fined not more than $1000 or imprisoned not more than one year, or both . . . 18 U.S.C. §242

In order for Rambeaux to be guilty of the federal crime, the following elements must be shown:

1. That he acted under color of law;
2. That he acted willfully;
3. That he deprived someone of his Constitutional rights, or
4. That he inflicted a different punishment because of the person's race or color.

II. ACTIONS UNDER COLOR OF LAW

The courts have often held that police officers acting in their capacity as law enforcement are acting under color of law and therefore are controlled by 18 U.S.C. § 242. *United States v. Reese,* 2 F.2d 870 (9th Cir. 1993). In this case, when Rambeaux made the traffic stop and ordered the occupants out of the car he was off duty. Therefore, a question arises as to whether he was acting under color of law. However, even off-duty police officers are considered to be acting under color of authority under certain situations. The case of *United States v. Tarpley,* 945 F.2d 806 (1991) explains. In the *Tarpley* case, defendant Tarpley, a deputy sheriff, learned of a past affair between his wife and Kerry Lee Vestal. He assaulted Vestal by inserting his service revolver in Vestal's mouth and told Vestal that he could get away with it because he was a cop. Tarpley also enlisted the aid of another sheriff's deputy to threaten Vestal. When they finally released Vestal, the officers followed him in a police vehicle. Tarpley was arrested and charged with violating 18 U.S.C. § 242. He was found guilty and appealed, claiming among other things, that he was not acting under color of authority at the time because he was off duty. The court of appeals found that even though he was off duty, he was still acting under color of authority because "the air of official authority pervaded the entire incident." *Tarpley,* 945 F.2d at 809. In like manner, the air of official authority pervaded the Rambeaux incident. Rambeaux was doing what police officers routinely do, stopping traffic offenders. He was acting on behalf of the state, attempting to enforce state laws. Thus, Rambeaux was acting under color of law, meeting the first element of the statute.

III. WILLFUL ACTIONS

The second requirement of 18 U.S.C. § 242 is that the actions of the defendant be willful. According to witnesses, all of the actions in this case were clearly willful. Rambeaux knew what he was doing and intended to do what he did. This was no accident. Thus, the second element is met.

IV. DEPRIVATION OF CONSTITUTIONAL RIGHTS

In making this traffic stop, Rambeaux violated the Constitutional rights of the driver. The Constitution guarantees that all persons have the right to be free from unreasonable searches and seizures. In this case, Rambeaux made a traffic stop and in doing this "seized" the persons in the vehicle, even if only temporarily. While Rambeaux may have been justified in making the stop, his conduct, as described by witnesses, during this seizure was clearly unreasonable. The use of physical force, such as occurred here, is not allowed in simple traffic stops where the offender neither uses any force nor threatens the officer with the use of force. Thus, if the witnesses are believed, the third element of the statute is met.

V. DIFFERENT PUNISHMENT, PAINS OR PENALTIES IMPOSED BECAUSE OF COLOR OR RACE

In addition to depriving another of Constitutional rights, the facts also suggest that Rambeaux used force on the victims because of their race. In doing this it could be argued that he inflicted punishment, pain or penalties because of color or race, providing an alternative basis for criminal responsibility. According to the witnesses, Rambeaux made the statement, "Why don't you guys go back where you belong. This country is for Americans." This is strong evidence of the fact that Rambeaux's actions were racially motivated.

CONCLUSION

In conclusion, if the witnesses in this case are believed, the facts support a finding of criminal responsibility on the part of Rambeaux. Even though he was off-duty, he was still in uniform and performing a routine police task. He was clearly acting under color of law. His actions were willful and constituted both a deprivation of a Constitutional right and an infliction of punishment, pain or penalty because of race or color.

A POINT TO REMEMBER

When you write a legal memorandum, you must follow the directions of your supervising attorney. If you are asked to research an issue, research that issue in a complete and objective manner. Do not research an issue that you think is more interesting or more important. If you are not sure what your supervising attorney wants, be sure to ask before you spend hours researching and writing.

SEC. 5-5 PERSUASIVE WRITING

Some of the documents you draft will need to be persuasive, that is, the document must persuade the reader to adopt the writer's point of view. Examples of such documents are trial briefs, points and authorities in support of motions, declarations, and demand letters. In persuasive writing every word, every phrase, every sentence must be carefully drafted. The writer must consider the impact the document will have on the reader. This goes beyond informative writing.

The following are excerpts from briefs filed with the U.S. Supreme Court in the *Minnesota v. Dickerson* case. The first excerpt is from the opening argument section of the brief filed for the United States as amicus curiae supporting the Petitioner.

ARGUMENT

I. OFFICER ROSE WAS CONDUCTING A LAWFUL PAT-DOWN SEARCH WHEN HE ACQUIRED PROBABLE CAUSE TO BELIEVE THAT RESPONDENT POSSESSED CONTRABAND

The Minnesota Supreme Court not only declined as a general matter to recognize a "plain feel" corollary to the "plain view" doctrine: it also held that the crack seized from respondent's pocket would not be admissible under a "plain feel" analysis in any event. The latter holding was based on the court's view that, in the course of determining that the object in respondent's pocket was crack, Officer Rose exceeded the scope of the protective pat-down search authorized under *Terry v. Ohio*. To the contrary, we submit that Officer Rose was acting within the scope of *Terry* when he developed probable cause to believe that respondent was in possession of contraband.

At the outset, we agree with the premise underlying the state court's *Terry* holding: a "plain feel" corollary to the "plain view" doctrine would not authorize a police officer to seize evidence without a warrant if the police officer violated the Fourth Amendment in the course of developing probable case to support the seizure. An "essential predicate" of a seizure based on "plain feel," like one based on "plain view," is that "the officer did not violate the Fourth Amendment in arriving at the place from which the evidence could be plainly [felt]." *Horton*

> *v. California*, 496 U.S. 128, 136 (1990). Thus, if a police officer reaches into a suspect's pocket without reasonable suspicion or probable cause and feels an object that the officer knows to be contraband, the seizure of that object cannot be justified on the ground that the seizure was the product of a "plain feel" of the object. In *Sibron v. New* York, 392 U.S. 40, 65 (1968), this Court held that such an intrusion was unlawful, because the intrusion was not justified by reasonable suspicion or probable cause to believe that the suspect had contraband or a weapon in his pocket. The Court therefore ordered suppression of the contraband found in the course of that search.
>
> Officer Rose's conduct, however, was a far cry from the sort of intrusion held to violate the Fourth Amendment in *Sibron*. This was not a case of retroactively justifying a search by what it turned up: rather, because the pat-down search was lawful, the fruits of that search could be considered in determining the lawfulness of Officer Rose's further investigative steps.

The second excerpt is from the opening argument section of the brief filed for the American Civil Liberties Union and the Minnesota Civil Liberties Union as amici curiae in support of Respondent.

> ***ARGUMENT***
>
> I. THE WARRANTLESS SEARCH OF RESPONDENT'S POCKET CONTRAVENED THE FOURTH AMENDMENT BY EXCEEDING THE SCOPE OF *TERRY*.
>
> A. A *Terry* frisk is limited solely to a narrowly-tailored search for weapons.
>
> In *Terry v. Ohio*, this Court set forth the standard governing pat-downs of temporarily detailed suspects: an officer can only conduct a limited protective search for weapons (a "frisk") when there is "reason to believe that he is dealing with an armed and dangerous individual. . . ." 392 U.S. at 27. Although subsequent cases have extended *Terry*'s reach to other contexts, this Court has never deviated from the fundamental rule that a frisk is singularly limited to weapon searches, and thus, cannot be conducted simply to locate contraband or evidence of crime.
>
> These principles were reaffirmed in *Ybarra v. Illinois*: "The *Terry* case created an exception to the requirement of probable cause, an exception whose 'narrow scope' this Court 'has been careful to maintain.' Under that doctrine a law enforcement officer, for his own protection and safety, may conduct a pat-down to find weapons that he reasonably believes or suspects are then in the possession of the person he has accosted. . . . Nothing in *Terry* can be understood to allow a generalized 'cursory search for weapons' or, indeed, any search whatever for anything but weapons."

Both briefs go on for many pages. Both are convincing. Compare and contrast these two opening arguments.

Featured Web Site: www.lectlaw.com/ref.html

This is the 'Lectric Law Library Web site.

Go Online

List the topics available in the Reference Room. Look under the "Legal Topic Areas."

Chapter Summary

Once the relevant primary law has been identified, the fourth step (you will recall that the first three steps are covered in Chapter 4) is the application of the law to your client's facts. This is the legal analysis. After analyzing the facts, the issues, and the law, you may be asked to write a legal memorandum. This memorandum includes the facts of your client's case; a statement of the legal issues; a summary of the relevant law; a discussion or analysis of the facts, the issues, and the law; and the conclusions to be drawn from the research analysis.

Terms to Remember

legal analysis
case brief
question presented
adjudicate
concurring opinion
dissenting opinion
legal memorandum

Questions for Review

1. What is the purpose of a thesis paragraph?
2. What makes a paragraph effective?
3. List the elements of a case brief.
4. What is the "notes in the margin" technique?
5. What are the elements of a legal memorandum?

Questions for Analysis

1. What was the Court's holding in *Powell v. Alabama*? (See the *Gideon v. Wainwright* case in this chapter.)
2. Reread the paragraphs taken from the argument made by the United States in support of the petitioner in *Minnesota v. Dickerson*. What tools did the author of these paragraphs use to make this argument persuasive?

Assignments and Projects

1. Write a brief for *Marvin v. Marvin*, 18 Cal. 3d 660, 124 Cal. Rptr. 815, 557 P.2d 106 (1976). Be sure to include the judicial history, facts, issues, rules/laws, the court's analysis, and the holding. The case is found in Appendix V.
2. Apply the *Marvin* case to the Tran case found in the Case File at the beginning of the chapter.

CHAPTER

LAWS

CIVIL VS. CRIMINAL

Technology Corner

Web Address	Name of Site
www.house.gov/judiciary/crim00.pdf	Federal Rules of Criminal Procedure
www.law.cornell.edu/rules/frcp	Federal Rules of Civil Procedure
www.washlaw.edu/	Washburn University School of Law
www.law.indiana.edu/v-lib/	Virtual Law Library—Indiana University School of Law
www.alllaw.com/law/federal_law/	All Law—Federal
www.ilrg.com/subject_ref.html	Internet Legal Resource Guide

CASE FILE: *UNITED STATES V. HARDTACK* AND *MARTINEZ V. HARDTACK*

After an intensive investigation, the U.S. Attorney has filed criminal charges against Harry Hardtack under 18 U.S.C. §242. The charges stemmed from an allegation that Hardtack used excessive force in making two different arrests. In addition, a separate civil lawsuit has been filed against Hardtack by Jaime Martinez, one of the victims. This suit is based on 42 U.S.C. §1983. These sections read as follows:

> Whoever, under color of any law, statute, ordinance, regulation, or custom, willfully subjects any person in any State, Territory, Commonwealth, Possession, or District to the deprivation of any rights, privileges, or immunities secured or protected by the Constitution or laws of the United States, or to different punishments, pains, or penalties, on account of such person being an alien, or by reason of his color, or race, than are prescribed for the punishment of citizens, shall be fined under this title or imprisoned not more than one year, or both; and if bodily injury results from the acts committed in violation of this section or if such acts include the use, attempted use, or threatened use of a dangerous weapon, explosives, or fire, shall be fined under this title or imprisoned not more than ten years, or both; and if death results from the acts committed in violation of this section or if such acts include kidnapping or an attempt to kidnap, aggravated sexual abuse, or an attempt to commit aggravated sexual abuse, or an attempt to kill, shall be fined under this title, or imprisoned for any term of years or for life, or both, or may be sentenced to death. (18 U.S.C. §242)
>
> Every person who, under color of any statute, ordinance, regulation, custom, or usage, of any State or Territory or the District of Columbia, subjects, or causes to be subjected, any citizen of the United States or other person within the jurisdiction thereof to the deprivation of any rights, privileges, or immunities secured by the Constitution and laws, shall be liable to the party injured in an action at law, suit in equity, or other proper proceeding for redress, except that in any action brought against a judicial officer for an act or omission taken in such officer's judicial capacity, injunctive relief shall not be granted unless a declaratory decree was violated or declaratory relief was unavailable. For the purposes of this section, any Act of Congress applicable exclusively to the District of Columbia shall be considered to be a statute of the District of Columbia. (42 U.S.C. §1983)

SEC. 6–1 INTRODUCTION

As you can tell from the two code sections in the Case File, the same act can result in both a criminal case and a civil case. The reason that we have two separate code sections for the same acts is that criminal cases are different from civil cases. Most people have some notion of the general difference between a criminal case and a civil case. A criminal case is often described as an offense against the state or society as a whole, whereas a civil case is normally described as a private dispute between parties. Consider the following three examples and determine whether each is civil or criminal:

1. Foreman drives a car (somewhat ineffectively) after consuming five martinis in one hour. Foreman is not involved in any accident and no one is injured as a result of the driving.
2. Meyers, while driving a car, is momentarily distracted by the two children sitting in the backseat who are fighting with each other. Meyers does not notice that the car in front has suddenly and unexpectedly stopped. The vehicles collide and the occupant of the first car is injured.

3. While driving an automobile in a drunken state, Stein rear-ends a vehicle driven by Silvers; as a result Silvers is injured.

Example 1 is a criminal case. Driving an automobile while under the influence of alcohol is conduct that is not accepted by society, and it has been made a crime. This is true even though no one was actually injured. Example 2 is an example of a civil action (in particular a tort, which is discussed more fully in Chapter 7). A private dispute might now arise between Meyers and the driver of the other vehicle regarding who caused the accident and who should pay for the bills. What about example 3? Is this a civil case? Or is it a criminal case? Is it an offense against the state or against Silvers individually? If you say both, you are correct. The traditional definitions of a criminal case and a civil case make it clear that both kinds of cases can result from the same factual situation. However, if one incident results in both a civil and criminal case, the cases must be handled separately; there are numerous differences in the way in which each is handled.

SEC. 6–2 WHERE CRIMINAL AND CIVIL LAWS ARE FOUND

substantive laws
Laws that define our rights and obligations.

procedural laws
Laws that dictate how we enforce our rights and obligations.

Before reviewing where the various criminal and civil laws are found, it is important to consider the difference between substantive and procedural laws. **Substantive laws** define the rights and duties of parties. They generally define what the law is and establish the legal basis for any lawsuit. **Procedural laws** relate to the enforcement of the substantive rights and duties. They dictate how a case should be handled once a dispute arises under the substantive law. For example, a law that makes burglary a crime is a substantive law. A law that gives anyone accused of burglary the right to a jury trial is a procedural law. Each of the two major categories of laws, civil and criminal, is divided into substantive principles and procedural rules. Both substantive principles and procedural rules are important in our legal system. If the substantive law does not support a party's position, then the court has no basis for granting that party any legal remedy. Likewise, if the party does not follow the procedural rules, the court might not afford legal remedies even if they are allowed under substantive legal principles.

For example, suppose Peters, driving inattentively, runs a red light and collides with a truck driven by McDonald. Peters is injured but McDonald is not. Peters wishes to sue for his damages. Peters would not prevail in any lawsuit because the substantive law does not support his claim. This kind of action is governed by tort law, in particular the law of negligence, which requires that one pay for damages that he or she negligently causes. In this case, since it is Peters and not McDonald who was negligent, the court cannot make McDonald pay for Peters's injuries. On the other hand, if McDonald was injured, the court could impose liability on Peters for those injuries.

statute of limitations
A law that places a time limit on when a lawsuit can be filed.

Assume, however, that the accident happens in a state that has a one-year **statute of limitations**. A statute of limitations is a time limit that a person has to file a lawsuit in court. If McDonald waits three years after the accident to sue, the court will probably dismiss the action because McDonald has not followed the procedural rules of the state.

Substantive laws exist for both criminal and civil actions, as do procedural rules. One of the differences between criminal and civil actions concerns the sources of these laws.

Substantive Laws—Criminal

crime
An act in violation of a criminal statute.

Substantive criminal laws deal with crimes. **Crimes** are types of behavior that society has declared illegal and has decided to punish. Standard punishments include jail or fines. Before a person can be tried and punished for any criminal offense, that person is entitled to *due process of law* under the U.S. Constitution. The concept of due process includes the requirement that individuals accused of crimes must be able to know ahead of time that their conduct constitutes a crime. In other words, there must be a law that prohibits the conduct in question and that law must be sufficiently certain and clear so that individual is capable of knowing what is permissible and what is illegal. Therefore, crimes are most commonly defined in statutes. Furthermore, these statutes must be sufficiently detailed and specific in order to meet constitutional requirements. In addition to adequately describing the proscribed conduct, criminal statutes must also specifically describe the penalty to be imposed in the event that one is found to have violated the statute. For example, in researching the possible crimes committed by Hardtack, the following state statutes might be applicable:

> ***Battery Defined***
>
> A battery is any willful and unlawful use of force or violence upon the person of another.
>
> ***Punishment for Battery***
>
> A battery is punishable by a fine not exceeding two thousand dollars ($2,000), or by imprisonment in a county jail for a term not exceeding six months, or by both the fine and imprisonment.
>
> ***Interfering with a Person's Civil Rights***
>
> (a) No person, whether or not acting under color of law, shall by force or threat of force, willfully injure, intimidate, interfere with, oppress, or threaten any other person in the free exercise of enjoyment of any right or privilege secured to him or her by the Constitution of the United States because of the other person's race, color, religion, ancestry, national origin, disability, gender, or sexual orientation.
>
> (b) Any person convicted of violating this section shall be punished by imprisonment in a county jail not to exceed one year, or by a fine not to exceed five thousand dollars ($5,000), or by both that imprisonment and fine.

ex post facto
"After the fact"; refers to laws that impose criminal responsibility for acts that were not crimes at the time the acts occurred.

If criminal laws stemmed from case law instead of statutes, problems with due process would arise. Since a court cannot make any decision until and unless an actual case is brought before it, an individual's conduct would be judged and determined to be criminal after the fact rather than before. This is known as **ex post facto** and is prohibited by the Constitution. Hence, it is often said that there are no common-law crimes in the United States. However, this does not mean that case law has no applicability to criminal law. Cases frequently are needed to interpret words or phrases found in statutes. For example, suppose that Brady kisses Jones without Jones's consent. Has Brady committed a battery? Is an unwanted kiss an act of force or violence? Case law might be needed to resolve this issue.

A POINT TO REMEMBER

All substantive criminal law, or crimes, must meet constitutional due process requirements. The laws must be specific and not vague. The punishment for violation of the law must also be found in the law.

Substantive Laws—Civil

Substantive civil laws cover a variety of different topics. Laws regulating contracts, torts, corporations, and family law are examples of some of these topics. Some areas of civil law, like areas of criminal law, are controlled primarily by statutory laws and are as detailed and specific as criminal law. For example, consider the California statutory law regarding libel and slander:

> ***California Civil Code §45: Libel***
>
> Libel is a false and unprivileged publication by writing, printing, picture, effigy, or other fixed representation to the eye, which exposes any person to hatred, contempt, ridicule, or obloquy, or which causes him to be shunned or avoided, or which has a tendency to injure him in his occupation.
>
> ***California Civil Code §46: Slander***
>
> Slander is a false and unprivileged publication, orally uttered, and also communications by radio or any mechanical or other means which:
>
> 1. Charges any person with crime, or with having been indicted, convicted, or punished for crime;
> 2. Imputes in him the present existence of an infectious, contagious, or loathsome disease;
> 3. Tends directly to injure him in respect to his office, profession, trade, or business, either by imputing to him general disqualification in those respects which the office or other occupation peculiarly requires, or by imputing something with reference to his office, profession, trade, or business that has a natural tendency to lessen its profits;
> 4. Imputes to him impotence or want of chastity; or
> 5. Which, by natural consequences, causes actual damage.

On the other hand, some substantive civil laws are much less specific in the type of conduct they regulate. For example, consider the California statute regarding civil liability that establishes liability for torts:

> Every one is responsible, not only for the result of his willful acts, but also for an injury occasioned to another by his want of ordinary care or skill in the management of his property or person, except so far as the latter has, willfully or by want of ordinary care, brought the injury upon himself (California Civil Code §1714).

This type of statute could include liability for automobile accidents, liability based on manufacturing products, liability based on a business negligently maintaining its premises, or liability of a parent who fails to properly supervise a child who injures someone. This type of statute merely provides for liability in the event that conduct is "negligent." It is normally up to a jury to decide specifically if one's behavior is negligent, within guidelines that have been established by our courts (case law). In doing this, the courts are exercising their traditional role of interpreting the law. However, within the field of civil law, the courts are allowed considerable latitude and discretion, even to the point of defining conduct that constitutes the basis of civil liability. For an example of a case dealing with civil law, read the case *Sommer v. Gabor.*

Sommer v. Gabor

40 Cal. App. 4th 1455, 48 Cal. Rptr. 2d 235 (1995)

Defendant Zsa Zsa Gabor and her husband, defendant Frederic Von Anhalt, appealed from a judgment in favor of plaintiff Elke Sommer in her action for defamation. On appeal, defendants contended (1) that the court erred in applying California, rather than German, defamation law; (2) that the statements attributed to them were not actionable as a matter of law because they were opinions; (3) and that the damages were excessive.

Derogatory statements concerning plaintiff and attributed to Gabor and her husband were published in two German magazines. In the first instance, the statements were made in Germany, although the magazine did have a few California subscribers. In the second instance, the statements were allegedly made in Southern California. The statements alleged to be defamatory included statements that she frequented sleazy bars, that she was broke, that nobody would have anything to do with her, and that she was at least 60 years old. The lawsuit was filed in California and the California court applied California rather than German law.

The appellate court held that California law was properly applied since all parties were residents of the United States and some statements were made in the United States. Furthermore, defendant failed to raise this issue at trial and failed to show that the result would have been different if German law were applied. The court also said that there were sufficient factual statements to support a judgment for defamation. Finally, the court held that there was no evidence that the damages were excessive. The following is an excerpt from the appellate court's opinion.

OPINION

Defendant Zsa Zsa Gabor and her husband, defendant Frederic Von Anhalt, appeal from a judgment on a special verdict in favor of plaintiff Elke Sommer in her action for defamation. On appeal, defendants contend the court erred in applying California, rather than German, defamation law. Defendants also contend that the statements attributed to them are opinions and are not actionable as a matter of law, and that the damages are excessive.

Facts

Sommer, who was born in Germany in November 1940, began playing the romantic lead in films in Europe in 1958; in 1962, she made an American movie filmed in London; in 1963 she made her first Hollywood movie and played the lead with Paul Newman. From 1958 to 1991, Sommer made about 67 films; in the early 1970s, she began television work and live theater; although Sommer made no movies in Hollywood from 1983 to 1990, she appeared in stage productions and television series. According to her publicist in the 1960s, Richard Guttman, press coverage affects the reputation of a celebrity. Sommer's reputation as an actress is international and is of someone "attractive, charming, pleasant. Someone you are going to have in your house." Such a reputation must be maintained by positive publicity, not through negative publicity.

In the February 22, 1990, issue of the German language weekly magazine, *Freizeit Revue*, a "women's publication" with a worldwide circulation of about 1,300,000, including 310 in Southern California, writer Anna Amlong reported that Zsa Zsa Gabor (Gabor) said that Sommer was broke, had to sell her house in Hollywood, now lived in the worst section, hung out in sleazy bars, lived from selling her handknit sweaters for $150, and nobody wanted to have anything to do with her anymore. The article also attributed to Gabor a statement that she (Gabor) found "offending," a statement Sommer allegedly had made six years earlier after one of Gabor's performances on a horse, that "Zsa Zsa has such a big behind that she could not even manage to get on the horse by herself." The article in *Freizeit Revue* also reported that Sommer was upset by Gabor's statements and Sommer said that knitting was a hobby and that she had assets worth 30 million Marks.

According to Anna Amlong, a journalist for *Freizeit Revue*, she was in the lobby of a hotel in Germany where Gabor was also staying during rehearsals for a show; Amlong and a freelance photographer sat down at a breakfast table with Gabor and Von Anhalt; the photographer took pictures of Gabor; Von Anhalt, who had known Amlong for a long time, introduced Amlong to Gabor as a journalist; Amlong spoke to Von Anhalt and Gabor in German; Gabor spoke fluent German; Amlong brought up the subject of Sommer, and Gabor kept talking about her; Amlong told Gabor that "it was extremely interesting and that would make a good story." Gabor told Amlong that it would not matter, that "Sommer was so ruined that it would not matter." Von Anhalt also said the whole thing "was even worse, that Ms. Sommer was completely ruined and broke and also that . . . she hardly had any hair on her head. And she would be at least 60 years old." Amlong spoke to Sommer by telephone before the article was published; Sommer told her that all the information given by Gabor was incorrect and provided true details of her financial situation.

Sommer's business manager testified that in February 1990, and in 1992, Sommer was not broke and her bills were being paid on time. Sommer admitted, however, that she was suing her former United States business manager for mismanagement; in July 1992 she did not have enough ready cash in the United States to make a large purchase, but she still had a house and cash in Germany, and a condo in Spain.

According to Sommer, when a woman reporter telephoned her at her home in California and told her about Gabor's statements in February 1990, she hung up the phone and started crying; she was in terrible shock, "like I got stuck between two trucks," and "did not want to believe that somebody could just say something like that about another human being." Sommer told the reporter that there was no truth to the statements. According to Sommer, the statements were "demeaning, taking all your little bit of dignity away." Sommer suffered sleeplessness, headaches, and was sick to her stomach; she saw a psychiatrist twice.

According to Von Anhalt, he was the one who spoke to Amlong about Sommer; Gabor did not talk to Amlong about Sommer and Gabor was not familiar with the German dialect spoken by Amlong. Von Anhalt made statements about Sommer, but "not the way it was written, no"; he denied saying anything except that he never sees Sommer in their group of friends or society in America and she was not doing very much lately.

Gabor denied saying anything about Sommer "in my life in the press," and denied being interviewed by any reporter from *Freizeit Revue*. Gabor testified that she did not learn about the statements attributed to her until Sommer sued her. Gabor admitted that in 1990, she did not know whether Sommer was broke, whether she went to bars, where she lived, whether she sold her house, whether she knitted, and whether or not anyone in Hollywood wanted to have anything to do with her.

In April 1990, a German language daily newspaper, *Bild*, with a daily circulation in Germany of about 3,900,000, asked a foreign correspondent, Carolin Dendler, in Los Angeles, to talk to Von Anhalt to get both sides of the story about Gabor and Sommer; Dendler talked to Von Anhalt by telephone and sent a memo of her interview to *Bild*. According to Dendler, Von Anhalt told her that Sommer could not buy a $500 ticket for a charity benefit, Sommer's bills were not being paid, in Hollywood no one recognized her on the street anymore, Sommer was lying about her age in that she was not 48 but 62, and that Sommer looked like a 100-year-old grandmother. Articles in the German daily newspaper *Bild* on April 28 and 30, 1990, reported the foregoing statements by Von Anhalt, in addition to attributing the statement to him that he saw Sommer recently and [that] she had almost no hair left on her head.

Sommer testified that she was devastated by the *Bild* articles, which intensified her earlier distress, insomnia and "incredible uneasiness"; at trial, she still suffered from the same symptoms; but "sometimes if I get lucky they are gone a week or ten days that [I] don't think about it constantly."

Although Sommer admitted that no employer ever told her that she was not hired because of the articles, publicist Richard Guttman testified that it is common for actresses not to know what work they lost as a result of negative publicity; the statements published in *Freizeit Revue* and *Bild* were damaging to Sommer's reputation as an actress. The statement that no one wants to have anything to do with her is damaging because "the thing that creates the best work atmosphere, employment atmosphere, is the knowledge that people do want to have something to do with you; so if you are presented in disregard, then other people tend to disregard you." The statement that Sommer lied about her age and that she was 62 was damaging because "she's an actress who has always had a highly sexual identification. She's certainly a glamour star, and one tends to be regarded less glamourously as you get older."

The issue of punitive damages was bifurcated from all other issues and tried to the jury last. After instructions on defamation, general damages, and malice, the jury rendered a verdict finding in favor of Sommer and against Gabor and awarding Sommer general damages of $800,000; the jury also found in favor of Sommer and against Von Anhalt and awarded Sommer general damages of $1.2 million against him. The jury also returned a special finding that, by clear and convincing evidence, both defendants were guilty of malice in the conduct upon which the jury had based its finding of liability for defamation.

Trial then continued as to the issue of punitive damages. Gabor admitted that her net worth was $6.2 million, although she was then living off her capital, not income; her liquid assets were only $165,000. Von Anhalt testified that he had assets in Europe worth 2.5 million German Marks; he also owned 51 percent of a champagne business which he purchased in 1982 for 1.5 million German Marks. German news companies also pay him about $60,000 per year for news. After instruction and deliberation, the jury returned verdicts awarding Sommer punitive damages of $450,000 against Gabor and $850,000 against Von Anhalt. A judgment on a special verdict was entered against Gabor for a total of $1,250,000 and against Von Anhalt for a total of $2,050,000.

Defendants moved for new trial on numerous grounds, including excessive damages, insufficiency of the evidence, and error in failing to apply German law to plaintiff's claims. The court denied the motion for new trial. Defendants filed timely notice of appeal from the judgment.

No Error in Failing to Apply German Law of Defamation

Appellants contend that the trial court erred in applying California defamation damages law and "in refusing to apply German defamation damages law that would have precluded recovery of presumed and punitive damages."

Respondent contends that appellants failed properly to raise the choice of law issue in the trial court, and in any event, the court properly applied California law to the action.

Appellants failed below, and still fail here, adequately to address the issue of Germany's interest in applying its law to the instant dispute, involving parties who are all residents of the United States, and involving defamatory statements by Von Anhalt in Los Angeles to a *Bild* correspondent also in Los Angeles. Assuming *arguendo* that there is a true conflict of laws in this case, one court has remarked that "[a]lthough the two potentially concerned states have different laws, there is still no problem in choosing the applicable rule of law where only one of the states has an interest in having its law applied. 'When one of two states related to a case has a legitimate interest in the application of its law and policy and the other has none, there is no real problem; clearly the law of the interested state should be applied.'" *Hurtado v. Superior Court, supra,* 11 Cal. 3d at 580. Appellants fail to cite any authority addressing the issue of whether, or to what extent, Germany has an interest in the instant dispute. Hence, we are unable to conclude that appellants should prevail.

Inasmuch as there has been a trial on the merits, we also note that appellants have not established prejudicial error. In other words, assuming *arguendo* that it was error not to apply German law, appellants fail to establish that under German law it would have been more probable than not that the judgment would have been any different. For all of the foregoing reasons, we find to be without merit appellants' contention that German law applies to the instant case.

No Excessive Damages

Appellants contend that the awards of presumed and punitive damages are excessive. Appellants claim that in light of the fact that there were no special damages in this case, as acknowledged by Sommer's counsel below, the award of general damages is excessive. As to the award of punitive damages, appellants contend that the punitive damage award falls if the compensatory damage award is vacated; further, appellants argue that punitive damage awards in defamation cases "are routinely reduced on appeal, especially where the actual injury is small." It is well settled that damages are excessive only where the recovery is so grossly disproportionate to the injury that the award may be presumed to have been the result of passion or prejudice.

With respect to punitive damages, appellants fail to establish that there was not clear and convincing evidence to support the jury's finding of malice. Both appellants admitted at trial that they had no knowledge of the true age of Sommer or of the details of her financial condition. Although Gabor denied making the statements attributed to her in the press, and Von Anhalt admitted some statements but challenged their context, the jury obviously believed the testimony of the journalists and concluded that they in fact made the false statements with malice. Appellants thus fail to establish that the awards of punitive damages were excessive or the result of passion and prejudice.

Whether Statements Were Nonactionable Opinions

Without merit is appellants' contention that all of the statements attributed to Gabor are subjective opinions and not provably false as a matter of law. Only two particular statements of Gabor are addressed in the briefs: the statement that Sommer hangs out in sleazy bars, and the statement that she lives in the worst part of town. Appellants claim that "sleazy" and "worst" express subjective opinions that are not actionable. However, the import of Gabor's statements was not so limited. The *Freizeit Revue* article attributed to Gabor the statements that "[s]he is broke, had to sell her house in Hollywood, now lives in the worst section, hangs out only in the seediest bars. She now lives from handknit pullovers that she sells for 150 dollars." The evidence in this case established that Sommer did not frequent bars of whatever nature, was not broke, did not have to sell her house in Hollywood, and did not move, whether to the "best" or "worst" part of town. Thus, the statements were indeed proven to be false in their broad sense, so that it did not matter what kind of bars were described or to what part of town she was alleged to have moved. Thus, taken in context, the statements were defamatory not because of the adjectives used in the statements, but because even without the adjectives, they attributed characteristics to Sommer's lifestyle which exposed her to contempt, ridicule and disgrace. Thus, Gabor has not established that any of the statements attributed to her were not actionable as a matter of law.

DISPOSITION

The judgment is affirmed. Respondent is entitled to her costs on appeal.

CASE ANALYSIS

1. Which substantive law(s) do you think apply to this case?
2. What procedural law(s), if any, apply to this case?
3. Could the defendant have been charged with any crimes as a result of this case?
4. If a party committed a crime in Germany, could the trial take place in California if both the defendant and the victim were California residents?

PROCEDURAL RULES—CRIMINAL

local rules of court
Procedural rules adopted by an individual court for practice in that specific court.

As described earlier, procedural laws or rules tell us how we enforce substantive rights. Often, these rules deal with the court process. Where should a lawsuit be filed, what is the time limit for filing the action, and what type of papers must be filed in court are all questions of procedural law. The answers to these types of procedural questions are generally found in statutory law or rules of court. **Rules of court** are laws that are adopted by various courts with power given to the courts by the legislature.

In criminal law, however, procedural rules are not limited to the technical questions of how the court process is handled. The U.S. Constitution, specifically in the Bill of Rights and the Fourteenth Amendment, grants certain basic rights or safeguards to anyone accused of committing a crime. These rights or safeguards affect the procedures that are used by police and by the courts in investigating and prosecuting crime. However, the statement of rights found in the Bill of Rights is very general and provides very little guidance in the day-to-day functions of criminal investigation and prosecution. For example, the Fourth Amendment to the Constitution gives people the right to be free from "unreasonable searches and seizures." Unfortunately it does not define *unreasonable*, nor does it define the terms *search* and *seize*. This leaves open the practical questions that arise when police are doing their job. For example, is it an unreasonable search or seizure to set up a roadblock to check for drunk drivers? Is it an unreasonable seizure to stop and question someone who looks out of place in a neighborhood? The answers to these types of questions are found in case law that interprets the Constitution. Case law is thus the major source of criminal procedural rules, at least those rules required by the Constitution. For an example of a criminal case, read the case of *People v. Sirhan Sirhan*, which follows.

PROCEDURAL RULES—CIVIL

rules of court
Procedural rules adopted by all courts regulating practice in the court.

The rules for civil procedure are found primarily in statutes and rules of court. Within the federal system, the Federal Rules of Civil Procedure, the United States Code, and **local rules of court** control. Local rules of court are rules adopted by the individual courts that dictate procedures that must be followed within that court. States have comparable statutes and rules. In addition, a considerable body of case law, both state and federal, interprets and explains the various statutes.

People v. Sirhan Sirhan

7 Cal. 3d 710, 102 Cal. Rptr. 385, 497 P.2d 1121 (1972)

The following relates to the case of Sirhan Sirhan, the assassin of Robert Kennedy. A jury found the defendant guilty of first-degree murder of Senator Kennedy and fixed the penalty at death. The court denied a motion for a new trial and the defendant's automatic appeal was heard by the California Supreme Court.

Defendant contended that (1) the death penalty was cruel or unusual punishment; (2) in view of proof of his diminished capacity, the evidence was insufficient to support the first-degree murder conviction; (3) he was denied a fair trial as a result of certain publicity; and (4) his right to be secure against unreasonable searches and seizures and his privilege against self-incrimination were violated by the receipt of evidence found in his bedroom.

The California Supreme Court referred to a prior California case that had recently found the death penalty in California in violation of the California Constitution. It therefore (1) reduced the sentence to life in prison, and then addressed the other issues. The court found (2) that there was sufficient psychiatric testimony and other evidence to support the first-degree murder conviction, (3) that although there was extensive publicity, there was no evidence that it prejudiced the trial, and (4) that the warrantless search of his premises was reasonable due to exigent circumstances. The court also found no violation of the right against self-incrimination. The following is an excerpt of the California Supreme Court's opinion.

OPINION

A jury found defendant guilty of first degree murder of Senator Robert Kennedy and fixed the penalty at death. The court denied a motion for a new trial, and defendant's automatic appeal is now before us.

Defendant contends that (1) the death penalty is cruel or unusual punishment; (2) in view of proof of his diminished capacity the evidence is insufficient to support the first degree murder conviction; (3) he was denied a fair trial as a result of certain publicity; (4) his right to be secure against unreasonable searches and seizures and his privilege against self-incrimination were violated by the receipt of evidence found in his bedroom; . . .

People v. Anderson, 6 Cal. 3d 628, 100 Cal. Rptr. 152, 493 P.2d 880, holds that the death penalty violates our state constitutional provision against cruel or unusual punishment (Cal. Const., art. I, § 6). The first of defendant's contentions thus is meritorious. We have concluded that the other contentions set forth above cannot be upheld and that the judgment should be modified to provide for life imprisonment and as so modified affirmed.

At the trial it was undisputed that defendant fired the shot that killed Senator Kennedy. The principal defense relied upon by defendant was that of diminished capacity. Extensive evidence was presented of the circumstances surrounding the shootings and of defendant's mental condition, which evidence may be summarized as follows:

About 8:30 p.m. on June 2, 1968, two days before defendant shot Senator Kennedy, the senator made a speech in the Coconut Grove at the Ambassador Hotel in Los Angeles, following which he delivered a second speech outside the hotel. Defendant was seen at the hotel about 8:45 that night by an acquaintance.

During the day on June 4, 1968, defendant practiced firing at a gun range for several hours and had also practiced shooting at ranges on several prior occasions. On June 4 he engaged in rapid fire with the .22 revolver he used a few hours later to kill Senator Kennedy.

A person who talked with defendant at the gun range on June 4 testified that defendant stated he was "going to go on a hunting trip with his gun," that he told defendant it was not permissible to use pistols for hunting "because of the accuracy," and that defendant said, "Well, I don't know about that. It could kill a dog."

Shortly before midnight on the same day defendant asked hotel employees if Senator Kennedy was going to come through the pantry, and they told him that they did not know. One of the employees observed defendant for about a half hour in the pantry and noticed nothing unusual about his manner or activity.

About midnight on June 4, Senator Kennedy made a speech in the Embassy Ballroom announcing his victory as a Democratic candidate for president in the California primary. Following the speech he and his entourage proceeded toward the hotel's Colonial Room, which was then being used as a press room. En route the senator stopped in the pantry to shake hands with the kitchen staff. Suddenly defendant darted toward the senator, pulled out a revolver, and fired several shots. The senator fell. Pandemonium ensued.

A hotel employee grabbed defendant around the wrist of the hand holding the gun, but defendant, who was still able to move that hand, continued shooting. Several persons joined in the struggle and succeeded in restraining defendant, and one took the gun from him. When asked, "Why did you do it?" defendant replied something to the effect of "I can explain."

The senator was taken to a hospital where he underwent surgery. He subsequently died on June 6, 1968. Expert testimony indicated that the gun was an inch and a half or less from the senator's head when the fatal bullet was fired and in contact with him or within a few inches when the other wounds were inflicted.

Around the time that the senator was taken to the hospital the police arrived at the hotel and took custody of defendant. Two officers, defendant, and Jesse Unruh got into a car and drove to the police station. En route the officers advised defendant of his constitutional rights. Subsequently Unruh asked defendant, "Why did you shoot him?" and defendant replied, "You think I am crazy? You think I will tell you so you can use it as evidence against me?" Unruh also heard defendant say, "I did it for my country." Unruh believed that defendant was not intoxicated, and police officers who were with defendant at the time of his arrest or shortly thereafter reached the same conclusion.

About 12:45 A.M., minutes after defendant arrived at the police station, he was seen by Officer Jordan. The officer estimated that he was with defendant between four and five hours on this occasion. Jordan stated that defendant never appeared irrational and that in the officer's many years on the force, defendant was "one of the most alert and intelligent people I have ever attempted to interrogate." Jordan initially identified himself and asked defendant his name but received no response. The officer then advised defendant of his constitutional rights, and defendant, after asking a few questions, indicated he wished to remain silent.

The police found various items on defendant's person, including a newspaper article which in part noted that in a recent speech Senator Kennedy "favored aid to Israel 'with arms if necessary' to meet the threat of the Soviets."

The prosecution also introduced documents found by the police at defendant's home. The documents contain statements in defendant's handwriting regarding various matters including killing Senator Kennedy. Defendant, testifying in his own behalf, admitted having shot Senator Kennedy, but claimed that he did not remember having done so. He conceded, however, that he stated, "I killed Robert Kennedy willfully, premeditatively, with twenty years of malice aforethought."

Defendant also described in detail his views regarding the Arab-Israeli conflict and his hatred of the Zionists. Additional evidence was introduced by the defense regarding the bombings in Old Jerusalem during the period defendant resided there, the various gruesome matters he saw during his childhood, and his poor living conditions in that city.

In support of his defense of diminished capacity, defendant called to the stand two psychiatrists and two psychologists who administered psychological tests to defendant and four psychologists who evaluated the tests administered to defendant. According to both psychiatrists, defendant lacked the capacity to maturely and meaningfully reflect upon the gravity of the contemplated act of murder and to comprehend his duty to govern his actions in accord with the duties imposed by law, and they explained the reasons for their conclusion. They further testified concerning the origin, development, and manifestations of the illness.

In rebuttal the prosecution called to the stand Seymour Pollack, M.D., a professor of psychiatry and law at the University of Southern California. Dr. Pollack interviewed defendant eight times, spending about 24 hours with him. The doctor also observed defendant in the courtroom during preliminary proceedings that began June 28, 1968, and during the trial. In addition he interviewed members of defendant's family; reviewed the psychological tests given to defendant and numerous other matters such as the grand jury transcript and tapes of defendant's conversations after his apprehension; and attended a conference with other psychiatrists and psychologists concerning the case. The overall time Dr. Pollack spent on the case was close to 200 hours.

He testified, "In my opinion when Sirhan shot Kennedy, Sirhan's mental capacity was not impaired to the extent of diminished capacity to maturely and meaningfully premeditate and deliberate and reflect upon the gravity of the contemplated act of shooting the Senator" and that Sirhan "did not have . . . diminished mental capacity to harbor malice aforethought." The doctor explained that he considered the following "functions" in reaching the foregoing conclusions: he found no evidence of any altered state of consciousness or dissociate state, and various matters indicated to the contrary.

1. SUFFICIENCY OF EVIDENCE TO SUPPORT FIRST DEGREE MURDER CONVICTION

Defendant contends that in view of proof of his diminished capacity the evidence is insufficient to support his conviction of first degree murder and that he should have been convicted of manslaughter or at most second degree murder.

The recited evidence, including, among other things, the expert testimony introduced by the prosecution and proof of the circumstances surrounding the crime, is sufficient to support the jury's implied finding that defendant committed the killing with malice.

We turn next to whether the evidence is also sufficient to support the jury's implied finding that the murder was willful, deliberate and premeditated. Here, defendant had ample time to reflect upon the killing, and, although the evidence is conflicting, the summarized evidence constitutes substantial proof that at the time of the shooting defendant was not a paranoid schizophrenic, in a dissociate state, or intoxicated. Also, as we have seen, Dr. Pollack, who examined defendant on eight occasions as well as having reviewed extensive materials and interviewed members of defendant's family, testified that although defendant was mentally ill, defendant did not have diminished capacity to harbor malice aforethought or to maturely and meaningfully reflect upon the gravity of his contemplated act, and the doctor explained the reasons for his conclusions. There was also evidence that the assassination was politically motivated, and defendant's actions in carrying out the crime are, of course, additional proof of his then mental state. We conclude that the evidence is sufficient to support the first degree murder conviction.

2. ALLEGED DENIAL OF FAIR TRIAL AS A RESULT OF PUBLICITY

The publicity on the subject was massive. In the words of the trial judge, "Everybody knows it has been on the radio every hour; it has been in the newspapers, . . . in the most important spot. . . ."

Here neither prejudice to defendant from the publicity nor a probability thereof is shown by the record, even if it be assumed that the jurors were unable to disregard the matters they had heard or seen relating to a guilty plea by defendant.

3. ASSERTED VIOLATION OF RIGHT TO BE SECURE AGAINST UNREASONABLE SEARCHES AND SEIZURES AND PRIVILEGE AGAINST SELF-INCRIMINATION

Defendant contends that his right to be secure against unreasonable searches and seizures (U.S. Const., 4th and 14th Amends.; Cal. Const., art. I, § 19), and privilege against self-incrimination (U.S. Const., 5th and 14th Amends.) were violated by the introduction by the prosecution of several pages from two of his notebooks and an envelope that were found in his bedroom on June 5, 1968.

A. Alleged illegal search and seizure on June 5, 1968

On the morning of June 5, 1968, defendant's brothers, Adel and Munir, upon seeing a newspaper picture of defendant in connection with the Kennedy shooting, went to the police station, where Adel was interviewed by Sergeant Brandt, one of the officers who made the search. Adel advised the officer of the suspect's identity and stated that he (Adel), his two younger brothers, Sirhan and Munir, and their mother lived at a specified address in Pasadena and that their father was in another country. The officer asked if they could search the home, and Adel replied that "as far as he was concerned [they] could, however it was his mother's house." When asked if he wanted the police to call her for permission, Adel replied that she did not know what had happened and he did not want to alarm her.

Sergeant Brandt, accompanied by two other officers and Adel, then went to the Sirhan residence, arriving about 10:30 A.M. on June 5, 1968. Brandt testified that they "were interested in evidence of possible conspiracy in that there might be other people that were not yet in custody." He stated that there was nothing which "indicated [defendant] was engaged in any conspiracy" but that there was no evidence "there was not a conspiracy." Adel admitted the officers into the house. They asked which bedroom belonged to defendant, and Adel directed them to a back bedroom. There the officers opened a closed dressing table drawer and found an envelope bearing the notation "RFK must be disposed of like his brother was." On the floor in plain sight they saw a closed notebook. They opened it to see its contents; it contained a prediction of America's downfall, an attack upon its leaders, and comments relating to "doing away" with those leaders. On top of the dressing table they saw a second notebook which looked "like a school book." They looked through it, and in it were notations such as "R.F.K. must be assassinated" and "Ambassador Goldberg must die." The envelope and pages from the two notebooks containing the foregoing comments were introduced into evidence by the prosecution. The handwriting on the envelope and in the notebooks was identified as defendant's. Since the search was without a warrant, the burden was on the People to show proper justification therefor. *People v. Edwards,* 71 Cal. 2d 1096, 1099 (80 Cal. Rptr. 633, 458 P.2d 713).

The Attorney General asserts that there was a pressing emergency to ascertain the existence of a possible conspiracy to assassinate presidential candidates or high government officials, and he relies on the emergency exception to the warrant requirement. Defendant, on the other hand, argues that no emergency was shown justifying the search, and he points to testimony that the officers had no evidence of a conspiracy.

We turn next to a consideration of whether the theory is a valid one. In *Johnson v. United States,* 333 U.S. 10, 14–15, 92 L. Ed. 436, 440–441, 68 S. Ct. 367, a case involving narcotics law violations, the court declared that "[t]here are exceptional circumstances in which, on balancing the need for effective law enforcement against the right of privacy, it may be contended that a magistrate's warrant for search may be dispensed with."

The Attorney General urges that the "exigencies of the situation" in this case made it imperative for the officers to follow the course they took. The heretofore recited evidence indicates that the officers believed that there might be a conspiracy, and although none of the officers mentioned the object thereof they undoubtedly contemplated the obvious possibility of a conspiracy to assassinate political leaders in this country. It also may be inferred from the recited evidence that they believed that an emergency existed and that prompt action on their part was necessary.

Their beliefs were entirely reasonable. The crime was one of enormous gravity, and the "gravity of the offense" is an appropriate factor to take into consideration. The victim was a major presidential candidate, and a crime of violence had already been committed against him. The crime thus involved far more than possibly idle threats. Although the officers did not have reasonable cause to believe that the house contained evidence of a conspiracy to assassinate prominent political leaders, we believe that the mere possibility that there might be such evidence in the house fully warranted the officers' actions. It is not difficult to envisage what would have been the effect on this nation if several more political assassinations had followed that of Senator Kennedy.

We conclude that the trial court did not err in admitting the evidence found in defendant's bedroom. . . .

The judgment is modified to provide a punishment of life imprisonment instead of death for the murder and as so modified is affirmed.

CASE ANALYSIS

1. Who was the plaintiff in this case?
2. What did the California Supreme Court do?
3. With what crime was the defendant charged?
4. What procedural questions were raised on appeal by the defendant?

SEC. 6–3 HOW CRIMINAL AND CIVIL CASES ARE HANDLED

The major difference between civil and criminal laws is the way in which each of these types of cases is handled. Recall the example of Stein and Silvers where Stein, while driving an automobile in a drunken state, rear-ends a vehicle driven by Silvers, as a result of which Silvers is injured. Remember that this factual situation could give rise to both a criminal and a civil action. In such an event the cases would be handled separately. The following discussion points out the differences and similarities that would exist in the two cases.

THE PARTIES

In any kind of case, civil or criminal, one party, the *plaintiff*, brings the action, and another party, the *defendant*, is sued. Since a crime is considered an offense against the state, the plaintiff in the criminal case is always some government representative. Sometimes the plaintiff is referred to as "The People of the State of __________." If a federal crime is involved, the plaintiff is usually referred to as "United States" or "U.S." In a civil case, the plaintiff is normally the injured party or the one who has sustained some kind of damage.

In the preceding example, which involves both a criminal case and a civil action, in the civil case Silvers would be the plaintiff. In the criminal action, the plaintiff would be the People of the State. Silvers would be only a witness in the case. The defendant in both the civil and criminal cases would, of course, be Stein. The name of the criminal case would be *People v. Stein*. The name of the civil case would be *Silvers v. Stein*.

A POINT TO REMEMBER

Most cases, civil and criminal, have a plaintiff, the one who sues, and the defendant, the one who is sued. In a criminal case, the plaintiff is always the representative of the government.

The Court

The next question that arises concerns which court has jurisdiction to hear the civil and criminal actions. Even though both cases stem from the same factual situation, they will not necessarily be handled in the same court. The laws of each state determine which state court has proper jurisdiction to hear a matter. This is often affected by the amount of damages requested in a civil case or the nature of the criminal charge in a criminal case.

Even if the civil and criminal actions were brought in the same court, they would never be handled together. They would always be tried separately. Because of the right to a speedy trial in a criminal case, in all likelihood, the criminal action will be heard much sooner than the civil case, where no right to a speedy trial exists.

The Right to a Jury

The right to a jury in a criminal trial is guaranteed under the Sixth and Fourteenth Amendments to the U.S. Constitution. These provisions apply to actions in federal court as well as in state court.

case at law
A civil action in which one party is seeking money damages.

case in equity
A civil case in which one party is seeking equitable or specific relief, such as specific performance of a contract or an injunction.

In civil cases, whether a right to a jury exists often depends on whether the case is a **case at law** or a **case in equity**. The distinction between law and equity originated in early common law. Originally, severe technical pleading requirements existed. Furthermore, only limited types of remedies were available. In civil cases, this often meant that a court could only award money damages. In order to prevent the harshness and unfairness that resulted because of "technicalities," a separate court system developed known as the *Chancery Courts*. The Chancery Courts filled the void left by the technical requirements of the other courts. The Chancery Courts were able to consider fundamental fairness or "equity." Today, we no longer have two separate court systems; one court system handles both kinds of cases. However, the distinction between actions at law and actions in equity remains, and that distinction is still important. The difference between actions at law and actions in equity is seen primarily in the type of remedy that is available. In an action at law, normally the court can award only money damages, whereas in an action in equity the court can afford specific relief (such as specific performance of a contract or dissolution of a marriage). Conversely, the type of legal remedy that is being sought usually determines whether the case is one at law or one in equity.

In civil actions at law, the parties are often entitled to a jury. In fact, the Seventh Amendment to the U.S. Constitution also provides for juries in certain kinds of these cases: "In Suits at common law, where the value in controversy shall exceed twenty dollars, the right of trial by jury shall be preserved." Unlike the provision for a criminal jury, the constitutional right to a jury in a civil case applies only to federal cases. It is up to the individual states to determine the right to a jury trial in a state civil case. On the other hand, juries are seldom allowed for cases in equity.

Even when juries are allowed in civil cases, however, some distinctions between the civil and criminal jury exist. First, in a criminal case, the jury must be provided at the expense of the state. In a civil case, the party requesting the jury must pay for it. Second, the number of jurors who must agree before a verdict is reached is sometimes different, at least in state practice. Federal rules require unanimous agreement for both civil and criminal practice, but this is not always the case in state practice. Some states provide for less-than-unanimous verdicts in both civil and criminal cases, while other states provide for less-than-unanimous verdicts only in civil cases.

Thus, in the Stein example, in a criminal case Stein would be entitled to a jury at state expense. Whether the jury would have to be unanimous in its decision is a matter of state law. In a civil case, either Stein or Silvers could request a jury. However, the state would not pay for the jury. The number of jurors who must agree before a verdict is rendered is a matter of state law.

The Right to an Attorney

indigent
Without funds or assets and therefore unable to afford an attorney.

The Sixth Amendment to the U.S. Constitution guarantees that the defendant has the right to have an attorney in a criminal case. If the defendant is **indigent** and cannot afford an attorney, the state must provide one for him or her, free of cost (these are often public defenders). No corollary right exists in civil cases; as a rule, defendants who cannot afford an attorney either represent themselves or do not contest the lawsuit. Occasionally, a defendant in a civil lawsuit will receive aid from some sort of legal-aid society. However, no right to a free attorney exists.

Thus, in our example, in the criminal case Stein is entitled to a court-appointed attorney if he cannot afford his own lawyer. If he is not indigent, however, he must pay for his own lawyer. In the civil case, Stein is not entitled to any free legal services.

A POINT TO REMEMBER

The right to a free attorney exists only in criminal trials where the defendant is indigent and cannot afford to pay an attorney. There is no right to court-appointed counsel in civil cases.

Burden of Proof

burden of proof
The necessity of establishing a particular fact or the necessity of going forward with the evidence.

complaint
A document filed in a civil or criminal lawsuit that describes the allegations of the plaintiff and the basis for the lawsuit.

preponderance of the evidence
The amount of proof necessary for most civil cases; more likely than not.

beyond a reasonable doubt
The amount of proof necessary for a conviction in a criminal case.

Another distinction between civil and criminal cases involves the **burden of proof**. Burden of proof has two separate aspects. First is the determination of which party must prove the allegations that have been made. Second is the determination of how much proof is needed. In all cases the plaintiff always has the burden of proving the allegations that are made in the **complaint**. The complaint is a document filed in both civil and criminal cases that describes the plaintiff's basis for suing. The plaintiff must prove the case. (If the defendant has alleged certain types of defenses, then the defendant has the burden of proving these.) However, the amount of proof needed varies from civil to criminal cases. In a civil case, the burden of proof is usually said to be "a preponderance of the evidence," whereas in a criminal case, the burden of proof is normally defined as "beyond a reasonable doubt." A **preponderance of the evidence** means that there is more evidence on one side than on the other, that is, the allegations are true with more than a 50/50 probability. **Beyond a reasonable doubt** requires a much higher degree of certainty in the mind of the juror. It is impossible to equate this with mathematical exactness.

In our example, in the criminal case, the prosecutor will have to present enough evidence against Stein so that the jurors are convinced of his guilt beyond a reasonable doubt. In the civil case, however, Silvers will win if the allegations in the complaint are proved to the jury by a preponderance of the evidence.

THE VERDICT

acquittal
A finding of *not guilty* in a criminal case.

hung jury
A jury that cannot attain the necessary consensus or majority to reach a verdict.

liable
A finding of responsibility in a civil case.

The decision in a case is known as the *verdict*. In a criminal case, the verdict can be either *guilty* or *not guilty*. A *not guilty* verdict is sometimes called an **acquittal**. If the required number of jurors cannot agree on a verdict, then a **hung jury** occurs. At this point, the judge declares a mistrial and the case can be later retried in front of a new jury.

In a civil case, the term **liable** is usually used rather than *guilty*. Just as with criminal cases, if the required number of jurors cannot agree on a verdict, then a hung jury exists, a mistrial is declared, and the case can be retried.

In our example, in the criminal case, if all the jurors believe that Stein did in fact commit the crime, he will be found guilty. If all of the jurors do not believe that his guilt has been proved beyond a reasonable doubt, then he will be found not guilty or acquitted. If the jurors cannot agree, then a hung jury results and the case can be retried.

In the civil case, assuming that the jury consists of twelve individuals, and that state law requires a three-fourths majority for a verdict, only nine out of the twelve must agree before Stein is found liable or not liable. If nine jurors cannot agree, then the civil case will end in a hung jury. A mistrial will be declared and the case can be retried.

THE PUNISHMENT

If the defendant in a criminal case is found guilty, some sort of punishment will be imposed. In a criminal case, this can be a fine, imprisonment, probation, or a combination of the three. As mentioned earlier, the punishment for any particular crime is set in the statute defining the crime. However, the judge imposes the precise punishment in any case. If a fine is imposed, the money will go to the state, not to the victim of the crime.

If the defendant is found liable in a civil case, then normally *damages* will be assessed. Damages in a civil case are either compensatory or punitive. *Compensatory damages* are intended to compensate the plaintiff for the loss sustained. They include out-of-pocket expenses such as medical bills (called *special damages*). They also include compensation for general loss such as pain and suffering (*general damages*). In some instances, courts also allow *punitive damages*. These are meant to punish the defendant for particularly offensive or malicious conduct. In recent years, punitive damages have come under a great deal of criticism, and some states have passed laws limiting them. If the case was tried by a jury, then normally the jury determines the amount of compensatory or punitive damages. The damages are payable to the plaintiff. In some kinds of civil cases, other types of relief are awarded, such as specific performance of a contract, a marital dissolution, or child support. Neither a jail sentence nor probation can be ordered in a civil case.

If the defendant does not pay a civil judgment, he or she cannot normally be put in jail. The plaintiff can follow certain collection proceedings such as wage garnishment or property attachment. If the defendant has no assets, then the plaintiff probably will not recover any money on his or her judgment. On the other hand, in a criminal case, a defendant who refuses to pay a fine can be put in jail, as long as he or she has the ability to pay. Even in a criminal case, though, if the defendant cannot pay a fine, he or she cannot be put in jail as a substitute.

Thus, in our example, Stein could be fined, jailed, or put on probation if found guilty in the criminal case. If Stein is found liable in the civil case, a money judgment can be awarded to Silvers, but Stein cannot be jailed.

The Right to Appeal

Our legal system gives most litigants the right to appeal a case if they do not win at the trial level. This is true in both criminal and civil cases with one major exception. If a defendant is found not guilty in a criminal case, the prosecutor is not allowed to appeal the decision, regardless of any legal errors that may have occurred at trial. This is because of the double jeopardy clause in the U.S. Constitution.

ETHICAL CHOICES

Assume that you work in a law office. You are interviewing a client who has retained your firm to represent him as a result of legal problems stemming from an automobile accident. Your client, who was drunk at the time, caused the accident. Your firm is representing him in the criminal action. He has been sued civilly, but his insurance company has provided an attorney to handle this case. The client is confused about the nature of the legal proceedings and asks you to explain the difference between the civil and criminal case. Can you tell him or would you be giving legal advice?

The following cases deal with similar factual situations. Pay close attention to whether they are civil cases or criminal cases

Coon v. Joseph

192 Cal. App. 3d 1269, 237 Cal. Rptr. 873 (1987)

The following case is a tort action based on a violation of a civil rights statute providing that all persons have the right to be free from any violence, intimidation or threat thereof "committed against their persons" because of their race, religion, sex, or sexual orientation. In this case, plaintiff saw a municipal bus driver harass and assault plaintiff's male partner. The complaint establishes that no violence or intimidation was committed or threatened against appellant's person and thus no cause of action exists in his own right. The trial court dismissed the complaint. The appellate court affirmed. This is an excerpt from the appellate court's decision.

Appellant Gary Coon appeals from a judgment of dismissal to his complaint.

The complaint here alleges as follows. On September 23, 1984, in San Francisco, appellant and a male friend [Ervin] attempted to board a municipal bus of respondent City and County of San Francisco. Appellant had been living with his friend for a year, and they had an intimate, stable and "emotionally significant" relationship. The bus driver "denied [appellant] entry to the number 19 Polk bus, but allowed [Ervin] onto said bus." Bus driver, in full view of appellant, verbally abused Ervin and struck his face. When appellant observed the assault on his friend, he suffered great mental and emotional distress. The complaint alleges four causes of action: intentional infliction of emotional distress, negligent infliction of emotional distress, negligence, and violation of appellant's civil rights.

As to appellant's claim of violation of civil rights, a brief review of the statute upon which he relies establishes he has no claim. That section provides that all persons have the right to be free from any violence, intimidation or threat thereof "committed against their persons" because of race, religion, sex or sexual orientation. The unambiguous language of this section gives rise to a cause of action in favor of a person against whom violence or intimidation has been committed or threatened. The complaint establishes that no violence or intimidation was committed or threatened against appellant's person and thus no cause of action exists in his own right. Following appellant's argument, any person would have the right to recover damages for himself or herself whenever the rights of any other human being of similar race, religion, sex, or sexual orientation were threatened. Such intent of the Legislature cannot be reasonably inferred. For these reasons, we affirm the judgment of dismissal.

CASE ANALYSIS

1. Who filed this case in the trial court?
2. What type of relief was the plaintiff seeking in this case?
3. Who is appealing this case?
4. Is this a civil case or a criminal case?
5. In the Hardtack case, if Martinez had a friend with him and that friend had watched Hardtack assault Martinez, would the friend have a case for a civil rights violation? Why or why not? Suppose that instead of a friend, Martinez's wife had watched her husband being assaulted. Would she have a case for a civil rights violation?

Buranen v. Hanna

623 F. Supp. 445 (1985)

OPINION

This matter is before the Court on the motions of defendant for dismissal.

Plaintiffs in this action, Candace Lee Buranen and Robert Francis Buranen, are a wife and husband who assert that police officers unjustifiably arrested them and used excessive force in the process.

The events in this case surround a high school hockey game. The Buranens were in attendance as spectators, while the defendants were at the game in their official capacity as police officers. During the game, an assistant coach for the visiting team, Jeffrey Smith, climbed up on the boards to yell at the referee about a mistake on the time clock. Defendants approached Smith. Apparently the two officers were unaware that Smith was an assistant coach. Plaintiffs state that the two officers physically removed Smith from the boards, put Smith in an arm bar, and proceeded to escort Smith out of the arena.

Candace Buranen saw the police taking Smith out of the arena, and she followed to inform them that they were making a mistake. When she approached the officers and Smith, defendant stepped in front of her and put arm out to stop her. Candace Buranen stopped and started to ask defendant where Smith was being taken. Defendant did not respond. She next tried to walk around Hanna in order to speak with Officer Beltrand. At this point, Hanna grabbed her, threw her against the wall, and wrestled her to the ground. Once she was on the ground, Hanna sat on her, placed a knee on her chest, placed a hand on her face and pushed her face to the ground.

In the meantime, Robert Buranen came to see what was happening because a bystander had informed him that his wife was in trouble. When he approached the officers, he saw defendant Hanna kneeling on top of his wife and he heard his wife crying out for help. Robert Buranen shouted at Hanna to let his wife go. Robert Buranen approached his wife and Hanna, but before he could reach them, officers grabbed him. Robert Buranen asked what was happening, but the officers only responded by telling him to shut up. The defendants proceeded to arrest plaintiffs and take them outside to the police cars. Robert Buranen was placed in an arm bar, and when he reached the patrol car, one of the officers grabbed his hair and slammed his face on the hood.

The defendants ultimately released Smith. Defendant, however, took plaintiffs to the police station where they were charged with assault and obstructing justice. Plaintiffs' trial took place in Municipal Court. Plaintiffs were each represented by a different attorney at the hearing. The defendant police officers were the only witnesses at the hearing; plaintiffs did not testify. The trial followed, and it resulted in the jury acquitting plaintiffs of all charges.

Subsequently, plaintiffs commenced the present action alleging violations of their civil rights in contravention of 42 U.S.C. §1983. Plaintiffs have also asserted a number of state tort claims.

Discussion

In order to establish a cause of action based on 42 U.S.C. §1983, plaintiffs must show that defendants acted under color of state law and that the defendants' conduct deprived plaintiffs of a right protected by the United States Constitution or federal law. As on-duty police officers, defendants were unquestionably acting under color of state law. Defendants acknowledge that they were acting under color of state law.

Defendants argue, however, that assuming plaintiffs' version of the facts is true, defendants still have not deprived plaintiffs of a federally protected right.

The plaintiffs in the present action are alleging violations of substantive constitutional rights as well as violations of procedural due process. Plaintiffs are claiming that defendants violated their Fourth Amendment right to be arrested only upon probable cause. Plaintiffs can clearly maintain a section 1983 action for being arrested without probable cause. Police officers' use of excessive force is [also] conduct actionable under section 1983.

It is further ordered that defendants' motion to dismiss is denied.

CASE ANALYSIS

1. Is this a civil case or a criminal case?
2. How can you tell?
3. Did the facts in this case give rise to a criminal case? If so, who were the parties in that case? Does the decision in the criminal case have any bearing on the outcome of this case?

People v. Lashley

1 Cal. App. 4th 938, 2 Cal. Rptr. 2d 629 (1991)

OPINION

Defendant Mark Shane Lashley was convicted in a court trial of attempted murder, assault with a firearm, civil rights violations and brandishing a weapon. Defendant was sentenced to state prison for an aggregate term of 14 years and 9 months.

Facts

Prosecution's Evidence

This sad tale of racial asperity began June 26, 1988, when Terence Goudeau and his three cousins, Dennis, Kelvin, and Trenton Wilson, decided to fish along the shore of Ballona Creek in Marina Del Rey. As they passed an adjacent apartment complex, defendant yelled out, "What kind of fish you gonna catch, black fish?" Goudeau caustically replied that he and his companions, each of whom [is] black, were planning to catch "white fish." Apparently angered by the answer, defendant, who [is] white, retorted with several racial epithets. After countering with an obscenity of his own, Goudeau and the others attempted to ignore the slurs but to no avail. Defendant, who had been joined on the balcony by several of his friends, persisted in taunting the group.

Shortly thereafter, one of the defendant's cohorts, Christopher Flores, appeared at the scene and walked toward where the men were fishing. Appearing heavily intoxicated, Flores confronted 12-year-old Trenton Wilson, challenging him to fight. Goudeau, carrying a pocket knife he had been using to cut bait, essentially told Flores that neither he nor Trenton would fight. Noticing the knife, Flores retreated but not before warning the group that he would "show them a real knife." As he staggered away, both Goudeau and Trenton returned to fishing.

Some five minutes later both Goudeau and Trenton turned toward the apartment building and saw defendant posed on the balcony aiming a .22-caliber rifle in their direction. Before Goudeau could move out of range, however, a shot rang out, striking the upper portion of his left arm and piercing his lung.

Defense Evidence

Testifying for the defense at trial, Flores essentially claimed that he, not Goudeau, had been the victim of an unprovoked and racially motivated attack. When Flores declined a challenge to fight, Goudeau pulled a buck knife from behind his back and made a stabbing motion in the air. Two of the men who had been fishing also drew knives and, along with Goudeau, surrounded Flores, blocking his escape.

While attempting to move toward the apartment building, Flores heard a "pop" and then saw the men scatter in the direction of the water. Defendant, along with several other defense witnesses, essentially testified in support of Flores's account of the shooting and the events preceding it. Denying any racial motivation for his actions, defendant maintained that upon seeing Flores threatened at knife point by Goudeau and the others he felt compelled to defend his friend. He insisted, however, that in firing the rifle his intent was not to kill Goudeau but only to wound him.

Discussion

Sufficiency of the Evidence to Support Defendant's Convictions for Civil Rights Violations

Defendant's next contention concerns the nature and quantum of evidence required to sustain his convictions for civil rights violations under sections 422.6 and 422.7.

Although the foregoing statutes have yet to be construed by any court of this state, both parties maintain that a conviction under either section requires proof of a specific intent to deprive an individual of the right secured by federal and/or state law. We agree. Both sections are modeled after the federal criminal civil rights statute presently codified in 18 United States Code section 242. The statutes, however, have broader application than the federal law because they apply to private as well as state action. The Supreme Court found that the term "wilfully," as used in the statute, meant acting with "a purpose to deprive a person of a specific constitutional right made definite by decision or other rule of law." [Citation omitted.]

With these principles in mind, we consider defendant's claim that the evidence elicited at trial is insufficient to support any finding of specific intent under either section 422.6 or 422.7.

The right to be free from violence, or the threat of it, is clearly within the purview of sections 422.6 and 422.7, is well established, and is plainly applicable to the facts of this case. The trial court reasonably could find that the defendant's brandishing of the rifle against Trenton Wilson, followed by his shooting of Goudeau, constituted acts of violence and intimidation motivated by racial hatred.

Whether defendant acted with the specific intent to deprive the victims of their right to be free from such attacks was a question of fact that the court obviously resolved against him. Based upon our review of the record we can only conclude that the record supports that determination.

CASE ANALYSIS

1. Is this a civil case or a criminal case? How can you tell?
2. Assume that the Hardtack case took place in this state. Also assume that the allegations against Hardtack using unnecessary force are true. Would Hardtack be guilty of violating the state statutes mentioned in the case? Do you think Hardtack would be guilty of violating 18 U.S.C. §242?
3. How do the state laws involved in this case differ from the state law mentioned in the *Coon* case?

ETHICAL CHOICES

You work as a paralegal for a sole practitioner, Bryan Anderson, who has a very busy practice. The *Hanley* case, a criminal action, is set for a pretrial conference at 10:00 A.M. on Tuesday. Unfortunately, the attorney also has a divorce case set for the same time in another courthouse. Your attorney tells you to appear in the divorce court and to introduce yourself and tell the court you are from the Anderson Law Firm. He tells you that if the judge asks if you are an attorney, do not lie about it, but do not volunteer any information either. What should you do?

Sec. 6–4 QUASI-CRIMINAL CASES

contempt
Willful disregard of a court order.

Some cases have elements of both civil and criminal cases. For example, suppose Dick and Jane divorce. Jane gets custody of the children and Dick is ordered to pay child support for their minor children. Dick intentionally refuses to pay, even though he has the ability to do so. Jane takes him to court on a **contempt** proceeding over the unpaid child support. A contempt proceeding determines whether an individual has willfully violated a court order. This case has elements of both civil and criminal actions. It is a dispute between two private individuals. The state is not a party. The action can be brought by Jane, an individual, through her own attorney. On the other hand, if Dick is found in contempt, he could be sentenced to jail. Thus, he is usually given the right to counsel and, if he is indigent, an attorney will be provided. Cases like this are referred to as *quasi-criminal.*

Featured Web Site: www.usdoj.gov/

The U.S. Department of Justice handles both civil and criminal cases. Its Web site describes the different divisions of the department and contains numerous legal documents.

Go Online

1. Describe the different divisions of the Department of Justice and indicate whether the division handles civil cases, criminal cases or both.
2. Locate and identify by name at least three documents from a civil case and three documents from a criminal case.

Chapter Summary

Laws are categorized as either criminal or civil. Criminal laws relate to behavior that is made illegal by society and for which a punishment is prescribed. The punishment often includes fines, jail, or probation. The area of criminal law and criminal procedure is subject to many constitutional requirements, especially the requirement of due process of law. Civil laws relate to private disputes between parties. The rules that govern criminal cases and the rules that govern civil cases differ in such matters as the parties to the action, the courts that have jurisdiction, the right to a jury, the right to an attorney, the burden of proof, the types of verdicts, the possible punishment, and the right to appeal.

Terms to Remember

substantive laws
procedural laws
statute of limitations
crime
local rules of court
rules of court
ex post facto
case at law
case in equity
indigent
burden of proof
complaint
preponderance of the evidence
beyond a reasonable doubt
acquittal
hung jury
liable
contempt

Questions for Review

1. Where are substantive criminal laws found?
2. What effect does the U.S. Constitution have on the rules of criminal procedure?
3. Compare the role of case law regarding substantive criminal laws with the role of case law regarding substantive civil laws.
4. Who are the parties to a criminal case?
5. If the same factual situation results in both a criminal case and a civil case, what will be the differences with regard to the parties to the lawsuit, the courts having jurisdiction, the right to a jury, the right to an attorney, the burden of proof, the types of verdicts, the possible punishment, and the right to appeal?

Questions for Analysis

1. Compare the two code sections at the beginning of the chapter, 18 U.S.C. §242 and 42 U.S.C.§1983. Which is a criminal statute and which is a civil statute? Are they equally specific as to the conduct that is forbidden? Are they equally specific as to the punishment that can be imposed? Which is less specific in this area?
2. The following are documents in connection with the Hardtack cases. Indicate whether each document belongs in the civil file or the criminal file:
   a. A letter from the prosecutor's office requesting copies of statements of any witnesses whom Hardtack plans to call at trial
   b. A request for trial signed by the attorney for Jaime Martinez
   c. Copies of medical bills from Martinez
   d. A document entitled "Complaint for Damages"
   e. A copy of a jury instruction entitled "Reasonable Doubt Defined"
   f. A legal memorandum comparing sentencing under state battery statutes with state civil-rights violations
3. Consider the Hardtack criminal and civil cases. Identify the following for the Hardtack criminal case:
   a. Parties (plaintiff and defendant)
   b. Possible punishment should Hardtack be found guilty
   c. Who could appeal the case

   Do the same for the civil case.
4. Review the Ethical Choices boxes in this chapter. Which NALA and/or NFPA rules or guidelines apply to the situations? Review your state's ethical rules. (*Hint*: Go to http://www.nala.org/ and find a link.) Which of those rules apply?
5. Review the summary of *U.S. v. Morrison* in Appendix VII. Is this a civil case or a criminal case? Explain.

Assignments and Projects

1. Read your local newspaper for one week. Make a list of all legal cases reported. Indicate whether they are civil or criminal cases.
2. Access the Web site http://www.courttv.com/. Find examples of three civil cases and three criminal cases.

CHAPTER 7

PERSONAL INJURY PRACTICE

TORT LAW AND WORKERS' COMPENSATION

Technology Corner

Web Address	Name of Site
www.abanet.org/tips/home.html	ABA Tort and Insurance Practice Section
www.findlaw.com/01topics/22tort/index.html	FindLaw Injury and Tort Law
www.hg.org/torts.html	Hieros Gamos Guide to Tort Law
www.rxlist.com/	Internet Drug Index
www.expertpages.com/	Expert Pages
www.experts.com/	Experts.com
www.claims.com/online.html	National Directory of Expert Witnesses
www.osha.gov/	OSHA

CASE FILE: THE GREENLY PERSONAL INJURY CASE

Lee Greenly, a customer service agent at Brentwood Department Store, tripped and fell on a piece of loose carpeting at work. Brentwood hired Carpets Etc. to install new carpeting one month prior to the accident. Within a few days after the carpet was installed, several employees, including Greenly, complained to Brentwood about the loose carpeting. Nothing was done. As a result of the fall, Greenly suffered a broken arm.

SEC. 7-1 INTRODUCTION

In the last chapter, you saw how our laws are divided into civil laws and criminal laws. Substantive civil laws are further divided or categorized by subject matter. Because of the complexities of the law, legal practitioners today tend to specialize within specific areas of law rather than engage in a general practice of law. A detailed discussion of all of the substantive legal principles that form the basis for the various areas of practice is obviously beyond the scope of this book. However, a brief introduction to some of the more common legal concepts is important to an understanding of the legal system and legal practice. One important area of legal practice is the area related to tort law. A **tort** is sometimes defined as a noncontractual civil wrong. Tort law forms the basis of numerous civil lawsuits between parties. If Greenly sued Carpets Etc. for damages, that lawsuit would be based on legal principles found in tort law. Because this accident happened at work, Greenly might also have a workers' compensation claim. This chapter introduces you to the area of law that forms the basis of personal injury practice and to the related area of **workers' compensation**, the laws that apply to those who are injured at work. Subsequent chapters cover some of the more common areas of law that form the basis for family practice, business practice, and criminal practice.

tort
A noncontractual civil wrong.

workers' compensation
Laws that apply to those who are injured at work.

SEC. 7-2 TORT LAW IN GENERAL

Personal injury practice deals with lawsuits or claims for money damages for injuries that people suffer. The most common type of personal injury case involves automobile accidents. For example, if Marshall runs a red light and collides with a car driven by Ng and Ng is injured as a result of the accident, Ng might make a monetary claim against Marshall to compensate Ng for medical expenses, lost earnings, and the pain and suffering that Ng experienced. The underlying substantive law that allows for this type of claim is known as *tort law*. A tort is a civil wrong that usually results in some sort of injury. The injury can be a physical injury, emotional distress, or damage to one's reputation or business. It can also be property damage. As a result of the tort, the wrongdoer, also known as the **tortfeasor**, becomes liable to the victim for money damages. Most often these money damages are intended to compensate for the injury, although in some instances they are also intended to punish the tortfeasor for the wrongdoing. These types of damages are known as **punitive damages**. Punitive damages are also known as **exemplary damages**.

Tort law is one of the oldest types of law, having its foundation in early common law. Today, tort law is found primarily in statutes and case law. Although differences exist from state to state, many common tort principles and concepts also

tortfeasor
One who commits a tort.

punitive damages
Damages meant to punish.

exemplary damages
Another term for *punitive damages*.

exist. In general, three types of torts exist: intentional torts, negligence, and strict liability. Each tort consists of various elements or legal requirements. In any situation, if the facts satisfy or support each of the elements, then the victim has a case or cause of action based on that tort. A **cause of action** is a legally recognized right to relief or damages. However, even if all of the elements of a tort are present, the cause of action or right to claim damages can be defeated if certain defenses exist. Tort defenses are facts that justify or excuse what would otherwise be a tort. The types of defenses that exist vary depending on the type of tort.

cause of action
The basis upon which a lawsuit may be brought to the court.

SEC. 7–3 INTENTIONAL TORTS

intentional tort
A tort that is willful and meant to cause harm.

An **intentional tort**, as the name suggests, is one in which the party committing the tort intends to do the act knowing it will cause an injury. Many intentional torts existed at common law. Some of the more common intentional torts that remain important include assault, battery, false imprisonment, defamation, invasion of privacy, intentional infliction of emotional distress, misrepresentation, conversion, and trespass. In addition, several other intentional torts have been created by modern statutes or case law. These include sexual harassment, civil rights violations, and a series of business torts. Many intentional torts are also crimes. In situations where the same act is both a tort and a crime, remember that the cases are handled separately in our legal system. You should also know that even where the same term is applied to acts that are both torts and crimes, sometimes the specific elements of the tort differ from the specific elements of the crime.

PERSONAL TORTS

Assault and Battery

Assault and battery are actually two distinct torts. An *assault* is an intentional act that causes fear or apprehension of some immediate harmful or offensive contact or touching of another. A *battery* is an intentional act that consists of a harmful or offensive contact or touching of another. Many times, one course of conduct results in the commission of both of these torts. For example, suppose that in the course of a fight, Adams points a gun at Braun and shoots, hitting Braun. At the moment Braun becomes aware of the gun pointed at him, the tort of assault occurs because Adams committed an intentional act that puts Braun in apprehension of immediate harmful contact, that is, a bullet hitting him. At the moment Braun is shot, a battery occurs because Adams committed an intentional act that caused harmful contact or touching of Braun.

While the tort of battery is frequently committed in the course of some kind of fight, it is not limited to that situation. It is often applied to situations involving medical treatment to which proper consent is not given. The medical treatment is considered to be a touching or contact. Although it is not harmful in the traditional sense, the medical treatment is offensive if not authorized. The tort of battery is also used to form the basis of lawsuits stemming from nonconsensual sexual contact or sexual assault. In fact, some states adopted specific laws governing this.

Assault and *battery* are terms that are used to describe both torts and crimes. In some cases the same act may be both. For example, the situation in which Adams shoots Braun is both a tort and a crime. However, suppose that Adams points an unloaded gun at Braun. This is still the tort of assault, because Braun is in apprehension of harmful contact if he does not know that the gun is unloaded. However, the crime of assault usually requires that the perpetrator have the actual ability to carry out the threat. If the gun is unloaded, there is no actual ability to do this. (However, many, if not all, states have laws that make pointing a gun at a person a separate crime, but it is not the common-law crime of assault.)

False Imprisonment and False Arrest

False imprisonment is an intentional act that involves the unlawful violation of the personal liberty of another. Individuals are falsely imprisoned if they are intentionally confined or restrained to an area by one who has no legal right to do so. Since an arrest always involves some sort of detention or confinement, a *false arrest* is a type of false imprisonment in which the confinement or restraint is done by one claiming the authority to make a lawful arrest. The most obvious example of a false imprisonment is the situation in which a victim is kidnapped and held against his or her will. However, in practice, lawsuits for false imprisonment rarely stem from this type of situation. Causes of action for false imprisonment and false arrest are alleged where businesses restrain individuals thought to have shoplifted or where an innocent person is arrested, either by police or by a private citizen. However, the torts of false imprisonment or false arrest are not always committed if the person restrained happens to be innocent of any crime. Businesses are usually allowed to make a reasonable detention and investigation if they have reasonable grounds to believe that someone has shoplifted. This is known as the **shopkeeper's privilege**. A resulting restraint on someone's liberty is thus not unlawful and therefore not a tort. Likewise, police and private citizens are not held to a standard of absolute certainty in making arrests. Police must comply with constitutional safeguards and state laws in making arrests, but this does not mean that police must always be right. A reasonable mistake in making an arrest, as long as it does not violate the victim's constitutional rights or state laws, will not give rise to a cause of action for false arrest. The same is true for a citizen's arrest, although the state laws may be different when an arrest is made by a private citizen rather than a police officer.

shopkeeper's privilege
The right of a merchant to make reasonable detention of a patron where there is probable cause to believe that shoplifting has occurred.

Defamation

Defamation involves the unprivileged publication of a factual statement that is untrue and defamatory or injurious to a person's reputation. The term *defamation* is used to describe two separate torts, *libel* and *slander*. The key difference between libel and slander is the manner of publication. Libel is written publication, while slander is oral. The term *publication* means communication to a third person. Before any statement is deemed defamatory, it must be untrue and it must be a statement of fact rather than opinion. Regardless of how injurious a statement is, if it is true it is not defamatory. Furthermore, generally it must be a statement of fact and not an opinion. The statement of fact must also be believable. A satirical article written about an individual and containing untrue defamatory-type statements is not a tort if the reader would reasonably interpret the article as being satirical and not true. Another distinction between libel and slander concerns the type of damages that must be proved. If the defamation is libel, then most states do not require the proof of actual out-of-pocket damages by the plaintiff. Damages are presumed by the written publication of the untrue statement. Slander is somewhat different. If a statement

slander per se
A statement that on its face is defamatory.

is slanderous on its face (referred to as **slander per se**), then damages are presumed by the publication of the untrue statement. On the other hand, if the statement is not slanderous on its face, then the plaintiff must prove actual monetary losses before a cause of action arises. A statement is slanderous on its face, or slander per se, when anyone hearing the statement would know that injury to one's reputation is intended. For example, the statement that "Francis Farmington, mayor of this city, was a paying customer of Monique Munro, a well-known madam" is defamatory on its face (assuming it is not true). On the other hand, a statement that Francis Farmington was seen keeping company with Monique Munro is not injurious to Farmington's reputation unless the reader knows that Monique is a madam.

The tort of defamation sometimes presents problems when contrasted with the First Amendment right of the press to publish news articles. Although defamation is an intentional tort, the intentional element is met if the tortfeasor intentionally communicates the defamatory statement. An act need not be malicious to be intentional. Traditionally, there was no requirement that the tortfeasor have any malicious purpose in making a defamatory statement. However, because of First Amendment rights to free speech, the U.S. Supreme Court held that special rules apply to the news media. The rules that apply depend on whether the victims of the defamatory statements are public officials or private persons. News media cannot be held liable for defamation where they print an untrue and injurious statement about a public figure unless it is shown by clear and convincing evidence that the statement was published with malice or a reckless disregard of the truth. *Malice* is a difficult term to define but generally means "ill will" or "hatred." Where a statement is made about a private person, it must be shown that the news media were at least negligent in not checking the truth or falsity of the statement.

Invasion of Privacy

Invasion of privacy is an intentional tort that involves intentionally and offensively intruding upon the solitude of another or upon his or her private affairs or concerns. The gist of this tort is the intrusion into a person's right to be left alone. This tort can be based on different types of conduct. First is the public disclosure of private facts. For example, suppose a movie producer films a story based on the life of a prostitute, and without her consent, uses her real name. This is an example of invasion of privacy. Note that the tort of defamation does not apply because the statements are true. Disclosing private facts about an individual does not always result in the tort of invasion of privacy, however. If the information is "newsworthy," it can be published even if it might cause embarrassment. If the victim is a public person, facts that might ordinarily be private may become items of legitimate public interest and thus not a basis for an invasion-of-privacy tort. Second, the tort of invasion of privacy can also be based on other types of conduct. These include appropriating a person's name or likeness for the benefit of the tortfeasor, intruding into someone's private affairs, and placing the victim in a false light. Appropriation usually involves using a famous person's name or likeness in connection with the advertisement of a product without the consent of the famous person. Intruding into one's private affairs might involve something like illegal electronic eavesdropping. Placing a person in a false light is similar to defamation and often exists with that tort. An example of this type of conduct was shown in a case where a newspaper featured an article on the family of a man who was killed in a major catastrophe. The article portrayed the family as living in poverty and in dilapidated home conditions. Some parts of the article were false. The court found that this was sufficient to support a cause of action for invasion of privacy based on placing a person in a false light.

Intentional Infliction of Emotional Distress

Intentional and outrageous conduct that causes mental suffering forms the basis of the tort of *intentional infliction of emotional distress*. The courts have always been reluctant to recognize this tort, primarily because of the possibility of abuse and false claims. A cause of action for intentional infliction of emotional distress requires outrageous conduct that is intentional or at least reckless. This tort is associated with the mental suffering incurred as a result of intentional mishandling of dead bodies, outrageous and cruel collection tactics, and insurance company tactics in refusing to pay benefits that are due. In recent years, this tort has often been associated with harassment in the workplace because of sex, age, race, or sexual orientation.

Hustler Magazine and Larry C. Flynt v. Jerry Falwell

485 U.S. 46 (1987)

Hustler *magazine (published by Larry Flynt) published an ad parody ridiculing Jerry Falwell and suggesting that his first sexual experience involved his mother and an outhouse. Falwell sued for damages for invasion of privacy, libel, and intentional infliction of emotional distress. The trial court directed a verdict for the defendant on the privacy claim. The jury found for* Hustler *and Flynt on the defamation claim, but awarded damages based on intentional infliction of emotional distress.* Hustler *and Flynt appealed, claiming that the First Amendment gave them the right to publish a parody of a public figure and thus protected them against an action for intentional infliction of emotional distress. The Supreme Court agreed and found for* Hustler *and Flynt, saying that a public figure cannot recover for this type of action unless he can prove that a false statement of fact was published with actual malice. The following is an excerpt from the Supreme Court's decision.*

OPINION

Petitioner Hustler Magazine, Inc., is a magazine of nationwide circulation. Respondent Jerry Falwell, a nationally known minister who has been active as a commentator on politics and public affairs, sued petitioner and its publisher, petitioner Larry Flynt, to recover damages for invasion of privacy, libel, and intentional infliction of emotional distress. The District Court directed a verdict against respondent on the privacy claim, and submitted the other two claims to a jury. The jury found for petitioners [*Hustler* and Flynt] on the defamation claim, but found for respondent [Falwell] on the claim for intentional infliction of emotional distress and awarded damages. We now consider whether this award is consistent with the First and Fourteenth Amendments of the United States Constitution.

The inside front cover of the November 1983 issue of *Hustler* magazine featured a "parody" of an advertisement for Campari Liqueur that contained the name and picture of respondent and was entitled "Jerry Falwell talks about his first time." This parody was modeled after actual Campari ads that included interviews with various celebrities about their "first times." Although it was apparent by the end of each interview that this meant the first time they sampled Campari, the ads clearly played on the sexual double entendre of the general subject of "first times." Copying the form and layout of these Campari ads, *Hustler's* editors chose respondent as the featured celebrity and drafted an alleged "interview" with him in which he states that his "first time" was during a drunken incestuous rendezvous with his mother in an outhouse. The *Hustler* parody portrays respondent and his mother as drunk and immoral, and suggests that respondent is a hypocrite who preaches only when he is drunk. In small print at the bottom of the page, the ad contains the disclaimer, "ad parody—not to be taken seriously." The magazine's table of contents also lists the ad as "Fiction: Ad and Personality Parody."

Soon after the November issue of *Hustler* became available to the public, respondent brought this action. Respondent stated in his complaint that publication of the ad parody in *Hustler* entitled him to recover damages for libel, invasion of privacy, and intentional infliction of emotional distress. The case proceeded to trial. At the close of the evidence, the District Court granted a directed verdict for petitioners on the invasion of privacy claim. The jury then found against respondent on the libel claim, specifically finding that the ad parody could not "reasonably be understood as describing actual facts about [respondent] or actual events in which [he] participated." The jury ruled for respondent on the intentional infliction of emotional distress claim, however, and stated that he should be awarded $100,000 in compensatory damages, as well as $50,000 each in punitive damages from petitioners.

This case presents us with a novel question involving First Amendment limitations upon a State's authority to protect its citizens from the intentional infliction of emotional distress. We must decide whether a public figure may recover damages for emotional harm caused by the publication of an ad parody offensive to him, and doubtless gross and repugnant in the eyes of most. Respondent would have us find that a State's interest in protecting public figures from emotional distress is sufficient to deny First Amendment protection to speech that is patently offensive and is intended to inflict emotional injury, even when that speech could not reasonably have been interpreted as stating actual facts about the public figure involved. This we decline to do.

At the heart of the First Amendment is the recognition of the fundamental importance of the free flow of ideas and opinions on matters of public interest and concern. We have therefore been particularly vigilant to ensure that individual expressions of ideas remain free from governmentally imposed sanctions.

The sort of robust political debate encouraged by the First Amendment is bound to produce speech that is critical of those who hold public office or those public figures who are "intimately involved in the resolution of important public questions or, by reason of their fame, shape events in areas of concern to society at large." *Associated Press v. Walker*, decided with *Curtis Publishing Co. v. Butts*, 388 U.S. 130, 164 (1967). Justice Frankfurter put it succinctly in *Baumgartner v. United States*, 322 U.S. 665, 673–674 (1944), when he said that "one of the prerogatives of American Citizenship is the right to criticize public men and measures." Such criticism, inevitably, will not always be reasoned or moderate; public figures as well as public officials will be subject to "vehement, caustic and sometimes unpleasantly sharp attacks." *New York Times Co. v. Sullivan*, 376 U.S. 254 at 270 (1964). "The candidate who vaunts his spotless record and sterling integrity cannot convincingly cry 'foul!' when an opponent or an industrious reporter attempts to demonstrate the contrary." *Monitor Patriot Co. v. Roy*, 401 U.S. 265, 274 (1971).

Of course, this does not mean that any speech about a public figure is immune from sanction in the form of damages. Since *New York Times Co. v. Sullivan*, we have consistently ruled that a public figure may hold a speaker liable for the damage to reputation caused by publication of a defamatory falsehood, but only if the statement was made "with knowledge that it was false or with reckless disregard of whether it was false or not."

Respondent argues, however, that a different standard should apply in this case because here the State seeks to prevent not reputational damage, but the severe emotional distress suffered by the person who is the subject of an offensive publication. In respondent's view, so long as the utterance was intended to inflict emotional stress, was outrageous, and did in fact inflict serious emotional distress, it is of no constitutional import whether the statement was a fact or an opinion, or whether it was true or false. It is the intent to cause injury that is the gravamen of the tort, and the State's interest in preventing emotional harm simply outweighs whatever interest a speaker may have in speech of this type.

Generally speaking, the law does not regard the intent to inflict emotional distress as one which should receive much solicitude, and it is quite understandable that most if not all jurisdictions have chosen to make it civilly culpable where the conduct in question is sufficiently "outrageous." But in the world of debate about public affairs, many things done with motives that are less than admirable are protected by the First Amendment. While a bad motive may be deemed controlling for purposes of tort liability in other areas of the law, we think the First Amendment prohibits such a result in the area of public debate about public figures.

Were we to hold otherwise, there can be little doubt that political cartoonists and satirists would be subjected to damages awards without any showing that their work falsely defamed its subject. The appeal of the political cartoon or caricature is often based on exploration of unfortunate physical traits or politically embarrassing events—an exploration often calculated to injure the feelings of the subject of the portrayal. The art of the cartoonists is often not reasoned or evenhanded, but slashing and one-sided.

Respondent contends, however, that the caricature in question here was so "outrageous" as to distinguish it from more traditional political cartoons. There is no doubt that the caricature of respondent and his mother published in *Hustler* is at best a distant cousin of the political cartoons described above, and a rather poor relation at that. If it were possible by laying down a principled standard to separate the one from the other, public discourse would probably suffer little or no harm. But we doubt that there is any such standard, and we are quite sure that the pejorative description "outrageous" does not supply one.

We conclude that public figures and public officials may not recover for the tort of intentional infliction of emotional distress by reason of publications such as the one here at issue without showing in addition that the publication contains a false statement of fact which was made with "actual malice," *i.e.*, with knowledge that the statement was false or made with reckless disregard as to whether or not it was true. This is not merely a blind application of the *New York Times* standard, it reflects our considered judgment that such a standard is necessary to give adequate "breathing space" to the freedoms protected by the First Amendment.

The judgment of the Court of Appeals is accordingly reversed.

CASE ANALYSIS

1. What was the factual basis for Falwell's claim against *Hustler* for intentional infliction of emotional distress?
2. Why did Falwell lose this lawsuit?

Malicious Prosecution and Abuse of Process

Filing an unjustified criminal complaint against an individual leads to the tort of malicious prosecution. A criminal complaint is not justified where there is no probable cause to believe that the defendant committed the crime. This tort requires that the outcome of the criminal case be favorable to the defendant as well as a malicious intent on the part of the tortfeasor. Maliciously instituting a civil action is also a tort requiring the same elements as malicious prosecution. The action must have no factual or legal basis, it must be maliciously filed, and it must terminate favorably for the defendant (the victim of the tort). Although the term *malicious prosecution* technically refers only to initiating criminal actions, the term is widely used to include civil actions. Malicious prosecution, for both criminal and civil actions, relates to the wrongful initiating of the action. A similar tort exists for misusing other aspects of legal proceedings. This tort is known as *abuse of process*. These torts impose liability on the party who maliciously initiated a legal action or who misused a legal proceeding. They may also impose liability on the attorney for that party.

Civil Rights Violations

In recent years, tort practice has included numerous actions based on violations of constitutional rights. In some cases these actions are based on Title 42, Section 1983 of the United States Code, which provides:

> Every person who, under color of any statute ordinance, regulation, custom, or usage, of any State or Territory or the District of Columbia, subjects, or causes to be subjected, any citizen of the United States or other person within the jurisdiction thereof to the deprivation of any rights, privileges, or immunities secured by the Constitution and laws, shall be liable to the party injured in an action at law, suit in equity, or other proper proceeding for redress.

This section usually applies only when a person is suing a governmental agency or employee and is used in lawsuits against police and police departments for excessive use of force. Some states enacted laws creating liability even where the wrongdoer is not acting under any color of authority.

In addition to this section, the United States Code (Title 42, Section 2000e *et seq.*) and many state codes provide remedies for job discrimination or harassment. As mentioned earlier, these actions are often combined with other torts such as infliction of emotional distress.

Business Torts

disparagement
Another term for the business torts of slander of title and trade libel.

Not all torts result in personal damage to the victim. Some are geared toward damage to a person's property or business interests. These include slander of title, trade libel, inducing a breach of contract, and interference with prospective economic advantage. Slander of title and trade libel are sometimes referred to as **disparagement**. These torts are distinguished from slander and libel in that defamation is a tort that damages a person's reputation, whereas disparagement damages the salability or value of one's property or business. Like defamation, disparagement involves publication of an untrue statement of fact. Unlike defamation, disparagement relates to a property interest and requires an actual pecuniary or monetary loss. *Slander of title* is the publication of an untrue statement of fact regarding ownership of property that results in actual monetary loss. *Trade libel* is the publication of an untrue statement of fact regarding the quality of one's property that results in actual monetary loss. Examples of slander of title include recording a false lien against a parcel of real property or failing to remove a recorded lien that was paid. Examples of trade libel include statements that a business's merchandise consists of seconds or was made with inferior materials.

While businesses certainly have the right to compete with one another, a tort is committed when one induces another to breach a contract that was entered into with another, as a result of which damage is suffered. This tort lies only against the third person who induces the breach, not against the breaching party. The remedy against the breaching party is a contract action for breach of contract, not a tort. For example, suppose Alvarez and Baker have a contract for a commercial lease in which Baker agrees to lease Alvarez's premises for five years for $5,000 per month plus a percentage of the gross income from Baker's business. Chao, knowing of this contract, approaches Baker with a better rent offer and induces Baker to move out and stop paying rent, as a result of which Alvarez suffers damages. Chao committed the tort of inducing Baker to breach a contract. Baker committed no tort, but is liable for damages for breach of contract. A related tort is interference with prospective economic advantage. This tort extends liability to interfering with business relations that are not yet subject to any contractual agreement but are prospective in nature. Obviously a fine line exists between this tort and the right to compete in the business environment. Before a tort will be found, one must use an intentional and improper method of soliciting another's business. Usually this intentional and improper method of competition will be a violation of some other tort or some state or federal law limiting business practices. Such laws are generally referred to as *consumer protection statutes*.

Property Torts

Two intentional torts are directed at protecting a person's property rights. These are *conversion* and *trespass*. Trespass is a tort against real property, whereas conversion is a tort against personal property. Real property, which is discussed in Chapter 10, is land and anything that is permanently fixed to the land. Personal property is property that is movable. The tort of trespass involves the unauthorized interference with or encroachment onto the real property of another. The tortfeasor need not intrude onto the land personally. The tort of trespass occurs when an individual allows such things as trees or roots to encroach on a neighbor's property. Damage to the property is not required; the trespassing person is liable for nominal damages even where no injury to the property occurred.

Conversion is the wrongful exercise of control over the personal property of another. The exercise of control can involve taking the property, destroying it, damaging it, or substantially interfering with the owner's use of the property. The acts that constitute the tort of conversion also frequently constitute a crime (primarily theft).

intellectual property
Property rights in the *result* of one's thoughts, ideas, or inventions; includes patents, copyrights, and trademarks.

infringement
Improper interference in the intellectual property rights of another.

A type of property that has become very important today is **intellectual property**. Intellectual property, which is really a type of personal property, includes such things as trademarks, tradenames, copyrights, and patents. Although the unlawful interference with such property rights would usually fall under the traditional definition of conversion, special statutory law has been created to apply to this area. Taking or interfering with intellectual property is usually referred to as **infringement**. Violations of these statutes have increased since the advent of the Internet, especially in the area of copyright infringement of music. Technology allowed sites such as the famous Napster and MP3 sites to make music CDs available to visitors who could download and copy the music without cost. As a result, numerous music companies and artists filed suits alleging copyright infringement. Intellectual property law is covered in more detail in Chapter 10.

Fraud

Although the term *fraud* is often associated with contract law, fraud is a tort. This tort consists of a misrepresentation made with the intent to deceive, where the misrepresentation is justifiably relied upon and causes damages. Normally, fraud requires that the misrepresentation be as to a matter of fact, not opinion, on the theory that we should not rely on opinions of others. However, where an opinion is expressed by someone who is an expert or who is in a special relationship with the victim, an opinion can form the basis of fraud. Since fraud is an intentional tort, it also requires that the statement be knowingly false and be made with the intent to deceive. Statements that are negligently made can form the basis of a negligent tort (negligent misrepresentation) but not fraud. The person to whom the misrepresentation is made must justifiably rely on the statement. If the victim knows that the statement is false, then there is no tort. Finally, fraud requires damages. The victim must suffer some financial loss because of the reliance on the misrepresentation.

Defenses to Intentional Torts

The two major defenses to intentional torts are *consent* and *privilege*. If the victim consents to the acts of another, then no tort occurs as long as the consent is knowingly and freely given by one with the power to consent. For example, recall how medical treatment can become a battery if the patient does not consent. If the patient agrees to the treatment, then there is no tort. However, if the patient is not informed of all of the possible risks of the treatment, the consent is not knowingly made and consent ceases to be a defense. Likewise, if the patient is twelve years old, the consent may not be valid because minors do not always have the power to give consent. Unless special circumstances exist, consent must come from a parent or guardian.

Privilege is a much more complicated defense because of the wide variety of privileges that exist. Privilege means that the law allows a person to engage in an activity that would be a tort if that act were not specially permitted. The types of privileges that exist vary depending on the specific tort. For example, a parent has the privilege or right to discipline a child. Thus, spanking a child is not a battery. A doctor has the privilege to render treatment in an emergency without consent if a victim is incapable of giving consent. A person has the right or privilege to enter the property of another in an emergency situation such as a fire. Individuals may also engage in activities that are reasonably necessary to defend themselves or others, even if such activities would otherwise be tortious. The key here is that the conduct must always be reasonable when compared with the threat.

Another defense to intentional torts, which is also sometimes a defense to other torts, is *immunity*. Governments and government officials sometimes are immune from liability for torts. Governmental immunity is determined by laws of the government in question. In other words, immunity of the federal government is determined by federal law; immunity of the state governments is determined by state laws. State and federal laws are not always consistent regarding this question. In all jurisdictions, however, immunity is limited. That is, no government is totally immune from all tort liability. Appropriate laws must be consulted before determining whether immunity exists.

A POINT TO REMEMBER

Every intentional tort consists of various requirements or elements. In analyzing any factual situation you should list the elements of potential torts and determine if your factual situation satisfies each of the elements. If your factual situation does satisfy every element of the tort, then you must consider all possible defenses. Only then can you determine if tort liability exists.

SEC. 7–4 NEGLIGENCE

NEGLIGENCE IN GENERAL

negligence
A tort; failure to act as a reasonably prudent person would act under the same or similar circumstances.

The most common basis for tort liability is **negligence**. The term *negligence* is used in two contexts in tort law. On one hand, the term *negligence* is the name given to a tort. This tort involves causing an injury to another by failing to act as a reasonably prudent person would act under the same or similar circumstances. On the other hand, the term *negligence* is also used in its everyday meaning of "carelessness." Carelessness is not a tort unless other elements are present. More specifically, the tort of negligence occurs when the following elements can be shown:

1. The tortfeasor was under a duty to use due care.
2. The tortfeasor breached that duty of due care.
3. The tortfeasor's act was the actual cause of injuries or damages.

4. The tortfeasor's act was the proximate cause of injuries or damages.
5. Damages were incurred.

Duty of Due Care

Generally speaking, we are all under a duty to act in such a way as not to injure those around us. No special relationships or circumstances are required. Thus, when a person drives a car on a public road, that person is under a duty to use due care to avoid injuries to other motorists and pedestrians. The issue of whether there is a duty of due care often arises, however, when a person is sued not for doing something but for failing to do something. For example, a motorist owes a duty not to drive carelessly, but if the motorist sees someone injured in an automobile accident, does that motorist have a duty to stop and help? Traditionally the law says that there is no duty to act in these situations unless a special relationship or circumstance exists. For example, if a motorist is involved in an accident resulting in an injury, the motorist is under an obligation to at least call for help even if the accident was not caused by the motorist's carelessness.

Breach of the Duty of Due Care

The breach of the duty of due care is the negligent or careless act. For most circumstances it is failing to act as a reasonably prudent person would act under the same or similar circumstances. In a jury trial, the jury is allowed to determine how a reasonably prudent person would act. However, if the activity requires the special expertise of a professional, then the breach of the duty is different. It is failing to act according to the standards of the profession. For example, in performing a surgical procedure, the breach of duty of due care is not how a reasonably prudent person performs the procedure, but how a trained surgeon does it. Since jurors cannot be presumed to know the standards of various professions, establishing whether there was a breach of duty under these circumstances often requires the testimony of expert witnesses, that is, other professionals. Of course, in some circumstances even a layperson knows that a doctor acted negligently. For example, if a patient is scheduled for an amputation and the doctor amputates the wrong leg, it does not take another doctor to tell a jury that negligence occurred. These types of situations are sometimes referred to as **res ipsa loquitur**. Literally translated, this means "the thing speaks for itself." In other words, anyone can tell that there was negligence or a breach of duty simply from the fact that the incident occurred.

res ipsa loquitur
"The thing speaks for itself"; negligence is implied from the fact that the incident happened.

In some cases, the act that is a breach of duty is also a violation of a statute. For example, consider the situation where Davis runs a red light and causes a collision, injuring Edelman. Applying traditional concepts of breach of duty, you could say that Davis failed to act as a reasonably prudent person in running the red light and therefore breached her duty. However, using this analysis, a jury is allowed to consider whether running a red light is failing to act as a reasonably prudent person. However, if the tortfeasor's act is also a violation of a statute, then the doctrine of **negligence per se** often applies. This legal doctrine provides that where an act is a violation of a statute, then the act is negligent per se. This means that the act is not weighed against the reasonable-person standard. The jury is told that the act is deemed to be a negligent act or a breach of duty simply because it is a violation of a statute.

negligence per se
Negligence that is presumed because the tortfeasor has violated a statute.

Actual Cause

Actual cause refers to the fact that the negligent act, the breach of duty, was what caused the injury. In most situations this is obvious and is determined by asking the question, "If not for the negligent act, would the injury have occurred?" For example, suppose Francis runs a red light and hits Gianni, a pedestrian crossing with a green light, injuring Gianni, who suffers a broken leg. If Francis had not run the red light, he would not have hit Gianni and no injury would have resulted. Francis is the actual cause of Gianni's injuries. This is sometimes referred to as the *"but for" test*. However, life is not always this simple. Suppose that Francis's vehicle barely brushes against Gianni, causing no real physical injury. However, Gianni, who suffers from a weak heart, is so shocked by the incident that he suffers a heart attack and dies. Is Francis's negligent act the cause of Gianni's death, or was the death caused by Gianni's heart disease? These questions are not always easy to answer, and ultimately are questions that a trier of fact (either a jury or judge) must determine. In analyzing this type of situation, the "but for" test does not always work, and the law uses another type of analysis. If the negligent act is a substantial factor in causing the injury, then the requirement of actual causation is met. The *substantial-factor test* asks the question, "Was the defendant's negligent act a substantial factor in causing the injury?" This test is used when two or more tortfeasors separately act to bring about one injury.

Proximate Cause

The concept of proximate cause is probably one of the most complicated legal concepts in existence. Sometimes negligent acts actually cause injuries that are so remote and so unforeseeable that the law refuses to impose liability on the individual who actually caused the injury. For example, suppose that Hussein negligently causes an automobile accident with a car driven by Irwin. Hussein and Irwin exit their respective vehicles to exchange insurance information. A bolt of lightning strikes Irwin, killing him. Is Hussein liable for his death? Analyzing this situation, you see that Hussein had a duty to Irwin, another motorist. He breached the duty by driving negligently. Were it not for the accident, Irwin would not be standing at the side of the road and would not be hit by the bolt of lightning. But should Hussein be liable? This is such a remote and unforeseeable consequence that the law would probably say no liability exists. The main consideration in determining proximate cause is the question of foreseeability of what happened.

Damages

Damages are a required element of the tort of negligence. If there is no injury, there is no tort. The injury, however, can be physical injury to a person or property damage. In some cases it can also be an emotional injury to a person. Thus, suppose that when Jackson runs a red light he manages to avoid hitting Keller, a pedestrian in the crosswalk. Although Keller is momentarily frightened, she suffers no physical injury nor any lasting emotional distress. No tort has occurred. Proving damages often involves reviewing medical records and reports. Knowledge of medical terminology is critical. Many good medical dictionaries can be found on the Internet.

Palsgraf v. Long Island Railroad Co.

248 N.Y. 339, 162 N.E. 99 (1928)

The following is a famous case dealing with the issues of duty of due care and proximate cause in negligence actions. In this case, the plaintiff sued a railroad company for the alleged negligence of one of its employees. The dissenting opinion written by Justice Andrews has become more important than the opinion itself and is the law generally followed in the United States today. The facts of the case are as follows: Plaintiff was standing on a railroad platform. A man, carrying a small unidentifiable package, jumped aboard a railroad car. A guard on the car, trying to help him board the train, dislodged the package from his arm. The package contained fireworks, which exploded when they fell. The explosion caused scales at the other end of the platform to fall, injuring plaintiff. The issue in this case was whether plaintiff had a cause of action for negligence. The majority opinion (Cardozo) approaches the question from the perspective of duty of care, stating that the plaintiff must show that "as to him" the negligent act was dangerous. Since this couldn't be done, the case was dismissed. The dissent (Andrews) takes a different view and approaches the issue from the perspective of proximate cause. Andrews states that the duty of care required for negligence should not be a duty owed to individual persons, but a duty owed to society to protect it from unnecessary danger. The question of liability thus becomes a question of proximate cause, rather than duty of care. Proximate cause, he says, depends in each case upon many considerations. In general however, proximate cause means that because of public policy, or a rough set of justice, the law refuses to extend liability beyond a certain series of events.

OPINION

Plaintiff was standing on a platform of defendant's railroad after buying a ticket to go to the Rockaway Beach. A train stopped at the station, bound for another place. Two men ran forward to catch it. One of the men reached the platform of the car without mishap, though the train was already moving. The other man, carrying a package, jumped aboard the car. A guard on the car, who had held the door open, reached forward to help him in, and another guard on the platform pushed him from behind. In this act, the package was dislodged, and fell upon the rails. It was a package of small size, about fifteen inches long, and was covered by a newspaper. In fact it contained fireworks, but there was nothing in its appearance to give notice of its contents. The fireworks when they fell exploded. The shock of the explosion threw down some scales at the other end of the platform, many feet away. The scales struck the plaintiff, causing injuries for which she sues.

The conduct of the defendant's guard, if a wrong in its relation to the holder of the package, was not a wrong in its relation to the plaintiff, standing far away. Relatively to her it was not negligence at all. Nothing in the situation gave notice that the falling package had in it the potency of peril to persons thus removed. Negligence is not actionable unless it involves the invasion of a legally protected interest, the violation of a right.

What the plaintiff must show is a "wrong" to herself, *i.e.*, a violation of her own right, and not merely a wrong to someone else.

Negligence is not a tort unless it results in the commission of a wrong, and the commission of a wrong imports the violation of a right, in this case, we are told, the right to be protected against interference with one's bodily security. But bodily security is protected, not against all forms of interference or aggression, but only against some. One who seeks redress at law does not make out a cause of action by showing without more that there has been damage to his person. If the harm was not willful, he must show that the act as to him had possibilities of danger so many and apparent as to entitle him to be protected against the doing of it though the harm was unintended.

The judgment of the Appellate Division and that of the Trial Term should be reversed, and the complaint dismissed.

DISSENT

Andrews, J. (Dissenting).

Assisting a passenger to board a train, the defendant's servant negligently knocked a package from his arms. It fell between the platform and the cars. Of its contents the servant knew and could know nothing. A violent explosion followed. The concussion broke some scales standing a considerable distance away. In falling they injured the plaintiff, an intending passenger.

Upon these facts may she recover the damages she has suffered in an action brought against the master? The result we shall reach depends upon our theory as to the nature of negligence. Is it a relative concept—the breach of some duty owing to a particular person or to particular persons? Or where there is an act which unreasonably threatens the safety of others, is the doer liable for all its proximate consequences, even where they result in injury to one who would generally be thought to be outside the radius of danger? If we adopt the second hypothesis we have to inquire only as to the relation between cause and effect. We deal in terms of proximate cause, not of negligence. Negligence may be defined roughly as an act or omission which unreasonably does or may affect the rights of others, or which unreasonably fails to protect oneself from the dangers resulting from such acts. There must be both the act or the omission, and the right. It is the act itself, not the intent of the actor, that is important.

But we are told that "there is no negligence unless there is in the particular case a legal duty to take care, and this duty must be one which is owed to the plaintiff himself and not merely to others." This, I think too narrow a conception. Where there is the unreasonable act, and some right that may be affected, there is negligence whether damage does or does not result. That is immaterial. Should we drive down Broadway at a reckless speed, we are negligent whether we strike an approaching car or miss it by an inch. The act itself is wrongful. It is wrong not only to those who happen to be within the radius of danger but to all who might have been there—a wrong to the public at large. As was said by Mr. Justice Holmes many years ago, "the measure of the defendant's duty in determining whether a wrong has been committed is one thing, the measure of liability when a wrong has been committed is another." Due care is a duty imposed on each one of us to protect society from unnecessary danger, not to protect A, B or C alone.

The proposition is this. Every one owes to the world at large the duty of refraining from those acts that may unreasonably threaten the safety of others. Such an act occurs. Not only is he wronged to whom harm might reasonably be expected to result, but he also who is in fact injured, even if he be outside what would generally be thought the danger zone. There needs be duty due the one complaining but this is not a duty to a particular individual because as to him harm might be expected. Harm to someone being the natural result of the act, not only that one alone, but all those in fact injured may complain. Unreasonable risk being taken, its consequences are not confined to those who might probably be hurt.

The right to recover damages rests on additional considerations. The damages must be so connected with the negligence that the latter may be said to be the proximate cause of the former. What is a cause in a legal sense, still more what is proximate cause, depends in each case upon many considerations, as does the existence of negligence itself.

What we do mean by the word "proximate" is, that because of convenience, or public policy, or a rough sense of justice, the law arbitrarily declines to trace a series of events beyond a certain point. This is not logic. It is practical politics.

Take the illustration given in an unpublished manuscript by a distinguished and helpful writer on the law of torts. A chauffeur negligently collides with another car which is filled with dynamite, although he could not know it. An explosion follows. A, walking on the sidewalk nearby, is killed. B, sitting in a window of a building opposite, is cut by flying glass. C, likewise sitting in a window a block away, is similarly injured. And a further illustration. A nursemaid, ten blocks away, startled by the noise, involuntarily drops a baby from her arms to the walk. We are told that C may not recover while A may. As to B it is a question for court or jury. We will all agree that the baby might not. Because, we are again told, the chauffeur had no reason to believe his conduct involved any risk of injuring either C or the baby. As to them he was not negligent.

But the chauffeur, being negligent in risking the collision, his belief that the scope of the harm he might do would be limited is immaterial. His act unreasonably jeopardized the safety of anyone who might be affected by it. C's injury and that of the baby were directly traceable to the collision. Without that, the injury would not have happened. C had the right to sit in his office, secure from such dangers. The baby was entitled to use the sidewalk with reasonable safety.

The true theory is, it seems to me, that the injury to C, if in truth he is to be denied recovery, and the injury to the baby is that their several injuries were not the proximate result of the negligence. And here not what the chauffeur had reason to believe would be the result of his conduct, but what the prudent would foresee, may have a bearing.

There are some hints that may help us. The proximate cause must be something without which the event would not happen. The court must ask itself whether there was a natural and continuous sequence between cause and effect. Was the one a substantial factor in producing the other? Was there a direct connection between them, without too many intervening causes? Is the effect of cause on the result not too attenuated? Is the cause likely, in the usual judgment of mankind, to produce the result? Or by the exercise of prudent foresight could the result be foreseen? Is the result too remote from the cause (and here we consider remoteness in time and space)?

The act upon which defendant's liability rests is knocking an apparently harmless package onto the platform. The act was negligent. For its proximate consequences the defendant is liable. If its contents were broken, to the owner; if it fell upon and crushed a passenger's foot, then to him. If it exploded and injured one in the immediate vicinity, to him also. Mrs. Palsgraf was standing some distance away. How far cannot be told from the record—apparently twenty-five or thirty feet. Perhaps less. Except for the explosion, she would not have been injured. We are told by the appellant in his brief, "it cannot be denied that the explosion was the direct cause of the plaintiff's injuries." So it was a substantial factor in producing the result—there was here a natural and continuous sequence—direct connection. The only intervening cause was that instead of blowing her to the ground, the concussion smashed the weighing machine which in turn fell upon her. There was no remoteness in time, little in space. And surely, given such an explosion as here it needed no great foresight to predict that the natural result would be to injure one on the platform at no greater distance from its scene than was the plaintiff. Injury in some form was most probable.

The judgment appealed from should be affirmed, with costs.

CASE ANALYSIS

1. Why did Justice Andrews dissent from the majority opinion?
2. According to Justice Andrews, what is proximate cause?

Types of Negligence Actions

Unlike the intentional torts, where different intentional acts are labeled as distinct intentional torts, the tort of negligence is not broken down into several different torts. There are, however, some common factual situations that give rise to the tort of negligence. While many of these factual situations are given specific and identifying legal terms, these factual situations are all variations of the tort of negligence. Some common examples of the tort of negligence follow.

Automobile Accidents

Probably the most common situation giving rise to the tort of negligence is the automobile or vehicle accident. An automobile accident stemming from the negligent operation or maintenance of the vehicle is based on the tort of negligence.

Liability of Landowners

Another common factual situation creating the tort of negligence is the negligent or careless maintenance of one's real property. A storekeeper who allows torn carpeting to remain where the public walks and a homeowner whose front steps are broken may both be liable for the tort of negligence if someone is injured. Sometimes the term *premises liability* is applied to these situations. More colloquially, these types of accidents are also called "slip and fall." In some jurisdictions, landowners' liability poses some special legal issues regarding the question of duty of care. Some courts hold that the duty of care a landowner owes to people coming onto the property is dependent on the status of the person coming onto the property. Those coming onto the property are categorized as business invitees, licensees, or trespassers. A business invitee is someone invited onto the property for a business purpose. A licensee is generally a social guest, even though he or she might be invited. A trespasser is one who is not legally on the premises. The highest duty of due care is owed to the business invitee and the lowest duty of due care to the trespasser. In general, the duty owed to a trespasser depends on whether the trespasser is known. If the trespasser is unknown, the landowner has only the duty to refrain from intentional harms or willful and wanton injury. No duty is owed to keep the premises in a safe condition, nor to warn of dangerous conditions. If the trespasser is known, then the landowner has a duty to warn of concealed dangers known to the landowner and to exercise reasonable care in conducting activities. If the trespasser is a child who comes onto the property because of special inducement (such as a tree house) on the property, a different rule applies. The landowner then owes that child a higher duty of due care even though the child may be trespassing. This is known as the **attractive nuisance** doctrine. A landowner owes an invitee a duty similar to that owed to known trespassers. There is a duty to warn of known dangerous conditions and to exercise reasonable care in conducting activities. The duty owed to the business invitee is the highest duty owed. Here the landowner is required not only to warn of known dangers on the property, but to inspect the property for dangerous conditions.

attractive nuisance
A condition on land that appeals to children; a doctrine that requires homeowners to use reasonable care to avoid injury to trespassing children.

Some jurisdictions abolished the distinct duties owed to invitees, licensees, and trespassers and now hold that landowners owe a duty to maintain their premises as a reasonably prudent person would under the same or similar circumstances. They do allow a jury to consider the status of the person coming onto the property as a circumstance, but the person's status does not in itself determine the duty of due care.

Professional Negligence

Professionals such as doctors, lawyers, accountants, and engineers are required to exercise such care consistent with the standards of the professional community. When they do not and when injury results, they face liability for their negligence. These kinds of cases are often referred to as **malpractice** cases.

malpractice
Professional negligence.

Negligent Infliction of Emotional Distress

Where the resulting injury of a negligent act is emotional distress rather than a physical injury, the tort of negligence may or may not have occurred. Where the negligent act causes physical harm as well as emotional distress, the law will usually allow recovery for the emotional distress. However, where no physical injury has occurred, the law is reluctant to allow tort recovery. In part, this is because of the opportunity for abuse in claiming such an injury. A special situation exists, however, where one person witnesses an injury to another caused by a negligent act and suffers emotional distress. In general, unless there is some special relationship between the injured party and the person claiming emotional distress, the courts will deny recovery. The courts also require that the person claiming emotional distress must have witnessed the accident. Learning later that a child has been hit by a car is not enough to support a claim by a parent for negligent infliction of emotional distress.

Defective Products

Lawsuits for injuries caused by defective products are often based on multiple legal theories, including the torts of negligence and strict liability. Negligence applies if the plaintiff claims that a product was *negligently* manufactured, designed, or distributed. The term **product liability** is used to describe lawsuits based on defective products. Product liability is not a separate tort, but rather a term used to describe the type of action filed. As discussed later in this chapter, product liability is not limited to the tort of negligence. It also includes strict liability.

product liability
Liability of manufacturers and distributors for defective products that cause injury.

Loss of Consortium

Consortium is the society, comfort, conjugal fellowship, and sexual relations between married people. When one spouse is physically injured because of the tortious conduct of another, the noninjured spouse may have an action for loss of

consortium
Companionship, comfort, and society given by one spouse to another.

consortium. While this type of action can be based on any tort, it is frequently associated with negligence actions.

Defenses to Negligence

Common defenses to negligence include contributory negligence, comparative negligence, and assumption of the risk. The concept of immunity, discussed earlier, may also apply.

Contributory Negligence

contributory negligence
Negligence of a plaintiff that contributes to the injury; a doctrine that is a defense to negligence.

Contributory negligence refers to negligence on the part of the plaintiff or the person claiming damages. The doctrine of contributory negligence provides that if the plaintiff was also negligent and contributed to his or her own injuries to any degree, then that plaintiff cannot recover any damages from the defendant. This is true even if the defendant's negligence caused most of the injuries. To avoid this harsh result, another concept, known as last clear chance, developed. This concept provides that even if the plaintiff is contributorily negligent, if the defendant had the **last clear chance** to avoid the accident, then the doctrine of contributory negligence does not apply.

last clear chance
A doctrine that prevents the harsh result that follows from the doctrine of contributory negligence; if a negligent defendant had the last opportunity to avoid an accident, the contributory negligence of the plaintiff will not be a bar to recovery.

comparative negligence
A doctrine that compares the negligence of the plaintiff and the defendant and allows recovery based on apportionment of fault.

Comparative Negligence

The doctrine of contributory negligence does not apply in all states. Many have adopted a different rule called **comparative negligence**. Comparative negligence also refers to negligence on the part of the plaintiff. However, this doctrine allows a court to compare the negligence of both the plaintiff and the defendant and to award damages in proportion to fault. Thus, if a defendant is 90 percent at fault and the plaintiff is 10 percent at fault, then the plaintiff recovers 90 percent of his or her damages. Some states limit the concept of comparative negligence by providing that a plaintiff cannot recover anything if he or she is more than 50 percent at fault.

Assumption of the Risk

assumption of the risk
Knowingly and voluntarily assuming a risk; a defense to negligence.

The doctrine of **assumption of the risk** provides that where people knowingly and voluntarily agree to assume a particular risk, they cannot later sue for injuries that occurred because of the risk. For example, spectators in a golf tournament know that there is a risk of being hit by a golf ball and, by attending the match, knowingly and voluntarily assume that risk. They may be asked to sign a release or waiver, in which case the assumption is express. But even if they do not expressly say they assume the risk, their conduct does so by implication. In either case, the doctrine of assumption of the risk is a defense to a negligence action they might bring if they are hit by a golf ball.

Immunity

The doctrine of immunity discussed earlier also applies to negligence actions. Any time a governmental agency is accused of negligence, the question of immunity must be considered. Although governmental entities are often liable for injuries resulting from automobile accidents or premises liability, they may be immune if the negligence is related to a discretionary act. For example, a motor vehicle department would probably be immune from liability for not revoking a license of a habitually negligent driver who causes injuries.

A POINT TO REMEMBER

The law of negligence is found primarily in state laws. Statutory and case law must always be consulted. However, whether an individual is negligent in a particular circumstance is usually a factual question for a jury. Careful gathering and preserving of evidence in cases is therefore critical to any case. Photographs, diagrams, and witness statements that can help prove what happened are important.

Baum v. New York Central Railroad

12 Misc. 2d 622, 175 N.Y.S. 2d 628 (1958)

While appearing on stage with a horse, a television actor was injured when the horse stepped on his hand. The actor sued, claiming damages as a result of negligence and breach of warranty. The complaint was dismissed because there was no evidence of any vicious or unruly propensities known by the owner of the animal and thus no evidence of negligence. Neither was there any evidence of breach of warranty. The horse acted like a horse. This case illustrates that damages alone are not enough for a lawsuit. Negligence or some other legal basis must be shown.

OPINION

At the beginning of the trial, this action as against the New York Central Railroad was discontinued and at the conclusion of the entire case a motion to dismiss the complaint as against the Columbia Broadcasting System, Inc., was granted, leaving as the sole defendant Frederick Eric Birkner, individually, and doing business as Chateau Riding Academy—Theatrical Division.

The plaintiff, a television actor, was engaged by the Music Corporation of America or an affiliate thereof, to perform in a certain television production called the Medallion Theatre to be transmitted from Studio 42 of the Columbia Broadcasting System, Inc., a tenant of the Grand Central Terminal Building.

By means of a telephonic communication by one Mr. Abrams of the Music Corporation of America, the defendant Birkner was advised that a horse was required to be on stage in connection with this production and subsequently the plaintiff and Mr. Medford, the director of the production, arrived at the stable and were shown a mare by the name of "T-V Rose." The plaintiff asserts that Birkner assured him that the horse had been performing on numerous occasions with well-known television personalities. The plaintiff's contention is that the defendant, in effect, guaranteed that the horse was safe and sound and fit for the purposes of the particular production which required the plaintiff and one Charles Heston to crawl under the horse in the course of a fight scene.

The original complaint is founded in negligence and the amended complaint includes additional allegations of breach of warranty of fitness for use and misrepresentation. At the end of the entire case the court granted a motion to conform the pleadings to the proof. Assuming plaintiff's right to recover as a general proposition under any theory, the plaintiff must establish that the defendant failed to exercise reasonable care either—

(1) to ascertain it was a suitable horse, having in mind all the existing and foreseeable conditions or
(2) to ascertain the habits of the animal with respect to its safety and suitability for the purposes hired.

Immediately after the first rehearsal, the plaintiff complained to the director, Medford, "that the horse moved slightly and that something should be done." On the second run-through, which was at a much faster pace, the plaintiff crawled under the horse and as he arose or attempted to arise, the horse stepped on his left hand, crushing two fingers badly.

There being no evidence of any vicious or unruly propensities known or likely to be known by the owner of this animal, I can find no basis for plaintiff's claim in negligence.

Even assuming the plaintiff could receive the benefit of the contractual obligation involved in the hiring of this horse, there is no proof of any breach of warranty or misrepresentation on the defendant's part. The horse neither kicked, reared nor acted in any unusual manner. The defendant did not, nor can it be assumed that he did, guarantee the horse to act in any manner different or contrary to its natural behavior.

The plaintiff was obligated to use the reasonable care of a prudent person, knowing by his own testimony that the horse had moved on the first so-called run-through. The court cannot find that such a movement or even a prancing on the hind legs is an unnatural act of the animal.

Even in this modern era in the great city of New York, discounting the esteemed and sometimes maligned thoroughbred and standard-bred, there are still mounted police and odd drays to be seen and any casual observer cannot fail to note that they do not stand absolutely immobile.

The complaint is, accordingly, dismissed on the merits.

CASE ANALYSIS

1. Review the elements for a cause of action for negligence. Which element or elements were missing here?
2. What would the plaintiff have had to prove in order to win?

SEC. 7–5 STRICT LIABILITY

strict liability
Liability without fault.

The third type of tort is **strict liability**. Both intentional torts and negligence are based on the concept of fault. If a person does something wrong, either intentionally or negligently, and causes injuries, that person must pay. However, the concept of strict liability is not based on fault, but rather on public policy. When individuals engage in certain types of activities or conduct and that conduct causes an injury, then the individuals must compensate the injured party. This is true even though there is no intentional wrongdoing or negligence. The activities that give rise to strict liability are (1) maintaining a dangerous animal, (2) engaging in an ultrahazardous activity, and (3) manufacturing or distributing a defective product.

DANGEROUS ANIMALS

If a person has a dangerous animal and that animal injures another person, the animal owner must compensate the injured person. Dangerous animals fall into two categories: wild animals who by their nature are dangerous, and domestic animals who for some reason become dangerous. Liability for maintaining a wild animal is absolute. However, liability for a dangerous domestic animal may not arise until the owner learns about the dangerous propensities of the animal. At common law, it was said that every dog was entitled to one bite. Until the dog had bitten someone, there were no known dangerous propensities and hence no liability. However, many states today have special dog-bite statutes that impose liability even when no prior acts have occurred.

ULTRAHAZARDOUS ACTIVITIES

ultrahazardous activity
A dangerous activity; one who engages in an ultrahazardous activity is strictly liable to those who may be injured as a result.

Ultrahazardous activities are generally dangerous types of activities where the risk of injury is high even if all due care is used. For example, dynamiting is a dangerous activity in which people are sometimes injured, even when the person engaging in the activity is very careful. In imposing liability in these circumstances, the law is saying that compensating injured persons is simply a cost of doing business.

DEFECTIVE PRODUCTS

As discussed earlier, if a product is negligently manufactured or sold, the negligent party is liable for injuries. However, negligence need not be shown. Anyone who manufactures or distributes a defective product that causes injuries is responsible for the injuries as long as the product was being used in a foreseeable manner. Strict liability applies to both the manufacturer and the distributor. This is true even though the distributor or seller has nothing to do with the making of the product and even though the distributor is a completely separate entity from the manufacturer. However, liability arises only where there is a defect in the product. Furthermore, some states require that the defect render the product unreasonably dangerous. The defect can be in the design of the product, in the way it was made, or in the warnings that may accompany the product. Products include almost anything that can be purchased by a consumer, such as automobiles, appliances, and even drugs. Liability extends to the individual who purchased the product, to one who uses the product, or to a bystander who is injured by the product. Before liability attaches, the injured party must show that he or she was using the product in a foreseeable manner. It does not necessarily have to be used in the intended manner. For example, a chair is intended for sitting. But it is foreseeable that one will stand on a chair. If the chair were to collapse when an individual stood on it, assuming that all the other elements were present, strict liability would still apply. In addition to negligence and strict liability in tort, product liability cases are sometimes based on a breach of an implied or express warranty. Proving that products are defective often requires the use of experts. Experts can often be located at local colleges and universities, as well as on the Internet. Three sites that can help you locate an expert are www.expertpages.com/, www.experts.com/, and //www.claims.com/online.html.

DEFENSES TO STRICT LIABILITY

The most common defense to strict liability is assumption of the risk. If a person knows a product is dangerously defective and uses it anyway, there will be no liability. Some jurisdictions allow comparative negligence as a defense, even though no negligence need be shown on the part of the manufacturer or distributor.

SEC. 7–6 DAMAGES

special damages
Out-of-pocket losses.

general damages
Damages not based on a monetary loss; includes items such as pain and suffering.

The main purpose of awarding damages in a personal injury or tort case is to compensate the injured party for the loss that was sustained. Such damages are called *compensatory*. Compensatory damages include special damages and general damages. **Special damages** are actual out-of-pocket expenses, such as medical bills and lost earnings. **General damages** are damages for losses that have no absolute or precise value. The most common type of general damage is pain and suffering. General damages also include damages for loss of use of a limb and permanent disfigurement. In a jury trial, the jurors determine the value of special and general damages. In addition to compensatory damages, some torts allow for punitive or exemplary damages. Punitive damages are means to punish a defendant for some particularly reprehensible action. *Punitive damages* are allowed in intentional torts if malice or ill will can be shown. Since by their nature these torts are intentional, it is not unusual to see a request or an award for punitive damages with intentional torts. Punitive damages are allowed in negligence actions only if the negligence rises to the level of gross negligence. It is difficult to define gross negligence, but generally it is conduct that is reckless and wanton.

Some intentional torts can be maintained even though the victim suffers no actual loss. These torts allow for nominal damages. As a practical matter, pursuing such an action would not be worth the time and cost involved.

Burnett v. National Enquirer, Inc.

144 Cal. App. 3d 991, 193 Cal. Rptr. 206 (1983)

In this case, plaintiff, Carol Burnett, sued the defendant, the National Enquirer, *for compensatory and punitive damages as a result of an article published in a defendant magazine. The article claimed that she became drunk in a public restaurant, had an argument with Henry Kissinger, and disturbed other guests. A jury awarded the plaintiff $300,000 in compensatory damages and $1.3 million as punitive damages. The trial judge reduced the amounts to $50,000 for compensatory and $750,000 for punitive damages. On appeal, the appellate court found the punitive damages still excessive. Defendant's net worth was estimated to be $2.6 million and its net income for the period under consideration was about $1.56 million. The amount of compensatory damages was upheld. The following is an excerpt from the appellate court decision.*

OPINION

On March 2, 1976, appellant caused to appear in its weekly publication, the *National Enquirer*, a "gossip column" headlined "Carol Burnett and Henry K. in Row," wherein a four-sentence item specified in its entirety that: "In a Washington restaurant, a boisterous Carol Burnett had a loud argument with another diner, Henry Kissinger. Then she traipsed around the place offering everyone a bite of her dessert. But Carol really raised eyebrows when she accidentally knocked a glass of wine over one diner and started giggling instead of apologizing. The guy wasn't amused and 'accidentally' spilled a glass of water over Carol's dress."

Maintaining the item was entirely false and libelous, an attorney for Ms. Burnett, by telegram the same day and by letter one week later, demanded its correction or retraction. In response to the demand, appellant on April 6, 1976, published the following retraction, again in the *National Enquirer's* gossip column: "An item in this column on March 2 erroneously reported that Carol Burnett had an argument with Henry Kissinger at a Washington restaurant and became boisterous, disturbing other guests. We understand these events did not occur and we are sorry for any embarrassment our report may have caused Miss Burnett."

On April 8, 1976, respondent, dissatisfied with this effort in mitigation, filed her complaint for libel in the Los Angeles Superior Court. Trial before a jury resulted in an award to respondent of $300,000 compensatory damages and $1.3 million in punitive damages. The trial court thereafter [reduced] judgment in respondent's favor for $50,000 compensatory and $750,000 punitive damages. This appeal followed.

As formulated by appellant, the issues here are whether the damage award and penalty specified in the judgment can stand.

Prior to addressing the merits of appellant's contentions and in aid of our disposition, we set out the following further facts pertaining to the publication complained of and descriptive of the nature and character of the *National Enquirer*, which were adequately established in the proceedings below.

On the occasion giving rise to the gossip column item hereinabove quoted, respondent, her husband, and three friends were having dinner at the Rive Gauche restaurant in the Georgetown section of Washington, D.C. The date was January 29, 1976. Respondent was in the area as a result of being invited to be a performing guest at the White House. In the course of the dinner, respondent had two or three glasses of wine. She was not inebriated. She engaged in banter with a young couple seated at a table next to hers, who had just become engaged or were otherwise celebrating. When curiosity was expressed about respondent's dessert, apparently a chocolate soufflé, respondent saw to it the couple were provided with small amounts of it on plates they had passed to her table for that purpose. Perhaps from having witnessed the gesture, a family behind respondent then offered to exchange some of their baked Alaska for a portion of the soufflé, and they, too, were similarly accommodated. As respondent was later leaving the restaurant, she was introduced by a friend to Henry Kissinger, who was dining at another table, and after a brief conversation, respondent left with her party.

There was no "row" with Mr. Kissinger, nor any argument between the two, and what conversation they had was not loud or boisterous. Respondent never "traipsed around the place offering everyone a bite of her dessert," nor was she otherwise boisterous, nor did she spill wine on anyone, nor did anyone spill water on her and there was no factual basis for the comment that she ". . . started giggling instead of apologizing."

The impetus for what was printed about the dinner was provided to the writer of the item, Brian Walker, by Couri Hays, a freelance tipster paid by the *National Enquirer* on an ad hoc basis for information supplied by him which was ultimately published by it, who advised Walker he had been informed respondent had taken her Grand Marnier soufflé around the restaurant in a boisterous or flamboyant manner and given bites of it to various other people; that he had further but unverified information that respondent had been involved in the wine-water spilling incident; but that, according to his sources, respondent was "specifically, emphatically" not drunk. No mention was made by Hays of anything involving respondent and Henry Kissinger. Having received this report, Walker spoke with Steve Tinney, whose name appears at the top of the *National Enquirer* gossip column, expressing doubts whether Hays could be trusted. Tinney voiced his accord with those doubts. Walker then asked Gregory Lyon, a *National Enquirer* reporter, to verify what Walker had been told by Hays. Lyon's inquiry resulted only in his verifying respondent had shared dessert with other patrons and that she and Kissinger had carried on a good-natured conversation at the restaurant.

In spite of the fact that no one had told him respondent and Henry Kissinger had engaged in an argument, that the wine-water spilling story remained as totally unverified hearsay, that the dessert-sharing incident was only partially bolstered, and that respondent was not under any view of the question inebriated, Walker composed the quoted item and approved the "row" heading. . . .

Was there error associated with the award to respondent of $750,000 in punitive damages? Yes.

We accept the proposition it is our duty to intervene in instances where punitive damages are so palpably excessive or grossly disproportionate as to raise a presumption that they resulted from passion or prejudice. In viewing the record in light of these principles, and assuming, as we will hereinafter decide, that the award of compensatory damages was proper, we are of the opinion that the award to respondent of $750,000 in order to punish and deter appellant was not justified.

[W]e set out preliminarily the following considerations and principles fundamental to our conclusions.

Nearly 20 years ago, it was announced in *New York Times Co. v. Sullivan*, (1964) 376 U.S. 254, that: "The constitutional guarantees [relating to protected speech] require, we think, a federal rule that prohibits a public official from recovering damages for a defamatory falsehood relating to his official conduct unless he proves that the statement was made with actual malice—that is, with knowledge that it was false or with reckless disregard of whether it was false or not."

The constitutional privilege thus defined was extended three years later . . . to include within its protection not only public officials but also "public figures," such that: "Those who, by reason of the notoriety of their achievements or the vigor and success with which they seek the public's attention, are properly classed as public figures and those who hold governmental office may recover for injury to reputation only on a clear and convincing proof that the defamatory falsehood was made with knowledge of its falsity or with reckless disregard for the truth."

[W]e are persuaded the evidence fairly showed that while appellant's representatives knew that part of the publication complained of was probably false and that the remainder of it in substance might very well be, appellant was nevertheless determined to present to a vast national audience in printed form statements which in their precise import and clear implication were defamatory, thereby exposing respondent to contempt, ridicule and obloquy and tending to injure her in her occupation. We are also satisfied that even when it was thought necessary to alleviate the wrong resulting from the false statements it had placed before the public, the retraction proffered was evasive, incomplete and by any standard, legally insufficient. In other words, we have no doubt the conduct of appellant respecting the libel was reprehensible and was undertaken with the kind of improper motive which supports the imposition of punitive damages.

Nevertheless, evidence on the point of appellant's wealth adequately established appellant's net worth to be some $2.6 million and its net income for the period under consideration to be about $1.56 million, such that the penalty award, even when substantially reduced by the trial court based on its conclusion that the jury's compensatory verdict was "clearly excessive and . . . not supported by substantial evidence," continued to constitute about 35 percent of the former and nearly half the latter.

Such being the case, and in the effort required of us to find acceptable only that balance between the gravity of a defendant's illegal act and a penalty necessary to properly deter such conduct, we hold the exemplary award herein to be excessive and require either that it be reduced to the sum of $150,000 or that appellant be granted a new trial on that issue.

We also reject the claim the malice in fact established herein should not have been attributed to appellant, since it is clear to us from the record that the acts of the individuals involved in publishing the defamatory statements were ratified.

Was there error associated with the award to respondent of $50,000? No.

We have previously recited those considerations, both legal and factual, which underlie our conclusion appellant's liability herein was established upon clear and convincing evidence. It remained nevertheless for respondent to establish the actual damage she had suffered as a result of the publication involved. Whether such damage necessarily encompassed both special and general damages was a matter dependent upon whether the publication was or was not libelous on its face. . . . A libel which is defamatory of the plaintiff without the necessity of explanatory matter, such as an inducement, innuendo or other extrinsic fact, is said to be a libel on its face. Defamatory language not libelous on its face is not actionable unless plaintiff alleges and proves that he has suffered special damage as a proximate result thereof.

That what was printed here was libelous on its face seems abundantly clear, in that the message conveyed was that respondent had been boisterous and loudly argumentative in a public dining place, and had "raised eyebrows" when she boorishly giggled instead of apologizing after spilling wine on another, a message which reasonably carried the implication respondent's actions were the result of some objectionable state of inebriation. Nor is the character of the publication altered by the consideration it might have been interpreted innocently.

Accordingly, it was incumbent upon respondent to show only those general damages caused by appellant's wrong, *i.e.*, damages arising from respondent's loss of reputation, shame, mortification and injured feelings. In this regard her own testimony was to the following effect:

"Q. What was your reaction?
A. Well, I was absolute—I was stunned. . . . I felt very, very angry. I started to cry. I started to shake.
Q. Why such a reaction to this article?
A. Well, it portrays me as being drunk. It portrays me as being rude. It portrays me as being uncaring. It portrays me as being physically abusive. It is disgusting, and it is a pack of lies. I—It hurts. It hurts, because words, once they are printed, they've got a life of their own. Words, once spoken, have a life of their own. How was I going to explain to my kids, my family, the people I care about? How am I going to go talk to do things . . . against alcoholism? . . .
Q. You mentioned something about work against alcoholism. What is that?
A. It didn't start out as any kind of crusade at all. I think I must have spoken about it many years ago. . . ."

The foregoing, in our view, when combined with the further evidence of respondent's prominence in the public eye, her professional standing and the fact the *National Enquirer* is read by some 16 million persons, was sufficient to support an award of $50,000 in compensatory damages.

CASE ANALYSIS

1. The award of $50,000 was for compensatory damages. Were these for general damages or special damages?
2. Why did the court reduce the amount of punitive damages? Why was the *National Enquirer*, as opposed to its employees, held responsible for the punitive damages?
3. Why did the plaintiff in this case recover both compensatory and punitive damages, while the respondent in the *Hustler* magazine case recovered nothing?

SEC. 7–7 LIABILITY FOR TORTS OF ANOTHER

respondeat superior
The responsibility of an employer for torts of employees that are committed in the course and scope of employment.

vicarious liability
Liability for the acts of another.

independent contractor
One who does work for another but who is not subject to control of the one who has hired him or her.

The person who commits a tort is known as a tortfeasor and that person is responsible for the consequences of his or her torts. Sometimes, the law will also impose liability on another person. In particular, if an individual commits a tort while in the course and scope of his or her employment, the employer is liable for the tort. Generally this applies in negligence situations. This doctrine is known as **respondeat superior**. The liability imposed is sometimes called **vicarious liability**. Vicarious liability does not generally apply if the employee is an **independent contractor** rather than an employee. This is because an employer has no right to control the activities of an independent contractor. On the other hand, the law will not allow a person to escape liability for dangerous activities by simply hiring an independent contractor to perform them. Where an independent contractor is hired to perform a particularly dangerous activity, the employer remains liable. This is known as the **peculiar risk doctrine**.

peculiar risk doctrine
A doctrine that makes an employer liable for the acts of an independent contractor when the independent contractor has been engaged to perform a nondelegable duty.

A POINT TO REMEMBER

In any personal injury case you must review all police reports and investigative reports carefully to determine whether the doctrine of *respondeat superior* will apply. If a defendant was working at the time of the incident, the employer may also be liable. Failure to name all parties in a lawsuit could result in a malpractice claim against the law firm.

SEC. 7–8 PERSONAL INJURY PRACTICE

contingent fee
A fee based on a fixed percentage of whatever amount is recovered by the attorney on behalf of the client.

Lawyers who practice tort law are more commonly known as *personal injury* or *P.I.* lawyers. Attorneys who represent plaintiffs generally handle cases on a **contingent fee** arrangement, taking as their fee a percentage of any recovery. Attorneys who represent defendants typically are hired by the defendant's insurance company. In many cases, defendants who commit torts, especially negligent or strict liability torts, are covered by insurance. The insurance company provides the defendant with an attorney and pays any judgment or settlement. However, the insurance company is not the defendant in the lawsuit. The defendant is the person who committed the tort. For obvious reasons, the practice of tort law not only involves the legal questions about the tort but frequently involves questions of insurance law.

A POINT TO REMEMBER

Lawyers cannot share fees with nonlawyers. If you or some other nonattorney refers a personal injury case to an attorney, that attorney cannot pay a referral fee. Lawyers can share fees only with other lawyers.

SEC. 7–9 THE FUTURE OF TORT LAW AND PERSONAL INJURY PRACTICE

In recent years, personal injury practice in the courts has come under tremendous criticism by numerous groups. The overcrowding of the courts, the outrageousness of some judgments, and the increasing costs of insurance have all contributed to the movement to reform tort practice. Various changes have been proposed, including a system of no-fault automobile insurance, limiting or abolishing punitive damages, limiting general damages, and limiting attorney fees. In some states, some of these proposals have been adopted as law.

ETHICAL CHOICES

You are working in a law office with an attorney who is preparing a client for a deposition. You are present taking notes. The client tells the attorney that he was not wearing a seat belt. The attorney tells the client, "If you say that during the deposition, the value of your case instantly diminishes." Should you do anything?

SEC. 7–10 WORKERS' COMPENSATION

Injuries that occur on the job are usually subject to a different set of rules than other injuries, even where the job-related injury was caused by an employer's negligence. All states have rules that regulate this area of law. In general, injured workers cannot sue employers under tort law. Instead, a special procedure allows injured workers to recover money to compensate them for their medical expenses and loss of earnings. Money for general damages is not allowed, but workers are compensated for any permanent disability that interferes with the ability to work. If a dispute arises, it generally cannot be resolved in court. A special board exists to resolve the disputes. This system protects all workers, whether the injury was the result of the employer's negligence or not. It even protects the worker if the injury was a result of the worker's own negligence. Of course, if a worker is injured due to the tort of someone other than the employer, the worker can sue that third party under the appropriate tort theory, while also filing a workers' compensation claim. The action against the tortfeasor is referred to as a *third-party action*. Double recovery is not allowed, however. One very important Web site for workers' compensation cases is maintained by the Occupational Safety and Health Administration (OSHA) at www.osha.gov/.

ETHICAL CHOICES

A young woman, a plaintiff in your office, sued a local fast-food chain. She scalded her mouth on a cup of very hot chocolate. She asks you how much her injuries are worth. You know that your office just settled the same type of case with comparable injuries for $5,000. What do you tell her?

Chapter Summary

A tort is a civil wrong not arising out of a contract. Tort law forms the basis of one of the most important areas of legal practice, commonly known as personal injury practice. Parties who are injured because of a tort committed by another are usually entitled to recover damages for their injuries. There are three major categories of torts: intentional torts, negligence, and strict liability. Intentional torts require that an individual intentionally do an act knowing that it will cause harm or acting in a reckless disregard of its consequences. Intentional torts include assault, battery, false imprisonment, false arrest, defamation, invasion of privacy, intentional infliction of emotional distress, malicious prosecution, abuse of process, trespass, conversion, and fraud. In addition, a series of business torts and actions based on

Featured Web Site: www.osha.gov/

The Occupational Safety and Health Administration of the U.S. Labor Department maintains a Web site describing how it helps prevent injuries to workers.

Go Online

1. Read through the site. What is the function and mission of OSHA?
2. Many states also have job safety and health programs. These states are listed on this site. Check to see whether your state has a plan. If so, link to that plan and summarize it. If not, select a state near you and do the same.

civil rights violations also exist. The second general category of torts is negligence. Negligence is a tort that results from damages caused by one who fails to act as a reasonably prudent person would act under the same or similar circumstances. This is the most common tort that gives rise to lawsuits; it stems from many different factual situations, including automobile accidents, medical and other professional malpractice, accidents occurring on premises, and defective products. The third category of torts is strict liability. Strict liability imposes liability on parties even though they did nothing wrong. It applies to injuries resulting from keeping dangerous animals, engaging in ultrahazardous activities, and manufacturing or distributing defective products.

Although victims of torts are normally entitled to sue the tortfeasor for money damages, a major exception occurs in injuries that are work related. State legislation often prevents an employee from suing his or her employer for job-related injuries. However, these laws provide that the employer must carry insurance, known as workers' compensation insurance, that provides medical care and reimbursement for lost wages. In addition, the employee receives compensation for any permanent disability. A special agency or board is often established to handle disputes that occur between employers (or their insurance carriers) and employees. This area of law is known as workers' compensation. Workers' compensation laws prevent lawsuits against employers but do not prevent lawsuits if the tortfeasor is someone other than the employer.

Terms to Remember

tort
workers' compensation
tortfeasor
exemplary damages
punitive damages
cause of action
intentional tort
shopkeeper's privilege
slander per se
disparagement
intellectual property
infringement
negligence
res ipsa loquitur
negligence per se
attractive nuisance
malpractice
product liability
consortium
contributory negligence
last clear chance
comparative negligence
assumption of the risk
strict liability
ultrahazardous activity
special damages
general damages
respondeat superior
vicarious liability
independent contractor
peculiar risk doctrine
contingent fee

Questions for Review

1. What is a tort?
2. Identify the three major categories of torts.
3. What is the difference between compensatory damages and punitive damages?
4. Distinguish intentional torts from negligence.
5. Explain the following terms:
   negligence per se
   res ipsa loquitur
   respondeat superior
   vicarious liability
   peculiar risk doctrine
   loss of consortium
6. What are some of the defenses to negligence?
7. Explain the types of situations for which there is strict liability in tort.
8. What is workers' compensation?

Questions for Analysis

1. Analyze the following factual situations and discuss possible torts.
   a. Peters points a gun at Quentin's back, Quentin being unaware of what is happening. Peters then shoots and hits Quentin.
   b. Jones consents to a blood transfusion, providing the doctor uses blood from a designated donor. The doctor does the transfusion using a general supply of blood. No injury results.
   c. Smith is late for an appointment and runs a red light, thinking that there was no cross traffic. Unfortunately, Smith collides with a vehicle that he had not seen. The driver of the other vehicle is injured.
   d. Roberts, a supervising attorney with a county prosecutor's office, consistently makes sexual remarks to James, a paralegal in the office. On several occasions she has also invited him out for drinks after work. James always declines the invitations and has asked Roberts to stop the remarks. Recently Roberts gave James a poor job review, even though his work is very good.
2. Review the Case File at the beginning of the chapter. Write a memo discussing the possible tort liability of Carpets Etc.
3. Review the Ethical Choices boxes in this chapter. Which NALA and/or NFPA rules or guidelines apply to the situations? Review your state's ethical rules. (*Hint*: Go to www.nala.org/ and find a link.) Which of those rules apply?
4. Read the case of *United States v. Morrison* in Appendix VII. What common law torts could plaintiff claim in this case?

Assignments and Projects

1. Prepare a chart listing each tort discussed in this chapter. For each tort listed, include in the chart the elements of a cause of action and the possible defenses. You should be able to identify the elements of a cause of action from the definition of the tort.
2. Review the Web sites maintained by Napster (www.napster.com/) and MP3 (www.MP3.com/). Are the sites still active? Can individuals still download music for free or are fees charged? Does it appear that copyright infringement lawsuits have had any effect on these sites?

CHAPTER 8

FAMILY LAW

Technology Corner

Web Address	Name of Site
www.nolo.com/	Nolo—Law for All (browse the topics for family law–related material)
www.divorcenet.com/	Divorce Net

CASE FILE: THE HOLMES FAMILY LAW MATTER

Mr. Holmes is retaining your office to represent him in a divorce proceeding and in a separate paternity action. Your supervising attorney asks you to set up an interview with Mr. Holmes as soon as possible. You are to collect as much information as possible. Mr. Holmes told the attorney the following. He has been married for fourteen years and has two children by this marriage. He also mentioned that he and his wife lived together for three years before marrying. Sixteen years ago he started a computer company that has grown and become very successful. Two weeks ago he was sued by his prior administrative assistant, who claims that he is the father of her nine-month-old child. Mr. Holmes denies paternity and says that his administrative assistant has been married for five years. In any event, Mr. Holmes has just been served with papers from his wife asking for a divorce. She also requests custody of the children, spousal and child support, and one-half of all of the property they own, including the business.

SEC. 8–1 INTRODUCTION

domestic relations
The area of law that deals with family law issues such as divorce, custody, and support.

Family law, or **domestic relations** as it is sometimes called, deals with legal issues that affect personal relationships. The most common type of family law matter deals with divorce and the related custody, support, and property issues. However, family law is not limited to divorce. Many parties today see lawyers even before they marry in order to protect themselves with prenuptial or premarital agreements. Family law is not limited to traditional family relationships. Family law practitioners may be involved in handling paternity actions, child custody, and support actions for couples who have children but have never married. In some states, unmarried couples who live together and then separate may also have support and property rights that become subjects of dispute. A few states continue to recognize the legal status of the common-law marriage. Today, laws are being passed that affect the rights of "domestic partners."

Laws regarding family and personal relationships are generally found in state statutes and cases. However, because of the mobility of the American people, interstate cooperation is necessary to protect the interests of the parties, especially the children. Consequently, most states have adopted uniform sets of laws regulating premarital agreements, payment of child support, jurisdiction for custody disputes, and paternity actions.

SEC. 8–2 PRENUPTIAL AGREEMENTS

premarital agreement
An agreement entered into before a couple marries; it often explains how the property belonging to each prospective spouse is to be characterized or distributed upon death or dissolution/divorce. This term is often used interchangeably with the term *prenuptial agreement*.

prenuptial agreement
Another term for premarital agreement.

Arranging a marriage used to include reserving the church, hiring a caterer, and arranging for flowers. Today it often includes retaining lawyers to draft **premarital** (or **prenuptial**) **agreements.** People often marry later in life (for the first or second time), bringing with them substantial property. They wish to protect these assets in the event that the marriage terminates either by legal action or by death. One way to achieve some protection is for the couple to enter into an agreement before marriage. Each state adopts its own laws regarding these agreements, but may pattern its laws after the Uniform Premarital Agreement Act. In general, this act provides that the agreement must be in writing and may cover the following:

- Rights and obligations regarding any property
- Rights to manage and control any property
- Disposition of property upon termination of the marriage by death or legal action
- Making of wills or trusts
- Choice of law to govern the agreement
- Any other matter, including personal rights and obligations, not in violation of public policy or the law

However, the right of a child to child support cannot be adversely affected by this agreement.

A prenuptial agreement between Robert Holmes and his wife might cover such matters as ownership of the business or Mr. Holmes's rights as to spousal support.

SEC. 8–3 TERMINATING A MARRIAGE

Terminating a marriage (other than by death) requires a court action. Three different types of court actions exist to accomplish this: annulment, divorce (sometimes referred to as *dissolution*), and legal separation.

NULLITY

An **annulment** or **nullity** proceeding is used to obtain a court declaration that no legal marriage ever existed. The court may find the marriage **void** or **voidable.** If the marriage is found to be void, it means that there was never a valid marriage. An example of a void marriage would be one in which one party was already married—in other words, a bigamous marriage. A voidable marriage is one that is a valid marriage until and unless a court declares it invalid. A marriage in which one party is a minor is an example of this. The court has the power to nullify this marriage. However, if no one brings a court action, the marriage remains valid. In order to obtain a judgment of nullity, a party must show specific grounds or reasons, such as bigamy, minority, or fraud.

DIVORCE/DISSOLUTION

A **divorce** or **dissolution** action acknowledges that a valid marriage existed, but the parties now wish to end the marital contract. While some states may require that a party requesting a divorce show that the other party has done something wrong (such as adultery or mental cruelty), many states have adopted a no-fault system. If Robert Holmes lives in such a state, whether he had an affair with his assistant or not is irrelevant to the question of divorce. Personal accusations and blame are not issues in the case. (However, some issues, such as physical abuse, may be relevant to custody issues.) In all divorce actions, the court will address all custody, support, and property issues. When a divorce involves numerous and complicated issues (usually related to the nature and value of property) the court may **bifurcate** the issues. This means that the court terminates the marriage, but the remaining issues are heard separately after the marriage is terminated. The parties are free to remarry once the marriage is officially terminated by order of the court, even if all property and support issues have not been decided.

LEGAL SEPARATION

A **legal separation** asks the court to grant the parties something short of a final termination of the marital contract. The couple wish to remain married, but they want the court and the state to view them as "legally separated." There are understandable reasons for this particular type of action. For religious reasons, some couples feel that they cannot completely terminate their marriage. Other couples choose to live apart and wish to accumulate separate property during this time period. When the state statutes allow a legal separation, the courts may enter a final judgment of legal separation. Couples who are legally separated are not free to remarry. Should the parties later choose to terminate their marriage, they must again petition the court and request a divorce or dissolution.

annulment
To annul something is to nullify it or make it void; the term is often used in connection with a marriage.

nullity
An action seeking a nullity of marriage requests the court to find that the "marriage" is null and void.

void
Having no binding effect or legal force, such as a marriage or a contract.

voidable
Having a defect that can be cured; often said of a marriage or a contract. If the defect is not cured, the marriage or contract can be nullified.

divorce
The total dissolving of a marriage.

dissolution
The dissolving or termination of a marriage; the terms *divorce* and *dissolution* are often interchangeable. Some states, such as California, no longer use the legal term *divorce*, but call the termination of a marriage a *dissolution of marriage*.

bifurcate
To sever from the trial; in family law, it means that the divorce or dissolution may be granted, but the parties will need to come back to court to adjudicate another issue—for example, their property issues.

legal separation
An order granted by the court when a couple wish to live separately but do not wish to dissolve or terminate their marriage.

Whenever a court terminates a marriage, the legal issues it must resolve usually concern child custody, support, and division of property.

SEC. 8–4 CHILD CUSTODY

Parents have certain legal responsibilities to care for their children. In all family law matters, the court will be most interested in the welfare of the children. The court will look for solutions that are in the best interest of the child or children. The following code section sets forth the factors a court could consider when making **child custody** decisions that are designed to be in the best interest of the child.

child custody
The immediate control and care of a minor; the court will determine which spouse will have custody of a child.

Illinois Marriage and Dissolution of Marriage Act
750 ILCS 5/602
Section 602: Best Interest of Child

(a) The court shall determine custody in accordance with the best interest of the child. The court shall consider all relevant factors including:

(1) the wishes of the child's parent or parents as to his custody;

(2) the wishes of the child as to his custodian;

(3) the interaction and interrelationship of the child with his parent or parents, his siblings and any other person who may significantly affect the child's best interest;

(4) the child's adjustment to his home, school and community;

(5) the mental and physical health of all individuals involved;

(6) the physical violence or threat of physical violence by the child's potential custodian, whether directed against the child or directed against another person;

(7) the occurrence of ongoing abuse as defined in Section 103 of the Illinois Domestic Violence Act of 1986 [750 ILCS 60/103], whether directed against the child or directed against another person; and

(8) the willingness and ability of each parent to facilitate and encourage a close and continuing relationship between the other parent and the child.

This statute, from the Illinois Marriage and Dissolution of Marriage Act, is typical of most state statutes that address the custody issue in light of the best interest of the child.

When a marriage dissolves and the parties have children, the court assists the parents in determining a custody arrangement that is in the best interest of the children. Child custody is not limited to marital relationships. Courts today recognize that both natural parents have rights even if the couple is not married. Each state code explains the various forms of child custody:

Physical Custody	*Legal Custody*
Sole physical custody	Sole legal custody
Joint physical custody	Joint legal custody

Following is a Florida case. The court in *Wages v. Wages* addresses child custody and visitation issues. Notice the court's discussion of the "best interest of the child" issue.

Wages v. Wages

660 So. 2d 797 (1995)

The trial court erred when it changed the custody of a child from the mother to the father. When the parents dissolved their marriage, the mother was designated as the primary residential parent and the father was to pay child support. When the mother wanted to relocate out of state, she requested a modification of the original visitation schedule. The father responded with a request for a change of custody or in the alternative that he no longer be required to pay child support. The trial court found that it would be in the "best interest" of the child to be placed into the custody of the father. On appeal, the court reversed the lower court's decision. It agreed that the out-of-state move may have constituted a "substantial change in circumstances." However, there was no evidence that it would have been in the child's "best interest" to be relocated with the father. The reviewing court found that the father did not meet "the evidentiary burden required to change custody in a modification contest."

OPINION

The issue on appeal concerns whether the trial court erred in changing the custody of the minor child from the mother to the father.

BACKGROUND

Arden M. Wages, the mother, filed a petition for dissolution of marriage and on October 28, 1993, the trial court entered a final judgment of dissolution which incorporated an agreement between the parties which designated the mother as the primary residential parent and provided that the father, Aubry D. Wages, pay child support.

Some months later, the mother relocated to Kentucky with her new husband and two children. Because the required alternate weekend visitation was excessively burdensome in light of the mother's relocation, she moved the court for a modification of the visitation schedule. In her motion, the mother stated that her relocation was based upon her well-founded belief that the move was in the best interest of the parties' daughter as it would improve the general quality of life for the family and the child. The mother further stated that she recognized that substitute visitation between the minor child and the father "must be provided for in order to foster a continuing meaningful relationship between the child and the former husband" and that she was willing to comply with any reasonable substitute visitation.

The father responded with a letter to the trial court, treated as a motion to change custody, in which he made numerous allegations regarding the mother's life prior to the dissolution of marriage. He further alleged that the mother's new husband had left her on two different occasions and that the mother had had two different jobs in the preceding few months. The father went on to include positive statements about his own background and lifestyle, again referring to time periods preceding the dissolution of marriage. The father concluded by suggesting to the court that he be given full custody or, in the alternative, that he no longer be required to pay child support or provide hospitalization insurance on the child and that the child live with him from the day school is out in the summer until two days prior to school resuming in the fall of each year.

HOLDING OF THE TRIAL COURT

The trial court granted the father's motion to modify custody for the following reasons, as set forth in the order:

> "The former wife has remarried and has relocated to Kentucky. The former wife has been married several times and has lived what could best be described as a transient lifestyle.
>
> The former husband has had the same job for approximately thirty (30) years with the Florida East Coast Railroad, owns his own home and has already raised one family.
>
> It is clear that the former husband is the more suitable of the two parents. The former husband has numerous relatives, co-workers and close friends, who are willing to help him care for the child, including his now grown children by previous marriages.
>
> The Court finds that it would be in the best interest of the minor child to be placed in the custody of the former husband.
>
> The Court further finds that the former wife's marriage and move to the state of Kentucky indicates a substantial change in circumstances."

FINDINGS OF THE APPELLATE COURT

The mother appeals; we reverse.

While we agree that the mother's move to Kentucky may well have constituted a "substantial change in circumstances," there was no evidence—and certainly no finding by the trial court—which indicated that such change so adversely affected the welfare of the child that it would have been in the child's "best interest" to be relocated with the father. *See Schweinberg v. Click,* 627 So. 2d 548 (Fla. 5th DCA 1993) (focus in modification proceedings is on how post-dissolution changes adversely affect the child; changes not affecting the child do not necessitate a change in custody).

It is apparent from the trial court's order that it conducted the hearing as though it were making the initial custody determination. Had he been, his ruling may well have been appropriate. However, the father did not meet the evidentiary burden required to change custody in a modification context. *See Schweinberg; Ackerson v. Murphy,* 622 So. 2d 154 (Fla. 5th DCA 1993) (modification of custody requires showing of substantial change in circumstances and that welfare of child would be promoted by change); *Wiggins v. Wiggins,* 411 So. 2d 263 (Fla. 1st DCA 1982), rev. denied, 418 So. 2d 1281 (1982) (detriment to the child is crucial to a modification adjudication).

The judgment is reversed with directions to deny the motion to change custody and instead to set an appropriate visitation schedule based on the present facts.

Reversed and remanded.

CASE ANALYSIS

1. Why did the appellate court reverse the decision of the trial court?
2. Explain the facts that brought about the father's letter to the court.

Rules for determining custody are found in state laws. Therefore, when the parents live in different states special problems can arise, especially concerning the question of jurisdiction. Which state has the right to determine the custody issues? To promote consistency and to protect the rights of children, many states have adopted the Uniform Child Custody Jurisdiction Act. The act is meant to assure that litigation concerning the custody of a child ordinarily takes place in the state with which the child and the family have the closest connection and where evidence concerning custody issues is most available.

SEC. 8–5 SUPPORT

CHILD SUPPORT

support
The court, in a family law matter, may award child or spousal support. Such awards are designed to ensure that housing, food, and clothing—the necessities of daily living—are available for children or a spouse who is unable to earn an adequate living. All states have statutes explaining support guidelines and rules.

jurisdiction
The power or authority to act in a certain situation; the power of a court to hear cases and render judgments.

Parents have a legal duty to **support** their children. Once all issues of paternity have been resolved, the court determines whether child support is to be awarded to the custodial parent. Many states and even some counties have predetermined guidelines for setting child support amounts. The attorneys for each party in a divorce prepare recommendations for the court concerning child support amounts. The court retains **jurisdiction** over the issue of child support.

Some states have adopted the Uniform Support of Dependents Law. For example, the state of New York includes the following statute in its Domestic Relations Code.

N.Y. C.L.S. Dom. Rel. Section 34
Section 34: Jurisdiction and Powers of Court

. . . 2. The court of the responding state shall have the power to order the Respondent to pay sums sufficient to provide necessary food, shelter, clothing, care, medical or hospital expenses, expenses of confinement, expenses of education of a child, funeral expenses and such other reasonable and proper expenses of the Petitioner, as justice requires, having due regard to the circumstances of the respective parties. Where Petitioner's needs are so urgent as to require it, the court may make a temporary order for support pending a final determination.

McCord v. McCord

910 P.2d 85 (Colo. App. 1995)

The McCord *case involves the issue of modification of child support after the father wins $2,000,000 in the Colorado lottery.*

OPINION

FACTS

In this post–dissolution of marriage proceeding, David L. McCord (father) appeals the order modifying his child support obligation and awarding Deborah A. McCord (mother) her attorney fees. We dismiss the appeal in part, affirm the trial court's order, and remand the cause for further proceedings.

The parties' marriage was dissolved in 1988. Custody of their minor child was awarded to mother, and father was ordered to pay $300 per month in child support. At the time of the dissolution, father was employed as a construction worker and was earning approximately $16,400 per year. Mother was earning approximately $14,500 per year as a clerical worker.

In April 1994, father won an annuity worth $2 million in the Colorado State Lottery and received his first installment payment of $50,000.

Mother thereafter filed a motion seeking a modification in child support, alleging that father's increased income constituted a material change in circumstances. She also requested that the magistrate order father to pay his share of the child's unreimbursed medical expenses in the amount of $1,721.02.

After an initial hearing on June 3, 1994, not attended by father or his counsel, the magistrate ordered father to pay $1,452 of the unreimbursed medical expenses. However, because father had not appeared for the hearing, the magistrate did not address mother's request for a modification in child support.

At a hearing on June 24, father and his counsel appeared and presented evidence regarding father's lottery winnings and his decision, upon learning of his good fortune, to quit his job and become "self-employed." Mother testified regarding her employment and financial resources. She also presented evidence regarding the attorney fees she had incurred in seeking a modification of child support.

Based on the evidence presented at the hearing, the magistrate concluded that mother's gross monthly income was $952. The magistrate determined that father was voluntarily unemployed and imputed to him the annual income he had earned before his resignation. The magistrate further found that father's lottery winnings constituted gross income for purposes of calculating child support and that his gross monthly income from his lottery proceeds and employment totalled $5,538. Applying the child support guidelines, the magistrate increased father's child support obligation to $781 per month and, in addition, ordered father to pay $1,300 of mother's attorney fees.

On petition by father, the district court affirmed the magistrate's findings and order.

ISSUE I

Father first contends that the magistrate erred in ordering him to pay $1,452 of the uninsured portion of the child's extraordinary medical expenses. We dismiss this portion of the appeal.

The powers of magistrates and appellate review of their decisions are governed by the Colorado Rules for Magistrates (C.R.M.). C.R.M. 6(e)(5) provides that a party to a proceeding conducted by a district court magistrate shall not be entitled to appellate review of any order or judgment entered in that proceeding, unless that party has first filed a timely motion for district court review of the magistrate's order. *See also In re Estate of Burnford,* 746 P.2d 51 (Colo. App. 1987). Such a motion for review must be filed within 15 days of the date of the magistrate's order. C.R.M. 6(e)(2).

Here, the magistrate entered a written order on June 3, 1994, directing father to pay his portion of the child's extraordinary medical expenses "forthwith." Father did not seek district court review of the order within the applicable 15-day period. Nor did father seek review of the June 3 order in his motion for district court review of the magistrate's subsequent order regarding modification of child support. Indeed, at the June 24 hearing father indicated that he had "no problem with paying that debt" and that he would do so immediately.

Under these circumstances, we do not have jurisdiction to consider his claims in this regard. *See* C.R.M. 6(e)(5); *see also In re Estate of Burnford.*

ISSUE II

Father next contends that the magistrate erred in modifying his child support obligation because mother failed to show a change of circumstances warranting such a modification. We disagree.

A parent's child support obligation may be modified upon a showing of changed circumstances that are substantial and continuing.

Here, father acknowledges that his financial resources increased dramatically and that his increase in income constitutes a substantial and continuing change in circumstances. He claims, however, that his increased income alone was insufficient to establish changed circumstances justifying a modification and that mother also should have been required to demonstrate an increased economic need on the child's part. We are not persuaded.

If the party requesting modification demonstrates that an increase in the obligor's income would result in at least a 10 percent change in the amount of child support, the child's increased needs are presumed. *See In re Marriage of Larsen,* 805 P.2d 1195 (Colo. App. 1991); *In re Marriage of Anderson,* 761 P.2d 293 (Colo. App. 1988).

Moreover, nothing in the statute precludes the trial court from ordering a support payment that exceeds the known needs of the child. *In re Marriage of Nimmo,* 891 P.2d 1002, 1007 (Colo. 1995) ("The guidelines were not enacted to prevent an increase in a child's standard of living by denying a child the fruits of one parent's good fortune").

Here, father conceded that mother had demonstrated a substantial change in the parties' financial circumstances and he did not present any evidence rebutting the presumption of need of the child. Accordingly, the magistrate correctly determined that father's increased income constituted a change of circumstances warranting modification of his child support obligation. *See In re Marriage of Larsen.*

Issue III

Father next contends that the magistrate erred in concluding that he is voluntarily unemployed and in imputing to him the annual income he had earned prior to his resignation. We are not persuaded.

If a parent is voluntarily unemployed or underemployed, child support must be calculated based on the parent's potential income. However, a parent may not be considered voluntarily unemployed if he or she is physically or mentally incapacitated. A parent who is employed but is earning less than he or she is capable of earning shall not be deemed underemployed if:

> (A) The employment is temporary and is reasonably intended to result in higher income within the foreseeable future; or
>
> (B) The employment is a good faith career choice which is not intended to deprive a child of support and does not unreasonably reduce the support available to a child; or
>
> (C) The parent is enrolled in an educational program which is reasonably intended to result in a degree or certification within a reasonable period of time and which will result in a higher income, so long as the educational program is a good faith career choice which is not intended to deprive the child of support and which does not unreasonably reduce the support available to a child. Section 14-10-115(7)(b)(III), C.R.S. (1995 Cum. Supp.).

Here, father maintains that he was incapable of performing physical labor and that his decision to resign from his job was a good faith career choice. Accordingly, he maintains that the magistrate erred in imputing to him his potential income from employment.

The record shows that, before winning the lottery, father earned approximately $16,400 per year as a construction worker. Father testified that he injured his back in January 1992 and that the injury affected his ability to work in a physically demanding job. He indicated that, although he continued to work as a construction laborer for over a year after he was injured, he quit his job immediately upon winning the lottery because his back injury made it too difficult for him to work. He did not present any evidence, however, to support his assertion that he was physically incapable of working.

With respect to his current employment, father testified that he was "self-employed" and that this "employment" consisted of investing his winnings and "trying to figure out what type of business I want to be in."

This evidence amply supports the magistrate's determination that father quit his job because he won the lottery, that he was physically capable of working but was voluntarily unemployed, and that his decision to resign from his job was not a good faith career choice. Thus, the magistrate did not err in imputing to father the annual income he had earned prior to his resignation.

We reject father's contention that as long as his lottery winnings provide him with the same or more income than he earned when he was employed, the court may not impute to him the annual income he earned before quitting his job and that a gross income figure that combines his imputed income and his lottery winnings is excessive.

The statute provides that income may come "from any source," and the definition of "gross income" expressly includes gifts and prizes. Section 14-10-115(7)(a)(I)(A), C.R.S. (1995 Cum. Supp.). In our view, lottery winnings constitute gifts or prizes within the meaning of the statute and are therefore includable as gross income.

Thus, there was no abuse of discretion in the conclusion that father's potential income from employment as well as his lottery winnings are includable as income for purposes of calculating child support, even though his gross income after winning the lottery exceeds the income he earned when he was employed. *See In re Marriage of Nimmo; In re Marriage of Armstrong,* 831 P.2d 501 (Colo. App. 1992).

The portion of the appeal challenging the award of extraordinary medical expenses is dismissed. The order entered following the hearing on June 24, 1994, is affirmed and the cause is remanded for the trial court's consideration of an award of attorney fees to mother for this appeal.

CASE ANALYSIS

1. Explain the "changed circumstances" cited by the appellate court in upholding the ruling of the magistrate.
2. Write a brief summary of the court's discussion of the "voluntarily unemployed" issue (Issue III).

Because of the mobility of the American people, interstate cooperation is necessary to protect the interests of children of broken marriages. Consequently, most states have adopted a uniform set of laws regulating the payment of child support. This is known as the Uniform Reciprocal Enforcement of Support Act (URESA).

Spousal Support

spousal support
The court, in a family law matter, may award spousal support. Such support awards are designed to ensure that housing, food, and clothing—the necessities of daily living—are available for a spouse who is unable to earn an adequate living. All states have statutes explaining support guidelines and rules.

Spousal support, sometimes called *alimony,* may be awarded when two people end their marriage. The standards for setting spousal support vary widely and are found in each state code. Following is the California Family Code section listing the factors to be considered before the court awards spousal support:

Cal. Fam. Code Section 4320
Circumstances to Be Considered in Ordering Spousal Support

In ordering spousal support under this part, the court shall consider all of the following circumstances:

(a) The extent to which the earning capacity of each party is sufficient to maintain the standard of living established during the marriage taking into account all of the following:

(1) The marketable skills of the supported party; the job market for those skills; the time and expenses required for the supported party to acquire the appropriate education or training to develop those skills; and the possible need for retraining or education to acquire other, more marketable skills or employment.

(2) The extent to which the supported party's present or future earning capacity is impaired by periods of unemployment that were incurred during the marriage to permit the supported party to devote time to domestic duties.

(b) The extent to which the supported party contributed to the attainment of an education, training, a career position, or a license by the supporting party.

(c) The ability to pay of the supporting party, taking into account the supporting party's earning capacity, earned and unearned income, assets, and standard of living.

(d) The needs of each party based on the standard of living established during the marriage.

(e) The obligations and assets, including the separate property, of each party.

(f) The duration of the marriage.

(g) The ability of the supported party to engage in gainful employment without unduly interfering with the interests of dependent children in the custody of the party.

(h) The age and health of the parties.

(i) The immediate and specific tax consequences to each party.

(j) Any other factors the court determines are just and equitable.

ETHICAL CHOICES

In a complicated divorce case, both parties have come to a settlement agreement through their attorneys. You are the paralegal working on this case. Your supervising attorney gave you her notes regarding the settlement and told you that the other attorney was preparing the papers. When the settlement papers arrive, you review them and note that the other attorney made a substantial error in the spousal support provision. This error is in your client's favor. You bring this to the attention of your attorney, who tells you not do to anything about it. What do you do?

SEC. 8–6 PROPERTY CONCERNS

When a couple ends a marriage there may be property to be divided. Depending on the state, the way in which it is divided often depends on the type of property involved. Marital property may fall into three broad categories:

separate property
Property that belongs solely to one party; includes property acquired by gift or inheritance.

community property
Property owned jointly by married persons; not all states recognize community property.

quasi-community property
Property that would be considered community property if it had been acquired while the married couple were living in a community property state.

1. *Separate property*—**Separate property** belongs solely to one party. It is property in which the marital partner has no legal interest. Stated simply, depending on the state involved, one may acquire separate property before marriage, after the date the parties legally separate, from an inheritance, or through any number of other means. This property is not divided when the parties divorce.
2. *Community property*—**Community property** is owned jointly. Each of the parties owns a one-half interest in the item. In general, property acquired during marriage, with community property funds and/or efforts, is usually considered community property. This commonly includes wages, anything purchased with wages, and pension plans. It also includes debts. This property is equally divided during the property settlement phase of a divorce action. (Community property is recognized only in the "community property" states.)
3. *Quasi-community property*—**Quasi-community property** is property that would be considered community property if it had been acquired while the parties were living in a community property jurisdiction or state. This usually refers to property the parties acquired while they were *domiciled,* that is, living in another state. Once the item is determined to be quasi-community property, it will be treated as though it is community property for purposes of division.

VALUE AND DIVISION OF PROPERTY

retain
To employ or engage the services of a person.

expert
A person who, through education or experience, has special expertise or knowledge in a particular field.

characterize
To determine whether an item is separate, community, or quasi-community property.

When a court divides property it is bound by state laws. In some cases the court must divide the property equally. Unless the court orders that the parties sell all of their assets, it cannot make an even distribution of property without knowing the value of the property. In many cases, the parties dispute the value of certain property. In trying to persuade a court to accept a certain value on property, such as businesses, homes, retirement funds, or stock portfolios, attorneys may **retain experts.** In some cases, the court may also appoint its own expert. Once a court has determined the value of property and has **characterized** the property as separate or community, it will divide the property (including debts) according to the state law.

SEC. 8–7 FAMILY LAW COURT PROCEEDINGS

complaint
A document filed in a civil or criminal lawsuit that describes the allegations of the plaintiff and the basis for the lawsuit.

answer
The pleading used by the defendant to respond to the plaintiff's complaint.

petition
In a family law matter, the initial pleading filed by the petitioner; a family law petition will request a divorce/dissolution, nullity of marriage, or legal separation.

petitioner
The person who files a petition with the court.

respondent
The person who answers the petition.

Procedurally, family law disputes often differ somewhat from other civil actions. In most civil disputes, as will be explained in Chapter 13, the plaintiff files a **complaint** in which he alleges that the defendant has done certain things. The defendant usually files an **answer** denying that he or she has done anything wrong. If the parties cannot settle their dispute, the matter goes to trial before a judge, and sometimes a jury, where the dispute is finally resolved. If one of the parties is dissatisfied with the result, that party can pursue the case further in the appellate courts. Once a case has been tried, and the appellate remedies have been exhausted, the case is over.

Family law cases, however, are frequently different. Many states have abolished the concept of blame or fault in divorce proceedings. Under such laws, neither party can file a complaint alleging that the other party caused the breakup. Instead of a complaint, one party would file a **petition** asking the court to dissolve the marriage and settle property and support issues. The parties may be known as **petitioner** and **respondent** rather than *plaintiff* and *defendant.* An example of such a petition is shown in Figure 8–1.

Family law proceedings differ from other civil actions in another way. In the typical civil action, such as an automobile accident case, if the disputing parties settle their dispute, a court action is not necessary. In order to terminate a marriage, however, a court decree is needed, even if the parties are in complete agreement about all issues. If parties do settle all issues they can put their agreement in writing, referred to as a *marital settlement agreement.* This agreement is usually submitted to the court for approval. If the parties do settle all issues, the proceeding is referred to as *uncontested.* On the other hand, if the parties cannot agree on all property, custody, and support issues, the proceeding is referred to as a *contested proceeding* (even if both parties agree that they want the marriage to end).

Unlike civil cases, not all matters are always finally resolved at trial. As long as there are minor children, the court retains jurisdiction and the parties can continue to come back to the court to change custody, visitation, or support, even after they have been divorced for several years. Such changes are also sometimes true for spousal support.

THE PLEADINGS

A family law action typically begins with a petition filed by the petitioner with the court. The petition is served on the petitioner's spouse. The spouse, often referred to as the respondent, serves and files a response or answer. These papers must be filed in a court that has jurisdiction to hear family law matters. In some states, special family law courts have been established. In other states, certain trial courts have this power.

MOTIONS AND ORDERS

motion
A request made to a court; for example, a motion could request temporary support or a change in custody.

Following the initial pleadings, any number of **motions** may be served and filed by the parties to a family law matter. A motion is a request to a judge for an order. A family law action such as a divorce may take months to get to trial. In the meantime, one party may refuse to allow the other to visit the children. Or one party may be threatening to destroy property. Or each party might be harassing and

ATTORNEY OR PARTY WITHOUT ATTORNEY *(Name and Mailing Address)*: TELEPHONE NO.:	*FOR COURT USE ONLY*
ATTORNEY FOR *(Name)*:	
SUPERIOR COURT OF CALIFORNIA, COUNTY OF STREET ADDRESS: MAILING ADDRESS: CITY AND ZIP CODE: BRANCH NAME:	
MARRIAGE OF PETITIONER: RESPONDENT:	
PETITION FOR ☐ **Dissolution of Marriage** ☐ **And Declaration Under Uniform Child Custody Jurisdiction Act** ☐ **Legal Separation** ☐ **Nullity of Marriage**	CASE NUMBER:

1. RESIDENCE (Dissolution only) ☐ Petitioner ☐ Respondent has been a resident of this state for at least six months and of this county for at least three months immediately preceding the filing of this Petition for Dissolution of Marriage.

2. STATISTICAL FACTS
   a. Date of marriage:
   b. Date of separation:
   c. Period between marriage and separation
      Years: Months:

3. DECLARATION REGARDING MINOR CHILDREN OF THIS MARRIAGE FOR WHOM SUPPORT MAY BE ORDERED OR WHO MAY BE SUBJECT TO CUSTODY OR VISITATION ORDERS
   a. ☐ There are no minor children.
   b. ☐ The minor children are:

Child's name	Birthdate	Age	Sex

   c. IF THERE ARE MINOR CHILDREN, COMPLETE EITHER (1) OR (2)
      (1) ☐ Each child named in 3b is currently living with ☐ petitioner ☐ respondent in the following county *(specify)*:
      During the last five years each child has lived in no state other than California and with no person other than petitioner or respondent or both. Petitioner has not participated in any capacity in any litigation or proceeding in any state concerning custody of any minor child of this marriage. Petitioner has no information of any pending custody proceeding or of any person not a party to this proceeding who has physical custody or claims to have custody or visitation rights concerning any minor child of this marriage.
      (2) ☐ A completed Declaration Under Uniform Child Custody Jurisdiction Act is attached.

4. ☐ **Petitioner requests** confirmation as separate assets and obligations the items listed ☐ in Attachment 4 ☐ below:

Item	Confirm to

NOTICE: Any party required to pay child support must pay interest on overdue amounts at the "legal" rate, which is currently 10 percent. This can be a large added amount.

(Continued on reverse)

Form Adopted by Rule 1281
Judicial Council of California
1281 [Rev. January 1, 1995]

PETITION
(Family Law)

Family Code, §§ 2330, 3409
Calif. Rules of Court, rule 1215

FIGURE 8–1 Family law petition form.

MARRIAGE OF *(last name, first name of parties)*:	CASE NUMBER:

5. DECLARATION REGARDING COMMUNITY AND QUASI-COMMUNITY ASSETS AND OBLIGATIONS AS CURRENTLY KNOWN
   a. ☐ There are no such assets or obligations subject to disposition by the court in this proceeding.
   b. ☐ All such assets and obligations have been disposed of by written agreement.
   c. ☐ All such assets and obligations are listed ☐ in Attachment 5 ☐ below *(specify)*:

6. **Petitioner requests**
   a. ☐ Dissolution of the marriage based on
      (1) ☐ irreconcilable differences. FC 2310(a)
      (2) ☐ incurable insanity. FC 2310(b)
   b. ☐ Legal separation of the parties based on
      (1) ☐ irreconcilable differences. FC 2310(a)
      (2) ☐ incurable insanity. FC 2310(b)
   c. ☐ Nullity of void marriage based on
      (1) ☐ incestuous marriage. FC 2200
      (2) ☐ bigamous marriage. FC 2201
   d. ☐ Nullity of voidable marriage based on
      (1) ☐ petitioner's age at time of marriage. FC 2210(a)
      (2) ☐ prior existing marriage. FC 2210(b)
      (3) ☐ unsound mind. FC 2210(c)
      (4) ☐ fraud. FC 2210(d)
      (5) ☐ force. FC 2210(e)
      (6) ☐ physical incapacity. FC 2210(f)

7. **Petitioner requests** that the court grant the above relief and make injunctive (including restraining) and other orders as follows:

	Petitioner	**Respondent**	**Joint**	**Other**
a. Legal custody of children to	☐	☐	☐	☐
b. Physical custody of children to	☐	☐	☐	☐
c. Child visitation be granted to	☐	☐	☐	☐
☐ supervised as to *(specify)*:				
d. Spousal support payable by (wage assignment will be issued)	☐	☐		
e. Attorney fees and costs payable by	☐	☐		

   f. ☐ Terminate the court's jurisdiction (ability) to award spousal support to respondent.
   g. ☐ Property rights be determined.
   h. ☐ Wife's former name be restored *(specify)*:
   i. ☐ Other *(specify)*:

8. If there are minor children of this marriage, the court will make orders for the support of the children without further notice to either party. A wage assignment will be issued.

9. **I have read the restraining orders on the back of the Summons, and I understand that they apply to me when this petition is filed.**

I declare under penalty of perjury under the laws of the State of California that the foregoing is true and correct.

Date:

▶ ______________________________
(SIGNATURE OF PETITIONER)

....
(TYPE OR PRINT NAME OF ATTORNEY)

▶ ______________________________
(SIGNATURE OF ATTORNEY FOR PETITIONER)

NOTICE: Please review your will, insurance policies, retirement benefit plans, credit cards, other credit accounts and credit reports, and other matters you may want to change in view of the dissolution or annulment of your marriage, or your legal separation. However, some changes may require the agreement of your spouse or a court order (see Family Code sections 231–235).

1281 [Rev. January 1, 1995]

PETITION
(Family Law)

Page two

FIGURE 8–1 Continued

threatening the other. In such cases, the parties can make a motion to the court for an immediate ruling.

Before making any ruling, the court usually requires that notice be given to the opposing side. The court then schedules a brief hearing. Any ruling or order that the court makes prior to the actual trial will usually be in effect only until the time of trial. These orders are often referred to as *temporary orders, temporary support orders, temporary custody orders,* or **temporary restraining orders (TROs).** Of course, at the time of trial the court may make the order more permanent. In some cases, family law concerns are so urgent that a party may be unable to give even a few days' notice to the other side before requesting a court order. For example, if one spouse discovers that the other is planning to take the children out of the country in less than 24 hours and wants an order preventing this, notice would be impossible. In such a case a party can approach a judge with the request without giving notice.

temporary restraining order (TRO)
An emergency remedy of short duration granted after the judge is assured that immediate and irreparable damage will be incurred by the party applying for the order. At the earliest possible date, both parties appear before the court for a full hearing on the matter.

Motions in family law matters are not limited to pretrial requests. If a party wants a court to modify a support or custody order after final judgment, a motion is also made. In the Holmes case, it will be necessary to determine whether any immediate problems exist. Are the parties working out a reasonable custody and visitation arrangement for the children? Is Mrs. Holmes threatening to close any bank accounts or is she interfering in any way with the operation of the business? If so, motions for temporary orders might be appropriate. An example of a temporary restraining order form is shown in Figure 8–2.

Discovery

Family law matters often require the use of certain **discovery** tools. Legal support staff play an important role in the discovery process. In discovery, the parties request information from each other. This information might include wage earnings records and retirement information. The most common discovery tools used in family law are the following:

1. *Interrogatories*—Interrogatories are written questions sent to a party involved in a lawsuit. Answers are written and sent back to the party who **propounded** the interrogatories. The questions are answered under penalty of perjury. Each state's code sets forth very specific rules regarding the use and numbers of interrogatories. A sample set of "form interrogatories" is shown in Figure 8–3. Many states have simplified the basic questions asked repeatedly in discovery through the use of standard forms. There are rules explaining the format of the questions, the time period in which a party must respond to each specific discovery tool, and the objections a party may make to specific questions.
2. *Depositions*—A **deposition** is a formal meeting. Depositions, unlike interrogatories, may be taken of nonparties. Attorneys for both parties are present. A **court reporter** records the entire proceeding, word for word, in a **transcript.** The party whose deposition has been requested, the **deponent,** is **deposed** by the attorney who requested the deposition. This oral question-and-answer session allows the attorney asking the questions to see and hear spontaneous responses to questions. After the deposition, the court reporter provides a written transcript or, if the attorney prefers, a computer disk containing the transcript. A member of the legal support staff then reads and summarizes the testimony contained in the deposition transcript. The transcript and the summary become part of the client's file.

discovery
A pretrial process of acquiring information; the most common discovery tools are written interrogatories, depositions, and requests for production of documents and things.

propound
To propose or offer.

deposition
The testimony of a witness, given under oath, outside the courtroom and taken before a court reporter; the *deponent* (the person whose deposition is being taken) will be asked questions by the attorney who requested the deposition.

court reporter
A person who records (electronically or stenographically) the testimony that takes place during the open court proceedings; the court reporter will produce a transcript.

transcript
The document produced by the court reporter; the official record of the proceedings.

deponent
The person whose testimony is given under oath during a deposition.

depose
To give evidence at a deposition.

MARRIAGE OF *(last name, first name of parties)*:	CASE NUMBER:

TEMPORARY RESTRAINING ORDERS
(Attachment to Order to Show Cause)

The person restrained in the first three orders is ***(name)*****:**

Race: Date of birth: Sex:

1. THE RESTRAINED PERSON

a. ☐ shall NOT contact, molest, attack, strike, threaten, sexually or otherwise assault, batter, telephone, or otherwise disturb the peace of the other party.

b. ☐ shall move out immediately and shall not return to the family dwelling at *(address)*:

☐ taking only clothing and personal effects needed until the hearing.

c. ☐ (1) must stay at least *(specify)*: yards away from the other party and the following places:

(a) ☐ Residence of *(name)*:
(address optional):

(b) ☐ Place of work of *(name)*:
(address optional):

(c) ☐ The children's school *(address optional)*:

(d) ☐ Other *(specify)*:

☐ (2) may make contact relating to pickup and delivery of children pursuant to a court order for visitation or a stipulation of the parties arrived at during mediation.

- ***Any person subject to any of these three restraining orders is prohibited by Penal Code section 12021 from purchasing or receiving or attempting to purchase or receive a firearm. Such conduct may be punishable by a $1,000 fine, imprisonment up to one year, or both.***
- ***Taking or concealing a child in violation of this order may be a felony and punishable by confinement in state prison, a fine, or both.***
- ***Other violations of these orders may also be punishable by fines, imprisonment, or both.***

2. This order is effective when made. The law enforcement agency shall enforce it immediately upon receipt. It is enforceable anywhere in California by any law enforcement agency that has received the order, is shown a copy of it, or has verified its existence on the California Law Enforcement Telecommunications System (CLETS). If proof of service on the restrained person has not been received, the law enforcement agency shall advise the restrained person of the terms of the order and then shall enforce it.

3. These orders expire on the date of the court hearing unless extended by the court.

4. **NOTICE TO RESTRAINED PERSON:** If you do not appear at the court hearing specified herein, the court may grant the requested orders for a period of up to three years without further notice to you.

5. ☐ PROPERTY RESTRAINT

a. ☐ Petitioner ☐ Respondent is restrained from transferring, encumbering, hypothecating, concealing, or in any way disposing of any property, real or personal, whether community, quasi-community, or separate, except in the usual course of business or for the necessities of life.

☐ The other party is to be notified of any proposed extraordinary expenditures and an accounting of such is to be made to the court.

(Continued on reverse)

Form Adopted by Rule 1285.05
Judicial Council of California
1285.05 [Rev. January 1, 1995]

TEMPORARY RESTRAINING ORDERS
(Family Law)

Family Code, §§ 2045, 6224, 6226, 6302, 6320–6326, 6380–6383

FIGURE 8–2 Temporary restraining order form.

(continued)

MARRIAGE OF *(last name, first name of parties)*:	CASE NUMBER:

b. ☐ Both parties are restrained and enjoined from cashing, borrowing against, canceling, transferring, disposing of, or changing the beneficiaries of any insurance or other coverage including life, health, automobile, and disability held for the benefit of the parties or their minor child or children.

c. ☐ Neither party shall incur any debts or liabilities for which the other may be held responsible, other than in the ordinary course of business or for the necessities of life.

6. ☐ PROPERTY CONTROL
   a. ☐ Petitioner ☐ Respondent is given the exclusive temporary use, possession, and control of the following property the parties own or are buying *(specify)*:

   b. ☐ Petitioner ☐ Respondent is ordered to make the following payments on liens and encumbrances coming due while the order is in effect:

Debt	Amount of payment	Pay to

7. ☐ MINOR CHILDREN
   a. Neither party shall remove the minor child or children of the parties
      (1) ☐ from the State of California.
      (2) ☐ other *(specify)*:

   b. ☐ Petitioner ☐ Respondent shall have the temporary physical custody, care, and control of the minor children of the parties, ☐ subject to the other party's rights of visitation as follows:

8. By the close of business on the date of this order, a copy of this order shall be delivered by the protected person to the law enforcement agency having jurisdiction over the residence of the protected person, who shall provide information to assist in identifying the restrained person. Proof of service of this order on the restrained person shall also be provided to the law enforcement agency. The law enforcement agency having jurisdiction over the plaintiff's residence is *(name and address of agency)*:

9. ☐ A copy of this order shall be given to the additional law enforcement agencies listed below as follows:
   a. ☐ Plaintiff shall deliver. b. ☐ Plaintiff's attorney shall deliver. c. ☐ The clerk of the court shall mail.

Law enforcement agency	Address

10. ☐ OTHER ORDERS *(specify)*:

Date:

____
JUDGE OF THE SUPERIOR COURT

11. **The date of the court hearing is** *(insert date when known)*:

CLERK'S CERTIFICATE

I certify that the foregoing is a true and correct copy of the original on file in my office.

[SEAL]

Date: Clerk, by ________________________, Deputy

1285.05 [Rev. January 1, 1995] **TEMPORARY RESTRAINING ORDERS** **(Family Law)** Page two

FIGURE 8–2 Continued

ATTORNEY OR PARTY WITHOUT ATTORNEY *(Name and Address)*:	TELEPHONE NO.:
ATTORNEY FOR *(Name)*:	
SUPERIOR COURT OF CALIFORNIA, COUNTY OF	
SHORT TITLE OF CASE:	
FORM INTERROGATORIES—Family Law **Asking Party:** **Answering Party:** **Set No.:**	CASE NUMBER:

Sec. 1. Instructions to Both Parties

These interrogatories are intended to provide for the exchange of relevant information without unreasonable expense to the answering party. They do not change existing law relating to interrogatories nor do they affect the answering party's right to assert any privilege or make any objection. **Privileges must be asserted.**

Sec. 2. Definitions

Words in **BOLDFACE CAPITALS** in these interrogatories are defined as follows:

(a) **PERSON** includes a natural person, partnership, any kind of business, legal, or public entity, and its agents or employees.

(b) **DOCUMENT** means all written, recorded, or graphic materials, however stored, produced, or reproduced.

(c) **ASSET or PROPERTY** includes any interest in real estate or personal property. It includes any interest in a pension, profit-sharing, or retirement plan.

(d) **DEBT** means any obligation including debts paid since the date of separation.

(e) **SUPPORT** means any benefit or economic contribution to the living expenses of another person, including gifts.

(f) If asked to **IDENTIFY A PERSON**, give the person's name, last known residence and business address, telephone numbers, and company affiliation at the date of the transaction referred to.

(g) If asked to **IDENTIFY A DOCUMENT**, attach a copy of the document unless you explain why not. If you do not attach the copy, describe the document, including its date and nature, and give the name, address, telephone number, and occupation of the person who has the document.

Sec. 3. Instructions to the Asking Party

Check the box next to each interrogatory you want the answering party to answer.

Sec. 4. Instructions to the Answering Party

You must answer these interrogatories under oath within 30 days, in accordance with Code of Civil Procedure section 2030.

You must furnish all information you have or can reasonably find out, including all information (not privileged) of your attorneys or under your control. If you don't know, say so.

If an interrogatory is answered by referring to a document, the document must be attached as an exhibit to the response and referred to in the response. If the document has more than one page, refer to the page and section where the answer can be found.

If a document to be attached to the response may also be attached to the Schedule of Assets and Debts form, the document should be attached only to the response, and the form should refer to the response.

If an interrogatory cannot be answered completely, answer as much as you can, state the reason you cannot answer the rest, and state any information you have about the unanswered portion.

Sec. 5. Oath

Your answers to these interrogatories must be under oath, dated, and signed. Use the following form *at the end of your answers:*

"I declare under penalty of perjury under the laws of the State of California that the foregoing answers are true and correct.

(DATE) ______________ (SIGNATURE) ______________

(Continued on reverse)

Form Approved by Rule 1292.10 Judicial Council of California 1292.10 [New July 1, 1990]

FORM INTERROGATORIES (Family Law)

Code of Civil Procedure, §§ 2030(c), 2033.5

FIGURE 8–3 Family law form interrogatories.

(continued)

☐ 1. ***Personal History.*** State your full name, current residence address and work address, social security number, any other names you have used, and the dates between which you used each name.

☐ 2. ***Agreements.*** Are there any agreements between you and your spouse made before or during your marriage or after your separation that affect the disposition of **ASSETS, DEBTS,** or **SUPPORT** in this proceeding? If your answer is yes, for each agreement, state the date made and whether it was written or oral, and attach a copy of the agreement or describe its content.

☐ 3. ***Legal Actions.*** Are you a party or do you anticipate being a party to any legal or administrative proceeding other than this action? If your answer is yes, state your role and the name, jurisdiction, case number, and a brief description of each proceeding.

☐ 4. ***Persons Sharing Residence.*** State the name, age, and relationship to you of each **person** at your present address.

☐ 5. ***Support Provided Others.*** State the name, age, address, and relationship to you of each **PERSON** for whom you have provided **SUPPORT** during the past 12 months and the amount provided per month for each.

☐ 6. ***Support Received for Others.*** State the name, age, address, and relationship to you of each **PERSON** for whom you have received **SUPPORT** during the past twelve months and the amount received per month for each.

☐ 7. ***Current Income.*** List all income you received during the past 12 months, its source, the basis for its computation, and the total amount received from each. Attach your last three pay check stubs.

☐ 8. ***Other Income.*** During the past three years have you received cash or other property from any source not identified in 7? If so, list the source, the date, and the nature and value of the property.

☐ 9. ***Tax Returns.*** Attach copies of all tax returns and schedules filed by or for you in any jurisdiction for the past three calendar years.

☐ 10. ***Schedule of Assets and Debts.*** Complete the Schedule of Assets and Debts form served with these interrogatories.

☐ 11. ***Separate Property Contentions.*** State the facts that support your contention an asset or debt is separate property.

☐ 12. ***Property Valuations.*** Have you had written appraisals or offers to purchase during the past 12 months on any of the assets listed on your completed Schedule of Assets and Debts. If your answer is yes, **IDENTIFY THE DOCUMENT.**

☐ 13. ***Property Held by Others.*** Is there any **PROPERTY** held by any third party in which you have any interest or over which you have any control? If your answer is yes, indicate whether the property is shown on the Schedule of Assets and Debts completed by you. If it is not, describe and identify each such asset and state its present value and the basis for your valuation, and **IDENTIFY THE PERSON** holding the asset.

☐ 14. ***Retirement and Other Benefits.*** Do you have an interest in any disability, retirement, profit sharing, or deferred compensation plan? If your answer is yes, **IDENTIFY** each plan and provide the name, address, and telephone number of the administrator and custodian of records.

☐ 15. ***Claims of Reimbursement.*** Do you claim the legal right to be reimbursed for any expenditures of your separate or community property? If your answer is yes, state all supporting facts.

☐ 16. ***Credits.*** Do you claim reimbursement credits for payments of community debts since the date of separation? If your answer is yes, **IDENTIFY** the source of payment, the creditor, the date paid, and the amount paid. State whether you have added to the debt since the separation.

☐ 17. ***Insurance.*** **IDENTIFY** each health, life, automobile, and disability insurance policy or plan that you now own or that covers you, your children, or your assets. State the policy type, policy number, and name of company. **IDENTIFY** the agent and give the address.

☐ 18. ***Health.*** Is there any physical or emotional condition that limits your ability to work? If your answer is yes, state each fact on which you base your answer.

☐ 19. ***Children's Needs.*** Do you contend your children have any special needs? If so, identify the child with the need, the reason for the need, its cost, and its expected duration.

☐ 20. ***Attorney Fees.*** State the total amount of attorney fees and costs incurred by you in this proceeding, the amount paid, the source of money paid, and describe the billing arrangements.

☐ 21. ***Gifts.*** List any gifts you have made without the consent of your spouse in the past 24 months, their value, and the recipients.

1292.10 [New July 1, 1990] **FORM INTERROGATORIES (Family Law)** Page two

FIGURE 8–3 Continued

3. *Request for production and inspection of documents and things*—This discovery tool, propounded to parties to the lawsuit, allows the party to see and copy specific documents or things that are relevant to the lawsuit. In family law, one party might request copies of W-2s and retirement account statements. This information is used to substantiate the answers provided in the interrogatories.

SEC. 8–8 SETTLEMENT AND TRIAL

mediation
An informal, out-of-court dispute resolution process; a *mediator*, or neutral person, assists the parties in reaching an agreement.

conciliation
The settlement of disputes in a nonadversary manner.

Many parties are able to resolve the various issues in their family law case. In such instances, the attorneys will usually prepare a marital settlement agreement that is signed by both parties. Generally, these agreements require court approval. The court may also require that at least one party appear in court before terminating the marriage. In some states, if the parties cannot resolve their issues, the court may require counseling, **mediation,** or **conciliation,** especially where there are minor children. If the parties cannot settle all matters, the case will eventually go to trial.

SEC. 8–9 FAMILY LAW MATTERS AND UNMARRIED PARTIES

Not all family law cases concern married parties. The number of children born to single mothers has skyrocketed, along with the number of lawsuits concerning custody and support of these children. Many states have adopted a uniform act known as the Uniform Parentage Act. The law recognizes that both natural parents have certain rights and obligations regarding their children. Parents have an obligation to support their children and have rights regarding custody and/or visitation. All of these rights and obligations depend, however, on the determination that a parent-child relationship exists. Usually this is a problem only with paternity. Today, actions to determine paternity are filed by both parents, mothers wanting support, or fathers wishing to establish visitation and custody rights.

presumption
An inference in support of a specific fact.

Scientific developments in DNA testing have made these actions much more straightforward, although sometimes scientific proof of paternity must give way to public policy regarding paternity. Many states have laws creating **presumptions** of paternity when a child is born to a married couple who are cohabitating. In such a case, a court might not even consider scientific proof that another man is the father of the child. In Robert Holmes's case, state law must be consulted to determine what presumptions exist. It might also be necessary to determine whether Holmes's assistant was actually living with her husband at the time of conception.

Once a court determines that a parent-child relationship exists, it must then consider support, custody, and visitation issues. These matters are resolved in much the same way as between married parents.

In addition to paternity actions, courts today are asked to decide support or property questions between unmarried parties, sometimes referred to as *domestic partners*. A number of legal issues are presented in these cases. Any client interview will go more smoothly if the interviewer uses a good questionnaire. After basic information is gathered, specific areas of interest to family law will follow. See the following client questionnaire form for examples.

Family Information Questionnaire

About Your Spouse:

Full Name of Spouse:
Social Security Number of Spouse:
Date of Birth:
Education:
Occupation:
Job Title:
Employer of Spouse:
  Address:
  Phone(s):
Number of Years Employed:
Monthly Gross Income:
Monthly Net Income:
Other Sources of Income:
Employment History since Date of Marriage:
Existing Retirement Plans:
Existing Life Insurance:

About Your Children:

Name:
Date of Birth:
Special Needs:
Child Care:

Name:
Date of Birth:
Special Needs:
Child Care:

Name:
Date of Birth:
Special Needs:
Child Care:

About Your Expenses:

Monthly Rent or Mortgage:
Food:
Utilities (water, phone, gas & electric, garbage):
Clothing:
Transportation:
Child Care:
Credit Card Debt:
Union Dues:
Incidentals:

Featured Web Site: www.law.cornell.edu/topics/Table_Divorce.htm

This site offers easy access to the divorce/dissolution laws of the fifty states.

Go Online

1. Choose your state.
2. Summarize the materials available for your state.

Chapter Summary

Family law is a challenging legal specialty. It encompasses marriage, divorce, children and support, child abuse, and many more issues. The family law statutes vary from state to state. Be sure to become familiar with the statutes in your state.

Most states have approved sets of forms that are used exclusively in family law matters. This allows people to fill in their own forms when they are not using the services of a family law office. However, family law can be a complicated legal specialty, and most people feel the need for legal advice.

Terms to Remember

domestic relations
premarital agreement
prenuptial agreement
annulment
nullity
void
voidable
divorce
dissolution
bifurcate
legal separation
child custody
support
jurisdiction
spousal support
separate property
community property
quasi-community property
retain
expert
characterize
complaint
answer
petition
petitioner
respondent
motion
temporary restraining order (TRO)
discovery
propound
deposition
court reporter
transcript
deponent
depose
mediation
conciliation
presumption

Questions for Review

1. What is a legal separation?
2. Summarize the Illinois Marriage and Dissolution of Marriage Act, Section 602, set forth in this chapter.
3. According to California Family Code Section 4320, set forth in this chapter, what circumstances are to be considered before the court awards spousal support?
4. Explain the differences between separate property and community property.
5. How do family law disputes differ from other civil actions?
6. State and discuss three discovery tools often used in family law.

Questions for Analysis

1. State the issues presented to the Court in *McCord v. McCord*.
2. Locate and summarize two family law statutes that address the issue of child custody. Provide the title of the code and the section number in your summary. Use Appendix IV to guide you in proper citation format. The index to the code

will enable you to go directly to the appropriate statutes. Choose your vocabulary carefully before going to the index, to provide focus on the topic.

Assignments and Projects

1. Create a two-page client questionnaire for a law office that has just begun to practice family law.
2. Based on the following facts, write a letter to a client who has neglected to provide your office with some critical information. Remember, legal correspondence is formal writing. Try to avoid creating a document that reads like a form letter.

   Ms. Eugene F. Voorhies is a family law client. The office must have the exact date of her marriage to Mr. Thomas C. Voorhies. This information is vital on at least one document. She has not responded to two messages left on her recorder. Her address, as stated on the client intake sheet, is 1234 First Street #60, Heartland City, Missouri 88888. (You may create the appropriate law office letterhead and the name of the law firm.) This letter will go out under your signature.

3. Write a summary of the *Wages v. Wages* case. Include the facts, issues, rules, analysis, and conclusion. See Chapter 5 to review how to summarize or brief a case.

CHAPTER 9

WILLS, TRUSTS, AND PROBATE

Technology Corner

Web Address	Name of Site
www.nolo.com/	Nolo—Law for All (browse through the topics related to wills, trusts, probate, and estate planning)
www.seniorlaw.com/	SeniorLaw Home Page

CASE FILE: *HOLMES V. HOLMES*

The Holmes divorce and paternity actions (Chapter 8) are proceeding. A paralegal working on the case received the following memorandum:

> Robert Holmes is coming in to see me next week concerning his will. Now that his wife has filed for divorce he is anxious to change some of the provisions. Since the value of his business has skyrocketed, he is also concerned about large estate taxes and probate costs. I will be talking to him about various types of estate plans. Please review his divorce file and make a list of all property owned by Holmes. Also, I know that he has a vacation home in another state.

SEC. 9-1 INTRODUCTION

The practice of law does not always involve disputes, such as divorce cases. Sometimes it involves helping clients handle their personal or business affairs. Estate planning and probate are such areas. Estate planning usually includes the preparation of documents, such as wills or trusts, that dispose of or transfer property. The type of estate plan that is best for an individual depends on circumstances such as the wishes of the individual, the value of the estate, and the family circumstances. For example, since Robert Holmes is in the process of a divorce, he probably does not want to leave property to his wife, should he die before the divorce is final. He also must consider the legal rights of an illegitimate child, should he lose the paternity action. If his business is worth millions of dollars, tax consequences and probate costs must be considered.

Probate is a related area of law. Probate occurs after the death of a person and involves the identification of that person's assets and debts, the payment of debts and taxes from the estate, and finally, the distribution of the remaining assets to the heirs. Probate is supervised by the court.

SEC. 9-2 WILLS

witnessed
A document is witnessed when the witness signs his or her name attesting that he or she observed the execution of a particular document or instrument.

real property
Land, including anything affixed to the land or growing upon the land.

personal property
Goods and money; in general, property is either real or personal.

testator/testatrix
A person who has made a will; a *testator* is a man, while a *testatrix* is a woman.

holographic will
A will written entirely by the testator; the handwritten document is not witnessed. Not all states recognize holographic wills.

nuncupative will
An oral will; not all states recognize nuncupative wills.

subscribe
To sign one's name at the end of a document.

acknowledge
To affirm that a document is genuine.

beneficiary
A person named in a will who will benefit from a transfer of specific property.

A *will* is a document in which an individual provides for the distribution of his or her property upon his or her death. In some cases it also names guardians to care for minor children. Wills come in all shapes and sizes. Many are drafted by lawyers; some are handwritten by the person creating the will. Some will be **witnessed,** others will not. Each state has specific laws (statutes) that establish the rules for the disposition of **real** and **personal property** by will. The law relating to wills is determined generally by the state in which the **testator** (or **testatrix**) resides. When real property is involved, the laws of the state in which the property is located cannot be ignored.

Wills fall into three broad categories: formal, **holographic,** and **nuncupative**. A *formal will* is the type usually prepared by attorneys. It is a written will, **subscribed** and **acknowledged** by the testator and witnessed by individuals who are not **beneficiaries** under the will. The number of witnesses required is a matter of state law, generally two or three.

A *holographic will* is handwritten by the testator. It must be signed and dated; witnesses are not required. A *nuncupative will* is an oral will made by one on his or her deathbed. This is sometimes referred to as a *soldier's will.*

Generally, anyone over the age of majority and of sound mind can make a will. The legislature of the state of California has even adopted a form will known as the California Statutory Will. This will, shown in Figure 9–1, is found in California Probate Code Section 6240.

Wills allow people to choose how their estate will be divided and disposed of after death. With a few exceptions, they may leave their assets to anyone they designate in the will. A well-drafted will may eliminate legal entanglements over a person's property after death. Similarly, a will should be written to accurately reflect the testator's intent. Usually, the testator wants the will to set out clearly all real and personal property assets and to whom those assets are to be distributed after the testator's death.

§6240. Form for California Statutory Will.
The following is the California statutory will form:

QUESTIONS AND ANSWERS ABOUT THIS CALIFORNIA STATUTORY WILL

The following information, in question and answer form, is not a part of the California Statutory Will. It is designed to help you understand about Wills and to decide if this Will meets your needs. This Will is in a simple form. The complete text of each paragraph of this Will is printed at the end of the Will.

1. *What happens if I die without a Will?* If you die without a Will, what you own (your "assets") in your name alone will be divided among your spouse, children, or other relatives according to state law. The court will appoint a relative to collect and distribute your assets.

2. *What can a Will do for me?* In a Will you may designate who will receive your assets at your death. You may designate someone (called an "executor") to appear before the court, collect your assets, pay your debts and taxes, and distribute your assets as you specify. You may nominate someone (called a "guardian") to raise your children who are under age 18. You may designate someone (called a "custodian") to manage assets for your children until they reach any age between 18 and 25.

3. *Does a Will avoid probate?* No. With or without a Will, assets in your name alone usually go through the court probate process. The court's first job is to determine if your Will is valid.

4. *What is community property?* Can I give away my share in my Will? If you are married and you or your spouse earned money during your marriage from work and wages, that money (and the assets bought with it) is community property. Your Will can only give away your one-half of community property. Your Will cannot give away your spouse's one-half of community property.

5. *Does my will give away all of my assets?* Do all assets go through probate? No. Money in a joint tenancy bank account automatically belong to the other named owner without probate. If your spouse or child is on the deed to your house as a joint tenant, the house automatically passes to him or her. Life insurance and retirement plan benefits may pass directly to the named beneficiary. A Will does not necessarily control how these types of "nonprobate" assets pass at your death.

6. *Are there different kinds of Wills?* Yes. There are handwritten Wills, typewritten Wills, attorney-prepared Wills, and statutory Wills. All are valid if done precisely as the law requires. You should see a lawyer if you do not want to use this statutory Will or if you do not understand this form.

7. *Who may use this Will?* This Will is based on California law. It is designed only for California residents. You may use this form if you are single, married, or divorced. You must be age 18 or older and or sound mind.

8. *Are there any reasons why I should NOT use this statutory Will?* Yes. This is a simple Will. It is not designed to do reduce death taxes or other taxes. Talk to a lawyer to do tax planning, especially if (i) your assets will be worth more than $600,000 at your death, (ii) you own business related assets, (iii) you want to create a trust fund for your children's education or other purposes, (iv) you own assets in some other state, (v) you want to disinherit your spouse or descendants, or (vi) you have valuable interests in pension or profit sharing plans. You should talk to a lawyer who knows about estate planning if this Will does not meet your needs. This Will treats most adopted children like natural children. You should talk to a lawyer if you have stepchildren or foster children whom you have not adopted.

9. *May I add or cross out any words on this Will?* No. If you do, the Will may be invalid or the court may ignore the crossed out or added words. You may only fill in the blanks. You may amend this Will by a separate document (called a codicil). Talk to a lawyer if you want to do something with your assets which is not allowed in this orm.

10. *May I change my Will?* Yes. A Will is not effective until you die. You may make and sign a new Will. You may change your Will at any time, but only by an amendment (called a codicil). You can give away or sell your assets before your death. Your Will only acts on what you own at death.

11. *Where should I keep my Will?* After you and the witnesses sign the Will, keep your Will in your safe deposit box or other safe place. You should tell trusted family members where your Will is kept.

12. *When should I change my Will?* You should make and sign a new Will if you marry or divorce after you sign this Will. Divorce or annulment automatically cancels all property stated to pass to a former husband or wife under this Will, and revokes the designation of a former spouse as executor, custodian, or guardian. You should sign a new Will when you have more children, or if your spouse or a child dies. You may want to change your Will if there is a large change in the value of your assets.

13. *What can I do if I do not understand something in this Will?* If there is anything in this Will you do not understand, ask a lawyer to explain it to you.

14. *What is an executor?* An "executor" is the person you name to collect your assets, pay your debts and taxes, and distribute your assets as the court directs. It may be a person or it may be a qualified bank or trust company.

15. *Should I require a bond?* You may require that an executor post a "bond." A bond is a form of insurance to replace assets that may be mismanaged or stolen by the executor. The cost of the bond is paid from the estate's assets.

16. *What is a guardian?* Do I need to designate one? If you have children under age 18, you should designate a guardian of their "persons" to raise them.

17. *What is a custodian?* Do I need to designate one? A "custodian" is a person you may designate to manage assets for someone (including a child) who is between ages 18 and 25 and who receives assets under your Will. The custodian manages the assets and pays as much as the custodian determines is proper for health, support, maintenance, and education. The custodian delivers what is left to the person when the person reaches the age you choose (between 18 and 25). No bond is required of a custodian.

18. *Should I ask people if they are willing to serve before I designate them as executor, guardian, or custodian?* Probably yes. Some people and banks and trust companies may not consent to serve or may not be qualified to act.

19. *What happens if I make a gift in this Will to someone and they die before I do?* A person must survive you by 120 hours to take a gift under this Will. If they do not, then the gift fails and goes with the rest of your assets. If the person who does not survive you is a relative of you or your spouse, then certain assets may go to the relative's descendants.

20. *What is a trust?* There are many kinds of trusts, including trusts created by Wills (called "testamentary trusts") and trusts created during your lifetime (called "revocable living trusts"). Both kinds of trusts are long-term arrangements where a manager (called a "trustee") invests and manages assets for someone (called a "beneficiary") on the terms you specify. Trusts are too complicated to be used in this statutory Will. You should see a lawyer if you want to create a trust.

FIGURE 9–1 The California statutory will.

INSTRUCTIONS

1. READ THE WILL. Read the whole Will first. If you do not understand something, ask a lawyer to explain it to you.

2. FILL IN THE BLANKS. Fill in the blanks. Follow the instructions in the form carefully. Do not add any words to the Will (except for filling in blanks) or cross out any words.

3. DATE AND SIGN THE WILL AND HAVE TWO WITNESSES SIGN IT. Date and sign the Will and have two witnesses sign it. You and the witnesses should read and follow the Notice to Witnesses found at the end of this Will.

CALIFORNIA STATUTORY WILL OF

Print Your Full Name

1. Will. This is my Will. I revoke all prior Wills and codicils.

2. Specific Gift of Personal Residence (Optional—use only if you want to give your personal residence to a different person or persons than you give the balance of your assets to under paragraph 5 below). I give my interest in my principal personal residence at the time of my death (subject to mortgages and liens) as follows:
(Select one choice only and sign in the box after your choice).

a. Choice One: All to my spouse, if my spouse survives me; otherwise to my descendants (my children and the descendants of my children) who survive me. [ ]

b. Choice Two: Nothing to my spouse; all to my descendants (my children and the descendants of my children) who survive me. [ ]

c. Choice Three: All to the following person if he or she survives me: (Insert the name of the person): [ ]

____

d. Choice Four: Equally among the following persons who survive me: (Insert the names of two or more persons):

____
____
____
______________________ [ ]

3. Specific Gift of Automobiles, Household and Personal Effects (Optional—use only if you want to give automobiles and household and personal effects to a different person or persons than you give the balance of your assets to under paragraph 5 below). I give all of my automobiles (subject to loans), furniture, furnishings, household items, clothing, jewelry, and other tangible articles of a personal nature at the time of my death as follows:
(Select one choice only and sign in the box after your choice).

a. Choice One: All to my spouse, if my spouse survives me; otherwise to my descendants (my children and the descendants of my children) who survive me. [ ]

b. Choice Two: Nothing to my spouse; all to my descendants (my children and the descendants of my children) who survive me. [ ]

c. Choice Three: All to the following person if he or she survives me: (Insert the name of the person): [ ]

____

d. Choice Four: Equally among the following persons who survive me: (Insert the names of two or more persons):

____
____
____
______________________ [ ]

4. Specific Gifts of Cash. (Optional) I make the following cash gifts to the persons named below who survive me, or to the named charity, and I sign my name in the box after each gift. If I don't sign in the box, I do not make a gift. (Sign in the box after each gift you make.)

Name of Person or Charity to receive gift (name one only—please print)	Amount of Cash Gift
	Sign your name in this box to make this gift

Name of Person or Charity to receive gift (name one only—please print)	Amount of Cash Gift
	Sign your name in this box to make this gift

Name of Person or Charity to receive gift (name one only—please print)	Amount of Cash Gift
	Sign your name in this box to make this gift

Name of Person or Charity to receive gift (name one only—please print)	Amount of Cash Gift
	Sign your name in this box to make this gift

Name of Person or Charity to receive gift (name one only—please print)	Amount of Cash Gift
	Sign your name in this box to make this gift

5. Balance of My Assets. Except for the specific gifts made in paragraphs 2, 3 and 4 above, I give the balance of my assets as follows:
(Select one choice only and sign in the box after your choice. If I sign in more than one box or if I don't sign in any box, the court will distribute my assets as if I did not make a Will).

a. Choice One: All to my spouse, if my spouse survives me; otherwise to my descendants (my children and the descendants of my children) who survive me. [ ]

b. Choice Two: Nothing to my spouse; all to my descendants (my children and the descendants of my children) who survive me. [ ]

c. Choice Three: All to the following person if he or she survives me: (Insert the name of the person): [ ]

____

d. Choice Four: Equally among the following persons who survive me: (Insert the names of two or more persons):

____
____
____
______________________ [ ]

6. Guardian of the Child's Person. If I have a child under age 18 and the child does not have a living parent at my death, I nominate the individual named below as First Choice as guardian of the person of such child (to raise the child). If the First Choice as does not serve, then I nominate the Second Choice, and then the Third Choice, to serve. Only an individual (not a bank or trust company) may serve.

FIGURE 9–1 Continued

Name of First Choice for Guardian of the Person

Name of Second Choice for Guardian of the Person

Name of Third Choice for Guardian of the Person

7. Special Provision of Property of Persons Under Age 25. (Optional—Unless you use this paragraph, assets that go to a child or other person who is under age 18 may be given to the parent of the person, or to the guardian named in paragraph 6 above as guardian of the person until age 18, and the court will require a bond; and assets that go to a child or other person who is age 18 or older will be given outright to the person. By using this paragraph you may provide that a custodian will hold the assets for the person until the person reaches any age between 18 and 25 which you choose). If a beneficiary of this Will is between age 18 and 25, I nominate the individual or bank or trust company named below as First Choice as custodian of the property. If the First Choice does not serve, then I nominate the Second Choice, and then the Third Choice, to serve.

Name of First Choice for Custodian of Assets

Name of Second Choice for Custodian of Assets

Name of Third Choice for Custodian of Assets

Insert any age between 18 and 25 as the age for the person to receive the property:
(If you do not choose an age, age 18 will apply.)

8. I nominate the individual or bank or trust company named below as First Choice as executor. If the First Choice does not serve, then I nominate the Second Choice, and then the Third Choice, to serve.

Name of First Choice for Executor

Name of Second Choice for Executor

Name of Third Choice for Executor

9. Bond. My signature in this box means a bond is not required for any person named as executor. A bond may be required if I do not sign in this box:

No bond shall be required.

(Notice: You must sign this Will in the presence of two (2) adult witnesses. The witnesses must sign their names in your presence and in each other's presence. You must first read to them the following two sentences.)

This is my Will. I ask the persons who sign below to be my witnesses.

Signed on ________ (date) at ________ (city), California

Signature of Maker of Will

(Notice to Witnesses: Two (2) adults must sign as witnesses. Each witness must read the following clause before signing. The witnesses should not receive assets under this Will.)

Each of us declares under penalty of perjury under the laws of the State of California that the following is true and correct:

a. On the date written below the maker of this Will declared to us that this instrument was the maker's will and requested us to act as witnesses to it;

b. We understand this is the maker's Will;

c. The maker signed this Will in our presence, all of us being present at the same time;

d. We now, at the maker's request, and in the maker's and each other's presence, sign below as witnesses;

e. We believe the maker is of sound mind and memory;

f. We believe that this Will was not procured by duress, menace, fraud or undue influence;

g. The maker is age 18 or older; and

h. Each of us is now age 18 or older, is a competent witness, and resides at the address set forth after his or her name.

Dated: ________

Signature of witness	Signature of witness
Print name here:	Print name here:
Residence Address:	Residence Address:

AT LEAST TWO WITNESSES MUST SIGN
NOTARIZATION ALONE IS NOT SUFFICIENT

FIGURE 9–1 Continued

SEC. 9-3 PREPARATION OF A WILL

In the modern law office, wills are created with the assistance of a computer. Common clauses are stored and used in many documents. Software packages such as Shepard's Drafting Wills and Trusts on CAPS offer sample wills and sample clauses. These packages help legal professionals draft a document that meets the client's needs, without starting with a blank computer screen or a blank piece of paper. The computer enables the drafter to create a document quickly and easily.

Elements that are common to most wills include the following:

- the opening clauses
- the body of the will
- the fiduciary clause
- the closing clauses

THE OPENING CLAUSES

exordium clause
The introductory part of a document.

revoke
To take back or to make void.

The first opening clause usually identifies the testator. This is called the **exordium clause.** The exordium clause also includes the testator's residence, the intent to create a last will and testament, and the intent to **revoke** any prior wills and codicils.

Another opening clause may explain funeral arrangements or give cremation instructions. The testator's instructions on the payment of any outstanding debts are often included in the opening clauses.

THE BODY OF THE WILL

bequest
A gift by will of specific personal property.

devise
A gift by will of specific real property.

general legacy
A gift of a specific amount of money.

demonstrative legacy
A gift of a specified amount of money in which the testator includes directions as to exactly which fund will be used to fulfill the legacy.

The testator disposes of his property in the body of the will. There are three basic forms of gifts. A gift may be specific, general, or demonstrative.

A specific **bequest** is a gift of specific property. Examples of such gifts might be a ruby necklace, an automobile, a piece of art, a table, or a computer. All property *except* real estate may be given as a specific bequest. When the testator wishes to make a gift of real property, the correct term for the gift is a specific **devise.**

A **general legacy** is a gift of a specific amount of money. This gift of money is taken from the assets of the general estate. In contrast, a **demonstrative legacy** is a gift of a specific amount of money, but the testator includes directions as to exactly which fund will be used to fulfill the gift. For example, the testator might designate a specific bank or savings account.

The *residuary clause* distributes all property not disposed of in the other clauses of the main body of the will. Everything that has not been disposed of through specific, general, or demonstrative gifts will fall into the residuary clause. Remember, this is necessary because a will should be drafted so that it distributes all of the testator's property.

disinheritance clause
A clause used to deprive an heir of the right to inherit.

Other clauses will be included in the main body of many wills. A will is a very personal document; since each person is different and estates contain different property, each individual's needs will vary greatly. The testator may choose not to leave anything to a certain heir. A **disinheritance clause** is appropriate in this instance.

THE FIDUCIARY CLAUSE

fiduciary
A person whose duties involve trust and good faith.

executor/executrix
A person chosen by a testator/testatrix to carry out the directions in the will; an executor is a man, while an executrix is a woman.

guardian
A person who has the duty of taking care of a person and that person's property.

trustee
A person who holds property in trust; a trust is created by a grantor for the benefit of specific beneficiaries.

testimonium clause
A clause that includes the date on which the document was executed and who signed the document.

attestation clause
A clause at the end of a will wherein all witnesses declare that the document was executed before them.

publish
To make something known to people.

codicil
An addition or change to a will. A codicil does not contain the entire will; it simply supplements the original document.

A **fiduciary** is a person appointed by the testator. This person owes a duty of trust to the estate. **Executors** (or **executrixes**), **guardians,** and **trustees** are all considered fiduciaries. The fiduciaries assist with the administration of the estate or care for the testator's dependents. A testator may grant certain powers to the fiduciaries. For example, a fiduciary may be given the power to sell property or distribute assets without prior consent of the court.

THE CLOSING CLAUSES

In general, two clauses are used to end or close the will. The **testimonium clause** comes just before the testator's signature and the date. This clause signals the end of the will. The next clause is the **attestation clause.** This clause will be set just above the signatures of the witnesses. The attestation clause states that the witnesses understand that this is the last will and testament of the testator. This clause is customary but not actually required.

CHANGING THE WILL

A will may be changed. Wills are often revoked or changed. Such revocation or change may take place any time after the will is properly created and before death. There are no rules about how many times a person may change his or her will. Some people have several wills in their lifetime. Circumstances change, assets are acquired and disposed of, heirs are born and die; all of these are reasons to change an existing will or create a new will. In some instances, a totally new will is not necessary. The changes may be **published** in a **codicil.** This is a separate document. A codicil, in some way, changes one or more provisions of an existing will.

WHERE THERE IS NO WILL

intestate succession
When a person dies without a will, his or her estate will be disposed of under the laws of intestate succession. The laws of intestate succession will dispose of the property under the state laws of descent and distribution.

decedent
A person who has died; a deceased person.

When a person dies without a will, the law of **intestate succession** will be applied. This law is created by state statute. The actual wishes of the **decedent** are not taken into account; instead, the statute explains how the decedent's real and personal property is to be distributed. Sometimes people believe that they have no need for a will because they own very little. However, if their financial status improves before they die and they have no will, the state will decide who receives the property. A simple will avoids this problem. Review the following probate code.

Probate Code Section 6402
Intestate Share of Heirs Other Than Surviving Spouse

Except as provided in Section 6402.5, the part of the intestate estate not passing to the surviving spouse under Section 6401, or the entire intestate estate if there is no surviving spouse, passes as follows:

(a) To the issue of the decedent, the issue taking equally if they are all of the same degree of kinship to the decedent, but if of unequal degree those of more remote degree take in the manner provided in Section 240.

(b) If there is no surviving issue, to the decedent's parent or parents equally.

(c) If there is no surviving issue or parent, to the issue of the parents or either of them, the issue taking equally if they are all of the same degree of kinship to the decedent, but if of unequal degree those of more remote degree take in the manner provided in Section 240.

(d) If there is no surviving issue, parent or issue of a parent, but the decedent is survived by one or more grandparents or issue of grandparents, to the grandparent or grandparents equally, or to the issue of such grandparents if there is no surviving grandparent, the issue taking equally if they are all of the same degree of kinship to the decedent, but if of unequal degree those of more remote degree take in the manner provided in Section 240.

(e) If there is no surviving issue, parent or issue of a parent, grandparent or issue of a grandparent, but the decedent is survived by the issue of a predeceased spouse, to such issue, the issue taking equally if they are all of the same degree of kinship to the predeceased spouse, but if of unequal degree those of more remote degree take in the manner provided in Section 240.

(f) If there is no surviving issue, parent or issue of a parent, grandparent or issue of a grandparent, or issue of a predeceased spouse, but the decedent is survived by next of kin, to the next of kin in equal degree, but where there are two or more collateral kindred in equal degree who claim through different ancestors, those who claim through the nearest ancestor are preferred to those claiming through an ancestor more remote.

(g) If there is no surviving next of kin of the decedent and no surviving issue of a predeceased spouse of the decedent, but the decedent is survived by the parents of a predeceased spouse or the issue of such parents, to the parent or parents equally, or to the issue of such parents if both are deceased, the issue taking equally if they are all of the same degree of kinship to the predeceased spouse, but if of unequal degree those of more remote degree take in the manner provided in Section 240.

SEC. 9-4 TRUSTS

WHAT IS A TRUST?

A *trust* is a document or instrument in which one makes provisions for the disposition of one's property either during one's lifetime or after one's death. A trust involves placing legal title to property in a person, the *trustee,* who then holds that property for the benefit of another. Usually the trust establishes certain terms and conditions regarding the use of the property and the duties and obligations of the trustee.

HOW TO CREATE A TRUST

legal title
Title that is enforceable in a court of law; legal title involves the full ownership of the trust property.

equitable title
A trust beneficiary holds equitable title; the person holding equitable title has the right to benefit from the trust property.

Technically a trust is a situation in which the title to property is divided into two parts: **legal title** and **equitable title.** The trustee has the legal title. This involves full ownership of the property in the trust. However, the trustee will not take personal gain from the trust property. The beneficiary holds equitable title. This is the right to benefit from the trust property.

Although there are many types of trusts, in general, they fall into two categories: *express trusts* and *implied trusts.*

EXPRESS TRUSTS

settlor
The person who creates a trust.

Express trusts may be written or oral. In order to create an express trust, the **settlor** (the person creating the trust) must clearly intend to create a trust. All express trusts will have these four elements: (1) a settlor, (2) a trustee, (3) trust property, and (4) at least one beneficiary. The most common types of express trusts are *living trusts* and *testamentary trusts.*

Living Trusts

living trust
A trust that is operative during the lifetime of the settlor.

probate court
A court that has jurisdiction over the probate of a will and the administration of a decedent's estate.

testamentary trust
A trust created by a will.

A **living trust** becomes effective during the life of the settlor. This type of trust does not fall under the supervision or control of a **probate court.** This provides privacy for the settlor and the beneficiary.

Testamentary Trusts

A **testamentary trust** is created by will and is effective only upon the death of the settlor. It is essential that the settlor clearly separate the legal and equitable title to the property. The settlor must also convey the legal title to a trustee for a specific beneficiary's benefit.

IMPLIED TRUSTS

constructive trust
A trust created by law; the court may determine that a person has by actual or constructive fraud or duress obtained a legal right to property that he or she should not in good faith possess.

Implied trusts are often called *involuntary trusts.* These trusts are created by law. For example, if a person acquires legal title to property as a result of some wrongdoing, the court may impose a trust on the individual holding the legal title. The court may declare that the title is held in trust for the benefit of the person who should possess the title. This is a **constructive trust.**

SEC. 9-5 PROBATE

probate
The judicial procedure by which a will is proved valid or invalid; includes distributing property to the heirs and paying debts and taxes.

Probate is a court-supervised process that takes place after a person dies. The court appoints an individual, known as an *executor* or *administrator,* to be responsible for this process. (An executor is a person who has been named in a will to do this. An administrator is a person named by the court.) The executor or administrator identifies the assets and debts, including estate or inheritance taxes. After paying all debts and taxes, the executor or administrator distributes the property either in accordance with the will, or in accordance with the laws of intestate succession if there is no will. Probate results in title to the decedent's property being passed to the heirs.

Not all property is probate property. In other words, probate is not the only way that property can pass to heirs. Property placed in a living trust or property held in joint tenancy passes to other trust beneficiaries or surviving joint tenants without court supervision. Other common examples of nonprobate property include life insurance benefits with named beneficiaries and individual retirement accounts with named beneficiaries. It is important to note, however, that avoiding probate does not necessarily avoid estate or inheritance taxes.

Legal support staff are often heavily involved in the probate process. They interact with executors and heirs in identifying and valuing property. They draft court documents under attorney supervision. They also interact with accountants and tax preparers.

SEC. 9-6 CASE LAW EXAMPLES

The following four cases involve the same legal issue. The heirs of Agatha Christie, Marilyn Monroe, Groucho Marx, and Elvis Presley have sued various defendants over the "right of publicity," which is a somewhat new legal concept. These four cases, which span nine years, provide a framework for you to understand how law develops or evolves in the American judicial system. Notice how the latter cases rely on the earlier cases.

A POINT TO REMEMBER

You will see language in cases that may seem confusing at first. Most of the cases you will read are appellate decisions. This means that there has already been a trial in a lower court. You may see language at the end of the case that says the case is *remanded* to the trial court. This means that the court whose decision you are reading is sending the case back to the trial or lower court.

In some cases, the court uses the term *we* to identify the court. When you write about or paraphrase a case, use "the court" to refer to the judge or panel of judges who heard the case on appeal.

Hicks v. Casablanca Records

464 F. Supp. 426 (1978)

This is an action brought by the heirs of Agatha Christie against a movie company and book publisher who wanted to distribute a movie and book, entitled Agatha, *that gave a fictionalized account of a true incident in the life of Agatha Christie. At one point in her life, Ms. Christie disappeared for eleven days. No one knows why, although the movie and book suggest that she did this because she was emotionally unstable and was plotting to kill her husband's mistress. The petitioners requested a preliminary injunction while the respondents moved to dismiss the case.*

The issues in this case involve the right of heirs to assert the right of publicity value of the name or likeness of the decedent and whether that right exists at all in connection with movies or books rather than with the sale of merchandise.

OPINION

Plaintiffs, the heir and assignees of the late Agatha Christie, seek an order enjoining the defendant movie producers, Casablanca Records, Filmworks, First Artists and Warner Brothers (hereinafter referred to as the "movie case") from distributing or showing the motion picture *Agatha.* Plaintiffs, in a related case, similarly seek an order enjoining defendant publisher, Ballantine Books (hereinafter referred to as the "book case") from distributing or making the book *Agatha* available to the public.

The defendants in both cases oppose the plaintiffs' applications for injunctive relief, and have separately moved to dismiss plaintiffs' claims on the ground that they fail to state claims upon which relief could be granted pursuant to Rule 12(b) (6) Fed. R. Civ. P.

The defendant in the book case has separately moved to dismiss the complaint pursuant to Rule 12(b)(6). The plaintiffs have cross-moved for a preliminary injunction. On July 11, 1978, a hearing on plaintiffs' motion for a preliminary injunction in the movie case was held along with oral argument on defendant Ballantine Books' motion to dismiss. With consent of the parties, evidence was taken in the book case. The Court reserved decision.

Accordingly, this opinion addresses the motions to dismiss made by the defendants in each case, and plaintiffs' motions for preliminary injunction made in each.

Background

Plaintiffs' decedent and assignor was the late Dame Agatha Christie, one of the best-known mystery writers in modern times. Her career spanned five decades until her death in 1976, and culminated in the production of scores of mystery novels, not the least famous of which are *Murder on the Orient Express* and the short story "Witness for the Prosecution." Although Mrs. Christie attempted to shun publicity with respect to her personal life, professionally, she cultivated the name "Agatha Christie" in such a way as to make it almost synonymous with mystery novels. Thus, during her life, she agreed to the use of her name in connection with various motion pictures and plays based on her works. Upon her death, the rights in her works descended to plaintiff, Rosalind Christie Hicks, Mrs. Christie's sole legatee, and plaintiffs, Agatha Christie, Ltd. and William Collins Sons & Co., Ltd., her assignees.

In the winter of 1977, defendants in the movie case began the filming of a movie entitled *Agatha* which, like the book in the related case, presents a fictionalized account of a true incident which occurred during the life of Mrs. Christie. The book is scheduled for distribution shortly. Although both the movie and the book are entitled *Agatha*, it is not disputed by defendants in either case that both concern the late mystery writer.

Plaintiffs, in seeking preliminary injunctions, have asserted their right to recover on the basis of the recently developing law of the right of publicity.

It appears that on or about December 4, 1926, Mrs. Christie, then married to Colonel Archibald Christie, disappeared from her home in England. This disappearance was widely publicized and, although a major effort was launched to find her, everyone was at a loss to explain her disappearance. However, eleven days after she was reported missing, Mrs. Christie reappeared, but her true whereabouts and the reasons for her disappearance are, to this day, a mystery.

In view of the death of Mrs. Christie, the public may never know the facts surrounding this incident, but should the defendants prevail herein, the public will have a fictionalized account of this disappearance as set forth in the movie and in the book. In each instance, Mrs. Christie is portrayed as an emotionally unstable woman, who, during her eleven-day disappearance, engages in a sinister plot to murder her husband's mistress, in an attempt to regain the alienated affections of her husband. Given this portrayal of their decedent and assignor, plaintiffs, mindful of the personal nature of defamation and privacy actions, bring the instant actions alleging unfair competition and infringement of the right of publicity.

Discussion

This Circuit has recently addressed the parameters of the right of publicity in *Factors Etc., Inc. v. Pro Arts, Inc.*, 579 F.2d 215 (2d Cir. 1978) (hereinafter cited as *Factors*). In *Factors*, the Court found that the right of publicity, *i.e.*, the right in the publicity value of one's name or likeness, is a valid property right which is transferable and capable of surviving the death of the owner. *Id.* at 220–21. However, the Court went on to state that this interest survives only if it is found that the owner "exploited" the right during his or her lifetime. *Id.* at 222 n. 11; *accord, Guglielmi v. Spelling-Goldberg Prods.*, 73 Cal. App. 3d 436, 140 Cal. Rptr. 775 (1977). While the *Factors* opinion does not define "exploitation," it would appear that a party claiming the right must establish that the decedent acted in such a way as to evidence his or her own recognition of the extrinsic commercial value of his or her name or likeness, and manifested that recognition in some overt manner, *e.g.*, making an *inter vivos* transfer of the rights in the name *(Factors)*, or posing for bubble gum cards *(see Haelan Laboratories, Inc. v. Topps Chewing Gum, Inc.*, 202 F.2d 866 [2d Cir. 1953]).

In applying the *Factors* analysis to the cases at bar, this Court finds for purposes of the present motions that plaintiffs have established that Mrs. Christie "exploited" her name during her lifetime. The plaintiffs have established that Mrs. Christie assigned rights to her literary works to plaintiff, Agatha Christie Ltd., and also bequeathed similar rights by testamentary disposition. The Court notes that this evidence, when considered together with evidence of contracts entered into by Mrs. Christie for the use of her name during her lifetime in connection with movies and plays based on her books, sufficiently establishes "exploitation." Thus, it seems clear as it pertains to the present motions that her right of publicity survived her death and was properly transferred to the plaintiffs as her heirs and assignees.

However, unlike the *Factors* case, our inquiry here does not end upon this finding that plaintiffs possess valid property rights. Here, the Court is faced with the novel and rather complex question of "[Does] the right of publicity [attach] where the name or likeness is used in connection with a book or movie?" The question is novel in view of the fact that more so than posters, bubble gum cards, or some other such "merchandise," books and movies are vehicles through which ideas and opinions are disseminated and, as such, have enjoyed certain constitutional protections, not generally accorded "merchandise." It is complex because this Court is unaware of any other cases presenting a similar fact pattern or similar constitutional question with respect to this issue of the right of publicity. Thus, in search of guidance to resolve the issue presented herein, the Court has looked to cases involving the right of privacy. While the right of publicity is not statutory, nevertheless both the rights of privacy and of publicity are intertwined due to the similarity between the nature of the interests protected by each. Further, as a result of earlier interpretations of these rights it would appear that judicial interpretations with respect to the limits of the right of privacy could be helpful in determining the limitations, if any, to be placed on the right of publicity.

The New York privacy statute, Civil Rights Law § 51, provides in pertinent part:

> "Any person whose name, portrait or picture is used within this state for advertising purposes or for the purposes of trade without the written consent first obtained . . . may maintain an equitable action. . . ."

In interpreting this provision, the New York State Supreme Court, Appellate Division, has held that: "engrafted upon (the statute are) certain privileged uses or exemptions . . . (*i.e.*) matters of news, history, biography, and other factual subjects of public interest despite the necessary references to the names, portraits, identities, or histories of living persons." *Spahn v. Julian Messner, Inc.*, 23 A.D.2d 216, 219, 260 N.Y.S.2d 451, 453 (1st Dep't 1965) (hereinafter cited as *Spahn*).

This Court finds that the same privileges and exemptions "engrafted" upon the privacy statute are engrafted upon the right of publicity.

In addressing defendants' argument that the book *Agatha* is a biography protected under *Spahn*, this Court, while noting that the affidavit of the author of the book details her investigation with respect to the "facts" surrounding the disappearance, finds the book to be fiction, not biography. Indeed, defendant Ballantine Books' use of the word "novel" on the cover of the book, as well as the notable absence of any cited source or reference material therein, belie its contention that the book is a biography. Moreover, the only "facts" contained in the book appear to be the names of Mrs. Christie, her husband, her daughter, and Ms. Neeley; and that Mrs. Christie disappeared for eleven days. The remainder is mainly conjecture, surmise, and fiction. Accordingly, the Court finds that the defendants in both cases cannot avail themselves of the biography privilege in connection with the book or movie. Further, since the book and the movie treat these few scant facts about the disappearance of Mrs. Christie as mere appendages to the main body of their fictional accounts, neither can be considered privileged as "fair comment" or as "newsworthy" or historical.

Thus, finding none of the *Spahn* privileges available to the defendants herein, the Court must next inquire as to whether the movie or the novel, as fictionalizations, are entitled to any constitutional protection. In so doing, it is noted that other courts, in addressing the scope of First Amendment protections of speech, have engaged in a balancing test between society's interest in the speech for which protection is sought and the societal, commercial or governmental interests seeking to restrain such speech. And unless there appears to be some countervailing legal or policy reason, courts have found the exercise of the right of speech to be protected. Thus, for instance, such a balancing test was employed by the Supreme Court in *New York Times Co. v. Sullivan,* 376 U.S. 254, 84 S. Ct. 710, 11 L. Ed. 2d 686 (1964) with respect to the law of defamation in relation to public figures. There, the Court found that speech, even though false, was protected unless it was shown that it was published "with knowledge that it was false or with reckless disregard of whether it was false or not." *Id.* at 280, 84 S. Ct. at 727. Here, this Court is of the opinion that the interests in the speech sought to be protected, *i.e.*, the movie and the novel, should be protected and that there are no countervailing legal or policy grounds against such protection.

The *Spahn* case, like the book case here, involved the distribution of a book which was presented by the defendant as being a biography of the well-known baseball player Warren Spahn. However, presented in the book were deliberate falsifications of events represented to be true, manufactured dialogue, and erroneous statistical data. Defendant argued that this material was presented in an effort to make the book more attractive to youngsters. Plaintiff sued on the ground that the book constituted a violation of his right of privacy. The New York Court of Appeals agreed, stating:

> "We hold in conformity with our policy of construing sections 50 and 51 so as to fully protect free speech, that, before recovery by a public figure may be had for an unauthorized presentation of his life it must be shown, in addition to the other requirements of the statute, that the presentation is infected with material and substantial falsification . . . or with a reckless disregard for the truth." *Spahn v. Julian Messner, Inc.,* 21 N.Y.2d 124, 127, 286 N.Y.S.2d 832, 834, 233 N.E.2d 840, 842 (1967).
>
> "To hold that this research effort (on the part of the author) entitled the defendants to publish the kind of knowing fictionalization presented here would amount to granting a literary license which is not only unnecessary to the protection of free speech but destructive of an individual's right albeit a limited one in the case of a public figure to be free of the commercial exploitation of his name. . . ." *Id.* at 129.

A case involving Notre Dame and the distribution of a movie entitled *John Goldfarb, Please Come Home* satirized modern-day events, people, and institutions, including a football team, identified as that of Notre Dame. Notre Dame University and its president, Father Hesburg, brought suit against the defendant pursuant to the New York Civil Rights Act and the common law on unfair competition. *Notre Dame v. Twentieth Century–Fox Film Corp.*, 22 A.D.2d 452, 256 N.Y.S.2d 301 (1965). The Appellate Division, in denying the relief requested, stated:

> "Motion pictures, as well as books, are 'a significant medium for the communication of ideas'; their importance 'as an organ of public opinion is not lessened by the fact that they are designed to entertain as well as to inform'; and like books, they are a constitutionally protected form of expression notwithstanding that 'their production, distribution and exhibition is a large-scale business conducted for private profit.'" *Notre Dame,* 22 A.D.2d at 457, 256 N.Y.S.2d at 306.

In applying the holdings of these two cases to those at bar, it would appear that the later-decided *Spahn* case, which curiously did not cite *Notre Dame,* would dictate the result herein. However, upon closer scrutiny of *Spahn,* this Court is of the opinion that the *Spahn* holding should be and was intended to be limited to its facts, and that the result here should follow the holding in the *Notre Dame* case. The Court reaches this conclusion based on the very language of the New York Court of Appeals' decision in *Spahn.* In essence, the Court in *Spahn* stressed the fact that the lower court had found that the defendant had engaged in deliberate falsifications of the circumstances surrounding the life of plaintiff and that such falsifications, which the reader might accept as true, were capable of presenting plaintiff in a false light. *Spahn v. Julian Messner, Inc.*, 18 N.Y.2d 324, 328, 274 N.Y.S.2d 877, 880, 221 N.E.2d 543 (1966). Thus, the Court of Appeals in *Spahn* balanced the plaintiff's privacy rights against the First Amendment protection of fictionalization qua falsification and, after finding there to be no such protection, held for the plaintiff. Conversely, in the *Notre Dame* case, the Appellate Division, as affirmed by the New York Court of Appeals, found that the defendant had not represented the events in the movie to be true and that a viewer of the film would certainly know that the circumstances involved therein were fictitious; thus, the finding for the defendants.

It is clear from the review of these two cases that the absence or presence of deliberate falsifications, or an attempt by a defendant to present the disputed events as true, determines whether the scales in this balancing process shall tip in favor of or against protection of the speech at issue. Since the cases at bar are more factually similar to the *Notre Dame* case, *i.e.,* there were no deliberate falsifications alleged by plaintiffs, and the reader of the novel in the book case by the presence of the word "novel" would know that the work was fictitious, this Court finds that the First Amendment protection usually accorded novels and movies outweighs whatever publicity rights plaintiffs may possess and for this reason their complaints must be dismissed.

The foregoing shall constitute the Court's findings of fact and conclusions of law in accordance with Rule 52(a) Fed. R. Civ. P.

So ordered.

CASE ANALYSIS

1. What is a "right to publicity"?
2. Why does the court cite so many cases in the *Hicks v. Casablanca Records* decision?

Frosch v. Grosset & Dunlap, Inc.

75 A.2d 768, 427 N.Y.2d 828 (1980)

The executor of the estate of Marilyn Monroe brought this action against various defendants as a result of the Norman Mailer book, Marilyn. *The book purported to be a biography, although plaintiff disputed this characterization. The trial court granted summary judgment. The court of appeals affirmed, saying that it did not matter whether the book was truly a biography or not. The right of publicity applied to commercial advertisements for the sale of goods or services. It does not apply to any literary works.*

OPINION

The executor of the estate of the famous film actress Marilyn Monroe sues to recover damages for invasion of the "right of publicity" alleged to adhere in the decedent's name, personality, photographs, etc. Plaintiff claims that this right of publicity is infringed by the publication of a book entitled *Marilyn,* written by defendant Norman Mailer and published by defendant publishers.

The book was written and published some years after the death of Marilyn Monroe. The statutory right of privacy applies to the name, portrait or picture of "any living person"; and it is thus on its face not applicable to the present book. Plaintiff, however, claims that there is an additional property right, a right of publicity which survives the death of Miss Monroe and belongs to the estate. No such non-statutory right has yet been recognized by the New York State courts.

The lower court held that the book here involved is what it purports to be, a biography, and as such did not give rise to a cause of action in favor of the estate for violation of a right of publicity. Plaintiff disputes the characterization of the book as a biography. We think it does not matter whether the book is properly described as a biography, a fictional biography, or any other kind of literary work. It is not for a court to pass on literary categories, or literary judgment. It is enough that the book is a literary work and not simply a disguised commercial advertisement for the sale of goods or services. The protection of the right of free expression is so important that we should not extend any right of publicity, if such exists, to give rise to a cause of action against the publication of a literary work about a deceased person.

The defendant's motion for summary judgment dismissing the complaint is unanimously affirmed.

CASE ANALYSIS

1. Explain the plaintiff's argument.
2. According to the court in this case, does a right of publicity survive the death of Marilyn Monroe? Explain.

Groucho Marx Productions, Inc. v. Day and Night Company

523 F. Supp. 485 (S.D.N.Y. 1981)

Plaintiffs are the heirs and assignees of three Marx brothers, Groucho, Chico, and Harpo. They brought this action alleging that defendants appropriated the right of publicity in their names, by producing a musical play. The court discusses two main issues. First, does the right to publicity exist under New York law? Second, after establishing that the right to publicity did in fact exist, did it descend to the heirs and assignees of the Marx brothers in this case?

OPINION AND ORDER

This action arises out of the production of the musical play *A Day in Hollywood/A Night in the Ukraine* by defendants, Day and Night Company, Inc., Alexander Cohen and the Shubert Organization. (Plaintiffs' claims against the Shubert Organization have now been otherwise resolved.) Plaintiffs, Groucho Marx Productions, Inc. and Susan Marx, as Trustee under the will of Harpo Marx, claim, *inter alia,* that defendants have appropriated their rights of publicity in the names and likenesses of Groucho, Harpo and Chico Marx. In their amended complaint plaintiffs also allege causes of action under Section 43(a) of the Lanham Act, 15 U.S.C. § 1125(a), for misappropriation of proprietary rights, for interference with contractual relations, and for infringement of common law copyright and unfair competition.

Background

Plaintiffs acquired what rights, if any, they have in the Marx Brothers characters in three ways. Plaintiff Susan Marx claims standing as trustee of the residuary trust under the last will and testament of Adolph ("Harpo") Marx.

Plaintiff Marx Productions claims its rights through contractual assignments. On October 2, 1976, Julius ("Groucho") Marx assigned to plaintiff all right, title and interest in the name, likeness and style of the character Groucho, both as an individual and as a member of the Marx Brothers. Subsequently, on June 13, 1979, Marx Productions executed a similar agreement with the estate of Leo ("Chico") Marx by his widow, Mary Marx Fusco. The will of Leo Marx does not expressly devise any intangible rights; Mary Marx Fusco claimed these rights as the residuary beneficiary of the will.

Plaintiffs assert that these rights have been infringed by the play, which originally opened in the New End Theatre in London, England, on January 10, 1979. The play made several other stops before opening on Broadway on May 1, 1980. Plaintiffs take issue with the second half of the play which features performers simulating the unique appearance, style and mannerisms of the Marx Brothers.

The Right of Publicity in New York

Despite burgeoning activity in this area, New York courts have never explicitly recognized a non-statutory right of publicity. *See Brinkley v. Casablancas,* 80 A.D.2d 428, 438 N.Y.S.2d 1004 (1st Dept. 1981). The right of publicity, as defined by other courts, represents the right of an individual to control the commercial value of his name and likeness and to prevent their unauthorized exploitation by others.

See Estate of Elvis Presley v. Russen, 513 F. Supp. 1339, 1353 (D.N.J. 1981). Although the right of publicity developed as an offshoot of the law of privacy, the right differs in that it protects the plaintiff's commercial interests rather than noneconomic interests such as freedom from public embarrassment or scorn.

New York does provide statutory protection against the invasion of privacy of living persons. See N.Y. Civil Rights Law §§ 50 and 51. This statutory right is neither descendible, nor assignable, and applies only to limited situations. Because the present case involves the publicity rights of deceased celebrities, such rights, if they exist, must stem from the common law.

Although no state court has ruled on the issue, several federal courts, including the Second Circuit, have concluded that a right of publicity does exist in New York. *See Factors Etc., Inc. v. Pro Arts, Inc.,* 579 F.2d 215, 220–21 (2d Cir. 1978), cert. denied, 440 U.S. 908, 99 S. Ct. 1215, 59 L. Ed. 2d 455 (1979).

The Second Circuit first considered whether a claim for the commercial infringement of one's likeness is cognizable outside of the privacy statute in *Haelan Laboratories v. Topps Chewing Gum, Inc.,* 202 F.2d 866, cert. denied, 346 U.S. 816, 74 S. Ct. 26, 98 L. Ed. 343 (1953). In *Haelan* the question was whether a contract signed by a ballplayer for the exclusive right to use his photo constituted a release of liability under the privacy statute or an assignment of a property right in his likeness. *Id.* at 867. The court held that the contract was a valid assignment of the right to market the ballplayer's likeness and stated:

> "(w)e think that, in addition to and independent of that right of privacy (which in New York derives from statute), a man has a right in the publicity value of his photograph, . . .
>
> "This right might be called a 'right of publicity.' For it is common knowledge that many prominent persons (especially actors and ballplayers), far from having their feelings bruised through public exposure of their likenesses, would feel sorely deprived if they no longer received money for authorizing advertisements, popularizing their countenances, displayed in newspapers, magazines, busses, trains and subways. This right of publicity would usually yield them no money unless it could be made the subject of an exclusive grant which barred any other advertiser from using their pictures. . . . The right, having been distinguished from a right personal to the individual, is capable of being transferred by him for commercial purposes." *Id.* [at 868.]

Following *Haelan,* other cases decided in this district have recognized a right of publicity under New York law. *See Hicks v. Casablanca Records,* 464 F. Supp. 426 (S.D.N.Y. 1977); *Price v. Hal Roach Studios, Inc.,* 400 F. Supp. 836 (S.D.N.Y. 1975). Moreover, in *Factors Etc., Inc. v. Pro Arts,* 579 F.2d 215 (2d Cir. 1978), cert. denied, 440 U.S. 908, 99 S. Ct. 1215, 59 L. Ed. 2d 455 (1979), the Second Circuit, assuming at the time the applicability of New York law, reaffirmed its conclusion that New York recognizes a right of publicity as a transferable interest. *Id.* at 221.

Given the Second Circuit's clearly stated opinion on this issue, this Court need only examine state cases decided after *Factors* in order to determine whether there is any new indication that those courts disagree with the federal interpretation of New York law.

In two cases decided after *Factors,* the First Department has discussed, but not decided, the issue of the existence of a common law right of publicity. In *Frosch v. Grosset & Dunlap, Inc.,* 75 A.D.2d 768, 427 N.Y.S.2d 828 (1st Dept. 1980), the court considered claims by Marilyn Monroe's estate that a fictional biography published after Ms. Monroe's death infringed her rights of privacy and publicity. The court rejected the privacy claim because the Civil Rights Law applies only to "any living person." As to the right of publicity claim, the court, instead of disposing of it as part of the statutory claim, dismissed on the separate ground that, even if the estate possessed such rights, First Amendment considerations would prevail and would preclude a finding of liability. *Id.* 427 N.Y.S.2d at 829.

The First Department again had occasion to discuss the right of publicity in *Brinkley v. Casablancas,* 80 A.D.2d 428, 438 N.Y.S.2d 1004 (1st Dept., 1981). *Brinkley* involved a suit by a model to enjoin the sale of an unauthorized poster bearing her likeness and to recover damages under the privacy statute. The defendants claimed that the plaintiff's damages were of a commercial nature and thus her claim was not within the ambit of Section 51. The court held that the statutory right of privacy embraces a public figure's commercial interest in the exploitation of his personality. Although the court noted the state and federal cases discussing an independent, non-statutory right of publicity, it decided that those cases were inapposite where the statute covered the activity complained of. The court concluded that "irrespective of whether a separate and distinct common law right of publicity exists" in New York, the privacy statute provides monetary relief for the invasion of commercial value in one's likeness. The decision, therefore, cannot be read as casting doubt on the New York courts' willingness to recognize the commercial value in a name and likeness. Accordingly, this Court finds, in line with other courts in this Circuit, that a suit for infringement of publicity is cognizable under New York law.

The Descendency of the Right

In deciding whether the right of publicity survives death this Court again finds guidance in prior decisions of the Second Circuit. In *Factors Etc., Inc. v. Pro Arts, Inc.,* 579 F.2d 215 (2d Cir. 1978), cert. denied, 440 U.S. 908, 99 S. Ct. 1215, 59 L. Ed. 2d 455 (1979), the Second Circuit, assuming the governance of New York law, considered whether the right of publicity survived Elvis Presley's death. During Presley's lifetime the commercial rights to his likeness were marketed through Boxcar Enterprises, a corporation controlled by Presley and his manager. *Id.* at 217. Two days after Presley's death, these rights were assigned to Factors. The court held that the assigned right of publicity survived Presley's death, reasoning that "[t]he death of Presley, who was merely the beneficiary of an income interest in Boxcar's exclusive right, should not in itself extinguish Boxcar's property right. Instead, the income interest, continually produced from Boxcar's exclusive right of commercial exploitation, should inure to Presley's estate at death like any other intangible property right. To hold that the right did not survive Presley's death, would be to grant competitors of Factors, such as Pro Arts, a windfall in the form of profits from the use of Presley's name and likeness. At the same time, the exclusive right purchased by Factors and the financial benefits accruing to the celebrity's heirs would be rendered virtually worthless." *Id.* at 221.

In reaching its decision in *Factors,* the Second Circuit analyzed another case from this district, *Price v. Hal Roach Studios, Inc.,* 400 F. Supp. 836 (S.D.N.Y. 1975). In *Price* the court applied New York law in determining whether the right to exploit the names and likenesses of Laurel and Hardy survived their deaths. The plaintiff corporation had been assigned the pair's commercial rights by Stan Laurel (during his lifetime), by Oliver Hardy's widow (who claimed her rights as Hardy's sole heir) and by Laurel and Hardy Productions. After the death of both Laurel and Hardy, the plaintiff sued to protect against infringement of its rights by the defendants. The court found that, unlike the situation obtaining with respect to the right of privacy, there is "no logical reason" to terminate the publicity right upon the death of the person protected.

> "Since the theoretical basis for the classic right of privacy, and of the statutory right in New York, is to prevent injury to feelings, death is a logical conclusion to any such claim. In addition, based upon the same theoretical foundation, such a right of privacy is not assignable during life. When determining the scope of the right of publicity, however, one must take into account the purely commercial nature of the protected right. Courts and commentators have done just that in recognizing the right of publicity as assignable. There appears to be no logical reason to terminate this right upon death of the person protected. It is for this reason, presumably, that this publicity right has been deemed a 'property right.'" *Id.* at 844.

In *Factors,* the Second Circuit ruled that the right survived Presley's death because it had been exploited during his lifetime. Although the *Factors* court did not define "exploitation," the term has been interpreted to mean that "a party claiming the right must establish that the decedent acted in such a way as to evidence his or her own recognition of the extrinsic commercial value of his or her name or likeness, and manifested that recognition in some overt manner, *e.g.,* making an *inter vivos* transfer of the rights in the name (*Factors*), or posing for bubble gum cards (*see Haelan Laboratories, Inc. v. Topps Chewing Gum, Inc.,* 202 F.2d 866 (2d Cir.), cert. denied, 346 U.S. 816, 74 S. Ct. 26, 98 L. Ed. 343 (1953))." *Hicks v. Casablanca Records,* 464 F. Supp. 426, 429 (S.D.N.Y. 1978).

In the present case, defendants assert that the Marx Brothers did not exploit their rights of publicity during their lifetimes. Defendants contend that exploitation means commercial use other than the celebrity's main commercial activity. Thus, defendants argue, the inquiry should be directed not to the Marx Brothers' activities as stage, movie, television or night club performers, but to their activities, if any, in product endorsements and the like.

In support of this argument, defendants rely on a case decided by the California Supreme Court, *Lugosi v. Universal Pictures,* 25 Cal. 3d 813, 160 Cal. Rptr. 323, 603 P.2d 425 (1979) (*en banc*). In *Lugosi* the widow and surviving son of actor Bela Lugosi, who played the title role in the 1930 film *Dracula,* brought suit to recover profits made by the defendant movie company in its licensing of the "Count Dracula" character. The Lugosi court broadly held that the right to exploit one's name and likeness is personal and must be exercised, if at all, during the owner's lifetime. 160 Cal. Rptr. at 329, 603 P.2d at 431. The court stated, however, that "Lugosi could have created during his lifetime through the commercial exploitation of his name, face and/or likeness in connection with the operation of any kind of business or the sale of any kind of product or service a general acceptance and good will for such business, product or service among the public, the effect of which would have been to impress such business, product or service with a secondary meaning, protectable under the law of unfair competition. The tie-up of one's name, face and/or likeness with a business, product or service creates a tangible and saleable product in much the same way as property may be created by one who organizes under his name a business to build and/or sell houses according to a fixed plan or who writes a book, paints a picture or creates an invention." *Id.* 160 Cal. Rptr. at 326, 603 P.2d at 428.

Turning to the resolution of the exploitation issue in the present case, there is little question that Julius Marx demonstrated a recognition of and the intent to capitalize on the value of the name and likeness of the character Groucho. Julius Marx made an *inter vivos* transfer of his rights, an action similar to that taken by Elvis Presley. *See Factors,* 579 F.2d at 217. Moreover, Julius Marx also included a testamentary disposition of his rights in his will.

Neither Leo nor Adolph Marx made any *inter vivos* or specific testamentary disposition of their rights. This fact does not end the inquiry, however, since other acts taken by the two comedians may manifest the requisite intent to exploit the commercial value in the names and likenesses of Chico and Harpo Marx.

As a common sense matter, it must be noted that Leo and Adolph Marx, no less than Julius, earned their livelihoods by exploiting the unique characters they created. The Marx Brothers' fame arose as a direct result of their efforts to develop instantly recognizable and popular stage characters, having no relation to their real personalities. Here there can be no question of intent to capitalize on the commercial value of artificial personalities created for entertainment purposes. Every appearance, contract and advertisement involving the Marx Brothers signified recognition by the performers of the commercial value of unique characters they portrayed. To suggest, as defendants do, that the right of publicity was not exploited because the Marx Brothers did not endorse dance studios, candy bars or tee shirts is wholly illogical.

For the foregoing reasons, this Court finds that the Marx Brothers exploited their rights of publicity in their self-created characters and therefore those rights are properly asserted here.

So ordered.

CASE ANALYSIS

1. How did each plaintiff acquire rights of publicity?
2. How did Julius Marx demonstrate an intent to capitalize on the value of the name and likeness of the character Groucho?

State ex. rel. The Elvis Presley International Memorial Foundation v. Crowell

733 S.W.2d 89 (1987)

This case involves a dispute between two nonprofit corporations concerning their respective rights to use Elvis Presley's name as part of their corporate name. Plaintiff was known as the Elvis Presley International Memorial Foundation and defendant was known as the Elvis Presley Memorial Foundation. After the death of Elvis Presley, his estate incorporated Elvis Presley Enterprises, Inc. This corporation monitors and sells the right to the name and likeness of Elvis Presley. In 1981 a group of Presley fans incorporated the Elvis Presley International Memorial Foundation, a nonprofit corporation supporting a trauma center that was part of the Memphis and Shelby County hospital system. Although they had approached the Presley estate for permission to use the Presley name, permission was denied. They incorporated anyway. A few years later, the Presley estate incorporated a different nonprofit corporation called the Elvis Presley Memorial Foundation. Plaintiff sued to dissolve this corporation, claiming that it constituted unfair competition. Defendant corporation claimed that it had the right to use the Presley name under agreement with the Presley estate. Plaintiff claimed, that upon his death, the name of Elvis Presley entered the public domain and that no descendible property right existed. They were therefore free to use the name. The trial court entered summary judgment in favor of defendant. Ultimately, the appellate court concluded that the right to use the Presley name was a property right that was descendible.

OPINION

This appeal involves a dispute between two not-for-profit corporations concerning their respective rights to use Elvis Presley's name as part of their corporate names. The case began when one corporation filed an unfair competition action in the Chancery Court for Davidson County to dissolve the other corporation and to prevent it from using Elvis Presley's name. Elvis Presley's estate intervened on behalf of the defendant corporation. It asserted that it had given the defendant corporation permission to use Elvis Presley's name and that it had not given similar permission to the plaintiff corporation.

The trial court determined that Elvis Presley's right to control his name and image descended to his estate at his death and that the Presley estate had the right to control the commercial exploitation of Elvis Presley's name and image. Thus, the trial court granted the defendant corporation's motion for summary judgment and dismissed the complaint.

The plaintiff corporation has appealed. Its primary assertion is that there is no descendible right of publicity in Tennessee and that Elvis Presley's name and image entered into the public domain when he died. It also asserts that the trial court should not have granted a summary judgment because there are disputed factual issues and that the trial court should not have permitted the corporation representing Elvis Presley's estate to intervene. We concur with the trial court's determination that Elvis Presley's right of publicity is descendible under Tennessee law. However, for the reasons stated herein, we vacate the summary judgment and remand the case for further proceedings.

Issue I

Elvis Presley's career is without parallel in the entertainment industry. From his first hit record in 1954 until his death in 1977, he scaled the heights of fame and success that only a few have attained. His twenty-three-year career as a recording star, concert entertainer and motion picture idol brought him international recognition and a devoted following in all parts of the nation and the world.

Elvis Presley was aware of this recognition and sought to capitalize on it during his lifetime. He and his business advisors entered into agreements granting exclusive commercial licenses throughout the world to use his name and likeness in connection with the marketing and sale of numerous consumer items. As early as 1956, Elvis Presley's name and likeness could be found on bubble gum cards, clothing, jewelry and numerous other items. The sale of Elvis Presley memorabilia has been described as the greatest barrage of merchandise ever aimed at the teenage set. It earned millions of dollars for Elvis Presley, his licensees and business associates.

Elvis Presley's death on August 16, 1977 did not decrease his popularity. If anything it preserved it. Now Elvis Presley is an entertainment legend, somewhat larger than life, whose memory is carefully preserved by his fans, the media and his estate.

The demand for Elvis Presley merchandise was likewise not diminished by his death. The older memorabilia are now collector's items. New consumer items have been authorized and are now being sold. Elvis Presley Enterprises, Inc., a corporation formed by the Presley estate, has licensed seventy-six products bearing his name and likeness and still controls numerous trademark registrations and copyrights. Graceland, Elvis Presley's home in Memphis, is now a museum that attracts approximately 500,000 paying visitors a year. Elvis Presley Enterprises, Inc. also sells the right to use portions of Elvis Presley's filmed or televised performances. These marketing activities presently bring in approximately fifty million dollars each year and provide the Presley estate with approximately $4.6 million in annual revenue. The commercial exploitation of Elvis Presley's name and likeness continues to be a profitable enterprise. It is against this backdrop that this dispute between these two corporations arose.

A group of Elvis Presley fans approached Shelby County officials sometime in 1979 concerning the formation of a group to support a new trauma center that was part of the Memphis and Shelby County hospital system. This group, calling themselves the Elvis Presley International Memorial Foundation, sought a charter as a Tennessee not-for-profit corporation in October, 1980. The Secretary of State denied their application on November 12, 1980 stating that "the name Elvis Presley cannot be used in the charter."

Lawyers representing the group of fans and the Presley estate met to discuss the group's use of Elvis Presley's name following the Secretary of State's rejection of the charter application. In December, 1980, the Presley estate and its trademark counsel formally declined to give the group the unrestricted right to use Elvis Presley's name and likeness. However, the Presley estate offered the group a royalty-free license to use Elvis Presley's name and likeness if the group agreed to abide by eight conditions limiting the group's activities. The group declined the offer of a royalty-free license.

The Presley estate incorporated Elvis Presley Enterprises, Inc. on February 24, 1981. Two days later on February 26, 1981, the Secretary of State, reversing its original decision, granted the fan group's renewed application and issued a corporate charter to the Elvis Presley International Memorial Foundation (International Foundation). The International Foundation raises funds by charging membership fees and dues and by sponsoring an annual banquet in Memphis. It uses its funds to support the trauma center of the new City of Memphis Hospital which was named after Elvis Presley and to provide an annual award of merit.

The Presley estate and Elvis Presley Enterprises, Inc. incorporated the Elvis Presley Memorial Foundation, Inc. (Foundation) as a Tennessee not-for-profit corporation on May 14, 1985. The Foundation is soliciting funds from the public to construct a fountain in the shopping center across the street from Elvis Presley's home.

The International Foundation's heretofore amicable relationship with the Presley estate and Elvis Presley Enterprises, Inc. deteriorated after the formation of the Foundation. On July 17, 1985, the International Foundation filed this action seeking to dissolve the Foundation and to enjoin it from using a deceptively similar name.

Issue II

Elvis Presley's right of publicity

We are dealing in this case with an individual's right to capitalize upon the commercial exploitation of his name and likeness and to prevent others from doing so without his consent. This right, now commonly referred to as the right of publicity, is still evolving and is only now beginning to step out of the shadow of its more well known cousin, the right of privacy.

The confusion between the right of privacy and the right of publicity has caused one court to characterize the state of the law as a "haystack in a hurricane." *Ettore v. Philco Television Broadcasting Corp.*, 229 F.2d 481, 485 (3d Cir. 1956). This confusion will not retard our recognition of the right of publicity because Tennessee's common law tradition, far from being static, continues to grow and to accommodate the emerging needs of modern society. *Powell v. Hartford Accident & Indemnity Co.*, 217 Tenn. 503, 509–10, 398 S.W.2d 727, 730–31 (1966).

A

The right of privacy owes its origin to Samuel Warren's and Louis Brandeis' now famous 1890 law review article. Warren & Brandeis, "The Right to Privacy," 4 Harv. L. Rev. 193 (1890). The authors were concerned with the media's intrusion into the affairs of private citizens and wrote this article to vindicate each individual's "right to be left alone." The privacy interest they sought to protect was far different from a celebrity's interest in controlling and exploiting the economic value of his name and likeness.

Writing in 1890, Warren and Brandeis could not have foreseen today's commercial exploitation of celebrities. They did not anticipate the changes that would be brought about by the growth of the advertising, motion picture, television and radio industries. American culture outgrew their concept of the right of privacy and soon began to push the common law to recognize and protect new and different rights and interests.

It would be difficult for any court today, especially one sitting in Music City U.S.A. practically in the shadow of the Grand Ole Opry, to be unaware of the manner in which celebrities exploit the public's recognition of their name and image. The stores selling Elvis Presley tee shirts, Hank Williams, Jr. bandannas or Barbara Mandrell satin jackets are not selling clothing as much as they are selling the celebrities themselves. We are asked to buy the shortening that makes Loretta Lynn's pie crusts flakier or to buy the same insurance that Tennessee Ernie Ford has or to eat the sausage that Jimmy Dean makes.

There are few everyday activities that have not been touched by celebrity merchandising. This, of course, should come as no surprise. Celebrity endorsements are extremely valuable in the promotion of goods and services. *Carson v. Here's Johnny Portable Toilets, Inc.*, 698 F.2d 831, 834 (6th Cir. 1983). They increase audience appeal and thus make the commodity or service more sellable. *Uhlaender v. Henricksen*, 316 F. Supp. 1277, 1278 (D. Minn. 1970). These endorsements are of great economic value to celebrities and are now economic reality.

The concept of an independent right of publicity did not achieve immediate recognition. Dean Prosser, in his authoritative discussions of the right of privacy, continued to include the right of publicity as one of the four distinct interests protected by the right of privacy. W. Prosser, *Handbook of the Law of Torts* § 97 at 637 & 639 (2d ed. 1955). In his later writings, Prosser characterized the right of publicity as an exclusive right in the individual plaintiff to a species of trade name, his own, and a kind of trade mark in his likeness. It seems quite pointless to dispute over whether such a right is to be classified as "property"; it is at least clearly proprietary in nature. W. Prosser, *Handbook of the Law of Torts* § 117 at 807 (4th ed. 1971). *See also* W. Keeton, Prosser and Keeton on *The Law of Torts* § 117 at 854 (5th ed. 1984).

The legal experts have consistently called for the recognition of the right of publicity as a separate and independent right. In 1977, the United States Supreme Court recognized that the right of publicity was distinct from the right of privacy. *Zacchini v. Scripps-Howard Broadcasting Co.*, 433 U.S. 562, 571–74, 97 S. Ct. 2849, 2855–56, 53 L. Ed. 2d 965 (1977). Now, courts in other jurisdictions uniformly hold that the right of publicity should be considered as a free standing right independent from the right of privacy.

B

The status of Elvis Presley's right of publicity since his death has been the subject of four proceedings in the Federal courts. The conflicting decisions in these cases mirror the difficulty other courts have experienced in dealing with the right of publicity.

The first case originated in Tennessee and involved the sale of pewter statuettes of Elvis Presley without the exclusive licensee's permission. The United States District Court recognized Elvis Presley's independent right of publicity and held that it had descended to the Presley estate under Tennessee law. *Memphis Development Foundation v. Factors Etc., Inc.*, 441 F. Supp. 1323, 1330 (W. D. Tenn. 1977). The United States Court of Appeals for the Sixth Circuit reversed. Apparently without considering Tennessee law, the court held that Tennessee courts would find that the right of publicity would not survive a celebrity's death. *Memphis Development Foundation v. Factors Etc., Inc.*, 616 F.2d 956, 958 (6th Cir.), cert. denied, 449 U.S. 953, 101 S. Ct. 358, 66 L. Ed. 2d 217 (1980).

The courts have recognized the existence of Elvis Presley's right of publicity. The courts also recognized that this right was descendible upon Elvis Presley's death.

C

The appellate courts of this State have had little experience with the right of publicity. The Tennessee Supreme Court has never recognized it as part of our common law or has never undertaken to define its scope. However, the recognition of individual property rights is deeply embedded in our jurisprudence. These rights are recognized in Article I, Section 8 of the Tennessee Constitution and have been called "absolute" by the Tennessee Supreme Court. *Stratton Claimants v. Morris Claimants*, 89 Tenn. 497, 513–14, 15 S.W. 87, 90 (1891). This Court has noted that the right of property "has taken deep root in this country and there is now no substantial dissent from it." *Davis v. Mitchell*, 27 Tenn. App. 182, 234–35, 178 S.W.2d 889, 910 (1943).

The concept of the right of publicity is multi-faceted. It has been described as a bundle of rights or legally protected interests. These rights or interests include: (1) the right of possession, enjoyment and use; (2) the unrestricted right of disposition; and (3) the power of testimonial disposition. *Weiss v. Broadway National Bank,* 204 Tenn. 563, 571, 322 S.W.2d 427, 431 (1959).

Our courts have recognized that a person's "business," a corporate name, a trade name and the good will of a business are species of intangible personal property. *M. M. Newcomer Co. v. Newcomer's New Store,* 142 Tenn. 108, 118–19, 217 S.W. 822, 825 (1919) [trade name].

Tennessee's common law thus embodies an expansive view of property. Unquestionably, a celebrity's right of publicity has value. It can be possessed and used. It can be assigned, and it can be the subject of a contract. Thus, there is ample basis for this Court to conclude that it is a species of intangible personal property.

D

Today there is little dispute that a celebrity's right of publicity has economic value. Courts now agree that while a celebrity is alive, the right of publicity takes on many of the attributes of personal property. It can be possessed and controlled to the exclusion of others. Its economic benefits can be realized and enjoyed. It can also be the subject of a contract and can be assigned to others.

What remains to be decided by the courts in Tennessee is whether a celebrity's right of publicity is descendible at death under Tennessee law. Only the law of this State controls this question. *Hartman v. Duke,* 160 Tenn. 134, 137, 22 S.W.2d 221–22 (1929) and *Jones v. Marable,* 25 Tenn. (6 Humph.) 116, 118 (1845).

We have also concluded that recognizing that the right of publicity is descendible promotes several important policies that are deeply ingrained in Tennessee's jurisprudence. First, it is consistent with our recognition that an individual's right of testamentary distribution is an essential right. If a celebrity's right of publicity is treated as an intangible property right in life, it is no less a property right at death. *See Price v. Hal Roach Studios, Inc.,* 400 F. Supp. 836, 844 (S.D.N.Y. 1975).

Second, it recognizes one of the basic principles of Anglo-American jurisprudence that "one may not reap where another has sown nor gather where another has strewn."

Third, recognizing that the right of publicity is descendible is consistent with a celebrity's expectation that he is creating a valuable capital asset that will benefit his heirs and assigns after his death. It is now common for celebrities to include their interest in the exploitation of their right of publicity in their estate. While a celebrity's expectation that his heirs will benefit from his right of publicity might not, by itself, provide a basis to recognize that the right of publicity is descendible, it does recognize the effort and financial commitment celebrities make in their careers. This investment deserves no less recognition and protection than investments celebrities might make in the stock market or in other tangible assets.

Fourth, concluding that the right of publicity is descendible recognizes the value of the contract rights of persons who have acquired the right to use a celebrity's name and likeness. The value of this interest stems from its duration and its exclusivity. If a celebrity's name and likeness were to enter the public domain at death, the value of any existing contract made while the celebrity was alive would be greatly diminished. *Factors Etc., Inc. v. Pro Arts, Inc.,* 579 F.2d 215, 221 (2d Cir. 1978), cert. denied, 440 U.S. 908, 99 S. Ct. 1215, 59 L. Ed. 2d 455 (1979) and *Martin Luther King, Jr. Center for Social Change, Inc. v. American Heritage Products, Inc.,* 250 Ga. 135, 296 S.E.2d 697, 705 (1982).

Fifth, recognizing that the right of publicity can be descendible will further the public's interest in being free from deception with regard to the sponsorship, approval or certification of goods and services. Falsely claiming that a living celebrity endorses a product or service violates Tenn. Code Ann. § 47-18-104(b)(2), (3), and (5). It should likewise be discouraged after a celebrity has died.

Finally, recognizing that the right of publicity can be descendible is consistent with the policy against unfair competition through the use of deceptively similar corporate names.

The legal literature has consistently argued that the right of publicity should be descendible. A majority of the courts considering this question agree.

The summary judgment granted in favor of Elvis Presley Enterprises, Inc. is vacated and the case is remanded for further proceedings consistent with this opinion. The costs of this appeal are taxed in equal portions to the Elvis Presley International Memorial Foundation and Elvis Presley Enterprises, Inc. and their respective sureties for which execution, if necessary, may issue.

CASE ANALYSIS

1. Is there a descendible right of publicity in Tennessee?
2. Summarize each of the three issues in *State ex rel. The Elvis Presley International Memorial Foundation v. Crowell.*

Featured Web Site: www.courttv.com/people/wills/

The Court TV site offers a good collection of the wills of famous or newsworthy people.

Go Online

1. Browse through the short summaries.
2. Open up the will of someone who interests you.
3. Summarize the will.

Chapter Summary

Wills and trusts are basic estate planning tools. A will is one of the documents an individual may use to provide for the distribution of his or her property upon his or her death. A trust is an instrument or document in which one makes provisions for the disposition of property either during his or her lifetime or after his or her death. Probate is the process by which an heir must prove title to the decedent's property. All of this falls under the broad topic of estate planning. Estate planning is one of many specialty areas of law.

Terms to Remember

witnessed
real property
personal property
testator/testatrix
holographic will
nuncupative will
subscribe
acknowledge
beneficiary
exordium clause
revoke
bequest
devise
general legacy
demonstrative legacy
disinheritance clause
fiduciary
executor/executrix
guardian
trustee
testimonium clause
attestation clause
publish
codicil
intestate succession
decedent
legal title
equitable title
settlor
living trust
probate court
testamentary trust
constructive trust
probate

Questions for Review

1. What is the purpose of a will?
2. What is the purpose of a trust?
3. How do wills and trusts differ?
4. What is intestate succession?
5. What is probate?

Questions for Analysis

1. State the issues presented to the Court in *Groucho Marx Publications, Inc. v. Day and Night Company.*
2. How is the right of publicity different from the right of privacy? (*See* the Elvis Presley case in this chapter.)

Assignments and Projects

1. Write a summary of the *Hicks v. Casablanca Records* case.
2. Reread the Case File at the beginning of the chapter. Assume that you have spoken to Mr. Holmes on the phone and have set an appointment one week from today. Write a letter confirming the appointment and describing documents and information you want him to bring to the appointment.

CHAPTER 10

BUSINESS PRACTICE

CONTRACT LAW AND PROPERTY LAW

Technology Corner

Web Address	Name of Site
www.fedmarket.com/	The Federal Marketplace
www.law.indiana.edu/v-lib/	Virtual Law Library (Browse Topic: Contract Law)
www.catalaw.com/topics/Contract.shtml	CataLaw: Contract and Remedy Law
www.hg.org/commerc.html	Hieros Gamos: Commercial and Contract Law
www.findlaw.com/01topics/07contracts/index.html	FindLaw: Contracts Law
www.hg.org/realest.html	Hieros Gamos: Property Law
www.law.cornell.edu/topics/landlord_tenant.html	LII Landlord-Tenant Law
www.law.emory.edu/LAW/refdesk/subject/prop.html	Emory Law Library: Property & Real Estate Law
www.findlaw.com/01topics/23intellectprop/index.html	FindLaw: Intellectual Property Law
www.uspto.gov/	U.S. Patent and Trademark Office
www.loc.gov/copyright/	U.S. Copyright Office
www.ce9.uscourts.gov/web/sdocuments.nsf/civ	Model Civil Jury Instructions (including infringement)

Case File: The Kersch Matter

Brian Kersch has developed a new computer chip. He believes that this chip will be widely used by computer manufacturers. In fact, he is now negotiating with two large computer companies that want to use his product. He is concerned about several matters. First, he wants to protect his design against "copycats." Second, he needs written agreements with the computer companies detailing their terms. Finally, he needs to either lease or purchase a building for his business.

Sec. 10-1 INTRODUCTION

Not all types of law practice involve court proceedings. In fact, much of the work done by lawyers relates to handling business matters for clients. This might involve incorporating businesses, drafting partnership agreements, and negotiating sales of property or commercial leases. This type of work is often referred to as *transactional work*. One area of law that affects all of these tasks is contract law. Partnership agreements, real estate sales agreements, leases, and licensing agreements are all types of contracts. Contract law, however, is not limited to business matters. It also relates to personal matters. Recall from Chapter 8 that parties contemplating marriage often enter into premarital agreements, and parties going through divorce proceedings may settle their disputes in a marital settlement agreement. Both of these documents are contracts. In the Case File you see how different areas of law often overlap and affect individuals engaged in business. A law firm representing Brian Kersch must deal with issues of contract law, real property law, and intellectual property law. In this chapter you will be introduced to some of the more common concepts of these areas of law. In Chapter 11 you will read about important concepts of the law of business organizations and the law of bankruptcy, both of which play an important role in a business practice.

Sec. 10-2 CONTRACT LAW

Uniform Commercial Code A uniform set of laws dealing with contracts for the sale of goods; adopted by most states.

Laws regarding *contracts*, or agreements between parties, are among the oldest laws that we have. These laws originated and developed through English common law; many of the rules we have today are the same as they were years ago. Today these rules are found in state and federal statutes and cases. However, modern business transactions and practices have required that changes be made in order to address contemporary problems. In particular, there has been a very significant addition to the common law in the area of contracts that deal with the sale of goods. Contracts for the sale of goods are generally regulated by state laws that have been patterned after the **Uniform Commercial Code.** These laws are intended to reflect the way that businesses deal with one another in the marketplace. Furthermore, because the individual states have patterned their laws after the same uniform law, businesses can deal with one another across state lines with relative certainty about the law. The U.C.C. can be found on the Internet at *www.law.cornell.edu/ucc/ucc.table.html.*

Contracts for the sale of goods are not the only types of contracts requiring special legislation. Both the federal government and state governments have enacted laws regulating a number of consumer contracts, especially in areas where fraudulent or abusive practices have occurred. For example, special laws may regulate contracts for extending credit, home solicitation, automated payment, home improvement, and health studios. In spite of special legislative enactments, certain well-established contract principles still exist.

Formation of Contracts

A contract is an agreement between two or more persons that is enforceable by law, usually containing four elements: mutual consent, consideration, capable parties, and legal subject matter.

- **Mutual consent**—The agreement usually arises when one party, the *offeror,* makes an offer to enter into a contract and that offer is accepted in a timely manner by the *offeree.* This agreement can be express or it can be implied by the conduct of the parties.
- **Consideration**—All contracts must be supported by consideration. Loosely translated, this means you cannot get something for nothing. Each party to the contract must give up something. For example, take the most simple contract. A consumer goes into a store to buy an item of merchandise. The consumer gives up money (the purchase price) for the item. The store gives up the item for the money. In many contracts, the consideration for the contract is the *promise* to do something, rather than the act itself. For example, if Mulcahy and Gates agree that Mulcahy will sell his house to Gates for $100,000, and Gates agrees to pay that sum, a contract is created even before the money is paid or the house is transferred. The promises are the consideration and each promise is the consideration for the other promise. Where both parties make promises, the contract is referred to as a **bilateral contract.** When one party makes a promise and the other party does nothing, the result is a gift. A promise to make a gift is normally not an enforceable contract.

bilateral contract
A contract in which both parties have made promises to perform.

- **Capable parties**—In order to be able to enter into a contract, a party must normally be of sound mind and an adult. Lacking a sound mind can be a permanent condition or a temporary one. For example, an individual who is drunk would lack contractual capacity while in that state. Children also generally lack contractual capacity, although there are exceptions to this rule. The age at which a person achieves contractual capacity depends on the age of majority determined by the state. Exceptions to this rule include contracts for the purchase of necessities of life (assuming that the parents were not providing these necessities), and contracts of emancipated minors. Contracts by people who lack contractual capacity are usually *voidable* contracts. A voidable contract is one that is enforceable until the parties lacking capacity, or their representative, act to disaffirm or **rescind** the contract. In some instances, contracts by incapacitated individuals may be *void.* A void contract is one that is never enforceable. Contracts by individuals who have been adjudicated (judged by a court) to be insane or incapacitated are often void.

rescind
To undo a contract, usually when the contract is voidable.

- **Legal subject matter**—No court will enforce a contract between parties where the subject matter of the contract is illegal. For example, if two people enter into a contract to form a partnership to run a gambling hall in a state where gambling is illegal, such a contract would not be enforceable. Sometimes, courts take this further and refuse to enforce contracts that they believe are against public policy. Public policy is a difficult concept to define even by the courts, but it does relate to a public sense of morality. Recall the *Marvin* case in Appendix V.

In addition to an agreement meeting the four basic elements, whether or not a valid and enforceable contract exists can be affected by other legal principles. Some of the more common of these follow.

Statute of Frauds

Statute of Frauds
A law based on English common law requiring certain types of contracts to be evidenced by a writing.

Unless some special rule exists, contracts need not be in writing to be enforceable. One such rule, which stems from English common law, is known as the **Statute of Frauds.** This rule lists several types of contracts that must be evidenced by something in writing. These include contracts that cannot be performed within one year, contracts for the sale of real property, contracts in contemplation of marriage, and contracts that cannot be performed within the lifetime of the promisor. While the Statute of Frauds requires that these contracts be evidenced by a writing, it does not require a formal written contract signed by both parties. The Statute of Frauds requires a written memorandum of the essential terms signed by the party to be charged. (The party to be charged would be the defendant in any lawsuit, that is, the party who is claimed to have breached the contract.) A written memorandum can consist of any type of writing (handwritten or printed). It can be a letter or a note. It must contain a sufficient description of the agreement so that a court could enforce it. Finally, it need not be signed by both parties, only the party to be charged.

A POINT TO REMEMBER

In adopting the English common-law Statute of Frauds, state legislatures may have changed the types of contracts included or the details of any writings required. It is important that you check your state law to see how the Statute of Frauds applies in your state.

Special Legislative Requirements

Both federal and state laws regulate certain types of contracts, often dealing with consumer rights. These laws usually require that the contract be in writing and, unlike the Statute of Frauds, contain very specific requirements for the writing. A memorandum containing the essential terms will not meet these requirements. Additionally, these statutes frequently give the consumer a right to rescind or reject the contract within a certain time frame (usually three days).

Parol Evidence Rule

parol evidence rule
A rule of contract law stating that when parties have put their agreement in writing, evidence of prior or contemporaneous statements regarding the agreement are not admissible if a dispute arises and the parties go to trial.

At times, parties agree that a contract was formed but disagree about the terms of that agreement. The **parol evidence rule** limits the types of evidence that can be used to prove the terms of the agreement. This rule provides that if the parties have a written agreement that is intended to be a complete expression of their agreement, then written or oral evidence of prior or contemporaneous agreements is not admissible evidence. Evidence of subsequent changes to the agreement is admissible. In part, this rule exists to give certainty to written agreements and to eliminate some of the complications that could arise where there has been a great deal of negotiation and changes in terms prior to the agreement. In order to make certain that the parol evidence rule will apply, many contracts contain a provision stating that "this contract is intended to be a full and complete statement of the agreement of the parties." This type of clause is referred to as an **integration clause.**

integration clause
A clause in a contract that indicates that the contract is meant to embody all of the terms of the parties' agreement.

quasi contract
A contract imposed by law; a transaction that will be treated as a valid contract even though one or more elements may be missing, because it is the equitable thing to do.

Quasi Contract

Quasi contract is a legal doctrine that allows the court to treat a certain situation as if a contract exists, even where one of the elements to the formation of the contract may be missing (usually the mutual assent). This is based on an equitable principle that under the circumstances the contract should exist because if it does not, one party will unjustly benefit or be "unjustly enriched." For example, suppose Summers purchases a television set from Evans Electronics and Evans is to deliver the television. When it is delivered, the store makes a mistake and leaves it with Summers's neighbor, Yardly. When the error is discovered, Yardly refuses to allow the store to pick up the television. Even though Yardly never agreed to pay for the set, the law will treat this situation as if a contract does exist and require Yardly to pay for the television if he wants to keep it. In this situation, it is important that the television set was delivered in error. If a merchant intentionally sends unsolicited merchandise to a consumer, the consumer will probably not be required to pay for it. State law may even give consumers the right not to return the merchandise but allow them to keep it without requiring any payment.

Promissory Estoppel/Detrimental Reliance

As mentioned earlier, a promise to make a gift does not normally create an enforceable promise or a contract. As with most legal principles, however, exceptions exist. Suppose, for example, that Byers, a noted philanthropist, promises to donate $1 million to the Centerville Paralegal School for a computer laboratory to be named in honor of his mother. He sends a check for $100,000, promising the remainder in 60 days. In reliance on this promise, the school signs a binding contract with a general contractor to begin construction. The cost of the project will be $1 million. After work has begun, Byers notifies the school that he will not donate any more than the $100,000 already given. Because the school has justifiably relied on the promise to its detriment, the promisor may be estopped from reneging on the promise to make a gift. The promise may be enforceable. This concept is known as either *promissory estoppel* or *detrimental reliance.*

A POINT TO REMEMBER

To determine whether a valid enforceable contract exists, check state statutes and case law. Because different types of contracts are governed by different laws, you must first identify the type of contract involved so that you check the appropriate law.

Performance of Contracts

Breach of Contract

breach of contract
The failure of one party to a contract to perform his or her obligations under the contract.

specific performance
A court order requiring one party to fulfill his or her obligations under a contract.

Once an enforceable contract has been created, each party to the contract is obligated to perform something. The performance may include such tasks as delivery or sale of merchandise, performance of work, or payment of money. When parties fail to perform their promises or fail to perform them in a satisfactory manner, then a **breach of contract** has occurred. When a breach occurs, the nonbreaching party has various remedies. The most common remedy is money damages to compensate for any loss sustained. In addition to money damages, the nonbreaching party might also seek a court order requiring the breaching party to perform his or her promise. Such a remedy is known as **specific performance.** For example, suppose Delia and Young enter into a contract in which Delia agrees to sell to Young a home, and Young agrees to buy the home for a purchase price of $100,000. When the transfer is to take place, Delia backs out and refuses to sell the home. At the time when performance was to take place, assume that the value of the house had increased to $105,000. Young has various remedies. Young can claim money damages for the loss. This would include the difference between the contract price and the fair market value at the time the home was to be transferred—in this case, $5,000. There might also be other incidental damages or losses. Young has another remedy, however. Young could seek a court order requiring Delia to sell the home under the agreed-upon terms.

The Uniform Commercial Code

A special problem regarding nonperformance or unsatisfactory performance arises under contracts that are regulated by the Uniform Commercial Code (U.C.C.). Under the U.C.C., contracts for the sale of goods often contain an implied promise that the goods are of a certain quality. This is known as an *implied warranty of merchantability.* Contracts for the sale of goods also are subject to an implied warranty or promise that the goods are suitable for the purpose for which they are bought. This is known as the *implied warranty of fitness for use.* Since these are implied warranties, they are not stated in the contract. Nevertheless, if the implied promise applies, a party may seek damages where the goods do not meet a certain standard of quality. The case of *Keith v. Buchannan,* which follows, illustrates some of these concepts.

Unenforceable Contracts

restitution
To make restitution is to return consideration that was given.

Sometimes, when parties fail to perform promises under a contract, they fail to do so because they claim that the contract is not enforceable or is voidable. For example, suppose Clark and Dreyer agree that Dreyer will purchase Clark's stereo for $1,000, and Dreyer gives Clark a $100 down payment. Dreyer, however, is sixteen years old. Dreyer then refuses to go through with the sale and wants the $100 back. If Dreyer were an adult, Dreyer would be held to the promise that was made. Dreyer would be obligated to purchase the stereo for the agreed-upon price or would be liable for damages. Because Dreyer is a minor, however, Dreyer has the right to disaffirm the contract and to be reimbursed for any amounts already paid. To disaffirm the contract, Dreyer could rescind the contract. To recover the down payment, Dreyer would have the remedy known as **restitution.**

Keith v. Buchannan

173 Cal. App. 3d 13, 220 Cal. Rptr. 392 (1985)

This is an action based on breach of express and implied warranties arising out of the purchase of a yacht by plaintiff. Plaintiff purchased a boat intended to be used for long distances on the ocean. In purchasing the vessel, plaintiff stated that he relied on representations made by the sales representative and representations contained in printed literature that the boat would be seaworthy for such use. Plaintiff also had a friend who was involved in a boat-building enterprise inspect the vessel before it was purchased. The trial court found that the written statements in the brochure were opinions and therefore no express warranty was created. It also found that no implied warranty of fitness was created because plaintiff relied on his own experts.

The appellate court discusses the law of express and implied warranties as found in the Uniform Commercial Code (as adopted in California). Under the U.C.C., express warranties are created by any affirmation of fact relating to the goods that becomes part of the basis of the bargain and any description of the goods that is made part of the basis of the bargain. The court finds that statements found in a brochure can create express warranties. In this case, the vessel purchased was described in the brochure as a "picture of sure-footed seaworthiness" and a "carefully well-equipped and very seaworthy vessel." Furthermore, seller was aware that appellant was looking for a vessel sufficient for long-distance oceangoing cruises. The statements were statements of fact. The court also discussed what the "part of the basis of the bargain" test means. The court stated that a buyer need not show that he would not have entered into the agreement without the warranty or even that it was a dominant factor. It only needs to be part of the basis or merely a factor or consideration inducing the buyer to enter into the bargain. The facts in this case indicate that it was a factor.

As to the issue of implied warranty of fitness, the court points out that the main issue is whether the buyer relies on the skill and judgment of the seller. In this case, the buyer relied on his own expert. The trial court's judgment regarding express warranty was reversed. The finding on implied warranty was affirmed. The following is an excerpt from the court's actual opinion.

OPINION

This breach of warranty case is before this court after the trial court granted defendants' motion for judgment at the close of plaintiff's case during the trial proceedings.

Statement of Facts

Plaintiff, Brian Keith, purchased a sailboat from defendants in November 1978 for a total purchase price of $75,610. Even though plaintiff belonged to the Waikiki Yacht Club, had attended a sailing school, had joined the Coast Guard Auxiliary, and had sailed on many yachts in order to ascertain his preferences, he had not previously owned a yacht. He attended a boat show in Long Beach during October 1978 and looked at a number of boats, speaking to sales representatives and obtaining advertising literature. In the literature, the sailboat which is the subject of this action, called an "Island Trader 41," was described as a seaworthy vessel. In one sales brochure, this vessel is described as "a picture of sure-footed seaworthiness." In another, it is called "a carefully well-equipped, and very seaworthy live-aboard vessel." Plaintiff testified he relied on representation in the sales brochures in regard to the purchase. Plaintiff and a sales representative also discussed plaintiff's desire for a boat which was ocean-going and would cruise long distances.

Plaintiff asked his friend, Buddy Ebsen, who was involved in a boat-building enterprise, to inspect the boat. Mr. Ebsen and one of his associates, both of whom had extensive experience with sailboats, observed the boat and advised plaintiff that the vessel would suit his stated needs. A deposit was paid on the boat, a purchase contract was entered into, and optional accessories for the boat were ordered. After delivery of the vessel, a dispute arose in regard to its seaworthiness.

Plaintiff filed the instant lawsuit alleging causes of action in breach of express warranty and breach of implied warranty. The [trial] court found that no express warranty was established by the evidence. It found that the written statements produced at trial were opinions or commendation of the vessel. The court further found that no implied warranty of fitness was created because the plaintiff did not rely on the skill and judgment of defendants to select and furnish a suitable vessel, but had rather relied on his own experts in selecting the vessel.

DISCUSSION

I. Express Warranty

California Uniform Commercial Code section 2313 provides that express warranties are created by (1) any affirmation of fact or promise made by the seller to the buyer which relates to the goods and becomes part of the basis of the bargain, and (2) any description of the goods which is made part of the basis of the bargain. Formal words such as "warranty" or "guarantee" are not required to make a warranty, but the seller's affirmation of the value of the goods or an expression of opinion or commendation of the goods does not create an express warranty.

California Uniform Commercial Code section 2313, regarding express warranties, was enacted in 1963 and consists of the official text of Uniform Commercial Code section 2313 without change. In deciding whether a statement made by a seller constitutes an express warranty under this provision, the court must deal with three fundamental issues. First, the court must determine whether the seller's statement constitutes an "affirmation of fact or promise" or "description of the goods" under California Uniform Commercial Code section 2313, subdivision (1)(a) or (b) or whether it is rather "merely the seller's opinion or commendation of the goods" under section 2313, subdivision (2). Second, assuming the court finds the language used susceptible to creation of a warranty, it must then be determined whether the statement was "part of the basis of the bargain." Third, the court must determine whether the warranty was breached.

A warranty relates to the title, character, quality, identity, or condition of the goods. The purpose of the law of warranty is to determine what it is that the seller has in essence agreed to sell.

A. Affirmation of Fact, Promise or Description versus Statement of Opinion, Commendation or Value

The determination as to whether a particular statement is an expression of opinion or an affirmation of a fact is often difficult, and frequently is dependent upon the facts and circumstances existing at the time the statement is made. Recent decisions have evidenced a trend toward narrowing the scope of representations which are considered opinion, sometimes referred to as "puffing" or "sales talk," resulting in an expansion of the liability that flows from broad statements of manufacturers or retailers as to the quality of their products. Courts have liberally construed affirmations of quality made by sellers in favor of injured consumers.

Statements made by a seller during the course of negotiation over a contract are presumptively affirmations of fact unless it can be demonstrated that the buyer could only have reasonably considered the statement as a statement of the seller's opinion. Several factors tend to indicate an opinion statement. These are (1) a lack of specificity in the statement made, (2) a statement that is made in an equivocal manner, or (3) a statement which reveals that the goods are experimental in nature.

It is clear that statements made by a manufacturer or retailer in an advertising brochure which is disseminated to the consuming public in order to induce sales can create express warranties. In the instant case, the vessel purchased was described in a sales brochure as "a picture of sure-footed seaworthiness" and "a carefully well-equipped and very seaworthy vessel." The seller's representative was aware that appellant was looking for a vessel sufficient for long-distance ocean-going cruises. The statements in the brochure are specific and unequivocal in asserting that the vessel is seaworthy. Nothing in the negotiation indicates that the vessel is experimental in nature. The representations regarding seaworthiness made in sales brochures regarding the Island Trader 41 were affirmations of fact relating to the quality or condition of the vessel.

B. "Part of the Basis of the Bargain" Test

Under former provisions of the law, a purchaser was required to prove that he or she acted in reliance upon representations made by the seller. California Uniform Commercial Code section 2313 indicates only that the seller's statement must become "part of the basis of the bargain." According to official comment 3 to this Uniform Commercial Code provision, "no particular reliance need be shown in order to weave [the seller's affirmations of fact] into the fabric of the agreement. Rather, any fact, which is to take such affirmations, once made, out of the agreement requires clear affirmative proof."

A buyer need not show that he would not have entered into the agreement absent the warranty or even that it was a dominant factor inducing the agreement. The representation need only be part of the basis of the bargain, or merely a factor or consideration inducing the buyer to enter into the bargain.

Where a buyer inspects the goods before purchase, he may be deemed to have waived the seller's express warranties. But, an examination or inspection by the buyer of the goods does not necessarily discharge the seller from an express warranty if the defect was not actually discovered and waived.

Appellant's inspection of the boat by his own experts does not constitute a waiver of the express warranty of seaworthiness. Prior to the making of the contract, appellant had experienced boat builders observe the boat, but there was no testing of the vessel in the water. Such a warranty (seaworthiness) necessarily relates to the time when the vessel has been put to sea and has been shown to be reasonably fit and adequate in material, construction, and equipment for its intended purposes.

In this case, appellant was aware of the representations regarding seaworthiness by the seller prior to contracting.

He also had expressed to the seller's representative his desire for a long-distance ocean-going vessel. Although he had other experts inspect the vessel, the inspection was limited and would not have indicated whether or not the vessel was seaworthy. It is clear that the seller has not overcome the presumption that the representations regarding seaworthiness were part of the basis of this bargain.

II. Implied Warranty

Appellant also claimed breach of the implied warranty of fitness for a particular purpose in regard to the sale of the subject vessel. An implied warranty of fitness for a particular purpose arises when "seller at the time of contracting has reason to know any particular purpose for which the goods are required and that the buyer is relying on the seller's skill or judgment to select or furnish suitable goods," which are fit for such purpose. An implied warranty of fitness for a particular purpose arises only where (1) the purchaser at the time of contracting intends to use the goods for a particular purpose, (2) the seller at the time of contracting has reason to know of this particular purpose, (3) the buyer relies on the seller's skill or judgment to select or furnish goods suitable for the particular purpose, and (4) the seller at the time of contracting has reason to know that the buyer is relying on such skill and judgment.

The reliance elements are important to the consideration of whether an implied warranty of fitness for a particular purpose exists. The major question in determining the existence of an implied warranty of fitness for a particular purpose is the reliance by the buyer upon the skill and judgment of the seller to select an article suitable for his needs.

The trial court found that the plaintiff did not rely on the skill and judgment of the defendants to select a suitable vessel, but that he rather relied on his own experts. A review of the record reveals ample evidence to support the trial court's finding. Appellant had extensive experience with sailboats at the time of the subject purchase. He looked at a number of different vessels, reviewed their advertising literature, and focused on the Island Trader 41 as the object of his intended purchase. He also had friends look at the boat before making the final decision to purchase. The trial court's finding that the buyer did not rely on the skill or judgment of the seller in the selection of the vessel in question is supported by substantial evidence.

The trial court's judgment that no express warranty existed in this matter is reversed. The trial court's judgment is affirmed in all other respects.

CASE ANALYSIS

1. Why does this case depend on the Uniform Commercial Code and not general contract law?
2. Does a careful shopper risk the loss of warranties?
3. What is the difference between an express warranty and an implied warranty?

arbitration
An out-of-court hearing before a neutral party who listens to two or more disputing parties and renders a decision resolving the dispute.

Traditionally, remedies relating to nonperformance of a contract have been sought by filing an appropriate lawsuit in court. However, more and more, parties are choosing to reject court proceedings in favor of **arbitration.** If both parties to a contract agree, any dispute can be resolved through an arbitration proceeding rather than a court proceeding. In fact, many contracts contain provisions that in the event of a dispute, the contract will be settled through an arbitration proceeding. Arbitration is discussed in more detail in Chapter 15. However, briefly, arbitration involves an out-of-court hearing before a neutral third party selected by the disputing parties. The neutral third party, known as an *arbitrator,* listens to both sides and makes a decision. In contract arbitration hearings, the decision is usually binding.

Assignment of Contract Rights

assignment
The transfer of one's rights under a contract.

assignor
The person who makes a transfer or assignment of rights under a contract.

assignee
The person to whom a transfer or assignment is made.

Occasionally after parties enter into a contract, they want to transfer their rights or obligations under the contract. A transfer of one's rights under a contract is known as an **assignment.** Consider the following situation. Suppose Reese sells an automobile to Noonan for $5,000 with an agreement that Noonan will pay Reese the sum of $500 per month until paid in full. Noonan fails to make three payments and Reese turns the matter over to a collection agency. In this case an assignment has been made. Reese, the **assignor,** has *assigned* or transferred the right to receive payment to the collection agency, the **assignee.** Once Noonan is informed of this assignment, Noonan is obligated to make payment to the collection agency. A common example of an assignment is the situation in which a party to a contract has not been paid money due him or her under the contract and then turns the matter over to a collection agency.

delegation
The transfer of obligations under a contract.

Occasionally, a party to a contract attempts to transfer his or her obligations under a contract. This is known as a **delegation** of duties. For example, suppose that in the situation between Reese and Noonan, Noonan is owed $5,000 by Jeffers, and Noonan instructs Jeffers to pay the money to Reese. In such a case, Noonan has delegated the obligation to pay to Jeffers. Generally, the law allows parties to delegate their duties subject to certain restrictions. First, parties cannot delegate duties under contracts that call for their personal services if the transfer would change the basic agreement of the parties. For example, if a party hired a noted artist to do a portrait, that artist could not delegate the duty to paint the portrait to another painter. This would greatly change the original agreement. Also, even if obligations or duties are delegated, the original promisor remains liable under the original contract unless specifically released from liability by the other party.

SEC. 10-3 REAL PROPERTY LAW

In business transactions, many situations involve both contract law and real property law. For example, if a transfer of real property is to take place, the parties usually execute a document called a *contract of sale* in which they set out the terms and conditions of the transfer. In landlord/tenant law, an important area of real property law, leases and rental agreements involve both contract and real property issues. Like contract law, real property law has its origins in early English common law. Today, the law is found in state statutes or codes and case law. Property is classified as real property or personal property. **Real property** is land and anything that is permanently attached to or growing on the land. *Personal property* is property that is movable. For example, a tree is considered real property while it is growing in the ground. However, if it is cut down, it becomes movable and thus becomes personal property.

real property
Land, including anything affixed to the land or growing upon the land.

Real property law, as the name suggests, deals with issues surrounding real property, such as ownership of real estate and transfer of ownership and nonownership interests in land. It can also deal with such issues as zoning and use. An important area of real property law deals with the landlord/tenant relationship.

OWNERSHIP INTERESTS IN REAL PROPERTY

fee simple
Outright ownership of land.

life estate
The right to use real property for the term of someone's life.

An outright ownership of a parcel of real estate is known as ownership in **fee simple.** An ownership in fee simple allows the owner complete power over the property and is the most common type of ownership. A lesser ownership interest is a **life estate.** A life estate gives the holder the right to use the property during the lifetime of the holder or some other individual. Sometimes this is used as an estate-planning device. Ownership of real estate is fairly simple where only one person holds title. Where more than one has an ownership interest, then other legal issues develop. Many of these legal issues are determined by the way in which the owners hold title to the property. The most common ways of holding title are as joint tenants, as tenants in common, and, in community property states, as community property. In each of these forms of joint ownership, the joint owners have an *undivided interest* in the real estate. This means that they all have a say in how the entire piece of property is to be used and they all have equal rights to possess all of the property.

joint tenancy
Co-ownership of property characterized by a right of survivorship.

tenants in common
A term that describes co-ownership of property carrying no right of survivorship.

community property
Property owned jointly by married persons; not all states recognize community property.

deed
A document that evidences title to real property; it is also used to convey property.

The key feature of **joint tenancy** is the right of survivorship. That is, if one of the joint tenants dies, the remaining joint tenant or tenants inherit the property. Generally, this cannot be changed by a will. With **tenants in common,** no right of survivorship exists; if one tenant in common dies, the property passes to the tenant's heirs. **Community property** is a method of holding property between spouses in a community property state. Although one spouse is free to leave his or her share of the property to anyone in a will, if no will exists, the surviving spouse will inherit. In addition to these differences, the manner of holding title to real estate may affect the tax basis of the property should one tenant die.

Regardless of how title is held to real property, title is usually manifested by a **deed,** which is a document that describes the property and lists the owners. The description found in a deed is called the *legal description* of the property and might look something like the following:

> LOT 182, TRACT NO. 6215 THE RIOS RANCH UNIT NO. 2, FILED AUGUST 1, 1986 IN BOOK 467 OF MAPS, AT PAGE(S) 9, 10, AND 11, SANTA CLARA COUNTY RECORDS.

This deed is *recorded,* usually in the county where the property is located. When recorded, the deed puts everyone on notice regarding ownership of the property, gives protection to the listed owners, and prevents an original owner from conveying property more than once. If title to real estate is ever in dispute, the court will look to the recorded deeds to see who was the earliest to record. While this does not always determine ownership, it is important evidence.

Transfer of Ownership

warranty deed
A type of deed used in some states that implies certain representations regarding title.

grant deed
A type of deed used in some states that implies certain representations regarding title.

quitclaim deed
A deed that implies no representations or warranties regarding title.

easement
The right to a limited use of a portion of another's property.

Deeds do more than just indicate who owns a parcel of property. They are also the documents used to accomplish a legal transfer of property. Different kinds of deeds can be used, each one carrying with it different implied warranties regarding the title conveyed. Not all types of deeds are used in all states. The most common types of deeds are warranty deeds, grant deeds, and quitclaim deeds. In a **warranty deed,** the grantor guarantees title to the property. In a **grant deed,** the grantor represents that he or she has not previously transferred the property. In a **quitclaim deed,** the grantor makes no representation regarding title.

While transfer of property is accomplished by signing and delivering a deed to the buyer or grantee, in order to protect the new owner the deed should be recorded to create a public record reflecting the transfer of ownership. Title companies search this record when checking a piece of property.

Non-Ownership Interests in Real Property

Not all interests in real property involve ownership. A person may have the right to use property that is owned by another, a right referred to as an **easement.** For example, if Morgan owns property that can only be accessed by passing over property owned by Sanchez, Morgan probably has the right to travel across Sanchez's property. Morgan has a limited right to use Sanchez's property. Other examples of easements are the utility or cable lines that run across property. The utility and cable companies have the right to use someone else's property for their equipment.

mortgage
An encumbrance against real property.

A second type of non-ownership interest is a lien or **mortgage.** A lien or mortgage secures a debt owed to a person by a landowner. As long as the property owner pays the debt, the creditor has no claim to the property. However, if the debtor/landowner fails to pay the debt, the creditor can eventually have the property sold and the debt paid from the proceeds of the property. This is known as **foreclosure.** In some states, a lien is evidenced by a recorded document known as a **deed of trust.** However evidenced, notice of the lien or mortgage must be recorded to protect the creditor should the landowner decide to sell the property or borrow more money against the property. Often a landowner will owe several debts that are secured by the property. In such cases, the creditors have priority according to the dates their liens were recorded.

foreclosure
A legal proceeding involving the sale of encumbered or mortgaged property when the owner fails to pay the debt.

deed of trust
A document that evidences a debt secured by real property.

tenancy
The right to use another's property for a limited time.

A third type of non-ownership interest in real property is a **tenancy.** A tenancy creates the right of an individual (the *tenant*) to occupy premises owned by another (the *landlord*) for a period of time. This type of interest is regulated by an area of real estate law known as landlord/tenant law. Since a large portion of society rents or leases property, either for personal use or business use, this important area of law is practiced by many lawyers.

Landlord/Tenant Law

One of the most important areas of real estate law is the law that governs the relationship between landlords and tenants. Tenants have the right to occupy premises owned by the landlord under an agreement that they have. This agreement can give the tenant the right to occupy the premises for an indefinite amount of time. In such a case, the tenancy is usually referred to as a *month-to-month tenancy.* Normally this type of tenancy continues until either party gives the other thirty days' notice that he or she intends to terminate the tenancy. Such a tenancy agreement need not be in writing, but, of course, many problems are avoided if it is. This type of agreement is referred to as a *rental agreement.* Rather than being for an indefinite time, a rental agreement can be for a specified amount of time. Such an agreement is often referred to as a **lease.** Whether a lease must be in writing depends on state law and usually depends on the length of time of the lease. Under the English common-law Statute of Frauds, leases for more than one year had to be in writing; those for under a year could be oral.

lease
An agreement between an owner of property and another in which the owner of the property gives the other person the right to use the property for a set period of time.

At common law, the parties were free to determine the terms of their rental agreements, especially those specifying rent. Today, these terms may be subject to local rent control ordinances. Additionally, the right to rent or lease premises is often controlled by laws that prohibit any type of discrimination in the selection of the tenant.

The termination of the tenancy arrangement sometimes leads to serious legal problems, especially when one party wishes to end the tenancy relationship and the other does not. Before either side decides it wants to end the tenancy, that party must consult the rental agreement or lease. If one side acts to end the relationship contrary to the provisions of the agreement, it has breached the contract and is liable for damages. Landlords must be particularly careful if they want to evict a tenant. They cannot use "self-help." Changing locks on doors or moving out a tenant's belongings will subject the landlord to severe penalties. If a tenant fails to move out of the premises voluntarily, the landlord must file a lawsuit in court, sometimes called an **unlawful detainer** action, in order to evict the tenant.

unlawful detainer
A lawsuit to evict a tenant.

ETHICAL CHOICES

A friend of yours, who is a paralegal, has asked you to come and work with her. She owns and operates Paralegal Eviction Services, a company that helps landlords evict tenants. The firm employs no attorneys. You do not enjoy your present job in a law office and would like to find another job. Your friend has even offered you a partnership interest in the business. What should you do?

SEC. 10-4 INTELLECTUAL PROPERTY LAW

intellectual property
Property rights in the result of one's thoughts, ideas or inventions; includes patents, copyrights, and trademarks.

infringement
Improper interference in the intellectual property rights of another.

A type of property having great importance in today's commercial environment is intellectual property. **Intellectual property** consists of the *result* of one's thoughts, ideas or inventions. It is not the thought or idea itself, but the result, such as a book or a computer chip. Intellectual property law deals with obtaining protection for one's work, licensing others to use one's work, and enforcing one's rights. Obtaining protection for intellectual property often includes registration with the proper government agency. Licensing one's work involves negotiating and drafting contracts. Enforcing one's rights often means filing a lawsuit known as an **infringement** action. Intellectual property law includes the law that relates to copyrights, patents, trademarks, and trade names.

COPYRIGHT LAW

Copyright Protection

Copyright is a method of protecting "original works of authorship" against misappropriation. Types of materials that can be copyrighted include literary, dramatic, musical, artistic, and certain other intellectual works. Included in literary material is computer software. Included in dramatic works are movies and plays. Included in musical works are records, tapes, and compact discs. Copyright protection is available to both published and unpublished works. The laws governing copyrights are federal and are found in Title 17 of the United States Code (known as the 1976 Copyright Act). In general the owner of copyright has the exclusive right to the work. The Copyright Act gives the author of the work the exclusive right to do and to authorize others to do the following:

- *To reproduce the work*
- *To prepare derivative works based upon the work*
- *To distribute copies of the work* to the public by sale or other transfer of ownership, or by rental, lease, or lending

- *To perform the work publicly,* in the case of literary, musical, dramatic, and choreographic works; pantomimes; and motion pictures and other audiovisual works
- *To display the copyrighted work publicly,* in the case of literary, musical, dramatic, and choreographic works; pantomimes; and pictorial, graphic, or sculptural works, including the individual images of a motion picture or other audiovisual work
- *In the case of sound recordings, to perform the work publicly* by means of a digital audio transmission.

A party who interferes with the author's rights to copyrighted material can be sued. It is important to note that there is no copyright violation unless a work is actually copied. If a similar work is independently created, there is no copyright violation.

There are also several exceptions or limitations to these rights. One major limitation is the doctrine of "fair use." Fair use allows others to use the work for purposes such as criticism, comment, news reporting, teaching, scholarship, or research. Another exception is the right to resell a work that has been purchased. For example, you are allowed to resell your textbooks at the end of the course. However, you are not allowed to copy the textbook and sell a copy to another person.

Claiming a Copyright

Copyright protection exists from the time the work is created in a fixed or permanent form and *immediately* becomes the property of the author who created the work. Only the author or those receiving rights through the author can rightfully claim copyright. This rule does not apply to works created by an employee in the scope of employment. In such a case, the work is referred to as "a work made for hire"; the employer, not the employee, is entitled to claim the copyright.

What Is Not Protected

Types of work that are generally not eligible for federal copyright protection include the following:

- Works that have *not* been fixed in a tangible form of expression (for example, improvisational speeches or performances that have not been written or recorded)
- Titles, names, short phrases, and slogans; familiar symbols or designs; mere variations of typographic ornamentation, lettering, or coloring; mere listings of ingredients or contents
- Ideas, procedures, methods, systems, processes, concepts, principles, discoveries, or devices, as distinguished from a description, explanation, or illustration
- Works consisting *entirely* of information that is common property and containing no original authorship (for example: standard calendars, height and weight charts, tape measures and rulers, and lists or tables taken from public documents or other common sources)

License

The holder of a copyright has the right to allow another to use the copyrighted material. This right is usually conveyed through a contract. One such type of agreement is a *license agreement,* which gives the non-author the right to use the product. Most often limitations are placed on how the product can be used. License agreements are common with software. When an individual purchases a piece of software, the accompanying license agreement allows the purchaser to use the software on limited computers. Allowing friends to load software on their computers is a copyright violation. It is no different than purchasing a book and making copies of the book for your friends.

Obtaining a Copyright

A copyright automatically exists when the work is first created in a fixed way. No documents must be filed. However, the law does provide for a manner of formally registering a copyright, and registration does provide some benefits. If any copyright violation is alleged, no lawsuit can be filed until the copyright is registered. To formally register a copyright, the holder fills out the proper form and sends it along with the filing fee to the United States Copyright Office. See Figure 10–1 for an example of a form used to register a literary work. The following are acceptable ways of giving notice that the author is claiming a copyright: © followed by a date and name; "copyright" followed by a date and name; and "copr." followed by a date and name. The United States Copyright Office maintains a Web site at http://www.loc.gov/copyright/ with a great deal of valuable information, including a database of existing copyrights.

Length of Copyright Protection

A work is protected from the moment of its creation and is ordinarily given a term enduring for the author's life plus an additional seventy years after the author's death. For works made for hire, and for anonymous and pseudonymous works (unless the author's identity is revealed in Copyright Office records), the duration of copyright will be ninety-five years from publication or 120 years from creation, whichever is shorter.

Lawsuits for copyright infringement have become more prevalent in recent years. Read the case following Figure 10–1 dealing with that issue.

Patent Law

Patent Protection

Just as a copyright protects the property rights of an author, a patent is a way of protecting the property rights of an inventor. A patent gives the inventor the exclusive right to the product or process that is the subject of the patent and prevents others from unauthorized use of the product or process. Like copyright law, patent law is also federal; it is found in the U.S. Constitution, Article I, Section 8 and in Title 35 of the U.S. Code. The U.S. Code specifies the subject matter for which a patent may be obtained and the conditions for patentability. The law also establishes the Patent and Trademark Office, which grants patents and maintains patent records.

FEE CHANGES
Fees are effective through June 30, 2002. After that date, check the Copyright Office Website at www.loc.gov/copyright or call (202) 707-3000 for current fee information.

FORM TX
For a Nondramatic Literary Work
UNITED STATES COPYRIGHT OFFICE

REGISTRATION NUMBER

TX TXU

EFFECTIVE DATE OF REGISTRATION

Month Day Year

DO NOT WRITE ABOVE THIS LINE. IF YOU NEED MORE SPACE, USE A SEPARATE CONTINUATION SHEET.

1

TITLE OF THIS WORK ▼

PREVIOUS OR ALTERNATIVE TITLES ▼

PUBLICATION AS A CONTRIBUTION If this work was published as a contribution to a periodical, serial, or collection, give information about the collective work in which the contribution appeared. Title of Collective Work ▼

If published in a periodical or serial give: Volume ▼ Number ▼ Issue Date ▼ On Pages ▼

2

a NAME OF AUTHOR ▼ DATES OF BIRTH AND DEATH Year Born ▼ Year Died ▼

Was this contribution to the work a "work made for hire"? ☐ Yes ☐ No

AUTHOR'S NATIONALITY OR DOMICILE Name of Country OR { Citizen of ▶ Domiciled in ▶

WAS THIS AUTHOR'S CONTRIBUTION TO THE WORK Anonymous? ☐ Yes ☐ No Pseudonymous? ☐ Yes ☐ No If the answer to either of these questions is "Yes," see detailed instructions.

NATURE OF AUTHORSHIP Briefly describe nature of material created by this author in which copyright is claimed. ▼

b NAME OF AUTHOR ▼ DATES OF BIRTH AND DEATH Year Born ▼ Year Died ▼

Was this contribution to the work a "work made for hire"? ☐ Yes ☐ No

AUTHOR'S NATIONALITY OR DOMICILE Name of Country OR { Citizen of ▶ Domiciled in ▶

WAS THIS AUTHOR'S CONTRIBUTION TO THE WORK Anonymous? ☐ Yes ☐ No Pseudonymous? ☐ Yes ☐ No If the answer to either of these questions is "Yes," see detailed instructions.

NATURE OF AUTHORSHIP Briefly describe nature of material created by this author in which copyright is claimed. ▼

c NAME OF AUTHOR ▼ DATES OF BIRTH AND DEATH Year Born ▼ Year Died ▼

Was this contribution to the work a "work made for hire"? ☐ Yes ☐ No

AUTHOR'S NATIONALITY OR DOMICILE Name of Country OR { Citizen of ▶ Domiciled in ▶

WAS THIS AUTHOR'S CONTRIBUTION TO THE WORK Anonymous? ☐ Yes ☐ No Pseudonymous? ☐ Yes ☐ No If the answer to either of these questions is "Yes," see detailed instructions.

NATURE OF AUTHORSHIP Briefly describe nature of material created by this author in which copyright is claimed. ▼

NOTE
Under the law, the "author" of a "work made for hire" is generally the employer, not the employee (see instructions). For any part of this work that was "made for hire" check "Yes" in the space provided, give the employer (or other person for whom the work was prepared) as "Author" of that part, and leave the space for dates of birth and death blank.

3

a YEAR IN WHICH CREATION OF THIS WORK WAS COMPLETED This information must be given in all cases. ◀ Year

b DATE AND NATION OF FIRST PUBLICATION OF THIS PARTICULAR WORK Complete this information ONLY if this work has been published. Month ▶ Day ▶ Year ▶ ◀ Nation

4

COPYRIGHT CLAIMANT(S) Name and address must be given even if the claimant is the same as the author given in space 2. ▼

See instructions before completing this space.

TRANSFER If the claimant(s) named here in space 4 is (are) different from the author(s) named in space 2, give a brief statement of how the claimant(s) obtained ownership of the copyright. ▼

DO NOT WRITE HERE OFFICE USE ONLY
APPLICATION RECEIVED
ONE DEPOSIT RECEIVED
TWO DEPOSITS RECEIVED
FUNDS RECEIVED

MORE ON BACK ▶ • Complete all applicable spaces (numbers 5-9) on the reverse side of this page. • See detailed instructions. • Sign the form at line 8.

DO NOT WRITE HERE
Page 1 of ____ pages

FIGURE 10–1 Copyright registration form.

EXAMINED BY — FORM TX

CHECKED BY

☐ CORRESPONDENCE Yes

FOR COPYRIGHT OFFICE USE ONLY

DO NOT WRITE ABOVE THIS LINE. IF YOU NEED MORE SPACE, USE A SEPARATE CONTINUATION SHEET.

5

PREVIOUS REGISTRATION Has registration for this work, or for an earlier version of this work, already been made in the Copyright Office?
☐ **Yes** ☐ **No** If your answer is "Yes," why is another registration being sought? (Check appropriate box.) ▼
a. ☐ This is the first published edition of a work previously registered in unpublished form.
b. ☐ This is the first application submitted by this author as copyright claimant.
c. ☐ This is a changed version of the work, as shown by space 6 on this application.
If your answer is "Yes," give: **Previous Registration Number** ▶ **Year of Registration** ▶

6

DERIVATIVE WORK OR COMPILATION
a **Preexisting Material** Identify any preexisting work or works that this work is based on or incorporates. ▼

See instructions before completing this space.

b **Material Added to This Work** Give a brief, general statement of the material that has been added to this work and in which copyright is claimed. ▼

7

a **DEPOSIT ACCOUNT** If the registration fee is to be charged to a Deposit Account established in the Copyright Office, give name and number of Account.
Name ▼ **Account Number** ▼

b **CORRESPONDENCE** Give name and address to which correspondence about this application should be sent. Name/Address/Apt/City/State/ZIP ▼

Area code and daytime telephone number ▶ Fax number ▶
Email ▶

8

CERTIFICATION* I, the undersigned, hereby certify that I am the
Check only one ▶
☐ author
☐ other copyright claimant
☐ owner of exclusive right(s)
☐ authorized agent of ______
Name of author or other copyright claimant, or owner of exclusive right(s) ▲

of the work identified in this application and that the statements made by me in this application are correct to the best of my knowledge.

Typed or printed name and date ▼ If this application gives a date of publication in space 3, do not sign and submit it before that date.

Date ▶

Handwritten signature (X) ▼

X ______

9

Certificate will be mailed in window envelope to this address:

Name ▼
Number/Street/Apt ▼
City/State/ZIP ▼

YOU MUST:
- Complete all necessary spaces
- Sign your application in space 8

SEND ALL 3 ELEMENTS IN THE SAME PACKAGE:
1. Application form
2. Nonrefundable filing fee in check or money order payable to *Register of Copyrights*
3. Deposit material

MAIL TO:
Library of Congress
Copyright Office
101 Independence Avenue, S.E.
Washington, D.C. 20559-6000

As of July 1, 1999, the filing fee for Form TX is $30.

*17 U.S.C. § 506(e): Any person who knowingly makes a false representation of a material fact in the application for copyright registration provided for by section 409, or in any written statement filed in connection with the application, shall be fined not more than $2,500.
June 1999—200,000
WEB REV: June 1999
PRINTED ON RECYCLED PAPER
☆U.S. GOVERNMENT PRINTING OFFICE: 1999-454-879/49

FIGURE 10–1 Continued

ProCD, Inc. v. Zeidenberg

908 F. Supp. 640 (1996)

Plaintiff created a comprehensive national directory of residential and business listings and sold these on CD-ROM. Defendant downloaded data from the CD-ROM and made it available over the Internet. He did not, however, download the software that plaintiff had developed and used on the CD-ROM. Plaintiff filed an action seeking an injunction prohibiting defendant from distributing the material on the Internet. Each party made a motion for summary judgment. Defendant was granted summary judgment. The appellate court affirmed, stating that federal copyright law controlled this situation. Under federal copyright law, public data such as phone numbers are not subject to copyright protection. The court also considered a Wisconsin Computer Crimes Act that made it unlawful to modify, destroy, access, take, or copy computer data willfully, knowingly and without authorization. In this case, however, federal law preempts. Read the decision.

OPINION AND ORDER

This is a civil action for injunctive and monetary relief brought pursuant to the federal Copyright Act, 17 U.S.C. §§ 101–1010, the Wisconsin Computer Crimes Act, Wis. Stat. § 943.70, and Wisconsin contract and tort law. The facts are not in dispute. Defendant Zeidenberg, a one-person corporation formed by Zeidenberg, purchased copies of plaintiff's Select Phone™ CD-ROM software program, downloaded telephone listings stored on the CD-ROM discs to Zeidenberg's computer and made the listings available to Internet users by placing the data onto an Internet host computer. Plaintiff contends that defendant's actions constitute copyright infringement, and breach of the express terms of the parties' software licensing agreement, a violation of Wisconsin's Computer Crimes Act. Defendant argues that the data [he] downloaded from plaintiff's Select Phone™ program were not protected by copyright, that defendant did not use Select Phone™ in a manner inconsistent with plaintiff's copyright, that [he is] not bound by the software licensing agreement and that plaintiff's state law claims are preempted by federal copyright law.

The case is before the court on the parties' cross motions for summary judgment. Jurisdiction is present under 28 U.S.C. § 1331, because plaintiff's copyright claim arises under federal law, and under 28 U.S.C. § 1332, because there is complete diversity of citizenship among the parties and more than $50,000 is at issue.

I conclude that defendant is entitled to summary judgment in his favor. First, defendant did not infringe plaintiff's copyright. Although the software plaintiff developed for its Select Phone™ program is protected by copyright, that protection does not extend to the telephone listings included on the CD-ROM discs. Second, defendant used the protected software for his own individual purposes, consistent with plaintiff's copyright, and distributed only unprotected data. Defendant never assented to the license agreement included in the Select Phone™ user guide and is not bound by it. Even if defendant had assented, the license agreement is preempted by federal copyright law to the extent plaintiff intended it to apply to uncopyrightable data. Finally, plaintiff's remaining state law claims are preempted by the Copyright Act because they are attempts to avoid federal copyright law.

From the facts proposed by the parties, I find that the following facts are not in dispute.

Undisputed Facts

Plaintiff ProCD, Inc., is a Delaware corporation with its principal place of business in Danvers, Massachusetts. Defendant Zeidenberg is a Wisconsin citizen residing in Madison, Wisconsin, and working on a Ph.D. in computer science.

Plaintiff spent millions of dollars creating a comprehensive, national directory of residential and business listings. Plaintiff compiled over 95,000,000 residential and commercial listings from approximately 3,000 publicly available telephone books. The listings include full names, street addresses, telephone numbers, zip codes and industry or "SIC" codes where appropriate. Plaintiff sells these listings on CD-ROM discs under the trademark "Select Phone™," as well as under other trade names and trademarks.

Each of plaintiff's CD-ROM discs contains both telephone listings and a software program used to access, retrieve and download the data. Plaintiff sells Select Phone™ in boxes containing a set of discs and a user guide. The user guide includes a series of terms entitled, "Single User License Agreement." The agreement states in its opening paragraph: "Please read this license carefully before using the software or accessing the listings contained on the discs. By using the discs and the listings licensed to you, you agree to be bound by the terms of this License. If you do not agree to the terms of this License, promptly return all copies of the software, listings that may have been exported, the discs and the User Guide to the place where you obtained it." The license informs the user that plaintiff's software is copyrighted and that copying the software is authorized only for particular purposes and uses. Once the product is installed on the user's computer, the computer screen reminds the user that use of the product and the data is subject to the Single User License Agreement and that the products are licensed for authorized use only. Before a user can access the listings a field appears on the computer screen, stating: "The listings contained within this product are subject to a License Agreement. Please refer to the Help menu or to the User Guide." In addition, most screens contain the following warning:

> "The listings on this product are licensed for authorized users only. The user agreement provides that copying of the software and the data may be done only for individual or personal use and that distribution, sublicense or lease of the software or the data is prohibited. The agreement provides expressly that: You will not make the Software or the Listings in whole or in part available to any other user in any networked or time-shared environment, or transfer the Listings in whole or in part to any computer other than the computer used to access the Listings."

In late 1994, defendant Zeidenberg purchased a copy of Select Phone™ at a local retail store. In February or March 1995, defendant Zeidenberg decided he could download data from Select Phone™ and make it available to third parties over the Internet for commercial purposes. Zeidenberg purchased an updated version of Select Phone™ in March 1995, and in April 1995 incorporated Silken Mountain Web Services, Inc. for the purpose of making a database of telephone listings available over the Internet. In April and May 1995, after incorporation, Silken Mountain Web Services, Inc., began assembling its own telephone listings database, part of which contained data from Select Phone™ and part of which involved data from another company's product. Defendants were aware of the computer screen warning message notifying them that Select Phone™ was subject to the agreement contained in the user guide. Defendant disregarded the screen warnings because he did not believe the license to be binding.

Defendant Zeidenberg is the sole shareholder, sole employee and sole officer of Silken Mountain Web Services, Inc. Defendant compiled his database by installing Select Phone™ on Zeidenberg's personal computer, thereby making a copy of the software onto Zeidenberg's computer's hard drive. Defendant used the software on this hard disk copy to download data from the Select Phone™ discs to contribute to the corporation's own database. Every time defendant downloaded data from the discs, an additional copy of Select Phone™ software was copied into the random access memory (RAM) of Zeidenberg's computer.

Silken Mountain Web Services, Inc., wrote its own computer program to allow users to search its database. No person who accessed the Silken Mountain Web Services, Inc. home page used or copied plaintiff's Select Phone™ software. The software that defendant created permits searches based only on name or standard industrial code while plaintiff's software can search a number of "fields," such as name, address, telephone number, area code, zip code, or any combination of the above.

In May 1995, defendant entered into a contract with Branch Information Systems pursuant to which Branch provided defendant with access to the Internet. Defendant uploaded his database onto Branch Information Systems' computer and provided access to the database to third parties via the Internet. Plaintiff discovered this activity and demanded that defendant discontinue his actions immediately. Zeidenberg wrote to plaintiff and admitted downloading listings from Select Phone™ and making some of those listings available over the Internet but explained that he would continue his project.

After learning of plaintiff's displeasure, Branch Information Services stopped doing business with defendant. In August 1995, defendant entered into a contract with Ivory Tower Information Services for Internet access. The parties contemplated that plaintiff would complain and they provided in the contract that Ivory Tower Information Services was required to continue providing defendant Internet access until ordered by a court to stop.

Pursuant to this contract, defendant made his database available over the Internet until this court issued a preliminary injunction on September 22, 1995. Prior to entry of the preliminary injunction, defendant's database was receiving approximately 20,000 "hits" per day on the Internet. (A hit occurs each time a new screen is displayed on a user's computer screen during a search of the database. Each search tends to generate multiple hits.) For each search of defendant's database, users are permitted to extract up to 1,000 listings. Because the public could access defendant's database for free, plaintiff believed its ability to sell Select Phone™ was jeopardized.

Opinion

Plaintiff commenced this lawsuit in September 1995 and immediately sought a preliminary injunction barring the defendant from distributing Select Phone™ telephone listings over the Internet. At the hearing on its motion for a preliminary injunction, plaintiff's arguments for protection of its entrepreneurial effort were sufficiently compelling to secure the injunction. Nonetheless, it was clear then, as it is now, that plaintiff had no valid claim to federal copyright protection for the raw data contained on its Select Phone™ CD-ROM discs. Now, after the parties have briefed the issues more fully, it has become evident that plaintiff cannot prevail on its copyright claim even with respect to its protected software and that its state law claims are similarly unavailing. Plaintiff's arguments boil down to the proposition that it is unfair and commercially destructive to allow the defendant to take the information plaintiff assembled with a significant investment of time, effort and money and use it for commercial purposes without paying any compensation to plaintiff. Although the proposition has substantial equitable appeal, it is one that the United States Supreme Court rejected specifically in a nearly identical context four years ago. In *Feist Publications, Inc. v. Rural Telephone Service Co., Inc.,* 499 U.S. 340, 113 L. Ed. 2d 358, 111 S. Ct. 1282 (1991), the court held that telephone listings are not protected by copyright law and denied the claim of a telephone company that sought to prevent competitors from using the data it had compiled and published in its directories. If this result seems perverse, the remedy lies with Congress. *See* Maureen A. O'Rourke, 41 Fed. B. News & J. 511 (1994) (rapidly expanding Internet use will force Congress to address difficult question of appropriate level of protection for on-line fact-based databases); Jane C. Ginsburg, "No Sweat"? Copyright and Other Protection of Works of Information after *Feist v. Rural Telephone,*" 92 Colum. L. Rev. 338 (suggesting a federal misappropriation statute to prevent commercial copying of non-copyrightable databases by other compilers if public access to information were assured through collective licensing).

It is not surprising that the recent explosive growth of the Internet would give rise to lawsuits concerning the ownership of the data available through that system. *See* Jane C. Ginsburg, "Putting Cars on the 'Information Superhighway': Authors, Exploiters, and Copyright in Cyberspace," 95 Colum. L. Rev. 1466 (1995). Defendant Zeidenberg is not the first computer student to find himself involved in a legal dispute after downloading information and offering it over the Internet. In *United States v. LaMacchia,* 871 F. Supp. 535 (D. Mass. 1994), a Massachusetts Institute of Technology student set up a computer bulletin board and encouraged his correspondents to upload copyrighted software that other users could download for free. The United States charged the student with criminal copyright infringement under the federal wire fraud statute, 18 U.S.C. § 1343. The district court noted the impropriety of the defendant's actions but held that his conduct was not punishable under the wire fraud statute; copyright law provided the full range of penalties for criminal infringement actions and copyright law did not cover defendant's noncommercial activities. *Id.* at 544–45. The *LaMacchia* decision appears to have generated congressional interest. On August 4, 1995, Senator Patrick Leahy introduced a bill (S. 1122) to ensure better copyright protection for creative works available on-line. "Bill to Stiffen Criminal Penalties for Copyright Infringement Introduced," 7 *Journal of Proprietary Rights* 26 (1995). The executive branch is also well aware of these problems. A presidential study group formed in 1993 recently released a report entitled, "Intellectual Property and the National Information Infrastructure." The report suggests that the Internet will not flourish if significant protection against theft and copyright abuse is not offered. Guy Alvarez, "New Legal Issues on the Net," Am. Law. 28, 29 (Dec. Supp. 1995). Against this background, I will take up plaintiff's federal copyright claim.

Copyright Infringement

Select Phone™ is comprised of two elements: 1) the software that allows users to access and retrieve the data contained on the CD-ROM discs; and 2) the data itself. The difference between these two elements is critical.

Plaintiff contends that the defendant infringed plaintiff's copyright when [he] copied and used Select Phone™ for purposes of commercially distributing the listings on the Internet because copyright protection extends to both the telephone listings and to its software. Defendant argues that the Select Phone™ data is not copyrightable but acknowledges that plaintiff has a valid copyright in the Select Phone™ software. Nonetheless, defendant contends, copyright law permits him to make a copy of the program as long as it is essential to his personal use of the program and is not used in a manner inconsistent with plaintiff's copyright.

Select Phone™ Data

In *Feist Publications, Inc. v. Rural Telephone Service Co. Inc.,* 499 U.S. 340, 113 L. Ed. 2d 358, 111 S. Ct. 1282, the Supreme Court held that a telephone company's white pages were not entitled to copyright protection because the raw data contained in the listings were not arranged in an original manner and lacked the minimal degree of creativity necessary to constitute a copyrightable compilation of facts. *Id.* at 362. As the Court noted, *Feist* concerned "the interaction of two well-established propositions. The first is that facts are not copyrightable; the other, that compilations of facts generally are." *Id.* at 344. Even a modicum of originality may suffice to make a compilation of fact copyrightable, but the alphabetical listing of telephone subscriber addresses and telephone numbers does not achieve even this minimal degree of creativity. *Id.* at 345. To the argument that it was unfair for the publishing company to use the fruits of the telephone company's labor without compensating it, the Court gave short shrift. "The primary objective of copyright is not to reward the labor of authors, but 'to promote the Progress of Science and Useful Arts.'" *Id.* at 349 (citing U.S. Const. art. I, § 8, cl. 8). In reaching this conclusion, the Court rejected a line of cases applying a "sweat of the brow" theory that offered copyright protection to factual compilations as a reward for the hard work that goes into compiling facts. *Id.* at 352. The Court explained that the 1976 Copyright Act overruled the "sweat of the brow" cases. *Id.* at 354–55. The Court's overruling of the "sweat of the brow" theory can be viewed as implementation of Congressional intent with respect to federal copyright law.

Plaintiff does not suggest that the phone listings contained in Select Phone™ are any different from those in *Feist* for purposes of copyright protection. As a collection of facts arranged in a commonplace, non-original fashion, the Select Phone™ listings themselves are not copyrightable. Without originality, time and effort do not factor into the copyright equation. *Feist's* result may well serve as a disincentive to companies considering the compilation of factual databases (*see* Philip H. Miller, Note, "Life after *Feist:* Facts, the First Amendment and the Copyright Status of Automated Databases," 60 Fordham L. Rev. 507, 521–23 [1991] [*Feist* chills incentive to create databases]), but *Feist* struck the "careful balance" between fact and expression in copyright law by allowing facts to be copied at will in order to advance the development of science and art. That disincentives might result was not considered important.

Therefore, based on the *Feist* decision and the reasons set forth above, there has been no copyright infringement.

Wisconsin Computer Crimes Act Claim

The Wisconsin Computer Crimes Act makes it unlawful to modify, destroy, access, take, or copy computer data willfully, knowingly and without authorization. Wis. Stat. 943.70(2)(a). Under the statute, "data" are property and include representations of information, knowledge or facts prepared in formalized manners and intended to be processed in a computer system. Wis. Stat. 943.70(1) (f). Under the act, the Select Phone™ telephone listings qualify as data and defendant's distribution of that data is made unlawful.

Again, the question is whether federal copyright law preempts the statute as it applies to defendant's actions. Plaintiff points to a recent Wisconsin appellate court decision in which the court held that the law was not preempted by the Copyright Act. In *State v. Corcoran,* 186 Wis. 2d 616, 522 N.W.2d 226 (Ct. App.), review denied, 527 N.W.2d 335 (1994), the Wisconsin Court of Appeals upheld a conviction under the Wisconsin Computer Crimes Act of a computer software programmer who destroyed data stored on the computer of his former employer by inserting "booby traps" into programs he had written for the employer. *Id.* at 620, 522 N.W.2d at 228. The court explained that it did not need to consider the defendant's argument that federal copyright law preempted the Wisconsin act because the data the defendant was accused of destroying could not be protected by copyright. *Id.* at 628, 522 N.W.2d at 231.

Plaintiff argues that the court reached its holding in *Corcoran* because the destroyed data were not copyrightable and therefore did not meet the first requirement of the preemption test, that the material falls within the subject matter of copyright. This is a reasonable interpretation of the court's holding, but not the only one. The court of appeals did not hold explicitly that such data does not "fall within the subject matter of copyright for purposes of preemption analysis." In fact, the court's footnote seems to indicate that the court's understanding of the preemption test focused solely on the second, or "extra element prong of the analysis." *See* 186 Wis. 2d at 628 n. 11, 522 N.W.2d at 231 ("The analysis applied by the federal courts requires a determination if the state-created cause of action contains an 'extra element' in addition to the acts of reproduction or distribution"). The court's discussion of the issue lacks specific mention of the subject matter test. As seen in *Baltimore Orioles,* 805 F.2d 663, an inquiry into the subject matter of copyright requires more than just determining whether given material is a proper recipient of copyright protection. It is unlikely that the court's single sentence mention of subject matter in *Corcoran* was meant to foreclose future application of a more comprehensive subject matter test.

Applying the preemption test to plaintiff's claim that defendant violated the Wisconsin Computer Crimes Act, it becomes evident that the claim should be preempted for the same reasons as plaintiff's breach of contract and misappropriation claims. The first prong is satisfied because the telephone listings fall within the subject matter of copyright and the second is met because plaintiff seeks merely to prohibit the copying and distribution that it could not prevent under federal copyright law. In reaching this conclusion that federal law preempts plaintiff's claim under the Wisconsin Computer Crimes Act, I do not hold or intend to imply that the Wisconsin Computer Crimes Act is preempted in all instances. Preemption would not occur in a *Corcoran*-like situation when an individual destroys another's data purposefully. In those situations, the right sought to be enforced differs greatly from the copying and distribution rights covered by copyright law. What this conclusion does mean is that plaintiff cannot succeed on its underlying copyright claim by dressing it in other clothing. Plaintiff's efforts to establish a right under the Wisconsin Computer Crimes Act conflicts directly with the federal copyright law's directive to keep unoriginal factual compilations in the public domain. It would undermine the public access to facts and ideas if states could block such access with their own legislation.

Order

It is ordered that the motion for summary judgment of defendant Zeidenberg is granted and that the motion for summary judgment of plaintiff ProCD, Inc. is denied.

CASE ANALYSIS

1. Explain the plaintiff's argument.
2. Explain the defendant's argument.
3. Discuss the *Feist* case relied upon by the court.

According to the U.S. Code, "any new and useful process, machine, manufacture, or composition of matter, or any new and useful improvement thereof" may be the subject of a patent. The word *process* is defined by law as a process, act, or method, and primarily includes industrial or technical processes. The term *manufacture* refers to articles that are made, and includes all manufactured articles. The term *composition of matter* relates to chemical compositions and may include mixtures of ingredients as well as new chemical compounds. Obviously the code definition includes almost everything made by humans and the processes for making the products. A second requirement for items capable of being patented is that they be "useful." This means that the subject matter has a useful purpose and it must work or operate the way it is intended to. The statutes defining the subject matter that can be patented have been interpreted by courts.

What Is Not Protected

Courts have held that the laws of nature, physical phenomena, and abstract ideas are not patentable subject matter. Furthermore a patent cannot be obtained upon a mere idea or suggestion. The patent is always on the product or process resulting from the idea. Even if a product would otherwise qualify for a patent, a patent will not be granted if the invention was (1) known or used by others in this country before the invention by the applicant for patent, (2) patented or described in a printed publication in this or a foreign country, before the invention by the applicant for patent, (3) patented or described in a printed publication in this or a foreign country more than one year prior to the application for patent in the United States, or (4) in public use or on sale in this country more than one year prior to the application for patent in the United States. It doesn't matter whether the publication, prior use, or prior patent was by the inventor. In order for a patent to be granted, the item must be new. If the subject matter is related to something that has previously been patented, it must be sufficiently different from what has been used or described before.

Obtaining a Patent

In most instances only the inventor may apply for a patent. If a person who is not the inventor applies for a patent, the patent, if it is obtained, is invalid. An application for a patent is filed with the U.S. Patent and Trademark Office and is made to the Assistant Commissioner for Patents. The application includes the following:

1. A written document that comprises a specification (description and claims) and an oath or declaration
2. A drawing in those cases in which a drawing is necessary
3. The filing fee

See Figure 10–2 for an example of a declaration for a patent. The U.S. Patent and Trademark Office maintains an informative Web site at www.uspto.gov/.

Length of Patent Protection

The term of the patent is twenty years from the date on which the application for the patent was filed in the United States subject to the payment of maintenance fees as provided by law. A maintenance fee is due 3½, 7½ and 11½ years after the original grant for all patents issuing from the applications filed on and after December 12, 1980. Once a patent has expired, anyone may make, use, offer for sale, or sell or import the invention without permission of the patentee, provided that matter covered by other unexpired patents is not used. The terms can be extended by law.

TRADEMARK LAW

Trademark Protection

If someone were to show you a picture of the "Golden Arches" you would undoubtedly associate the picture with McDonald's. This symbol or picture is uniformly recognized as belonging to the restaurant. It is an example of a trademark. Trademarks include words, phrases, symbols or designs, and combinations of words, phrases, symbols or designs, that identify and distinguish goods or services of one party from those of others. A trademark is different from a copyright or a patent. A copyright protects an original artistic or literary work; a patent protects an invention.

A business establishes trademark rights either by using the mark or by filing the proper application to register a mark in the U.S. Patent and Trademark Office. Federal registration is not required. However, federal registration does provide benefits that might not otherwise exist. One important benefit is that the owner of a federal registration is presumed to be the owner of the mark for the goods and services specified in the registration, and to be entitled to use the mark *nationwide.* The right to use a trademark that is not registered is limited to the geographical area in which it is actually used.

Trademark protection exists under both federal and state laws. The federal law is found in Title 15 of the U.S. Code (the Lanham Act); the trademark rules, 37 C.F.R. Part 2; and the *Trademark Manual of Examining Procedure* (2d ed., 1993).

What Is Not Protected

A trademark must distinguish an owner's goods or services from those of another. A term that merely describes a product is not protected. For example, the term "high heel" is not protectible as a trademark for shoes because it only describes a general category of shoes. It doesn't distinguish one owner's product from that of another. Geographical terms are also not protectible, for example, "Florida" used in conjunction with orange juice.

One major difference between copyrights and patents and trademarks is that trademark protection does not necessarily give the owner the exclusive right to use the mark. Trademark protection exists only against the use of a trademark that is likely to cause confusion, mistake, or deception among consumers. If the same or a similar symbol or mark is used by owners of two very different products and the public would not be confused, there would be no protection. However, determining whether there is confusion is up to the courts. Read the case printed in this chapter concerning the terms "King Kong" and "Donkey Kong" (*Universal City Studios, Inc. v. Nintendo Co.*) to see what criteria the courts use to do this.

Federal Trademark Registration

Trademarks are registered with the U.S. Patent and Trademark Office. An applicant may apply for federal registration in three principal ways: (1) An applicant who

Please type a plus sign (+) inside this box → ☐

PTO/SB/01 (10-00)
Approved for use through 10/31/2002. OMB 0651-0032
U.S. Patent and Trademark Office; U.S. DEPARTMENT OF COMMERCE
Under the Paperwork Reduction Act of 1995, no persons are required to respond to a collection of information unless it contains a valid OMB control number.

DECLARATION FOR UTILITY OR DESIGN PATENT APPLICATION (37 CFR 1.63)

☐ Declaration Submitted with Initial Filing **OR** ☐ Declaration Submitted after Initial Filing (surcharge (37 CFR 1.16 (e)) required)

Attorney Docket Number	
First Named Inventor	
COMPLETE IF KNOWN	
Application Number	/
Filing Date	
Group Art Unit	
Examiner Name	

As a below named inventor, I hereby declare that:

My residence, mailing address, and citizenship are as stated below next to my name.

I believe I am the original, first and sole inventor (if only one name is listed below) or an original, first and joint inventor (if plural names are listed below) of the subject matter which is claimed and for which a patent is sought on the invention entitled:

(Title of the Invention)

the specification of which

☐ is attached hereto

OR

☐ was filed on (MM/DD/YYYY) ______ as United States Application Number or PCT International Application Number ______ and was amended on (MM/DD/YYYY) ______ (if applicable).

I hereby state that I have reviewed and understand the contents of the above identified specification, including the claims, as amended by any amendment specifically referred to above.

I acknowledge the duty to disclose information which is material to patentability as defined in 37 CFR 1.56, including for continuation-in-part applications, material information which became available between the filing date of the prior application and the national or PCT international filing date of the continuation-in-part application.

I hereby claim foreign priority benefits under 35 U.S.C. 119(a)-(d) or 365(b) of any foreign application(s) for patent or inventor's certificate, or 365(a) of any PCT international application which designated at least one country other than the United States of America, listed below and have also identified below, by checking the box, any foreign application for patent or inventor's certificate, or any PCT international application having a filing date before that of the application on which priority is claimed.

Prior Foreign Application Number(s)	**Country**	**Foreign Filing Date (MM/DD/YYYY)**	**Priority Not Claimed**	**Certified Copy Attached? YES**	**NO**
			☐	☐	☐
			☐	☐	☐
			☐	☐	☐
			☐	☐	☐

☐ Additional foreign application numbers are listed on a supplemental priority data sheet PTO/SB/02B attached hereto:

I hereby claim the benefit under 35 U.S.C. 119(e) of any United States provisional application(s) listed below.

Application Number(s)	**Filing Date (MM/DD/YYYY)**	
		☐ Additional provisional application numbers are listed on a supplemental priority data sheet PTO/SB/02B attached hereto.

[Page 1 of 2]

Burden Hour Statement: This form is estimated to take 21 minutes to complete. Time will vary depending upon the needs of the individual case. Any comments on the amount of time you are required to complete this form should be sent to the Chief Information Officer, U.S. Patent and Trademark Office, Washington, DC 20231. DO NOT SEND FEES OR COMPLETED FORMS TO THIS ADDRESS. SEND TO: Assistant Commissioner for Patents, Washington, DC 20231.

FIGURE 10–2 Declaration for a patent.

Please type a plus sign (+) inside this box → ☐

PTO/SB/01 (10-00)
Approved for use through 10/31/2002. OMB 0651-0032
U.S. Patent and Trademark Office; U.S. DEPARTMENT OF COMMERCE
Under the Paperwork Reduction Act of 1995, no persons are required to respond to a collection of information unless it contains a valid OMB control number.

DECLARATION — Utility or Design Patent Application

Direct all correspondence to: ☐ Customer Number or Bar Code Label [ ]	OR ☐ Correspondence address below	
Name		
Address		
Address		
City	State	ZIP
Country	Telephone	Fax

I hereby declare that all statements made herein of my own knowledge are true and that all statements made on information and belief are believed to be true; and further that these statements were made with the knowledge that willful false statements and the like so made are punishable by fine or imprisonment, or both, under 18 U.S.C. 1001 and that such willful false statements may jeopardize the validity of the application or any patent issued thereon.

NAME OF SOLE OR FIRST INVENTOR :	☐ A petition has been filed for this unsigned inventor		
Given Name (first and middle [if any])	Family Name or Surname		
Inventor's Signature	Date		
Residence: City	State	Country	Citizenship
Mailing Address			
Mailing Address			
City	State	ZIP	Country

NAME OF SECOND INVENTOR:	☐ A petition has been filed for this unsigned inventor		
Given Name (first and middle [if any])	Family Name or Surname		
Inventor's Signature	Date		
Residence: City	State	Country	Citizenship
Mailing Address			
Mailing Address			
City	State	ZIP	Country

☐ Additional inventors are being named on the ____supplemental Additional Inventor(s) sheet(s) PTO/SB/02A attached hereto.

[Page 2 of 2]

FIGURE 10–2 Continued

has already commenced using a mark in commerce may file based on that use (a "use" application). (2) An applicant who has not yet used the mark may apply based on a bona fide intention to use the mark in commerce (an "intent to use" application). The use in commerce must be in good faith and not made merely to reserve a right in a mark. If an applicant files based on a bona fide intention to use in commerce, the applicant will have to use the mark in commerce and submit an allegation of use to the PTO before the PTO will register the mark. (3) Under certain international agreements, an applicant from outside the United States may file in the United States based on an application or registration in another country. A U.S. registration provides protection only in the United States and its territories.

The application must be filed in the name of the owner of the mark—usually an individual, corporation, or partnership. The owner may submit and prosecute its own application for registration, or may be represented by an attorney.

When the application is filed, the Patent and Trademark Office will conduct a search of its files to determine whether any conflicts exist. To determine whether there is a conflict between two marks, the office determines whether there would be likelihood of confusion. Factors to be considered in reaching this decision are the similarity of the marks and the commercial relationship between the goods and services identified by the marks. To find a conflict, the marks need not be identical, and the goods and services do not have to be the same. The Patent and Trademark Office does not conduct any type of public search. Thus, if someone else is already using the mark but has not registered it, the Patent and Trademark Office would allow the registration. However, common-law trademark rights still exist and the one to be the first to use the mark might still have the rights to the trademark. These rights would have to be determined by a court in an infringement action. The fact that one party was the first to register the mark does not mean that they will win the lawsuit. In order to prevent unnecessary litigation, a party seeking to register a trademark should probably conduct its own search prior to filing the application. This search should include a search of the records of the Patent and Trademark Office as well as any other sources that might reveal the use of a trademark (such as the Internet).

Length of Trademark Protection

Unlike copyrights or patents, trademark rights can last indefinitely if the owner continues to use the mark to identify its goods or services. The term of a federal trademark registration is ten years, with ten-year renewal terms. However, between the fifth and sixth year after the date of initial registration, the registrant must file an affidavit setting forth certain information to keep the registration alive. If no affidavit is filed, the registration is canceled.

State Protection

Trademarks, as well as trade names or service marks, used within a state can also be registered pursuant to that state's law. A *trade name* is a work, name, or symbol used by a person to identify his or her business. A *service mark* is a mark used in the sale or advertising of services to identify the services of that person. See Figure 10–3 for a copy of a state registration of trademark or service mark.

State of California
Secretary of State

REGISTRATION OF TRADEMARK OR SERVICE MARK

Pursuant to Business and Professions Code Section 14230

NOTICE: READ ACCOMPANYING INSTRUCTIONS BEFORE COMPLETING THIS FORM

REGISTRATION APPLICATION FOR: ☐ TRADEMARK ☐ SERVICE MARK

1. APPLICANT NAME

2. STREET ADDRESS (PROVIDE CALIFORNIA BUSINESS ADDRESS IF SERVICE MARK)
3. CITY AND STATE
4. ZIP CODE

5. BUSINESS STRUCTURE (CHECK ONE)

☐ LIMITED PARTNERSHIP
☐ LIMITED LIABILITY COMPANY
☐ GENERAL PARTNERSHIP
☐ CORPORATION (STATE OF INCORPORATION) ____________
☐ SOLE PROPRIETOR
☐ HUSBAND AND WIFE, AS COMMUNITY PROPERTY
☐ OTHER (DESCRIBE) ____________

6. NAMES OF THE GENERAL PARTNERS, IF APPLICANT IS A PARTNERSHIP
7. NAMES OF MEMBER(S) OR MANAGER(S), IF APPLICANT IS A LIMITED LIABILITY COMPANY

8. **NAME AND/OR DESIGN OF MARK.** (FOR DESIGN PROVIDE A BRIEF WRITTEN DESCRIPTION THAT CAN BE PICTURED IN THE MIND WITHOUT REFERENCE TO THE SPECIMENS. DO NOT DRAW THE DESIGN ON APPLICATION)

DISCLAIMER (IF APPLICABLE) NO CLAIM IS MADE TO THE EXCLUSIVE RIGHT TO USE THE TERM:

9. DATE THE MARK WAS FIRST USED IN CALIFORNIA

DATE THE MARK WAS FIRST USED ANYWHERE

10. IF A TRADEMARK, LIST SPECIFIC GOODS. IF A SERVICE MARK, LIST SPECIFIC SERVICE.

CLASS NUMBER ____________ (ONE CLASSIFICATION NUMBER ONLY)

11. **RETURN ACKNOWLEDGMENT TO:** (TYPE OR PRINT)

NAME
ADDRESS
CITY
STATE
ZIP CODE

THIS SPACE FOR FILING OFFICER USE

TRADE/SERVICE MARK

REG. NO. ____________

CLASS NO. ____________

SEC/STATE LP/TM 101 (REV. 2/97) FILING FEE: $70.00

(OVER)

FIGURE 10–3 State registration of trademark or service mark.

(continued)

12. **MANNER OF MARK USE.**

CHECK ALL THAT APPLY

FOR TRADEMARKS ONLY

- ☐ ON LABELS AND TAGS AFFIXED TO THE GOODS.
- ☐ ON LABELS AND TAGS AFFIXED TO CONTAINERS OF THE GOODS.
- ☐ BY PRINTING IT DIRECTLY ONTO THE GOODS.
- ☐ BY PRINTING IT DIRECTLY ONTO THE CONTAINERS FOR THE GOODS.
- ☐ OTHER________________________

FOR SERVICE MARKS ONLY

- ☐ ON BUSINESS SIGNS.
- ☐ ON ADVERTISING BROCHURES.
- ☐ ON ADVERTISING LEAFLETS.
- ☐ ON BUSINESS CARDS.
- ☐ ON LETTERHEADS.
- ☐ ON MENUS.
- ☐ OTHER________________________

13. **SPECIMENS**

CHECK ONE BOX BELOW. ENCLOSE THREE (3) IDENTICAL ORIGINAL SPECIMENS.

FOR TRADEMARKS ONLY

- ☐ ACTUAL LABELS.
- ☐ ACTUAL TAGS.
- ☐ PHOTOGRAPHS OF THE GOODS/CONTAINERS SHOWING THE TRADEMARK.
- ☐ FRONT PANELS OF A PAPER CONTAINER BEARING THE TRADEMARK.
- ☐ OTHER________________________

FOR SERVICE MARKS ONLY

- ☐ BUSINESS CARDS.
- ☐ ADVERTISING BROCHURES.
- ☐ ADVERTISING LEAFLETS.
- ☐ MENUS SHOWING THE MARK.
- ☐ OTHER________________________

14. **DECLARATION OF OWNERSHIP**

APPLICANT HEREWITH DECLARES THAT HE/SHE HAS READ THE ABOVE AND FOREGOING APPLICATION AND KNOWS THE CONTENTS THEREOF AND THAT THE FACTS SET OUT HEREIN ARE TRUE AND CORRECT AND THAT THE THREE SPECIMENS OF THE MARK SUBMITTED ARE TRUE AND CORRECT, AND TO HIS/HER BEST KNOWLEDGE AND BELIEF NO OTHER PERSON, FIRM, CORPORATION, UNION OR ASSOCIATION HAS THE RIGHT TO USE SAID MARK IN THIS STATE, EITHER IN IDENTICAL FORM OR IN SUCH NEAR RESEMBLANCE THERETO AS MIGHT BE CALCULATED TO DECEIVE OR CONFUSE.

NAME OF CORPORATION/PARTNERSHIP/LIMITED LIABILITY COMPANY (IF APPLICABLE)	
SIGNATURE OF APPLICANT	IF PARTNER, MANAGER OR CORPORATE OFFICER, INCLUDE TITLE
TYPE OR PRINT NAME OF APPLICANT	DATE

TYPE OR PRINT THE NAME AND ADDRESS OF THE PERSON OR FIRM TO RECEIVE THE ACKNOWLEDGEMENT OF THE FILING. SEND THE SIGNED APPLICATION WITH ORIGINAL SIGNATURE(S) TO THE SECRETARY OF STATE, TRADEMARK UNIT, P.O. BOX 944225, SACRAMENTO, CA 94244-2250 WITH THE $70.00 FILING FEE.

FIGURE 10–3 Continued

Universal City Studios, Inc. v. Nintendo Co.

746 F.2d 112 (1984)

This is a case concerning trademark infringement brought by Universal, who owned the rights to the name and character of King Kong, against Nintendo, who produced the famous game Donkey Kong. Universal claimed that Donkey Kong infringed on the name and character of King Kong. After comparing and inspecting both the Donkey Kong game and the King Kong movies, the trial court found that the differences between the two were great and that Donkey Kong was clearly a parody of King Kong. The trial court found that there was no likelihood of consumer confusion between the two and therefore granted summary judgment. The appellate court agreed. The following is an excerpt from the appellate court's opinion.

OPINION

BACKGROUND

Nintendo Co., and its wholly owned subsidiary Nintendo of America, has engaged in the design, manufacture, importation, and sale of the extraordinarily successful video game known as "Donkey Kong." Nintendo has realized over $180 million from the sale of approximately 60,000 video arcade machines in the United States and Canada. Donkey Kong requires the player to maneuver a computerized man named Mario up a set of girders, ladders and elevators to save a blond pigtailed woman from the clutches of a malevolent, yet humorous gorilla, while simultaneously avoiding a series of objects such as barrels and fireballs hurled at him by the impish ape.

Universal, a giant in the entertainment industry, maintains that it owns the trademark in the name, character and story of "King Kong."

Universal filed its complaint against Nintendo in 1982, approximately nine months after Nintendo began marketing Donkey Kong. Universal alleged that the Donkey Kong name, character and story constituted false designation of origin in violation of 15 U.S.C. § 1125(a) because Nintendo's "actions falsely suggest to the public that [its] product originates with or is authorized, sponsored or approved by the owner of the King Kong name, character and story." Universal also asserted claims based upon common law unfair competition, trademark and trade name principles.

After extensive discovery, Nintendo moved for summary judgment. The motion was granted by the district court. Specially, the court held that any trademark that Universal purported to own could not be the basis of a successful action under the Lanham Act because it lacked "secondary meaning" as a matter of law; even if Universal's trademark had secondary meaning, there was no question of fact as to whether consumers were likely to confuse Donkey Kong and King Kong; and the common law trademark, trade name and unfair competition claims should be dismissed. This appeal followed.

DISCUSSION

We turn first to what Universal labels the "main" issue, whether the district court's decision that Universal failed to raise a question of fact as to the likelihood of consumer confusion concerning the origin of Donkey Kong was erroneous.

It is well settled that the crucial issue in an action for trademark infringement or unfair competition is whether there is any likelihood that an appreciable number of ordinarily prudent purchasers are likely to be misled, or indeed simply confused, as to the source of the goods in question.

Where the products are different, the prior owner's chance of success is a function of many variables: the strength of his mark, the degree of similarity between the two marks, the proximity of the products, the likelihood that the prior owner will bridge the gap, actual confusion and the reciprocal of defendant's good faith in adopting its own mark, the quality of defendant's product and the sophistication of the buyers. Even this extensive catalogue does not exhaust the possibilities—the court may have to take still other variables into account.

The district court conducted a visual inspection of both the Donkey Kong game and the King Kong movies and stated that the differences between them were "great." It found the Donkey Kong game "comical" and the Donkey Kong gorilla character "farcical, childlike and nonsexual." In contrast, the court described the King Kong character and story as "a ferocious gorilla in quest of a beautiful woman." The court summarized that "Donkey Kong creates a totally different concept and feel from the drama of King Kong" and that "at best, Donkey Kong is a parody of King Kong." Indeed, the fact that Donkey Kong so obviously parodies the King Kong theme strongly contributes to the dispelling confusion on the part of the consumers.

We agree with the district court that the two characters and stories are so different that no question of fact was presented on the likelihood of consumer confusion. The two properties have nothing in common but a gorilla, a captive woman, a male rescuer and a building scenario. Universal has not introduced any evidence indicating actual consumer confusion. Where, as here, the two properties are so different, Universal's claim cannot stand without some indication of actual confusion or a "survey of consumer attitudes under actual market conditions."

Universal argues that the district court's analysis ignored its "primary" contention, "whether Donkey Kong is confusingly similar to the name King Kong." It maintains that it has presented evidence which raises questions of fact on the likelihood of confusion regarding the two names. After reviewing this evidence, we are satisfied that no question of fact exists and thus the decision below should be affirmed.

Universal points to the similarity of the two names, claiming that the use of the word "Kong" raises a question of fact on the likelihood of confusion. We disagree. In order to determine if confusion is likely, each trademark must be compared in its entirety; juxtaposing fragments of each mark does not demonstrate whether the marks as a whole are confusingly similar. The "Kong" and "King Kong" names are widely used by the general public and are associated with apes and other objects of enormous proportions. Nintendo's use of the prefix "Donkey" has no similarity in meaning or sound with the word "King." When taken as a whole, we find as a matter of law that "Donkey Kong" does not evoke or suggest the name of King Kong.

In sum, we find that Universal failed to raise a question of fact whether there was any likelihood that an appreciable number of prudent purchasers are likely to be misled or confused as to the source of Donkey Kong. Consequently, the district court properly granted summary judgment to Nintendo on Universal's Lanham Act claim.

The district court also correctly dismissed the common law claims because, as discussed above, Universal failed to raise a question of fact on the likelihood of confusion.

The judgment of the district court is affirmed.

CASE ANALYSIS

1. Who are the parties to this case? What type of business organization is each party? How do you know?
2. Why did Universal sue Nintendo?
3. How did the court distinguish "King Kong" from "Donkey Kong"?

TRADE SECRET LAW

Unlike other forms of intellectual property, laws governing trade secrets are state rather than federal. Many states have adopted the Uniform Trade Secret Act. Under this act, a trade secret includes items such as "information, including a formula, pattern, compilation, program, device, method, technique or process" that are kept secret by the owner, that have value because they are kept secret, and that would have value to another if disclosed. One of the most common types of trade secret is the customer list. Also, unlike other forms of intellectual property, there is no registration process for a trade secret.

In general, the Uniform Trade Secret Act prevents misappropriation of a trade secret and provides for civil damages, sometimes including punitive damages, if misappropriation is shown. Misappropriation includes both acquiring the trade secret through improper means and disclosing the trade secret under improper circumstances. Thus, if a disgruntled employee sells a customer list to a competing business, both the employee and the competing business are liable for damages.

ETHICAL CHOICES

Assume that you work in a law firm. A complex intellectual property litigation case is set for trial in one week. In organizing the file before trial, you locate a document that was not produced during discovery because no one knew of its existence. The document is obviously relevant, but is very harmful to your client's position. The client is your neighbor. What should you do?

Featured Web Site: www.uspto.gov/

The Web site for the U.S. Patent and Trademark Office contains a great deal of important information about patents and trademarks. The site provides downloadable forms, information about filing fees, and searchable databases.

Go Online

1. List the various searchable databases.
2. What are the address and phone number for the U.S. Patent and Trademark Office?

Chapter Summary

Contract law stems from early English common law but has been modified by many different statutes. A contract is an agreement between parties who are capable of contracting. There must also be consideration and a legal subject matter. If one party fails to perform under a contract, a breach of contract results unless some recognized defense exists. Where a party fails to perform, the nonbreaching party can sue for money damages for the breach, or in some cases for equitable relief. The most common type of equitable relief is specific performance. Special contract rules exist when the contract is for the sale of goods. These rules are found in the Uniform Commercial Code. Many states have also adopted special contract rules to protect consumers in certain kinds of contracts.

Real property is defined as the land and anything permanent attached to it. Real property law involves anything that affects real property. This includes the manner of holding title to property, the various types of interests in real property, and the transfer of real property. Outright ownership of property is known as fee simple. Where more than one person owns the property, title can be held as joint tenants, tenants in common, and, in some states, as community property. Ownership of property is manifested by a document known as a deed. In order to protect title to property, deeds are generally recorded. An important area of real property law is the law that deals with the relationship between landlords and tenants.

Intellectual property law relates to copyrights, patents, trademarks, and trade secrets. The law protects the results of a person's thoughts, ideas, or inventions against unauthorized infringement by others. In some cases intellectual property is protected by common law. It exists without taking any special action. Copyright, patent, and trademark protection can also be obtained by proper registration. A copyright is registered with the U.S. Copyright Office. Patents and trademarks are registered with the U.S. Patent and Trademark Office. A trade secret is protected by keeping it secret.

Terms to Remember

Uniform Commercial Code
bilateral contract
rescind
Statute of Frauds
parol evidence rule
integration clause
quasi contract
breach of contract
specific performance
restitution
arbitration
assignment
assignor
assignee
delegation
real property
fee simple
life estate
joint tenancy
tenants in common

community property
deed
warranty deed
grant deed
quitclaim deed
easement
mortgage
foreclosure
deed of trust
tenancy
lease
unlawful detainer
intellectual property
infringement

Questions for Review

1. Explain the necessary elements for the formation of a contract.
2. Define the following: *Statute of Frauds, parol evidence rule,* and *quasi contract.*
3. What is the effect of the U.C.C. on contract law?
4. What is the difference between real property and personal property?
5. What is the purpose of recording a deed?
6. Describe the various non-ownership interests in real property.
7. How does one protect rights in intellectual property?
8. What items are protected by copyrights?
9. What items are protected by patents?
10. What is a trade secret?

Questions for Analysis

1. Review the Case File at the beginning of the chapter. How would Kersch protect his computer chip?
2. Assume that Kersch enters into an oral agreement to lease a building for eleven months. Three months into the lease, Kersch decides to buy a building. Can he cancel the lease without penalty?
3. Review the Ethical Choices boxes in this chapter. Which NALA and/or NFPA rules or guidelines apply to the situations? Review your state's ethical rules. (*Hint:* Go to www.nala.org/ and find a link.) Which of those rules apply?

Assignments and Projects

1. Review the Case File at the beginning of the chapter. In a law library or on the Internet locate forms:
   a. that would be appropriate for use by Kersch for the sale of computer monitors.
   b. that would be appropriate for Kersch to use to lease premises for his company.
2. If you own your own home, review your deed. What kind of deed is it? Where are deeds recorded in your area? If you are renting, review your rental agreement or lease. Summarize the terms of the agreement.

CHAPTER 11

BUSINESS PRACTICE
THE LAW OF BUSINESS ORGANIZATIONS AND BANKRUPTCY

Technology Corner

Web Address	Name of Site
www.abiworld.org/	American Bankruptcy Institute
http://bankrupt.com/	Internet Bankruptcy Library
www.agin.com/lawfind/	Bankruptcy Lawfinder
www.sec.gov/	Securities and Exchange Commission
www.sec.gov/edgarhp.htm	SEC Edgar Database
www.hoovers.com	Hoover's Online
www.irs.gov/	Internal Revenue Service
www.taxresources.com/	TaxResources

Case File: The Hoppat's Business Matter

Patrick Blackthorne and Hope Escobedo operate a computer business known as Hoppat's. Their business consists of manufacturing and selling computer chips. To date they have operated as a partnership. At this point they are worried about their personal liability for business debts. Also, the business is growing rapidly and they may want to take in additional investors to raise more capital.

Sec. 11-1 INTRODUCTION

Business clients such as Hoppat's often have legal problems that involve several different areas of law. In Chapter 10 you saw how the laws of contracts and real property are involved in everyday legal problems for businesses. The law of business organizations and bankruptcy can also be of major concern. In this case, for example, the clients must carefully review the law of partnership and corporations before choosing a type of business organization. Furthermore, any business like Hoppat's always faces potential bankruptcy problems either as a *creditor*, someone to whom money is owed, or as the bankrupt *debtor*. This chapter will explore some of the major concepts of these two areas of law.

Sec. 11-2 BUSINESS ORGANIZATIONS

security
A financial interest in a business.

uniform act
A set of laws proposed by a group of legal scholars and submitted to the legislatures of the various states for adoption.

The law relating to business organizations is mostly a result of statutory law and case decisions interpreting that law. Each state has adopted its own statutes and laws regulating the various areas of business organizations. In general, these laws regulate the formation, operation, and dissolution of a business. State laws also regulate the sale of securities within the state. **Securities** is a term used to describe an interest in a business. It commonly refers to shares of stock in a corporation, but it includes many other types of interests. Many states have patterned their laws after some **uniform acts** (Uniform Partnership Act, Uniform Limited Partnership Law, Model Business Act). Uniform acts are laws written by experts in a particular area of law and submitted for adoption to the various state legislatures. Until adopted by a state legislature, a uniform act has no binding authority in the state. In addition to state laws, federal rules may apply where securities are sold through any national exchange or through any means of interstate commerce. The Securities and Exchange Commission, a federal agency, has adopted rules that must be followed by corporations and other businesses that engage in such transactions.

Sec. 11-3 SOLE PROPRIETORSHIPS

sole proprietorship
A business owned and operated by one person.

Several forms of business organizations exist: sole proprietorships, partnerships, limited partnerships, and corporations. In recent years, two new forms have grown in popularity: limited liability partnerships and limited liability companies. A **sole proprietorship** is a business owned and operated by one individual. There is a unity of the individual owner and the business itself. In other words, the individual owner is fully liable for any business debts and, conversely, the business is liable for any individual debts. The owner files one tax return, in which business and nonbusiness income is listed. When the owner dies, the sole proprietorship terminates. Of course, the business may continue as a new sole proprietorship under someone else's ownership.

Starting a business as a sole proprietorship requires few, if any, formalities. A person starting a sole proprietorship can usually obtain information from local small business associations and rarely needs the services of an attorney. The requirements for starting this type of business might include obtaining a city business license, a tax identification number, a tax reseller's license (if the business involves selling taxable goods), and complying with any fictitious-name laws. A city business license is obtained from the city in which the individual does business and probably would require no more than paying the appropriate fee. A tax identification (I.D.) number is obtained by requesting one from the Internal Revenue Service. A reseller's license is obtained from the state taxing authority. Any necessary financial forms are usually handled by the sole proprietor or by his or her accountant.

One type of legal procedure that might be handled by an attorney is compliance with fictitious-name laws. Many businesses (of all forms, not only sole proprietors) use clever or unusual names (such as *Hoppat's*). When a business does not use the last name of the owners of that business, the law may require the owners to file and/or publish that information so that consumers can learn the true names if necessary. (Corporations may be required to do the same if they do not use the name that appears in their articles of incorporation.) If a business has a trade name or trademark that it wants to safeguard from use by other businesses, it may want to register the trade name or trademark. This can be done under both federal and state law, as described in the previous chapter.

SEC. 11-4 GENERAL PARTNERSHIPS

partnership
A business operated by two or more individuals for profit.

agent
One who acts on behalf of another.

actual authority
The power given in fact to an agent by the principal or employer.

apparent authority
Authority created by conduct that leads a third person to believe that authority exists.

A **partnership** consists of two or more people who are co-owners of a business for profit. Two kinds of partnerships exist, which are really very different kinds of business organizations: the general partnership and the limited partnership. In a *general partnership*, unless they agree to the contrary, the partners have equal rights in management and control and equal rights in sharing profits and losses. As in the sole proprietorship, there is a unity between the partnership form of business and the individual. A key characteristic of a partnership is the fact that in conducting partnership business, each partner is the **agent** of the other partners. An agent is one who acts for another and whose actions can bind or obligate another. In terms of partnerships, this means that a contract entered into by one partner will bind the other partners and the partnership if the contract was authorized. The contract is authorized if the partner has **actual authority** to enter into the agreement or if that authority is *apparent*. Actual authority means that the other partners have approved the contract. **Apparent authority** exists when the contract has not been actually approved by the other partners but their conduct or actions have reasonably led third parties to believe that such authority exists. The agency relationship also makes partners and the partnership liable or responsible for torts of one party that are committed in the course and scope of the partnership business.

In a partnership, each of the partners is fully and personally liable for all partnership debts. Partnership income is taxed to the individual partners along with nonpartnership income (although the partnership is required to file an informational tax return). When one partner dies, the partnership dissolves and terminates, unless the partners have agreed to the contrary. The parties can form a partnership by adopting a formal written agreement or an informal oral agreement. The only other formalities required are the same as those required of a sole proprietorship.

Many states have adopted laws found in the Uniform Partnership Act. These laws cover such topics as the rights and liabilities of partners, formation of partnerships, management of partnerships, and dissolution of partnerships.

Lawyers and paralegals who deal with partnerships may be involved in negotiating and drafting partnership agreements. Other times, attorneys and paralegals become involved in partnerships when disputes arise among the partners. If these disputes cannot be resolved, the partners may sue one another in court. The legal team also becomes involved in partnerships when the partnership business has floundered and the partnership business considers filing bankruptcy.

SEC. 11-5 LIMITED PARTNERSHIPS

limited partnership
A partnership meeting certain legal formalities and including at least one *general partner* and at least one *limited partner*; the limited partner's liability is limited to the extent of his or her capital contribution.

A **limited partnership** is a different type of business organization. Like a general partnership, it consists of two or more people who are co-owners of a business for profit. However, unlike a general partnership, not all of the co-owners of the business are involved in the management and operation of the business. A limited partnership has both general partners and limited partners. It must have at least one general partner and one limited partner. The *general partner* or partners are similar to partners in a general partnership. They have the right to manage and control the business, and have full personal liability for any partnership debts. The *limited partners,* however, differ. Limited partners must make a cash or property contribution to the business. Their liability for partnership debts is limited to this contribution. Along with this, however, they are restricted from participating in the daily management of the business. The creation of a limited partnership is strictly regulated by law. Written agreements are required, and generally some document must be filed with an agency of the state government, usually the secretary of state. The sale of limited partnership interests may also be considered a sale of a security and be further regulated by securities laws. These laws are discussed later in this chapter. See Figure 11–1 for a sample certificate of limited partnership, which must be filed with the secretary of state in order to form a limited partnership in California.

SEC. 11-6 CORPORATIONS

corporation
A business that is a legal entity unto itself and is formed according to the corporate laws of one state.

business corporation
A corporation formed for any business purpose.

nonprofit corporation
A corporation formed for a charitable, religious, educational, or like purpose; it uses all income for the stated purpose.

Corporations are organizations that are created by following statutory guidelines enacted by the state. Once incorporated, these organizations have legal existence. A corporation is sometimes referred to as an *artificial person* and even has some constitutional rights. Corporations can be formed for many different purposes. The two main types of corporations are business corporations and nonprofit corporations. **Business corporations** are formed for a business purpose—that is, to engage in a business for the purpose of making a profit that can be distributed to the owners of the corporation. A **nonprofit corporation** is formed to serve some public purpose—often charitable, religious, or educational. While nonprofit corporations sometimes

State of California
Secretary of State
Bill Jones

CERTIFICATE OF LIMITED PARTNERSHIP

A $70.00 filing fee must accompany this form.
IMPORTANT-- Read instructions before completing this form

This Space For Filing Use Only

1. NAME OF THE LIMITED PARTNERSHIP (END THE NAME WITH THE WORDS "LIMITED PARTNERSHIP" OR THE ABBREVIATION "L.P.")

2. STREET ADDRESS OF PRINCIPAL EXECUTIVE OFFICE — CITY AND STATE — ZIP CODE

3. STREET ADDRESS OF CALIFORNIA OFFICE WHERE RECORDS ARE KEPT — CITY — CA — ZIP CODE

4. COMPLETE IF LIMITED PARTNERSHIP WAS FORMED PRIOR TO JULY 1, 1984 AND IS IN EXISTENCE ON THE DATE THIS CERTIFICATE IS EXECUTED.
THE ORIGINAL LIMITED PARTNERSHIP CERTIFICATE WAS RECORDED ON ____________ 19 ____ WITH THE RECORDER
OF ____________ COUNTY. FILE OR RECORDATION NUMBER ____________

5. NAME THE AGENT FOR SERVICE OF PROCESS AND CHECK THE APPROPRIATE PROVISION BELOW:
____________ WHICH IS
[ ] AN INDIVIDUAL RESIDING IN CALIFORNIA. PROCEED TO ITEM 6.
[ ] A CORPORATION WHICH HAS FILED A CERTIFICATE PURSUANT TO SECTION 1505. PROCEED TO ITEM 7.

6. IF AN INDIVIDUAL, CALIFORNIA ADDRESS OF THE AGENT FOR SERVICE OF PROCESS:
ADDRESS:
CITY: STATE: CA ZIP CODE:

7. NAMES AND ADDRESSES OF ALL GENERAL PARTNERS: (ATTACH ADDITIONAL PAGES, IF NECESSARY)
A. NAME:
ADDRESS:
CITY: STATE: ZIP CODE:
B. NAME:
ADDRESS:
CITY: STATE: ZIP CODE:

8. INDICATE THE NUMBER OF GENERAL PARTNERS' SIGNATURES REQUIRED FOR FILING CERTIFICATES OF AMENDMENT, RESTATEMENT, MERGER, DISSOLUTION, CONTINUATION AND CANCELLATION. [ ]

9. OTHER MATTERS TO BE INCLUDED IN THIS CERTIFICATE MAY BE SET FORTH ON SEPARATE ATTACHED PAGES AND ARE MADE A PART OF THIS CERTIFICATE BY CHECKING THIS BOX. OTHER MATTERS MAY INCLUDE THE PURPOSE OF BUSINESS OF THE LIMITED PARTNERSHIP E.G. GAMBLING ENTERPRISE. [ ]

10. TOTAL NUMBER OF PAGES ATTACHED, IF ANY: [ ]

11. I CERTIFY THAT THE STATEMENTS CONTAINED IN THIS DOCUMENT ARE TRUE AND CORRECT TO MY OWN KNOWLEDGE. I DECLARE THAT I AM THE PERSON WHO IS EXECUTING THIS INSTRUMENT, WHICH EXECUTION IS MY ACT AND DEED.

SIGNATURE — POSITION OR TITLE — PRINT NAME — DATE

SIGNATURE — POSITION OR TITLE — PRINT NAME — DATE

SEC/STATE (REV. 11/98)

FORM LP-1 – FILING FEE: $70.00
Approved by Secretary of State

FIGURE 11–1 Certificate of limited partnership.

generate income, this income is not distributed to individual owners. It is used by the corporation for its stated purpose.

Business Corporations

A business corporation is a legal entity separate from its owners. Its legal existence does not depend on the life of its owners, and the corporation is liable for its own debts and pays its own taxes. A corporation is formed by complying with statutory requirements. Business corporations come in all sizes. Some may have only one owner or shareholder; others have thousands. Regardless of the size, however, certain characteristics are the same. All corporations are formed by filing a document known as *articles of incorporation* with the secretary of state of some state. Usually this is the state in which the business is primarily operating, but it need not be. Articles of incorporation give the corporation its legal existence. This usually very simple document describes the name and general powers that are given to the business. (See Figure 11–3 for an example.) Businesses can incorporate in one state and do business as a corporation in other states. There may be documents they must file in these states to qualify to do business, but they need to incorporate in only one state. When a corporation does this, it is said to be qualified as a **foreign corporation**. A foreign corporation is one that does business within a state but is not incorporated within that state.

foreign corporation
A corporation incorporated in one state and doing business in another.

bylaws
The internal rules and regulations for a corporation.

Corporations are governed by a set of rules or policies known as **bylaws**. Bylaws are the internal regulations for the corporation. They describe such things as the powers of the corporation and the duties and responsibilities of the directors and officers. Bylaws are kept at the corporate office; they are not filed with any government agency.

shareholders
The owners of a corporation.

dividends
Profits of a corporation that are distributed to the shareholders.

Three groups of parties play an important role in all corporations: shareholders, directors, and officers. **Shareholders** are the owners of the business. They usually have invested money, property, or services in the business and in return they share in profits that the business makes. Profits are usually distributed to the shareholders in the form of **dividends**. When shareholders invest in the business they are purchasing a security; these purchases are regulated by securities regulations, discussed later in this chapter. Even though shareholders are the owners of the business, unlike other forms of business, these owners do not have the right to directly manage and operate the business. Their power is usually limited to electing the directors, although they do have the right to approve certain types of business decisions made by the directors. Shareholders are usually required to meet at least once a year and hold a regular meeting. Minutes of these meetings are prepared.

directors
The individuals who exercise general management and control of a corporation.

Directors or the *board of directors* are the group that have general management power over the corporation. They are responsible for setting general business policies. Directors are sometimes also shareholders. This is especially true of corporations that have only a few shareholders. Like shareholders, the directors are required to hold a regular meeting at least once a year. They are also allowed to hold special meetings whenever necessary. Written minutes are always kept of their meetings. Directors are not responsible for the day-to-day operation of the business; day-to-day management is the responsibility of the officers of the corporation. The **officers** are chosen by the directors.

officers
The individuals who are responsible for the day-to-day management of a corporation.

Corporations can have various officers. The traditional officers are president, vice-president, secretary, and treasurer. Today the president and treasurer are usually referred to as the chief executive officer (CEO) and the chief financial officer (CFO). In smaller corporations, the officers of the corporation are also shareholders and directors.

For examples of various statutes governing corporations, see Figure 11–2.

Delaware Code General Corporation Law

§ 101. Incorporators; how corporation formed; purposes

(a) Any person, partnership, association or corporation, singly or jointly with others, and without regard to his or their residence, domicile or state of incorporation, may incorporate or organize a corporation under this chapter by filing with the Division of Corporations in the Department of State a certificate of incorporation which shall be executed, acknowledged, filed and recorded in accordance with § 103 of this title.

(b) A corporation may be incorporated or organized under this chapter to conduct or promote any lawful business or purposes, except as may otherwise be provided by the Constitution or other law of this State.

(c) Corporations for constructing, maintaining and operating public utilities, whether in or outside of this State, may be organized under this chapter. But corporations for constructing, maintaining and operating public utilities within this State shall be subject to, in addition to this chapter, the special provisions and requirements of Title 26 applicable to such corporations.

§ 106. Commencement of corporate existence

Upon the filing with the Secretary of State of the certificate of incorporation, executed and acknowledged in accordance with § 103 of this title, the incorporator or incorporators who signed the certificate, and his or their successors and assigns, shall, from the date of such filing, be and constitute a body corporate, by the name set forth in the certificate, subject to subsection (d) of § 103 of this title and subject to dissolution or other termination of its existence as provided in this chapter.

§ 109. Bylaws

(a) The original or other bylaws of a corporation may be adopted, amended or repealed by the incorporators, by the initial directors if they were named in the certificate of incorporation, or, before a corporation has received any payment for any of its stock, by its board of directors. After a corporation has received any payment for any of its stock, the power to adopt, amend or repeal bylaws shall be in the stockholders entitled to vote, or, in the case of a nonstock corporation, in its members entitled to vote; provided, however, any corporation may, in its certificate of incorporation, confer the power to adopt, amend or repeal bylaws upon the directors, or, in the case of a nonstock corporation, upon its governing body by whatever name designated. The fact that such power has been so conferred upon the directors or

FIGURE 11–2 Selected sections of Delaware corporation law.

(continued)

governing body, as the case may be, shall not divest the stockholders or members of the power, nor limit their power to adopt, amend or repeal bylaws.

(b) The bylaws may contain any provision, not inconsistent with law or with the certificate of incorporation, relating to the business of the corporation, the conduct of its affairs, and its rights or powers or the rights or powers of its stockholders, directors, officers or employees.

§ 121. General powers

(a) In addition to the power enumerated in § 122 of this title, every corporation, its officers, directors and stockholders shall possess and may exercise all the powers and privileges granted by this chapter or by any other law or by its certificate of incorporation, together with any powers incidental thereto, so far as such powers and privileges are necessary or convenient to the conduct, promotion or attainment of the business or purposes set forth in its certificate of incorporation.

(b) Every corporation shall be governed by the provisions and be subject to the restrictions and liabilities contained in this chapter.

§ 122. Specific powers

Every corporation created under this chapter shall have power to:

(1) Have perpetual succession by its corporate name, unless a limited period of duration is stated in its certificate of incorporation;

(2) Sue and be sued in all courts and participate, as a party or otherwise, in any judicial, administrative, arbitrative or other proceeding, in its corporate name;

(3) Have a corporate seal, which may be altered at pleasure, and use the same by casing it or a facsimile thereof, to be impressed or affixed or in any other manner reproduced.

(4) Purchase, receive, take by grant, gift, devise, bequest or otherwise, lease, or otherwise acquire, own, hold, improve, employ, use and otherwise deal in and with real or personal property, or any interest therein, whenever situated, and to sell, convey, lease, exchange, transfer or otherwise dispose of, or mortgage or pledge, all or any of its property and assets, or any interest therein, wherever situated;

(5) Appoint such officers and agents as the business of the corporation requires and to pay or otherwise provide for them suitable compensation;

(6) Adopt, amend and repeal bylaws;

(7) Wind up and dissolve itself in the manner provided in this chapter;

(8) Conduct its business, carry on its operations and have offices and exercise its powers within or without this State;

(9) Make donations for the public welfare or for charitable, scientific or educational purposes, and in time of war or other national emergency in aid thereof;

(10) Be an incorporator, promoter or manager of other corporations of any type of kind;

(11) Participate with others in any corporation, partnership, limited partnership, joint venture or other association of any kind, or in any transaction,

FIGURE 11–2 Continued

undertaking or arrangement which the participating corporation would have power to conduct by itself, whether or not such participation involves sharing or delegation of control with or to others;

(12) Transact any lawful business which the corporation's board of directors shall find to be in the aid of governmental authority;

(13) Make contracts, including contracts of guaranty and suretyship, incur liabilities, borrow money at such rates of interest as the corporation may determine, issue its notes, bonds and other obligations, and secure any of its obligations by mortgage, pledge or other encumbrance of all or any of its property, franchises and income, and make contracts of guaranty and suretyship which are necessary or convenient to the conduct, promotion or attainment of the business of (a) a corporation all of the outstanding stock of which is owned, directly or indirectly, by the contracting corporation, or (b) a corporation which owns, directly or indirectly, all of the outstanding stock of the contracting corporation, or (c) a corporation all of the outstanding stock of which is owned, directly or indirectly, by a corporation which owns, directly or indirectly, all of the outstanding stock of the contracting corporation, which contracts of guaranty and suretyship shall be deemed to be necessary or convenient to the conduct, promotion or attainment of the business of the contracting corporation, and make our contracts of guaranty and suretyship which are necessary or convenient to the conduct, promotion or attainment of the business of the contracting corporation;

(14) Lend money for its corporate purposes, invest and reinvest its funds, and take, hold and deal with real and personal property as security for the payment of funds so loaned or invested;

(15) Pay pensions and establish and carry out pension, profit sharing, stock options, stock purchase, stock bonus, retirement, benefit, incentive and compensation plans, trusts and provisions for any or all of its directors, officers and employees, and for any or all of the directors, officers and employees of its subsidiaries;

(16) Provide insurance for its benefit on the life of any of its directors, officers or employees, or on the life of any stockholder for the purpose of acquiring at his death shares of its stock owned by such stockholder.

FIGURE 11–2 Continued

PROFESSIONAL CORPORATIONS

professional corporation A corporation formed for the purpose of engaging in certain professions, such as medicine or law.

A special type of business corporation is the **professional corporation**. These are corporations formed by certain professional groups, such as doctors, lawyers, accountants, and dentists. The formation and organization is similar to that of any business corporation. In addition to general corporate rules, these corporations are usually subject to the rules of the profession involved. One difference between these and other corporations relates to ownership. The professional organization may prohibit nonprofessionals from owning an interest (being a shareholder) in a professional corporation.

Close Corporations vs. Public Corporations

close corporation
A small corporation whose shares of stock are not available to the public.

public corporation
A corporation whose shares of stock can be purchased by anyone.

Most corporate businesses are small businesses owned by a few shareholders. Ownership, management, and control is kept confined to those few individuals who created and operate the business. Investment in the business is not open or available to others. This type of corporation is sometimes called a **close corporation**. On the other hand, some corporations allow anyone to invest in the business by buying shares of stock or other securities. These corporations are known as **public corporations**.

Nonprofit Corporations

A nonprofit corporation is created for religious, educational, or other charitable purposes. It is formed in the same way as a business corporation: by filing articles of incorporation with the state's secretary of state. It may have directors and officers who operate the corporation, but because it is not a business, it does not have owners in the same way that a business corporation does. Instead of shareholders, nonprofit corporations usually have members, who do not share in any profits that are made by the corporation. Being a nonprofit corporation does not in itself give the organization any tax advantages. In order for the corporation to gain tax-exempt status, it must apply separately with the Internal Revenue Service and the state tax agency. A nonprofit corporation is not guaranteed tax benefits.

A POINT TO REMEMBER

A corporation is a legal entity that is treated as a person. It pays taxes, can own property, and can sue and be sued in its own name. It has legal status separate and apart from its owners. If the owners should die, the corporation continues.

Piercing the Corporate Veil

One of the chief characteristics of the corporate form is the separation of the corporate entity from the individuals who own or manage the business. In particular, a corporation is responsible for its own debts; ordinarily, shareholders bear no liability for corporate debts. This rule may change, however, under certain circumstances. If a corporation fails to operate as an entity that is separate from its owners, the owners or shareholders can be held personally liable for corporate debts. When this happens, the creditor is said to "pierce the corporate veil." In deciding whether to pierce the corporate veil, the court may look at such factors as:

- Did the corporation observe corporate formalities such as holding meetings?
- Did the corporation keep separate bank accounts?
- Were corporate funds used for corporate and not personal purposes?
- Was the corporation undercapitalized?

SECURITY REGULATIONS

equity security
An ownership interest in a business; an interest whose value is determined by the net worth of the business.

debt security
A certificate indicating that the holder is owed money by a business.

The term *security* describes a variety of types of investments in a business. The most common type of security is a share of stock in a corporation, but there are many other types of securities. For example, a loan to a corporation may also constitute a type of investment and thus be a security. Shares of stock are known as **equity securities**. Loans are known as **debt securities**. Since the great stock market crash of 1929, government has had a strong interest in the regulation of securities. This interest has resulted in state laws that regulate the sale or transfer of securities within that state, as well as federal laws that regulate securities on a national level. Although we tend to think of securities as investments in the corporate form of business, securities and securities regulations are not limited to corporations. Investments in any type of business may be deemed a security.

Federal Regulation

The federal government created the Securities and Exchange Commission (SEC) and enacted two separate major federal acts to regulate certain securities: the Securities Act of 1933 and the Securities Exchange Act of 1934. These acts prohibit fraudulent practices in connection with the sale of securities and also require that certain corporations register a great deal of information and data on the business with the SEC before sales transactions occur. This is a particularly cumbersome process when a closely held corporation decides to go public or to make its shares of stock available to the general public. Such a process is referred to as an *initial public offering* (IPO). The federal rules also require periodic reports from these corporations. The federal rules do not apply to all corporations. Small corporations that do not sell stock through any means of interstate commerce are exempt from most provisions of the law.

State Rules

blue-sky laws
State securities regulations.

State laws govern the sale or transfer of securities within the state (intrastate). These laws are known as **blue-sky laws**, the term *blue sky* coming from a case written by a judge who described a fraudulent stock scheme as having no more substance than the blue sky above. Blue-sky laws are found in the codes or statutory law of the individual states. Although some variances exist from state to state, blue-sky laws usually contain requirements similar to those of federal law. The sale or transfer of securities may have to be registered, corporate reports may have to be filed, and fraudulent practices are outlawed.

ETHICAL CHOICES

Assume that you work as a member of the support staff in a corporate law firm. Your supervising attorney asks you to prepare minutes of regular meetings of a board of directors for a corporation for the past five years. The attorney explains that over the past five years, the corporation, which is owned entirely by a husband, a wife, and their son, failed to actually hold their board of directors meetings or keep minutes. The corporation has recently been sued and the attorney is afraid that the plaintiff will try to pierce the corporate veil. Should you prepare five years' worth of minutes for board of directors meetings that never took place?

Corporate Practice

Lawyers who practice in the area of business organizations usually are involved in the organization and operation of businesses. Many firms specialize in corporate practice. These firms are involved in all aspects of corporate law, including formation (preparing articles or certificates of incorporation, bylaws, and initial minutes), operation (preparing annual minutes of directors' and shareholders' meetings), and compliance with all securities regulations. Since much of this work does not involve giving legal advice or appearing in court, it is easily relegated to a paralegal or legal secretary. See Figure 11–3 for a sample set of articles of incorporation.

Articles of Incorporation of Hoppat's, Inc.

I

The name of this corporation is HOPPAT's, INC.

II

The purpose of this corporation is to engage in any lawful act or activity for which a corporation may be organized under the General Corporation Law of California other than the banking business, the trust company business, or the practice of a profession permitted to be incorporated by the California Corporation Code.

III

The name and address in the state of California of this corporation's initial agent for service of process is:

Patrick Blackthorne
1234 Main St.
Centerville, CA 98765

IV

This corporation is authorized to issue only one class of shares of stock; and the total number of shares which the corporation is authorized to issue is one hundred thousand (100,000).

Dated: January 10, ____

____
Hope Escobedo, Incorporator

I hereby delcare that I am the person who executed the foregoing Articles of Incorporation, which execution is my act and deed.

____
Hope Escobedo, Incorporator

FIGURE 11–3 Sample articles of incorporation.

SEC. 11-7 LIMITED LIABILITY PARTNERSHIPS

limited liability partnership
An organization that provides limited liability to the partners without the restrictions imposed by a limited partnership; may be limited to certain types of professions.

In recent years two new forms of business organizations, limited liability partnerships and limited liability companies, have gained popularity. A **limited liability partnership** provides limited liability to the partners without the restrictions imposed by a limited partnership. In a limited liability partnership, limited liability is available even to partners who participate in the business. This form of business is used by professionals, including lawyers. Like limited partnerships, this form of business is regulated; it is formed by filing appropriate documents with the state's secretary of state. See Figure 11–4 for a sample of such forms. State laws also generally require a professional, such as a lawyer, who wishes to obtain limited liability to maintain a specified amount of malpractice insurance. Failure to do so results in loss of the limited liability.

SEC. 11-8 LIMITED LIABILITY COMPANIES

limited liability company
A type of business organization that provides limited liability to its owners, similar to a corporation, but not taxed as a corporation.

A **limited liability company** is a cross between a sole proprietorship or partnership and a corporation, having characteristics of each. One of the appeals of the corporate form is the fact that the corporation itself is liable for its own debts. Unless the corporate veil has been pierced, the shareholders, officers, and directors are not personally liable for corporate debts. On the other hand, the way that corporations are taxed is often detrimental to small businesses. The limited liability company offers a compromise. In this business form, the company is liable for its own debts. The individuals behind the company are not personally liable for company debts. The business is taxed as a sole proprietorship (if only one person owns the company) or as a partnership (if more than one owner exists). A limited liability company is formed by filing appropriate forms with the state's secretary of state. See Figure 11–5 for a sample of such forms. Operation and management of these businesses is generally much less formal than that of a corporation. Meetings and minutes are not required, although they do occur in some businesses.

SEC. 11-9 BANKRUPTCY LAW

A legal practice concerned with general business matters will probably in one way or another be involved in bankruptcy proceedings, either with debtors or with creditors. Bankruptcy law concerns the procedures used by debtors and creditors when debtors cannot pay their obligations. The primary goal of a bankruptcy proceeding is generally to relieve debtors of the burdens of being unable to pay debts, while protecting the rights of creditors to any nonexempt assets that the debtor might have. *Nonexempt assets* are those assets of the debtor that must be turned over to satisfy debts. *Exempt assets* are those that the debtor can keep even though bankruptcy was filed.

discharge
To relieve or forgive.

Several different bankruptcy procedures exist for accomplishing the goals of a bankruptcy proceeding. These procedures are found in different chapters of the bankruptcy law. In the most common type of bankruptcy proceeding, the debtors file petitions in bankruptcy court asking the court to **discharge** or excuse their debts. While many debts are dischargeable, the law does hold that some debts are

State of California
Bill Jones
Secretary of State

File #____________________

This Space For Filing Use Only

REGISTERED LIMITED LIABILITY PARTNERSHIP REGISTRATION

A $70.00 filing fee must accompany this form.
IMPORTANT – Read instructions before completing this form.

1. Name of the registered limited liability partnership or foreign limited liability partnership:
(End the name with the word "Registered Limited Liability Partnership" or "Limited Liability Partnership" or one of the abbreviations "L.L.P.", "LLP", "R.L.L.P.", or "RLLP.")

2. ☐ Domestic (California) **OR** ☐ Foreign (Not in California) | 3. Jurisdiction

4. Address of the principal office: City State Zip Code

5. Name the Agent for Service of Process in this state and check the appropriate provision below:
_______________________________________ which is
[ ] an individual residing in California. Proceed to item 6.
[ ] a corporation which has filed a certificate pursuant to California Corporations Code Section 1505. Proceed to item 7.

6. If an individual, California address of the agent for service of process:
Address
City State **CA** Zip Code

7. Indicate the business in which the limited liability partnership shall engage: (check one)
☐ Practice of Architecture ☐ Practice of Public Accountancy
☐ Practice of Law ☐ Related:______________________

8. By filing this Registered Limited Liability Partnership (LLP-1) with the Secretary of State, the partnership named above is registering as a domestic registered limited liability partnership or foreign limited liability partnership. **(DO NOT ALTER)**

9. Indicate whether the limited liability partnership is complying with the alternative security provisions:
☐ Yes. Attach Alternative Security Provision (LLP-3) ☐ No

10. Future Effective Date Month Day Year

11. Other matters to be included in this registration may be set forth on separate attached pages and are made a part of this registration.

12. Total number of pages attached, if any:

13. **Declaration:** I declare that I am the person who executed this instrument, which execution is my act and deed.

_______________________________ _______________________________
Signature of Authorized Partner/Person Type or Print Name of Authorized Partner/Person Date

14. **RETURN TO:**
NAME
FIRM
ADDRESS
CITY/STATE
ZIP CODE

SEC/STATE (REV. 1/99) FORM LLP-1 – FILING FEE $70
Approved by Secretary of State

FIGURE 11–4 Registered liimited liability partnership registration.

State of California
Bill Jones
Secretary of State

File#________________________

This Space For Filing Use Only

LIMITED LIABILITY COMPANY ARTICLES OF ORGANIZATION

A $70.00 filing fee must accompany this form.
IMPORTANT – Read instructions before completing this form.

1. Name of the limited liability company (end the name with the words "Limited Liability Company," " Ltd. Liability Co.," or the abbreviations "LLC" or "L.L.C.")

2. The purpose of the limited liability company is to engage in any lawful act or activity for which a limited liability company may be organized under the Beverly-Killea limited liability company act.

3. Name the agent for service of process and check the appropriate provision below:

   ______________________________ which is

   [ ] an individual residing in California. Proceed to item 4.

   [ ] a corporation which has filed a certificate pursuant to section 1505. Proceed to item 5.

4. If an individual, California address of the agent for service of process:
   Address:

   City: State: **CA** Zip Code:

5. The limited liability company will be managed by: **(check one)**

   [ ] one manager [ ] more than one manager [ ] single member limited liability company [ ] all limited liability company members

6. Other matters to be included in this certificate may be set forth on separate attached pages and are made a part of this certificate. Other matters may include the latest date on which the limited liability company is to dissolve.

7. Number of pages attached, if any:

8. Type of business of the limited liability company. (For informational purposes only)

9. **DECLARATION:** It is hereby declared that I am the person who executed this instrument, which execution is my act and deed.

   ______________________________ ______________________________
   Signature of Organizer Type or Print Name of Organizer

   ____
   Date

10. **RETURN TO:**
   NAME
   FIRM
   ADDRESS
   CITY/STATE
   ZIP CODE

SEC/STATE (REV. 12/99)

FORM LLC-1 – FILING FEE $70.00
Approved by Secretary of State

FIGURE 11–5 Limited liability company articles of organization.

not dischargeable. That is, there are some obligations that a person must pay, such as child support and taxes. Recent changes in the bankruptcy laws have increased the number of non-dischargeable debts. If the debtor has assets, they must be turned over to a trustee if the assets are not exempt. The *trustee* in a bankruptcy proceeding is a person specially appointed to take charge of any nonexempt assets, to sell those assets, and to make proper distribution of the proceeds to creditors. Of course, in many cases, the debtor has no assets. If the court grants the debtor's petition, the debts are discharged and the debtor is relieved of any obligation to pay those debts. In other types of bankruptcy proceedings, the debtor does not ask to be totally relieved of paying debts. Rather, the debtor asks the court to approve a payment plan or schedule, which may include payment of a lesser amount than is owed. See Figure 11–6 for a sample bankruptcy petition.

In the United States, bankruptcy law is governed primarily by federal law, specifically the Bankruptcy Code found in the United States Code. Additionally, bankruptcy proceedings are heard in special courts known as bankruptcy courts. These courts are adjuncts to the federal district courts. Today most bankruptcy courts maintain Web sites where you can find information about the court, rules, and procedures about filing bankruptcy. From many of the sites you can download necessary forms. To find the Web site for the bankruptcy court near you go to http://www.uscourts.gov/links.html.

In re Tia Carrere, Debtor

UNITED STATES BANKRUPTCY COURT FOR THE CENTRAL DISTRICT OF CALIFORNIA

64 Bankr. 156; Bankr. L. Rep. (CCH) P71, 279; 15 Collier Bankr. Cas. 2d (MB) 407; 14 Bankr. Ct. Dec. (CRR) 977

JULY 16, 1986 FILED

The issue in this bankruptcy proceeding is whether a debtor who was under a personal service contract is entitled to reject the contract after filing bankruptcy. In this case, the debtor, a movie and television actress, was under a contract to appear in a soap opera. She also entered into a separate agreement to appear in a different television program (The A Team) *for more money. The second agreement was in the nature of an option. The actress subsequently filed bankruptcy and requested release from the first, binding contract. Under bankruptcy law, the trustee may assume contracts that are advantageous to the estate and reject contracts that are not. The bankruptcy court found that under bankruptcy law, personal service contracts are not part of the bankrupt estate. Furthermore, in this case, the court was concerned with the good faith issue. The following is an excerpt from the court's findings.*

STATEMENT OF FACTS

In August, 1985, Tia Carrere ("Carrere") entered into a personal services contract with American Broadcasting Company ("ABC") whereby she agreed to perform in the television series *General Hospital* from that time until August, 1988 ("ABC Contract"). Under the terms of the contract, Carrere was guaranteed employment on the average of 1½ performances per week. She was to be paid between $600 and $700 for each 60-minute program in which she performed.

While the contract with ABC was still in effect, Carrere agreed to make an appearance on the show *A Team*. Under the terms of her agreement with Steven J. Cannell Productions ("*A Team* Contract"), if she became a regular on *A Team*, she would make considerably more money over the life of the contract than if she remained on *General Hospital.*

Although a state court suit was filed by ABC against Carrere for breach of contract due to her agreement with *A Team,* it appears that no actual breach of the ABC contract will take place until the option in the *A Team* Contract has been exercised.

On March 4, 1986, Carrere filed her voluntary petition under Chapter 11. The next day she filed a Notice of Rejection of Executory Contract, seeking to reject the ABC Contract. A motion to reject the ABC Contract was filed by the debtor, and the matter was set for hearing. In her declaration in support of the motion to reject, Carrere makes it clear that her primary motivation in seeking the protection of this Court was to reject the contract with ABC so as to enter into the more lucrative contract with *A Team.* In fact, she claims she did not enter into the contract with *A Team* until she had obtained advice that the bankruptcy would allow her to reject the contract with ABC. In her schedules she claims unsecured debt only. Her stated liabilities are $76,575 and her assets are $13,191.

ANALYSIS

The key issue to be determined by this Court is whether a debtor, who is a performer under a personal services contract, is entitled to reject the contract by virtue of the provisions of 11 U.S.C. § 365. If so, what criteria must be applied?

A Personal Services Contract Is Not Property of the Estate in Chapters 7 or 11

The concept of § 365 is that the trustee, in administering the estate, may assume (and even assign) contracts which are advantageous to the estate and may reject contracts which are not lucrative or beneficial to the estate. 2 *Collier on Bankruptcy* (15th Ed.), para. 365.01. It is not the trustee's duty to benefit the debtor's future finances, but he is to maintain the property of the estate for the benefit of the creditors. The threshold issue to be determined is whether the ABC contract is "property of the estate." If it is not, the trustee has no standing to assume or reject it.

When the Bankruptcy Code became operable in 1979, it radically expanded the concept of property of the estate. The Bankruptcy Code begins with the concept that everything is property of the estate unless it is specifically excluded or unless the debtor thereafter exempts it. 11 U.S.C. § 541(a)(6) states that property of the estate does not include "earnings from services performed by an individual debtor after the commencement of the case." The post-petition earnings from personal services contracts are thus excluded from the Chapter 7 or Chapter 11 estate. Does this exclude the contract itself?

Under the Code, it has been held that a contract for personal services is excluded from the estate pursuant to both § 541(a) (6) and § 365(c). *In re Bofill,* 25 Bankr. 550 (Bankr. S.D.N.Y. 1982). The foremost recent opinion on this matter is *In re Noonan,* 17 Bankr. 793 (Bankr. S.D.N.Y. 1982), which is cited by both sides in support of their respective positions. While *Noonan* is usually cited for the proposition that a debtor may not be forced to assume a personal services contract, it also deals with the personal services contract as property of the estate.

In *Noonan* the debtor was also a performer. He had entered into a personal services contract with a recording company, which wished to exercise its option and require him to record new albums. Noonan, a debtor-in-possession, sought to reject the contract. When the recording company vigorously opposed Noonan's motion, Noonan converted to Chapter 7, knowing that the trustee could not assume the contract, nor could he force the debtor to perform. Therefore the contract would be automatically rejected.

The recording company moved to reconvert to Chapter 11 and to be allowed to confirm a creditor's plan requiring Noonan to assume the contract and perform under it. The Court denied the motion. Among the grounds for denial was the holding that a personal services contract is not property of the estate. The *Noonan* case did not deal with the issue of rejection of a personal services contract, for the debtor's motion to reject was never heard. But the case clearly held that a personal services contract is not property of the estate. The Court finds this line of reasoning to be persuasive.

Since the trustee has no interest in the contract, he cannot assume or reject the contract.

The Rights of a Debtor-in-Possession Are No Greater Than Those of a Trustee

In her role as debtor-in-possession, she has no interest in the proceeds of the personal services contract, nor in the contract itself. The contract never comes under the jurisdiction of the Bankruptcy Court. The Court has no interest, the estate has no interest.

It Would Be Inequitable to Allow the Contract to be Rejected

Beyond the legal arguments described above, the Court is concerned about the good faith issue of allowing a debtor to file for the primary purpose of rejecting a personal services contract. A personal services contract is unique and money damages will often not make the employer whole. In weighing the rights of the employer to require performance against the rights of the performer to refuse to perform, California courts have allowed the employer to seek an injunction against the performer so that she could not breach the negative promises not to compete. *Warner Bros. Pictures v. Brodel,* 31 Cal. 2d 766, 192 P. 2d 949 (1948). It is this very remedy that Carrere seeks to avoid. For that reason this Court finds that there is not "cause" to reject this contract, if the major motivation of the debtor in filing the case was to be able to perform under the more lucrative *A Team* contract. It is clear that for Carrere this is the major motivation, even if it is not the sole motivation.

Therefore, rejection is denied for lack of cause.

CASE ANALYSIS

1. Why did Carrere file bankruptcy?
2. What is a personal services contract?
3. Under bankruptcy law, what is meant by the term *estate*?

ETHICAL CHOICES

Assume that you are working as a paralegal in a bankruptcy law firm. You are helping a client fill out a bankruptcy petition. During this process, the client tells you that since he first contemplated filing bankruptcy, approximately six months ago, he has been putting aside cash from each paycheck and now has about $3,000 cash. The client tells you not to list this as an asset on the bankruptcy petition. What do you do?

Featured Web Site: www.sba.gov

The Small Business Administration has always provided valuable information to anyone starting a business. That information is now available through their Internet site.

Go Online

1. What types of matters should be considered by a person who is starting a new business?
2. What kind of information pertaining to your state is accessible through this site?

(Official Form 1) (9/97)

FORM B1 United States Bankruptcy Court ____________District of____________	Voluntary Petition
Name of Debtor (if individual, enter Last, First, Middle):	Name of Joint Debtor (Spouse) (Last, First, Middle):
All Other Names used by the Debtor in the last 6 years (include married, maiden, and trade names):	All Other Names used by the Joint Debtor in the last 6 years (include married, maiden, and trade names):
Soc. Sec./Tax I.D. No. (if more than one, state all):	Soc. Sec./Tax I.D. No. (if more than one, state all):
Street Address of Debtor (No. & Street, City, State & Zip Code):	Street Address of Joint Debtor (No. & Street, City, State & Zip Code):
County of Residence or of the Principal Place of Business:	County of Residence or of the Principal Place of Business:
Mailing Address of Debtor (if different from street address):	Mailing Address of Joint Debtor (if different from street address):
Location of Principal Assets of Business Debtor (if different from street address above):	

Information Regarding the Debtor (Check the Applicable Boxes)

Venue (Check any applicable box)

☐ Debtor has been domiciled or has had a residence, principal place of business, or principal assets in this District for 180 days immediately preceding the date of this petition or for a longer part of such 180 days than in any other District.

☐ There is a bankruptcy case concerning debtor's affiliate, general partner, or partnership pending in this District.

Type of Debtor (Check all boxes that apply)

☐ Individual(s) ☐ Railroad
☐ Corporation ☐ Stockbroker
☐ Partnership ☐ Commodity Broker
☐ Other ____________

Chapter or Section of Bankruptcy Code Under Which the Petition is Filed (Check one box)

☐ Chapter 7 ☐ Chapter 11 ☐ Chapter 13
☐ Chapter 9 ☐ Chapter 12
☐ Sec. 304 - Case ancillary to foreign proceeding

Nature of Debts (Check one box)

☐ Consumer/Non-Business ☐ Business

Filing Fee (Check one box)

☐ Full Filing Fee attached
☐ Filing Fee to be paid in installments (Applicable to individuals only) Must attach signed application for the court's consideration certifying that the debtor is unable to pay fee except in installments. Rule 1006(b). See Official Form No. 3.

Chapter 11 Small Business (Check all boxes that apply)

☐ Debtor is a small business as defined in 11 U.S.C. § 101
☐ Debtor is and elects to be considered a small business under 11 U.S.C. § 1121(e) (Optional)

Statistical/Administrative Information (Estimates only)

☐ Debtor estimates that funds will be available for distribution to unsecured creditors.
☐ Debtor estimates that, after any exempt property is excluded and administrative expenses paid, there will be no funds available for distribution to unsecured creditors.

THIS SPACE IS FOR COURT USE ONLY

Estimated Number of Creditors	1-15	16-49	50-99	100-199	200-999	1000-over
	☐	☐	☐	☐	☐	☐

Estimated Assets							
$0 to $50,000	$50,001 to $100,000	$100,001 to $500,000	$500,001 to $1 million	$1,000,001 to $10 million	$10,000,001 to $50 million	$50,000,001 to $100 million	More than $100 million
☐	☐	☐	☐	☐	☐	☐	☐

Estimated Debts							
$0 to $50,000	$50,001 to $100,000	$100,001 to $500,000	$500,001 to $1 million	$1,000,001 to $10 million	$10,000,001 to $50 million	$50,000,001 to $100 million	More than $100 million
☐	☐	☐	☐	☐	☐	☐	☐

FIGURE 11–6 Voluntary bankruptcy petition.

(Official Form 1) (9/97)

Voluntary Petition *(This page must be completed and filed in every case)*	Name of Debtor(s):	**FORM B1,** Page 2
Prior Bankruptcy Case Filed Within Last 6 Years (If more than one, attach additional sheet)		
Location Where Filed:	Case Number:	Date Filed:
Pending Bankruptcy Case Filed by any Spouse, Partner or Affiliate of this Debtor (If more than one, attach additional sheet)		
Name of Debtor:	Case Number:	Date Filed:
District:	Relationship:	Judge:

Signatures

Signature(s) of Debtor(s) (Individual/Joint)

I declare under penalty of perjury that the information provided in this petition is true and correct.

[If petitioner is an individual whose debts are primarily consumer debts and has chosen to file under chapter 7] I am aware that I may proceed under chapter 7, 11, 12 or 13 of title 11, United States Code, understand the relief available under each such chapter, and choose to proceed under chapter 7.

I request relief in accordance with the chapter of title 11, United States Code, specified in this petition.

X ______________________________
Signature of Debtor

X ______________________________
Signature of Joint Debtor

____
Telephone Number (If not represented by attorney)

____
Date

Signature of Attorney

X ______________________________
Signature of Attorney for Debtor(s)

____
Printed Name of Attorney for Debtor(s)

____
Firm Name

____
Address

____

____
Telephone Number

____
Date

Exhibit A

(To be completed if debtor is required to file periodic reports (e.g., forms 10K and 10Q) with the Securities and Exchange Commission pursuant to Section 13 or 15(d) of the Securities Exchange Act of 1934 and is requesting relief under chapter 11)

☐ Exhibit A is attached and made a part of this petition.

Exhibit B

(To be completed if debtor is an individual whose debts are primarily consumer debts)

I, the attorney for the petitioner named in the foregoing petition, declare that I have informed the petitioner that [he or she] may proceed under chapter 7, 11, 12, or 13 of title 11, United States Code, and have explained the relief available under each such chapter.

X ______________________________
Signature of Attorney for Debtor(s) Date

Signature of Debtor (Corporation/Partnership)

I declare under penalty of perjury that the information provided in this petition is true and correct, and that I have been authorized to file this petition on behalf of the debtor.

The debtor requests relief in accordance with the chapter of title 11, United States Code, specified in this petition.

X ______________________________
Signature of Authorized Individual

____
Printed Name of Authorized Individual

____
Title of Authorized Individual

____
Date

Signature of Non-Attorney Petition Preparer

I certify that I am a bankruptcy petition preparer as defined in 11 U.S.C. § 110, that I prepared this document for compensation, and that I have provided the debtor with a copy of this document.

____
Printed Name of Bankruptcy Petition Preparer

____
Social Security Number

____
Address

____

Names and Social Security numbers of all other individuals who prepared or assisted in preparing this document:

If more than one person prepared this document, attach additional sheets conforming to the appropriate official form for each person.

X ______________________________
Signature of Bankruptcy Petition Preparer

____
Date

A bankruptcy petition preparer's failure to comply with the provisions of title 11 and the Federal Rules of Bankruptcy Procedure may result in fines or imprisonment or both 11 U.S.C. §110; 18 U.S.C. §156.

FIGURE 11–6 Continued

FORM B6B
(10/89)

In re ____, Case No. ____________________
Debtor (If known)

SCHEDULE B - PERSONAL PROPERTY

Except as directed below, list all personal property of the debtor of whatever kind. If the debtor has no property in one or more of the categories, place an "x" in the appropriate position in the column labeled "None." If additional space is needed in any category, attach a separate sheet properly identified with the case name, case number, and the number of the category. If the debtor is married, state whether husband, wife, or both own the property by placing an "H," "W," "J," or "C" in the column labeled "Husband, Wife, Joint, or Community." If the debtor is an individual or a joint petition is filed, state the amount of any exemptions claimed only in Schedule C - Property Claimed as Exempt.

Do not list interests in executory contracts and unexpired leases on this schedule. List them in Schedule G - Executory Contracts and Unexpired Leases.

If the property is being held for the debtor by someone else, state that person's name and address under "Description and Location of Property."

TYPE OF PROPERTY	NONE	DESCRIPTION AND LOCATION OF PROPERTY	HUSBAND, WIFE, JOINT, OR COMMUNITY	CURRENT MARKET VALUE OF DEBTOR'S INTEREST IN PROPERTY, WITHOUT DEDUCTING ANY SECURED CLAIM OR EXEMPTION
1. Cash on hand.				
2. Checking, savings or other financial accounts, certificates of deposit, or shares in banks, savings and loan, thrift, building and loan, and homestead associations, or credit unions, brokerage houses, or cooperatives.				
3. Security deposits with public utilities, telephone companies, landlords, and others.				
4. Household goods and furnishings, including audio, video, and computer equipment.				
5. Books; pictures and other art objects; antiques; stamp, coin, record, tape, compact disc, and other collections or collectibles.				
6. Wearing apparel.				
7. Furs and jewelry.				
8. Firearms and sports, photographic, and other hobby equipment.				
9. Interests in insurance policies. Name insurance company of each policy and itemize surrender or refund value of each.				
10. Annuities. Itemize and name each issuer.				

FIGURE 11–6 Continued

Chapter Summary

Lawyers who concentrate on handling business clients often deal in many different areas of law. Some of the more common areas include the law of business organizations, the law of real property, and the law of bankruptcy. The law of business organizations deals primarily with the laws regulating the formation, operation, and dissolution of partnerships, limited partnerships, and corporations.

A partnership is a business owned and managed by two or more individuals. The partners can have any agreement among themselves regarding management rights and sharing of profits and losses, but each partner is fully liable for all partnership debts. A partner's personal assets are liable for partnership debts. The partnership agreement can be a formal written agreement or an informal oral agreement. A limited partnership is a special type of partnership with at least one general partner and one limited partner. General partners manage and control the business and are fully liable for partnership debts. Limited partners have no management rights and are liable for partnership debts only to the extent of their initial capital contribution. Legal formalities are required for the formation of a limited partnership.

A corporation is a legal entity created by filing articles of incorporation with the state's secretary of state. A corporation is owned by shareholders whose ownership interest is in the form of shares of stock. General policy decisions for a corporation are made by a board of directors; the corporation is managed on a day-to-day basis by officers. A corporation is a legal person.

Two new forms of business entities are the limited liability partnership and limited liability company. In a limited liability partnership, the partners can all participate in the business and still maintain limited liability. In some states this form is limited to certain professions that must carry a minimum level of malpractice insurance. A limited liability company has many of the characteristics of a corporation, including a separation of the business and the individuals for purposes of debts. However, the business income is taxed as if the business were a sole proprietorship or partnership.

Bankruptcy, which is regulated by the federal government rather than the states, is a proceeding in which debtors are legally relieved of certain debts.

Terms to Remember

- security
- uniform act
- sole proprietorship
- partnership
- agent
- actual authority
- apparent authority
- limited partnership
- corporation
- business corporation
- nonprofit corporation
- foreign corporation
- bylaws
- shareholders
- dividends
- directors
- officers
- professional corporation
- close corporation
- public corporation
- equity security
- debt security
- blue-sky laws
- limited liability partnership
- limited liability company
- discharge

Questions for Review

1. Describe the key characteristics of a sole proprietorship.
2. Compare and contrast a general partnership and a limited partnership.
3. Describe the different types of corporations.
4. Explain the roles of directors, officers, and shareholders in a business corporation.
5. What are blue-sky laws?
6. Which governmental agencies are involved with corporations?
7. Describe a limited liability partnership.

8. Describe a limited liability company.
9. What is the goal of bankruptcy?

Questions for Analysis

1. Refer to the quoted sections of the Delaware corporation laws in Figure 11–2 and answer the following questions, referring to the section in which you found the answer.
   a. Must a business be doing business in Delaware in order to incorporate in that state?
   b. Who is responsible for adopting bylaws for a corporation?
   c. List at least five powers of a corporation.
2. Review Figures 11–4 (limited liability partnership registration) and 11–5 (limited liability company, articles of organization). List the information that you would need to obtain from Hoppat's if they were considering a limited liability partnership and a limited liability company as possibilities for their business.
3. Review the Ethical Choices boxes in this chapter. Which NALA and/or NFPA rules or guidelines apply to the situations? Review your state's ethical rules. (*Hint*: Go to www.nala.org/ and find a link.) Which of those rules apply?

Assignments and Projects

1. Find a sample partnership agreement in a form book for your state. Also find a sample form for articles of incorporation.
2. Find the Web site for the office of secretary of state for your state. (*Hint*: Start with the home page for your state and look for state agencies.) What business forms, if any, are available?
3. Go on the Internet and find sample partnership and other business forms. Try the following site to get you started: www.findlaw.com/. Go to the legal topics section of this Web site.
4. Locate the Web site for the closest bankruptcy court. Describe the type of information that is available on the site.

CHAPTER 12

CRIMINAL PRACTICE

CRIMINAL LAW AND JUVENILE LAW

Technology Corner

Web Address	Name of Site
http://faculty.ncwc.edu/toconnor/	Criminal Justice MegaLinks
www.cybercrimes.net/	Cybercrimes
www.fbi.gov/	Federal Bureau of Investigation

Case File: The Simmons Criminal Matter

Mr. Jacob Simmons believes that he will be charged with several crimes. He describes the events as follows:

"I had been playing pool and drinking beer in Sam's Billiards Hall for about two hours when Ron Opal walked in. He is dating Kathy Smith. Kathy and I were engaged until about two weeks ago when she said she needed some space. When Ron swaggered past me, toward the bar, he asked me if I liked the 'space' Kathy had given me. That really made me mad. I am not seeing anyone and I had a bad couple of weeks. I told him to stay away from me. He came back and poked his index finger into my chest and told me to get a life. I slapped his hand away. He didn't scare me. Then he went over to the bar and got a beer. The more I thought about him and Kathy and his attitude I just lost my temper and yelled out, 'You are no good and everyone knows it. Stay away from me or you will be sorry.' He came back up to me and began yelling at me. I got so mad I threw my beer bottle at him. It broke when it hit him on the shoulder, he had a pretty good cut on the top of his right shoulder. Then the bartender came over and got between us. He told us to leave. The last thing Ron said to me was that he was going to report it to the cops. A friend who works at County Hospital told me today that Ron has been in the hospital since that night; he is a 'bleeder' or something and lost a lot of blood and is in real serious condition. My friend says he could actually die. I am really worried."

SECTION I: CRIMINAL LAW

Sec. 12-1 INTRODUCTION TO CRIMINAL PRACTICE

crime
An act in violation of a criminal statute.

Model Penal Code
A collection of criminal statutes; it was created for the states to adopt in whole or in part, and has helped create uniformity in criminal law.

presumption
An inference in support of a specific fact.

rebuttable presumption
An inference that may be rebutted or challenged.

A criminal law office can be an exciting place to work. In a criminal practice the client, in many instances, will have been charged with the commission of a **crime.** A crime is a social wrong or social evil. Crimes are punishable under the law, that is, the criminal statute. A primary goal of criminal law is to prevent socially undesirable or unacceptable behavior. All states, as well as the federal government, have criminal codes. The **Model Penal Code** has been adopted in whole or in part by many states. This code was drafted by legal scholars in a largely successful attempt to create consistent criminal laws.

A research assistant working in a criminal law office researches the case law and the statutes applicable to the client's case. In addition, the assistant reviews the paperwork for potential flaws in the pleadings or flaws in the laws relied upon in the pleadings. This person might interview witnesses to determine the facts of the case. Remember, new laws must be placed under very strict scrutiny. They must be carefully analyzed and reviewed for potential ambiguities.

People who practice criminal law and the staff who work with them carry a tremendous burden. The penalties in criminal law may be severe. Most of these penalties involve the loss, if the defendant is convicted, of one or more of the defendant's personal freedoms. The drafters of the Constitution of the United States understood what it meant to lose one's liberty or one's freedom. The Constitution was carefully drafted so as to protect people and citizens from unfair laws and unfair governmental practices. In criminal law, there is a **presumption** that the defendant is innocent until proven guilty. This is a **rebuttable presumption,** which means that the presumption may be disproved by the facts.

SEC. 12-2 PURPOSES OF CRIMINAL LAW

It is incomplete to say that the purpose of criminal law is to prevent socially unacceptable or undesirable behavior. The purpose also involves punishment. Our criminal justice system relies, in part, on punishment to prevent socially undesirable behavior.

DETERRENCE

deter
To stop, discourage, or prevent a person from performing a certain act.

For example, some criminal punishments are designed to **deter** people from committing crimes. Once individuals understand that they will be punished for certain acts, they will be deterred from committing those acts.

REHABILITATION

rehabilitation
The process of helping a person attain or regain his or her potential as a citizen; may take the form of counseling or therapy.

Rehabilitation is often cited as the purpose for punishing people convicted of committing crimes. In theory, the criminal benefits from programs offering education, counseling, training, and treatment. However, there are serious concerns about the success of rehabilitation programs.

INCAPACITATION

incapacitation
The act of restraining a person from taking certain actions.

Another purpose for the punishment of crimes is **incapacitation.** If a person who is dangerous to society is placed in prison or jail, that person cannot injure members of the general public. The criminal is literally restrained or incapacitated from injuring others. This restraint may take the form of extended incarceration or even death.

RETRIBUTION

retribution
Punishment for a crime.

Retribution takes place when society, through the criminal justice system, takes revenge on criminals who violate criminal statutes. The punishment of the criminal must take place through the criminal justice system. Victims of crime or the families of victims of crime must not seek their own retribution. The criminal statutes help to serve this purpose.

SEC. 12-3 THE ELEMENTS OF A CRIME: *MENS REA* AND *ACTUS REUS*

Most crimes have two basic elements. First, there is a mental element: the guilty state of mind. Second, there is a physical element: the physical act by the criminal defendant.

MENS REA

mens rea
The mental element of a crime; sometimes called the "guilty mind."

The mental element is known as the ***mens rea,*** or mental state, of the defendant. Sometimes this is referred to as the "guilty mind" of the defendant, or the defendant's criminal intent. Under the Model Penal Code, four states of mind fulfill the *mens rea* requirement: purposeful, knowing, reckless, and negligent.

A Purposeful Act

purposeful act
An act that is performed willfully or voluntarily.

A **purposeful act** occurs when the defendant acts with the desire to cause the result. For example, suppose the defendant shot a gun at the victim, intending to shoot him. This is a purposeful act.

A Knowing Act

knowing act
An act that is performed consciously or with knowledge.

A **knowing act** occurs when the defendant acts with the knowledge that the result is almost certain to occur. The difference between a purposeful act and a knowing act is that the knowing actor is not acting to cause the result. For example, suppose a defendant fired a gun into a crowded room. He knew that he would almost certainly shoot a person. However, he did not intend harm to any specific victim. This is thus a knowing act rather than a purposeful act.

A Reckless Act

reckless act
An act in which a person is careless or indifferent to the consequences of the action.

A **reckless act** occurs when the defendant acts with a conscious disregard that a substantial and unjustifiable risk will result. For example, suppose that at the public park on the Fourth of July, the defendant fired his gun into the air and the falling bullet struck and injured a child. This is a reckless act.

A Negligent Act

negligent act
An act in which a person acts with a substantial and unjustifiable risk.

A **negligent act** occurs when the defendant acts with a substantial and unjustifiable risk. However, there is no conscious disregard of the risk. For example, suppose the defendant's 1,000-acre ranch was clearly posted with No Trespassing signs; no one should have been on the ranch on the Fourth of July. The defendant fired his gun into the air and the falling bullet struck and injured a trespasser. This is a negligent act.

inference
A logical conclusion of a fact that is not supported by direct evidence; a deduction made by a judge or a jury, based on common sense and the evidence presented in the trial.

The prosecution bears the burden of proving the defendant's mental state when the act in question was committed. Proving *mens rea* can be difficult because we are talking about proving what a person was actually thinking when a specific event or act occurred. In many instances, the prosecutor will use **inferences** to prove the *mens rea* of the defendant. Inferences are conclusions that a jury or judge may make after full consideration of the facts. For example, suppose a woman walks up to her estranged husband and shoots him in the chest. She later says she intended only to wound him. The husband dies as a result of the gunshot injury. In some jurisdictions, to sustain a first-degree murder charge, the prosecutor must show that the defendant intended to kill the victim. In this instance, the jury would be allowed to infer that the wife intended to kill her husband, based on the seriousness of her action.

ACTUS REUS

actus reus
The physical element of a crime; the guilty act or the physical aspect of the crime.

Actus reus is the second element of a crime: the guilty act or the physical aspect of the crime. In most cases, an act is a volitional physical act. In the example of the woman who shot her estranged husband, the act of pulling the trigger of the gun is the act, or the *actus reus,* of the crime.

voluntary act
An unconstrained act.

One further aspect of *actus reus* is vital: The action must be a **voluntary act.** The Model Penal Code provides the following guidance on what is a voluntary act.

> ***Article 2: General Principles of Liability***
> ***Section 2.01: Requirement of Voluntary Act; Omission as Basis of Liability; Possession as an Act***
>
> (1) A person is not guilty of an offense unless his liability is based on conduct which includes a voluntary act or the omission to perform an act of which he is physically capable.
>
> (2) The following are not voluntary acts within the meaning of this Section:
> (a) a reflex or convulsion;
> (b) a bodily movement during unconsciousness or sleep;
> (c) conduct during hypnosis or resulting from hypnotic suggestion;
> (d) a bodily movement that otherwise is not a product of the effort or determination of the actor, either conscious or habitual.
>
> (3) Liability for the commission of an offense may not be based on an omission unaccompanied by action unless:
> (a) the omission is expressly made sufficient by the law defining the offense; or
> (b) a duty to perform the omitted act is otherwise imposed by law.
>
> (4) Possession is an act, within the meaning of this Section, if the possessor knowingly procured or received the thing possessed or was aware of his control thereof for a sufficient period to have been able to terminate his possession.

United States v. Falkowski

900 F. Supp. 1207 (Alaska 1995)

In this criminal case, defendant Falkowski was indicted on charges related to the cultivation and distribution of marijuana. The day following the criminal indictment, the government filed civil forfeiture proceedings against real property obviously used in the commission of the crime. The sequence of the events following is important. On October 14, defendant was arrested. On November 5, the United States sought entry of default in the civil forfeiture case. On November 13, defendant pleaded guilty to some of the criminal charges pursuant to a plea agreement. On December 2, the government made a second request to enter default in the civil forfeiture action. On December 14, the clerk entered default in the civil forfeiture proceeding. On February 2, the United States moved for a decree of forfeiture. On July 28, defendant was sentenced in the criminal case. Defendant appealed the criminal conviction, claiming that the civil forfeiture and criminal sentence constituted double jeopardy and because the sentence was the last to be imposed, the conviction must be set aside. The court stated that there were three reasons why the attack on the criminal case must fail. First, jeopardy attached in the criminal case before the default judgment was entered in the civil proceeding. Second, by entering a plea of guilty, the defendant waived or forfeited the right to collaterally attack his conviction and sentence on double jeopardy. Third, the civil forfeiture was not based upon the same offense for which defendant was criminally prosecuted.

OPINION

Statement of Relevant Facts

On October 6, 1992, Falkowski and co-defendants were indicted on charges related to the cultivation and distribution of marijuana in the Fairbanks area. Falkowski was charged as part of a continuing conspiracy headed by John Collette, and with conducting a continuing criminal enterprise and related offenses. The indictment contained criminal forfeiture counts addressing property in which Falkowski was alleged to claim an interest.

On October 7, 1992, the day following the return of the indictment, the government filed civil forfeiture proceedings against real property located at 1804 Caribou Way in Fairbanks, Alaska. This property had also been listed in the indictment. The criminal case was brought in Anchorage while the civil case proceeded in Fairbanks. Falkowski was served but did not file a claim regarding the civil forfeiture of the Caribou Way property, while others with interest in the real estate did file claims.

On October 14, 1992, Falkowski was arrested and simultaneously served with notice of the arrest of the property at 1804 Caribou Way.

On November 5, 1992, the United States sought entry of default against Falkowski in the civil forfeiture case. The request made no reference to the pending criminal prosecution.

On November 13, 1992, Falkowski pled guilty to some of the charges in the indictment pursuant to a plea agreement anticipating that the other counts would be dismissed. The charges to which Falkowski pled included conducting a continuing criminal enterprise, money laundering, and investing drug proceeds in a business enterprise. As part of the plea agreement, Falkowski agreed to forfeit any property (1) which he acquired as a result of drug trafficking and (2) to assist the government in locating and seizing any such property. The plea agreement did not specify whether the property at 1804 Caribou Way would be forfeited civilly or criminally. In fact, the plea agreement made no specific reference to the Caribou Way property or the civil forfeiture proceeding.

On December 2, 1992, the government made a second request to enter default against Falkowski in the civil forfeiture action. On December 14, 1992, the clerk entered a default against all defendants or claimants in the forfeiture action who had not filed claims, answers or responses. The defaulted parties included Falkowski.

On February 2, 1993, the United States moved for a decree of forfeiture, relying in part on the declaration and order of default. The 1804 Caribou Way property was ordered forfeited to the United States by an order entered on February 10, 1993.

On July 28, 1993, the district court sentenced Falkowski to identical concurrent seventy-two-month sentences on each of the counts of conviction. The judgment of conviction makes no reference to forfeiture of the Caribou Way property.

Discussion

Falkowski contends that the civil forfeiture of some of his property coupled with his significant prison sentence constitutes multiple punishments for the "same offense" which is barred by the double jeopardy clause of the United States Constitution. He contends that the default judgment forfeiting his property preceded his sentence and, therefore, his criminal sentence should be vacated. The Fifth Amendment provides that "No person shall . . . be subject for the same offense to be twice put in jeopardy of life or limb. . . ." The double jeopardy clause protects against a second prosecution for the same offense after acquittal, a second prosecution for the same offense after conviction, and multiple punishments for the same offense. *See North Carolina v. Pearce*, 395 U.S. 711, 717, 23 L. Ed. 2d 656, 89 S. Ct. 2072 (1969). Although the text mentions only harm to life or limb, the Fifth Amendment covers imprisonment and monetary penalties as well. *See United States v. Halper*, 490 U.S. 435, 104 L. Ed. 2d 487, 109 S. Ct. 1892 (1989). A civil forfeiture proceeding is not a criminal prosecution. *United States v. One Assortment of 89 Firearms*, 465 U.S. 354, 361–62, 104 S. Ct. 1099, 79 L. Ed. 2d 361 (1984). Thus, this Court is only concerned in this case with the punishment prong of the rule.

There are three reasons why Falkowski's attack on his criminal sentence must fail: First, jeopardy attached in the criminal case before the default judgment was entered in the civil proceeding. Second, by entering a plea of guilty, Falkowski waived or, more accurately, forfeited the right to collaterally attack his conviction and sentence on double jeopardy grounds. Third, the civil forfeiture proceeding was not based upon the same offense for which Falkowski was criminally prosecuted.

The Relative Timing of Plea and Forfeiture

Where a defendant contends that he was subject to multiple punishments for the same offense, it is necessary to determine the point at which jeopardy attaches because first in time is apparently first in right. *See, e.g., United States v. Faber*, 57 F.3d 873 (9th Cir. 1995). Jeopardy attaches in a criminal case when the jury is sworn or, as in this situation, when the case settles without trial, jeopardy attaches when a plea is accepted. *Faber*, 57 F.3d at 874–5. In the instant case, Falkowski entered an unconditional plea on November 13, 1992. While there is some uncertainty regarding the point at which jeopardy "attaches" in a civil forfeiture proceeding, the consensus seems to be that the earliest jeopardy attaches is when an answer is filed in the civil forfeiture proceeding. *See also United States v. Wong*, 62 F.3d 1212, slip op. at 9925 (9th Cir. 1995). Falkowski never filed an answer, so jeopardy never attached. *Accord United States v. Torres*, 28 F.3d 1463 (7th Cir. 1994). Alternatively, the only other significant date would be the entry of default judgment against Falkowski on February 10, 1993. Until final judgment was entered, Falkowski could still seek to reclaim the property. *United States v. A Parcel of Land, Buildings, Appurtenances and Improvements, Known as 92 Buena Vista Ave., Rumson, New Jersey*, 507 U.S. 111, 113 S. Ct. 1126, 1136, 122 L. Ed. 2d 469 (1993) (until judgment entered, the government does not own property). The civil forfeiture of the Caribou Way property does not impact Falkowski's criminal sentence.

The Civil Forfeiture Was Not Based upon the Same Offense

The Fifth Amendment prevents *inter alia* multiple punishments for the same offense. Falkowski argues that his civil forfeiture and criminal prosecution comprised the same offense and relies upon *United States v. $405,089.23 United States Currency*, 33 F.3d 1210 (9th Cir. 1994). That decision does not, however, specifically address the issue or discuss the definitive decision determining whether two offenses are the same for double jeopardy purposes. *See United States v. Dixon*, 125 L. Ed. 2d 556, 113 S. Ct. 2849 (1993). In *Dixon*, the Supreme Court overruled *Grady v. Corbin*, 495 U.S. 508, 109 L. Ed. 2d 548, 110 S. Ct. 2084 (1990) and disapproved the dictum suggested in *Illinois v. Vitale*, 447 U.S. 410, 65 L. Ed. 2d 228, 100 S. Ct. 2260 (1980), that prosecuting someone a second time based on evidence used to convict him of a related crime on another occasion would implicate double jeopardy. *Dixon*, 113 S. Ct. at 2861–2863. The Court held that to determine whether successive prosecutions involve the same offense, the Supreme Court will look only to the same elements test derived from *Blockburger v. United States*, 284 U.S. 299, 304, 76 L. Ed. 306, 52 S. Ct. 180 (1932) (holding that "where the same act or transaction constitutes a violation of two distinct statutory provisions, the test to be applied to determine whether there are two offenses or only one is whether each provision requires proof of an additional fact which the other does not"). *Id. Dixon*, by overruling *Grady*, cast doubt on using *Vitale* to create lesser included offenses by reference to evidence and conduct rather than basic elements. *Id.*

What then are the elements of a criminal offense and, by extension, of a civil claim? The elements of a claim or charge constitute the minimum which the plaintiff must prove to prevail. Generally, the elements of a criminal charge are sketched in the indictment, and the elements of a civil claim are suggested in the complaint. But, at least in this Court, neither the indictment nor the complaint go to the jury nor control what the government must prove to prevail. In both situations, the elements are sent to the jury in the jury instructions.

What then is the minimum the government must prove to obtain a forfeiture? *See* 21 U.S.C. § 881(a). The government must prove that there is probable cause to believe that there is a substantial connection between the property and some violation of one or more of the laws prohibiting drug trafficking. For example, probable cause that the property was either purchased with the proceeds of drug offenses or was used to commit or facilitate the violation of various drug statutes. In each case, the elements of the claim focus on specific property. In contrast, none of the criminal statutes require the use of any specific property to prove guilt. Thus, the civil claim has an element not shared by the criminal statutes. Consequently, it is not possible to find that the civil forfeiture and the criminal prosecution are identical offenses. *See United States v. Chick*, 61 F.3d 682, 687 (9th Cir. 1995) (holding that if criminal charges require proof of facts which the civil forfeiture action would not have required to be proven, then the criminal charges cannot be said to be based upon the same offense underlying the forfeiture action).

The only alternative allowed by *Dixon* would be a finding that one was a lesser offense and the other a greater offense. Clearly, the criminal offense could not be the greater because it does not completely include the elements of the civil forfeiture, the involvement of property. Therefore, some cases conclude, without analysis, that the civil forfeiture must be the greater offense and the criminal offenses must be lesser included offenses. *See, e.g., United States v. Ursery*, 59 F.3d 568, 574 (6th Cir. 1995). This seems wrong. The criminal cases all require the government to prove both an *actus reus* and *mens rea*, generally knowledge or intent; the civil forfeitures do not require the government to prove *mens rea*. True, the innocent owner defense injects additional elements into the case with superficial similarity to *mens rea*, but it is clear that Congress did not consider the claimant's burden to relate to elements of the offense. The claimant is given an affirmative "defense."

There is a clear distinction, however, between the elements of the offense and the elements of an affirmative defense. First, the claimant must disprove knowledge and consent and the government does not have to prove it as an element. *See United States v. 1980 Red Ferrari, VIN No. 9A0034335*, 827 F.2d 477, 478 (9th Cir. 1987). More important, to convict of the underlying crime, the government must prove that the defendant committed the *actus reus* with the complementary *mens rea*. The elements of the criminal case focus on the defendant and his actions. In contrast, to avoid forfeiture, the claimant must prove that he did not have knowledge that anyone was using his property in drug trafficking and that he tried, to the extent of his power, to prevent its use for such purposes; this is a significantly greater burden than the burden to prove that he was not an accomplice. Thus, the civil claim and the criminal offense each have an element not shared by the other. The civil claim requires the use of property; the criminal claim requires *mens rea*. The cases that conflate the civil claim and the criminal offense fail to see the significance of *Dixon*'s overruling of *Grady*. The United States Supreme Court clearly repudiated both a same conduct test and a same transaction test. More importantly, the Court made it clear that the same offense test means precisely the same thing whether courts are considering the successive prosecution strand of the double jeopardy clause or the successive punishment strand. *See Dixon* ("it is embarrassing to assert that the Fifth Amendment single term 'same offense' has two different meanings").

It is, of course, true that the government will typically rely on the same evidence to prove the charges in the indictment and the forfeiture claim. It is also true that the forfeiture will inevitably arise out of the same transaction or series of transactions as the criminal prosecution. But, as *Dixon* teaches, this is not enough. The confusion in the cases comes from the failure to distinguish between the allegations in the complaint or indictment, much of which may be surplusage, and the elements that must be proven. *See, e.g., United States v. McCaslin*, 863 F. Supp. 1299, 1303 (W.D. Wash. 1994) and *Oaks*, 872 F. Supp. at 823–24 (suggesting that, because proof of any violation of drug laws would permit a forfeiture, any forfeiture is the same offense as any violation of the drug laws). That confusion is compounded in forfeiture cases when the court, conducting an analysis of elements to determine whether a criminal prosecution and a civil claim have the same elements, focuses on the affidavit submitted in conjunction with the showing of probable cause necessary to seize the property in the first instance instead of focusing on the elements the government must prove to forfeit the property. It is probably true that the affidavit will set out virtually everything that is known about the defendant's criminal activities, but it does not determine what must be proven to accomplish a forfeiture. A single use of the property, in conjunction with a single violation, will suffice. *See, e.g.*, 21 U.S.C. § 881(a)(7).

As the Supreme Court made clear in *Felix*, 503 U.S. at 380–381, prosecution of a defendant for conspiracy does not violate the double jeopardy clause, where some of the overt acts relied upon by the government are based on substantive offenses for which the defendant has been previously convicted and punished. Consequently, prosecution for conspiracy or its twin, continuing criminal enterprise after the defendant has previously suffered a civil forfeiture based on similar evidence and arising out of the same transaction, does not violate the double jeopardy clause. *See United States v. Saccoccia*, 18 F.3d 795, 798 (9th Cir. 1994) ("A substantive crime and a conspiracy to commit that crime are not the same offense for double jeopardy purposes.") (citing *Felix*, 503 U.S. at 389). By the same token, the fact that the civil forfeitures and the criminal indictment charge violations of similar statutes is not determinative.

An example will illustrate the point. Assume that John Doe flies his Cessna 180 on the first of each month for thirty-six months between Mexico City and Los Angeles to pick up and deliver a shipment of cocaine. Clearly, each trip is a separate crime which could be separately prosecuted and separately punished. In addition, conspiracy counts would probably be sustained. The issue arises in that type of situation as to whether the government could prosecute him criminally for twenty trips and use one or more of the other sixteen as a predicate for forfeiture of the airplane. *See Felix*, 503 U.S. at 386–387 (suggesting that it could). It is not enough, however, to tie a particular forfeiture to a particular criminal statute. It is also necessary to tie it to a particular violation of that statute on a particular day and at a particular place charged in a particular indictment for the forfeiture and the prosecution to encompass the same offense. It is only then that an elements analysis can be made. *See, e.g., One 1978 Piper Cherokee Aircraft*, 37 F.3d at 494–95 (prosecution of defendant for drug offenses does not bar subsequent forfeiture tied to criminal act which did not result in specific prosecution). It is clear, for example, that jeopardy does not attach to dismissed counts. *See United States v. Vaughan*, 715 F.2d 1373 (9th Cir. 1983) (where defendant pleads to some charges in an indictment and others are dismissed, jeopardy only attaches to the counts to which the defendant pleads). In this case, a number of counts were dismissed as part of the plea bargain. Thus, any of the dismissed counts could form the basis for the civil forfeiture without impacting double jeopardy.

CASE ANALYSIS

1. Summarize the facts that lead up to the defendant's claim that he had been subjected to double jeopardy.
2. What was (were) the legal question(s) before the court?
3. Based on what you read in this case, what is civil forfeiture?

CONCURRENCE OF *ACTUS REUS* AND *MENS REA*

concur
To act together.

Not all crimes require a mental act; however, a physical act must always be shown. When mental and physical elements are required under the language of a criminal statute, they must **concur.** This concurrence is the joining of the physical and mental elements of the crime. The mental state must be the reason that the physical act occurred, and must occur before the physical act.

SEC. 12-4 CRIMES

Crimes can be committed against people, against property, and against the public. Crimes against people include murder, battery, assault, and rape. Crimes against property include burglary, embezzlement, and receiving stolen goods. Examples of crimes against the public include hate crimes, vagrancy, and disorderly conduct. A complete analysis of crimes is best covered in a criminal law course.

There are some relatively new developments in criminal justice. One such development is the Federal Electronic Communication Privacy Act (18 U.S.C. § 2510 *et seq.*), which punishes unauthorized interceptions of protected communications by imposing criminal and civil penalties on law enforcement and private parties who violate the act. Another federal law, the Privacy Protection Act (42 U.S.C. § 2000aa *et seq.*), limits the government's ability to use a search warrant or seize materials that have been prepared or acquired by people intending to disseminate information to the public—in other words, the media.

The effect of technology on the law is clearly illustrated in the legal community of Silicon Valley, the birthplace of modern technology. In that area (Santa Clara County, California), the prosecutor's office established a special unit of attorneys to handle criminal complaints stemming from the use of technology. In particular, this unit deals with crimes involving unlawful computer access (theft or destruction of information), theft of intellectual property (usually trade secrets), and theft of computer components. This type of law practice requires that the attorneys and their investigators be knowledgeable not only in the law but also in the technology. The legal and technical problems in this area are so specialized that one of the prosecuting attorneys, Kenneth S. Rosenblatt, has recently written a book entitled *High-Technology Crime: Investigating Cases Involving Computers* (KSK Publications, 1995). In this book, Mr. Rosenblatt explains:

> High technology crime investigation is comparatively new, and there are no clear legal signposts. Investigators working in this area are unusually vulnerable to legal assault, including lawsuits based on alleged damage to equipment and data, invasion of privacy, and violation of civil rights. . . . One law enforcement expert put it best when he urged the author to speak only in vague generalities: "Bill Gates is making changes faster than we are."

The following discussion represents an overview of some common crimes and their elements. Crimes are generally categorized into felonies, misdemeanors, and petty offenses. A *felony* is the most serious category of crime. A felony is often punishable with a minimum of one year's imprisonment. A *misdemeanor* is a less serious crime. Misdemeanors are punishable by a jail term of up to one year. In some misdemeanor cases, fines are also charged. A *petty offense* carries a maximum penalty of up to six months' incarceration.

A POINT TO REMEMBER

In order to adequately analyze a criminal law fact pattern, each crime must be broken down into its elements. The prosecution must prove, beyond a reasonable doubt, each element of a crime. Section 1.12 of the Model Penal Code states: "No person may be convicted of an offense unless each element of such offense is proved beyond a reasonable doubt. In the absence of such proof, the innocence of the defendant is assumed."

HOMICIDE

homicide
The taking of the life of a human being by another.

Homicide is the taking of the life of one person by another. Keep in mind that not all homicides are crimes. Before the criminal justice system affixes the term *crime* to a homicide, there must be a showing of criminal intent, or *mens rea.* The Model Penal Code provides the following definitions to be used in criminal homicide cases: (1) a "human being" means a person who has been born and is alive; (2) "bodily injury" means physical pain, illness, or any impairment of physical condition; (3) "serious bodily injury" means bodily injury that creates a substantial risk of death, or that causes serious, permanent disfigurement or protracted loss or impairment of the function of any bodily member or organ; and (4) "deadly weapon" means any firearm or other weapon, device, instrument, material, or substance, whether animate or inanimate, that in the manner in which it is used or is intended to be used is known to be capable of producing death or serious bodily injury.

first-degree murder
A homicide that is premeditated, willful, and deliberate.

manslaughter
A lesser crime than murder.

second-degree murder
A homicide that involves an impulsive act, rather than a premeditated act.

Statutory law divides the crime of homicide into degrees. **First-degree murder** is a homicide that is premeditated, willful, and deliberate. Premeditated, willful, and deliberate acts may indicate criminal intent. This is the highest form of murder and is severely punished. Any homicide that is not first degree murder and is not **manslaughter** is **second-degree murder.** Second degree murder often involves *impulsive acts,* which may include acts of passion or fear. Manslaughter is a lesser crime than murder. Some states divide manslaughter into the categories of *voluntary* and *involuntary.*

The Model Penal Code takes a somewhat different approach to defining homicide, murder, manslaughter, and negligent homicide. Section 210.1 states:

> (1) A person is guilty of criminal homicide if he purposely, knowingly, recklessly or negligently causes the death of another human being.
> (2) Criminal homicide is murder, manslaughter or negligent homicide.

Section 210.2 states:

> (1) Criminal homicide constitutes murder when
> (a) it is committed purposely or knowingly; or
> (b) it is committed recklessly under circumstances manifesting extreme indifference to the value of human life. Such recklessness and indifference are presumed if the actor is engaged or is an accomplice in the commission of, or an attempt to commit, or flight after committing or attempting to commit robbery, rape or deviate sexual intercourse by force or threat of force, arson, burglary, kidnapping or felonious escape.
> (2) Murder is a felony of the first degree.

Section 210.3 states:

> (1) Criminal homicide constitutes manslaughter when
> (a) it is committed recklessly; or
> (b) a homicide which would otherwise be murder is committed under the influence of extreme mental or emotional disturbance for which there is reasonable explanation or excuse. The reasonableness of such explanation or excuse shall be determined from the viewpoint of a person in the actor's situation under the circumstances as he believes them to be.
> (2) Manslaughter is a felony of the second degree.

Negligent homicide is explained in Section 210.4:

> (1) Criminal homicide constitutes negligent homicide when it is committed negligently.
> (2) Negligent homicide is a felony of the third degree.

Roy v. Gomez

55 F.3d 1483 (9th Cir. 1995)

This criminal case deals primarily with the felony murder rule. Defendant Roy and a friend, McHargue, were charged with two counts of robbery and two counts of first-degree murder. The facts leading to the charges are as follows. The two victims picked up both defendants, who were hitchhiking. The prosecutor argued that the defendants planned to drive to a remote location, rob and kill both victims, and steal their pickup truck. When defendants were arrested, a search of Roy produced a knife, cash, and a watch later identified as belonging to victim Mannix. Roy also made statements to fellow inmates in jail and these statements were admitted into evidence at trial. The facts indicated that Roy killed victim Clark while defendant McHargue was struggling with victim Mannix, and that after Roy had killed Clark, Roy helped McHargue rob and kill Mannix. The jury found Roy guilty of second-degree murder for killing Clark, but found him not guilty of robbing Clark. They found him guilty of first-degree murder in the killing of Mannix. Roy appealed, stating that the finding of second-degree murder in the Clark killing eliminated the theory of premeditation. The only way that the first-degree murder could stand would be under the theory of the felony murder rule. In connection with this, defendant claims that the court committed a Beeman *error in the instructions in that the court failed to tell the jury that an aider or abettor must not only know the unlawful purpose of the accomplice but must intend to encourage or facilitate the commission of the offense, in this case a robbery. The California Court of Appeal affirmed the felony murder verdict, stating that the* Beeman *error was harmless. The federal court agreed. The court felt that no jury could fail to find that Roy intended to aid McHargue in robbing Mannix.*

OPINION

FACTS

On September 13, 1981, Kenneth Roy and one Jesse McHargue, while hitchhiking near Gridley, California, met Archie Mannix and James Clark outside a liquor store and began drinking beer with them. A Gridley police officer observed the foursome in a pickup truck. The officer stopped the truck and advised the four not to drive.

Sometime after midnight, officers came upon the pickup truck nose down in a ditch. The bodies of Clark and Mannix were found. The bodies showed signs of stabbing. Mannix's body was partly submerged in the ditch water under the truck. His body later revealed evidence of drowning. Both bodies showed signs of having been stripped of clothing, and such clothing as was found showed the pockets turned out. Blood was found on bushes, and papers, not otherwise described, were found scattered near the truck. Roy and McHargue were not present, but were found about 3 A.M. in a nearby restaurant. Both men were wearing wet and muddy clothing.

Roy and McHargue were informed of their *Miranda* rights and consented to a search of their backpacks. McHargue's pack yielded Mannix's wet moccasins and his vest. After the two men were arrested, a search of Roy produced a Buck knife, $170.52 in cash, and a watch later identified as having belonged to Mannix. Roy was charged with two counts of robbery and two counts of first degree murder.

At trial, Roy did not testify, but the jury heard testimony from two jail inmates who swore Roy had told them of his participation in the killing of Clark and Mannix.

The state's case was structured on two theories to support first degree murder: premeditation and felony murder. The prosecutor argued that Roy and McHargue planned to drive to a remote location, rob and kill both victims, and steal their pickup truck. The prosecution argued that the physical evidence, the testimonial evidence that the victims had money and the defendants had none, and the testimony about admissions Roy allegedly made to jailed informers proved that Roy killed Clark while McHargue was struggling with Mannix, and that after Roy had killed Clark, Roy helped McHargue rob and kill Mannix. The evidence was sufficient to take both theories to the jury. The state also sought a verdict of special circumstances, based on the use of knives in the stabbing deaths of the two victims, but this issue was eliminated in state court proceedings.

The jury found Roy guilty of second degree murder for killing Clark, but found him not guilty of robbing Clark. The jury answered a special verdict "no" on the question whether Roy used his knife, but found him guilty of first degree murder in the killing of Mannix.

Roy now argues, and we agree, that the verdict of second degree murder of Clark eliminates the theory of premeditation in Roy's conviction of first degree murder. The validity of Roy's first degree murder conviction in the killing of Mannix thus depends on felony murder in the course of aiding and abetting the robbing of Mannix.

INSTRUCTIONS

The trial court instructed the jury orally and in writing, *inter alia*, "to find that the special circumstance, referred to in these instructions as murder in the commission of robbery, is true, it must be proved: [1] That the murder was committed while the defendant was engaged in or was an accomplice in the commission of a robbery. [2] That the murder was committed in order to carry out or advance the commission of the crime of robbery. . . . In other words, the special circumstance referred to . . . is not established if the . . . robbery was merely incidental to the commission of the murder."

The jury was also instructed "if a human being is killed by any one of several persons engaged in the perpetration of, or attempt to perpetrate, the crime of robbery, all persons who . . . with knowledge of the unlawful purpose of the perpetrator of the crime aid . . . its commission, are guilty of murder of the first degree, whether the killing is intentional, or accidental."

The jury was further instructed that one "who aids and abets is not only guilty of the particular crime that to his knowledge his confederates are contemplating committing, but he is also liable for the natural and reasonable or probable consequences of any act that he knowingly aided or encouraged."

Criminal Jury Instruction Number 301 as given, reads: "A person aids and abets the commission of a crime if, with knowledge of the unlawful purpose of the perpetrator of the crime, he aids, promotes, encourages or instigates by act or advice the commission of such crime."

The *Beeman* error [an error named after the case that first identified the error] in the above instruction consisted in the failure of the court to tell the jury that an aider and abettor (Roy) must not only know the unlawful purpose of the accomplice (McHargue), but must intend to encourage or facilitate the commission of the offense—in this case the robbery of Mannix.

On direct appeal, the California court of appeal affirmed the felony murder verdict on the theory of aiding and abetting in the robbery of Mannix. The court of appeal found the *Beeman* error harmless beyond a reasonable doubt, and the state supreme court denied post conviction relief in 1989.

The petition for habeas corpus in the district court followed. The district court again found the *Beeman* error harmless beyond a reasonable doubt, saying: "No rational juror could find that Roy aided McHargue, knowing what McHargue's purpose was, without also finding that Roy intended to aid McHargue in his purpose." We agree.

DISCUSSION

The appeal advances the argument that because no *Beeman* instruction was given on intent, an essential element of the crime, a new trial is required. We have in the § 2254 cases collected in *Martinez v. Borg*, 937 F.2d 422, 424 (9th Cir. 1991), refused to find the *Beeman* error harmless beyond a reasonable doubt. But the teaching of the *Carella* line of cases tells us to look to what the jury actually decided, not what we, as judges, believe the jury would have decided if they had been properly instructed. We have held that if jury instructions omit an element of the offense (in this case, specific intent), constitutional error results.

If the jury returned a verdict from which it could be said that the jury actually made the essential predicate fact finding, then we affirm. Here, the only rational way the jury could have found Roy guilty on a felony murder theory was by making a preliminary predicate factual finding that Roy intended to help McHargue rob Mannix, while knowing that McHargue intended to rob Mannix. It is therefore necessary for us to review the record, the instructions as a whole, and the verdict, to determine whether the jury, despite the incomplete instruction, had to find every material element of the offense in order to return the verdict it returned.

Roy argues the jury could have found that he knew McHargue intended to rob Mannix and helped him do so without necessarily finding that Roy intended to assist in the robbery. Roy, as noted, did not testify. His counsel put on expert evidence in an effort to prove that Roy's mental capacity was impaired by intoxication, as well as by his inherent immaturity and lack of mental acuity. This evidence was introduced to show the jury that Roy was unable to form any intent at all, much less an intent to help McHargue rob Mannix. The state put on evidence to the contrary. The jury was entitled to disbelieve Roy's experts.

Whether or not the *Beeman* instruction had been given, on the evidence in this case, no jury could fail to find that Roy intended to aid McHargue in subduing and robbing Mannix. There was no other rational explanation of the physical evidence and the testimony about Roy's admitted participation in the robberies and murders that could be consistent with the verdict.

Hypothetical and imaginary scenarios perhaps may be contrived to suggest that Roy did not intend to help McHargue rob Mannix. But the jury had before it the defense evidence that attempted to cast doubt on Roy's capacity to form any intent, criminal or otherwise, and the jury obviously did not believe that evidence. We conclude, as did the California courts and the District Court, that the only rational route which the jury could have followed to reach the verdict it reached in this case had to include the implicit finding that Roy intended to help McHargue, knowing McHargue's purpose. That verdict was supported by evidence, and was completely rational. [In] *O'Neal v. McAninch*, 130 L. Ed. 2d 947, 115 S. Ct. 992, 995 (1995), "[o]nly if the record demonstrates the jury's decision was substantially influenced by the trial error or there is grave doubt about whether an error affected a jury in this way will [Roy] be entitled to habeas relief."

Affirmed.

CASE ANALYSIS

1. Summarize the facts of the *Roy* case.
2. What is the legal issue in *Roy*?
3. Why did the court affirm the lower court's ruling?

BATTERY

battery
A reckless or intentional, harmful or offensive touching of another; it is both a crime and a tort.

A **battery** is a reckless or intentional, harmful or offensive touching of another. Battery may be broken into its elements in the following manner:

1. A reckless or intentional touching
2. of another person
3. that is harmful or offensive.

Once the crime is broken into its elements, it is easy to perform a factual analysis. For example, suppose Stuart throws a book at Darlene's back because he wants to get her attention. The book hurt her when it hit her and left a large bruise at the base of her spine. The *actus reus* of this battery is the touching of Darlene with the book. According to statute, the defendant in a battery case does not have to touch the person with his hands or body. In this instance, did Stuart commit a battery?

ASSAULT

assault
The placing of another in apprehension or fear of an imminent battery; it is both a crime and a tort.

Assault is placing another in apprehension or fear of an imminent battery. Unlike battery, a touching does not have to take place. The elements of assault could be broken down as follows:

1. Placing another person in apprehension or fear of
2. an imminent battery.

In many fact patterns, assault and battery will occur together. Under the preceding definition of assault, the person must experience fear or apprehension. Some statutes define assault as an attempted battery. This definition omits the knowledge element on the part of the victim.

KIDNAPPING AND FALSE IMPRISONMENT

kidnapping
The unlawful taking, confinement, and carrying away of another person, by threat, force, fraud, or deception.

Kidnapping is the unlawful taking, confinement, and carrying away of another person, by threat, force, fraud, or deception. The elements of kidnapping may be broken down as follows:

1. An unlawful taking,
2. confinement,
3. and carrying away
4. of another person
5. by threat, force, fraud, or deception.

false imprisonment
The intentional interference with another person's liberty through force or threat without authority.

Kidnapping is a very serious crime and is therefore considered a felony. All kidnappings involve **false imprisonment.** False imprisonment is often defined as the intentional interference with another person's liberty through force or threat without authority. False imprisonment does not involve the "carrying away" element of kidnapping. The Model Penal Code describes false imprisonment as follows: "A person commits a misdemeanor if he knowingly restrains another unlawfully so as to interfere substantially with his liberty."

Schweinle v. Texas

915 S.W.2d 17 (Tex. Crim. App. 1996)

In this criminal case, defendant was found guilty of aggravated kidnapping. The crime arose out of a situation involving a domestic dispute. After a fight, defendant "abducted" his girlfriend, beat her, and took her to his house where he kept her over night. Under Texas law, the offense of kidnapping occurs if a defendant intentionally or knowingly abducts another. Abduct *means to secrete or hold a person in a place where he is not likely to be found, or to use or threaten to use deadly force. Also under Texas law, the offense of false imprisonment is committed if a defendant knowingly restrains another person. At trial, the jury was instructed as to the crime of kidnapping but not as to the crime of false imprisonment. Defendant appealed, claiming that the jury should have been instructed as to false imprisonment because it is a lesser included offense of kidnapping and the facts in this case would have supported such a finding. The court of appeal affirmed the trial court finding, but the Texas high court granted discretionary review. It found that false imprisonment was a lesser included offense of kidnapping. The second issue required more discussion, but the court held that a jury could have found that no deadly force was used or threatened. The defendant testified that he did not touch the gun nor point it at the victim. Furthermore, he testified that he always carried the gun in his truck and that the victim knew this. The court reversed and remanded.*

OPINION

A jury convicted appellant of aggravated kidnapping and assessed his punishment at confinement for fifteen years in the penitentiary. The conviction was affirmed. We granted discretionary review to determine whether evidence of extraneous offenses and expert testimony regarding "battered woman syndrome" was improperly admitted in the guilt-innocence phase, and whether a lesser included offense was raised by the evidence.

Appellant and the complainant became engaged after a brief courtship, and the complainant, who had formerly lived with her parents, moved into appellant's house. However, the couple began arguing, and the complainant moved back to her parents' house, although she would occasionally spend the night with appellant. On October 23, 1991, they had planned that appellant would pick up some food for dinner, and the complainant would meet appellant at his father's liquor store, where appellant worked. The complainant was alone at her parents' house changing clothes when she heard a door slam. Appellant came into the bedroom, enraged because the complainant had not met him at the liquor store as planned. The complainant testified appellant told her she was coming with him, that he had some food in the car and she was going to eat every bite of it. He grabbed her by the arm, dragged her down the hall and slapped her. The complainant told appellant she did not want to go with him, but appellant insisted she was coming with him and walked her to the truck. As appellant was driving, he smeared a steak sandwich in the complainant's face and pointed a gun at her, telling her he would shoot her if she tried to escape. Appellant drove the truck to a subdivision near his house in which roads had been built but no houses constructed. There, he threw another sandwich at her and hit her in the stomach with his fist. He then drove to his house, where he continued to beat her with a belt and a rolled-up newspaper covered with duct tape. The next morning appellant took the complainant to her parents' house.

Appellant contends the Court of Appeals erred by holding that the lesser included offense of false imprisonment was not raised by the evidence. Whether a charge on a lesser included offense is required is determined by a two-pronged test. First, we must determine whether the offense constitutes a lesser included offense. In Texas an offense is a lesser included offense if, *inter alia,* "it is established by proof of the same or less than all the facts required to establish the commission of the offense charged." Second, the lesser included offense must be raised by the evidence at trial. In other words, there must be some evidence which would permit a rational jury to find that if guilty, the defendant is guilty only of the lesser offense. Anything more than a scintilla of evidence from any source is sufficient to entitle a defendant to submission of the issue. *Bignall v. State,* 887 S.W.2d 21 (Tex. Cr. App. 1994).

Under Texas Penal Code § 20.03, a person commits the offense of kidnapping if he intentionally or knowingly abducts another. "Abduct" means to restrain a person with intent to prevent his liberation by: (A) secreting or holding him in a place where he is not likely to be found; or (B) using or threatening to use deadly force." "'Restrain' means to restrict a person's movements without consent, so as to interfere substantially with his liberty, by moving him from one place to another or by confining him. Restraint is 'without consent' if it is accomplished by force, intimidation, or deception. . . ." Texas Penal Code, § 20.01.

A person commits the offense of false imprisonment if he "intentionally or knowingly restrains another person." Texas Penal Code, § 20.02. Kidnapping is accomplished by abduction, which includes restraint, but false imprisonment is committed by restraint only. Thus, false imprisonment is a lesser included offense of kidnapping and aggravated kidnapping.

The next step of the analysis is to determine whether there was evidence that if guilty, appellant was guilty only of restraining the complainant, without intending to prevent her liberation by either secreting or holding her in a place where she was not likely to be found or using or threatening to use deadly force. The Court of Appeals held appellant was required to rebut or negate both theories of abduction which could have occurred anytime during the ongoing offense. It noted that appellant argued he needed only to refute that he pointed the gun at the complainant in the truck and that he kept her at his house. It held that keeping the complainant isolated at the undeveloped subdivision constituted restraint in a place where she was not likely to be found. It determined that the only evidence which refuted this theory was appellant's testimony that the complainant freely chose to go with him and stayed in the truck of her own free will. However, it reasoned that because this evidence refuted both abduction and restraint, appellant failed to show if guilty, he was guilty of only the lesser included offense. *Schweinle,* 893 S.W.2d at 715.

The Court of Appeals' analysis is flawed in two respects. First, the Court of Appeals determined that the subdivision where appellant stopped his truck to throw more food on the complainant and beat her was a place where she was not likely to be found, without considering whether a rational jury could have reached the opposite conclusion under the evidence. In *Saunders v. State,* 840 S.W.2d 390 (Tex. Cr. App. 1992), this Court held that a lesser included offense may be raised if evidence either affirmatively refutes or negates an element establishing the greater offense, or the evidence on the issue is subject to two different interpretations, and one of the interpretations negates or rebuts an element of the greater. In the instant case, the Court of Appeals did not refer to any facts in the record which demonstrated that the subdivision was or was not a place where the complainant was not likely to be found.

Appellant testified that the complainant's parents lived on Woodforest, which was a main thoroughfare, and the subdivision where appellant lived was off Woodforest, two to three minutes away from the complainant's parents' house. Appellant described the area where he stopped his truck as a few blocks from his house and in his neighborhood. He testified he turned right off Woodforest going into his neighborhood, and "as we got around the corner there, I had to make another left to cut down to go to my house." He testified the area where he stopped was very small, "two or three streets there, it's all cleaned out." He further explained, "It's developed, there is just no houses there. . . . It's not really what I would call secluded." The complainant testified that the area was "not very far off Woodforest, but it's just a little—just a little bit secluded. There is like some trees and it's right by the school." Pictures of this area were admitted into evidence. From this evidence, a rational jury could have believed that the street where appellant stopped his truck was not a place where the complainant was not likely to be found.

Secondly, by holding that appellant did not raise the lesser included offense because his testimony refuted both the greater and lesser offenses, the Court of Appeals erred under *Bignall.* In that case, this Court held that the defendant was entitled to submission of the lesser included offense of theft based on defense testimony that no one had a gun, despite his evidence showing he was not guilty of any offense. This Court held that a rational jury could have believed that part of the State's evidence that Bignall was involved in the theft, and that part of Bignall's evidence that no one had a gun, and concluded that appellant was guilty only of theft. We pointed out that the defendant's denial of committing any offense does not automatically foreclose submission of a lesser included offense. *Bignall,* 887 S.W.2d at 24.

Applying those principles to this case, a rational jury could have believed the complainant's testimony that she did not go freely with appellant. Appellant testified that he did not threaten to shoot the complainant, did not touch the gun during the drive from her parents' house to his and did not point the gun at her at any time. He admitted that the gun was lying on the seat of his truck during the offense, but explained that he habitually carried the gun in his truck either on the seat next to him or on the floor next to the gearshift. He testified that when they reached his house, he retrieved the gun from the truck, took it inside as he always did, and placed it on his pinball machine where he often kept it. The complainant testified that she knew appellant kept a gun in his truck, and that it was not unusual for it to be lying on the seat. From this evidence, a rational jury could have found that despite the presence of a gun on the seat, appellant did not use or threaten to use deadly force to prevent the complainant's liberation.

Similarly, the jury could have believed that appellant held the complainant in his house against her will, but believed appellant's house was not a place where the complainant was not likely to be found. Evidence was presented that the complainant had a key to appellant's house, had formerly lived there, and had spent the night there the past three or four nights before the offense. In addition, the complainant's mother testified that when she came home on the night of the offense and found the house in disarray and her daughter missing, she became afraid for her daughter's safety and drove by appellant's house. From this evidence, a jury could have rationally concluded that the complainant was restrained at appellant's house, but his house was not a place where she was not likely to be found. In sum, the jury could have found that appellant had restrained but not abducted the complainant, and thus was guilty only of false imprisonment. Therefore, the Court of Appeals erred by holding this lesser included offense was not raised by the evidence. Accordingly, we reverse the judgment of the Court of Appeals and remand the cause to that court to conduct a harm analysis.

CASE ANALYSIS

1. Why did the court remand the case to the court of appeals?
2. According to what you read in *Schweinle,* what is a lesser included offense?
3. Under the Model Penal Code, did the appellant commit the crime of kidnapping? Explain, using the appropriate elements of the Model Penal Code set forth in the text.

BURGLARY

burglary
The unlawful entry of a structure or building for the purpose of committing a felony inside.

Burglary is the unlawful entry into a structure or building for the purpose of committing a felony once inside. Break this crime down into its elements. Now apply those elements to the following fact patterns.

1. Roberta breaks a window and enters the back door of her neighbor's residence. She is entering the residence because she was supposed to look after the neighbor's plants, but cannot find her key to the house. Is Roberta guilty of burglary?
2. Roberta decides that she wants her neighbor's CD player. She enters the unlocked side door when the neighbor is out shopping. Is Roberta guilty of burglary?

The Model Penal Code offers a more detailed definition of burglary:

Section 221.1 Burglary

(1) *Burglary Defined.* A person is guilty of burglary if he enters a building or occupied structure, or separately secured or occupied portion thereof, with purpose to commit a crime therein, unless the premises are at the time open to the public or the actor is licensed or privileged to enter. It is an affirmative defense to prosecution for burglary that the building or structure was abandoned.

(2) *Grading. Burglary.* Burglary is a felony of the second degree if it is perpetrated in the dwelling of another at night, or if, in the course of committing the offense, the actor:

(a) purposely, knowingly, or recklessly inflicts or attempt to inflict bodily injury on anyone; or

(b) is armed with explosives or a deadly weapon.

Otherwise, burglary is a felony of the third degree. An act shall be deemed to occur "in the course of committing" an offense if it occurs in an attempt to commit the offense or in flight after the attempt or commission.

Under the Model Penal Code, did Roberta commit a burglary in either of the preceding fact patterns? If she did commit a burglary, in what degree was the burglary?

SEC. 12-5 DEFENSES TO CRIMINAL CHARGES

defense
The explanation of why the person complaining should not prevail in his or her action.

The prosecution will charge the defendant with one or more crimes. The burden is on the prosecution to prove that the elements to each crime charged are fulfilled. But that does not mean that the defendant will necessarily be found guilty of the crimes. The defendant may plead *not guilty*. This is a factual *plea* that says the defendant did not commit the crime. The defendant may also offer a **defense,** such as diminished capacity, self-defense, or duress, to name just a few. Each defense has elements; the burden to prove each element is on the criminal defendant. An in-depth discussion of crimes and criminal defenses is best reserved for a criminal law course.

> **ETHICAL CHOICES**
>
> You are a case assistant. You sit in on an interview with a criminal defendant who admits to your supervising attorney that he did in fact commit the crime in question. At trial, the client takes the stand and testifies that he had nothing to do with the crime. Should you do anything about either the client or the attorney?

SECTION II: JUVENILE LAW

SEC. 12-6 INTRODUCTION TO JUVENILE LAW

The first section of this chapter deals with adult offenders and the laws that are applied to adults. Juveniles charged with crimes are often treated somewhat differently from adults. In some instances, the rules applied to juvenile offenders are very different from the rules applied to adults charged with crimes. The juvenile justice system was created to protect children. In recent years there has been a move toward treating juveniles who commit serious crimes as adults. For example, a juvenile charged with murder may, in some states, be prosecuted as an adult in an adult court and be subject to adult punishments, including the death penalty.

delinquent
A minor, as defined by law, who violates a criminal law.

The juvenile justice system has suffered heavy criticism in recent years. Prior to 1900, juvenile offenders received punishment comparable to that of adults. Because of changing mores, revisions to policies, and encouraged rehabilitation of youthful offenders, this trend lasted until the 1960s. In the past thirty years, the trend has once again been to punish juveniles who commit certain crimes with the same punishment as adults. Before 1960, juvenile offenders, or juvenile **delinquents,** were apprehended by law enforcement and handed over to the juvenile justice system. Once in the juvenile system, they were usually treated leniently, compared to their adult counterparts in the criminal justice system. In most instances, juveniles were placed in brief confinement in a juvenile correctional or detention facility. This is no longer true. Many states have adopted a "get tough" attitude toward juvenile offenders. Recent changes in statutory law show a growing trend toward holding juvenile offenders accountable, as adults, for serious crimes.

SEC. 12-7 THE JUVENILE COURT

There is no uniformity, among the states, in how the juvenile court system works. In some states, judges sitting in juvenile courts may hear only juvenile matters. In other states, judges who hear adult criminal matters also hear juvenile matters.

When our nation was founded, children were treated as adults in the criminal justice system. Just before the turn of the century, the United States decided that there was a need for a separate juvenile justice system. States began to create systems designed to work with and hopefully rehabilitate youthful offenders. The idea was to protect young offenders from the serious penalties applied to adults who commit crimes. Juveniles were placed in institutions whose purpose was to counsel and rehabilitate. Unfortunately, the group homes and detention centers did not meet the high expectations of the public.

In the 1960s, attitudes began to change. Laws were enacted enabling the relatively easy transfer of a youth from juvenile court to adult criminal court when a serious crime is charged. Today's juvenile courts are run much the same as the criminal courts. The process is almost identical, with the exception that there is no jury. The only obvious difference is that the statutes applied are different. All other rights guaranteed under the Constitution, except for bail, are applicable in juvenile delinquency hearings and proceedings. Preparation for a juvenile proceeding is the same as preparation for the criminal proceedings discussed earlier in this chapter and in more detail in Chapter 14 of this text.

SEC. 12-8 PROSECUTION OF JUVENILE OFFENDERS

In the most simplistic of terms, juveniles are delinquent when they commit a violation of the law. It is important to keep in mind that some violations that fall short of being "crimes" apply only to minors. Truancy from school and violating curfew rules are two examples. The juvenile courts address some problems that are not criminal in nature. However, most matters heard in the juvenile courts are criminal.

Proceedings against juveniles and adults are very similar. However, the stages of the process are often identified by differing terminology. For example, the state of California uses the following vocabulary to describe the justice process:

Juvenile Court	*Criminal Court*
Petition	Charges/complaint
Detention hearing	Arraignment
Jurisdictional hearing	Trial
Dispositional hearing	Sentencing

In the state of California, various dispositions are available to the juvenile court; they are listed below in increasing order of severity.

1. Dismissal of the case
2. Six months' probation
3. Wardship and probation
4. Relative home placement
5. Foster or group home placement
6. Private institution placement
7. County facility/program
8. California Youth Authority

In 1967, the U.S. Supreme Court addressed the issues of due process and the privilege against self-incrimination in a juvenile proceeding, *In re Gault.*

Eight years after the *Gault* case, the issue of the rights and protections of juveniles was once again before the U.S. Supreme Court. In *Breed v. Jones,* the issue of double jeopardy was addressed.

In re Gault

387 U.S. 1 (1967)

In Gault, *police arrested a juvenile for making obscene phone calls. After denying him substantial due process rights, Gault, age 15, was committed to an institution until he should reach his majority. The U.S. Supreme Court held that juveniles are entitled to several due process rights under the U.S. Constitution. Specifically, the juvenile and his parents are entitled to adequate written notice of the specific issues in the case, this notice must be given sufficiently in advance of the hearing to permit preparation. The child and his parents must be advised of their right to counsel and if unable to afford counsel, that one would be appointed. The constitutional privilege against self-incrimination is applicable.*

OPINION

Facts and Judicial History

Gerald Gault, 15 years old, was taken into custody as the result of a complaint that he had made lewd telephone calls. After hearings before a juvenile court judge, Gerald was ordered committed to the State Industrial Schools as a juvenile delinquent until he should reach majority. Gerald's parents brought a habeas corpus action in the state courts to challenge the constitutionality of the Arizona Juvenile Code and the procedure actually used in Gerald's case, on the ground of denial of various procedural due process rights. The State Supreme Court affirmed dismissal of the writ. Agreeing that juveniles are charged as delinquents, the court held that the Arizona Juvenile Code impliedly includes the requirement of due process in delinquency proceedings, and that such due process requirements were not offended by the procedure leading to Gerald's commitment.

Holding of the Court

(1) *Kent v. United States,* 383 U.S. 541, 562 (1966), held "[t]hat the [waiver] hearing must measure up to the essentials of due process and fair treatment." This view is reiterated, here in connection with a juvenile court adjudication of "delinquency," as a requirement which is part of the Due Process Clause of the Fourteenth Amendment of our Constitution. The holding in this case related only to the adjudicatory stage of the juvenile process, where commitment to a state institution may follow. When proceedings may result in incarceration in an institution of confinement, "it would be extraordinary if our Constitution did not require

the procedural regularity and exercise of care implied in the phrase 'due process.'"

(2) Due process requires, in such proceedings, that adequate written notice be afforded the child and his parents or guardian. Such notice must inform them "of the specific issues that they must meet" and must be given "at the earliest practicable time, and in any event sufficiently in advance of the hearing to permit preparation." Notice here was neither timely nor adequately specific, nor was there waiver of the right to constitutionally adequate notice.

(3) In such proceedings the child and his parents must be advised of their right to be represented by counsel and, if they are unable to afford counsel, that counsel will be appointed to represent the child. Mrs. Gault's statement at the habeas corpus hearing that she had known she could employ counsel, is not "an 'intentional relinquishment or abandonment' of a fully known right."

(4) The constitutional privilege against self-incrimination is applicable in such proceedings: "an admission by the juvenile may [not] be used against him in the absence of clear and unequivocal evidence that the admission was made with knowledge that he was not obliged to speak and would not be penalized for remaining silent." "The availability of the privilege does not turn upon the type of proceeding in which its protection is invoked, but upon the nature of the statement or admission and the exposure which it invites. . . . Juvenile proceedings to determine 'delinquency,' which may lead to commitment to a state institution, must be regraded as 'criminal' for purposes of the privilege against self-incrimination." Furthermore, experience has shown that "admissions and confessions by juveniles require special caution" as to their reliability and voluntariness, and "it would indeed be surprising if the privilege against self-incrimination were available to hardened criminals but not to children." "Special problems may arise with respect to waiver of the privilege by or on behalf of children, and . . . there may well be some differences in technique—but not in principle—depending upon the age of the child and the presence and competence of parent. . . ." Gerald's admissions did not measure up to these standards, and could not properly be used as a basis for the judgment against him.

(5) Absent a valid confession, a juvenile in such proceedings must be afforded the right of confrontation and sworn testimony of witnesses available for cross-examination.

CASE ANALYSIS

1. What constitutional right was Gerald denied during the adjudicatory stage of the juvenile process?
2. What does due process require in the adjudicatory stage of the juvenile process?
3. Does a juvenile have a privilege against self-incrimination? Discuss.

Breed v. Jones

421 U.S. 519 (1975)

In this case, a petition was filed in the Juvenile Division of the Superior Court, seeking to have the juvenile declared a ward of the court on the ground that he committed an act (armed robbery) that would have been a crime had he been an adult. At an adjudicatory hearing, the facts of the petition were found to be true. At that point, the juvenile court also found that the juvenile was not fit for juvenile proceedings and transferred the case to the Superior Court for him to be tried as an adult. The juvenile claimed that this was double jeopardy. Eventually, the case reached the U.S. Supreme Court, which held that even if there was no double punishment, double jeopardy applied because he was required to go through two trials for basically the same offense.

OPINION

Facts and Judicial History

We granted certiorari to decide whether the prosecution of respondent as an adult, after Juvenile Court proceedings which resulted in a finding that respondent had violated a criminal statute and a subsequent finding that he was unfit for treatment as a juvenile, violated the Fifth and Fourteenth Amendments to the United States Constitution.

On February 9, 1971, a petition was filed in the Superior Court of California, County of Los Angeles, Juvenile Court, alleging that respondent, then 17 years of age, was a person described by Cal. Welf. & Inst'ns Code § 602 (1966), in that, on or about February 8, while armed with a deadly weapon, he had committed acts which, if committed by an adult, would constitute the crime of robbery in violation of Cal. Penal Code § 211 (1970). The following day, a detention hearing was held, at the conclusion of which respondent was ordered detained pending a hearing on the petition. As of the date of filing of the petition in this case, Cal. Welf. & Inst'ns Code § 602 (1966) provided:

> "Any person under the age of 21 years who violates any law of this State or of the United States or any ordinance of any city or county of this State defining crime or who, after having been found by the juvenile court to be a person described by Section 601, fails to obey any lawful order of the juvenile court, is within the jurisdiction of the juvenile court, which may adjudge such person to be a ward of the court."

The jurisdictional or adjudicatory hearing was conducted on March 1. After taking testimony from two prosecution witnesses and respondent, the Juvenile Court found that the allegations in the petition were true and that respondent was a person described by § 602, and it sustained the petition. The proceedings were continued for a dispositional hearing, pending which the court ordered that respondent remain detained. At a hearing conducted on March 15, the Juvenile Court indicated its intention to find respondent "not . . . amenable to the care, treatment and training program available through the facilities of the juvenile court" under Cal. Welf. & Inst'ns Code § 707 (Supp. 1967). Respondent's counsel orally moved "to continue the matter on the ground of surprise," contending that respondent "was not informed that it was going to be a fitness hearing." The court continued the matter for one week, at which time, having considered the report of the probation officer assigned to the case and having heard her testimony, it declared respondent "unfit for treatment as a juvenile," and ordered that he be prosecuted as an adult.

Thereafter, respondent filed a petition for a writ of habeas corpus in Juvenile Court, raising the same double jeopardy claim now presented. Upon the denial of that petition, respondent sought habeas corpus relief in the California Court of Appeal, Second Appellate District. Although it initially stayed the criminal prosecution pending against respondent, that court denied the petition. *In re Gary J.*, 17 Cal. App. 3d 704, 95 Cal. Rptr. 185 (1971). The Supreme Court of California denied respondent's petition for hearing.

After a preliminary hearing respondent was ordered held for trial in Superior Court, where an Information was subsequently filed accusing him of having committed robbery, in violation of Cal. Penal Code § 211 (1970), while armed with a deadly weapon, on or about February 8, 1971. Respondent entered a plea of not guilty, and he also pleaded that he had "already been placed once in jeopardy and convicted of the offense charged, by the judgment of the Superior Court of the County of Los Angeles, Juvenile Court, rendered . . . on the 1st day of March, 1971." By stipulation, the case was submitted to the court on the transcript of the preliminary hearing. The court found respondent guilty of robbery in the first degree under Cal. Penal Code § 211a (1970) and ordered that he be committed to the California Youth Authority. No appeal was taken from the judgment of conviction.

On December 10, 1971, respondent, through his mother as guardian *ad litem*, filed the instant petition for a writ of habeas corpus in the United States District Court for the Central District of California. In his petition he alleged that his transfer to adult court pursuant to Cal. Welf. & Inst'ns Code § 707 and subsequent trial there "placed him in double jeopardy." The District Court denied the petition, rejecting respondent's contention that jeopardy attached at his adjudicatory hearing. It concluded that the "distinctions between the preliminary procedures and hearings provided by California law for juveniles and a criminal trial are many and apparent and the effort of [respondent] to relate them is unconvincing," and that "even assuming jeopardy attached during the preliminary juvenile proceedings . . . it is clear that no new jeopardy arose by the juvenile proceeding sending the case to the criminal court." 343 F. Supp. 690, 692 (1972).

The Court of Appeals reversed, concluding that applying double jeopardy protection to juvenile proceedings would not "impede the juvenile courts in carrying out their basic goal of rehabilitating the erring youth," and that the contrary result might "do irreparable harm to or destroy their confidence in our judicial system." The court therefore held that the Double Jeopardy Clause "is fully applicable to juvenile court proceedings." 497 F. 2d 1160, 1165.

Findings of the Court

The prosecution of respondent as an adult in California Superior Court, after an adjudicatory finding in Juvenile Court that he had violated a criminal statute and a subsequent finding that he was unfit for treatment as a juvenile, violated the Double Jeopardy Clause of the Fifth Amendment, as applied to the State through the Fourteenth Amendment.

(a) Respondent was put in jeopardy at the Juvenile Court adjudicatory hearing, whose object was to determine whether he had committed acts that violated a criminal law and whose potential consequences included both the stigma inherent in that determination and the deprivation of liberty for many years. Jeopardy attached when the Juvenile Court, as the trier of the facts, began to hear evidence.

(b) Contrary to petitioner's contention, respondent's trial in Superior Court for the same offense as that for which he had been tried in Juvenile Court violated the policies of the Double Jeopardy Clause, even if respondent "never faced the risk of more than one punishment," since the Clause "is written in terms of potential or risk of trial and conviction, not punishment." *Price v. Georgia*, 398 U.S. 323, 329. Respondent was subjected to the burden of two trials for the same offense; he was twice put to the task of marshaling his resources against those of the State, twice subjected to the "heavy personal strain" that such an experience represents.

(c) If there is to be an exception to the constitutional protection against a second trial in the context of the juvenile-court system, it must be justified by interests of society, reflected in that unique institution, or of juveniles themselves, of sufficient substance to render tolerable the costs and burdens that the exception will entail in individual cases.

(d) Giving respondent the constitutional protection against multiple trials in this context will not, as petitioner claims, diminish the flexibility and informality of juvenile-court proceedings to the extent that those qualities relate uniquely to the goals of the juvenile-court system. A requirement that transfer hearings be held prior to adjudicatory hearings does not alter the nature of the latter proceedings. More significantly, such a requirement need not affect the quality of decision making at transfer hearings themselves. The burdens petitioner envisions would not pose a significant problem for the administration of the juvenile-court system, and quite apart from that consideration, transfer hearings prior to adjudication will aid the objectives of that system.

CASE ANALYSIS

1. What is the legal issue in the *Breed* case?
2. Explain why the Court found that the double jeopardy clause of the Fifth Amendment was violated by the California courts.

Featured Web Site: www.hg.org/

This is the Hieros Gamos Web site—The Comprehensive Law and Government Portal.

Go Online

Summarize the types of materials available on this site.

Chapter Summary

One goal of criminal law is to prevent socially undesirable behavior. All jurisdictions have criminal statutes. Not everyone agrees on the purpose of criminal law; the most common theories are deterrence, rehabilitation, incapacitation, and retribution. Most crimes consist of two primary elements: *mens rea* and *actus reus.* There are many types of crimes; for example, there are crimes against people, crimes against property, and crimes against society. Criminal statutes are very carefully drafted because the potential penalties are so severe.

Juvenile law is a newcomer to the justice system. The juvenile justice system is very similar to the criminal justice system. Many states are enacting new laws that make it much easier to try children as adults when they commit serious crimes. The protections enumerated in the Constitution apply to juveniles as well as adults.

Terms to Remember

crime
Model Penal Code
presumption
rebuttable presumption
deter
rehabilitation
incapacitation
retribution
mens rea
purposeful act
knowing act
reckless act
negligent act
inference
actus reus
voluntary act
concur
homicide
first-degree murder
manslaughter
second-degree murder

battery
assault
kidnapping
false imprisonment
burglary
defense
delinquent

Questions for Review

1. What is the primary goal of criminal law?
2. Why do we need criminal law?
3. Discuss the purposes of criminal law.
4. What is *mens rea?* Provide an example.
5. What is *actus reus?* Provide an example.
6. Explain the difference between first-degree and second-degree murder.
7. Why do we have a juvenile justice system?
8. What does it mean to be delinquent?
9. Compare the stages of a criminal action with the stages of a juvenile action.
10. Briefly summarize the *Gault* case.

Questions for Analysis

1. Locate the juvenile court rules for your jurisdiction. Choose two statutes. Rewrite them, breaking them into their elements. Review the statutes for assault, battery, and kidnapping in this chapter to review how a statute is broken apart into elements.
2. Reread the Case File at the beginning of the chapter. What crimes has the client committed? Explain your answer by discussing the facts and the elements of the crimes.

Assignments and Projects

1. Create a hypothetical situation in which a person commits the crimes of assault and battery upon another person. Be sure to include facts that will address each element of each crime.
2. Create a hypothetical situation in which a person commits first degree murder. Identify the *mens rea* and *actus reus* necessary for this crime.
3. Make a field trip to your local criminal court. Watch a motion or a trial. Take notes and prepare a written report on what you witnessed.

CHAPTER 13

CIVIL PROCEDURE BEFORE TRIAL

Technology Corner

Web Address	Name of Site
www.law.cornell.edu/rules/frcp/	Federal Rules of Civil Procedure
www.house.gov/judiciary/appel00.pdf	Federal Rules of Appellate Procedure
www.expertpages.com/	Expert Pages
www.experts.com/	Experts.com
www.claims.com/online.html	National Directory of Expert Witnesses
http://pacer.psc.uscourts.gov/	PACER Service Center
www.courttv.com/legaldocs/	Court TV Legal Documents

CASE FILE: *MARTINEZ V. HARDTACK AND THE CITY OF CENTERVILLE*

Jaime Martinez has filed a lawsuit against Harry Hardtack claiming that Hardtack, a police officer, used excessive force in trying to arrest him. He is asking for money damages. Also joined in the lawsuit is the City of Centerville, which employs Hardtack. At this stage all of the pleadings have been filed and the attorneys are starting discovery. Interrogatories have been sent out and depositions are scheduled.

SEC. 13-1 INTRODUCTION TO CIVIL LITIGATION

Jaime Martinez, Harry Hardtack, and the City of Centerville are involved in civil litigation. That process began when Martinez filed a complaint in court and will continue until the case is settled or until it goes to trial. If one party decides to appeal from the trial, the process continues until all appeals have been decided. This chapter examines the various pretrial procedures that occur during the civil litigation process. Trial procedures are discussed in Chapter 17.

The area of substantive civil law governs the rights and obligations of parties to one another. At times, disputes arise regarding those rights and obligations. When that occurs, the parties must somehow resolve those disputes. Most often, the parties involved can resolve or settle their own disagreements without any legal intervention. Sometimes, attorneys or other third parties will help them settle their dispute in an informal manner. However, occasionally disputes cannot be settled and the parties must resort to legal procedures to resolve the dispute. Most often this involves filing a lawsuit and pursuing it through the courts, although other methods, such as **arbitration** or **mediation**, are used in some situations. Arbitration and mediation involve bringing in a neutral third party who listens to the facts of the case. In the case of arbitration, the third party then decides the dispute. In the case of mediation, the third party tries to get the parties to settle their dispute. Chapter 15 addresses alternative dispute resolution.

arbitration
An out-of-court hearing before a neutral party who listens to two or more disputing parties and renders a decision resolving the dispute.

mediation
An informal, out-of-court dispute resolution process; a mediator, or neutral person, assists the parties in reaching an agreement.

A basic outline of pretrial civil procedure steps follows:

- One party determines that a *cause of action* exists.
- The proper court is chosen.
- The plaintiff files a *complaint* in court and a *summons* is issued by the court.
- The defendant is *served* with a copy of the complaint and summons.
- The defendant either *defaults* or files an appropriate response to the complaint.
- Both sides prepare for trial, normally by conducting *discovery*.
- The trial date is set.

In federal court, civil procedure is regulated by the United States Code and the Federal Rules of Civil Procedure. The federal rules, or rules similar to them, have been adopted by many states. In state courts, civil procedure is regulated by the laws of the state.

A POINT TO REMEMBER

Federal and state codes and rules can be found on the Internet, on many different Web sites. Whenever you rely on a code section for an answer to a legal question, it is essential that the code be current. Always check the dates of any code sections found on the Internet. If they are more than one year old, do not rely on them.

SEC. 13-2 CAUSE OF ACTION

cause of action
The basis upon which a lawsuit may be brought to the court.

Before plaintiffs can recover in court, they must show that they have a cause of action. A **cause of action** is a factual situation that creates a legally recognized right to damages or other relief. Recall the discussions of torts from Chapter 7. Each tort listed had certain elements or requirements. When each of these requirements is met, we say that a cause of action exists. For example, the tort of battery is defined as the harmful or offensive touching of another without consent. One of the probable causes of action that would be found in a lawsuit against Harry Hardtack is battery. The plaintiff will maintain that Hardtack beat him (the touching), that it was harmful (it caused injuries), and certainly that there was no consent. A cause of action is stated when those facts are alleged or claimed to have happened. Hardtack will undoubtedly claim that the "touching" was privileged because Hardtack was involved in a lawful arrest and using reasonable force. This will be asserted as a defense to the cause of action. Before the plaintiff will be entitled to damages from Hardtack, the cause of action must be proved. At trial, the plaintiff will try to prove the elements of the cause of action and the defendant will try to prove that there is a valid defense. However, getting to trial requires that the parties follow certain procedures. These procedures are governed by the law of civil procedure. The first step is to select the appropriate forum or court to hear the dispute. The appropriate court is one that has both jurisdiction and venue.

SEC. 13-3 JURISDICTION

jurisdiction
The power or authority to act in a certain situation; the power of a court to hear cases and render judgments.

original jurisdiction
The power to first hear a case; court of original jurisdiction is where trial takes place.

Before any court can resolve a dispute between individuals, it must have the basic power or authority to hear the dispute and to render a decision. This is a question of **jurisdiction**. Jurisdiction is a legal concept that has many different facets. It can apply to a court's having authority to hear a trial versus an appeal. In the American legal system, different courts have different types of jurisdiction. Recall from Chapter 2 that the federal courts are organized in three tiers. At the top is the Supreme Court, in the middle are the courts of appeals, and at the bottom are the federal district courts. The federal district courts have authority to hear trials and the preliminary matters that lead to trial. This authority is referred to as **original jurisdiction**. The appellate courts and the Supreme Court are primarily courts of *appellate jurisdiction*. They review what happened at trial. Civil litigation begins in a trial court, a court of original jurisdiction.

Because the American legal system consists of both federal courts and state courts, a plaintiff must make a choice of court systems when filing a lawsuit. This choice is determined by laws regarding *subject matter jurisdiction* and laws regarding *personal jurisdiction*. A court has subject matter jurisdiction when it has authority to a particular type of case. A court has personal jurisdiction when it has power or authority over the defendant in the case.

SUBJECT MATTER JURISDICTION

subject matter jurisdiction
The power of a court to resolve the kind of dispute in question.

Subject matter jurisdiction first involves a determination as to whether a case belongs in federal court or in state court.

Federal Court Jurisdiction

federal question
A case that involves a federal law, either in statutes, in the Constitution, or in treaties.

diversity of citizenship
A basis for federal court jurisdiction where the plaintiff and defendant are residents of different states and the amount in controversy exceeds $75,000.

The federal courts have limited authority as to subject matter jurisdiction. They can hear cases only when a federal question is involved, when the United States is a party, or when diversity of citizenship exists. A **federal question** exists when the lawsuit is based on federal law, which can be found in federal statutes, treaties, or the U.S. Constitution. For example, suppose a large corporation sues a small corporation for a patent infringement. This must be brought in federal court because patent laws are federal.

Federal subject matter jurisdiction also can be based on **diversity of citizenship**. Diversity of citizenship means that the plaintiff and the defendant reside in different states. For jurisdiction to be based on diversity of citizenship, the amount in controversy must exceed $75,000.

exclusive jurisdiction
The sole power or authority to act in a certain situation.

concurrent jurisdiction
A term that describes situations where more than one entity has the power to regulate or act.

If a party determines that the federal courts have subject matter jurisdiction, it does not necessarily mean that the action must be brought in federal court. When the federal court has subject matter jurisdiction, sometimes that jurisdiction is exclusive. Other times it is concurrent with the jurisdiction of the state courts. **Exclusive jurisdiction** means that the action *must* be brought in federal court. Examples of federal court exclusive jurisdiction include maritime cases, patent cases, and bankruptcy cases. **Concurrent jurisdiction** means that the case can be brought either in federal court or in state court. In other words, both the federal court and the state court have jurisdiction over the subject matter. Concurrent jurisdiction commonly exists where federal jurisdiction is based on diversity of citizenship. Where a court has concurrent jurisdiction, the plaintiff chooses the court in which to initially file a complaint. However, the defendant has the right to ask the federal court to *remove*, or transfer, the case to the federal court.

pendent jurisdiction
The power of the federal court to hear an issue which would normally belong in state court, if that issue is incident to the adjudication of a federal question.

In addition to the kinds of subject matter jurisdiction already mentioned, the federal courts also have **pendent jurisdiction**. Pendent jurisdiction means that they can hear an issue that would normally belong in state court, if that issue is incident to the adjudication of a federal question.

Twentieth Century–Fox Film Corporation v. Taylor

239 F. Supp. 913 (1965)

This is a civil lawsuit brought by Twentieth Century–Fox against both Elizabeth Taylor and Richard Burton as a result of their actions during the filming of Cleopatra. *The complaint contained several causes of action, some against Taylor only, some against Burton only, and some against both of them. Taylor was a citizen of the United States, but not any individual state. Burton was a British resident. The action was first filed in the New York state court. The entire case was removed to federal court on the basis of diversity of citizenship between Burton and plaintiff, even though no diversity existed as to Taylor. Twentieth Century–Fox moved to remand the entire action back to the state court. The court found that four of the five causes of action were properly in federal court even though two of them were against Taylor only because there were common questions between these causes of action and the ones against Burton. Since the fifth cause of action contained no common questions, it was remanded. Read the following case carefully. The legal issues revolve around jurisdiction and breach of contract. The jurisdiction issues raise questions regarding diversity of citizenship, removal to federal court, and pendent jurisdiction.*

OPINION

The plaintiff, Twentieth Century–Fox Film Corporation, moves to remand this action to the New York State Supreme Court whence it was removed to this Court on the petition of the defendant Richard Burton. The action is one of a series of litigations arising out of the production of the motion picture *Cleopatra,* in which Burton and Elizabeth Taylor, now husband and wife, play principal roles. Twentieth Century–Fox seeks to recover substantial damages based upon five separate causes of action, the first and fifth of which are against Taylor individually, the second against Burton individually, and the third and fourth against them severally and jointly. Plaintiff, a Delaware corporation, alleges its principal place of business is New York. Taylor is a citizen of the United States, but is not a citizen of any state. Burton is a British subject, not resident in any state of the United States.

I. Removal of the Second Cause of Action

Had Burton, an alien, been named as the sole defendant, removability could not be questioned, since the case would be within the original diversity jurisdiction of this Court. And so, too, it is beyond challenge that had Taylor been named as the sole defendant, the action would have been nonremovable. However, the joinder of the claims against them enabled Burton to remove the entire case to this Court upon his allegation that the second cause of action, pleaded solely against him, came within the purview of 28 U.S.C. § 1441 (c) which provides:

> "Whenever a separate and independent claim or cause of action which would be removable is sued upon alone, is joined with one or more otherwise non removable claims or causes of action, the entire case may be removed and the district court may determine all issues therein, or, in its discretion, may remand all matters not otherwise within its original jurisdiction."

The first cause of action is against Taylor individually for breach of her contract, and specifies a series of acts and conduct which gives rise to the claim. These include allegations that she failed to perform her services with diligence, care and attention; that she reported for work in an unfit condition; that she allowed herself to become unphotographable and unfit to perform her services; that she failed to report for work; that she failed to report on time; that she suffered herself to be held up to scorn, ridicule and unfavorable publicity by her public conduct; and that she conspired with and induced others to breach their agreements with plaintiff.

The second cause of action against Burton for breach of his employment contract contains allegations of conduct identical to those charged against Taylor. There are, however, allegations that he breached the contract in other respects.

The third cause of action against Taylor and Burton, individually and jointly, charges that each induced the other, and others, to breach the respective employment agreements as set forth in the first and second causes of action; this cause of action specifies that each induced the other:

> "To engage in conduct with each other although each was to public knowledge at these times, married to another, so as to hold the other up to public scorn and ridicule;"
>
> "Not to abide by and observe reasonable and customary rules, directives, regulations and orders for conduct and deportment during the course of production. . . ."

The fourth cause of action against Taylor and Burton, individually and jointly, charges interference with and injury to plaintiff's business and property rights by the acts and conduct complained of in the prior causes of action.

The fifth cause of action is solely against Taylor and alleges that she is the alter ego of MCL Films, S.A. and seeks a declaratory judgment that any money due from Twentieth Century–Fox to MCL may be set off against any judgment against Taylor.

Basically there are two separate and distinct employment contracts, one with each defendant, for services of a highly specialized and individual nature. This circumstance at once negates rather than supports plaintiff's position that individual breaches of the two separate contracts give rise to a single wrong and a single claim for damages.

The contracts were entered into on different dates. Taylor performed services almost a year before Burton entered into his agreement. Each alleged breach, predicated upon individual acts, gives rise to a separate wrong and a separate claim for damages unrelated to the breach of the employment contract with the other defendant. The fact that the services were to be rendered by each performer in the production of one film does not coalesce violations of the two separate contracts into a single wrong. While it is true that the same kind or type of conduct is asserted to constitute the breach of each separate contract, it does not follow that the acts resulted, as plaintiff charges, in the "simultaneous breach of two employment agreements." For example, it is alleged that each defendant rendered himself or herself unfit to perform required services; failed to report for work; failed to report on time; and refused to follow directions. But it is not alleged, and it does not appear from the complaint, that one defendant's violation of contractual duty is necessarily related to the other; that their alleged absences from work or tardiness in appearing, or refusal to follow directions occurred simultaneously, at the same place or under similar circumstances. Moreover, as already noted, there are some allegations of breaches different in the one cause of action from the other. Thus, Taylor is charged with having permitted herself to become unphotographable. No such claim is made against Burton. On the other hand, charges are made against him that are not made against her—to wit, that he disabled himself from performing in the manner directed and at times and places required; that he failed or refused to perform to the best of his ability with due regard to the efficient production of the picture; that he circulated and disseminated news stories and issued other publicity without prior approval contrary to his agreement.

It is true that the individual acts alleged in support of the respective claims against each defendant for breach of his or her contract serve, upon additional allegations of joint conduct, as the basis for the third and fourth causes of action—the tort claims. However, these allegations of joint conduct which underlie the tort claims do not destroy the independent character of the cause of action against Burton for breach of his individual agreement—the single wrong attributed to Burton still remains one of the plaintiff's separate claims.

The claim against him individually is not governed by the operative facts required to establish, nor does it turn upon, any other cause of action. The amount of damages claimed from Burton for his alleged breach is $5,000,000; that sought from Taylor for her alleged breach is $20,000,000. A recovery by Twentieth Century–Fox in its suit against her for breach of her contract will not foreclose recovery against Burton for breach of his and vice versa. Thus, plaintiff's success or failure in one suit will not bar the other. Similarly with respect to the tort actions, a disposition of them will not necessarily be dispositive of the second cause of action against Burton. First, one cannot be charged with inducing a breach of his own contract. Then, should it be found there was no breach of the agreement, it would end any claim of inducement, and even should it be found that there has been a breach, it would not necessarily follow that it was the result of tortious conduct or inducement on the part of any third person. In sum, plaintiff here charges more than a single wrong; it seeks more than a single recovery.

What this Court said in a somewhat parallel situation, where there were three plaintiffs, employees of one defendant, each suing upon his separate and individual employment agreement, is applicable here:

> "The complaint alleges three separate and entirely independent contracts, one by each plaintiff with the defendant. Two were made on the same day, although not necessarily at the same time, and the third some months later. The terminal date of the third is different from that of the other two. Neither the complaint nor the petition alleges any fact or circumstance which would warrant the conclusion that the three agreements were based upon a common understanding or that proof of the same operative facts would establish the right of each plaintiff to recover. The fact that the plaintiffs were engaged by a common employer who agreed to pay them the same rate of compensation does not destroy the separate and independent nature of their respective claims. Even if we were to assume, that which is not revealed by the complaint or petition, that there are common questions of fact or that the claims arose out of the same occurrences, this would not change the separate and independent character of each plaintiff's claim." [Citation omitted.]

And finally, in no respect has the second cause of action any relationship whatsoever to the fifth cause of action involving the status of Taylor and a Swiss corporation. The motion to remand on the ground that the suit was not removable under Section 1441 (c) is denied.

II. The Remaining Causes of Action

The plaintiff further moves, in the event the second cause of action is deemed separate and independent, that the Court remand the other four claims, nonremovable in and of themselves, to the State Court. It urges that such a course is constitutionally compelled and, if not, is justified as a matter of discretion. Neither ground is persuasive.

Plaintiff's constitutional contention may be summarized as follows: Article III, Section 2, of the Constitution authorizes the Federal courts to adjudicate only those controversies arising between parties of diverse citizenship or cases involving Federal questions; Twentieth Century–Fox and defendant Taylor are not of diverse citizenship within the meaning of the Article; the claims or causes of action asserted against Taylor clearly raise no Federal question; therefore they cannot be carried into the Federal courts on the coattails of the separate and independent cause of action which plaintiff brought against defendant Burton; to the extent Section 1441 (c) authorizes the transfer of the separate nondiversity, nonfederal question claims against Taylor, it confers jurisdiction upon the Federal courts in excess of the judicial power authorized in Article III, Section 2. The unconstitutionality of this grant of jurisdiction, argues plaintiff, is underscored by the fact that the 1948 requirement of a separate and independent cause of action as a predicate for removal necessarily means that such a claim or cause of action is so "unrelated," "disassociated," or "isolated" from the joined and otherwise nonremovable claims as to foreclose the application of pendent and ancillary jurisdiction doctrines to justify Federal retention of such claims—in sum that only the diversity and "separate and independent claim" can constitutionally be removed, leaving to the State the nondiversity, nonfederal claims.

Although this constitutional attack on Section 1441 (c) has been accepted by some commentators and noticed by some courts, this Court finds the arguments to the contrary more convincing.

First, the presumption of constitutionality which cloaks all legislation is, in this instance, strengthened by nearly a century of usage and judicial decisions upholding the jurisdiction of Federal courts to remove not only a controversy between diverse citizens, but the entire case, including nonfederal, nondiversity claims of other citizens. And while it may readily be acknowledged that few courts have dealt explicitly with the constitutional issue, that the issue is readily avoided and has been avoided, and that many of the decisions antedate the 1948 revision of the separate and independent requirement, the fact is that until 1948 retained jurisdiction of nonremovable claims was generally accepted. With the 1948 amendment thus favored by the presumption of constitutionality and a history of decisions implicitly recognizing the constitutionality of removal of nonfederal, nondiverse controversies, a heavy burden is cast upon those seeking to overturn it.

Finally, Section 1441 (c) finds support in Congressional power under the "necessary and proper" clause of Article I, Section 8. Since 1875 Congress has manifested concern lest the removal jurisdiction result in the fragmentation of litigation. As the Supreme Court said in *Barney v. Latham*:

> "It was often convenient to embrace in one suit all the controversies which were so far connected by their circumstances as to make all who sue, or are sued, proper, though not indispensable parties. Rather than split up such a suit between courts of different jurisdictions, Congress determined that the removal of the separable controversy to which the judicial power of the United States was, by the Constitution, expressly extended, should operate to transfer the whole suit to the Federal Court."

Although Congress in 1948 narrowed the category of removable claims, requiring of them a greater degree of disassociation than was true of the "separable controversies" referred to in *Barney v. Latham*, it still retained power to effectuate a policy against fragmentation of litigation. While the "necessary and proper" clause is not without limitation, it has been applied to supply constitutional authority to support legislative policy where otherwise such authority might be doubtful. Where considerations of convenience and economy of litigation dictated, the expansive "necessary and proper" clause frequently has been relied upon to sustain judicial power beyond the strict limits of Article III, assuming *arguendo* that the Article commands complete diversity. *Barney v. Latham*'s approval of the Separable Controversy Act of 1875 appears to be such an instance. And the whole notion of removal, nowhere provided for in the Constitution, is itself a creature of Congressional power "to make all Laws which shall be necessary and proper for carrying into Execution . . . all Powers vested by this Constitution." Analogous extensions may be found in the doctrines of ancillary and pendent jurisdiction under which the Federal courts adjudicate many kinds of claims for which there is no independent jurisdictional basis rooted in Article III. To the extent that "separate and independent" claims relate to the same transaction or series of transactions and thus involve overlapping items of proof, as in the instant case, retention of them by this Court places no greater strain on Article III than do many accepted applications of the ancillary jurisdiction doctrine. Since the power of Congress to make a Federal forum available to a diversity litigant in Burton's position is unquestioned, this Court is of the view that Congress has the concomitant power to provide that, once the litigant exercises his right to remove, he may be relieved of the burden of multiple trials in different jurisdictions, at least where some degree of duplication is involved. In this connection it might be noted that Section 1441 (c) is in some way a more sensitive instrument to effectuate Congressional policy than was the 1875 provision approved by the Supreme Court in *Barney v. Latham*. The 1875 statute required retention of the entire case; the 1948 enactment permits remand of nonfederal issues which the Court decides ought not to be tried with the removable matter—a discretion which the Court exercises with respect to the fifth cause of action as noted hereinafter.

As to plaintiff's alternative motion addressed to the Court's discretion, it is abundantly clear that, despite the "separate and independent" quality of the second cause of action, at least the first four claims have some common problems. Items of proof may overlap and the same witnesses may be called to testify with relation to all four claims. To splinter the case and to require a separate trial in this Court, and another in the State Court as to those claims, would needlessly waste the time and effort of all concerned—litigants, witnesses, counsel and courts. The parties are already embroiled in enough litigation here and in California; it would be unreasonable further to proliferate the litigation. Accordingly, the alternative motion to remand the first, third and fourth causes of action is denied. As to the fifth cause of action for declaratory judgment against Taylor alone, this has no relationship of any kind to the individual claims against Burton, or for that matter to the claims asserted against him and Taylor jointly and severally. The motion for remand of the fifth claim is granted.

CASE ANALYSIS

1. State each cause of action in a separate sentence.
2. Why were Elizabeth Taylor and Richard Burton sued by Twentieth Century–Fox Film Corporation?
3. Why was Richard Burton able to move the case to federal court?
4. What was the nature of the motion that was made in this case? Who made the motion?
5. Why did the federal court decide to retain jurisdiction over the first, third, and fourth causes of action, even though they involved no federal question nor diversity of citizenship?

State Court Jurisdiction

The state courts usually have general subject matter jurisdiction. Unless some law prohibits a state from hearing a particular type of case, it will have subject matter jurisdiction. Within individual states, however, certain courts may have limited jurisdiction. For example, a court may have only subject matter jurisdiction in criminal cases. In some states, certain courts have only jurisdiction to hear disputes involving a small amount of money. This varies from state to state. Even in states that have courts with limited subject matter jurisdiction, at least one court usually has general subject matter jurisdiction. If a court does not have proper subject matter jurisdiction, it does not have the power to resolve the dispute and any judgment rendered by the court is void.

PERSONAL JURISDICTION

personal jurisdiction Authority over the person of the defendant in a case.

Before a court's decision can obligate a defendant to pay money or affect other rights that the defendant might have, that court must have **personal jurisdiction** over the defendant. All courts, including federal courts, have personal jurisdiction over residents of the state in which the court is located. However, the right of a court to extend its power to nonresident defendants is always an issue. This is true even if the court is a federal district court. For example, suppose that Mary's mother sends her a sweater for her birthday. Mary lives in California and her mother lives in New York. The sweater was purchased at a small boutique in New York, and is guaranteed to be machine washable. When washed, however, the sweater shrinks. Mary now wants to sue, and since she lives in California, she would like to sue in a California court. Should she be allowed to sue the boutique owner in California, even though he does business exclusively in New York?

The issue of personal jurisdiction is first a question of fairness and due process. Under what circumstances is it fair to require nonresident defendants to appear before a court and defend themselves or risk a judgment by default? Consider the preceding example. Suppose that the boutique owner maintains that while the sweater is machine washable, the directions clearly indicate that it must be washed in cold water and that the reason it shrank was that Mary washed it in hot water. Should he be forced to come to California, a state with which he has no connection, to defend himself? The Supreme Court has held that the Fourteenth Amendment to the U.S. Constitution requires due process in civil cases. Generally, this means that if the defendant is not a resident of the state in which the action is filed, the defendant must have sufficient contacts with the state. This can include activities such as doing business within the state, entering a contract within the state, or causing an accident within the state. In this example, since the boutique owner has no connection with California, that state would not have personal jurisdiction over him.

In addition to meeting the constitutional requirement of due process, the exercise of personal jurisdiction must also be consistent with state law. States have the right to limit who can be sued within their state courts. Most states have enacted laws known as **long-arm statutes**, which specify when nonresident defendants can be sued in the state.

long-arm statutes State laws that describe the circumstances in which the state may exercise jurisdiction over nonresident defendants.

Personal jurisdiction is based on the defendant's constitutional right to due process. Like all constitutional rights, the defendant can waive this right and agree that any court having subject matter jurisdiction can hear the case. A defendant wishing to challenge personal jurisdiction must be very careful. Certain procedures must be followed; if they are not, the court will say that the defendant waived any problem with personal jurisdiction.

In Rem Jurisdiction and *Quasi in Rem* Jurisdiction

***in rem* jurisdiction**
Jurisdiction conferred on a court that may lack personal jurisdiction because the "thing" that is the subject of the dispute is located within the state.

***quasi in rem* jurisdiction**
Jurisdiction based on personal property located within the state; any judgment is limited to an amount equal to the value of the property.

If a court lacks personal jurisdiction, the court can still hear a case if parties are fighting over property that is located within the state. This is known as ***in rem* jurisdiction** and is a substitute in some cases for personal jurisdiction. For example, suppose Bob, a resident of Arizona, and Karen, a resident of Nevada, both claim ownership of real property located in Arizona. Bob sues to establish sole ownership, a quiet title action, naming Karen as a defendant. Because the property is located in Arizona, the courts in Arizona have jurisdiction over the property that is the subject of the lawsuit. They have *in rem* jurisdiction. Another substitute for personal jurisdiction is ***quasi in rem* jurisdiction**. *Quasi in rem* jurisdiction exists when the defendant owns property in the state that is not the subject of the lawsuit. To acquire this type of jurisdiction, the parties must first bring the property before the court through an attachment proceeding. The court can then hear any lawsuit, but the damages are limited to the value of the property before the court.

Sec. 13-4 VENUE

venue
The proper geographical court in which to file an action.

Often there is more than one court of proper jurisdiction for a case. This is particularly true in state courts, where the jurisdiction is statewide. In other words, if a trial court in any part of a state has subject matter and personal jurisdiction, then all the trial courts of that state have jurisdiction. Choosing the specific court is now a question of **venue**. Venue is a geographical determination. As a general rule, actions can be maintained in the judicial district in which the defendant resides or where the cause of action arose. When a lawsuit involves title to real property, the location of the property usually governs. If there is more than one possible judicial district, the plaintiff chooses where to file. The defendant can always ask the court to change venue, but a good reason would be required before a court would do this; venue can be changed only to a court that has proper jurisdiction.

Lawsuits should be filed and heard in a court that has proper venue. However, unlike jurisdiction, a court's lack of proper venue does not always render a judgment void. If a defendant does not object to improper venue, he or she waives the right to object to the judgment rendered by the court.

Sec. 13-5 PLEADINGS

pleadings
The formal written allegations filed with the court by both sides to a lawsuit; claims and defenses are clearly set out so that both parties are placed on notice of the position of the opposing party.

complaint
A document filed in a civil or criminal lawsuit that describes the allegations of the plaintiff and the basis for the lawsuit.

Before parties have the right to go before a judge or jury, appropriate pleadings must be filed in the court. **Pleadings** are written documents that describe the contentions and allegations of the parties—the plaintiff and the defendant. The two most common pleadings are the **complaint** and the **answer**. The complaint sets out the allegations of the plaintiff. The answer sets forth the defendant's response to these allegations. The Federal Rules of Civil Procedure also permit counterclaims, cross-claims, and third-party actions. A **counterclaim** is a claim that the defendant asserts against the plaintiff. A **cross-claim** is a claim that one defendant has against another defendant. A **third-party action** is a claim that a defendant has against a

answer
The pleading used by the defendant to respond to the plaintiff's complaint.

counterclaim
A pleading in which the defendant asks for damages or other relief from a plaintiff.

cross-claim
A pleading in which the defendant asks for damages or other relief from a co-defendant.

third-party action
A pleading in which the defendant asks for damages or other relief from a new party to the action.

new party. Usually, all of these claims have some relationship or connection to the initial complaint. In some jurisdictions, such as California, the term *cross-complaint* is used instead of *counterclaim, cross-claim,* or *third-party action*.

Once the pleadings have all been filed, the parties await their opportunity to present their evidence to a judge or jury. The opportunity, however, does not automatically present itself. One of the parties must specifically request that the case be given a trial date. Unless that is done, the case will sit indefinitely. Once a trial date is requested, the case is put on the *civil active list,* the list of all cases awaiting trial. The length of the wait on the civil active list depends on the judicial district in which the action is filed. In some busy metropolitan areas it takes years before the case gets a trial date.

When the matter goes to trial, the parties will attempt to prove the allegations contained in their pleadings. If a matter is not alleged in the pleadings either expressly or by implication, the parties could be prevented from presenting evidence. However, most jurisdictions are fairly liberal in allowing parties to amend their pleadings.

THE COMPLAINT

Once the proper court has been determined, the first step in initiating a civil lawsuit is the preparation and filing of a *complaint*. This is a formal document in which the plaintiff must state the basis for the lawsuit. For most types of cases, the federal rules require that the plaintiff state sufficient facts to put the defendant on notice as to why the defendant is being sued. This is sometimes referred to as *notice pleading*. On the other hand, some states require that a complaint state facts that constitute a cause of action. In other words, the complaint must contain factual allegations that satisfy each element of the cause of action. The elements of a cause of action, in turn, depend on the substantive area of law involved, and differ depending on the nature of the action. This type of pleading is based on early New York law found in the Field Code, and as a result is sometimes referred to as *code pleading*. Complaints are often complicated and involved. Most lawyers and paralegals who prepare complaints rely on form books for suggested format and language. For some kinds of cases, the federal rules give suggested forms.

A complaint consists of various parts:

- **The caption**—contains the names of the parties and description of the pleading
- **The allegations**—factual statements or claims that form the basis for the lawsuit and the basis for jurisdiction
- **The prayer**—a demand for relief
- **The date and the address, telephone number, and signature** of the attorney for the plaintiff

If the factual claims are numerous, the complaint might be divided into different causes of action or counts. Complaints vary from very simple documents where one plaintiff is suing one defendant, to very complicated documents where numerous plaintiffs are suing numerous defendants for a number of different reasons.

In some states complaints are occasionally *verified*. That is, the plaintiff swears under penalty of perjury that the statements contained in the complaint are true.

file
To turn a document over to the court clerk, along with any required filing fee.

docket number
The court's numerical designation for a case; used by the court to organize files.

Once a complaint has been prepared, it is taken to court to be **filed**. A complaint is filed by turning the document over to the court clerk, along with the proper filing fee. The original complaint is then taken by the court and given a **docket number**. The clerk then starts a new file for this action. Since files are kept not according to name, but according to docket number, all documents filed in connection with the case must contain the docket or case number. Figures 13–1 and 13–2 are examples of complaints.

Caption

SUPERIOR COURT OF CALIFORNIA
COUNTY OF SANTA CLARA

PETER PIPER Plaintiff vs.	)	No. ______
GEORGIE PORGIE, and DOES I–V, inclusive,	)	COMPLAINT FOR DAMAGES (BREACH OF CONTRACT)
Defendants ______________________	)	

Allegations

As and for a cause of action, plaintiff alleges:

1. Defendant Georgie Porgie is, and at all times herein mentioned was, a resident of Santa Clara County, California.

2. Plaintiff is ignorant of the true names and capacities of defendants sued herein as DOES I through V, inclusive, and therefore sues these defendants by such fictitious names. Plaintiff will amend this complaint to allege their true names and capacities when ascertained.

3. Plaintiff is informed and believes, and thereupon alleges, that each and every defendant is the agent, servant and employee of each of the remaining defendants and at all times mentioned herein was acting within the scope and authority of said agency and/or employment.

4. On or about September 1, ______, in the city of Gilroy, County of Santa Clara, State of California, plaintiff and defendants entered into a written agreement, a copy of which is attached hereto as Exhibit A and made a part hereof. Said agreement, in part, provided that Plaintiff agreed to sell and Defendant agreed to purchase for the sum of $50,000, five hundred pecks of pickled peppers. Delivery of said pickled peppers and payment therefore was to be performed on September 10, ______.

FIGURE 13–1 Complaint for breach of contract.

(continued)

Allegations	5. Plaintiff has at all times done and performed all the stipulations, covenants and agreements required by him on his part to be performed in accordance with the terms and conditions of the contract. 6. On or about September 10, ______, defendants failed and refused to perform said contract in that, even though they took delivery of the aforementioned pickled peppers, they refused to pay the sum of $50,000, or any amount, for the pickled peppers. Even though demand has been made by plaintiff for payment, defendants continue to refuse payment. 7. As a result of defendants' breach of the contract, plaintiff has sustained damages in the sum of $50,000, no part of which has been paid.
Prayer	WHEREFORE, plaintiff prays judgment against defendants, and each of them as follows: 1. For compensatory damages in the sum of $50,000; 2. For interest on the sum of $50,000, from and after September 10, ______; 3. For costs of suit herein incurred; and 4. For such other and further relief as the court may deem proper.
Date and Signature	Dated: October 1, ______ ______________________________ Kurt Rume, Attorney for Plaintiff

FIGURE 13–1 Continued

THE SUMMONS

summons
One of the documents used to begin a legal action; it is served on the defendant and tells the defendant to appear in court and respond to the charge or risk a default.

appear
As used in a summons, to appear means to file appropriate documents in the action.

default
Failure to appear.

At the same time that the plaintiff files the complaint, the court clerk will issue a **summons**. A summons is a form that explains to the defendant that he or she has been sued and has a certain amount of time in which to **appear**, or a **default** will be taken against him or her. The term *appear* as used in a summons does not mean to appear personally in court. Rather, it means the filing of appropriate documents in the action. If a default is entered against the defendant, the plaintiff becomes eligible for a *default judgment*, discussed later in this chapter. Figure 13–3 shows a sample of a summons used in federal court.

Rule 55 of the Federal Rules of Civil Procedure sets out the procedure to be followed in federal court when a party defaults. Many states have patterned their laws after this section.

IN THE UNITED STATES DISTRICT COURT
FOR THE DISTRICT OF NEW JERSEY

UNITED STATES OF AMERICA, Plaintiff

v.

STATE OF NEW JERSEY, and
DIVISION OF STATE POLICE OF THE
NEW JERSEY DEPARTMENT OF LAW AND PUBLIC SAFETY, Defendants.

CIVIL NO. 99-5970 (MLC)

COMPLAINT

The United States brings this action under 42 U.S.C. § 14141, and the Omnibus Crime Control and Safe Streets Act, as amended, 42 U.S.C. § 3789d(c)(3), to remedy a pattern or practice of racially discriminatory conduct by law enforcement officers of the Division of State Police, New Jersey Department of Public Safety, that deprives persons of rights, privileges, or immunities secured or protected by the Constitution or laws of the United States, including the Fourteenth Amendment and rights protected by the anti-discrimination provisions and implementing regulations of the Omnibus Crime Control and Safe Streets Act, as amended, 42 U.S.C. § 3789d(c).

The United States of America alleges:

DEFENDANTS

1. Defendant State of New Jersey is legally responsible for the operation of the Division of State Police, New Jersey Department of Public Safety, and for the activities of the troopers, employees, and agents of the Division of State Police.

2. Defendant Division of State Police, New Jersey Department of Law and Public Safety ("New Jersey State Police"), is responsible for highway enforcement of motor vehicle and criminal laws of the State of New Jersey, for providing police coverage in various areas of the State, and for providing other law enforcement services throughout the State.

JURISDICTION AND VENUE

3. This Court has jurisdiction of this action under 28 U.S.C. §§ 1331 and 1345.

4. The United States is authorized to initiate this action pursuant to 42 U.S.C. § 14141 and 42 U.S.C. § 3789d(c)(3).

FIGURE 13–2 Complaint for civil rights violation.

(continued)

5. Venue is proper in the District of New Jersey pursuant to 28 U.S.C. § 1391 because the claims set forth in this Complaint all arose in this District and defendants reside in this District.

FACTUAL ALLEGATIONS

6. The New Jersey State Police is a program or activity of the State of New Jersey funded, in part, by funds made available under the Omnibus Crime Control and Safe Streets Act, as amended ("Safe Streets Act").

7. Defendants have engaged in and continue to engage in a pattern or practice of performing vehicle stops and post-stop enforcement actions and procedures, including searches, of African American motorists traveling on New Jersey roadways, including the New Jersey Turnpike, that:

a. have the intent of discriminating on the basis of race; and

b. use criteria or methods of administration that have the effect of discriminating on the basis of race.

8. Defendants, through their acts or omissions, have tolerated and continue to tolerate racially discriminatory law enforcement by New Jersey State troopers, described in ¶ 7 above. These acts or omissions include, but are not limited to:

a. failing to implement and enforce policies related to vehicle stops that appropriately guide and limit the discretion of individual troopers;

b. failing to train troopers adequately to prevent racially discriminatory conduct related to vehicle stops;

c. failing to supervise troopers adequately to prevent racially discriminatory conduct related to vehicle stops;

d. failing to monitor troopers adequately who engage in or may be likely to engage in racially discriminatory conduct related to vehicle stops;

e. failing to establish a procedure whereby all civilian complaints are documented, and are investigated and adjudicated adequately; and

f. failing to discipline adequately troopers who engage in racially discriminatory conduct related to vehicle stops.

9. The pattern or practice, described in ¶¶ 7–8 above, constitutes intentional racial discrimination by defendants in performing vehicle stops and post-stop enforcement actions and procedures, including searches, of African American motorists traveling on New Jersey highways, including the New Jersey Turnpike.

FIGURE 13–2 Continued

CAUSES OF ACTION

10. Through the actions described in ¶¶ 7–9 above, defendants have engaged in and continue to engage in a pattern or practice of conduct by law enforcement officers that deprives persons traveling in New Jersey of rights, privileges, or immunities secured or protected by the Constitution or the laws of the United States, in violation of 42 U.S.C. § 14141.

11. Through the actions described in ¶¶ 7–9 above, defendants have engaged in and continue to engage in a pattern or practice of conduct that subjects persons traveling in New Jersey to discrimination on the basis of race in violation of the anti-discrimination provisions and implementing regulations of the Omnibus Crime Control and Safe Streets Act, as amended, 42 U.S.C. § 3789d(c).

PRAYER FOR RELIEF

12. The Attorney General is authorized under 42 U.S.C. § 14141 and 42 U.S.C. § 3789d(c)(3) to seek declaratory and equitable relief to eliminate a pattern or practice of law enforcement conduct that deprives persons of rights, privileges, or immunities secured or protected by the Constitution or laws of the United States, including the Fourteenth Amendment, and rights protected by the anti-discrimination provisions and implementing regulations of the Safe Streets Act.

WHEREFORE, the United States prays that the Court:

a. declare that defendants have engaged in a pattern or practice by New Jersey State troopers of depriving persons of rights, privileges, or immunities secured or protected by the Constitution or laws of the United States, in violation of 42 U.S.C. §14141 and the anti-discrimination provisions and implementing regulations of the Omnibus Crime Control and Safe Streets Act, as amended, 42 U.S.C. § 3789d(c), as described in ¶¶ 7–9 above;

b. order defendants to refrain from engaging in any of the predicate acts forming the basis of the pattern or practice of conduct as described in ¶¶ 7–9 above;

c. order defendants to adopt and implement policies and procedures to remedy the pattern or practice of conduct described in ¶¶ 7–9 above, and to prevent troopers of the New Jersey State Police from depriving persons of rights, privileges, or immunities secured or protected by the Constitution or laws of the United States, including rights protected by the anti-discrimination provisions and implementing regulations of the Omnibus Crime Control and Safe Streets Act, as amended, 42 U.S.C. § 3789d(c); and

d. order such other appropriate relief as the interests of justice may require.

Respectfully submitted,

JANET RENO
Attorney General of the United States

FIGURE 13–2 Continued

AO 440 (Rev. 10/93) Summons in a Civil Action

United States District Court

NORTHERN DISTRICT OF CALIFORNIA

SUMMONS IN A CIVIL CASE

CASE NUMBER:

V.

TO:

YOU ARE HEREBY SUMMONED and required to serve upon PLAINTIFF'S ATTORNEY

an answer to the complaint which is herewith served upon you, within days after service of this summons upon you, exclusive of the day of service. If you fail to do so, judgement by default will be taken against you for the relief demanded in the complaint. You must also file your answer with the Clerk of this Court within a reasonable period of time after service.

CLERK DATE

(BY) DEPUTY CLERK

FIGURE 13–3 Summons in a civil case.

Rule 55: Default and Judgment

(a) Entry. When a party against whom a judgment for affirmative relief is sought has failed to plead or otherwise defend as provided by these rules and that fact is made to appear by affidavit or otherwise, the clerk shall enter the party's default.

(b)Judgment. Judgment by default may be entered as follows:

(1) By the Clerk. When the plaintiff's claim against a defendant is for a sum certain or for a sum which can by computation be made certain, the clerk upon request of the plaintiff and upon affidavit of the amount due shall enter judgment for that amount and costs against the defendant, if the defendant has been defaulted for failure to appear and is not an infant or incompetent person.

(2) By the Court. In all other cases the party entitled to a judgment by default shall apply to the court therefor; but no judgment by default shall be entered against an infant or incompetent person unless represented in the action by a general guardian, committee, conservator, or other such representative who has appeared therein. If the party against whom judgment by default is sought has appeared in the action, the party (or, if appearing by representative, the party's representative) shall be served with written notice of the application for judgment at least 3 days prior to the hearing on such application. If, in order to enable the court to enter judgment or to carry it into effect, it is necessary to take an account or to determine the amount of damages or to establish the truth of any averment by evidence or to make an investigation of any other matter, the court may conduct such hearings or order such references as it deems necessary and proper and shall accord a right of trial by jury to the parties when and as required by any statute of the United States.

(c) Setting Aside Default. For good cause shown the court may set aside an entry of default and, if a judgment by default has been entered, may likewise set it aside in accordance with Rule 60(b).

SERVICE OF PROCESS

service of process
The actual process of giving the defendant a copy of the plaintiff's pleading.

serve
To deliver documents to another party in accordance with legal requirements.

Once a complaint has been filed, the plaintiff then has the obligation of giving notice to the defendant that a lawsuit has been filed. Generally, the court will not do this for the plaintiff. Notice is given through **service of process**. That is, the defendant is **served** with a copy of the complaint and a copy of the summons. Depending on the laws of the state, service can be accomplished in a number of different ways. The following are some standard methods of service:

- **Personal service**—In many jurisdictions, the preferred method of service is *personal service*, which involves delivering the documents to the defendant personally. Note that the defendant does not have to accept the documents. If the defendant refuses to take the documents in his or her hand, they can be dropped at his or her feet.
- **Substituted service**—Sometimes defendants are impossible to serve personally. They never seem to be at home or at work, and repeated attempts at personal service prove fruitless. In such cases, *substituted service* is permissible. The requirements for substituted service can vary, but generally this type of service involves leaving a copy of the complaint and summons at the defendant's home or workplace with a responsible person who appears to be over age 18. Some states may also require that a copy of the summons and complaint be mailed to the defendant.

- **Publication**—There are times when the defendant cannot be located at all. In such cases pursuing a lawsuit might be a complete waste of time and money, since any judgment probably could not be collected. However, in some kinds of cases, where money is not the main remedy sought, the plaintiff might still wish to pursue the matter. For example, suppose Robert and Jane, a married couple, decide to separate. They each go their separate ways and do not keep in contact with one another. Three years later, Jane wants a divorce, but has no idea where Robert is. The only thing Jane wants is a decree from the court that she is no longer married. She wants nothing from Robert. In such a case, Robert cannot be served personally or by substituted service, since his whereabouts are unknown. *Publication* would be the only manner in which he could be served. Service by publication seldom, if ever, results in actual notice to defendants that they have been sued. Therefore, before service by publication is allowed, a court order must first be obtained. After that is done, then notice of the lawsuit is published in a paper of general circulation.
- **Service by mail**—In some circumstances, documents can be served by certified mail, return receipt requested.
- **Waiver**—Many jurisdictions favor an informal service on the defendant with the defendant returning a document stating that he waives formal service. This is the method favored by the federal rules.

Who Can Serve

As mentioned earlier, the plaintiff has the responsibility of seeing that service takes place. But the plaintiff cannot serve the documents himself or herself. Generally, service can be accomplished by any person, not a party to the lawsuit, who is over age 18. Licensed process servers are people who serve papers professionally, but plaintiffs are not required to use them.

Date of Service

The date that service is completed is an important date, since it starts the time running in which the defendant must respond. In federal court, the defendant usually has twenty days from the date he or she is served in which to answer. In state court the time might be different. For example, in California a defendant has thirty days to respond. The date service is completed is not always synonymous with the date the defendant actually receives copies of the papers. In the case of personal service, service is completed when the defendant is given the papers. In the other types of service, it may differ. For example, in the case of substituted service, in some jurisdictions service is deemed completed ten days after the papers are deposited in the mail.

Proof of Service

proof of service
The document that details when and how the papers were served; it is signed under penalty of perjury by the person serving the papers.

Once the papers have been served, a document known as the **proof of service** must be filled out by the individual who served the papers. This document details when and how the papers were served and is signed under penalty of perjury by the person serving the papers. If a defendant fails to respond to the complaint, this document verifies to the court that the entry of a default is appropriate. Figure 13–4 shows a sample proof of service.

AO 440 (Rev. 10/93) Summons in a Civil Action

RETURN OF SERVICE

Service of the Summons and Complaint was made by me [1]	DATE
Name of SERVER (PRINT)	TITLE

Check one box below to indicate appropriate method of service

☐ Served Personally upon the Defendant. Place where served: ....
....

☐ Left copies thereof at the defendant's dwelling house or usual place of abode with a person of suitable age and ..... discretion then residing therein.
Name of person with whom the summons and complaint were left

☐ Returned unexecuted:

☐ Other *(specify)*:

STATEMENT OF SERVICE FEES

TRAVEL	SERVICES	TOTAL

DECLARATION OF SERVER

I declare under penalty of perjury under the laws of the United States of America that the foregoing information contained in the Return of Service and Statement of Service Fees is true and correct.

Executed on ____________________ ________________________________
Date *Signature of Server*

____
Address of Server

(1) As to who may serve a summons see Rule 4 of the Federal Rules of Civil Procedure.

FIGURE 13–4 Proof of service.

The Answer

Once defendants have been properly served with copies of the complaint and summons, the next step is up to them. They can either respond to the papers or ignore them. If defendants do nothing in response to the complaint within the allowable time, they default. The plaintiff can then obtain a *default judgment.* However, default judgments are not automatically given by the court. The plaintiff must first show the court that the defendant was properly served (this is done by filing the proof of service). The plaintiff must also prove to the court that the plaintiff is entitled to a judgment. This is normally done either by filing an affidavit with the court in which the plaintiff details, under penalty of perjury, the facts that show there is a right to a judgment. Alternatively, the plaintiff can appear in court and testify before a judge, again showing that the plaintiff is entitled to a judgment. At such a hearing, usually known as a *default hearing,* the defendant is not present.

In order to contest a lawsuit, the defendant must file appropriate documents with the court within allowable time limits. These time limits are set by statute, but may be extended by agreement of the parties or by court order. The most common response filed by a defendant is called an *answer.* In this pleading, the defendant normally denies the allegations of the complaint that are being challenged. Additionally, the defendant might set forth **affirmative defenses**. In a sense, an affirmative defense may admit by implication that the allegations of the complaint are true, but then give some reason why the plaintiff is still not entitled to win. For example, in the Hardtack case, Hardtack might assert as an affirmative defense to battery that he was privileged to use force because he was making a lawful arrest. Hardtack is admitting that there was a harmful unconsented touching. But he is saying that the plaintiff is still not entitled to any damages because of the affirmative defense of privilege.

affirmative defenses
Defenses raised by the defendant in the answer; reasons why the plaintiff should not recover even if all of the allegations of the complaint are true.

Two different kinds of answers are commonly used: the general denial and the specific denial. A **general denial** is a very simple responsive pleading that denies each and every allegation contained in the complaint. The federal rules state that such a denial should be used only when the defendant is in fact denying all of the allegations in the complaint, including the allegation regarding the jurisdiction of the court. Some states permit a wider use of this document and allow parties to deny allegations that are obviously true. As the name suggests, a **specific denial** is more detailed or specific. As opposed to simply denying all the allegations of the complaint, the various allegations of the complaint are addressed by number. Any paragraph or allegation that is not specifically denied, incidentally, is deemed admitted. As a practical matter, a specific denial often is no more enlightening to the plaintiff than a general denial.

general denial
A responsive pleading that denies each and every allegation contained in the complaint.

specific denial
A detailed or specific responsive pleading; it addresses each allegation by number.

Once an answer is prepared, it is filed in court, like the complaint. Also like the complaint, a filing fee is required before the court will accept the document. A copy of the answer is also served on the plaintiff, usually by mailing a copy of the answer to the plaintiff's attorney. See Figure 13–5 for a sample answer.

In addition to denying liability to the plaintiff, defendants might also feel that they are entitled to some sort of damages or other relief. Damages cannot be requested in an answer. To request damages, defendants must prepare a pleading in addition to the answer. In federal practice, this request is made either in a *counterclaim,* a *cross-claim,* or a *third-party action,* as described earlier in the chapter.

SUPERIOR COURT OF CALIFORNIA
COUNTY OF SANTA CLARA

PETER PIPER, Plaintiff vs. GEORGIE PORGIE, and DOES I–V, inclusive, Defendants	)))))))))	No. ________ ANSWER TO COMPLAINT

Defendant, Georgie Porgie, answers the complaint of plaintiff, Peter Piper, in this action as follows:

1. Answering paragraph 1, defendant admits that he is an individual residing in Santa Clara County, California. Defendant denies the remaining allegations in this paragraph.

2. Answering paragraph 2, defendant is without sufficient information or belief to admit or deny the allegations in this paragraph. Based on this lack of information or belief, defendant denies the allegations.

3. Answering paragraph 3, defendant denies each and every allegation contained therein.

4. Answering paragraph 4, defendant admits the allegations contained therein.

5. Answering paragraph 5, defendant denies the allegations in this paragraph, and in particular alleges that plaintiff failed to deliver any pecks of pickled peppers to defendant.

6. Answering paragraph 6, defendant denies the allegations in this paragraph.

7. Answering paragraph 7, defendant denies the allegations in this paragraph.

FIRST AFFIRMATIVE DEFENSE

Other Action Pending

8. This action is barred by a prior action pending before this Court which involves the same transactions, issues, parties, and property that are the subject of the complaint. The other action is presently pending in this branch, Case No. 123456, filed by defendant against plaintiff. Both parties to this complaint have appeared in the other action. Defendant requests that the Court take judicial notice of the other action under Evidence Code Section 452. A copy of the complaint in that action, filed __[date]__, is attached as Exhibit A.

SECOND AFFIRMATIVE DEFENSE

Fails To State Cause of Action

9. The complaint is barred by plaintiff's failure to state a cause of action against defendant.

FIGURE 13–5 Answer

(continued)

WHEREFORE, defendant requests judgment as follows:

1. That plaintiff take nothing by the complaint, which will be dismissed with prejudice.
2. That defendant recover from plaintiff costs in the amount to be proven.
3. That the Court order further reasonable relief.

Date: November 1, ______

____
Chance R. Rhee, Attorney for Defendant

FIGURE 13–5 Continued

Motions and Demurrers

Answers are filed by defendants when they wish to contest the substance or truth of the allegations in a complaint. In other words, if the plaintiff is claiming that the defendants breached a contract and therefore owe the plaintiff money, the defendants would file an answer to claim that they did not breach the contract. Sometimes, however, defendants wish to challenge the legal sufficiency of the complaint itself. Often this means that the defendants claim that the complaint does not contain any factual basis for the court to render a judgment.

demurrer
A pleading used in some states to challenge the legal sufficiency of the complaint.

In code pleading states, such as California, this is done in a pleading called a **demurrer**. The most common legal basis for filing a demurrer is that the complaint fails to state a cause of action. If the defendant files a demurrer to the complaint, then a brief court hearing is held, much as with a motion, to determine the merits of the demurrer. Even if the judge sustains a demurrer, the judge will often give the plaintiff the opportunity to amend the complaint.

Rather than a demurrer, sometimes *motions* are used to challenge a complaint. This is what happens in federal court. A motion is a request that the court take some action and issue a ruling or an order. There are many different types of motions, but common ones used to attack a complaint are motions to dismiss, motions for judgment on the pleadings, and motions for a more definite statement.

Sec. 13-6 PRETRIAL MOTIONS

Often, even before a case comes to trial, procedural disputes arise between the parties that they cannot resolve on their own. For example, one party might wish to amend a pleading and the other party might not be agreeable, or a problem with discovery might arise. Refer to the *Taylor* case found in this chapter. In that case, a motion was made to remand a case back to the state court. Court intervention is required when the parties cannot work out their problems. When one side makes such a request of the court, it is usually known as a *pretrial motion*. The party who makes the request, or the motion, is known as the *moving party*. The other side is known as the *responding party*. The moving party initiates a motion by requesting a court date for a hearing on the motion and by filing the appropriate documents in court. The appropriate documents consist of the following:

Notice of Motion—a document describing the nature of the motion and the time and place set for the hearing

Declaration in Support of Motion—a statement of fact, made under penalty of perjury, describing the factual basis for the motion

Memorandum of Points and Authorities in Support of Motion—A discussion of case law and statutes that provide legal basis for the motion

Prior to the hearing, the responding party is allowed to file opposing papers, which normally consist of the following:

Declaration in Opposition to Motion—a statement of fact, made under penalty of perjury, describing why the motion should be denied

Memorandum of Points and Authorities in Opposition to Motion—a discussion of case law and statutes that provide legal basis for denying the motion

Motions are usually heard on a special court calendar known as *law and motion*.

A POINT TO REMEMBER

Motions require court hearings. Be sure that all dates found in the notice of motion have been calendared.

The case of *MTV Network v. Curry* discusses various motions that can be made in federal court.

MTV Network v. Curry

867 F. Supp. 202 (1994)

Defendant Curry was a video disc jockey who worked for plaintiff MTV. He also engaged in activities not affiliated with MTV. While working for MTV he developed an Internet site, mtv.com. According to Curry, he discussed this with several officials of MTV and was told to go ahead with his development. Sometime later, MTV decided to set up an Internet site and brought this action against Curry on several grounds including trademark claims based on the use of registered MTV marks and breach of Curry's employment contract. Curry counterclaimed for breach of oral contact, fraud/negligent misrepresentation, and unfair competition. MTV made a motion to dismiss the counterclaims, claiming that any agreement violated the statute of frauds (it could not be performed within one year), that the allegations of fraud are not sufficiently pleaded in the complaint, and that the allegation of unfair competition was not clearly stated. The court denied plaintiff's motions as to the first two counterclaims, but granted a motion for a more definite statement as to the third counterclaim. Read the court's opinion and order.

OPINION: MEMORANDUM AND ORDER

Plaintiff, MTV Networks ("MTVN"), brought this action against Defendant, Adam Curry ("Curry"). Plaintiff now moves the Court to dismiss Curry's counterclaims, pursuant to Rules 9(b) and 12(b)(6) of the Federal Rules of Civil Procedure, or in the alternative, for a more definite statement of the counterclaims, pursuant to Rule 12(e). For the reasons stated below, Plaintiff's motion is granted in part and denied in part.

I. Legal Standard for 12(b)(6) Motion

In the course of resolving a motion to dismiss pursuant to Rule 12(b)(6), the Court reads the complaint generously, accepting the truth of, and drawing all reasonable inferences from, the well-pleaded factual allegations. When determining the sufficiency of plaintiff's claim for Rule 12(b)(6) purposes, consideration is limited to the factual allegations in the complaint, which are accepted as true, to documents attached to the complaint as an exhibit or incorporated in it by reference, to matters of which judicial notice may be taken, or to documents either in plaintiff's possession or of which plaintiff had knowledge and relied on in bringing suit.

The Court will only dismiss a complaint for failure to state a claim when the Court finds beyond a doubt that plaintiff "can prove no set of facts" to support the claim that plaintiff is entitled to relief. The standards for dismissing claims under Rule 12(b)(6) are identical to the standards for dismissing counterclaims.

Where, as here, the parties have submitted material outside the pleadings, the Court must either exclude those materials from consideration, or convert the motion to one for summary judgment. Fed. R. Civ. P. 12(c). The Court, in its discretion, has chosen to exclude these materials, and Plaintiff's motion is considered one for dismissal for failure to state a claim.

II.

A. Facts

The facts alleged in Curry's Answer and Counterclaims are as follows. Curry served as a video disc jockey ("VJ") for MTVN under a written contract through May 1, 1992. He continued to serve as an MTVN VJ through April, 1994, under "informal" terms. Curry also engaged in activities in the contemporary music industry that were not directly related to his MTVN employment, such as hosting radio programs and live entertainment events.

In approximately June, 1993, Curry met with MTVN Vice President Matthew Farber ("Farber") and discussed, *inter alia*, an Internet service he was developing with the Internet site address "mtv.com." Curry alleges that while Farber disclaimed any interest by MTVN in entering a joint venture, he indicated that Curry was free to continue development of the Internet site at his own expense.

By approximately August, 1993, Curry had announced the mtv.com address on MTVN broadcasts. On the afternoon of one August taping, Curry claims to have had a conversation about mtv.com with Joel Stillerman ("Stillerman"), a senior MTVN executive. In this conversation Stillerman "made clear that MTVN had no objection to Curry's use and development of the mtv.com address."

Curry alleges that between August, 1993, and April, 1994, he discussed the mtv.com site with other MTVN personnel on "numerous" occasions, receiving encouragement in his continuing development efforts. During the period August, 1993, to mid-January, 1994, Curry claims that MTVN programmers placed the graphic letters "mtv.com" on the television screen for viewers of the MTVN program "Top Twenty Countdown." In reliance on his discussions with MTVN executives and personnel, Curry continued to develop mtv.com at his own expense.

On January 19, 1994, MTVN formally requested that Curry cease use of the mtv.com address. However, Curry alleges not only that MTVN programming continued to make on air references to the address, but that Stillerman asked him, sometime in February, to include certain materials at the mtv.com site.

By the spring of 1994, Curry's mtv. com address had been accessed by millions of Internet users. Curry credits this success, in part, to a computer bulletin board that facilitates communication between performers and other music professionals—a service he claims to have discussed with MTVN personnel since August, 1993.

Curry argues that MTVN was exploiting his development efforts to "test the waters" for their own interactive service. During the second half of 1993, he alleges that MTVN and Viacom explored their options for developing online services. These efforts culminated in an agreement between MTVN and America Online ("AOL") to provide a computer link to MTVN for a fee. The AOL/MTVN service will include a performer-music professional bulletin board similar to the one Curry developed at mtv.com.

MTVN brought this action on several grounds, including trademark claims based on Curry's use of registered MTV marks and breach of Curry's employment contracts. Curry has counterclaimed for breach of oral contract, fraud/negligent misrepresentation, and unfair competition. The Court now considers MTVN's motion to dismiss these counterclaims.

B. Breach of Contract Counterclaim

Curry's breach of contract claim is grounded in his conversations with Farber, Stillerman and others, in which he was allegedly promised that MTVN would not interfere with his development of mtv.com. MTVN argues that the purported contract is void as it violates the relevant statute of frauds.

The statute provides in relevant part: "(a) Every agreement, promise or undertaking is void, unless it or some note or memorandum thereof be in writing, and subscribed by the party to be charged therewith, or by his lawful agent, if such agreement, promise or undertaking: By its terms is not to be performed within one year from the making thereof."

In New York, oral agreements violate the statute of frauds only if by their very terms [they] have absolutely no possibility in fact and law of full performance within one year. The question is not what the probable, or expected, or actual performance of the contract was; but whether the contract, according to the reasonable interpretation of its terms, required that it should not be performed within the year.

MTVN urges the following interpretation of the agreement outlined by Curry's pleadings: Curry would be free to terminate the development of his Internet site at will, but MTVN would forever be obliged not to interfere with Curry's use of the site name mtv.com. Under this view of the contract, Curry's obligations would be susceptible of completion within a year, but MTVN's obligations would continue indefinitely.

The more straightforward reading of Curry's pleadings suggest two performances that are susceptible of completion within one year: Curry's development of the Internet site terminable by him at any time; and MTVN's forbearance to assert any rights it might have in the site—for so long as the site continued. Under this interpretation the performances are of equal duration, each terminating upon Curry's unilateral decision to discontinue operation of the site.

The statute of frauds, "designed to guard against fraudulent claims supported by perjured testimony, was never meant to be used as 'a means of evading just obligations' based on contracts 'fairly, and admittedly, made.'" *Manhattan Fuel Co. v. New England Petroleum Corp.*, 422 F. Supp. 797, 801 (S.D.N.Y. 1976). Assuming, *arguendo*, that this contract involved one-sided obligations of indefinite duration, the Court is not convinced by the arguments submitted that the statute of frauds will bar Curry's claim. Development of the record to a fuller degree than what is presented on the present motion is warranted. In June or August, 1993, MTVN may simply have failed to appreciate the commercial potential of an Internet music site, and improvidently (in retrospect) granted Curry all of the rights he has alleged. MTVN now argues that Curry's purported agreement involves a "major property right" which would ordinarily be embodied in a writing, but this characterization may derive from the 20-20 vision of hindsight.

Finally, the Court notes that the statute of frauds does not present a bar to an agreement that may be characterized as a "joint venture." A joint venture is a "special combination of two or more persons where in some specific venture a profit is jointly sought without any actual partnership or corporate designation." *Forman v. Lumm*, 214 A.D. 579, 212 N.Y.S. 487, 490 (A.D. 1st Dept. 1925). It is widely recognized that the statute of frauds is generally inapplicable to joint ventures, because these agreements are terminable at will.

Although Farber expressly disclaimed MTVN's interest in a joint venture during the June meeting, he may have intended only to convey MTVN's lack of interest in funding the project. A joint venture does not, however, require financial support from the co-venturers. Curry has alleged MTVN contributions of various sorts, including advertising of the mtv.com address on MTVN broadcasts and permission (or at least a request by Stillerman) to place certain MTVN materials on Curry's Internet site.

As New York General Obligations Law § 5–701 presents no bar to this cause of action, defendant's breach of contract counterclaim survives plaintiff's motion to dismiss.

C. Fraud/Negligent Misrepresentation Counterclaim

Curry's second counterclaim is labeled "Fraud/Negligent Misrepresentation." Under Federal Rule of Civil Procedure 9(b), "in all averments of fraud or mistake, the circumstances constituting fraud or mistake shall be stated with particularity." A claim for fraud must be dismissed under Rule 12(b)(6) if it does not satisfy the Requirements of Rule 9(b). MTVN argues for dismissal of the fraud claim on the ground that Curry has merely set forth conclusory allegations of fraud "without clearly stating who said what and when." The Court finds that the details of the Farber and Stillerman conversations are sufficiently set forth in paragraphs 9–11 of Curry's Answer and Counterclaims to meet the Rule 9(b) standard.

MTVN next argues that Curry has failed to set forth a sufficient factual basis to establish fraudulent intent (scienter) when MTVN executives encouraged Curry to develop his computer service under the mtv.com name. While Rule 9(b) permits scienter to be demonstrated by inference, this "must not be mistaken for license to base claims of fraud on speculation and conclusory allegations." *Wexner v. First Manhattan Co.*, 902 F.2d 169, 172 (2d Cir. 1990).

Curry's fraud claim requires that MTVN personnel had fraudulent intent at the time that they made the statements at issue. MTVN argues that Curry's pleadings are deficient in this regard, as there is no suggestion that Farber or Stillerman intended, at the time of the June and August conversations, to break the promises they allegedly made.

The Court finds Curry's pleadings sufficient in this regard. Curry's August conversation with Stillerman was critical to his reliance and resulting damages. Curry alleges that "during the second half of 1993, MTVN and Viacom explored various options for development of interactive television or on-line computer services," resulting in an agreement with America Online to provide a computer link to MTVN. Since the "second half of 1993" encompasses August, 1993, the Court only need infer that Stillerman, a "senior executive" at MTVN, would be aware of MTVN's plans to develop a computer-based information service to find a sufficient basis for scienter in Curry's pleadings.

Questions of the reasonableness of reliance raise issues of fact that must be resolved at trial. The Court notes only that Curry's pleadings allege a period of services rendered to MTVN, from May, 1992, through April, 1994, that were not based upon a written contract. This oral employment contract may have set the stage for the oral agreement that Curry now asserts. The Court also takes judicial notice of the explosive growth in public and corporate awareness of the commercial potential of the Internet.

The Court therefore finds that Curry's fraud allegations are sufficient to withstand this motion to dismiss. The Court is similarly unpersuaded by the similar arguments that MTVN raises in opposition to Curry's negligent misrepresentation counterclaim.

D. Unfair Competition Claim

Curry's third counterclaim alleges the New York common law tort of unfair competition, which "bans 'any form of commercial immorality.' A cause of action for unfair competition requires unfairness and an unjustifiable attempt to profit from another's expenditure of time, labor and talent." *Coors Brewing Co. v. Anheuser-Busch Co.,* 802 F. Supp. 965, 975 (S.D.N.Y. 1992). This claim is grounded in Curry's theory that MTVN was using his Internet site as a no risk "test bed" for its own on-line service.

MTVN argues that it cannot determine how to interpret Curry's third counterclaim, which in paragraph 33 of his Answer and Counterclaims charges MTVN with "misappropriating the fruits of Curry's labors and expenditures." The Court agrees that Curry has failed to specify what it is that MTVN has allegedly misappropriated.

Unfair competition is an imprecisely defined cause of action in New York. There appear to be "few limits on this evolving tort." *Demetriades v. Kaufmann,* 698 F. Supp. 521, 525 (S.D.N.Y. 1988).

Rule 12(e) of the Federal Rules of Civil Procedure states in part: "If a pleading to which a responsive pleading is permitted is so vague or ambiguous that a party cannot reasonably be required to frame a responsive pleading, the party may move for a more definite statement. . . ." There is a tension between Rule 12(e) and Fed. R. Civ. P. 8, which requires only "a short and plain statement of the claim showing that the pleader is entitled to relief." While motions for more definite pleadings are generally disfavored, the opposing party must be given sufficient notice to frame a responsive pleading.

Applying this standard to the amorphous tort of unfair competition, the Court concludes that MTVN is entitled to clarification of Curry's third counterclaim. In particular, MTVN deserves amplification of the phrase in paragraph 33 that charges MTVN with misappropriation of "the fruits of Curry's labors and expenditures." These fruits might involve trademark issues, such as the use of the Internet address "mtv.com," or theft of Curry's idea, or perhaps theft of Curry's mtv.com audience. Given the broad range of defenses involved in opposing these claims, and the potential for unexpected claims at trial, MTVN is entitled to a clarification of Curry's pleadings. Recognizing that MTVN has not been provided with fair notice of Curry's third counterclaim, the Court grants MTVN's motion for a more definite statement.

III. Conclusion

For the foregoing reasons, plaintiff's motion with regard to counterclaims I and II is denied. As to counterclaim III, plaintiff's motion for a more definite statement is granted. Defendant shall have thirty (30) days from the date of this Order to file an amended third counterclaim. Plaintiff shall have thirty (30) days from the date of the filing of the amended counterclaim in which to file an answer or other appropriate response to the amended counterclaim.

So ordered.

The Court provided the following two informative footnotes:

1. The Internet is the world's largest computer network (a network consisting of two or more computers linked together to share electronic mail and files). The Internet is actually a network of thousands of independent networks, containing several million "host" computers that provide information services. *The Internet Unleashed 22–23* (Sams Publishing, 1994). An estimated 25 million individuals have some form of Internet access, and this audience is doubling each year. Philip Elmer-Dewitt, "Battle for the Soul of the Internet," *Time,* July 25, 1994, at 50. The Internet is a cooperative venture, owned by no one, but regulated by several volunteer agencies.

2. Each host computer providing Internet services ("site") has a unique Internet address. Users seeking to exchange digital information (electronic mail ["e-mail"], computer programs, images, music) with a particular Internet host require the host's address in order to establish a connection.

Hosts actually possess two fungible addresses: a numeric "IP" address such as 123.456.123.12, and an alphanumeric "domain name" such as microsoft.com, with greater mnemonic potential. See *The Internet Unleashed,* footnote 1. Internet domain names are similar to telephone number mnemonics, but they are of greater importance, since there is no satisfactory Internet equivalent to a telephone company white pages or directory assistance, and domain names can often be guessed. A domain name mirroring a corporate name may be a valuable corporate asset, as it facilitates communication with a customer base.

The uniqueness of Internet addresses is ensured by the registration services of the Internet Network Information Center ("Internic"), a collaborative project established by the National Science Foundation. *Id.* at 460. Internic "hands out the names for free under a very simple rule: First come, first served. Trademark violations are the requestor's responsibility." Joshua Quittner, "Making a Name on the Internet," *Newsday*, October 7, 1994 (discussing speculation in Internet addresses such as mcdonalds.com).

CASE ANALYSIS

1. Describe the motions that were made at trial.
2. What is the legal issue in the *MTV* case?
3. What are the various pleadings discussed in this case?

SEC. 13-7 DISCOVERY

Before the parties actually go to trial, they are allowed to find out, or *discover*, a great deal about the other side's case. Theoretically, this promotes settlement and, in those cases that do go to trial, results in a more efficient, orderly process. In general, each side is allowed to discover those facts and contentions that are relevant to the case and are not privileged. In conducting civil **discovery**, certain procedures or methods must be employed. The following is a brief description of the methods used in civil discovery.

discovery
A pretrial process of acquiring information; the most common discovery tools are written interrogatories, depositions, and requests for production of documents and things.

INTERROGATORIES

interrogatories
Written questions sent by one party to another party; must be answered under oath.

Interrogatories are written questions sent by one party to another party that must be answered under oath. These questions usually call for a narrative answer, for example, "Please describe in detail all injuries that you sustained in the accident that is the subject of this lawsuit." Where the parties are represented by attorneys, the documents are, of course, sent by one attorney to the other, although they are to be answered by the client. The following is a sample of the types of questions that might appear in a set of Interrogatories sent to Harry Hardtack by Jaime Martinez:

Interrogatories to Defendant

1. State your name, address, and date of birth.
2. State all names by which you have ever been known.
3. Give the name and address of all employers for the past 10 years, including dates of employment.
4. On what date were you first employed by the Centerville City Police Department?
5. Describe all job training that you were given at the time you were hired.
6. Describe all job training you have received since you were hired.
7. Have any complaints been lodged against you claiming that you used excessive force. If so, please state:
   a. The date of the complaint
   b. The name of the complainant
   c. The nature of the complaint
   d. Whether any disciplinary proceedings resulted from said complaint
   e. Whether any litigation resulted from said complaint

Requests for Admissions

request for admissions
A written request by one party to another to admit or deny the truth of a statement or the genuineness of a document.

Requests for admissions are written requests by one party (through his or her attorney, if represented) to another to admit or deny the truth of a statement or the genuineness of a document. These questions do not call for a narrative response, but rather a simple admission or denial, for example, "Do you admit that you owe the plaintiff $15,000?"

Requests to Produce or Inspect

request to produce or inspect
A written request by one party to another to allow one side to see and copy documents or to physically inspect real or personal property that is relevant to the lawsuit.

Requests to produce or inspect are a form of discovery that allows one side to see and copy documents in the possession of the other. It also allows one side to physically inspect any real or personal property that is relative to the lawsuit.

ETHICAL CHOICES

You are the paralegal in a litigation practice. Your next-door neighbor has sued a local police officer. The police officer is a client in your office. You have been assigned to the case. Should you do anything?

Depositions

deposition
The testimony of a witness, given under oath, outside the courtroom and taken before a court reporter; the deponent (the person whose deposition is being taken) will be asked questions by the attorney who requested the deposition.

A **deposition** is an oral proceeding in which one side personally questions another party or witness in a case. The questioning takes place before a court reporter and is under oath. All sides have the right to be present during questioning. After the deposition, the questions and answers are reduced to writing in a *deposition transcript*. This is the only form of discovery that can be used with people who are not parties to the lawsuit. An exerpt from a deposition transcript in the Hardtack matter might look like this:

Examination by Ms. Meyers

Q: Good afternoon, Mr. Hardtack. My name is Jeanne Meyers and I represent Jaime Martinez. I am going to be asking you questions related to a lawsuit that my client has filed against you. Would you state your name and address for the record.
A: Harry Hardtack. 3465 Alta Bates Rd., Centerville.
Q. By whom are you employed Mr. Hardtack?
A: The City of Centerville Police Department.
Q: How long have you been so employed?
A: For seven years.
Q: At present what is your position with the police department?
A: I am a patrol officer.
Q: What was your position with the police department on May 15 of last year?
A: The same.
Q: Please describe your duties as a patrol officer.

Of course, an actual deposition would be several pages.

Requests for Medical Examination

In cases where the physical condition of one of the parties is in question, the other side can request that the party be examined by a doctor of their choosing. This method of discovery, known as a *request for medical examination*, is most commonly found in personal injury cases and is referred to as a *defense medical.*

Disclosure

In addition to these methods of discovery, the federal rules also require the parties to disclose certain basic information to one another. This includes the identity of people who have relevant information, a description of relevant documents, a computation of all damages, and, eventually, the identity and qualifications of people expected to be called at trial as expert witnesses.

> **A POINT TO REMEMBER**
>
> Paralegals play an important role in the discovery process. They draft discovery documents, answer discovery documents, and keep track of the responses to the various discovery requests.

Sec. 13-8 PRETRIAL CONFERENCES AND SETTLEMENT

pretrial conference
A meeting between the attorneys and the judge that takes place before trial.

In many cases, before the matter actually goes to trial various **pretrial conferences** are held. One type of conference is held for the dual purpose of determining that the case really is ready for trial and then assigning a trial date. These conferences are known as *status conferences, pretrial conferences,* or *trial-setting conferences.* They are informal proceedings, but do involve the attorneys for all parties appearing in court before a judge.

settlement
A settlement occurs when the parties reach an agreement on some or all of the issues without actually going to trial; if settlement is on some issues, the remaining issues are litigated or tried.

compromise and release
A settlement agreement that ends a case.

Another type of conference frequently held before trial is the *settlement conference.* In this instance, the attorneys meet with the judge prior to the date set for trial and try to reach a **settlement**. Only a small percentage of lawsuits that are filed ever go to trial. Most of them settle sometime prior to trial. If the parties settle the case before a lawsuit has been filed, then the proceedings are fairly simple. The parties enter into an agreement, normally in writing, that details the terms of their agreement. Sometimes, this agreement is referred to as a **compromise and release**. If pleadings have been filed, then somehow the court file must reflect that the action is no longer pending. This is accomplished by the filing of a *dismissal with prejudice.* A dismissal with prejudice means that the case has been settled and cannot be refiled. Sometimes parties dismiss cases *without prejudice,* which allows them to refile. However, this is never done if the case has been settled.

Settlement is strongly encouraged by all courts. Many courts, including the federal courts, not only hold settlement conferences, but encourage or require that the parties attempt some form of nonbinding alternative dispute resolution such as mediation or arbitration. This procedure is discussed in Chapter 15.

ETHICAL CHOICES

Your supervising attorney tells you that for each case you refer, the firm will pay you a $100 bonus. In case of a contingent fee, the firm will pay you 10 percent of the fee. A case you referred to the office settles and the firm receives a contingent fee of $100,000. You do not ask for any referral fee, but the firm offers you $10,000. Do you accept it?

Featured Web Site: www.usdoj.gov/

The U.S. Department of Justice represents the United States in a variety of lawsuits, both civil and criminal. Its Web site describes the various divisions within the Department and contains several actual documents.

Go Online

1. Describe the different divisions that handle civil cases.
2. Find examples of at least one civil complaint, a civil motion, and a civil settlement agreement. Describe the contents of each.

Chapter Summary

The process of getting a civil case to trial is known as civil procedure. This process includes determining that a cause of action exists, selecting the proper jurisdiction and venue, preparing pleadings, conducting discovery, and, sometimes, making pretrial motions. A cause of action is a legally recognized factual basis for the lawsuit. Jurisdiction is the power or authority of a court to hear a case. A court must have subject matter and personal jurisdiction (or *in rem* or *quasi in rem* jurisdiction) before it can hear the case. The pleadings consist of the complaint and the answer. They might also include counterclaims, cross-claims, and third-party actions. Discovery includes the use of interrogatories, requests for admissions, requests for inspection of documents or other things, depositions, and requests for medical examinations. It also requires that parties disclose some information without a request.

Terms to Remember

arbitration
mediation
cause of action
jurisdiction
original jurisdiction
subject matter jurisdiction
federal question
diversity of citizenship
exclusive jurisdiction
concurrent jurisdiction
pendent jurisdiction
personal jurisdiction
long-arm statutes
in rem jurisdiction
quasi in rem jurisdiction
venue
pleadings
complaint
answer
counterclaim
cross-claim
third-party action
file
docket number

summons
appear
default
service of process
serve
proof of service
affirmative defenses
general denial
specific denial
demurrer
discovery
interrogatories
request for admissions
request to produce or inspect
deposition
pretrial conference
settlement
compromise and release

Questions for Review

1. What is a cause of action?
2. Explain the concepts of subject matter jurisdiction, personal jurisdiction, *in rem* jurisdiction, and *quasi in rem* jurisdiction.
3. Name and explain the uses of a complaint and an answer.
4. What is the purpose of a pleading?
5. What is the purpose of a summons?
6. Explain the various types of "service" that may take place.
7. What is a demurrer? When is a demurrer used?
8. List and explain the pretrial motions discussed in this chapter.
9. List and explain the discovery devices covered in this chapter.
10. Explain the legal result when a settlement is reached.

Questions for Analysis

1. Review the short excerpt from a deposition transcript found on page 306. Write a short summary of this transcript.
2. Review the interrogatories that might be used in the Hardtack case. Write a set of questions that might be sent to the plaintiff in this case.
3. Review the Ethical Choices boxes in this chapter. Which NALA and/or NFPA rules or guidelines apply to the situations? Review your state's ethical rules. (*Hint*: Go to http://www.nala.org/ and find a link.) Which of those rules apply?
4. Read the case *Good News Club v. Milford Central School* found in Appendix VII. What was the nature of the lawsuit filed in the trial court? What happened in the trial court?

Assignments and Projects

1. Locate the rules of civil procedure in your state. How many days does a person have to respond to a civil summons? Cite the section title and number for the code section you locate. You can probably find your state's rules of civil procedure online. (*Hint*: Start with www.findlaw.com/ and go to legal topics.)
2. Litigation documents related to famous people are often online. You can find these on the following sites: www.courttv.com/, www.thesmokinggun.com/, and www.cnn.com/.

CHAPTER 14

CRIMINAL PROCEDURE BEFORE TRIAL

Technology Corner

Web Address	Name of Site
www.ethics-justice.org/	Ethics and Justice
www.ilj.org/	Institute for Law and Justice
www.ckfraud.org/	National Check Fraud Center
www.ncjrs.org/	National Criminal Justice Reference Service

CASE FILE: THE DARWOOD CRIMINAL MATTER

The office has accepted a new client, Mr. Robert P. Darwood. Mr. Darwood was arrested and charged with the possession of (1) a controlled substance and (2) an illegal weapon.

Several weeks ago the police knocked on Mr. Darwood's door and requested entrance for the purpose of searching the residence. Mr. Darwood, who was home ill, denied the officers entrance. For the next four hours the police watched the residence. During this time search and arrest warrants were issued. The warrants named Mr. Robert Darwood as the person to be arrested and his residence as the place to be searched.

The police believed Mr. Darwood was responsible for the bombing of a church. The search warrant listed the materials needed for constructing a bomb. This turned out to be a case of mistaken identity. The Robert Darwood the police were searching for lives in

Union City. Our client lives in Pleasant Hills. The informant who called the police with the information on the bombing did not have an address; he only provided the police with a name.

When the police returned with the warrants, they did not wait for Mr. Darwood to answer the door when they knocked. After waiting about five seconds (according to Darwood), the police broke down the front and back doors of Mr. Darwood's home.

The cocaine and weapon were found during the widespread search of the house. When the police arrived with the warrant, they would not show it to Mr. Darwood and they would not let him use the phone to call an attorney.

SEC. 14-1 INTRODUCTION TO CRIMINAL PROCEDURE

Criminal procedure is a branch of constitutional law. Criminal procedure is (1) the process of facilitating criminal prosecutions and (2) the process of protecting the rights of criminal suspects and defendants. Several constitutional amendments play key roles in criminal procedure. The Fourth Amendment to the U.S. Constitution prohibits unreasonable searches and seizures. The Fifth Amendment contains a **due process clause** and the privilege against self-incrimination. The Sixth Amendment guarantees the right to counsel and numerous rights regarding trial, including the right to a speedy trial and a jury trial. The Eighth Amendment prohibits cruel and unusual punishments.

due process clause
A clause in the Fifth and Fourteenth Amendments to the U.S. Constitution that protects people from state actions which would deprive them of basic rights.

SEC. 14-2 THE CONSTITUTION AND THE CRIMINAL SUSPECT

DUE PROCESS

Due process refers to the system of rules and regulations designed to assure justice in the American legal system (see Figure 14–1). There are two areas of due process: procedural and substantive. *Procedural due process* ensures fair proceedings in the criminal justice system, such as the right to a speedy trial, the right to assistance of counsel, and the right to a jury trial. Procedural due process extends beyond the criminal justice system to other areas of the law. *Substantive due process* protects personal property from governmental interference or possession. On a simple level, due process is the right to notice and a hearing.

The Fifth and Fourteenth Amendments contain the due process clauses. Before the Fourteenth Amendment to the Constitution, due process was solely a federal procedure. The Fourteenth Amendment changed this with the concept of **incorporation.** Incorporation meant that the Bill of Rights (the first ten amendments) was now applicable to the state courts.

incorporation
When two ideas are incorporated, they become one concept.

SEARCH AND SEIZURE

The Fourth Amendment states:

> The right of the people to be secure in their persons, houses, papers and effects, against unreasonable searches and seizures, shall not be violated, and no Warrants shall issue, but upon probable cause, supported by Oath or affirmation, and particularly describing the place to be searched, and the person or things to be seized.

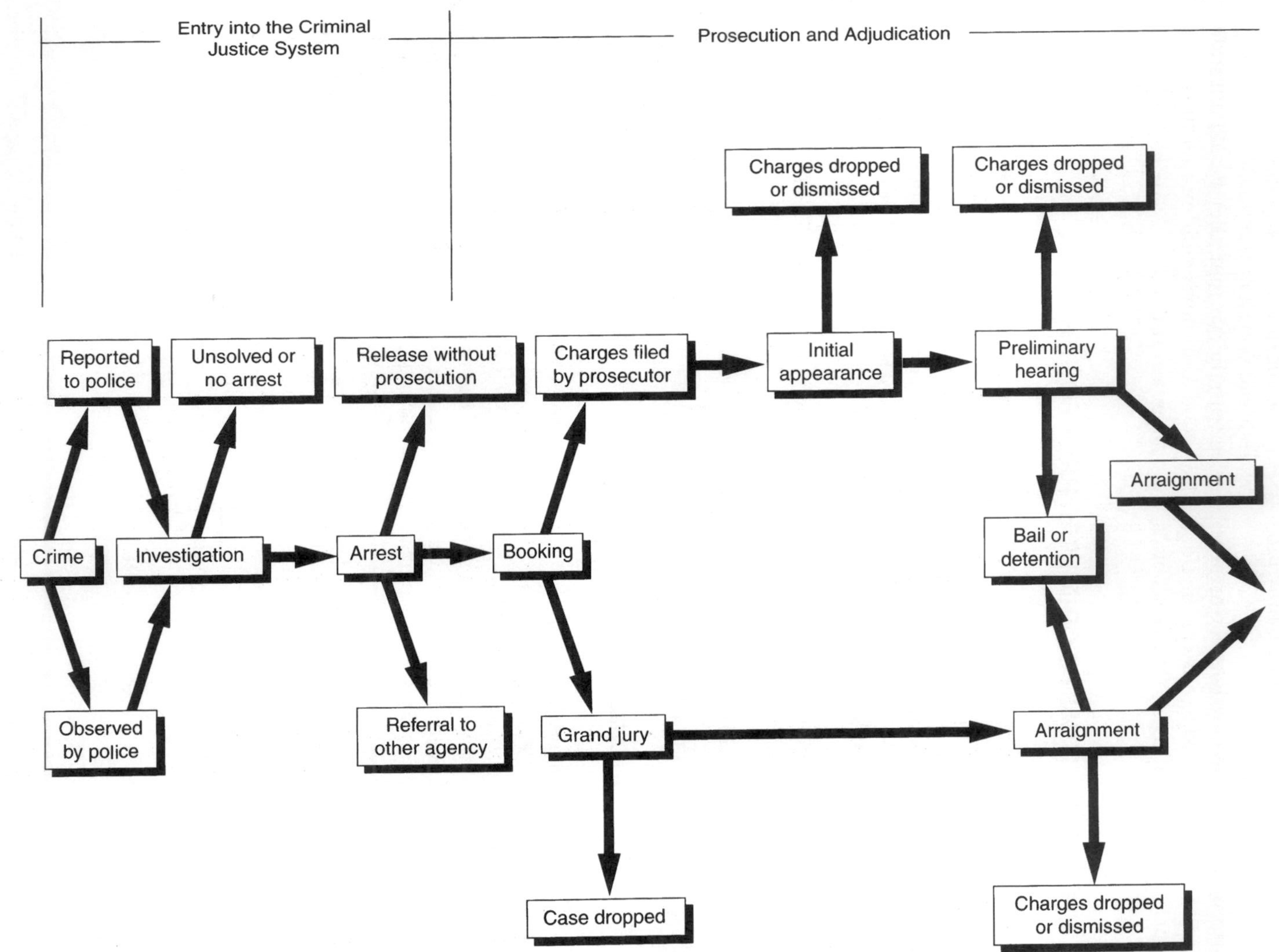

FIGURE 14–1 The process of criminal justice.

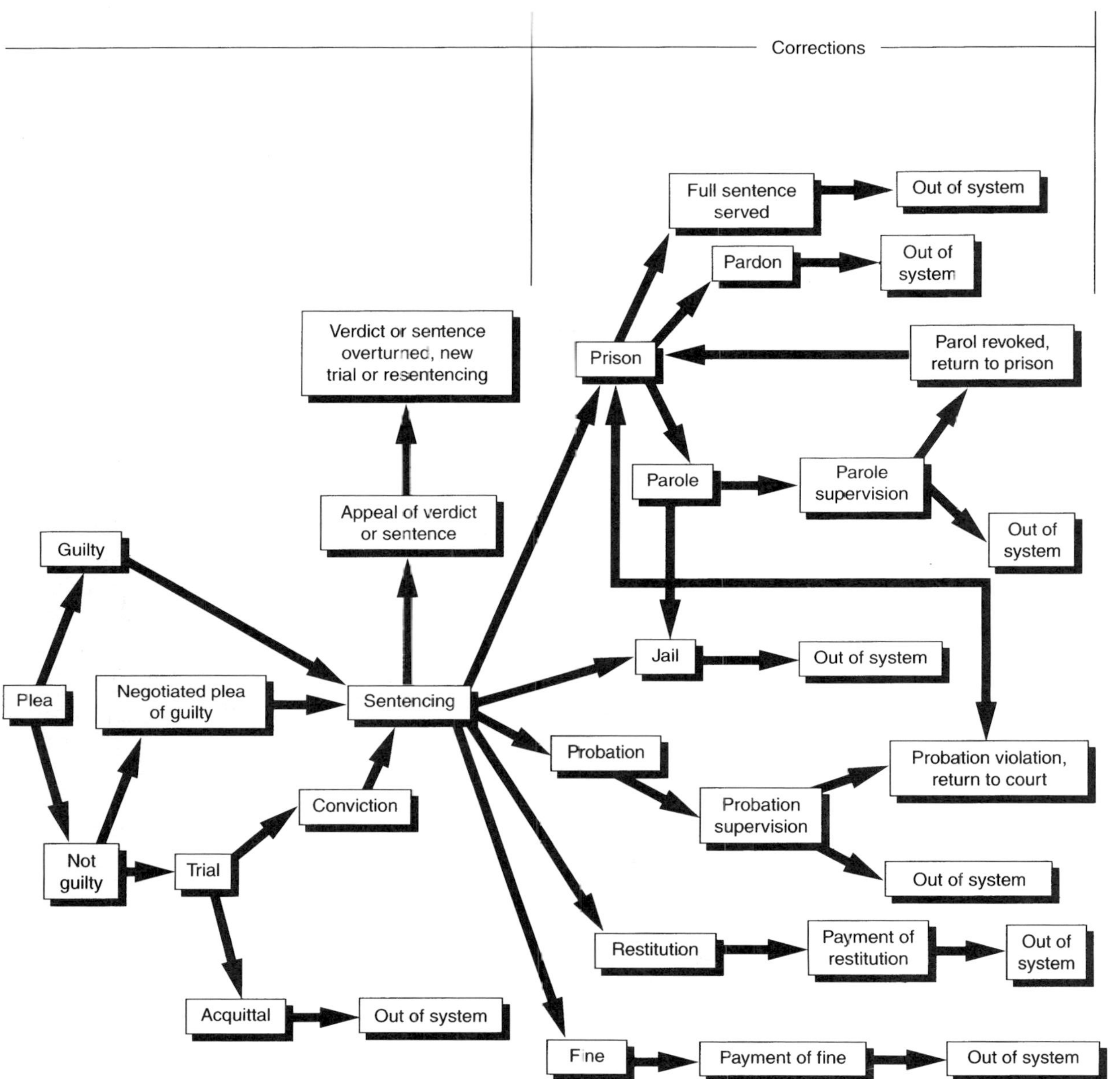

FIGURE 14–1 Continued

hearsay
An out-of-court statement offered in evidence to prove the truth of the matter asserted.

The Fourth Amendment prohibits unreasonable searches and seizures. While it does not expressly require a *warrant* for every search or seizure, it does set out the requirement for a warrant. Searches pursuant to a warrant are favored. In order to obtain a warrant from a neutral magistrate, the officer must have probable cause that the suspect has committed the crime. Under Federal Rule of Criminal Procedure 41(c)(1), an officer may present **hearsay** evidence to obtain a warrant, as well as information that may later be suppressed at trial. The officer must also be able to particularly describe the place, person, or thing to be searched. The "scope" requirement of warrants keeps officers from searching too broadly or seizing additional property. Relevant evidence includes evidence of the crime, contraband (items that are illegal to possess), or an object intended for criminal use.

Katz v. United States

389 U.S. 347 (1967)

In Katz v. United States, *the U.S. Supreme Court held that the Fourth Amendment "protects people, not places" and that what an individual "seeks to preserve as private, even in an area accessible to the public, may be constitutionally protected." This was the first case to hold that electronic eavesdropping could violate the Fourth Amendment.*

Petitioner was convicted of transmitting wagering information by telephone across state lines. Evidence in this case was obtained by FBI agents placing an electronic listening device on a public telephone without a warrant. The Supreme Court held that Katz had an expectation of privacy in his phone call and that the activities of the FBI constituted an unreasonable search since they failed to obtain a warrant.

SYLLABUS

Petitioner was convicted under an indictment charging him with transmitting wagering information by telephone across state lines in violation of 18 U.S.C. § 1084. Evidence of petitioner's end of the conversations, overheard by FBI agents who had attached an electronic listening and recording device to the outside of the telephone booth from which the calls were made, was introduced at the trial. The Court of Appeals affirmed the conviction, finding that there was no Fourth Amendment violation since there was "no physical entrance into the area occupied by" petitioner. Held:

1. The Government's eavesdropping activities violated the privacy upon which petitioner justifiably relied while using the telephone booth and thus constituted a "search and seizure" within the meaning of the Fourth Amendment.

(a) The Fourth Amendment governs not only the seizure of tangible items but extends as well to the recording of oral statements. *Silverman v. United States,* 365 U.S. 505, 511 P. 353.

(b) Because the Fourth Amendment protects people rather than places, its reach cannot turn on the presence or absence of a physical intrusion into any given enclosure. The "trespass" doctrine of *Olmstead v. United States,* 277 U.S. 438, and *Goldman v. United States,* 316 U.S. 129, is no longer controlling.

2. Although the surveillance in this case may have been so narrowly circumscribed that it could constitutionally have been authorized in advance, it was not in fact conducted pursuant to the warrant procedure which is a constitutional precondition of such electronic surveillance.

OPINION

The petitioner was convicted in the District Court for the Southern District of California under an eight-count indictment charging him with transmitting wagering information by telephone from Los Angeles to Miami and Boston, in violation of a federal statute. At trial the Government was permitted, over the petitioner's objection, to introduce evidence of the petitioner's end of telephone conversations, overheard by FBI agents who had attached an electronic listening and recording device to the outside of the public telephone booth from which he had placed his calls. In affirming his conviction, the Court of Appeals rejected the contention that the recordings had been obtained in violation of the Fourth Amendment, because "there was no physical entrance into the area occupied by [the petitioner]."

We granted certiorari in order to consider the constitutional questions thus presented.

The petitioner has phrased those questions as follows:

"A. Whether a public telephone booth is a constitutionally protected area so that evidence obtained by attaching an electronic listening and recording device to the top of such a booth is obtained in violation of the right to privacy of the user of the booth."

"B. Whether physical penetration of a constitutionally protected area is necessary before a search and seizure can be said to be violative of the Fourth Amendment to the United States Constitution."

We decline to adopt this formulation of the issues. In the first place, the correct solution of Fourth Amendment problems is not necessarily promoted by incantation of the phrase "constitutionally protected area." Secondly, the Fourth Amendment cannot be translated into a general constitutional "right to privacy." That Amendment protects individual privacy against certain kinds of governmental intrusion, but its protections go further, and often have nothing to do with privacy at all. Other provisions of the Constitution protect personal privacy from other forms of governmental invasion. But the protection of a person's general right to privacy—his right to be let alone by other people—is, like the protection of his property and of his very life, left largely to the law of the individual States.

Because of the misleading way the issues have been formulated, the parties have attached great significance to the characterization of the telephone booth from which the petitioner placed his calls. The petitioner has strenuously argued that the booth was a "constitutionally protected area." The Government has maintained with equal vigor that it was not. But this effort to decide whether or not a given "area," viewed in the abstract, is "constitutionally protected" deflects attention from the problem presented by this case. For the Fourth Amendment protects people, not places. What a person knowingly exposes to the public, even in his own home or office, is not a subject of Fourth Amendment protection. *See Lewis v. United States,* 385 U.S. 206, 210; *United States v. Lee,* 274 U.S. 559, 563. But what he seeks to preserve as private, even in an area accessible to the public, may be constitutionally protected. *See Rios v. United States,* 364 U.S. 253; *Ex parte Jackson,* 96 U.S. 727, 733.

The Government stresses the fact that the telephone booth from which the petitioner made his calls was constructed partly of glass, so that he was as visible after he entered it as he would have been if he had remained outside. But what he sought to exclude when he entered the booth was not the intruding eye—it was the uninvited ear. He did not shed his right to do so simply because he made his calls from a place where he might be seen. No less than an individual in a business office, in a friend's apartment, or in a taxicab, a person in a telephone booth may rely upon the protection of the Fourth Amendment. One who occupies it, shuts the door behind him, and pays the toll that permits him to place a call is surely entitled to assume that the words he utters into the mouthpiece will not be broadcast to the world. To read the Constitution more narrowly is to ignore the vital role that the public telephone has come to play in private communication.

The Government contends, however, that the activities of its agents in this case should not be tested by Fourth Amendment requirements, for the surveillance technique they employed involved no physical penetration of the telephone booth from which the petitioner placed his calls. It is true that the absence of such penetration was at one time thought to foreclose further Fourth Amendment inquiry, *Olmstead v. United States,* 277 U.S. 438, 457, 464, 466; *Goldman v. United States,* 316 U.S. 129, 134–136, for that Amendment was thought to limit only searches and seizures of tangible property. But "the premise that property interests control the right of the Government to search and seize has been discredited." *Warden v. Hayden,* 387 U.S. 294, 304. Thus, although a closely divided Court supposed in Olmstead that surveillance without any trespass and without the seizure of any material object fell outside the ambit of the Constitution, we have since departed from the narrow view on which that decision rested. Indeed, we have expressly held that the Fourth Amendment governs not only the seizure of tangible items, but extends as well to the recording of oral statements, overheard without any "technical trespass under . . . local property law." *Silverman v. United States,* 365 U.S. 505, 511. Once this much is acknowledged, and once it is recognized that the Fourth Amendment protects people—and not simply "areas"—against unreasonable searches and seizures, it becomes clear that the reach of that Amendment cannot turn upon the presence or absence of a physical intrusion into any given enclosure.

We conclude that the underpinnings of *Olmstead* and *Goldman* have been so eroded by our subsequent decisions that the "trespass" doctrine there enunciated can no longer be regarded as controlling. The Government's activities in electronically listening to and recording the petitioner's words violated the privacy upon which he justifiably relied while using the telephone booth and thus constituted a "search and seizure" within the meaning of the Fourth Amendment. The fact that the electronic device employed to achieve that end did not happen to penetrate the wall of the booth can have no constitutional significance.

The question remaining for decision, then, is whether the search and seizure conducted in this case complied with constitutional standards. In that regard, the Government's position is that its agents acted in an entirely defensible manner: They did not begin their electronic surveillance until investigation of the petitioner's activities had established a strong probability that he was using the telephone in question to transmit gambling information to persons in other States, in violation of federal law. Moreover, the surveillance was limited, both in scope and in duration, to the specific purpose of establishing the contents of the petitioner's unlawful telephonic communications. The agents confined their surveillance to the brief periods during which he used the telephone booth, and they took great care to overhear only the conversations of the petitioner himself.

Accepting this account of the Government's actions as accurate, it is clear that this surveillance was so narrowly circumscribed that a duly authorized magistrate, properly notified of the need for such investigation, specifically informed of the basis on which it was to proceed, and clearly apprised of the precise intrusion it would entail, could constitutionally have authorized, with appropriate safeguards, the very limited search and seizure that the Government asserts in fact took place. Only last Term we sustained the validity of such an authorization, holding that, under sufficiently "precise and discriminate circumstances," a federal court may empower government agents to employ a concealed electronic device "for the narrow and particularized purpose of ascertaining the truth of the . . . allegations" of a "detailed factual affidavit alleging the commission of a specific criminal offense." *Osborn v. United States,* 385 U.S. 323, 329–330. Discussing that holding, the Court in *Berger v. New York,* 388 U.S. 41, said that "the order authorizing the use of the electronic device" in *Osborn* "afforded similar protections to those . . . of conventional warrants authorizing the seizure of tangible evidence." Through those protections, "no greater invasion of privacy was permitted than was necessary under the circumstances." *Id.* at 57. Here, too, a similar judicial order could have accommodated "the legitimate needs of law enforcement" by authorizing the carefully limited use of electronic surveillance.

The Government urges that, because its agents relied upon the decisions in *Olmstead* and *Goldman,* and because they did no more here than they might properly have done with prior judicial sanction, we should retroactively validate their conduct. That we cannot do. It is apparent that the agents in this case acted with restraint. Yet the inescapable fact is that this restraint was imposed by the agents themselves, not by a judicial officer. They were not required, before commencing the search, to present their estimate of probable cause for detached scrutiny by a neutral magistrate. They were not compelled, during the conduct of the search itself, to observe precise limits established in advance by a specific court order. Nor were they directed, after the search had been completed, to notify the authorizing magistrate in detail of all that had been seized. In the absence of such safeguards, this Court has never sustained a search upon the sole ground that officers reasonably expected to find evidence of a particular crime and voluntarily confined their activities to the least intrusive means consistent with that end. Searches conducted without warrants have been held unlawful "notwithstanding facts unquestionably showing probable cause," *Agnello v. United States,* 269 U.S. 20, 33, for the Constitution requires "that the deliberate, impartial judgment of a judicial officer . . . be interposed between the citizen and the police. . . ." *Wong Sun v. United States,* 371 U.S. 471, 481–482. "Over and again this Court has emphasized that the mandate of the [Fourth] Amendment requires adherence to judicial processes," *United States v. Jeffers,* 342 U.S. 48, 51, and that searches conducted outside the judicial process, without prior approval by judge or magistrate, are per se unreasonable under the Fourth Amendment—subject only to a few specifically established and well-delineated exceptions.

It is difficult to imagine how any of those exceptions could ever apply to the sort of search and seizure involved in this case. Even electronic surveillance substantially contemporaneous with an individual's arrest could hardly be deemed an "incident" of that arrest. Nor could the use of electronic surveillance without prior authorization be justified on grounds of "hot pursuit." And, of course, the very nature of electronic surveillance precludes its use pursuant to the suspect's consent.

The Government does not question these basic principles. Rather, it urges the creation of a new exception to cover this case. It argues that surveillance of a telephone booth should be exempted from the usual requirement of advance authorization by a magistrate upon a showing of probable cause. We cannot agree. Omission of such authorization "bypasses the safeguards provided by an objective predetermination of probable cause, and substitutes instead the far less reliable procedure of an after-the-event justification for the . . . search, too likely to be subtly influenced by the familiar shortcomings of hindsight judgment." *Beck v. Ohio,* 379 U.S. 89, 96. And bypassing a neutral predetermination of the scope of a search leaves individuals secure from Fourth Amendment violations "only in the discretion of the police." *Id.* at 97.

These considerations do not vanish when the search in question is transferred from the setting of a home, an office, or a hotel room to that of a telephone booth. Wherever a man may be, he is entitled to know that he will remain free from unreasonable searches and seizures. The government agents here ignored "the procedure of antecedent justification . . . that is central to the Fourth Amendment," a procedure that we hold to be a constitutional precondition of the kind of electronic surveillance involved in this case. Because the surveillance here failed to meet that condition, and because it led to the petitioner's conviction, the judgment must be reversed.

It is so ordered.

CASE ANALYSIS

1. Summarize the facts in the *Katz* case.
2. Why did the Court rephrase the legal issues?
3. Explain the Court's decision in the *Katz* case.

Probable Cause

probable cause
Probable cause exists when an officer has a reasonable basis for the belief that a person should be searched or arrested.

Before a warrant may be issued under the Fourth Amendment, **probable cause** must be established. Probable cause is required for most warrantless searches and for all warrantless arrests. Simply stated, probable cause consists of known facts that allow a "reasonably prudent" person to infer certain conclusions. In other words, based on the known facts, would a reasonably prudent person believe that evidence will be found in a certain location or that a certain person committed a crime? If so, probable cause to search or to arrest exists. Although probable cause is based on "known" facts, a police officer seeking a warrant does not need first-hand knowledge of all the facts. Knowledge may be based on hearsay. In 1983, the Supreme Court decided *Illinois v. Gates,* 462 U.S. 213 (1983). This decision provides a new test for law enforcement reliance on the hearsay of an informer to establish probable cause. This test is known as the "totality of the circumstances" test. The court held that "probable cause is a fluid concept—turning on the assessment of probabilities in particular factual contexts—not readily, or even usefully reduced to a neat set of legal rules." The court recognized that one simple rule would not cover every situation. The *Gates* decision increased law enforcement's ability to search based solely on an informant's information.

The Warrant Requirement

warrant
A written order of a court allowing law enforcement officers to search a certain place, or search or arrest a certain person.

American courts have made it clear that whenever possible, law enforcement officers should search and seize under the authority of a search warrant. The **warrant** is intended to protect people from overeager law enforcement behavior. A warrant is issued by a neutral and detached person, usually a judge or a magistrate. The officer requesting the warrant must convince the judge or magistrate that there is enough probable cause to issue the warrant. This initial determination of probable cause does not bar the criminal defendant from attacking the validity of the warrant and moving to suppress the evidence collected as a result of the search and seizure.

The Fourth Amendment provides the requirements that must be met before a warrant will be issued:

1. The evidence submitted to the judge or magistrate must establish probable cause to believe that the items enumerated will be found in the location to be searched.
2. Probable cause must exist to believe that the items are in some way connected to criminal activity.
3. All items to be seized and areas to be searched must be specifically described.
4. The facts alleged to support the warrant must be supported by oath or affirmation.
5. The warrant must be issued by a neutral and detached magistrate.

The search and seizure warrants and affidavits shown in Figures 14–2 through 14–5 are representative of the documents used by law enforcement officers.

AO106 (Rev. 7/87) Affidavit for Search Warrant

UNITED STATES DISTRICT COURT

NORTHERN DISTRICT OF CALIFORNIA

In the Matter of the Search of
(Name, address or brief description of person, property or premises to be

APPLICATION AND AFFIDAVIT FOR SEARCH WARRANT

Case Number:

I, ______________________________ being duly sworn depose and say:

I am a(n) ______________________________ and have reason to believe
Official Title

that ☐ on the person of or ☐ on the property or premises known as (name, description and/or location)

in the Norther District of California

there is now concealed a certain person or property, namely (describe the person or property to be seized)

which is (state one or more bases for search and seizure set forth under Rule 41(b) of the Federal Rules of Criminal Procedure)

concerning a violation of Title __________ United States code, Section(s) ______________

The facts to support a finding of Probable Cause are as follows:

Continued on the attached sheet and made a part hereof: ☐ Yes ☐ No

____
Signature of Affiant

Sworn to before me and subscribed in my presence,

______________________________ at ______________________________
Date City and State

______________________________ ______________________________
Name and Title of Judicial Officer Signature of Judicial Officer

FIGURE 14–2 Affidavit for search warrant.

AO 93 (Rev. 5/85) Search Warrant

United States District Court

FOR THE NORTHERN DISTRICT OF CALIFORNIA

In the Matter of the Search of
(Name, address or brief description of the person or property to be searched))

SEARCH WARRANT

CASE NUMBER:

TO: ______________________________ and any Authorized Officer of the United States

Affidavit(s) having been made before me by ______________________________ who has reason to
Affiant

believe that ☐ on the person of or ☐ on the premises know as (name, description and/or location)

in the ______________________________ District of ______________________________ there is now concealed a certain person or property, namely (describe the person or property)

I am satisfied that the affidavit(s) and any record testimony establish probable cause to believe that the person or property so described is now concealed on the person or premises above-described and establish grounds for the issuance of this warrant.

YOU ARE HEREBY COMMANDED to search on or before ______________________________
Date
(not to exceed 10 days) the person or place named above for the person or property specified, serving this warrant and making the search (in the daytime--6:00 A.M. to 10:00 P.M.) (at any time in the day or night as I find reasonable cause has been established), and if the person or property be found there to seize same, leaving a copy of this warrant and receipt for the person or property taken, and prepare a written inventory of the person or property seized and promptly return this warrant to ______________________________
as required by law. U.S. Judge or Magistrate

______________________________ at ______________________________
Date and Time Issued City and State

______________________________ ______________________________
Name and Title of Judicial Officer Signature of Judicial Officer

FIGURE 14–3 Search warrant.

(continued)

AO 93 (Rev. 2/90) Search Warrant

RETURN		
DATE WARRANT RECEIVED	DATE AND TIME WARRANT EXECUTED	COPY OF WARRANT AND RECEIPT FOR ITEMS LEFT WITH
INVENTORY MADE IN THE PRESENCE OF		
INVENTORY OF PERSON OR PROPERTY TAKEN PURSUANT TO THE WARRANT		

CERTIFICATION

I swear that this inventory is true and detailed account of the person or property taken by me on the warrant.

____

Subcribed, sworn to, and returned before me this date.

______________________________ __________________

U.S. Judge or Magistrate Date

FIGURE 14–3 Continued

AO 108 (Rev. 2/90) Application for Seizure Warrant

United States District Court

FOR THE NORTHERN DISTRICT OF CALIFORNIA

In the Matter of the Seizure of
(Address or brief description of person, property or premises to be seized)

APPLICATION AND AFFIDAVIT FOR SEIZURE WARRANT

CASE NUMBER:

I ____ being duly sworn depose and say:

I am a(n) ____ and have reason to believe

that in the Northern District of California there is now certain property which is subject to forfeiture to the United States, namely (describe the property to be seized)

which is (state one or more bases for seizure under the United States code)

concerning a violation of Title ______________ United States code, Sections(s) ____________________
The facts to support a finding of Probable Cause for issuance of a Seizure Warrant are as follows:

Continued on the attached sheet and made a part hereof. ☐ Yes ☐ No

____
Signature of Affiant

Sworn to before me, and subscribed in my presence

______________________________ at ______________________________
Date City and State

______________________________ ______________________________
Name and Title of Judicial Officer Signature of Judicial Officer

FIGURE 14–4 Affidavit for seizure warrant.

AO 109 (Rev. 2/90) Seizure Warrant

United States District Court

FOR THE NORTHERN DISTRICT OF CALIFORNIA

In the Matter of the Seizure of
(Address or brief description of property or premises to be seized)

SEIZURE WARRANT

CASE NUMBER:

TO: ____ and any Authorized Officer of the United States

Affidavit(s) having been made before me by ____who has reason to
Affiant
believe that in the ______________________________District of__________________________there is now certain property which is subject to forfeiture to the United States, namely (describe the property to be seized)

I am satisfied that the affidavit(s) and any recorded testimony establish probable cause to believe that the property so described is subject to seizure and that grounds exist for the issuance of this seizure warrant.

YOU ARE HEREBY COMMANDED to seize within 10 days the property specified, serving this warrant and making the seizure (in the daytime-6:00 A.M. to 10:00 P.M.) (at any time in the day or night as I find reasonable cause has been established), leaving a copy of this warrant and receipt for the property seized, and prepare a written inventory of the property seized and promptly return this warrant to ________________________________
as required by law. U.S. Judge or Magistrate

____ at ______________________________________
Date and Time Issued City and State

____ ______________________________________
Name and Title of Judicial Officer Signature of Judicial Officer

FIGURE 14–5 Seizure warrant.

AO 109 (Rev. 2/90) Seizure Warrant

RETURN		
DATE WARRANT RECEIVED	DATE AND TIME WARRANT EXECUTED	COPY OF WARRANT AND RECEIPT FOR ITEMS LEFT WITH
INVENTORY MADE IN THE PRESENCE OF		
INVENTORY OF PROPERTY SEIZED PURSUANT TO THE WARRANT		

CERTIFICATION

I swear that this inventory is true and detailed account of the property seized by me on the warrant.

____

Subcribed, sworn to, and returned before me this date.

______________________________ ______________________________

U.S. Judge or Magistrate Date

FIGURE 14–5 Continued

Exceptions to the Warrant Requirement

There are certain well-defined circumstances in which a search warrant is not required. These circumstances usually involve an emergency. Following are some of the exceptions to the warrant requirement.

- A law enforcement officer may arrest a person without a warrant when that person is in the process of committing a misdemeanor. This "caught in the act" exception allows officers to respond quickly to lesser crimes in progress without having to leave the scene.
- Officers may arrest a person without a warrant when they have probable cause to believe he or she has committed a **felony.**
- **Exigent circumstances** arise when a situation requires immediate or unusual actions. Such situations do not allow time for the officer to obtain a warrant. Exigent circumstances include destruction of evidence, mobility of the suspect (such as being in a car), or the presence of weapons at a crime scene. The officers must have probable cause and they must act immediately to arrest, search, or seize the suspect or the evidence.
- A related warrant exception is **hot pursuit.** When an officer is actively involved in chasing down a suspect, just because the suspect enters a building does not mean that the officer has to stop and get a warrant. The officer may enter the building to continue his or her pursuit of the suspect.
- Another search warrant exception is the **plain-view doctrine.** An officer may seize any contraband (items that are illegal), such as cocaine. However, the officer must legally be in sight of the items to seize them. For example, if an officer illegally entered a house and found cocaine lying on the kitchen counter, that seizure of the cocaine is illegal, because the officer did not have the legal right to be in a position to see the cocaine.

felony
A serious crime; includes murder, robbery, burglary and arson; a crime designated as a felony is punishable by death or imprisonment for more than one year.

exigent circumstances
An emergency that requires immediate action; such situations do not allow time for law enforcement officers to obtain a search or arrest warrant.

hot pursuit
In some instances, law enforcement officers may follow a suspect into an otherwise protected area, such as a residence; when officers are in hot pursuit, they may make warrantless arrests and searches.

plain-view doctrine
Items are said to be in plain view if an officer has the legal right to be in sight of the evidence; such items are subject to warrantless seizure.

The Exclusionary Rule

The **exclusionary rule** is a criminal procedure rule stating that evidence obtained illegally cannot be used at trial. Illegally obtained evidence is *excluded;* this means that a jury will never hear or see the evidence. A doctrine that often works with the exclusionary rule is the "fruit of the poisonous tree" doctrine. This doctrine states that subsequently discovered evidence, derived from an initial illegal search and seizure, is not admissible. *Mapp v. Ohio,* 367 U.S. 643 (1961) is a landmark case involving Fourth Amendment issues. As you read the *Mapp* case, focus on the Supreme Court's discussion of the Fourth Amendment and its use of other cases to support and explain its decision in *Mapp*.

exclusionary rule
A rule that excludes evidence when it has been acquired in violation of constitutional protections.

Arrest

An **arrest** is the physical seizure of a person by the government. This seizure of the individual is a serious interference with that person's freedom or liberty. The Fourth Amendment limits the government's right to arrest. It also limits the right of police to detain or stop people, even on a temporary basis. Police frequently "pat down" suspects for weapons when they stop them; this practice is known as "stop and frisk." The Supreme Court in *Terry v. Ohio,* 392 U.S. 1 (1968), established the rules for when the seizure of a person is allowed.

arrest
The physical seizure of a person by the government.

Mapp v. Ohio

367 U.S. 643 (1961)

In this case, police searched the home of appellant without a warrant. They obtained evidence of obscene material and then arrested appellant. She was convicted of possession of lewd and lascivious material in violation of state law. She appealed, claiming that the evidence was obtained as a result of an illegal search and therefore should have been excluded at trial. The state claimed that even if the search were unreasonable, it should not be prevented from using the evidence at trial. The Supreme Court disagreed and held that the exclusionary rule applied to states.

OPINION

Appellant stands convicted of knowingly having had in her possession and under her control certain lewd and lascivious books, pictures, and photographs in violation of Ohio statutes. As officially stated in the syllabus to its opinion, the Supreme Court of Ohio found that her conviction was valid though "based primarily upon the introduction in evidence of lewd and lascivious books and pictures unlawfully seized during an unlawful search of defendant's home. . . ."

On May 23, 1957, three Cleveland police officers arrived at appellant's residence in that city pursuant to information that "a person [was] hiding out in the home, who was wanted for questioning in connection with a recent bombing, and that there was a large amount of policy paraphernalia being hidden in the home." Miss Mapp and her daughter by a former marriage lived on the top floor of the two-family dwelling. Upon their arrival at that house, the officers knocked on the door and demanded entrance but appellant, after telephoning her attorney, refused to admit them without a search warrant. They advised their headquarters of the situation and undertook a surveillance of the house.

The officers again sought entrance some three hours later when four or more additional officers arrived on the scene. When Miss Mapp did not come to the door immediately, at least one of the several doors to the house was forcibly opened and the policemen gained admittance. Meanwhile Miss Mapp's attorney arrived, but the officers, having secured their own entry, and continuing in their defiance of the law, would permit him neither to see Miss Mapp nor to enter the house. It appears that Miss Mapp was halfway down the stairs from the upper floor to the front door when the officers, in this highhanded manner, broke into the hall. She demanded to see the search warrant. A paper, claimed to be a warrant, was held up by one of the officers. She grabbed the "warrant" and placed it in her bosom. A struggle ensued in which the officers recovered the piece of paper and as a result of which they handcuffed appellant because she had been "belligerent" in resisting their official rescue of the "warrant" from her person. Running roughshod over appellant, a policeman "grabbed" her, "twisted [her] hand," and she "yelled [and] pleaded with him" because "it was hurting." Appellant, in handcuffs, was then forcibly taken upstairs to her bedroom where the officers searched a dresser, a chest of drawers, a closet and some suitcases. They also looked into a photo album and through personal papers belonging to the appellant. The search spread to the rest of the second floor including the child's bedroom, the living room, the kitchen and a dinette. The basement of the building and a trunk found therein were also searched. The obscene materials for possession of which she was ultimately convicted were discovered in the course of that widespread search.

At the trial no search warrant was produced by the prosecution, nor was the failure to produce one explained or accounted for. At best, "there is, in the record, considerable doubt as to whether there ever was any warrant for the search of defendant's home." The Ohio Supreme Court believed a "reasonable argument" could be made that the con viction should be reversed "because the 'methods' employed to obtain the [evidence] . . . were such as to 'offend "a sense of justice,"'" but the court found determinative the fact that the evidence had not been taken "from defendant's person by the use of brutal or offensive physical force against defendant."

The State says that even if the search were made without authority, or otherwise unreasonably, it is not prevented from using the unconstitutionally seized evidence at trial, citing *Wolf v. Colorado*, 338 U.S. 25 (1949), in which this Court did indeed hold "that in a prosecution in a State court for a State crime the Fourteenth Amendment does not forbid the admission of evidence obtained by an unreasonable search and seizure." *Id.* at 33. On this appeal, of which we have noted probable jurisdiction, it is urged once again that we review that holding.

I

Seventy-five years ago, in *Boyd v. United States*, 116 U.S. 616, 630 (1886), considering the Fourth and Fifth Amendments as running "almost into each other" on the facts before it, this Court held that the doctrines of those Amendments "apply to all invasions on the part of the government and its employees of the sanctity of a man's home and the privacies of life. It is not the breaking of his doors, and the rummaging of his drawers, that constitutes the essence of the offence; but it is the invasion of his indefeasible right of personal security, personal liberty and private property. . . . Breaking into a house and opening boxes and drawers are circumstances of aggravation; but any forcible and compulsory extortion of a man's own testimony or of his private papers to be used as evidence to convict him of crime or to forfeit his goods, is within the condemnation . . . [of those Amendments]." The Fourth Amendment states:

> The right of the people to be secure in their persons, houses, papers, and effects, against unreasonable searches and seizures, shall not be violated, and no Warrants shall issue, but upon probable cause, supported by Oath or affirmation, and particularly describing the place to be searched, and the persons or things to be seized.

Less than 30 years after *Boyd*, this Court, in *Weeks v. United States*, 232 U.S. 383 (1914), stated that "the Fourth Amendment . . . put the courts of the United States and Federal officials, in the exercise of their power and authority, under limitations and restraints [and] . . . forever secure[d] the people, their persons, houses, papers and effects against all unreasonable searches and seizures under the guise of law . . . and the duty of giving to it force and effect is obligatory upon all entrusted under our Federal system with the enforcement of the laws." *Id.* at 391–392.

Finally, the Court in that case clearly stated that use of the seized evidence involved "a denial of the constitutional rights of the accused." *Id.* at 398. Thus, in the year 1914, in the *Weeks* case, this Court "for the first time" held that "in a federal prosecution the Fourth Amendment barred the use of evidence secured through an illegal search and seizure." *Wolf v. Colorado*, at 28. This Court has ever since required of federal law officers a strict adherence to that command which this Court has held to be a clear, specific, and constitutionally required—even if judicially implied—deterrent safeguard without insistence upon which the Fourth Amendment would have been reduced to "a form of words." It meant, quite simply, that "conviction by means of unlawful seizures and enforced confessions . . . should find no sanction in the judgments of the courts . . . ," *Weeks v. United States*, at 392, and that such evidence "shall not be used at all."

There are in the cases of this Court some passing references to the *Weeks* rule as being one of evidence. But the plain and unequivocal language of *Weeks*—and its later paraphrase in *Wolf*—to the effect that the *Weeks* rule is of constitutional origin, remains entirely undisturbed.

II

In 1949, 35 years after *Weeks* was announced, this Court, in *Wolf v. Colorado*, again for the first time, discussed the effect of the Fourth Amendment upon the States through the operation of the Due Process Clause of the Fourteenth Amendment. It said: "We have no hesitation in saying that were a State affirmatively to sanction such police incursion into privacy it would run counter to the guaranty of the Fourteenth Amendment." *Id.* at 28.

While they are not basically relevant to a decision that the exclusionary rule is an essential ingredient of the Fourth Amendment as the right it embodies is vouchsafed against the States by the Due Process Clause, we will consider the current validity of the factual grounds upon which *Wolf* was based.

The Court in *Wolf* first stated that "the contrariety of views of the States" on the adoption of the exclusionary rule of *Weeks* was "particularly impressive"; and, in this connection, that it could not "brush aside the experience of States which deem the incidence of such conduct by the police too slight to call for a deterrent remedy . . . by overriding the [States'] relevant rules of evidence." *Id.* at 31–32. While in 1949, prior to the Wolf case, almost two-thirds of the States were opposed to the use of the exclusionary rule, now, despite the Wolf case, more than half of those since passing upon it, by their own legislative or judicial decision, have wholly or partly adopted or adhered to the Weeks rule. *See Elkins v. United States*, 364 U.S. 206 (1960).

It, therefore, plainly appears that the factual considerations supporting the failure of the *Wolf* Court to include the *Weeks* exclusionary rule when it recognized the enforceability of the right to privacy against the States in 1949, while not basically relevant to the constitutional consideration, could not, in any analysis, now be deemed controlling.

III

Today we once again examine *Wolf*'s constitutional documentation of the right to privacy free from unreasonable state intrusion, and, after its dozen years on our books, are led by it to close the only courtroom door remaining open to evidence secured by official lawlessness in flagrant abuse of that basic right, reserved to all persons as a specific guarantee against that very same unlawful conduct. We hold that all evidence obtained by searches and seizures in violation of the Constitution is, by that same authority, inadmissible in a state court.

IV

Since the Fourth Amendment's right of privacy has been declared enforceable against the States through the Due Process Clause of the Fourteenth, it is enforceable against them by the same sanction of exclusion as is used against the Federal Government. Therefore, in extending the substantive protections of due process to all constitutionally unreasonable searches—state or federal—it was logically and constitutionally necessary that the exclusion doctrine—an essential part of the right to privacy—be also insisted upon as an essential ingredient of the right newly recognized by the *Wolf* case. In short, the admission of the new constitutional right by *Wolf* could not consistently tolerate denial of its most important constitutional privilege, namely, the exclusion of the evidence which an accused had been forced to give by reason of the unlawful seizure. To hold otherwise is to grant the right but in reality to withhold its privilege and enjoyment. Only last year the Court itself recognized that the purpose of the exclusionary rule "is to deter—to compel respect for the constitutional guaranty in the only effectively available way—by removing the incentive to disregard it." *Elkins v. United States* at 217.

Indeed, we are aware of no restraint, similar to that rejected today, conditioning the enforcement of any other basic constitutional right. The right to privacy, no less important than any other right carefully and particularly reserved to the people, would stand in marked contrast to all other rights declared as "basic to a free society." *Wolf v. Colorado*, at 27. We find that, as to the Federal Government, the Fourth and Fifth Amendments and, as to the States, the freedom from unconscionable invasions of privacy and the freedom from convictions based upon coerced confessions do enjoy an "intimate relation" in their perpetuation of "principles of humanity and civil liberty [secured] . . . only after years of struggle. . . ."

V

Moreover, our holding that the exclusionary rule is an essential part of both the Fourth and Fourteenth Amendments is not only the logical dictate of prior cases, but it also makes very good sense. There is no war between the Constitution and common sense. Presently, a federal prosecutor may make no use of evidence illegally seized, but a State's attorney across the street may, although he supposedly is operating under the enforceable prohibitions of the same Amendment. Thus the State, by admitting evidence unlawfully seized, serves to encourage disobedience to the Federal Constitution which it is bound to uphold.

Federal-state cooperation in the solution of crime under constitutional standards will be promoted, if only by recognition of their now mutual obligation to respect the same fundamental criteria in their approaches. "However much in a particular case insistence upon such rules may appear as a technicality that inures to the benefit of a guilty person, the history of the criminal law proves that tolerance of shortcut methods in law enforcement impairs its enduring effectiveness." *Miller v. United States*, 357 U.S. 301, 313 (1958). Denying shortcuts to only one of two cooperating law enforcement agencies tends naturally to breed legitimate suspicion of "working arrangements" whose results are equally tainted.

As is always the case, however, state procedural requirements governing assertion and pursuance of direct and collateral constitutional challenges to criminal prosecutions must be respected.

The ignoble shortcut to conviction left open to the State tends to destroy the entire system of constitutional restraints on which the liberties of the people rest. Having once recognized that the right to privacy embodied in the Fourth Amendment is enforceable against the States, and that the right to be secure against rude invasions of privacy by state officers is, therefore, constitutional in origin, we can no longer permit that right to remain an empty promise. Because it is enforceable in the same manner and to like effect as other basic rights secured by the Due Process Clause, we can no longer permit it to be revocable at the whim of any police officer who, in the name of law enforcement itself, chooses to suspend its enjoyment. Our decision, founded on reason and truth, gives to the individual no more than that which the Constitution guarantees him, to the police officer no less than that to which honest law enforcement is entitled, and, to the courts, that judicial integrity so necessary in the true administration of justice.

The judgment of the Supreme Court of Ohio is reversed and the cause remanded for further proceedings not inconsistent with this opinion.

Reversed and remanded.

CASE ANALYSIS

1. Summarize the facts in the *Mapp* case.
2. What are the legal issues in *Mapp*?
3. How did the Court use the exclusionary rule in this case?

Terry v. Ohio

392 U.S. 1 (1968)

A police offer saw two men walking back and forth in front of a store and pausing to stare in the store window. He later saw a third man join them. The officer then approached them, identified himself and asked their names. They mumbled something, at which point the officer frisked one of the suspects and felt a weapon. He later removed the weapon. He also found a weapon on a second suspect. Both were charged with carrying a concealed weapon. They moved to suppress the evidence. The Court held that the Fourth Amendment does apply to stop-and-frisk procedures such as those followed in this case. However, where a reasonably prudent officer is warranted in believing that his safety or that of others is endangered, he may make a reasonable search for weapons. In this case, the officer's original stop was good. He had reason to think that they were contemplating a daylight robbery and were armed. He had the right to stop and investigate and do a pat-down for weapons.

This is a summary of the facts and the holding in the *Terry* case.

A Cleveland detective (McFadden), on a downtown beat which he had been patrolling for many years, observed two strangers (petitioner and another man, Chilton) on a street corner. He saw them proceed alternately back and forth along an identical route, pausing to stare in the same store window, which they did for a total of about 24 times. Each completion of the route was followed by a conference between the two on a corner, at one of which they were joined by a third man (Katz) who left swiftly.

Suspecting the two men of "casing a job, a stick-up," the officer followed them and saw them rejoin the third man a couple of blocks away in front of a store. The officer approached the three, identified himself as a policeman, and asked their names. The men "mumbled something," whereupon McFadden spun petitioner around, patted down his outside clothing, and found in his overcoat pocket, but was unable to remove, a pistol. The officer ordered the three into the store. He removed petitioner's overcoat, took out a revolver, and ordered the three to face the wall with their hands raised. He patted down the outer clothing of Chilton and Katz and seized a revolver from Chilton's outside overcoat pocket. He did not put his hands under the outer garments of Katz (since he discovered nothing in his pat-down which might have been a weapon), or under petitioner's or Chilton's outer garments until he felt the guns.

The three were taken to the police station. Petitioner and Chilton were charged with carrying concealed weapons. The defense moved to suppress the weapons. Though the trial court rejected the prosecution theory that the guns had been seized during a search incident to a lawful arrest, the court denied the motion to suppress and admitted the weapons into evidence on the ground that the officer had cause to believe that petitioner and Chilton were acting suspiciously, that their interrogation was warranted, and that the officer for his own protection had the right to pat down their outer clothing having reasonable cause to believe that they might be armed. The court distinguished between an investigatory "stop" and an arrest, and between a "frisk" of the outer clothing for weapons and a full-blown search for evidence of crime. Petitioner and Chilton were found guilty, an intermediate appellate court affirmed, and the State Supreme Court dismissed the appeal on the ground that "no substantial constitutional question" was involved. Held:

1. The Fourth Amendment right against unreasonable searches and seizures, made applicable to the States by the Fourteenth Amendment, "protects people, not places," and therefore applies as much to the citizen on the streets as well as at home or elsewhere.

2. The issue in this case is not the abstract propriety of the police conduct but the admissibility against petitioner of the evidence uncovered by the search and seizure.

3. The exclusionary rule cannot properly be invoked to exclude the products of legitimate and restrained police investigative techniques; and this Court's approval of such techniques should not discourage remedies other than the exclusionary rule to curtail police abuses for which that is not an effective sanction.

4. The Fourth Amendment applies to "stop and frisk" procedures such as those followed here.

(a) Whenever a police officer accosts an individual and restrains his freedom to walk away, he has "seized" that person within the meaning of the Fourth Amendment.

(b) A careful exploration of the outer surfaces of a person's clothing in an attempt to find weapons is a "search" under that Amendment.

5. Where a reasonably prudent officer is warranted in the circumstances of a given case in believing that his safety or that of others is endangered, he may make a reasonable search for weapons of the person believed by him to be armed and dangerous regardless of whether he has probable

cause to arrest that individual for crime or the absolute certainty that the individual is armed.

(a) Though the police must whenever practicable secure a warrant to make a search and seizure, that procedure cannot be followed where swift action based upon on-the-spot observations of the officer on the beat is required.

(b) The reasonableness of any particular search and seizure must be assessed in light of the particular circumstances against the standard of whether a man of reasonable caution is warranted in believing that the action taken was appropriate.

(c) The officer here was performing a legitimate function of investigating suspicious conduct when he decided to approach petitioner and his companions.

(d) An officer justified in believing that an individual whose suspicious behavior he is investigating at close range is armed may, to neutralize the threat of physical harm, take necessary measures to determine whether that person is carrying a weapon.

(e) A search for weapons in the absence of probable cause to arrest must be strictly circumscribed by the exigencies of the situation.

(f) An officer may make an intrusion short of arrest where he has reasonable apprehension of danger before being possessed of information justifying arrest.

6. The officer's protective seizure of petitioner and his companions and the limited search which he made were reasonable, both at their inception and as conducted.

(a) The actions of petitioner and his companions were consistent with the officer's hypothesis that they were contemplating a daylight robbery and were armed.

(b) The officer's search was confined to what was minimally necessary to determine whether the men were armed, and the intrusion, which was made for the sole purpose of protecting himself and others nearby, was confined to ascertaining the presence of weapons.

7. The revolver seized from petitioner was properly admitted into evidence against him, since the search which led to its seizure was reasonable under the Fourth Amendment.

CASE ANALYSIS

1. Summarize the Court's decision in the *Terry* case.
2. When may an officer make a reasonable search for weapons?

SEC. 14-3 INTERROGATIONS AND CONFESSIONS

Police officers routinely question criminal suspects. This questioning is an essential element of any law enforcement investigation. When an officer questions a person he or she believes to have committed a crime, this is **interrogation.** When a person claims to have committed a crime, this is a **confession.** The Fifth Amendment guarantees people the right to be free from **self-incrimination.** The well-known case of *Miranda v. Arizona,* 384 U.S. 436 (1966), addresses the issue of self-incrimination.

interrogation
The process used by law enforcement officers to elicit information from a criminal suspect.

confession
A voluntary statement made by a person charged with a crime, acknowledging that he or she is guilty of the charge.

self-incrimination
The Fifth Amendment to the Constitution prohibits the government from making a person become a witness against himself or herself.

arraignment
A hearing where the criminal defendant comes before the court to enter a plea; it is a hearing in open court where the information and/or indictment are read and the defendant is asked to plead.

plea
The criminal defendant's response to the charge against him or her.

RIGHT TO COUNSEL

The Sixth Amendment states: "In all criminal prosecutions, the accused shall enjoy the right . . . to have the Assistance of Counsel for his defense." This important right is applicable to all of the states. A federal criminal defendant has the right to have counsel present at all stages of trial, including **arraignment** and entering a **plea,** under Federal Rule of Criminal Procedure 44. For many years state courts were compelled to appoint counsel only when the defendant faced capital charges. In 1932, in *Powell v. Alabama,* 287 U.S. 45 (the "Scottsboro" case), the Court recognized a constitutional right for indigents to have counsel appointed to represent them. In *Powell,* nine young black men were charged with the rapes of two white women. The defendants were tried within one week of the arrests. Eight of the men were convicted and sentenced to death. On appeal the defendants claimed that the trial court should have appointed counsel to represent them. The U.S. Supreme Court agreed with the defendants. Later, in *Betts v. Brady,* 315 U.S. 455 (1942), the

Miranda v. Arizona

384 U.S. 436 (1966)

The Miranda *case was what is known as a consolidation of cases. Four cases were brought to the Supreme Court with essentially identical factual situations and identical legal issues. All four cases were decided under the one case name of* Miranda v. Arizona.

SYLLABUS (TAKEN FROM THE UNITED STATES SUPREME COURT)

In each of these cases the defendant while in police custody was questioned by police officers, detectives, or a prosecuting attorney in a room in which he was cut off from the outside world. None of the defendants was given a full and effective warning of his rights at the outset of the interrogation process. In all four cases the questioning elicited oral admissions, and in three of them signed statements as well, which were admitted at their trials. All defendants were convicted and all convictions, except in No. 584, were affirmed on appeal. Held:

1. The prosecution may not use statements, whether exculpatory or inculpatory, stemming from questioning initiated by law enforcement officers after a person has been taken into custody or otherwise deprived of his freedom of action in any significant way, unless it demonstrates the use of procedural safeguards effective to secure the Fifth Amendment's privilege against self-incrimination.

(a) The atmosphere and environment of incommunicado interrogation as it exists today is inherently intimidating and works to undermine the privilege against self-incrimination. Unless adequate preventive measures are taken to dispel the compulsion inherent in custodial surroundings, no statement obtained from the defendant can truly be the product of his free choice.

(b) The privilege against self-incrimination, which has had a long and expansive historical development, is the essential mainstay of our adversary system and guarantees to the individual the "right to remain silent unless he chooses to speak in the unfettered exercise of his own will," during a period of custodial interrogation as well as in the courts or during the course of other official investigations.

(c) The decision in *Escobedo v. Illinois,* 378 U.S. 478, stressed the need for protective devices to make the process of police interrogation conform to the dictates of the privilege.

(d) In the absence of other effective measures the following procedures to safeguard the Fifth Amendment privilege must be observed: The person in custody must, prior to interrogation, be clearly informed that he has the right to remain silent, and that anything he says will be used against him in court; he must be clearly informed that he has the right to consult with a lawyer and to have the lawyer with him during interrogation, and that, if he is indigent, a lawyer will be appointed to represent him.

(e) If the individual indicates, prior to or during questioning, that he wishes to remain silent, the interrogation must cease; if he states that he wants an attorney, the questioning must cease until an attorney is present.

(f) Where an interrogation is conducted without the presence of an attorney and a statement is taken, a heavy burden rests on the Government to demonstrate that the defendant knowingly and intelligently waived his right to counsel.

(g) Where the individual answers some questions during in custody interrogation he has not waived his privilege and may invoke his right to remain silent thereafter.

(h) The warnings required and the waiver needed are, in the absence of a fully effective equivalent, prerequisites to the admissibility of any statement, inculpatory or exculpatory, made by a defendant.

2. The limitations on the interrogation process required for the protection of the individual's constitutional rights should not cause an undue interference with a proper system of law enforcement, as demonstrated by the procedures of the FBI and the safeguards afforded in other jurisdictions.

3. In each of these cases the statements were obtained under circumstances that did not meet constitutional standards for protection of the privilege against self-incrimination.

CASE ANALYSIS

1. Discuss the pros and cons of the *Miranda* warning on the justice system.
2. Discuss the privilege against self-incrimination.

Supreme Court added "special circumstances" to the debate over appointed counsel. An example of a special circumstance was illiteracy. The Supreme Court in *Gideon v. Wainwright,* 372 U.S. 335 (1963), reversed itself, declaring that all felony defendants have the right to assistance of counsel at trial. The *Gideon* case extended the right to counsel to all state felony proceedings. The *Gideon* case is found in Chapter 4.

Federal Rule of Criminal Procedure 44(a) states:

> Every defendant who is unable to obtain counsel shall be entitled to have counsel assigned to represent him at every stage of the proceedings from his initial appearance before the Federal magistrate or the court through appeal, unless he waives such appointment.

The Sixth Amendment also lists several rights regarding a criminal trial. The defendant has the right to a jury trial of his or her peers, the right to a speedy trial, the right to a trial in the area where the crime occurred, and the right to subpoena witnesses for trial.

SEC. 14-4 PRETRIAL ACTIVITIES

investigation
The process of asking questions and locating evidence.

A great number of things will take place before a matter goes to trial. In fact, several things usually happen prior to an arrest. The **investigation** will begin as soon as the police are made aware of criminal activity.

DISCOVERY AND INVESTIGATION

The police are often notified by citizens that a crime has been committed. Sometimes, they are alerted even before the crime has taken place. Once they are on notice of criminal activity, law enforcement agents will begin to investigate and discover evidence. This discovery and investigation may take many forms. The police might question suspects and witnesses. They may place surveillance on a location or a person. Usually, this is done prior to making an initial arrest. At this point, the officers are looking to gather enough evidence to satisfy the probable-cause standard necessary to acquire a search or arrest warrant. Later they will pursue the evidence in an effort to gather enough evidence to convict the suspect.

THE ARREST

booking
The process after arrest when the police have entered formal charges against a defendant.

bail
An amount of money set by the court, payment of which is a condition of pretrial release from police custody.

The arrest is made after enough evidence has been collected to establish probable cause. Arrests may be made with or without a warrant, but there must always be probable cause to arrest. A criminal defendant will usually be searched at the time of the arrest. At the police station the defendant will be *booked*. The **booking** process involves fingerprinting and photographing the defendant. Background information on the defendant, such as full name, address, phone number, and so forth will also be collected. In most instances, the defendant will be allowed to make a phone call during or just after the booking process.

The defendant is searched again before he or she is placed in a jail cell. If the defendant's offense is minor, he or she may be allowed to post **bail** and appear before the judge at a later date. When the offense is not minor, the defendant will be held until the initial appearance; the judge sets the bail amount at this time. In some states, the amount of bail is set on the arrest warrant.

THE COMPLAINT

Federal Rule of Criminal Procedure 3 states:

> The complaint is a written statement of the essential facts constituting the offense charged. It shall be made upon oath before a magistrate.

affidavit
A non-oral statement of facts that is confirmed by affirmation or oath of the person making the statement.

After the arrest, the prosecutor decides whether to charge the person held with a criminal offense. A complaint will be filed if the prosecutor is convinced that the evidence supports the charge. The *criminal complaint* is the charging instrument. As such, it is the first document filed with the court. It is similar to a civil complaint in that it is a written statement explaining the significant facts of the case. Because the officer writing the complaint may not have firsthand knowledge of the facts alleged in the complaint, **affidavits** from witnesses and victims often accompany the complaint.

Compare the criminal complaints filed in the O. J. Simpson case (Figure 14–6) and the Terry Nichols case (the Oklahoma City bombing) (Figure 14–7).

Notice the detail in the affidavit supporting the complaint in the *Nichols* case.

State of California v. O. J. Simpson

June 17, 1994
Felony Complaint for Arrest Warrant, Case No. BA097211

The undersigned is informed and believes that:

COUNT ONE

On or about June 12, 1994, in the county of Los Angeles, the crime of murder, in violation of Penal Code Section 187(a), a Felony, was committed by Orenthal James Simpson, who did willfully, unlawfully, and with malice aforethought murder Nicole Brown Simpson, a human being.

Notice: The above offense is a serious felony within the meaning of Penal Code Section 1192.7(c)(1).

It is further alleged that in the commission and attempted commission of the above offense, the said defendant(s), Orenthal James Simpson, personally used a deadly and dangerous weapon(s), to wit, knife, said use not being an element of the above offense, within the meaning of Penal Code Section 12022(b) and also causing the above offense to be a serious felony within the meaning of Penal Code Section 1192.7(c)(23).

FIGURE 14–6 The Simpson criminal complaint.

COUNT TWO

On or about June 12, 1994, in the county of Los Angeles, the crime of murder, in violation of Penal Code Section 187(a), a Felony, was committed by Orenthal James Simpson, who did willfully, unlawfully, and with malice aforethought murder Ronald Lyle Goldman, a human being.

Notice: The above offense is a serious felony within the meaning of Penal Code Section 1192.7(c)(1).

It is further alleged that in the commission and attempted commission of the above offense, the said defendant(s), Orenthal James Simpson, personally used a deadly and dangerous weapon(s), to wit, knife, said use not being an element of the above offense, within the meaning of Penal Code Section 12022(b) and also causing the above offense to be a serious felony within the meaning of Penal Code Section 1192.7(c)(23).

It is further alleged as to Counts 1 and 2 the defendant has in this proceeding been convicted [*sic*] of more than one offense of murder in the first or second degree within the meaning of Penal Code 190.2(a)(3).

Further, attached hereto and incorporated herein are official reports and documents of a law enforcement agency which the undersigned believes establish probable cause for the arrest of defendant(s), Orenthal James Simpson, for the above-listed crimes. Wherefore, a warrant of arrest is requested for Orenthal James Simpson.

I declare under penalty of perjury that the foregoing is true and correct and that this complaint, Case Number BA097211, consists of 2 count(s).

Executed at Los Angeles, County of Los Angeles, on June 17, 1994.

Phillip Vannatter
(LAPD Robbery-Homicide detective)
Declarant and Complainant

FIGURE 14–6 Continued

UNITED STATES OF AMERICA *v.* TERRY LYNN NICHOLS

CASE NUMBER: M-95-105-H

UNITED STATES DISTRICT COURT
WESTERN DISTRICT OF OKLAHOMA
May 9, 1995, Filed

CRIMINAL COMPLAINT

I, the undersigned complainant being duly sworn state the following is true and correct to the best of my knowledge and belief. On or about April 19, 1995, in Oklahoma City, Oklahoma County, in the Western District of Oklahoma, defendant(s) did, maliciously damage and destroy by means of fire and an explosive, a building, vehicle, and other personal real property in whole or in part owned, possessed, and used by the United States, and departments and agencies thereof, in violation of Title 18, United States Code, Section(s) 844(f) and 2.

FIGURE 14–7 The Nichols criminal complaint and attached affidavit.

I further state that I am a(n) Special Agent of the Federal Bureau of Investigation and that this complaint is based on the following facts:

See attached Affidavit of Special Agent Henry C. Gibbons, Federal Bureau of Investigation, which is incorporated and made a part hereof by reference.

Continued on the attached sheet and made a part hereof: XX Yes No
/s/Henry C. Gibbons

Special Agent
Federal Bureau of Investigation
Sworn to before me and subscribed in my presence, on this 9th day of May, 1995, at Oklahoma City, Oklahoma.

Ronald L. Howland
UNITED STATES MAGISTRATE JUDGE

STATE OF OKLAHOMA
COUNTY OF OKLAHOMA

AFFIDAVIT

I, Henry C. Gibbons, being duly sworn, do hereby state as follows:

1. I am a Special Agent (SA) of the Federal Bureau of Investigation, have been so employed for approximately 26 years, and as such am vested with the authority to investigate violations of Title 18, United States Code, Section 844(f). I am presently assigned to the Oklahoma City Field Office, Oklahoma City, Oklahoma, and have been working on the investigation of the April 19, 1995, bombing of the Alfred P. Murrah Federal Building. This Affidavit is submitted in support of a criminal complaint against Terry Lynn Nichols. The following information was received by the Federal Bureau of Investigation during the period April 19, 1995, to May 9, 1995:

2. On April 19, 1995, a massive explosive device was detonated outside the Alfred P. Murrah Federal Building in Oklahoma City, Oklahoma, at approximately 9:00 A.M., causing numerous deaths and injuries, and extensive damage.

3. Investigation by Federal agents at the scene of the explosion has determined that the explosive was contained in a truck owned by Ryder Rental Company.

a. A partial vehicle identification number (VIN) was found at the scene of the explosion and determined to be from a part of the truck that contained the explosive.

b. The VIN, which was reconstructed, was traced to a truck owned by Ryder Rentals of Miami, Florida.

c. Ryder Rentals informed the FBI that the truck was assigned to a rental company known as Elliott's Body Shop, a Ryder truck rental establishment in Junction City, Kansas.

4. An employee at Elliott's Body Shop has advised the FBI that two persons rented the truck on April 17, 1995. The rental agreement contained the following information:

FIGURE 14–7 Continued

a. The person who signed the rental agreement identified himself as Bob Kling, Social Security No. 962–42–9694, South Dakota driver's license number YF942A6, and provided a home address of 428 Maple Drive, Omaha, Nebraska. The destination was reflected as Omaha, Nebraska.

b. Subsequent investigation conducted by the FBI determined the information to be false.

5. An employee of Elliott's Body Shop in Junction City, Kansas, identified Timothy McVeigh from a photographic array as the person who rented the Ryder truck on April 17, 1995, and signed the rental agreement.

6. The Alfred P. Murrah Federal Building is used by various agencies of the United States, including the Agriculture Department, Department of the Army, the Defense Department, Federal Highway Administration, General Accounting Office, General Services Administration, Social Security Administration, Housing and Urban Development, Drug Enforcement Administration, Labor Department, Marine Corps, Small Business Administration, Transportation Department, United States Secret Service, Bureau of Alcohol, Tobacco, and Firearms and Veterans Administration.

7. The detonation of the explosives in front of the Federal Building constitutes a violation of 18 U.S.C. 5844(f), which makes it a crime to maliciously damage or destroy by means of an explosive any building or real property, in whole or in part owned, possessed or used by the United States, or any department or agency thereof.

8. On April 21, 1995, a federal criminal complaint was filed charging Timothy James McVeigh with a violation of Title 18, United States Code, Section 844(f), based on his involvement in the bombing of the Alfred P. Murrah Federal building on April 19, 1995.

9. On April 21, 1995, investigators learned that at approximately 10:20 A.M., on April 19, 1995, Timothy James McVeigh was arrested in Noble County, Oklahoma, on traffic and weapon offenses, and was thereafter incarcerated on those charges in Perry, Oklahoma. McVeigh's arrest occurred approximately 60–70 miles north of Oklahoma City, Oklahoma, approximately one hour and 20 minutes after the April 19, 1995, explosion that damaged the Alfred P. Murrah Federal Building. When booked into jail following that arrest, McVeigh listed 3616 North Van Dyke Road, Decker, Michigan, as his address and James Nichols of Decker, Michigan, as a reference. The property at 3616 N. Van Dyke Road, Decker, Michigan is owned by the Nichols family. James Nichols is the brother of Terry Nichols.

10. On April 27, 1995, a preliminary hearing was held on the federal criminal complaint against McVeigh, evidence was presented, and the federal magistrate judge found that there was probable cause to believe that an offense had been committed and that McVeigh committed it.

11. Supervisory Special Agent (SSA) James T. Thurman, Chief, Explosives Unit—Bomb Data Center, FBI Laboratory, Washington, D.C., has advised as follows:

a. The bomb which detonated in front of the Murrah Federal Building on April 19, 1995, contained a high explosive main charge initiated by methods as yet unknown;

FIGURE 14–7 Continued

(continued)

b. An explosive device of the magnitude which exploded in Oklahoma City on April 19, 1995, would have been constructed over a period of time utilizing a large quantity of bomb paraphernalia and materials, which may have included, among other things, fertilizer, fuel oil, boosters, detonators (blasting caps), detonation cord, fusing systems, and containers;

c. The construction of the explosive device that caused the damage to the Alfred P. Murrah Federal Building would necessarily have involved the efforts of more than one person.

12. On April 21, 1995, at approximately 3:00 P.M., after hearing his name on the radio in connection with the Oklahoma City bombing, Terry Nichols voluntarily surrendered to the Department of Public Safety in Herington, Kansas. Herington authorities took no action and awaited the arrival of the FBI. Thereafter, a Special Agent of the FBI arrived and advised Nichols of his Miranda rights, which Nichols agreed to waive.

13. Terry Nichols was subsequently interviewed and provided the following information:

a. He first met McVeigh at U.S. Army Basic Training in 1988 in Georgia. He later served with McVeigh at Fort Riley, Kansas. Over the years they have occasionally lived together, operated a business together involving the sale of army surplus items and firearms at gun shows throughout the United States, and otherwise stayed in close contact.

b. Nichols was with McVeigh in downtown Oklahoma City, Oklahoma, on April 16, 1995.

c. On Tuesday, April 18, 1995, McVeigh and Nichols met in Junction City, Kansas, where Nichols said he loaned his dark blue 1984 GMC half-ton diesel pickup to McVeigh. Nichols said McVeigh had the vehicle for approximately 5 hours while Nichols attended an auction.

d. On Tuesday, April 18, 1995, McVeigh told Nichols he had items in a storage unit in Herington, Kansas, and that if McVeigh did not pick them up, Nichols should do it for him. On April 20, 1995, Nichols did pick up items, including a rifle, from the storage unit. Nichols described the location of the storage unit, which is further identified in paragraph 18.

e. Nichols knows how to make a bomb by blending ammonium nitrate with diesel fuel which could be detonated by blasting caps. Nichols also stated that he had ammonium nitrate at his residence until Friday, April 21, 1995, at which time he placed it on his yard as fertilizer. Nichols said that he did this after reading in several different newspapers that ammonium nitrate was used in the Oklahoma City bombing.

f. He had a fuel meter in his garage which he said he had purchased for resale.

g. Nichols stated several times that if they searched his residence, he hoped that agents "would not mistake household items" for bomb-producing materials. In particular, Nichols told agents that he had several containers of ground ammonium nitrate which he said he sells as plant food fertilizer at gun shows.

FIGURE 14–7 Continued

h. Nichols said he possessed numerous weapons scattered throughout his house and detached garage.

i. Nichols also stated that he has in the past rented storage facilities in Kansas and Nevada.

j. Nichols denied involvement in or knowledge of the bombing.

14. While Terry Nichols was being interviewed, he gave consent for agents to search his residence, 109 South Second Street, Herington, Kansas, and his pickup truck, VIN # 2GTEC14C9E1511984, described as a dark blue 1984 GMC Sierra Classic with a white topper, or camper shell. A search warrant was obtained and executed on Terry Nichols' residence in Herington, Kansas, on April 22, 1995. During that search, agents seized the following items:

a. Five 60-foot #8 primadet cords with non-electric blasting caps. According to FBI bomb experts, such cord can be used to initiate the explosion of a fertilizer—fuel oil bomb.

b. Four white barrels with blue lids made from material resembling the blue plastic fragments found at the bomb scene in Oklahoma City, Oklahoma.

c. One fuel meter (referred to in paragraph 13(f)). According to information provided by ATF bomb experts, such a device could be used to obtain the proper volume of diesel fuel to ammonium nitrate for a bomb.

d. One receipt from Mid-Kansas Cooperative Association, McPherson, Kansas, for 40 fifty-pound bags of 34-0-0 ammonium nitrate fertilizer.

e. Five gas cans of various sizes.

f. Several containers of ground ammonium nitrate. According to FBI bomb experts, this substance can be used as one ingredient of a booster for a fertilizer-fuel oil bomb.

15. On September 30, 1994, forty (40) fifty-pound bags of 34-0-0 ammonium nitrate fertilizer were purchased from Mid-Kansas Cooperative Association in McPherson, Kansas, by a "Mike Havens." A receipt for that purchase, referred to in paragraph 14(d), was found at the residence of Terry Nichols. The FBI has identified a fingerprint on the receipt as belonging to Timothy McVeigh.

16. On October 18, 1994, forty (40) additional fifty-pound bags of 34-0-0 ammonium nitrate fertilizer were purchased from Mid-Kansas Cooperative Association, McPherson, Kansas, by a "Mike Havens," who was driving a dark-colored pickup with a light-colored camper shell.

17. SSA Wallace Higgins, FBI Laboratory Explosives Unit, advises that 34-0-0 ammonium nitrate, fuel oil and #8 primadet cords can be used in the manufacture of a fertilizer—fuel oil bomb.

18. On September 22, 1994, a storage unit, identified as unit #2, was rented at Herington, Kansas, in the name Shawn Rivers. Unit #2 was rented approximately one week prior to the purchase of the ammonium nitrate fertilizer described in paragraph 15. This is the same storage unit described in paragraph 13(d).

FIGURE 14–7 Continued

(continued)

19. On October 17, 1994, a storage unit identified as unit #40, was rented at Council Grove, Kansas, in the name Joe Kyle. Unit #40 was rented one day prior to the purchase of the ammonium nitrate fertilizer described in paragraph 16. The FBI has obtained from Terry Nichols' home a document with the location of this storage unit and the name Joe Kyle.

20. On November 7, 1994, an additional storage unit, identified as unit #37, was rented at Council Grove, Kansas, in the name Ted Parker. The FBI has obtained from Terry Nichols' home a document with the location of this storage unit and the name Ted Parker.

21. The FBI has obtained a letter from Terry Nichols to Tim McVeigh, dated on or about November 22, 1994, the day Nichols left the United States for a visit to the Philippines. In the letter, Terry Nichols tells Timothy McVeigh that he will be getting this letter only in the event of Nichols' death. Nichols instructs McVeigh to "clear everything out of CG 37" and to "also liquidate 40." Terry Nichols also tells McVeigh he is on his own and to "Go for it!!"

22. Further investigation has revealed that "CG 37" refers to the Council Grove storage unit #37, rented by Terry Nichols on November 7, 1994, and that "Liquidate 40" refers to the Council Grove storage unit #40 rented by Terry Nichols on October 17, 1994.

23. On April 15, 1995, Terry Nichols purchased diesel fuel from a Conoco service station in Manhattan, Kansas.

24. On April 16, 1995, Terry Nichols purchased an additional 21.59 gallons of diesel fuel from a Conoco service station in Junction City, Kansas.

25. On April 17, 1995, a call was placed from Room 25 at the Dreamland Hotel to the residence of Terry Nichols in Herington, Kansas. Timothy McVeigh stayed at the Dreamland Hotel, in Room 25, from April 14, 1995, through April 18, 1995.

26. During the evening of April 17, 1995, a Ryder truck was seen parked behind the residence of Terry Nichols, 109 South 2nd Street, Herington, Kansas.

27. On April 17 or 18, 1995, an older model pickup with camper shell was seen backed up to the second garage door on the east end of the storage shed in Herington. This unit is #2. This is the storage unit which was previously discussed in paragraph 18.

28. During the week of April 17th, a Ryder truck was seen backed up to the east end of the storage shed in Herington near storage unit #2. This is the storage unit which was previously discussed in paragraph 18.

29. On the morning of April 18, 1995, a witness at the Geary State Fishing Lake, approximately six miles south of Junction City, Kansas, observed a yellow Ryder truck parked next to a pickup truck for several hours. Both vehicles were parked in an area which was not paved. The witness described the pickup truck as a dark blue or brown 1980–1987 Chevrolet or GMC truck and recalled that there was something white, possibly a camper shell, on the back of the pickup truck.

FIGURE 14–7 Continued

30. On April 28, 1995, the witness accompanied an FBI agent to Geary State Fishing Lake and took him to the area where the two vehicles had been parked. In that area, the agent observed a circular area of brown vegetation surrounded by green vegetation. Upon inspecting the area of brown vegetation, he noticed an oily substance and detected the distinct odor of diesel fuel.

Further your affiant sayeth not.

/s/HENRY C. GIBBONS
Special Agent
Federal Bureau of Investigation

Subscribed and sworn to before me this 9th day of May, 1995.

FIGURE 14–7 Continued

The Initial Appearance

Federal Rule of Criminal Procedure 5(a) states:

> In general. An officer making an arrest under a warrant issued upon a complaint or any person making an arrest without a warrant shall take the arrested person without unnecessary delay before the nearest available federal magistrate or, in the event that a federal magistrate is not reasonably available, before a state or local judicial officer authorized by 18 U.S.C. § 3041. If a person arrested without a warrant is brought before a magistrate, a complaint shall be filed forthwith which shall comply with the requirement of Rule 4(a) with respect to the showing of probable cause. . . .

magistrate
A judicial officer; federal magistrates are appointed by judges of federal district courts; magistrates have some of the powers of a judge.

initial appearance
The first court appearance of a criminal defendant after the arrest.

As soon as possible, the defendant is taken before a judge or **magistrate.** This usually occurs within twenty-four hours of the arrest. This **initial appearance** is short. The judge will determine that the defendant is the person named in the complaint. The defendant is told his or her rights at this time. These rights include the right to understand the charge, the right to counsel at all stages of the criminal process, and the right to bail. A preliminary hearing date is calendared, usually within ten days of the initial appearance. The court will decide whether the defendant may be released prior to the hearing date. If eligible for release, either the defendant will be released on a promise to appear, or bail will be set. The Eighth Amendment specifically prohibits the setting of excessive bail. Bail is designed to ensure the defendant's appearance in court. It is not to be used to punish a person accused of a crime.

The Preliminary Hearing

preliminary hearing
A defendant's second appearance before the court; the purpose is to establish that probable cause exists.

The **preliminary hearing** is the second time the defendant appears before a judge. Each state has rules dealing with the details involved in a preliminary hearing. The point of this hearing is to establish that probable cause exists. This hearing is similar

A POINT TO REMEMBER

Look again at Federal Rule of Criminal Procedure 5(a). Notice that the rule refers to the United States Code (18 U.S.C. § 3041) and to another rule of criminal procedure (Rule 4). If you are researching this rule or are planning to use this rule, you must read all rules or statutes (codes) mentioned in the text of the statute.

to a trial. Attorneys question witnesses and present arguments. Evidence is reviewed by the judge.

If probable cause is established, the criminal defendant is bound over for trial. However, a grand jury indictment is required in some jurisdictions. In these jurisdictions, the **grand jury** will make an independent assessment on the question of whether probable cause exists. If probable cause is not established, the criminal defendant is free to go home.

grand jury
A jury that is called upon to receive and review accusations and complaints in criminal matters; this jury will hear evidence and issue indictments.

FORMAL CHARGES

information
An accusation made by a prosecutor against a criminal defendant that does not involve a grand jury.

indictment
A written accusation given by a grand jury to the court in which it is impaneled; a criminal charge against a defendant that must be proved at trial.

Formal charges take two forms. An **information** is filed by the prosecutor. An **indictment** is filed by a grand jury. Both documents serve the same purpose. After the information or indictment is filed with the court, it replaces the criminal complaint. The information shown in Figure 14–8 was filed in the Oklahoma City bombing case.

The defendant makes another court appearance after the information or indictment has been filed with the court. This court appearance is known as the *arraignment*. At the arraignment, the charge is read and the defendant enters a plea. Rule 10 of the Federal Rules of Criminal Procedure states:

> Arraignment shall be conducted in open court and shall consist of reading the indictment or information to the defendant or stating to the defendant the substance of the charge and calling on the defendant to plead thereto. The defendant shall be given a copy of the indictment or information before being called upon to plead.

Criminal defendants may enter one of three pleas: (1) not guilty, (2) guilty, or (3) *nolo contendere*. When a criminal defendant enters a *not guilty* plea at the arraignment, the court will set a trial date. A *guilty* plea means that there will be no jury trial. When a *guilty* plea is entered, the court is careful to ensure that the defendant understands that the plea of *guilty* results in the waiver of rights. A *guilty* plea tells the court that the defendant admits the charges. A prosecutor may agree to reduce or dismiss one or more charges in exchange for the defendant's *guilty* plea. In such cases the prosecutor and the defendant's attorney will negotiate what is known as a *plea bargain*. Most criminal cases are settled using the plea bargaining process. The third possible plea is one of ***nolo contendere***. A plea of *nolo contendere* says to the court, "I will not contest it." This plea means that the defendant does not deny or admit the charges. The court will treat this as a *guilty* plea. A defendant might

nolo contendere
A criminal plea that means "I will not contest it." This plea means that the defendant does not deny or admit the charge.

choose a *nolo contendere* plea over a *guilty* plea because, in many states, the *nolo contendere* plea cannot be used against the defendant in a later civil suit. A plea of *guilty* can be used against a defendant in a later civil suit.

FORMAL DISCOVERY

The formal discovery process begins after the arraignment. Criminal discovery is quite limited when compared with civil discovery, and the rules differ in each jurisdiction. During discovery, the defendant's attorney and the prosecutor will exchange relevant information. The Supreme Court in *Brady v. Maryland*, 373 U.S. 83 (1962), fashioned an important rule applicable to state and federal courts. The prosecutor must produce any evidence that *exculpates*, or tends to prove the innocence of, the defendant. This is known as the *Brady* rule.

THE STATE OF OKLAHOMA *v.* McVEIGH

CASE NO.: CM-95-59

IN THE DISTRICT COURT IN AND FOR NOBLE COUNTY
STATE OF OKLAHOMA

May 11, 1995, Filed

INFORMATION

FOR:

COUNT 1—Transporting a Loaded Firearm
COUNT 2—Carrying a Concealed Weapon
COUNT 3—Carrying a Weapon
COUNT 4—No Tag
COUNT 5—No Security Verification Form

STATE OF OKLAHOMA, COUNTY OF NOBLE:

I, JOHN G. MADDOX, the undersigned District Attorney of said County, in the name and by the authority, and on behalf of the State of Oklahoma, give information that on or about the 19th day of April, 1995, and in said County of Noble and State of Oklahoma, one Timothy James McVeigh did then and there unlawfully, willfully, knowingly and wrongfully commit the crimes of Count 1: Transporting a Loaded Firearm, Count 2: Carrying a Concealed Weapon, Count 3: Carrying a Weapon, Count 4: No Tag, and Count 5: No Security Verification Form.

COUNT 1

Transporting Loaded Firearm 21 O.S. 1289.13

That is to say, the said defendant, on or about the 19th day of April, 1995,

FIGURE 14–8 The McVeigh information.

(continued)

while in Noble County, Oklahoma, did unlawfully, willfully, and wrongfully carry and transport a loaded firearm, to-wit: a .45 caliber pistol, in a motor vehicle over a public highway in Noble County, to-wit: Interstate Highway 35, 1 mile south of State Highway 15, said firearm not being then and there in a locked compartment of said motor vehicle, contrary to the form and the statute in such cases made and provided and against the peace and dignity of the State of Oklahoma.

COUNT 2

Carrying Concealed Weapon 21 O.S. 1289.8

That is to say, the said defendant, on or about the 19th day of April, 1995, while in Noble County, Oklahoma, did unlawfully, willfully, and wrongfully carry concealed on or about his person a certain weapon, to-wit: a .45 caliber pistol, on himself, said defendant not being then and there a person permitted to carry a concealed weapon under the provisions of the Oklahoma Firearms Act of 1971; contrary to the form and the statute in such cases made and provided and against the peace and dignity of the State of Oklahoma.

COUNT 3

Unlawful Carrying of a Weapon 21 O.S. 1272

That is to say, the said defendant, on or about the 19th day of April, 1995, while in Noble County, Oklahoma did knowingly, intentionally, and unlawfully carry on or about his person an offensive weapon, to-wit: a single blade knife, having a 5⅛ inch blade, contrary to the form and the statute in such cases made and provided and against the peace and dignity of the State of Oklahoma.

COUNT 4

Taxes Due (No Tag), 47 O.S. 1151

That is to say, the said defendant, on or about the 19th day of April, 1995, while in Noble County, Oklahoma, did willfully and knowingly drive a certain motor vehicle, to-wit: 1977 Mercury, on a public highway of this County and State, to-wit: Interstate Highway 35, 1 mile south of State Highway 15, without an Oklahoma license plate, contrary to the form and the statute in such cases made and provided and against the peace and dignity of the State of Oklahoma.

COUNT 5

No Security Verification Form, 47 O.S. 7–606

That is to say, the said defendant, on or about the 19th day of April, 1995, while in Noble County, Oklahoma, did unlawfully, willfully, knowingly, and wrongfully drive and operate a motor vehicle, to-wit: 1977 Mercury, in Noble County, Oklahoma, without carrying in said vehicle a current owner's security verification form listing said vehicle, contrary to the form and the statute in such cases made and provided and against the peace and dignity of the State of Oklahoma.

FIGURE 14–8 Continued

The Federal Rules of Criminal Procedure allow for very specific forms of discovery. The following are some of the rules.

F. R. Crim, P. 16 compels the prosecution to provide a copy of the defendant's criminal record to the defendant. It also compels the prosecution to make all statements made by the defendant available to the defense.

bill of particulars
A device used to provide a defendant with a statement of the facts enumerating the specific acts charged.

F. R. Crim. P. 7 gives the district court the power to order a prosecutor to file a **bill of particulars** with the court. A bill of particulars includes the details about the charges against the defendant. This device is used only when the information or indictment does not sufficiently state or particularize the charge.

Pretrial Motions

A wide variety of motions may be filed in criminal cases. A few of the most common pretrial motions are explained here.

Motion to Dismiss—This motion requests that the court dismiss the charges against the defendant. The most common bases for this motion include (1) that the charging instrument (the information or indictment) is fatally flawed (for example, the court lacks jurisdiction to hear the case), or (2) that the facts alleged in the charging instrument do not amount to criminal activity.

Motion for Change of Venue—This motion requests that the court change the location of the trial. A criminal defendant has a right to a fair and impartial trial. In some instances, pretrial publicity or community sentiment may make a fair and impartial trial unlikely or even impossible.

Motion to Suppress Evidence—A motion to suppress asks the court to *suppress* or "throw out" specific evidence. Evidence obtained in violation of the defendant's constitutional rights is often suppressed; that is, it will not be allowed into evidence. In a jury trial, this means that the jury will never know that the evidence exists.

In the Oklahoma bombing case, defendant McVeigh brought an interesting pretrial motion to preserve eyewitness identification evidence. The document shown in Figure 14–9 represents the prosecutor's response to the motion. Pay close attention to the grand jury material in the prosecutor's opposition.

After all of the pretrial motions have been heard and ruled upon, the case proceeds to trial. The trial process is discussed in Chapter 17. If the defendant is convicted, he or she may appeal. However, if the defendant is acquitted, the prosecutor cannot appeal.

ETHICAL CHOICES

You are interviewing a young man charged with burglary. He asks if you have to tell the attorney everything he tells you. What is your response and why?

United States v. McVeigh

IN THE UNITED STATES DISTRICT COURT FOR THE WESTERN DISTRICT OF OKLAHOMA

May 2, 1995, Filed

GOVERNMENT'S OPPOSITION TO MOTION TO PRESERVE EYEWITNESS IDENTIFICATION

COMES NOW the United States, by Merrick Garland, Associate Deputy Attorney General, Rozia McKinney-Foster, U.S. Attorney for the Western District of Oklahoma, and Arlene Joplin, Assistant U.S. Attorney, and hereby files its Opposition to Defendant's Motion to Preserve Eyewitness Identification.

Although Defendant styles his motion as one to "preserve" eyewitness identification evidence, the motion is clearly mislabeled. As the motion makes clear, what Defendant seeks is an order compelling the government either to permit defense counsel to monitor the ongoing progress of the grand jury investigation by requiring their presence at all out-of-court identifications, or to create evidence by requiring the government to videotape or audiotape all such identifications.

To the government's knowledge, no court has ever entered an order of the type requested here; and Defendant cites no such case. Indeed, under the Supreme Court's decision in *United States v. Williams*, 504 U.S. 36 (1992), this court is without authority to enter such an order. The government and the grand jury are currently conducting a nationwide investigation into the bombing of the Murrah Building, and a nationwide manhunt for others who may have been involved. The procedures demanded by the defendant would substantially interfere with the government's efforts to bring the perpetrators of this crime to justice.

Argument

1. While courts can and must pass upon the legality of the means by which the government acquired information it seeks to introduce at trial, there is no basis for the defendant's effort to monitor the conduct of an ongoing investigation or to require the creation of evidence of the way in which it was conducted. Due process principles regarding suggestive identifications "protect an evidentiary interest" at trial rather than any out-of-court right of the person identified. *Manson v. Brathwaite*, 432 U.S. 98, 113 (1977) (emphasis in original). A defendant may have "due process protections against the admission of evidence derived from suggestive identification procedures." *Id.* at 105; *but cf. Archuleta v. Kerby*, 864 F.2d 709, 711 (10th Cir.) ("Even if an identification procedure is suggestive, the introduction of the identification evidence does not necessarily violate a defendant's due process rights), *cert. denied.*, 490 U.S. 1084 (1989). However, "[u]nlike a warrantless search, a suggestive preindictment identification procedure does not in itself intrude upon a constitutionally protected interest." *Manson*, 432 U.S. at 113 n. 13.

FIGURE 14–9 The prosecutor's response to a motion filed by the defendant in the *McVeigh* case.

Accordingly, even where pretrial identification procedures may subsequently be found to have been unnecessary suggestive, there is no basis at the pretrial phase for prospectively regulating those procedures.

2. Defendant cites no case to support the order he seeks. His only citation to authority is a claim that the court may use its "supervisory powers" to prevent the "destruction" of evidence discoverable under Rule 16 and *Brady*. But notwithstanding the rhetoric he has chosen, "destruction" of evidence is not what his motion is about. Defendant does not allege that the government is destroying records; to the contrary, he wants the government to create a record of eyewitness identifications that it would not otherwise create. Neither Rule 16 nor *Brady* require the government to create such evidence. The government is not obligated to create potentially exculpatory material that does not exist. *United States v. Harvey*, 756 F.2d 636, 643 (8th Cir.), *cert. denied*, 474 U.S. 813 (1985). *See United States v. Sukumolachan*, 610 F.2d 685, 687 (9th Cir. 1980) ("*Brady v. Maryland* . . . does not require the government to create exculpatory material that does not exist.").

Nor can the defendant rely on the court's "supervisory powers" to oversee the present grand jury investigation. The Supreme Court has repeatedly stressed that judicial supervisory power "deal[s] strictly with the courts' power to control their own procedures." *United States v. Williams*, 112 S. Ct. 1735, 1741 (1992). Indeed, in *Williams*, the Court held that "because the grand jury is an institution separate from the courts, over whose functioning the courts do not preside, we think it clear that, as a general matter at least, no such 'supervisory' judicial authority exists and that the disclosure rule applied here exceeded the Tenth Circuit's authority" (emphasis added).

Exercising "supervisory" authority to create substantive standards of extrajudicial conduct for executive officers would contravene the Constitution's separation of powers. *See United States v. Simpson*, 927 F.2d 1088, 1090 (9th Cir. 1991) ("By penalizing executive conduct that violates neither the Constitution nor a federal statute, the court invaded the domain of the legislature, whose role it is to establish limits on such conduct by law; and it invaded the province of the executive, whose function it is, within legal limits, to decide how to enforce the law"). Put another way, a court's supervisory power does not allow a "chancellor's foot veto" over otherwise lawful activities of the executive branch. *United States v. Russell*, 411 U.S. 423, 435 (1973); *see also United States v. Payner*, 447 U.S. 727, 737 (1980) (judicial supervisory power cannot justify suppression of illegally seized evidence that the Fourth Amendment itself would not preclude).

3. Such case law as there is in this area is directly contrary to Defendant's claims. In *Simmons vs. United States*, 390 U.S. 377 (1968), the Supreme Court specifically declined to exercise supervisory oversight of the procedures followed by the Federal Bureau of Investigation with respect to out-of-court identifications from photographs. The Court in *Simmons* noted "hazards of initial identification by photograph" (*id.* at 384), and it agreed with the defendant that "the identification procedure employed [there] may have in some respects fallen short of the ideal" (*id.* at 385–386 & n. 6). Nonetheless, the Court was "unwilling to prohibit its employment, either in the exercise of our supervisory power or, still less, as a matter of constitutional requirement." *Id.* at 384.

FIGURE 14–9 Continued

(continued)

Similarly, in *United States v. Ash*, 413 U.S. 300 (1973), the Supreme Court was "not persuaded that the risks inherent in the use of photographic displays are so pernicious that an extraordinary system of safeguards is required." 413 U.S. at 321. And the Tenth Circuit has declined to require identification procedures beyond those required by Supreme Court case law. *See Hallmark v. Cartwright*, 742 F.2d 584, 585 (10th Cir. 1984) (though defendant is entitled under Supreme Court's rulings to have counsel present at post-indictment lineup, counsel is not entitled to be present at "post-indictment post-lineup interview").

4. Defendant will suffer no harm from the mere conducting of out-of-court identifications; if and when the prosecution seeks to introduce a witness' identification at trial, Defendant is free to challenge its admissibility or attack its weight. *Cf. Simmons*, 390 U.S. at 384 ("The danger that use of the [photographic identification] technique may result in convictions based on misidentification may be substantially lessened by a course of cross-examination at trial which exposes to the jury the method's potential for error").

By contrast, the investigation would be substantially impeded by the procedures Defendant seeks to require. There is an unquestionable and overwhelming public interest in permitting the nationwide investigation and manhunt to proceed as quickly as possible, before evidence is destroyed and witnesses and suspects disappear. The defendant's procedures would put that investigation in a straightjacket that would delay and complicate investigative efforts, and intimidate potential witnesses.

Accordingly, based on the foregoing arguments, Defendant's Motion to Preserve Eyewitness Identification should be denied.

FIGURE 14–9 Continued

Featured Web Site
www.co.eaton.mi.us/ecpa/process.htm

This Michigan site offers a step-by-step tour through a criminal prosecution.

Go Online

Summarize this material. Start with "Crime Committed" and work through to "Appeal."

Chapter Summary

Criminal procedure facilitates criminal prosecutions and protects the constitutional rights of criminal suspects and defendants. The Fourth, Fifth, Sixth, and Fourteenth Amendments to the Constitution play key roles in criminal procedure. The due process clause of the Fifth Amendment is designed to assure justice in our legal system. The Fourth Amendment prohibits unreasonable searches and seizures. The Sixth Amendment guarantees the right to counsel, the right to a speedy trial, and the right to a jury trial. The U.S. Supreme Court cases included in this chapter help explain the importance of the role of constitutional interpretation in case law. A criminal suspect has many rights; law enforcement must be cautious not to infringe upon those rights. In some instances, when a criminal defendant's rights have been violated, the evidence seized or the confession obtained will not be available for use at trial. In some cases, this means that the case must be dismissed. The Federal Rules of Criminal Procedure used in this chapter are representative of state criminal statutes. You will want to locate your local penal code and compare and contrast the state and federal rules.

Terms to Remember

due process clause
incorporation
hearsay
probable cause
warrant
felony
exigent circumstances
hot pursuit
plain-view doctrine
exclusionary rule
arrest
interrogation
confession
self-incrimination
arraignment
plea
investigation
booking
bail
affidavit
magistrate
initial appearance
preliminary hearing
grand jury
information
indictment
nolo contendere
bill of particulars

Questions for Review

1. What is due process?
2. What is probable cause?
3. Explain the Fourth Amendment requirements that must be met before a search warrant will be issued.
4. Why does the law allow certain exceptions to the warrant requirement?
5. Explain the exclusionary rule.
6. What is an indictment?
7. What is an information?
8. What happens at the arraignment?
9. Explain the three plea choices available to a criminal defendant.

Questions for Analysis

1. Discuss the differences between the complaints in the *Simpson* and *Nichols* cases.
2. Reread the Case File at the beginning of this chapter. Compare and contrast the case file facts with the facts of the *Mapp* case. Look for similar facts, differences, and factual gaps.

Assignments and Projects

1. Before a warrant may be issued under the Fourth Amendment, probable cause must be established. Create a hypothetical situation in which a court would find that probable cause exists to issue a search warrant for a person police believe to be responsible for the bombing of an empty church.
2. Discuss the strengths of the affidavit in support of the criminal complaint in the *Nichols* case.
3. Write a brief for the *Mapp* case.
4. Write a brief for the *Katz* case.
5. Describe the Fourth Amendment violations claimed by petitioner in the case of *Atwater v. Lago Vista* found in Appendix VII.

CHAPTER 15

ALTERNATIVE DISPUTE RESOLUTION

Technology Corner

Web Address	Name of Site
www.abanet.org/dispute/home.html	ABA Section of Dispute Resolution
www.adr.org/	American Arbitration Association
www.fmcs.gov/	Federal Mediation and Conciliation Service

CASE FILE: THE GRAHAM AUTOMOBILE ACCIDENT

Earlier this year Monica Graham was injured in an automobile accident caused by an uninsured drunk driver. Because Monica had uninsured motorist coverage on her own insurance policy she made a claim against her own insurance company. Monica incurred several thousand dollars in medical bills and lost earnings. She also suffered a great deal of pain because of neck and back injuries. Because her own insurance company refused to pay Monica a satisfactory settlement, Monica contacted a lawyer to handle the dispute. Monica thought that she might have to sue her own insurance company. However, when Monica contacted the attorney she was advised that her insurance policy required that this type of dispute be resolved through arbitration rather than a lawsuit.

SEC. 15-1 INTRODUCTION

alternative dispute resolution (ADR) Methods of resolving disputes outside the normal court process.

The American justice system has long been based on the philosophy that every person involved in a legal dispute should be able to have his or her day in court. Unfortunately, today a person's day in court is subject to lengthy delays and exorbitant costs. The cost and the overcrowding of our courtrooms is leading to major changes in the way that civil disputes are handled. Parties to disputes, as well as the courts themselves, have had to develop procedures to avoid lengthy delays and keep costs reasonable. In other words, parties and courts have developed "alternatives" to the traditional method of resolving disputes, that is, filing a lawsuit in court and eventually trying a case before judge or jury. These alternative methods of resolving disputes are referred to as **alternative dispute resolution (ADR)**. Alternative dispute resolution methods include such procedures as negotiation, arbitration, mediation, and the use of private judges. ADR has become a favored method of resolving disputes with the courts, with legislatures, and with parties to a dispute. It can reduce costs, eliminate unnecessary delays, and provide the parties with a degree of privacy not available once a lawsuit is filed.

SEC. 15-2 BINDING ADR VS. NONBINDING ADR

ADR may be binding or nonbinding on the disputing parties. In some cases the parties choosing alternative dispute resolution give up all right to have their dispute litigated in a court. Instead, they choose a method of alternative dispute resolution and agree to be bound by the decision. Binding ADR exists where parties have agreed to give up their right to court and to be bound by some method of ADR. The agreement to arbitrate is frequently contained in a written contract between two parties, such as with Monica Graham and her insurance company. Binding ADR becomes a complete substitute for the court process.

In other instances, ADR is nonbinding. That is, the parties agree to try to resolve their dispute through one of the means of ADR. If the parties are not successful in resolving the dispute, either party may pursue the claim through the traditional court process. Nonbinding arbitration is frequently ordered by a court in which a civil dispute has originated. The courts hope that forcing the parties to go through some type of alternative dispute resolution will enable them to resolve their dispute and avoid the necessity of a trial. However, if one of the parties is not satisfied with the result of the ADR process, then that party can request that the court action be resumed.

SEC. 15-3 NEGOTIATION

negotiation The process of discussing contested issues in an attempt to resolve disputes.

Negotiation involves the parties or their attorneys discussing the disputed issues and attempting to resolve their differences. It is a process that requires no formalities. Negotiation can take place at any time. Parties frequently try to settle disputes prior to retaining lawyers. Lawyers often try negotiation prior to filing lawsuits. Even after a lawsuit is filed, negotiation often continues. Successful negotiation results in settlement.

Madden v. Kaiser Foundation Hospitals

17 Cal. 3d 699, 131 Cal. Rptr. 882, 552 P.2d 1178 (1976)

The plaintiff, a retired state employee, was covered under a group medical plan with defendant Kaiser. The plan required that all disputes be resolved through binding arbitration. The plaintiff contends that she was not bound by this provision because she never agreed to it. This case discusses whether an agent or representative, contracting for medical services on behalf of a group of employees, has implied authority to agree to arbitration of malpractice claims of enrolled employees arising under the contract. The court found that the plaintiff was bound by the agreement because the board was her agent. The court's opinion follows.

OPINION

Defendants appeal from an order denying enforcement of an arbitration provision in a medical services contract entered into between the Board of Administration of the State Employees Retirement System (hereafter board) and defendant Kaiser Foundation Health Plan. Plaintiff, a state employee who enrolled under the Kaiser plan, contends that she is not bound by the provision for arbitration. The instant appeal presents the issue whether an agent or representative, contracting for medical services on behalf of a group of employees, has implied authority to agree to arbitration of malpractice claims of enrolled employees arising under the contract.

1. Summary of Proceedings

The board negotiated an agreement with Kaiser Foundation Health Plan, a corporation, to provide medical, hospital, and related health care benefits to state employees and their families. The agreement states that it is "subject to amendment by mutual agreement between [Kaiser] and the Board without the consent or concurrence of the members. By electing medical and hospital coverage pursuant to this Agreement, or accepting benefits hereunder, all Members agree to all terms, conditions and provisions hereof."

When plaintiff first enrolled under the Kaiser plan in 1965, it did not contain an arbitration provision. On April 1, 1971, however, the Kaiser Foundation Health Plan, anticipating the inclusion of an arbitration provision, mailed to all subscribers a brochure which, in describing the terms and benefits of the plan, stated that claims involving professional liability and personal injury must be submitted to arbitration. Shortly thereafter, on May 28, 1971, the Kaiser Foundation Health Plan and the board amended their contract in several respects and included a provision for binding arbitration of "any claim arising from the violation of a legal duty incident to this Agreement."

On August 1, 1971, plaintiff underwent a hysterectomy at the Kaiser Hospital in Los Angeles. During the surgery, her bladder was perforated; blood transfusions were required; plaintiff thereafter contracted serum hepatitis.

Plaintiff filed a malpractice complaint against Kaiser. Kaiser moved to stay the action and compel arbitration. Opposing this motion, plaintiff filed a declaration stating that because of absence from work by reason of illness she had not received the April 1971 brochure, that she was not aware of the execution of the arbitration agreement in May of 1971, and thus had no knowledge that the Kaiser plan, at the time of her operation, required arbitration of malpractice claims. The trial court denied the motion to compel arbitration.

2. The Board, as Agent for the Employees, Had Implied Authority to Provide for Arbitration of Malpractice Claims

Civil Code section 2319 authorizes a general agent "[t]o do everything necessary or proper and usual for effecting the purpose of his agency." We conclude that arbitration is a "proper and usual" means of resolving malpractice disputes, and thus that an agent empowered to negotiate a group medical contract has the implied authority to agree to the inclusion of an arbitration provision.

In *Crofoot v. Blair Holdings Corp.* (1953) 119 Cal. App. 2d 156, 183–184, Justice Peers summarized the evolution of legal attitudes toward arbitration. "Arbitration has had a long and troubled history. The early common law courts did not favor arbitration, and greatly limited the powers of arbitrators. But in recent times a great change in attitude and policy has taken place. Arbitrations are now usually covered by statutory law, as they are in California. Such statutes evidence a strong public policy in favor of arbitrations, which policy has frequently been approved and enforced by the courts." Subsequent decisions confirm the self-evident fact that arbitration has become an accepted and favored method of resolving disputes praised by the courts as an expeditious and economical method of relieving overburdened civil calendars.

The transformation of legislative and judicial attitudes toward arbitration has encouraged a dramatic development in the use of this procedure. A 1952 study estimated that "aside from personal injury cases and cases in which the government is a party, more than 70 percent of the total civil litigation is decided through arbitration rather than by the courts." In the following decades arbitration further expanded its role to encompass in certain circumstances disputes requiring evaluation of personal injury claims. California and many other states now require arbitration of uninsured motorist claims and proposals for no-fault automobile insurance frequently provide for arbitration.

The matter becomes even clearer if we narrow our focus to arbitration of disputes arising under group contracts. In collective bargaining agreements, which, like the present contract, are negotiated by elected representatives on behalf of a group of employees, arbitration has become a customary means of resolving disputes. Negotiators have invariably accepted without question the authority of the union representative to agree to such arbitration provisions. A New York decision confirms the equivalent right of a trade association representative to agree to an arbitration clause on behalf of employers.

Finally, we observe the growing interest in and use of arbitration to cope with the increasing volume of medical malpractice claims. The authority of an agent to agree to the arbitration of such claims finds an illustration in our decision in *Doyle v. Guiliucci*, 62 Cal. 2d 606 (1965). In *Doyle*, the father of an injured minor entered into a contract with the Ross-Loos Medical Group which provided for arbitration of tort and contract claims arising under the contract. In an unanimous opinion we held that the minor was bound by the provision of the agreement to submit her malpractice claim to arbitration. Rejecting the contention that the arbitration clause unreasonably limited the minor's rights, we replied, "The arbitration provision in such contracts is a reasonable restriction, for it does no more than specify a forum for the settlement of disputes."

We therefore conclude that an agent or other fiduciary who contracts for medical treatment on behalf of his beneficiary retains the authority to enter into an agreement providing for arbitration of claims for medical malpractice.

3. The Principles That Govern Contracts of Adhesion Do Not Bar Enforcement of the Arbitration Amendment

The concept that a contract of adhesion should be interpreted and enforced differently from an ordinary contract has evolved from cases which have involved contractual provisions drafted and imposed by a party enjoying superior bargaining strength—provisions which unexpectedly and often unconscionably limit the obligations and liability of the party drafting the contract. The Kaiser contract lacks those oppressive features which have characterized the contracts adjudicated in the prior decisions.

In the characteristic adhesion contract case, the stronger party drafts the contract, and the weaker has no opportunity, either personally or through an agent, to negotiate concerning its terms. The Kaiser plan, on the other hand, represents the product of negotiation between two parties, Kaiser and the board, possessing parity of bargaining strength. Although plaintiff asserts that the arbitration amendment promotes Kaiser's interest to the disadvantage of the members enrolled under the Kaiser plan, she overlooks the benefits of the arbitral forum. The speed and economy of arbitration, in contrast to the expense and delay of the jury trial, could prove helpful to all parties; the simplified procedures and relaxed rules of evidence in arbitration may aid an injured plaintiff in presenting his case. Plaintiffs with less serious injuries, who cannot afford the high litigation expenses of court or jury trial, disproportionate to the amount of their claim will benefit especially from the simplicity and economy of arbitration; that procedure could facilitate the adjudication of minor malpractice claims which cannot economically be resolved in a judicial forum.

4. Enforcement of the Arbitration Provision Does Not Violate Constitutional or Statutory Protections of the Right to Trial by Jury

The California Constitution permits the waiver of a jury trial in a civil action "by the consent of the parties, expressed as prescribed by statute."

When parties agree to submit their disputes to arbitration they select a forum that is alternative to, and independent of, the judicial—a forum in which, as they well know, disputes are not resolved by juries. Hence there are literally thousands of commercial and labor contracts that provide for arbitration but do not contain express waivers of jury trial. Courts have regularly enforced such agreements. . . .

6. Conclusion

Under the aegis of permissive legislation and favorable judicial decisions arbitration has become a proper and usual means of resolving civil disputes, including disputes relating to medical malpractice. We should not now turn the judicial clock backwards to an era of hostility toward arbitration.

We conclude that the trial court erred in denying Kaiser's motion to compel arbitration.

CASE ANALYSIS

1. If arbitration is so beneficial, why did the plaintiff oppose it in this case?
2. Since this case was decided by the California Supreme Court, is arbitration really an alternative to the court process? Explain.
3. According to the California Supreme Court, what are the advantages of arbitration?
4. The California Supreme Court ordered the parties to submit to arbitration in this case. Was it to be binding arbitration or nonbinding? Did the plaintiff in this case agree to be bound by an arbitration award?

A POINT TO REMEMBER

A case can never be settled without the client's consent. Attorneys cannot settle a case without client permission.

SEC. 15-4 ARBITRATION

arbitration
An out-of-court hearing before a neutral party who listens to two or more disputing parties and renders a decision resolving the dispute.

arbitrator
An individual who presides over an arbitration hearing and renders a decision.

arbitration award
The decision of the arbitrator in an arbitration hearing.

One of the earliest forms of alternative dispute resolution is the process known as **arbitration**. In an arbitration proceeding, parties present their case to a neutral individual or panel of individuals, known as **arbitrators**, who listen to each side and then make a decision regarding the dispute. The arbitrator need not be a lawyer, although many are. If the arbitration is binding, the arbitrator's decision, referred to as an **arbitration award**, resolves the dispute. Furthermore, appeal rights are severely restricted. Unless the arbitrator is shown to have some bias or prejudice, the award is generally not appealable. If the arbitration is nonbinding, then either of the parties can reject the award and pursue a trial in the appropriate court. Agreements to arbitrate disputes, rather than litigate them, are common in commercial contracts, employment contracts, contracts to provide medical care, and uninsured-motorist provisions of automobile policies.

Although binding arbitration relies on the agreement of the parties, many states, as well as the federal government, have adopted statutes that encourage, promote, and in part regulate the arbitration process. Furthermore, these laws generally provide for a method of enforcing an arbitration award. See the box titled "Federal Arbitration Statutes" for examples of federal statutes that provide for enforcement of arbitration agreements.

The actual arbitration process is subject to agreement by the parties. In most instances, there are no absolute rules that must be followed. Parties are free to adopt their own procedural rules for the arbitration process. If parties have agreed to arbitrate a dispute, they can agree between themselves who the arbitrator will be and what rules will be followed in arbitrating the dispute. To facilitate this process, a number of different organizations have been established that offer arbitration (as well as other ADR) services. One of the oldest organizations is the American Arbitration Association. Most alternative dispute resolution providers offer a variety of services. In some cases, these organizations have a complete set of rules in effect for the arbitration process that the parties can adopt. In fact, when some parties agree to arbitrate a case, they will also agree to adopt the rules of the American Arbitration Association for the specific type of arbitration involved.

If parties agree to arbitrate and use the services of a professional arbitration service, the first step in the arbitration process is usually to let the service know. This is often done by filing a form with the provider agreeing to submit the matter to arbitration. Many of the service providers have their own forms. See Figure 15–1 for a copy of a form used by the American Arbitration Association.

Even though a case going through arbitration avoids the court process, the parties still must prove their case to an arbitrator. This involves many of the same factual and legal issues that are involved in a trial. To gather and evaluate the evidence, attorneys handling arbitration cases use the same steps and procedures that are used in a civil action filed in court. In particular, the parties may send

American Arbitration Association
COMMERCIAL ARBITRATION RULES
DEMAND FOR ARBITRATION

***MEDIATION** is a nonbinding process. The mediator assists the parties in working out a solution that is acceptable to them. If you wish for the AAA to contact the other parties to ascertain whether they wish to mediate this matter, please check this box (there is no additional administrative fee for this service).* ❑

TO: Name			Name of Representative (if known)		Name of Firm (if applicable)
Address			Representative's Address		
City	State	Zip Code	City	State	Zip Code
Phone No.	Fax No.		Phone No.	Fax No.	

The named claimant, a party to an arbitration agreement contained in a written contract, dated ________________ and providing for arbitration under the Commercial Arbitration Rules of the American Arbitration Association, hereby demands arbitration thereunder.

THE NATURE OF THE DISPUTE

THE CLAIM OR RELIEF SOUGHT (the Amount, if Any)

DOES THIS DISPUTE ARISE OUT OF AN EMPLOYMENT RELATIONSHIP? ❑ Yes ❑ No

TYPES OF BUSINESS

Claimant ______________________________ Respondent ______________________________

HEARING LOCALE REQUESTED

You are hereby notified that copies of our arbitration agreement and this demand are being filed with the American Arbitration Association at its____________________office, with a request that it commence administration of the arbitration. Under the rules, you may file an answering statement within fifteen days after notice from the AAA.

Signature (may be signed by a representative)	Title

Name of Claimant			Name of Representative		Name of Firm (if Applicable)
Address (to Be Used in Connection with This Case)			Representative's Address		
City	State	Zip Code	City	State	Zip Code
Phone No.	Fax No.		Phone No.	Fax No.	

TO INSTITUTE PROCEEDINGS, PLEASE SEND TWO COPIES OF THIS DEMAND **AND THE ARBITRATION AGREEMENT**, WITH THE FILING FEE AS PROVIDED FOR IN THE RULES, TO THE AAA. SEND THE ORIGINAL DEMAND TO THE RESPONDENT.

Form C2-11/99

FIGURE 15–1 Demand for arbitration. (Reprinted with permission of the American Arbitration Association.)

interrogatories to one another, take depositions, and subpoena records. The attorneys may also have to research and brief important legal issues in the case. Finally, a hearing takes place before the arbitrator. This hearing is usually less formal than a trial, although the purpose is the same—to prove a case to a neutral party or parties.

Occasionally disputes arise between parties regarding the agreement to arbitrate. If one of the parties refuses to cooperate in pursuing the arbitration, the parties often find it necessary to file a lawsuit in court to force or compel the arbitration proceeding. In other cases, a party may challenge the validity or enforceability of an arbitration agreement and file an action in court. In such a case, the party seeking arbitration might file an action to stay the court proceeding. To **stay** a proceeding means to stop the proceeding.

stay
To delay or stop a proceeding.

The following are two federal statutes that deal with arbitration:

Federal Arbitration Statutes

Validity, Irrevocability, and Enforcement of Agreements to Arbitrate

A written provision in any maritime transaction or a contract evidencing a transaction involving commerce to settle by arbitration a controversy thereafter arising out of such contract or transaction, or the refusal to perform the whole or any part thereof, or an agreement in writing to submit to arbitration an existing controversy arising out of such a contract, transaction, or refusal, shall be valid, irrevocable, and enforceable, save upon such grounds as exist at law or in equity for the revocation of any contract. (9 U.S.C. § 2)

Stay of Proceedings Where Issue Therein Referable to Arbitration

If any suit or proceeding be brought in any of the courts of the United States upon any issue referable to arbitration under an agreement in writing for such arbitration, the court in which such suit is pending, upon being satisfied that the issue involved in such suit or proceeding is referable to arbitration under such an agreement, shall on application of one of the parties stay the trial of the action until such arbitration has been had in accordance with the terms of the agreement, providing the applicant for the stay is not in default in proceeding with such arbitration. (9 U.S.C. § 3)

In general, the courts tend to favor and support agreements to arbitrate, although there are exceptions. Read the following two cases for views from two different courts.

A POINT TO REMEMBER

When parties agree to arbitration in a contract it is a binding process. They cannot choose to go to court instead. Furthermore, the parties must accept whatever award was given.

Lawrence v. Walzer

207 Cal. App. 3d 1501, 256 Cal. Rptr. 6 (1989)

The plaintiff (Lawrence) sued defendants for legal malpractice. The defendants claimed that this matter should be subject to binding arbitration and asked the trial court to order the parties to submit to binding arbitration. The defendant's claim was based on the retainer agreement that plaintiff had signed. The agreement contained a provision requiring arbitration in the event of any dispute regarding fees, costs, or any other aspect of the attorney-client relationship. The plaintiff claimed that this provision did not cover malpractice claims. The court agreed with the plaintiff.

OPINION

The law firm of Walzer and Gabrielson and four attorneys associated with that firm are defendants in an action for legal malpractice brought by Margaret Drain Lawrence, a former client, and appeal from the denial of their petition to compel arbitration. Defendants contend the retainer agreement signed by plaintiff compels arbitration of this action for legal malpractice.

FACTS

In 1986 plaintiff retained defendants to represent her in the dissolution of her marriage. A retainer agreement, consisting of a three-page letter from defendants to plaintiff, states: "This letter sets forth the agreement concerning our representation of you." Thirteen numbered paragraphs follow. The first nine paragraphs concern the computation and payment of attorney's fees and costs. In paragraph 10, defendants promise to keep plaintiff informed of the progress of her case. Paragraph 11 then states: "In the event of a dispute between us regarding fees, costs or any other aspect of our attorney-client relationship, the dispute shall be resolved by binding arbitration. The prevailing party in any arbitration or litigation between us shall be entitled to reasonable attorney's fees and costs." The final two paragraphs contain a promise by defendants to conform "to the highest legal and ethical standards," and instructions to plaintiff to sign and return a copy of the letter. The letter was dated May 5, 1986 and was signed by plaintiff on May 8, 1986.

On February 9, 1987, plaintiff filed a complaint alleging causes of action for legal malpractice and willful breach of fiduciary duty. On April 27, 1987, defendants filed a petition to compel arbitration. In opposition, plaintiff submitted her declaration stating the retainer letter was handed to her by a paralegal employed by defendants who told her "to sign it, and return it, with $7,500.00 if she wanted the firm of Walzer and Gabrielson to act as her attorneys." Plaintiff's declaration said she "had no idea I was giving up my right to sue my attorneys in Superior Court, for their future malpractice, and that I was giving up my right to a jury trial." Plaintiff declared she would not have signed the agreement had she been told that she thereby "would be submitting the matter of their possible future malpractice to arbitration."

DISCUSSION

The fundamental assumption of arbitration is that it may be invoked as an alternative to the settlement of disputes through the judicial process "solely by reason of an exercise of choice by all parties." In other words, a party cannot be compelled to arbitrate a dispute he has not agreed to submit. And it has been held that to be enforceable, an agreement to arbitrate must have been "openly and fairly entered into."

Defendants contend that inclusion of the phrase "any other aspect of our attorney-client relationship" in the arbitration clause of the retainer agreement compels arbitration of "[any] dispute arising out of the attorney-client relationship," including a claim of legal malpractice. If this phrase is considered standing alone, defendants' argument would be compelling. The issue before us, however, is not whether the phrase "any other aspect of our attorney-client relationship," standing alone, would encompass an action for attorney malpractice, because in the retainer agreement at issue, these words do not stand alone. "In the event of a dispute between us regarding fees, costs or any other aspect of our attorney-client relationship, the dispute shall be resolved by binding arbitration." In this context, the arbitration clause appears to be limited to disputes concerning financial matters such as fees and costs and is most likely to be so viewed by a prospective client to whom the proposed agreement is tendered by the law firm.

An arbitration agreement constitutes a waiver of the right to a jury trial. "The right to select a judicial forum, *vis-à-vis* arbitration, is a substantial right, not lightly to be deemed waived." Although an express waiver of jury trial is not required, by agreeing to arbitration, the client does forfeit a valuable right. The law ought not to decree a forfeiture of such a valuable right where the client has not been made aware of the existence of an arbitration provision or its implications. Absent notification and at least some explanation, the client cannot be said to have exercised a "real choice" in selecting arbitration over litigation.

The arbitration clause in the present case was part of a retainer agreement drafted by defendant attorneys and presented to the plaintiff client for her signature. It was not the product of negotiation.

Accordingly, like the trial court, we conclude plaintiff did not agree to binding arbitration of her claims of legal malpractice and breach of fiduciary duty.

CASE ANALYSIS

1. Compare the attitude of this court toward arbitration to the attitude of the *Madden* court.
2. How do the facts of this case differ from the facts of the *Madden* case?

In the matter of the Arbitration between Freddie Prinze, Also Known as Freddie Pruetzel, Appellant, and David Jonas, Respondent
Court of Appeals of New York

38 N.Y.2d 570, 345 N.E.2d 295, 381 N.Y.S.2d 824 (1976)

The plaintiff, a minor, signed a contract employing the defendant as his personal manager. The contract provided for arbitration in the event of a dispute. A dispute arose regarding the enforceability of the contract itself. The plaintiff maintained that this issue should be decided by the court, not by arbitration. The defendant disagreed. The court decided that arbitration was the proper way to handle the dispute.

OPINION

The petitioner is a well-known entertainer in the television industry. The respondent is a "personal manager" in the entertainment profession. On January 16, 1974 they signed a contract whereby the petitioner agreed to employ the respondent as his agent for a period of three years. The contract is a standard form used and approved by the conference of personal managers in the entertainment industry. It contains an arbitration clause which provides that "[i]n the event of any dispute under or relating to the terms of this agreement, or the breach, validity or legality thereof, it is agreed that the same shall be submitted to arbitration." In addition to the standard features the contract contains a rider giving the respondent the option to extend the agreement for four more years.

When the petitioner signed these agreements he was 19 years old and thus, according to the law in effect at that time, he was legally an infant.

In October, 1974 petitioner advised respondent in writing that he disaffirmed the agreement "dated February 19, 1974 and any antecedent agreements on the ground that all such arrangements were entered into during my infancy." In November, 1974 respondent served a demand for arbitration indicating "Nature of Dispute: Freddie Prinze's alleged disaffirmance of contract."

Petitioner then applied to stay arbitration on the ground that there was no valid agreement to arbitrate. Specifically he urged that his disaffirmance invalidated the agreement in its entirety including the arbitration clause. Respondent argued that the petitioner did not have an absolute right to disaffirm since the law then provided that "a contract made by an infant after he has attained the age of eighteen years may not be disaffirmed by him on the ground of infancy, where the contract was made in connection with a business in which the infant was engaged and was reasonable and provident when made." Thus, he contends, validity of the disaffirmance depended upon the reasonableness of the agreement. Since this would determine the continuing validity of the agreement, the question of reasonableness should be decided by the arbitrators.

Prefactorily, it should be emphasized that in the absence of a compelling public policy, arbitration is a preferred means for the settlement of disputes. When arbitration is invoked the only questions to be resolved by the courts (unless the dispute is barred by the Statute of Limitations) are whether "a valid agreement was made" and whether such agreement was "complied with."

Petitioner urges that this State's public policy compels the submission of the total issue of disaffirmance to the courts. We do not agree. In lowering the age of majority to 18 years of age, the Legislature has indicated with significant clarity that protection of individuals over 18 years of age was not a "major State" policy. Since petitioner was 19 years of age when he signed the contract, the public policy protecting minors is really not, and cannot be, the issue here. Rather, the only issue is the reasonableness and providence of the contract pursuant to section 3-101 of the General Obligations Law.

In short we see no reason to depart from the general rule that the court's sole function is to determine the validity of the arbitration clause.

The final question, then, is whether the courts below were correct in holding that the arbitration clause was valid. The "valid agreement" referred to concerns a valid agreement to arbitrate. Thus even when it is alleged, as it is in this case, that the contract itself is invalid in its entirety, the court's role is still confined to determining the validity of the arbitration clause alone. If the arbitration agreement is valid, any controversy as to the validity of the contract as a whole passes to the arbitrators. In this case the courts below were correct in holding the arbitration clause valid. If the clause were unreasonable in nature, or had the mark of one wrongfully imposed upon an infant, its validity would be subject to question. However, again considering the age of petitioner, as well as the fact that this clause is standard, reasonable, and in common use between performers and their agents, the courts below properly concluded that it was valid and enforceable. Indeed, petitioner does not claim that the arbitration provision itself is unreasonable and there are no allegations that the arbitration agreement was procured by fraud, misrepresentation or overreaching.

Accordingly, the order of the Appellate Division should be affirmed.

CASE ANALYSIS

1. Did the court rule that the entire contract was valid? Could one provision in the contract be valid and enforceable while the rest of the contract was not valid?
2. What is the New York court's general attitude toward arbitration?

SEC. 15-5 MEDIATION

mediation
An informal, out-of-court dispute resolution process; a *mediator*, or neutral person, assists the parties in reaching an agreement.

Mediation is a process in which the parties discuss and negotiate the issues in dispute with the assistance of a neutral person, the *mediator*. In a traditional mediation process, the neutral mediator assists the parties in coming to an agreement. The mediator does not decide the disputed issues, but rather tries to get the parties to come to an agreement. Mediation is generally nonbinding since it is impossible to force parties to come to an agreement. However, in a form of binding mediation that is occasionally used, the parties attempt to resolve their dispute with the assistance of the mediator, but if they are unable to do so, they allow the mediator to determine unresolved issues.

Mediation has become a popular method of attempting to resolve family law disputes and labor problems. In these areas, the mediators often have special training and experience. Mediation is also used in landlord-tenant disputes and consumer complaints. Local governments sometimes establish mediation services that are available to the public at no cost. These services may be affiliated with local real estate boards or consumer groups. Frequently they are staffed by volunteers who receive some training.

A POINT TO REMEMBER

Many community mediation boards use the services of volunteers to act as mediators. Consider volunteering for such a position.

SEC. 15-6 MINI-TRIALS

A **mini-trial** is a procedure that is sometimes used to resolve disputes involving businesses and corporations. In this process, a panel of senior executives from all

mini-trial
A type of informal nonbinding trial in which disputing parties, usually businesses, present their side of the dispute to a jury of executives from the businesses.

of the disputing businesses are selected to act as a "jury." Attorneys for the corporations then present evidence to this jury. The executives then "deliberate" and try to come to some agreement regarding the disputed issues in much the same way as a regular jury would. The mini-trial is not an actual court process. It is a private proceeding that takes place by agreement of the parties.

SEC. 15-7 COURT-RELATED ADR

Not all alternative dispute resolution is initiated by the parties in an attempt to avoid litigation. Even after a lawsuit has been filed, most courts provide ADR opportunities and procedures for parties to resolve their dispute prior to trial. In many instances, the courts require that the parties use some of these procedures. Alternative dispute resolution that is court-related or court-ordered is always nonbinding unless the parties agree to the contrary. The court cannot order that the parties be bound by alternative dispute resolution without their agreement, because in many types of civil cases, parties have a right to a trial. Court-related alternative dispute resolution takes many forms; courts are still developing procedures that they hope will be successful. Among the common procedures used today are early neutral evaluation, mediation, nonbinding arbitration, and summary trials.

early neutral evaluation
A proceeding that takes place early in a civil case in which the disputing parties meet with a neutral person who evaluates the case in an attempt to settle the dispute.

Early neutral evaluation is a procedure employed at the beginning of a lawsuit that requires the parties to meet with a neutral person who discusses the case with the parties, and, with some objective input, tries to bring the parties to a settlement. This is a type of settlement conference that occurs early in the court proceeding. The procedure resembles mediation and the two are often combined. Mediation that is court-related is the same as mediation that has been agreed to by the parties.

nonbinding arbitration
A form of arbitration in which the parties are not obligated to accept the arbitrator's decision.

Another procedure that is recommended or required by courts is **nonbinding arbitration**. The process of nonbinding arbitration resembles binding arbitration, with the exception that the decision of the arbitrator can be rejected by either party. If the arbitration award is rejected, the case proceeds to trial.

summary trial
An informal nonbinding trial in which disputing parties present their case to a judge or jury in a way that circumvents the numerous rules of evidence.

Summary trials, which can take place before a judge or a jury, involve an abridged version of the trial. The parties present their evidence to the fact-finder in a summary fashion. Parties do not have to be concerned with all of the technical rules of evidence that sometimes take up a great deal of time at trial. The fact-finder, either the judge or jury, renders a nonbinding decision. Although the decision is not binding, it does give the parties a strong indication of what result will follow from a complete trial. The purpose of nonbinding arbitration and summary trials is to give the parties a realistic appraisal of the worth of the case, encouraging a reasonable settlement. See Figure 15–2 for an example of a form used to initiate court-related ADR.

SEC. 15-8 PRIVATE JUDGES

private judge
An individual hired by the parties to preside over a trial; often a retired judge.

Some states allow the use of a type of alternative dispute resolution that combines ADR features with the litigation process. This involves the use of **private judges** to preside over a trial. Parties file a lawsuit in court and begin the normal litigation process. Rather than trying the case before one of the regular judges on the court,

United States District Court
For the Northern District of California

IN THE UNITED STATES DISTRICT COURT
FOR THE NORTHERN DISTRICT OF CALIFORNIA

Plaintiff,

v.

Defendant.
_______________________________/

No. C

STIPULATION AND [PROPOSED] ORDER SELECTING ADR PROCESS

ADR CERTIFICATION

The parties stipulate to participate in the following ADR process:

Court Processes:

❑ Arbitration ❑ ENE ❑ Mediation

(To provide additional information regarding timing of session, preferred subject matter expertise of neutral, or other issues, please attach a separate sheet.)

Private Process:

❑ Private ADR (*please identify process and provider*)

____

Dated: _______________ _______________________________
Attorney for Plaintiff

Dated: _______________ _______________________________
Attorney for Defendant

IT IS SO ORDERED:

Dated: _______________ _______________________________
UNITED STATES DISTRICT JUDGE

STIPULATION AND ORDER SELECTING ADR PROCESS / ADR CERTIFICATION

N:\Adrpc3a.frm REV. 5/00

FIGURE 15–2 Stipulation and order selecting ADR process.

(continued)

SIGNATURE AND CERTIFICATION BY PARTIES AND LEAD TRIAL COUNSEL

Pursuant to Civ. L.R. 16 and ADR L.R. 3-5(b), each of the undersigned certifies that he or she has read either the handbook entitled "Dispute Resolution Procedures in the Northern District of California," or the specified portions of the ADR Unit's Internet site <www.adr.cand.uscourts.gov>, discussed the available dispute resolution options provided by the court and private entities, and considered whether this case might benefit from any of them.

(Note: This Certification must be signed by each party and its counsel.)

Dated: _____________ ____________________________________
[Typed name and signature of plaintiff]

Dated: _____________ ____________________________________
[Typed name and signature of counsel for plaintiff]

Dated: _____________ ____________________________________
[Typed name and signature of defendant]

Dated: _____________ ____________________________________
[Typed name and signature of counsel for defendant]

United States District Court
For the Northern District of California

STIPULATION AND ORDER SELECTING ADR PROCESS / ADR CERTIFICATION

N:\Adrpc3a.frm 2 REV. 5/00

FIGURE 15–2 Continued

however, the parties agree to use a private judge. A private judge is an individual who, by agreement of the parties, presides over the case. This individual is paid by the parties. Often this individual is a retired judge. The advantage of this procedure is that the parties are not subject to the normal court delays in being assigned to trial. Because of the backlog of cases, parties who have filed civil lawsuits often must wait years before their case comes to court. With a private judge, the parties can go to trial when they are ready, not when the court is ready. This method of ADR is often criticized as being justice for the rich.

SEC. 15-9 SPECIAL MASTERS AND DISCOVERY REFEREES

Another method of ADR that combines features of alternative dispute resolution with litigation is the use of *special masters* and discovery *referees*. In the course of any case in litigation, especially in complex cases, legal questions frequently arise in the preparation of the case for trial. For example, in Chapter 13 you read about the discovery process in litigation. During this process, disputes might arise regarding what documents are discoverable or what questions can be asked in a deposition. If the parties cannot resolve these disputes, the normal procedure is to file a motion in court, have a court hearing, and allow a judge to decide the issue. This can take weeks, even months. To avoid this, in some cases **special masters** or **referees** are appointed by the court with the agreement of the parties. These individuals, who are paid by the parties, resolve disputes that arise during the course of litigation, eliminating the need to make motions. Time and costs are saved by the parties.

special master
An individual hired by the parties to decide disputed pretrial matters in civil actions.

referee
An individual hired by the parties to decide disputed pretrial matters in civil actions.

SEC. 15-10 ADR AND CRIMINAL LAW

Alternative dispute resolution has traditionally been used to resolve civil disputes. In recent years, however, some governmental entities are attempting to resolve some criminal cases through this process. Obviously there are a number of different considerations with criminal cases. Defendants have constitutional rights that cannot be ignored. Society also has the right to see that criminals pay their debt for any criminal acts. Alternative dispute resolution is certainly not a viable alternative in any major crime. However, some types of infractions or misdemeanors can be handled outside the normal criminal court process. For example, consider the following neighborhood dispute. Adams and Brown live on the same block. Adams has a dog that he allows to wander without a leash. Unfortunately the dog is destroying Brown's lawn. Brown gets upset and sprays weed killer on Adams's lawn. In fact, both Adams and Brown may have violated local ordinances making this conduct a criminal infraction. Rather than filing criminal charges, a case like this might be better handled by a mediator working with the parties to resolve the underlying problems. In criminal cases where any property damage resulted, alternative dispute resolution could also require the party causing the property damage to pay damages. The criminal case is avoided and hopefully the parties have reached a better understanding.

SEC. 15-11 ARBITRATORS, MEDIATORS, AND OTHER NEUTRALS

Essential to the success of alternative dispute resolution are the individuals who help facilitate the process: the arbitrators, mediators, and other neutral parties. In most instances, there are no legal requirements that these individuals must meet. They need not be attorneys nor need they have special training. However, with the increase in alternative dispute resolution, more and more attention is being paid to these people. In fact, many arbitrators, mediators, and other neutrals are lawyers or retired judges. Furthermore, many have had special training in this area. It is becoming a new legal specialty, with attorneys advertising their services as specially trained arbitrators or mediators. In addition, businesses such as the American Arbitration Association are growing in number. These businesses offer arbitration, mediation, and other services, usually at a set hourly fee. They frequently employ experienced lawyers and retired judges to act as neutrals. The one requirement that all arbitrators, mediators, or neutrals must have is neutrality. The alternative dispute resolution process requires an objective neutral person in order for the process to work.

Neaman v. Kaiser Foundation Hospital

9 Cal. App. 4th 1170, 11 Cal. Rptr. 2d 879 (1992)

After an arbitration hearing, the petitioners learned that one of three arbitrators had a prior business relationship with the defendant. They moved to set aside the award. The court granted the motion.

FACTUAL AND PROCEDURAL BACKGROUND

The Neamans, who are the spouse and adult children of Freya Neaman, deceased, filed an action in superior court against Kaiser for medical malpractice in treating the decedent for lung cancer. The superior court action was stayed and the case was submitted to mandatory binding arbitration pursuant to the provisions of decedent's medical and hospital service agreement (the Agreement) with Kaiser. The arbitrators selected by the parties were P. Theodore Hammond (Hammond) on behalf of Kaiser and Albert Barouh (Barouh) on behalf of the Neamans. Retired Los Angeles Superior Court Judge Ralph Drummond (Drummond) served as a neutral arbitrator. The proceeding resulted in an award in favor of Kaiser.

The Neamans moved to vacate the award on the ground they discovered, after the arbitration hearing was concluded, Drummond had been named by Kaiser as its party arbitrator on a number of prior occasions. The Neamans urge Drummond thus failed to disclose a previous business relationship with Kaiser. . . .

DISCUSSION

1. STANDARD OF REVIEW

An arbitration award shall be vacated if the court determines that "(a) [t]he award was procured by corruption, fraud or other undue means; (b) there was corruption in any of the arbitrators."

The United States Supreme Court, interpreting the federal statutory grounds for vacating an arbitration award, ruled arbitrators must "disclose to the parties any dealings that might create an impression of possible bias." The court held failure to make such disclosure constitutes cause for vacating the award, even absent proof of actual fraud, corruption or bias on the part of the arbitrator.

Statutory grounds for vacation of an award in California are practically identical with the comparable federal grounds, and the "impression of possible bias" rule has been held applicable in this jurisdiction.

Justice Black observed that while arbitrators cannot be expected to sever all ties with the business world because they do not make their living out of deciding cases, the court should nevertheless be even more scrupulous to safeguard the impartiality of arbitrators than judges, since the former have completely free rein to decide the law as well as the facts and are not subject to appellate review.

In our case, although Drummond disclosed he previously had acted as an arbitrator in Kaiser matters, he failed to disclose that on five of those prior occasions, he was Kaiser's party arbitrator. While he had served in all capacities in his experience as an arbitrator in Kaiser matters and may well, as he claims, enjoy a reputation for fairness, his relationship with Kaiser was a substantial business relationship, and should have been fully disclosed to the Neamans. . . .

DISPOSITION

The judgment is reversed. The matter is remanded to the trial court which is directed to vacate the arbitrator's award and to order a rehearing before a new panel of arbitrators.

CASE ANALYSIS

1. Was the court concerned with the fairness of the arbitrator's award in this case?
2. Why did the court set aside the arbitration award?

ETHICAL CHOICES

Assume that you are conducting an initial interview with a client. Your attorney has asked you to have the client sign a retainer agreement, telling you that he has already explained the fee arrangement to the client. You give a copy of the retainer agreement to the client who proceeds to read the agreement. Before signing it, the client notices that there is a provision in the agreement stating that any dispute arising out of the attorney/client relationship, including fees, must be resolved through binding arbitration. The client asks you what that means. The client also asks you if it is a good idea to agree to such a provision. What do you tell the client?

Featured Web Site: www.guide.lp.findlaw.com/01topics/

Findlaw.com is a Web site that provides access to an extraordinary amount of legal material. One of the features of this site is the ability to search for information on a variety of legal topics. One of the topics listed is "Dispute Resolution and Arbitration."

Go Online:

Search for information on dispute resolution and arbitration. Locate at least two additional Web sites dealing with this topic. Summarize the information you find.

Chapter Summary

Alternative dispute resolution has become a popular method for resolving civil cases outside the court process. It provides a quicker and less expensive way of settling cases. Alternative dispute resolution can be binding or nonbinding. It is binding only if the parties agree that it will be. Binding arbitration is a complete substitute for the court process. Parties are obligated to accept the result. Under most circumstances, there are no appellate remedies. Nonbinding alternative dispute resolution does not obligate the parties. If any party is not satisfied with the result, the case can be pursued through the normal court process. Nonbinding arbitration is frequently recommended or required by a court in which an action is pending. Alternative dispute resolution methods include arbitration, mediation, mini-trials, early neutral evaluation, and summary trials. In some cases, features of alternative dispute resolution are combined with the litigation process. Special masters or referees are hired by the parties to resolve pretrial disputes; in some cases, the parties pay for private judges to preside over the trial. No special requirements exist for arbitrators, mediators, and other neutrals, although many are attorneys or retired judges. Although alternative dispute resolution is used primarily in civil cases, it does occasionally occur in minor criminal cases.

Terms to Remember

alternative dispute resolution (ADR)
negotiation
arbitration
arbitrator
arbitration award
stay
mediation
mini-trial
early neutral evaluation
nonbinding arbitration
summary trial
private judge
special master
referee

Questions for Review

1. What are the advantages of alternative dispute resolution?
2. Compare and contrast binding arbitration with mediation.
3. What is a mini-trial?
4. Discuss the various methods of court-related ADR.
5. Who may serve as arbitrators, mediators, and other neutrals?
6. What are some of the problems with alternative dispute resolution and criminal cases?

Questions for Analysis

1. Review the section of your automobile policy that deals with uninsured-motorist coverage. Describe these provisions.
2. Review the Ethical Choices box in this chapter. Which NALA and/or NFPA rules or guidelines apply to the situation? Review your state's ethical rules. (*Hint*: Go to www.nala.org/ and find a link.) Which of those rules apply?

Assignments and Projects

1. Locate alternative dispute resolution providers in your area and send for information regarding their services.
2. Determine whether your community sponsors any alternative dispute resolution boards or agencies for resolution of common problems such as consumer disputes, neighborhood disputes, or landlord-tenant problems.
3. Locate the Web site for your local United States District Court. (*Hint*: Go to www.uscourts.gov/ and link from there.) Summarize information on the site about ADR. Also copy any relevant forms.

CHAPTER 16

RULES OF EVIDENCE

Technology Corner

Web Address	Name of Site
www.fjc.gov/	Federal Judicial Center
www.fbi.gov/	Federal Bureau of Investigation
www.cia.gov/	Central Intelligence Agency

CASE FILE: THE RUTHERFORD MATTER

The Rutherford case is set for trial. The trial team is now organizing the evidence. They must do the following:

(1) Compile a list of the witnesses and a summary of the testimony we believe they will give.

(2) Identify the statements that may present evidentiary problems. Specifically, there is concern about the admissibility of the hearsay statements.

(3) Organize and prepare the demonstrative evidence.

SEC. 16-1 INTRODUCTION

Federal Rules of Evidence
The rules of evidence used in the federal courts.

The project in the Case File requires an understanding of the rules of evidence. The topic of evidence is governed by rules. Each state has an evidence code. This chapter focuses on the **Federal Rules of Evidence**, which govern evidence in federal courts. The concept of what is or what is not evidence arises in all areas of the law. A basic understanding of evidence provides a good foundation for understanding how our judicial system works. The rules of evidence encourage fairness, help avoid judicial delay, and assist in ascertaining the truth.

SEC. 16-2 WHAT IS EVIDENCE?

There are four basic types of evidence: the testimony of a witness, exhibits, facts that the attorneys have stipulated, and judicial notice.

TESTIMONY OF A WITNESS

witness
A person who testifies about something he or she observed.

lay witness
A person who gives testimony about a subject of which the witness has personal knowledge.

testimony
Evidence delivered under oath, either orally or through affirmation (by affidavit), by a competent witness.

expert witness
A person who, because of special qualifications, testifies about conclusions that may be drawn based on his or her expertise.

There are two types of **witnesses:** lay witnesses and expert witnesses. A **lay witness** gives **testimony** about a subject of which the witness has personal knowledge. For example, a lay witness might testify that he saw the red Camaro run the stop sign and hit the black BMW. An **expert witness** testifies about conclusions that may be drawn based on his or her expertise. For example, an accident reconstruction expert could testify, based on the length of the skid marks and the damage to both automobiles, that the red Camaro was traveling at approximately 45 mph when it struck the black BMW.

Federal Rule of Evidence 601: General Rule of Competency

> Every person is competent to be a witness except as otherwise provided in these rules. However, in civil actions and proceedings, with respect to an element of a claim or defense as to which State law supplies the rule of decision, the competency of a witness shall be determined in accordance with State law.

Rule 601 provides two basic pieces of information. First, every person may be a witness, except for the *exceptions* included in the Federal Rules of Evidence. Second, when state law supplies the rule to be applied in a civil matter, the competency of the witness will be determined under state law.

Federal Rule of Evidence 602: Lack of Personal Knowledge

> A witness may not testify to a matter unless evidence is introduced sufficient to support a finding that the witness has personal knowledge of the matter. Evidence to prove personal knowledge may, but need not, consist of the witness' own testimony. This rule is subject to the provisions of rule 703, relating to opinion testimony by expert witness.

foundation
A requirement for the admission of evidence at trial. Preliminary questions are asked to connect the legal issue with the evidence sought to be admitted; in connection with documentary evidence, questions are asked to determine the genuineness of the documents.

Rule 602 explains that a **foundation** must be built before the lay witness may testify. In the preceding automobile accident example, the witness who testified that the red Camaro ran the light would give this testimony after the attorney asking the questions has established that the witness was actually present when the collision took place. Further, the attorney might seek to establish (1) exactly what the witness was doing when the accident occurred, (2) that the witness had an unobstructed view of the collision, (3) the weather conditions that might affect the vision of the witness, and so forth.

A POINT TO REMEMBER

When you are faced with difficult statutory language, approach the statute sentence by sentence or phrase by phrase. Make sure you understand each word of the statute. Consider trying to write the statute in your own words. When you can do this, you understand the statutory language. Long statutes are sometimes best approached by rewriting them in outline format. Instead of looking at a very long paragraph, studying the outline may help you digest the information in a more understandable format.

Federal Rule of Evidence 701: Opinions and Expert Testimony

If the witness is not testifying as an expert, the witness' testimony in the form of opinions or inferences is limited to those opinions or inferences which are (a) rationally based on the perception of the witness and (b) helpful to a clear understanding of the witness' testimony or the determination of a fact in issue.

Federal Rule of Evidence 702: Testimony by Experts

If scientific, technical, or other specialized knowledge will assist the trier of fact to understand the evidence or to determine a fact in issue, a witness qualified as an expert by knowledge, skill, experience, training, or education may testify thereto in the form of an opinion or otherwise.

Exhibits

exhibit
A physical (tangible) piece of evidence that is offered to the court for consideration; for example, exhibits may be documents, charts, and photographs.

actual evidence
Also called *real evidence*; tangible evidence that may be admitted during a hearing on a motion or at trial.

tangible
Possessing physical form; tangible items can be seen and touched.

documentary evidence
A type of actual evidence including writings such as reports, business records, and correspondence.

There are three types of **exhibits:** actual evidence, documentary evidence, and demonstrative evidence.

Actual Evidence

Actual evidence (also referred to as *real evidence*) might include the weapon used in a crime or the purse that was stolen. These are **tangible** items that could be admitted into evidence during the hearing on a motion or at trial.

Documentary Evidence

Documentary evidence might include writings such as reports, business records, and correspondence. Much of this type of evidence will be gathered during the discovery process. Chapter 13 explains the basic civil discovery devices.

United States v. Lawson

653 F.2d 299 (1981)

During a criminal trial for extortion, a psychiatrist testified regarding defendant. His testimony and opinion were based primarily on information and reports from other doctors. Defendant was convicted and appealed, raising the contention that the admission of hearsay in the testimony of the psychiatrist violated his right to confront adverse witnesses. The court upheld the conviction, stating that the admission of hearsay was in accordance with Federal Rule of Evidence 703, which expressly permits experts to base their testimony on evidence that would otherwise be inadmissible, so long as it is of a type reasonably relied on by experts in the particular field in forming opinions. The admission of hearsay also did not violate the Constitutional right to confront witnesses, because the defendant had pretrial access to the hearsay information relied upon.

OPINION

I

Defendant Lawson appeals from his conviction on one count of extortion that affected interstate commerce and one count of assault of a federal officer with a deadly weapon. He argues that lay testimony on the issues of his sanity was improperly admitted, that hearsay evidence in the testimony of the Government's psychiatric expert denied him the right to confront adverse witnesses, and that he had a right to a government-appointed psychiatrist. We affirm his conviction.

In January 1980, the employees of the International Harvester Company were on strike. On January 29, the security officer for the plant received a telephone call from an unidentified male who told him that he had information about damage that was going to occur to one of the company's plants. The FBI was contacted and arrangements were made for future telephone calls to be recorded. The unidentified male, who was later identified as defendant Lawson, called again the next day. During this conversation, Lawson stated that "they're hitting every plant that's on strike." He said that a group of men were planning on doing between one and one-and-a-half million dollars damage to International Harvester plants. Lawson demanded $50,000 for the information he possessed. He mentioned that he had worked for International Harvester, but that he had been fired. The money, he said, was his way of gaining revenge.

When Lawson called again on February 1, he said that he would write out the information he had in detail, but that he would omit all names. He did not want to give any names in case one of the group backed out; he did not want them arrested. Lawson said the group had contacted him because of his expertise in the field of explosives. He agreed to meet with representatives of International Harvester. Specific instructions were given about the meeting place and the procedures. Lawson said his handle would be Mr. Spock, "just like Star Trek." The International Harvester men meeting him were to be Captain Kirk and Dr. McCoy.

The meeting took place on February 6, 1980. Lawson was wearing a blue ski mask, and he kept his right hand in his pocket. Unbeknownst to Lawson the men he met were two Special Agents of the FBI. Lawson handed over a note that read, "Gentlemen, in the course of human events there comes a time of distrust. I don't know if you are going to try or [are] even thinking of trying to rip us off. But be warned there are two 300 Winchester Magnums aimed at your heads right now. If you live up to your end, we will live up to ours. Thank you."

One of the agents told Lawson the money was three minutes away and that he would get it as soon as he had verified the information. The agent then read four pages of the information handed him by Lawson, who told him that he was the person who had made the telephone calls to International Harvester. When the agent finished reading, he signaled to another special agent to bring the briefcase containing the money. Lawson was shown the money; he then handed the agent the last page of the information. Lawson said that he saw a gun in the agent's belt. As Lawson stepped back and reached in his pocket, the agent shouted, "FBI," and dove for Lawson. In the ensuing scuffle Lawson fired at the agents and missed. Lawson was subdued. In addition to the .38-caliber handgun that was fired, the agents found another loaded .38 in Lawson's right coat pocket. Lawson waived his rights after arrest and admitted, among other things, that he was the one who had called International Harvester.

II

Lawson's principal contention is that the admission of hearsay in the testimony of the Government's expert psychiatrist violated his right to confront adverse witnesses. During the pretrial proceedings, Lawson was examined for three months at a Federal Medical Center. Dr. Sheldon, chief of psychiatry at the Center, testified on the Government's behalf at trial that Lawson evidenced no symptoms of mental illness and that he was aware his conduct during the extortion attempt was not in conformation with the law. Dr. Sheldon based his testimony on reports he received from staff physicians and other staff. He also stated that he relied on the results of tests administered at the Center, information received from the United States Marine Corps (of which Lawson had been a member), reports from the FBI, and "a large amount of information" furnished by the United States Attorney's Office. None of this information was ever introduced into evidence.

Lawson's trial attorney objected in a timely manner that Dr. Sheldon's opinion testimony was without foundation since "he would be placing the opinions of other persons not qualified (as an expert) and not before the Court (or) the jury." The district court overruled the objection and permitted Dr. Sheldon to state his opinion. Lawson now relied on *United States v. Bohle,* 445 F.2d 54, 69 (7th Cir. 1971), which held that a medical expert may not testify regarding his opinion if it is based on information obtained out of court from third persons, since such an opinion would depend upon hearsay. We agree with Lawson that the introduction of expert testimony based in large part on hearsay may raise serious constitutional problems if there is no adequate opportunity to cross-examine the witness. Under the circumstances in this case, however, Lawson had that opportunity, and his right to confront adverse witnesses was not violated.

The adoption of the Federal Rules of Evidence in 1975 expanded the scope of expert testimony. Rule 703 expressly permits experts to base their testimony on evidence that would otherwise be inadmissible, so long as it is "of a type reasonably relied on by experts in the particular field in forming opinions or inferences upon the subject." In this case, the information Dr. Sheldon relied on to reach his opinion, staff reports, interviews with other physicians, and background information from the Marine Corps and the United States Attorney's Office, were clearly of the type that psychiatrists would rely upon in making a similar professional judgment.

In criminal cases, a court's inquiry under Rule 703 must go beyond finding that hearsay relied on by an expert meets these standards. An expert's testimony that was based entirely on hearsay reports, while it might satisfy Rule 703, would nevertheless violate a defendant's constitutional right to confront adverse witnesses. The Government could not, for example, simply produce a witness who did nothing but summarize out-of-court statements made by others. A criminal defendant is guaranteed the right to an effective cross-examination. "Cross-examination is the principal means by which the believability of a witness and the truth of his testimony are tested." *Davis v. Alaska,* 415 U.S. 308 (1974).

In addition to the reasonable reliance requirement of Rule 703, a criminal defendant must therefore also have access to the hearsay information relied upon by an expert witness. Without such access, effective cross-examination would be impossible. Rule 705, which provides that an expert need not disclose the facts or data underlying his opinion prior to his testimony unless the court orders otherwise, recognizes this requirement.

The record in this case indicates that Lawson had sufficient access to the information Dr. Sheldon used to reach his opinion. The reports from the FBI and the United States Attorney's Office were provided pursuant to a standard *Brady* request, as was the final medical report from the Medical Center. It is true that Lawson's counsel did not have copies of the notes made by staff members at the Center that were placed in Lawson's file and were reviewed by Dr. Sheldon, but since he did have most of the data Dr. Sheldon relied on, he had an adequate opportunity to prepare his cross-examination. Furthermore, Dr. Sheldon had had at least some contact with Lawson himself, even though he never interviewed him in private. Under these circumstances, we hold that Dr. Sheldon's testimony did not violate Lawson's right to confront adverse witnesses.

Defendant's conviction is affirmed.

CASE ANALYSIS

1. Rule 703 was discussed in the *Lawson* case. Rule 703 states that "[t]he facts or data in the particular case upon which an expert bases an opinion or inference may be those perceived by or made known to the expert at or before the hearing. If of a type reasonably relied upon by experts in the particular field in forming opinions or inferences upon the subject, the facts or data need not be admissible in evidence." Explain why the *Lawson* court held that the opinion of Dr. Sheldon was admissible.
2. Prepare a brief for the *Lawson* case. Include the facts, issues, rules, analysis, and conclusion of the court.

Demonstrative Evidence

demonstrative evidence
A type of actual evidence or exhibits created for use in court; includes diagrams, charts, and photographs.

Demonstrative evidence is actually *created* for use in court. Demonstrative evidence could include diagrams and photographs. With the increased use of technology in the courtroom, demonstrative evidence has changed in recent years and is evolving on a daily basis. Of course, there are rules about what exhibits will be allowed into evidence. Federal Rule of Evidence 1001 is a typical statute setting forth the basic definitions

Federal Rule of Evidence 1001: Contents of Writings, Recordings, and Photographs

Definitions

For purposes of this article the following definitions are applicable:

(1) Writings and recordings. "Writings" and "recordings" consist of letters, words, or numbers, or their equivalent, set down by handwriting, printing, photostating, photographing, magnetic impulse, mechanical or electronic recording, or other form of data compilation.

(2) Photographs. "Photographs" include still photographs, X-ray films, video tapes, and motion pictures.

(3) Original. An "original" of a writing or recording is the writing or recording itself or any other part intended to have the same effect by a person executing or issuing it. An "original" of a photograph includes the negative or any print therefrom. If data are stored in a computer or similar device, any printout or other output readable by sight, shown to reflect the data accurately, is an "original."

(4) Duplicate. A "duplicate" is a counterpart produced by the same impression as the original, or from the same matrix, or by means of photography, including enlargements and miniatures, or by mechanical or electronic re-recording, or by chemical reproduction, or by other equivalent technique which accurately reproduces the original.

Stipulated Facts

stipulation
An agreement; when opposing counsel agree on an issue, the agreement is usually written or placed onto the record in the presence of the court reporter and binds all parties.

In some instances, there are facts that are not in dispute. When this occurs, the parties, through their lawyers, enter into agreements that are written for the court or are read to the trier of fact. These agreements are called **stipulations.**

For example, a jury could be instructed that "Counsel have stipulated that [____________________] shall be deemed to have been called and to have testified to certain matters. You must consider that stipulated testimony as if it had been given here in court." This is the California jury instruction for stipulated testimony. The blank line, in the brackets, in the instruction indicates that the court will fill in the appropriate factual language for the jury.

Judicial Notice

judicial notice
An action taken by the court; the recognition by the court of the existence and truth of specific facts that are universally accepted or are public records. For example, judicial notice is used to acknowledge the laws of a state, the Constitution, or geographical statistics.

Judicial notice is sometimes taken when the court believes that the information is common knowledge. *Common knowledge* refers to that of society as a whole.

For example, in *Texas v. Lyons*, 812 S.W.2d 336 (Tex. Crim. App. 1991), Thomas Lyons was convicted by a jury of driving while intoxicated and his punishment was a two-year probated jail sentence and a $600 fine. His behavior after his arrest was not videotaped. Lyons argued that he should have been videotaped. He further argued that the videotape was the only witness capable of contradicting the police officer's testimony on the intoxication issue.

Prior to 1991, Texas enacted an act that "shows a clear legislative intent for counties with a population of 25,000 or more to purchase and maintain video equipment. There is also a clear legislative intent that the state's failure to videotape a DWI arrestee is admissible at trial. That is the only sanction intended by the legislature for failure to videotape" (*Lyons* at 339). The trial court took judicial notice of the fact that the videotape statute applied in this case because the county in question had a population over 25,000. Because this was a commonly known fact, evidence on the size of the population was unnecessary. Ultimately, the court concluded that the statute did not mandate "use" of the video equipment in every case.

SEC. 16-3 TYPES OF EVIDENCE

DIRECT EVIDENCE

direct evidence
Evidence that proves a point; for example, the testimony of an eyewitness.

Evidence is either *direct* or *circumstantial.* **Direct evidence** actually proves a point. The testimony of an eyewitness is direct evidence. Consider the following statement: "I stole Susan's purse." This would appear to be a criminal confession. This statement is direct evidence. In a civil action, a statement admitting liability by a defendant is direct evidence. For example: "I am so sorry that I hit your car. I knocked over my coffee and looked down just for a minute. Is everyone okay?"

CIRCUMSTANTIAL EVIDENCE

circumstantial evidence
Indirect evidence that provides the jury with information from which inferences may be drawn.

inference
A logical conclusion of a fact that is not supported by direct evidence; a deduction made by a judge or a jury, based on common sense and the evidence presented in the trial.

Circumstantial evidence is more common. This form of evidence is indirect. Circumstantial evidence provides the trier of fact with information from which **inferences** may be drawn.

Consider the following facts: A baby-sitter leaves a plate of freshly baked brownies on the kitchen countertop while she answers the phone in another room. When she returns, the plate of brownies is missing. She locates six-year-old Tom, whose face and hands are smeared with chocolate. He is complaining of a tummy ache. Tom says he doesn't know anything about the missing brownies.

Certain inferences may be drawn from these circumstantial facts. This is indirect evidence.

A sample jury instruction regarding direct and circumstantial evidence follows.

> ***Direct and Circumstantial Evidence—Inferences***
>
> Evidence means testimony, writing, material objects or other things presented to the senses and offered to prove the existence or non-existence of a fact.
>
> Evidence is either direct or circumstantial. Direct evidence proves a fact without an inference and, if true, conclusively establishes that fact. Circumstantial evidence proves a fact from which an inference of the existence of another fact may be drawn.
>
> An inference is a deduction of fact that may logically and reasonably be drawn from another fact or group of facts established by the evidence.
>
> The law makes no distinction between direct and circumstantial evidence as to the degree of proof required; each is a reasonable method of proof. Each is respected for such convincing force as it may carry.

A POINT TO REMEMBER

Jury instructions are a good source of legal definitions and explanations. The instructions are written for a jury who have no legal vocabulary or training. Jury instructions are easily located in law libraries.

SEC. 16-4 RELEVANCY

relevancy
The standard by which testimony or physical evidence is evaluated; relates directly to the fact in question and proves, or has a tendency to prove, a particular legal theory.

According to the Federal Rules of Evidence, "Relevant evidence means evidence having any tendency to make the existence of any fact that is of consequence to the determination of the action more probable or less probable than it would be without the evidence." **Relevancy** involves a two-pronged test. First, ask whether the evidence tends to prove or disprove a fact of consequence. Second, ask whether the evidence should be withheld from the jury (*excluded*) because it is confusing or unfairly prejudicial.

Once the relevancy of a piece of evidence is established, the court will determine whether it is *admissible*. This means that the judge will decide whether the trier of fact will be allowed to consider this piece of evidence.

Federal Rule of Evidence 402: Relevant Evidence Generally Admissible; Irrelevant Evidence Inadmissible

All relevant evidence is admissible, except as otherwise provided by the Constitution of the United States, by Act of Congress, by these rules, or by other rules prescribed by the Supreme Court pursuant to statutory authority. Evidence which is not relevant is not admissible.

For example, in an action where the plaintiff seeks to establish that an accounting firm is guilty of malpractice, which of the following pieces of information are relevant in the accounting malpractice case?

- The accountant who worked on the plaintiff's books lied about having his Certified Public Accountant's license.
- The accounting firm lost the plaintiff's books.
- The owner of the accounting firm has been married nine times.
- The accountant who worked on the plaintiff's books had an affair with his secretary.

The first two pieces of evidence are relevant in an accounting malpractice case, and could be admitted into evidence. The second two pieces of evidence are interesting, but they are not relevant and would not be admitted into evidence for consideration by the trier of fact.

ETHICAL CHOICES

A client charged with armed robbery comes into the office with a small bundle wrapped in a kitchen towel. She asks you to hide the bundle. What should you do?

ETHICAL CHOICES

A client tells you he is going to shred certain relevant documents that are damaging to his case. What should you do?

SEC. 16-5 IMPEACHMENT

impeachment
A tool used to attack the credibility of a witness.

credibility
A witness's testimony is weighed by the jury; credibility of the witness is established when his or her testimony is found to be worthy of belief.

Impeachment is a tool used to attack a witness's **credibility.** There are numerous methods used to attack credibility. The most common attributes used to discredit a witness are the following:

- Personal bias
- Prior inconsistent statements
- Prior convictions
- Character for untruthfulness

Federal Rule of Evidence 607: Who May Impeach

The credibility of a witness may be attacked by any party, including the party calling the witness.

Federal Rule of Evidence 608: Evidence of Character and Conduct of Witness

(a) Opinion and reputation evidence of character. The credibility of a witness may be attacked or supported by evidence in the form of opinion or reputation, but subject to these limitations: (1) the evidence may refer only to character for truthfulness or untruthfulness, and (2) evidence of truthful character is admissible only after the character of the witness for truthfulness has been attacked by opinion or reputation evidence or otherwise.

(b) Specific instance of conduct. Specific instances of the conduct of a witness, for the purpose of attacking or supporting the witness' credibility, other than conviction of crime as provided in rule 609, may not be proved by extrinsic evidence. They may, however, in the discretion of the court, if probative of truthfulness or untruthfulness, be inquired into on cross-examination of the witness (1) concerning the witness' character for truthfulness or untruthfulness, or (2) concerning the character for truthfulness or untruthfulness of another witness as to which character the witness being cross-examined has testified.

The giving of testimony, whether by an accused or by any another witness, does not operate as a waiver of the accused's or the witness' privilege against self-incrimination when examined with respect to matters which relate only to credibility.

SEC. 16-6 HEARSAY

hearsay
An out-of-court statement offered in evidence to prove the truth of the matter asserted.

According to Federal Rule of Evidence 801, **hearsay** is "a statement, other than one made by the declarant while testifying at the trial or hearing, offered in evidence to prove the truth of the matter asserted." In other words, hearsay is a statement made while the speaker is not in court, not under oath; it is being offered to prove the truth of a statement.

Hearsay is not admissible evidence "except as proved by these rules [Federal Rules of Evidence] or by other rules prescribed by the Supreme Court pursuant to statutory authority or by Act of Congress" (Rule 802). The federal hearsay rules begin with a basic definition of hearsay, Rule 801(c). This definition is followed by a statement of what is not hearsay, Rule 801(d).

All of this *sounds* somewhat clear-cut. The language in the rules is easily understood. However, Federal Rules of Evidence 803 and 804 set forth more than twenty exceptions to the hearsay rule. Some of these exceptions include an excited utterance, a present sense impression, and statements for purposes of medical diagnosis or treatment. In Appendix VI, Federal Rules of Evidence 801 through 806 are set forth. Some of the exceptions make sense even to the casual observer. Others must simply be learned.

A POINT TO REMEMBER

Statements are hearsay only if they are offered to prove the truth of the statement. Always look to see why the statement is being offered. For example, suppose a bystander testifies that she heard a witness to the accident say, "The red car ran the light." This is hearsay, if the statement is offered in evidence to prove that the red car did actually run the red light. But suppose, on the other hand, that the accident witness says "I am immortal." If the statement is offered to prove that the accident witness was mentally incompetent when the statement was made, it is not hearsay. Remember, statements are hearsay only if they are offered to prove the truth of the statement.

The hearsay rule and its many exceptions are intended to ensure that testimony is reliable and accurate. In most instances, testimony based on out-of-court statements is not considered reliable. Such out-of-court statements do not allow cross-examination when they are made. It is best to have the actual speaker come into court and make the statement under oath. In the preceding example with the red car, instead of having the bystander tell what she heard a witness say, the actual witness should tell the court what she saw. In this way, the attorneys are offered the opportunity to seriously scrutinize the testimony.

Bowling v. Commonwealth of Virginia

12 Va. App. 166, 403 S.E.2d 375 (1991)

Defendant was convicted of murder, which occurred in the course of a robbery. At trial the following evidentiary issues arose: (1) Defendant attempted to introduce psychiatric testimony regarding his low IQ in an attempt to prove lack of premeditation. The court refused to allow the testimony. (2) The court admitted a recording of a 911 tape made by the victim minutes after the robbery and shooting. On the tape, the victim answered several questions. (3) The court admitted statements of the victim made to his wife in the emergency room as dying declarations. The victim also asked to see a minister and made several statements to his wife, indicating that he felt he was dying. The appellate court upheld all the trial court's rulings.

OPINION

Thomas Bowling appeals his convictions in a bench trial [no jury] for capital murder and use of a firearm during the commission of murder. His issues on appeal include (1) whether the trial court erred in prohibiting him from introducing evidence of his mental capacity at the time of the offense, (2) whether the trial court erred in admitting statements made by the victim immediately after the shooting, under the excited utterance exception to the hearsay rule, and (3) whether the trial court erred in admitting statements made by the victim at the hospital, under the dying declaration exception to the hearsay rule.

I

This case arises from a robbery of a Fisca station. The victim, Glenn West, was the manager of the station. On the evening of December 24, 1987 West called 911 and told the operator that he had been shot in the stomach with either a .25 or a .32 and robbed by a black male who ran off in the direction of the cinema. A tape of the call was admitted into evidence.

Mrs. West arrived at the station at 8:25 pursuant to arrangement she had made with West earlier in the day. When she arrived, there were several police vehicles, an ambulance, and medical personnel at the station. West was inside, lying on his back. West was taken out of the station on a stretcher. Mrs. West testified that he was in great pain at the time.

While at the hospital, West told his wife that he could not breathe. He asked her to say a prayer for him and requested a minister, requests that Mrs. West stated were out of character for West since he was not a religious person. West then told her that he was cold and that he could not stand the pain in his stomach.

After Mrs. West wrapped a blanket around him, he wished her a Merry Christmas and told her that the presents for her and their daughter were on the table at the station. Mrs. West told him they would wait Christmas until he got home, but West responded that he would not see Christmas. Mrs. West testified that she begged him not to die. West told her to take care of their daughter and to go on the best that they could. He then called his daughter over, wished her a Merry Christmas, and told her to be strong and take care of her mother.

While West was talking with his daughter, the minister arrived. West told the minister that he wanted to be saved and they prayed together. Mrs. West testified that she had never seen her husband pray before. Shortly thereafter, Officer McCane spoke with West about the robbery at the station.

West was then taken into surgery. He did not regain consciousness after surgery and died at approximately 2:50 A.M. The cause of death was determined to be hemorrhage and shock secondary to a .25 caliber gunshot wound to the abdomen.

While at the hospital, West told his wife that the robber had called him by name and knew that he was the manager of the station. When Officer McCane spoke with West, West indicated that while he was waiting for his wife to pick him up at the station, he saw somebody walking across the station driveway. The individual called West by name, asked him if he was the manager, and then asked him if he could open the safe. West told the individual that he was the manager but that he could not open the safe.

West informed McCane that the robber then told West to open the safe or he would shoot him. West told the robber that he could not open the safe because it had a time delay lock on it. The robber again told West to open the safe or he would shoot him. West begged the robber not to shoot him, then reached into his pocket and gave him approximately $50.00 that he had in his pocket. He again told the robber that he could not get the safe open and begged him not to shoot. The robber responded, "Well, I guess I will have to kill you then," and shot West in the stomach.

West described the individual who shot and robbed him as wearing a dark jacket and blue jeans, with short hair and no facial hair. He said the robber had a .32 or .25 automatic pistol and that he did not remember having seen the individual prior to that evening. West also told McCane that he saw a yellow van with mag wheels and some type of rack on top go up and down the street several times.

Steve Johnson testified that several days before Christmas Eve, he had spoken with Doc Hall about robbing the Fisca station. On the morning of the robbery, Hall, James Ward, Bowling and Tracy Brown pulled up in a yellow van and Brown told Johnson that Bowling had agreed to rob the station. About 7:00 P.M. that evening, Hall and Ward picked up Johnson and Brown in the van and drove to pick up Bowling. Thereafter, Ward drove the van to the cinema, circled around the parking lot a few times and parked across the street from the Fisca station.

While they were all in the van, Hall told Bowling that the manager's name was West. Hall also told Bowling that after the robbery, he should run through the cinema, go across the parking lot, and meet the van in front of the church. Ward gave Bowling a gun and told him that it was loaded. The gun was not cocked when Ward gave it to Bowling. Johnson testified that Bowling asked Hall: "What if I have to jinx him?" Hall responded: "I am not telling you to shoot him, but if you have to shoot him. . . ."

Bowling exited the van and crossed the street toward the station. Ward drove the van from the cinema to the church. Within five or six minutes, Bowling returned to the church. He told Hall that several customers came into the station so he just bought a soda and left. After some discussion Bowling agreed to try again.

After Bowling left, Ward drove the van along Timberlake Road, passing the station several times, before returning to the church. Bowling came back to the van, threw about $50.00 on the table and stated that he shot West. He told the others that West could not open the safe because it had some kind of lock on it. Bowling then gave the gun to Hall, who unloaded it. Johnson testified that as he unloaded the gun, Hall indicated that he had loaded the gun with seven rounds and only four remained.

Officer McCane spoke with Bowling at the police station on January 22, 1988. A tape recording of the conversation was admitted into evidence. Bowling told McCane that Ward, Hall and Brown picked him up in a black and yellow van on Christmas Eve. They drove over to the cinema, across the street from the Fisca station and Ward gave Bowling a .25 automatic.

Bowling stated that when he encountered West outside the station, he told him to open up the safe. Bowling indicated that he had the gun by his side. West told him that the safe could only be opened in the morning. Bowling again told West to open the safe, and West said that he could not. Bowling then asked West how much money he had in his pocket. West said about $45.00. Bowling told West to give him the money. He stated that as he was putting the gun back into his pocket, it went off, hitting West in the stomach. Bowling then ran across the street to the cinema and cut through the church yard.

Prior to trial, Bowling moved the trial court to admit evidence at trial concerning his mental state at the time of the offense. Counsel proffered that the evidence she sought to admit included the fact that Bowling functioned at the lower limits of the borderline range of the Adult Intelligence Scale and that Bowling did not have developed problem solving skills or elaborate abstract thinking capability. The trial court denied Bowling's motion.

II

Bowling argues that the trial court erred in denying his motion to introduce psychiatric evidence bearing on his mental state at the time of the offense. He claims that evidence of diminished capacity is relevant to the elements of premeditation and deliberation involved in capital cases. Thus, the trial court should have considered evidence of Bowling's borderline mental capacity in determining whether or not he acted with premeditation.

The court, quoting from *Stamper v. Commonwealth*, 228 Va. 707, 324 S.E.2d 682 (1985) stated: "For the purposes of determining criminal responsibility a perpetrator is either legally insane or sane; there is no sliding scale of insanity. The shifting and subtle gradation of mental illness known to psychiatry is useful only in determining whether the borderline of insanity has been crossed. Unless an accused contends that he was beyond that borderline when he acted, his mental state is immaterial to the issue of specific intent."

Bowling argues that this case is distinguishable from *Stamper* because the evidence he sought to introduce was intended to negate the element of premeditation. . . . The court rejects this argument.

In the case before us, Bowling sought to introduce evidence that he functioned at the lower limits of the adult intelligence range. At no time, however, did he put his sanity at issue nor did he present evidence in support of a finding that he was legally insane. Accordingly, in the absence of any claim of insanity, we find that the trial court did not err in denying Bowling's motion to introduce psychiatric evidence as to his mental state at the time of the offense.

Bowling next argues that the trial court erred in admitting the tape of West's initial conversation with the 911 operator. He claims that the Commonwealth failed to meet its burden of proving that the statements on the tape were "excited utterances." Bowling stresses that all but one of the statements made by West were made in response to questions posed by the 911 operator and were therefore outside the definition of an excited utterance.

The rule in Virginia is that "excited utterances prompted by a startling event, and not the product of premeditation, reflection, or design, are admissible, but the declaration must be made at such time and under such circumstances as to preclude the presumption that it was made as a result of deliberation." *Coins v. Commonwealth*, 218 Va. 466, 318 S.E.2d 382, 386 (1977).

In order to determine whether the Commonwealth has met this burden, a court must look to the passage of time between the event and the declaration, whether the statement was made spontaneously or in response to questions, and whether the statements were an admission against interest rather than self-serving declarations. The ultimate test is whether it appears that the facts are talking through the party or . . . the party is talking about the facts. [Citation omitted.]

In the case before us, West told Officer McCane at the hospital that after he was shot, he went into the office and called 911. The call was placed at approximately 8:13 P.M. Bowling told Officer McCane that the robbery occurred around 8:00 P.M. or a little after. Bowling told Officer McCane that after he shot West, he ran from the station back to the van. Steve Johnson testified that, by the time Bowling reached the van, they had already heard on a police scanner that West had been shot. From this evidence, the trial court properly concluded that West's call to 911 was made within minutes of the shooting.

Bowling argues that this is not determinative of the issue of admissibility because all but West's initial statements to the 911 operator were made in response to questions. Thus, he argues that they were not sufficiently spontaneous to be admitted under the excited utterance exception to the hearsay rule.

In *Martin v. Commonwealth*, 4 Va. App. 438, 358 S.E.2d 415 (1987), a panel of this court stated: "To pivot the admissibility of a subsequent statement, however spontaneous, on the questions of whether it was prompted by an equally spontaneous inquiry would serve no useful purpose. If the question or questioner suggested or influenced the response, then his declaration may lack the necessary reliability to be admitted." *Id.* at 442, 358 S.E.2d at 418. [Further citations omitted.] Considering the reliability of the statements in accordance with this standard, we find that West's statements were neither suggested by nor influenced by the questions posed by the 911 operator.

Upon consideration of all the circumstances surrounding West's statements to the 911 operator, we find that the trial court did not abuse its discretion in admitting the taped conversation under the excited utterance exception to the hearsay rule. At the time the statements were made, West was calling for help as he lay mortally wounded from a gunshot. West spoke with the 911 operator no more than ten minutes after the shooting and all the descriptive information regarding both his injury and his assailant was given spontaneously and not in response to direct questions posed by the operator. Based on the foregoing evidence, we find that West's statements to the 911 operator were not the result of premeditation, reflection or design, but a reaction to the startling events which resulted in West's death several hours later. Accordingly, the trial court did not err by admitting the tape of West's initial conversation with the 911 operator into evidence pursuant to the excited utterance exception to the hearsay rule.

Bowling likewise argues that the statements made by West to his wife while in the hospital emergency room were not admissible as dying declarations because the Commonwealth did not clearly establish that West had given up all hope of recovery at the time the statements were made. We find no error in the trial court's ruling that the statements were admissible under the dying declaration exception to the hearsay rule.

Bowling argues in the alternative that the statements, if admissible, were improperly considered by the trial court with respect to his guilt or innocence on the use of a firearm indictment, since dying declarations are admissible only in a homicide prosecution. We disagree.

The rule governing the admissibility of dying declarations has been stated as follows: "Dying declarations are admissible only in cases of homicide, when made by the person injured touching the cause of his death, while actually in extremis and conscious that he is so, under a sense of impending death, and without any expectation or hope of recovery." [Citation omitted.] The dying declarations were properly considered by the trial court in its determination of Bowling's guilt or innocence on that charge.

For these reasons we affirm the decision of the trial court.

CASE ANALYSIS

1. Using Appendix VI, find the Federal Rules of Evidence that might have been applicable to the *Bowling* case. Explain how each could be used.
2. Write a case brief for the *Bowling* case. Include the facts, issues, rules, analysis, and conclusion.

Featured Web Site: www.law.umich.edu/thayer/

This is the Evidence Site.

Go Online

1. Locate the most recent edition of the Evidence Section's Newsletter. Choose an article. Read and summarize the article.
2. Locate the "Relevant Links." Choose two. Open each and write a summary of the information found on each link.

Chapter Summary

Evidence is an important concept in all areas of the law. Evidence is governed by rules. These rules assist in ascertaining the truth, encourage fairness, and help to avoid judicial delay. There are four basic types of evidence: (1) the testimony of a witness, (2) exhibits, (3) facts that the attorneys have stipulated, and (4) judicial notice. Each type or piece of evidence will be either direct or circumstantial. All evidence must be relevant. In an attempt to ensure that testimony is reliable and accurate, the hearsay rule excludes statements made out of court that are offered for the truth of the matter asserted. There are many exceptions to the hearsay rule. These exceptions are listed in Federal Rule of Evidence 801, which is set forth in Appendix VI.

Terms to Remember

Federal Rules of Evidence	actual evidence	circumstantial evidence
witness	tangible	inference
lay witness	documentary evidence	relevancy
testimony	demonstrative evidence	impeachment
expert witness	stipulation	credibility
foundation	judicial notice	hearsay
exhibit	direct evidence	

Questions for Review

1. Explain the difference between a lay witness and an expert witness.
2. Name three types of evidence. Define each in a sentence.
3. What is relevancy?
4. What is character evidence?
5. Who is competent to testify?
6. What does it mean to impeach a witness? Give an example of impeachment.
7. What is hearsay?
8. What is the purpose of the hearsay rule?

Questions for Analysis

1. Read the following hypothetical situation after reviewing the Case File at the beginning of this chapter. Focus on the statements that may be hearsay.

   Tommy Rutherford and his family were staying at the lake for the summer. Tommy's family has a very small cabin built by his great-grandfather. The new home next door is quite large and the owner is almost never there. One weekend the next-door neighbor, Susan, came to the lake for a short stay. Tommy offered to cut her lawn and look after the outdoor plants on the back deck. Susan said that would be great. Susan also said, "Feel free to use the dock, the tennis courts, and the back deck any time."

   Late in the summer, Susan returned to find that the dock was badly damaged due to Tommy's inexpert docking of his family boat, and the net over the tennis court was ripped in half. When Susan asked about the damage, Tommy's sister Helen said, "Tommy said we could use the dock all we want, and besides, he is just learning to use a boat. The tennis court net was not my fault."

   Review Federal Rules of Evidence 801 through 806 in Appendix VI.

   a. Are any of these statements hearsay? Explain.
   b. Is there a nonhearsay use for any of the statements? Explain.
   c. What type of documentary evidence might be used in the Rutherford case?

Assignments and Projects

1. Locate the jury instructions for your state. Find the hearsay instruction. State the number and title of the instruction. Summarize the instruction.
2. Locate the federal jury instructions. Into what general topics or subjects are the instructions divided?
3. Summarize Federal Rules of Evidence 701 and 702. Reread the "Point to Remember" printed on page 367.
4. Summarize the dispute in *New York Times Co. Inc., v. Tasini*. The case syllabus (summary) is found in Appendix VII.

CHAPTER 17

THE TRIAL

Technology Corner

Web Address	Name of Site
http://oyez.nwu.edu/	U.S. Supreme Court Multimedia Database
www.ncsconline.org/	National Center for State Courts
www.osha.gov/	U.S. Department of Labor (OSHA)
vls.law.vill.edu/Locator/fedcourt.html	Federal Court Locator

CASE FILE: THE ACE AUTO REPAIR MATTER

The Ace Auto Repair matter is about to go to trial. A set of jury instructions must be prepared, including the following topics:

Negligence
Proximate cause
Damages
Respondent superior

SEC. 17-1 INTRODUCTION

trial
The open-court process where all parties present evidence, question witnesses, and generally put their case before the court.

A **trial** is a public process whereby parties involved in a legal dispute ask a judge, and often a jury, to decide the outcome of their legal matter. Many people play key roles in the trial process. A simple trial may last only a few hours. Some trials—for example, O. J. Simpson's criminal trial in 1995—last many months. Preparation for trial is similar to preparation for settlement. In each instance, discovery must be completed, research must be done, and witness lists and witness statements must be compiled. Legal support staff have many responsibilities along the road to the courtroom, where the trial will actually take place. Much of what takes place during a trial is the direct result of the efforts of the legal support staff back in the office. A basic understanding of the trial process is an essential component in any legal education.

ETHICAL CHOICES

In preparing for a trial, you come across a document at the bottom of a box of your client's documents. This document clearly indicates that your client has been untruthful with your office and the court. What should you do?

SEC. 17-2 ROLES OF TRIAL PARTICIPANTS

During the trial, each of the participants will play a particular and definite role.

Judge—The judge is in charge of the proceedings. As such, he or she makes all practical decisions such as when breaks are taken and at what time proceedings begin and end. The judge also has a more technical function. It is the judge's duty to decide all questions of law.

Plaintiff's attorney—The attorney for the plaintiff presents evidence and questions witnesses on behalf of the plaintiff. If the trial is criminal, the prosecutor presents the case on behalf of the victim and the state or jurisdiction.

Defendant's attorney—The attorney for the defendant presents evidence and questions witnesses on behalf of the defendant.

Court reporter—The court reporter "reports" every word of the open-court proceedings. A transcript (a paper copy or a diskette) is sometimes produced. After approval by the parties, the transcript becomes the official record of the trial.

Court clerk—A court clerk is assigned to the judge. The clerk assigns exhibit numbers, labels the evidence, and assists the judge as the need arises during the trial.

Jury—The jury is a group of citizens who decide the facts of the case.

Court deputy/bailiff—The court deputy or bailiff is the law enforcement officer assigned to the courtroom. This individual maintains order and protocol in the courtroom. The court deputy/bailiff is also in charge of the jury.

SEC. 17-3 PRETRIAL MOTIONS

brief
A written document that might contain a summary of the facts, issues, rules, and analysis used by a court and a comparison with a client's facts; a case brief is a short summary of a published case.

In civil and criminal trials, numerous pretrial motions may be made by either party. In a criminal trial, the defendant might move to suppress certain evidence. In a civil trial, either party might move for a summary judgment.

A motion for summary judgment requests that the judge decide the case on the legal issues without consideration of the factual issues. Such motions are made when the facts are not in dispute. If a motion for summary judgment is granted, there will be no trial. The judge will take the matter *under submission.* This means that both sides will **brief** the legal issues and submit their written findings to the judge. There will be no testimony by witnesses and there is no need for a jury when there are no factual questions to be decided.

Reuther v. Southern Cross Club, Inc.

785 F. Supp 1339 (1992)

The plaintiff hired the defendant to take him scuba diving. On the way to the dive site, a large wave struck the boat and plaintiff was injured. Prior to the dive, plaintiff signed a waiver and release, releasing defendant from all liability. The release referred to the "potential dangers incidental to scuba diving, instruction, or snorkeling." Defendant moved for summary judgment. Plaintiff claimed that his understanding of the agreement was that it applied only to the diving and not to the boat ride to the site. The court denied the motion for summary judgment.

I. BACKGROUND

"Just sit right back and you'll hear a tale" of what happened when David Reuther, while vacationing in the Cayman Islands at the Pirates Point Resort Hotel, decided to go scuba diving—"a fateful trip that started from this tropic port, aboard this tiny ship." Quoted with reference (and apologies) to the theme song from the syndicated 1960s sitcom television favorite, *Gilligan's Island:*

> Just sit right back and you'll hear a tale,
> a tale of a fateful trip,
> that started from this tropic port,
> aboard this tiny ship.
> The mate was a mighty sailing man,
> the skipper brave and sure,
> five passengers set sail that day,
> for a three hour tour,
> a three hour tour.
> The weather started getting rough,
> the tiny ship was tossed,
> if not for the courage of the fearless crew,
> the *Minnow* would be lost,
> the *Minnow* would be lost.
> The ship's aground on the shore of this
> uncharted desert isle,
> With Gilligan, the skipper too,
> The millionaire, and his wife,
> The movie star, the professor and Mary Ann,
> Here on Gilligan's Isle.

Pirates Point could not accommodate Reuther's desire to go diving and arranged—in accord with an informal standing agreement—for Reuther to dive with a nearby diving company, Southern Cross Club, Inc. Reuther and seven other passengers boarded Southern Cross' dive boat with the intention that the boat would take them to a scuba dive site. The dive boat started its short trip to the dive site, but as it entered a channel in the barrier reef that surrounds Little Cayman, "the weather started getting rough" (a huge wave struck the dive boat) and "the tiny ship was tossed." Although ultimately the boat neither "would be lost" nor stranded "on the shore of [an] uncharted desert isle," Reuther was injured when the wave struck the boat, and instead of a television show, this lawsuit was born. Reuther filed this action claiming the "skipper" of Southern Cross's dive boat should have waited until the "huge wave" passed before piloting the dive boat into the channel; that perhaps the "skipper" was too "brave and sure."

Prior to getting on the Southern Cross dive boat, Reuther had signed a form entitled "Waiver, Release and Indemnity Agreement." The release form stated in part:

> For and in consideration of permitting . . . David Reuther . . .
>
> To participate in scuba diving, instruction, snorkeling and any and all watersport activities . . . each of the above named persons by their signatures below hereby voluntarily releases, discharges, waives and relinquishes SCC . . . from any and all claims or causes of action for personal injury, property damages, wrongful death however caused and for himself . . . and hereby releases, waives, discharges and relinquishes any action . . . whether arising from the negligence of any such persons or otherwise. . . .
>
> Each of the undersigned persons acknowledges . . . that SCC does not maintain liability insurance for claims arising from scuba diving, instruction or snorkeling and is aware of the consequences of signing this document. . . .

Reuther claims that he signed the form quickly, that he did not get a copy of the signed form, that no one insisted that he read the form, and that no one explained the purpose or scope of the release. Reuther claims he understood the form to concern only the hazards of an actual scuba dive.

Southern Cross has moved for summary judgment arguing that Reuther released it from liability by signing the release form. Reuther objected to that motion, and Southern Cross replied to Reuther's response. Based on these filings, this court denies Southern Cross' motion for summary judgment.

II. DISCUSSION

Indiana's conflict of law rules instruct that this court must look to the laws of the Cayman Islands to determine the validity and scope of the release form.

The express wording of the Southern Cross release refers only to "the potential dangers incidental to scuba diving, instruction, or snorkeling." In particular, the last paragraph—the one directly above the signature, entirely in bold letters—describes specific dangers that are involved in scuba diving ("lung overexpansion") and warns potential scuba divers that they must be in "good health without physical ailments, disabilities, or abnormalities." The bolded paragraph further warns that the divers must be free from "respiratory ailment" so as to minimize the potential for injuries associated with a scuba dive—"diving injuries [that would] necessitate immediate and expensive emergency treatment." Nowhere does the release advise of the potential for injury while on the dive boat, nor are respiratory ailment or good health concerns relevant to the dangers of a simple boat ride.

Reuther's affidavit, a "recital," discloses that by signing the release form, he understood that it was an agreement not to sue Southern Cross for injuries that might have occurred in the context of a scuba dive:

> I believed that the release form I signed was strictly for the purpose of recognizing the unique risks of scuba diving. At no time did I acknowledge, intend, or contemplate that the short boat ride merely providing transportation to the scuba dive site would prove to be the real danger. Consequently, I did not contemplate nor intend to release to cover the boat pilot's negligence. I never thought that was the purpose of the release I signed.

Based on Reuther's (uncontradicted) recital of his understanding of the scope of the agreement, the absence of any written language in the release about the dangers of the boat ride, and the explicit warnings on the release that refer only to the "potential dangers incident to scuba diving," this court considers the scope of the release to be limited to injuries related to a scuba dive. However, by including specific dangers or events that may happen in the context of a scuba dive, the injury is not covered under the release. The "surrounding circumstances," "recitals," and "context" of the release leads this court to conclude that the "object and purpose" of the release was to waive liability for injuries incurred while scuba diving only.

Southern Cross argues that the dive boat ride was an integral part of the scuba dive experience, and that the release language, "For and in consideration of permitting . . . [David Reuther] . . . To participate in scuba diving," should be read reasonably to constitute a release for negligence that occurred during the dive boat ride. However, this release language is at best ambiguous as to Southern Cross' exposure to liability regarding dive boat negligence; it is not at all clear that the clause, "To participate in scuba diving" incorporates the preparatory boat ride. Because the release is ambiguous in this respect this court construes the release strictly against Southern Cross. We cannot state as a matter of law that the release protects Southern Cross from the type of negligence alleged in this litigation.

III. CONCLUSION

Accordingly, this court finds that the release form does not protect Southern Cross from liability for injuries that occurred on the boat ride while enroute to the dive site and therefore denies Southern Cross' motion for summary judgment.

It is so ordered.

CASE ANALYSIS

1. In the *Reuther* case, the Court did not grant the motion for summary judgment. Why?
2. Do you agree with the Court's interpretation of the language of the release signed by Mr. Reuther?

SEC. 17-4 JURY SELECTION

The jury selection process starts long before the actual day of the trial. The court must first obtain the names of potential jurors and command their presence in court. This group of people, from whom the actual trial jurors will be selected, is known as the *jury panel.* Whether the case is civil or criminal, potential jurors must be selected from the general public and must be representative of the community. There is no constitutionally prescribed method of jury selection, other than that it must not discriminate against any particular group of people. Popular sources of the jury panel include motor vehicle records and voter registration lists.

On the date set for trial, the jury panel will be commanded to appear in court. Since a number of people will be excused from jury duty, the number called will be considerably more than the number of jurors required.

JURY QUESTIONNAIRE

The following list represents the first 30 of the 302 questions given to the potential jurors in the O. J. Simpson criminal trial in Los Angeles, California, in September 1994.

List of Questions for Potential Simpson Jurors

9/30/94

The following is the partial text of the 75-page questionnaire filled out by prospective jurors in the O. J. Simpson murder case.

I. Family History—Background

1. Age
2. Are you male or female?
3. What is your race? (please circle)
   a. White-Caucasian?
   b. Black–African-American?
   c. Hispanic-Latino?
   d. Asian-Pacific Islander?
   e. Other? (please state)
4. Marital status:
   a. Single and never married?
   b. Single, but living with non-marital mate? For how long?
   c. Currently married? Length of marriage?
   d. Divorced? When divorced? Length of previous marriage? Did you initiate the divorce? Yes? No?
   e. Widowed? Length of marriage?
5. If you have children, please list (include children not living with you): Sex? Age? Does child live with you? Level of education? Occupation?
6. Do you have grown grandchildren? Yes? No? If yes: Sex? Age? Occupation?

(continued)

7. Do you have a medical or physical condition that might make it difficult for you to serve as a juror? (Please include any hearing or eyesight problem or difficulty in climbing stairs.) No? Yes? Please describe.
8. Are you presently taking any form of medication? If so, please list the medications you are taking, the reasons for taking them, and how often you take them.
9. Do you have any problems or areas of concern at home or at work that might interfere with your duties as a juror during trial? Yes? No? If yes, please describe.

II. Residential History

10. What part of Los Angeles County do you currently live in and what is your zip code? (If you live in the City of Los Angeles, please specify the area—for example, South Central, Crenshaw.)
11. How long have you lived at your present residence?
12. Which of the following best describes your current type of residence: Rental apartment? Own home? Rental house? Rental (other)? Other (specify)? Own apartment or condo? Own mobile home?
13. List areas of past residence within the last ten years and indicate how long you lived in each location.
14. Where were you born?
15. Where were you raised?
16. Is English your first language? Yes? No? If no, what is your language?
17. Do you speak any language other than English? Yes? What language(s)? No?
18. Do you have any difficulty:
    - **a.** Reading English? Yes? Sometimes? No?
    - **b.** Understanding spoken English? Yes? Sometimes? No?

III. Employment

19. Are you currently employed outside the home? Yes? No? If so, by whom are you employed? Full or part time? If part time, how many hours per week? How long have you been so employed?
20. What are your specific duties and responsibilities on the job?
21. Does your job involve management or supervisory duties? Yes? No? If your answer is yes, please describe your managerial responsibilities and state the number of employees you supervise.
22. Do you have the authority to hire and fire employees? Yes? No? If yes, is this a difficult decision to make? Yes? No? Please explain.
23. If not currently employed outside the home, please check the category that applies to your employment status: Homemaker? Unemployed—looking for work? Unemployed—not looking for work? Student? Retired? Disabled?
24. If you are not currently employed outside the home but were previously so employed, please describe your most recent form of employment, stating the name of your employer, whether you were employed full or part time, when and for how long you were so employed.

25. Please list your work experience over the past ten years and state when and for how long you were employed at each job. Please give a brief description of each job and the name of each employer. If additional space is needed please use the blank pages provided at the back of the questionnaire and put the number of this question next to your answer.

26. Have you ever worked in the entertainment industry in any capacity? No? Yes? If yes, please explain.

27. Do you have any close friends or relatives who either worked in the past or are currently working in any capacity in the entertainment industry? No? Yes? If yes, please indicate what relation s/he is to you and where s/he is or was so employed.

28. Have you ever worked in journalism or the news industry in any capacity? No? Yes? If yes, please state where and when you were so employed and give a brief description of your duties.

29. Do you have any close friends or relatives who either have worked or are currently working in journalism or in the news industry in any capacity? No? Yes? If yes, please state where and when s/he was so employed and give a brief description of his or her duties.

30. Have you ever worked in a laboratory or in any medical research or testing facility? No? Yes? If yes, please describe your duties and when and for how long you were so employed.

The jurors answered additional questions on the following subjects:

Education

Military service

Spouse or partner's background

Parents and siblings

Legal courtroom experience

Media coverage

Familiarity with Brentwood area of L.A.

Familiarity with judge, attorneys, parties, victims, witnesses

Familiarity with defendant O. J. Simpson

Domestic violence—use of force

Ethnic prejudice

DNA

Religion

Political views

"Expert" witness

Science and math courses

Victim or witness to crime

Contact with law enforcement agencies

Contact with prosecuting agencies

Contact with coroner's office

Leisure activities—entertainment—hobbies—miscellaneous

Sports

Sitting as a juror on this case

Concluding questions

As you can see, a juror questionnaire in a high-profile case covers a lot of material.

Voir Dire

Before any evidence can be presented, the actual jurors for the case must be selected. Since all parties to a case are entitled to a fair and impartial jury, potential jurors are questioned, under oath, by the judge and by the attorneys to learn if there is any bias or other reason that a person cannot sit as a juror. This questioning process is known as **voir dire.** This questioning process will take place in open court. Sample voir dire questions might include the following:

voir dire
The process of questioning the jury to determine their suitability to serve on a jury panel; the prospective jurors may be questioned by the court (the judge) and the attorneys for both parties.

"Do you know any of the parties or attorneys to this case?"

"Have you ever been involved in a similar case?"

If it appears that there is a bias or other legitimate reason that a person cannot sit as a juror, then that individual will be **excused for cause.** Since no party ever has to accept a biased individual on a jury, the number of potential jurors who can be excused (or challenged) for cause is unlimited.

excused for cause
Jurors may be excused for cause if it appears that there is bias or other legitimate reasons that a person cannot sit as a juror.

In addition to excuses or challenges for cause, each side is allowed a limited number of **peremptory challenges.** Peremptory challenges allow an attorney to excuse individuals without stating a reason.

peremptory challenge
The right of an attorney to challenge a prospective juror without stating a reason for the challenge.

When the attorneys have selected the proper number of jurors (which varies from six to twelve, depending on the state), the jurors are *sworn in;* that is, they take an oath to judge the facts of the case truly and fairly.

SEC. 17-5 OPENING STATEMENTS

opening statement
An attorney's first opportunity to address the jury with a summary of the case; it might include a summary of the facts and an outline of the evidence that the attorney plans to present.

Before any evidence is presented, each side is allowed to make an **opening statement.** These are the first statements made to the jury by the attorneys. An opening statement provides an initial picture of the case and the evidence that will be presented at trial. This is an important starting point in any case. The plaintiff will make the first opening statement. Following is a small portion of the opening statement made by defense counsel for Officer Laurence Powell in the Rodney King case. The format you see is what a transcript of court proceedings actually looks like.

People v. Powell

Transcript: Opening Statement of Defendant
Laurence M. Powell by Attorney Michael Stone
MARCH 5, 1992, THURSDAY

Opening statement by Mr. Stone:

Mr. Stone: May it please the court, good morning, ladies and gentlemen, my name is Michael Stone and I have the privilege in this proceeding of representing officer Laurence Powell.

Stand up, Larry, please. Thank you.

I hope in my brief remarks this morning in the form of an opening statement that what I have to say will be helpful to you during the course of this trial as you hear and see the evidence come in.

During the past month all of you have been subjected to jury selection where you have told us all about yourself and answered written questions, and before getting into the evidence, I would like just to take a minute and introduce you to defendant Laurence Powell.

He is a 29-year-old single man—

Mr. White: Objection, your honor.

The Court: All right.

Let's confine ourselves to the evidence at this point. You will have an opportunity to introduce other material as the trial progresses, Mr. Stone.

Mr. Stone: Thank you, your honor.

Joined the Los Angeles police department as a police reserve officer in 1984 and found that police work agreed with him.

Mr. White: Objection, Your Honor.

The Court: Yeah. Let's not get into that sort of editorializing. Let's confine ourselves to the evidence.

Mr. Stone: After serving as a reserve officer for three years he joined the regular police department entering the Police Academy.

Mr. White: Excuse me. Objection. We seem to be continuing the same line.

The Court: All right. This, as far as his experience and training, is relevant, but let's keep it confined to the bare bones.

You may proceed.

Mr. Stone: Graduated from the police academy, started serving on the Los Angeles Police Department as a patrol officer. He was promoted to police officer 3, became a Field Training Officer in 1991, and was assigned to Foothill Division as a Field Training Officer.

The job of a Field Training Officer is to instruct new police officers or rookies, as they're called, in field police work, and in fact on March 3rd, 1991, the date of this incident, he was assigned as a field training officer and had in his charge Officer Timothy Wind, another defendant in this case.

Turning to the evidence that you will see during this case, as Mr. White mentioned to you, it all began at about 12:30 in the morning on March 3rd, 1991.

(continued)

Officers Melanie and Tim Singer, California Highway Patrol, husband and wife, with Mrs. Singer driving the car westbound on the 210 freeway at normal speed.

Mrs. Singer will testify that she noticed the car approaching from the rear westbound at a high rate of speed. At this point the CHP cruiser was between Laguna Canyon Road and Sunland.

Wishing to get a clock on the car from behind, the Singers took the Sunland offramp and then immediately reentered the freeway heading westbound behind the car, which it develops is the white Hyundai driven by Rodney King and containing his two passengers.

By the time Mrs. Singer got up to speed on the freeway, Mr. King's car was already one mile ahead, and as Mr. White told you, she accelerated the CHP cruiser to the top speed and estimated that Mr. King was traveling in excess of 100 miles per hour.

Continuing on westbound on the freeway, Mr. King encountered slower moving traffic also traveling westbound so he had to slow to 80 miles an hour. At that point Mrs. Singer was able to catch Mr. King's car and pull the CHP cruiser to w/in 75 feet of Mr. King's car.

She activated the red lights and the emergency lights of the police car. No reaction from Mr. King. She tried the alternating headlights on the CHP cruiser. No reaction from Mr. King. She then activated the siren. Again no reaction from Mr. King.

Excuse me a minute.

(Brief pause.)

Mr. Stone: She continued to follow Mr. King at 75 feet, lights going, alternating headlights going, siren going, Mr. King does not yield. He continues at 80 miles an hour westbound and takes the Paxton Street offramp. The car speeds down the offramp, ignores the stop sign at the bottom of the offramp, turning left onto Paxton Street.

After turning left on Paxton the car passed through the Foothill Boulevard intersection again against a red light at 45 miles per hour, continued what would be southbound on Paxton toward the intersection of Glenoaks.

Now, ladies and gentlemen, the evidence is going to be that this entire chase covered a distance of 7.8 miles. Fully four miles of this chase was on surface streets where the speed limits did not exceed 34 miles per hour.

If you are not familiar with the area, it is no matter, we have a tape which you will see later in this case that will show you the route of the pursuit and you can see these various intersections that I'm going to talk to you about today.

As Mr. King drove southbound on Paxton Street, he reached speeds of 80 miles per hour. Again, remember the CHP cruiser is right behind him, red lights and sirens going, no reaction.

SEC. 17-6 PLAINTIFF'S CASE IN CHIEF

case in chief
The part of the trial where the plaintiff presents evidence.

rules of evidence
Statutes that govern the admissibility of evidence.

The plaintiff will present his or her **case in chief** through the testimony of various witnesses. Witnesses may include the injured person, eyewitnesses, physicians, experts, and the police. Each jurisdiction has **rules of evidence.** These rules make clear who may testify.

Factual Background

Maria applied her brakes but could not stop at a red light. She injured herself when she ran into a tree in an attempt to stop her car. She claims that her brakes did not work. Her brakes were serviced by Ace Auto Repair two days prior to the accident. Her brother, Stephan, took her to Ace and helped her explain the problem to Harry, who manages Ace. Stephan was also with Maria when she picked up her car and heard Harry tell Maria that her brakes "were just like new." Maria is suing Ace Auto Repair for the injuries she sustained in the accident and for the damage to her car. She claims that Ace was negligent in the repair of her car.

burden of proof
The necessity of establishing a particular fact or the necessity of going forward with the evidence.

cross-examination
Questioning that occurs when a witness is questioned by someone other than the direct examiner; in other words, questioning by opposing counsel, after the party who called the witness has completed his or her examination.

redirect examination
Examination of a witness that occurs when the direct examiner questions the witness after the cross-examination.

recross-examination
Examination of a witness that occurs when the cross-examiner questions the witness after the redirect examination.

rest
An attorney rests his or her client's case by telling the court that his or her presentation of evidence is complete.

In Maria's negligence case, she will testify about the repair work she paid to have done at Ace Auto Repair. Her attorney will call Stephan to the witness stand to explain what he saw and heard. The physician Maria saw after the accident may testify as to her injuries. The officer who first arrived at the accident may testify as to what Maria said to him just after the accident occurred.

BURDEN OF PROOF

The **burden of proof** falls upon the plaintiff. In a civil case, the plaintiff must prove (1) that a civil wrong was committed and (2) that a preponderance of the evidence shows that the defendant is liable for that wrong. In a criminal case, the prosecutor must prove (1) that a crime has been committed and (2) that the evidence shows that the defendant is guilty beyond a reasonable doubt. The civil standard of a preponderance of the evidence is a lesser standard of proof.

EXAMINATION OF WITNESSES

After this evidence has been presented by the plaintiff's attorney, the attorney for the defendant has the opportunity to conduct a **cross-examination** of any or all of the witnesses called by the plaintiff. If the attorney for the plaintiff feels that defense counsel has damaged the case through the questioning of the witnesses or has confused an issue, he or she may choose to do a **redirect examination** of one or more witnesses to clarify any necessary points. Finally, the defense has an opportunity to perform a **recross-examination** of any of the witnesses called by the plaintiff. At this point, the plaintiff **rests** his or her case.

People v. Martinez

207 A.2d 284, 615 N.Y.S.2d 383 (1994)

In this case the court discusses whether certain comments by the judge misled the jury about which party has the burden of proof during trial.

OPINION

Judgment rendered April 7, 1992, convicting defendant, after a jury trial, of the criminal sale of a controlled substance in the third degree and sentencing him, as a second felony offender, to an indeterminate term of from six to twelve years imprisonment, unanimously affirmed.

There is no merit to defendant's contention raised for the first time on appeal, that the trial court impermissibly shifted the burden of proof from the prosecution when, upon objection by the prosecutor to defense counsel's statement that ". . . the police, as you will learn, control everything that goes on in the streets and that comes into this courtroom," it interrupted the defense's opening statement to say "Mr. Stone, get to what you will show." Considered in the context of the defense's opening statement, and coupled with the fact that defense counsel went on with his opening to tell the jury how, in an effort to create a reasonable doubt in their mind, defendant would "show" how buy and bust operations are carefully orchestrated by the police who, according to counsel, "use scripts like on T.V.," the court's statement clearly constituted the proper exercise of its sound discretion in monitoring the conduct of the trial. Moreover, when considered in context, none of the court's other rulings or comments, now complained of, conveyed any opinion of the court regarding the case. The court also appropriately exercised its discretion in precluding the proposed defense pharmacological expert upon its finding, after a hearing, that defendant's offer of proof failed to establish or satisfy the standard for admissibility of his proposed testimony; *viz.,* that the principle espoused by the proposed expert witness enjoyed general acceptance in the field.

Finally, as to defendant's claims regarding allegedly improper comments by the prosecutor in her opening and closing arguments, none of these statements were objected to and such claims are both unpreserved for review and without merit.

CASE ANALYSIS

1. Explain the defendant's argument in this appeal.
2. Explain the court's reasoning and ultimate conclusion

SEC. 17-7 DEFENDANT'S CASE

In the preceding auto accident case, the attorney for Ace Auto Repair will call Harry to explain his version of what the parties said, what work was requested, and what work was performed.

EXAMINATION OF WITNESSES

In addition, the defendant's attorney might call to the stand the mechanic who actually performed the work on the car. After the defendant's case is presented, the attorney for the plaintiff will cross-examine the witnesses for the defense. In this case, Harry and the mechanic would be cross-examined. The defendant's attorney will then conduct a redirect examination, if necessary. The plaintiff's attorney may conduct a recross-examination of any of the defendant's witnesses.

SEC. 17-8 PLAINTIFF'S REBUTTAL CASE

rebuttal
Presentation of evidence and additional witnesses in response to evidence and issues raised in the defendant's case in chief.

At this point the plaintiff's attorney may present evidence in **rebuttal** to issues raised in the defendant's case. The evidence must be in response to evidence and issues raised in the defendant's case.

SEC. 17-9 CLOSING ARGUMENTS

closing argument
The argument given just prior to the judge instructing the jury; the attorney's last opportunity to address the court and the jury. It includes a summary of the facts, issues, evidence, and conclusions that may be drawn from the evidence.

Both of the parties have rested, or completed their cases. It is now time to close or summarize their arguments to the jury. In a **closing argument,** each attorney will try to highlight the evidence most favorable to his or her client. This is the last opportunity for the attorneys to address the jury on behalf of their clients. This can be crucial to ultimately persuading the jury to view their evidence favorably. The plaintiff usually closes first. The following is an excerpt from the closing argument given by the government in the Waco case.

United States v. Branch Davidians
FIRST CLOSING ARGUMENT ON BEHALF OF THE GOVERNMENT

MR. JOHNSTON: I speak today on behalf of the United States of America. The Defendants like to call us "the Government," "the Government." They want and they demand—they do—to be known as individuals. They don't want to be grouped or linked together, they want to be known as individuals, not a group or a cult. They want to be known as individuals, and in fact, they are individuals. They are individuals responsible for their own conduct, but we are individuals, too.

"Steve" Willis and "Rob" Williams and Conway LeBleu and Todd McKeehan are individuals, they are people. They are not the Government, they are people. And today I represent those four men, I argue on their behalf today.

Let me take just a—less than a moment to comment on your jury service. You have been an attentive and very patient jury. It's been a long haul here. You did not volunteer for this service, but yet when you were called, you served, and surely you will finish out your service with the dedication that you have shown thus far. And that's all I'm going to say about that, but it's been apparent—your dedication and patience has been very apparent.

I'm going to talk to you about the law that applies in this case, some of it. I obviously won't go over the whole thing again. I'm going to talk to you about just a couple of areas, and then I'm going to talk to you about the facts.

Now, we have had expert witnesses in this case, several, people who had a special skill or area that they really knew and could relate. Now you join their club today, because now—really, today and hereafter—you are the experts on the facts of this case. You may have recalled or you may remember that during the trial, at various points, a witness would say something, A, B and C, and immediately an attorney for whichever side would say, "Now,

(continued)

you just said A, B and F, isn't that right?" And maybe you had a quizzical look on your face and maybe today you wonder, "My gosh, can't anybody get these facts straight?" But at this point, you all are the experts on the facts. Don't let me or anybody else tell you, that is, force you to certain facts. You know what the facts are, you know what the facts are.

You remember the cross-examine—Judge Smith told you early on, questions of attorneys and arguments and so forth, that's not facts. Cross-examination questions aren't facts.

How many hours did we sit here and listen to cross-examination questions about things that were never proven? "You—you know that benzine—an element in the periodic table, benzine is in tear gas." "Nope." Next witness. "The old benzine and tear gas, right?" "Nope." As an example that, but many times, you heard cross-examination questions and argument and there was nothing to support that. Okay. That's just—those aren't facts. The facts are what you recall that witnesses stated that then you want to believe, because you can regard or disregard anything you heard, it is totally up to you. You are truly the experts on the facts, and like I say, don't let me or when other folks start arguing here this afternoon or here in a little bit, don't let anybody force you in your recollection. You will be surprised, individually and collectively—based on your memory and probably aided by your notes, you will be surprised, you will recall the facts, the facts necessary.

You may not remember every detail, and we don't have to prove every detail, folks. And everything mentioned in the Indictment in terms of the manner and means, we don't have to prove that. I think we have proven that, but we have to prove—

MR. TINKER: Your Honor, I object to him saying what he thinks he has proven. That's one of the instructions you gave them—

THE COURT: Sustain the objection.

MR. JOHNSTON: The evidence will indicate that those points have been proven. But it's only necessary that you find the things listed. And you—when you were read the instructions, it mentions, you know, one two, three and four, so forth. An overt act must be found by you. The evidence indicates that pretty well all of those things mentioned in the Indictment were proven. But at any rate, your memories will—will sustain you and you will be able to do your job, no doubt about it.

What about the law of conspiracy, the law of conspiracy? To some it might sound formal and complicated and worrisome. "My gosh, a conspiracy, a conspiracy, oh, a conspiracy." It's quite simple. Merely an implied understanding—merely an implied understanding to do something against the law can be a conspiracy. That's it, there is nothing weird or complicated about it. . . .

Notice the similarities and differences when you compare the closing statement in the Waco case with the opening statement given in the Rodney King case.

Windsor v. State of Alabama

683 So.2d 1021 (1994)

I. OPINION

Harvey Lee Windsor was convicted of capital murder under § 13A-5–40(a) (2), Ala. Code 1975, and was sentenced to death by electrocution. Windsor appealed the conviction and sentence to the Court of Criminal Appeals. That court reversed the conviction and remanded for a new trial, holding that the prosecutor had improperly referred to Windsor's failure to testify at trial and holding that the circuit clerk's practice of excusing potential jurors to whom jury service would prove burdensome constituted reversible error. We granted certiorari review. We reverse the judgment of the Court of Criminal Appeals and remand the case to that court for action consistent with this opinion.

II. DISCUSSION

During closing argument, the following exchange occurred:

> [Prosecution]: An intentional act—[the Judge] will tell you a person acts intentionally if his purpose is to cause that result or to engage in that conduct. That intent, whether Mr. Harvey Lee Windsor pulled the trigger of that sawed-off shotgun or whether Colan Lavon Guthrie did it, is still there. The intent to kill. Intent is a state of mind—something that is rarely capable of positive proof. I expect the Judge will tell you that. If we could get into that mind over there and put out here what is in there, we would have no reason for a jury.
>
> [Defense counsel]: Object, that is improper argument.
>
> [The Court]: Overruled.
>
> [Prosecution]: I'll tell you that he did have the intent to kill. If you find the intent to kill, there can be but one verdict. The state of mind—not capable of positive proof. How can you decide what his intent was? We have to prove—to find him guilty of capital murder—the intent. Intent can be inferred from his actions. Judge Austin will tell you in his charge that the intent can be inferred from his actions. Let's look at his actions. What did he do? How do we decide his intent? What are his actions?

As this Court recently held in *Ex parte Musgrove,* "[w]hen an accused contends that a prosecutor has made improper comments during a closing argument, the statements at issue must be viewed in the context of the evidence presented in the case and the entire closing arguments made to the jury. . . ." *Washington v. State,* 259 Ala. 104, 65 So. 2d 704 (1953). In this case, the prosecutor was explaining the difference between felony murder and capital murder, and arguing that the State had proven Windsor guilty of capital murder. In order to do so, the State had to prove Windsor's intent to kill.

In this narrow context, it is apparent that the prosecutor was referring not to Windsor's failure to testify, but rather to the State's own failure to produce direct evidence of Windsor's intent. The only way for the State to prove intent, and, therefore, to obtain a conviction on the capital murder charge, was to show that Windsor acted in accordance with an intent to kill. In a certain sense, what the prosecutor said was true. To mangle the maxim, it could be said that were we able to peer into the hearts of men, there would be no question of fact to be resolved by the jury concerning the specific issue of the defendant's state of mind at the time of the offense. However, resolution of that specific issue is certainly not the full extent of the jury's function, and even indirect comments on an accused's failure to testify have the potential to be highly prejudicial to the defense. *Musgrove.*

Alabama, by statute, specifically protects the privilege against self-incrimination from comment by the prosecution. § 12–21–220, Ala. Code 1975. A prosecutor must be extremely careful not to overstep the mark or to break with the established protocol regarding statements about that privilege. *Musgrove.* To improperly comment on that privilege would be a clear violation of the defendant's rights under Article I, § 6, Ala. Const. 1901, as well as the rights protected by the Fifth Amendment as that Amendment is incorporated into the Fourteenth Amendment to the United States Constitution.

In *Ex parte Wilson,* 571 So. 2d 1251, 1261 (Ala. 1990), this Court cited the standard endorsed by the United States Court of Appeals for the Eleventh Circuit:

> [A] statement by a prosecutor is improper if it was manifestly intended to be, or was of such a character that the jury would naturally and necessarily take it to be, a comment on the failure of the accused to testify. *Marsden v. Moore,* 847 F.2d 1536, 1547 (11th Cir.), cert. denied, 488 U.S. 983, 109 S. Ct. 534, 102 L. Ed. 2d 566 (1988).

We cannot say that the statement made in this case was intended to be a remark on Windsor's failure to testify; nor can we conclude that the natural and necessary reaction of the jury would be to conclude that the prosecutor was referring to Windsor's failure to take the stand in his own defense. We hold that the trial court properly overruled the objection to the prosecutor's statement.

CASE ANALYSIS

1. What is the legal issue before the court?
2. When is a statement by a prosecutor improper?

SEC. 17-10 JUDGE'S INSTRUCTIONS TO THE JURY

After meeting with the attorneys to consider which jury instructions will be given to the jury, the judge will instruct the jury. Both sides to the litigation will suggest certain instructions. The judge decides which instructions to give based upon (1) the legal and factual arguments, (2) the overall appropriateness of the instruction, (3) whether sufficient evidence was presented during the trial, and (4) recommended or pattern jury instructions for the jurisdiction.

Sample Jury Instructions

Weighing Conflicting Testimony

You are not bound to decide according to the testimony of a number of witnesses, which does not convince you, as against the testimony of a smaller number or other evidence, which is more convincing to you. The testimony of one witnesses worthy of belief is sufficient to prove any fact. This does not mean that you are free to disregard the testimony of any witness merely from caprice or prejudice, or from a desire to favor either side. It does mean that you must not decide anything by simply counting the number of witnesses who have testified on the opposing sides. The test is not the number of witnesses, but the convincing form of the evidence.

From the Committee on Standard Jury Instructions, Civil, of the Superior Court of Los Angeles, California

Employment Contract—Definition

A contract of employment is a contract by which one person, called the employer, engages another person, called the employee, to do something for the benefit of the employer or a third person for which the employee receives compensation. The contract may be oral or written.

From the Committee on Standard Jury Instructions, Civil, of the Superior Court of Los Angeles, California

As part of the jury instructions, the judge explains the jury process and the role of the jurors. The jury must follow the instructions, as the trier of fact. The judge will explain how the evidence presented is to be evaluated. The cause of action (in civil law) or the crime (in criminal law) will be defined and explained. The judge will explain the process of jury deliberation and any restrictions that will be placed on the jurors.

The following jury instructions were given in the *United States v. Koon* case. Pay close attention to how the judge attempts to make the law easy for the jury to understand. Each cause of action is broken down into simple, easy-to-follow elements. These jury instructions are only a portion of the instructions actually read to the jury in the *Koon* case.

United States v. Koon
TRANSCRIPT: JURY INSTRUCTIONS

April 10, 1993

THE COURT: Now, ladies and gentlemen, this is the time when the Court must instruct you on the law that applies to this case.

During the course of instructions, no one in the courtroom is permitted to leave. That is simply for the reason we don't want the distraction. The instructions are read only once. They are of extreme importance, and it's essential that the jurors not be distracted during this reading. So if you wish to leave, now is the time.

Members of the jury, now that you have heard all of the evidence and the arguments of attorneys, it is my duty to instruct you on the law which applies to this case. A copy of these instructions will be available for you in the jury room for you to consult if you find it necessary.

It is your duty to find the facts from all of the evidence in this case. To those facts, you will apply the law as I give it to you. You must follow the law as I give it to you, whether your agree with it or not. And you must not be influenced by any personal likes or dislikes, opinions, prejudices or sympathy. That means that you must decide the case solely on the evidence before you. You will recall that you took an oath promising to do so at the beginning of the case.

In following my instructions, you must follow all of them and not single out some and ignore others. They are all equally important. And you must not read into these instructions or into anything the Court may have said or done, any suggestion as to what verdicts you should return. That is a matter entirely up to you.

This is a criminal case brought by the United States government. Count 1 of the indictment charges that on or about March 3, 1991, Defendants Powell, Wind and Briseno, while acting under color of law, willfully violated Rodney King's constitutionally protected right to be free from the use of unreasonable force during arrest, and that Defendants Powell, Wind and Briseno aided and abetted each other in doing so.

Count 2 of the indictment charges that on or about March 3, 1991. Defendant Koon, while acting under color of law, willfully violated Rodney King's constitutionally protected right to be kept from harm while in custody.

All of the defendants have pleaded not guilty to the charges in the indictment. The indictment is not evidence. The defendants are presumed innocent, and do not have to testify or present any evidence to prove innocence.

(continued)

The government has the burden of proving every element of each charge beyond a reasonable doubt. If it fails to do so, you must return verdicts of not guilty.

You must presume that the defendants are innocent of the crimes charged against them. Thus, a defendant, although accused of a crime in the indictment, begins the trial with a clean slate, with no evidence against him.

The indictment is not evidence of any kind. The law permits nothing but legal evidence presented before the jury in court to be considered in support of any charge against an individual defendant. The presumption of innocence alone, therefore, is sufficient basis for a verdict of not guilty as to a defendant.

The burden is always upon the government to prove guilt beyond a reasonable doubt. This burden never shifts to a defendant, for the law never imposes upon a defendant the burden or duty of calling any witnesses or producing any evidence. The defendant is not even obligated to produce any evidence by cross-examining the witnesses for the government.

It is not required that the government prove guilt beyond all possible doubt. The test is one of reasonable doubt. A reasonable doubt is a doubt based upon reason and common sense, the kind of doubt that would make a reasonable person hesitate to act.

Proof beyond a reasonable doubt must therefore be proof of such a convincing character that a reasonable person would not hesitate to rely and act upon it in the most important of his or her own affairs.

If, after a careful and impartial consideration with your fellow jurors of all the evidence, you are not convinced beyond a reasonable doubt that an individual defendant is guilty, it is your duty to find such defendant not guilty.

On the other hand, if, after a careful and impartial consideration with your fellow jurors of all the evidence, you are convinced beyond a reasonable doubt that an individual defendant is guilty, it is your duty to find such defendant guilty.

It is not required that the government prove guilt beyond all possible doubt. The test is one of reasonable doubt. A reasonable doubt is a doubt based upon reason and common sense, and may arise from a careful and impartial considerations of all the evidence or from lack of evidence.

Proof beyond a reasonable doubt is proof that leaves you firmly convinced that a defendant is guilty.

Each defendant is on trial only for the crimes charged in the indictment, not for any other activities.

The indictment in this case contains two counts. Count 1 is against the Defendants Powell, Wind and Briseno.

Count 2 is against Defendant Koon only.

These instructions refer to "defendant" in the singular. This is because you must apply the instructions to each defendant individually. The fact that Count 1 contains charges against three defendants does not mean that you may consider the defendants collectively.

The government must prove every element of each offense against each defendant. If the government fails to prove each element of the offense charged beyond a reasonable doubt as to any individual defendant, you must find that defendant not guilty.

A separate crime has been charged against each defendant. The charges have been joined for trial. You must consider and decide the case of each defendant separately. Your verdict as to one defendant should not control your verdict as to any other defendant.

All of the instructions apply to each defendant, unless a particular instruction states that it applies only to a specific defendant.

Count 1 of the indictment charges that Defendants Powell, Wind and Briseno violated Section 242 of Title 18, United States Code, and aided and abetted each other in doing so.

Count 2 of the indictment charges that Defendant Koon violated Section 242 of Title 18, United States Code. The relevant portion of Section 242 reads as follows.

> "Whoever, under color of law, statute, ordinance, regulation or custom, willfully subjects an inhabitant of any state, territory or district to the deprivation of any rights, privileges or immunities secured or protected by the constitutional laws of the United States, shall be guilty of an offense against the United States."

The Fourth and Fourteenth Amendments of the Constitution of the United States guarantee certain rights relevant to this case.

The Fourth Amendment guarantees the right to be free from unreasonable searches and seizures. A use by police officers of unreasonable force during an arrest constitutes an unreasonable seizure within the meaning of the Fourth Amendment of the Constitution.

The Fourteenth Amendment of the Constitution guarantees that one will not be deprived of his liberty without due process of law. The right to due process of law includes the right to be kept from harm while in official custody.

At this time, I will read the indictment for you. Count 1 reads as follows:

On or about March 3, 1991, in Los Angeles, California, within the Central District of California, Defendants Laurence M. Powell, Timothy E. Wind and Theodore J. Briseno, then police officers with the Los Angeles Police Department, while acting under color of the laws of the State of California, aiding and abetting each other, did willfully strike with batons, kick and stomp Rodney Glen King, an inhabitant of the State of California, resulting in bodily injury to Rodney Glenn King, and thereby did willfully deprive Rodney Glenn King of the right to be preserved and protected by the Constitution of the United States not to be deprived of liberty without due process of law, including the right to be secure in his person, and free from the intentional use of unreasonable force by one making an arrest under color of law, all in violation of Title 18, United States Code Section 2 and 242.

(continued)

Count 2 reads as follows:

On or about March 3, 1991 in Los Angeles, California, within the Central District of California, Defendant Stacey C. Koon, then a sergeant with the Los Angeles Police Department, while acting under color of the laws of the State of California, did willfully permit other Los Angeles police officers in his presence and under his supervision, namely Laurence M. Powell, Timothy E. Wind and Theodore J. Briseno, unlawfully to strike with batons, kick and stomp Rodney Glenn King, an inhabitant of the State of California, while Rodney Glenn King was in the custody of those officers, and did willfully fail to prevent this unlawful assault, resulting in bodily injury to Rodney Glenn King, and thereby did willfully deprive Rodney Glenn King of the right preserved and protected by the Constitution of the United States not be deprived of liberty without due process of law, including the right to be kept free from harm while in official custody, all in violation of Title 18, United States Code, Section 242.

The government must prove beyond a reasonable doubt each of the following five elements to establish the offenses charged in Counts 1 and 2.

First, the person upon whom the alleged acts were committed must have been an inhabitant of a state, district or territory of the United States, here, the State of California.

Second, the defendant must have been acting under color of law.

Third, the conduct of the defendant must have deprived the inhabitant of some right secured or protected by the Constitution or laws of the United States.

Fourth, the defendant must have acted willfully; that is, with a specific intent to violate the protective constitutional right.

And fifth, the offense must have resulted in bodily injury.

The first element of the offenses charged in Counts 1 and 2 requires proof beyond a reasonable doubt that the victim is an inhabitant of a state or territory; here, California. A person is an inhabitant for these purposes if he is present within the State of California at the time of the offense.

If you find that Rodney King was physically present in California at the time of the incident in charge, then you may find that he was then an inhabitant of the state within the meaning of the statute.

The second element requires proof beyond a reasonable doubt that the defendant acted under color of law. The term "color of law" means that a defendant acted in his official capacity, or claimed to do so.

In order to convict the defendant, you must find beyond a reasonable doubt that at the time of the offense, he was acting or purporting to act, in his official capacity as a police officer.

The third element that the government must prove beyond a reasonable doubt is that the conduct of a defendant or defendants deprived the inhabitant of the right secured or protected by the constitutional laws of the United States.

Count 1 charges Defendants Powell, Wind and Briseno with violating certain constitutional rights, and Count 2 charges Defendant Koon with violating different constitutional rights.

Count 1 of the indictment charges Defendants Powell, Wind and Briseno with using unreasonable force. All persons present in the United States have the legal right, as guaranteed in the Fourth Amendment in the United States

Constitution, to be free from unreasonable seizures, which includes the right to be free from unreasonable use of force during an arrest.

A police officer may use that amount of force which is reasonable to make an arrest, or to defend himself or another from bodily harm. He may not, however, use more force than is reasonable to accomplish these purposes.

If you find that a defendant used force in this case, you should then consider whether the force used by that defendant was reasonable. Reasonable force is that which would appear reasonable to an ordinary, reasonable officer under the same circumstances.

To determine whether the defendants used reasonable force, you should consider all the circumstances as they would be viewed by a reasonable officer under the same circumstances.

A POINT TO REMEMBER

Jury instructions explain the law. They are an excellent source of simple explanations of the law. In your study of the law, remember that pattern/suggested jury instructions are available in most law libraries. They help you understand and analyze the law.

SEC. 17-11 JURY DELIBERATIONS AND THE VERDICT

deliberation
The process of analyzing and discussing the evidence heard during the course of the trial by the jury; it takes place in the jury room without the judge or the attorneys present.

sequester
To isolate; a jury may be isolated from contact with the media and the public during a trial.

The **deliberation** of the jury takes place in private. This allows the jurors to speak openly and work as a group. In most cases, the jury will retire to a *jury room* connected to the courtroom. In high-profile cases, such as the O. J. Simpson and Rodney King beating trials, the jury is **sequestered.** This means that when the jury are not actually deliberating, they are confined to a hotel. The bailiff will watch all jurors to be sure that they are not speaking to other jurors about the case outside of the deliberation room, or reading the newspaper, or watching the news, or speaking to nonjurors about the trial.

Featured Web Site: www.umkc.edu/famoustrials

A professor at the University of Missouri Law School has created a wonderful collection of resources from famous trials.

Go Online

1. Choose a trial.
2. Review the materials.
3. Create a summary of the trial.

In most cases, the jury is able to reach a decision. The number of jurors required for a decision is determined by the jurisdiction. When they are not able to agree, the rules of the specific jurisdiction will dictate what further instruction may be given to the jurors and whether or not a mistrial must be declared.

verdict
The formal decision of a jury.

Once the jury reaches a **verdict,** the court reconvenes. The verdict is first shown to the judge and is then read into the court record.

Chapter Summary

The American judicial system provides people with the opportunity to settle their disputes in a public forum. This is an essential element of what makes our legal system work. A typical trial will include a judge, a court clerk, a court reporter, the plaintiff's attorney (or, in a criminal matter, the prosecutor), the defendant's attorney, a jury, and a bailiff. There will also be parties to the action and witnesses. Some issues may be resolved before the trial begins through the use of pretrial motions. Once the parties and the court are prepared to proceed, a jury is selected. After the jury is impaneled, the parties will each present an opening statement. Opening statements are often used to acquaint the jury and the judge with the facts and the issues from the perspective of the party offering the opening statement. Remember, the prosecutor's opening statement may be quite different from the opening statement made by the defense attorney. Following the opening statements, the parties will present their cases. It is at this point that witnesses are called and evidence is presented. After each party has rested its case, the closing arguments are presented to the court and the jury. Finally, the judge instructs the jury and the jury then deliberates. After deliberation, the jury will deliver its verdict.

Terms to Remember

trial
brief
voir dire
excused for cause
peremptory challenge
opening statement
case in chief
rules of evidence
burden of proof
cross-examination
redirect examination
recross-examination
rest
rebuttal
closing argument
deliberation
sequester
verdict

Questions for Review

1. Describe the roles of the trial participants.
2. What is a jury questionnaire?
3. Explain the importance of an opening statement.
4. What is the prosecutor's burden of proof in a criminal case?
5. What is the plaintiff's burden of proof in a civil case?
6. Explain the importance of a closing statement.
7. What are jury instructions?
8. Why are some juries sequestered?

Questions for Analysis

1. Write a case brief for the *Windsor* case. Include the facts, issues, rules, analysis, and conclusion.
2. How do the responses to a jury questionnaire help an attorney choose jurors?

Assignments and Projects

1. A mock trial is located in Appendix III. Your class will actually prepare a criminal case for trial. A review of Chapters 10, 12, and 14 will help you with this project. Your instructor will provide additional instructions.

2. Locate the jury instructions for your state. Find the jury instructions listed in the Case File at the beginning of this chapter. Your instructor will be able to direct you to the proper resources. Make copies of your findings. Do not copy more than three for each.
3. Attend a local trial (civil or criminal). Write a summary of both opening arguments, the plaintiff's case in chief, the defendant's case, and both closing arguments.
4. What is the legal issue before the United States Supreme Court in *Texas v. Cobb*? The case syllabus (summary) is found in Appendix VII.

CHAPTER 18

TECHNOLOGY AND LAW PRACTICE

A PARALEGAL PERSPECTIVE

Technology Corner

Web Address	Name of Site
www.cyberbar.net/	Cyberspace Bar Association
www.epic.org/	Electronic Privacy Information Center
cyber.lp.findlaw.com/	Findlaw Cyberspace Law Center
www.gahtan.com/cyberlaw/	Cyberlaw Encyclopedia

CASE FILE: *MICRO INC. V. DOGGIE IN THE WINDOW RECORD CO.*

Micro Inc. set up a Web site where music fans share their music. Micro uses technology known as MP3, which allows users to easily download and copy their music. Doggie in the Window Record Co. has threatened to sue Micro Inc. for copyright infringement. Micro Inc. decided to seek legal advice. In preparation for their meeting with an attorney, the officers of Micro Inc. reviewed their files for relevant documents. Including contracts, written correspondence, and e-mails, they identified more than four thousand different documents. They are sure that there are many more.

SEC. 18-1 INTRODUCTION

A law firm is a business office, and anyone working in a law office must have basic office and computer skills. Today, even attorneys are often expected to have general office skills. Maintaining office files, being familiar with billing procedures, communicating with clients, and writing business letters are all important skills for working in a law firm. If you work in a law office, you must be comfortable using a computer to accomplish all of these tasks. This means that you must be familiar with appropriate computer hardware and software. You must also know how to navigate the Internet.

The modern law office looks nothing like the office of twenty years ago. The way that litigators try cases, the way that business lawyers prepare documents, and the way that all lawyers do their legal research is new. The law office of years ago could never effectively handle cases such as *Micro Inc. v. Doggie in the Window Record Co.*, the case described in the Case File. However, computers and appropriate software now make it possible to manage thousands and even hundreds of thousands documents. Computer technology is also essential to the sole practitioner who handles much smaller cases. Even the simplest documents are generated by computers. Accompanying the increased use of technology is the growing popularity and importance of the paralegal in the law office. Law firms that handle cases such as the one described in the Case File often hire dozens of paralegals to help with litigation tasks in a single case. Smaller offices often rely on one paralegal to work on multiple cases. Paralegals, like technology, are a valuable resource in all types of law firms. Previous chapters discussed the general nature of the paralegal profession as well as the effect of technology on the substantive law. This chapter discusses the day-to-day practice of law from a paralegal perspective. It also examines the role of technology in that practice.

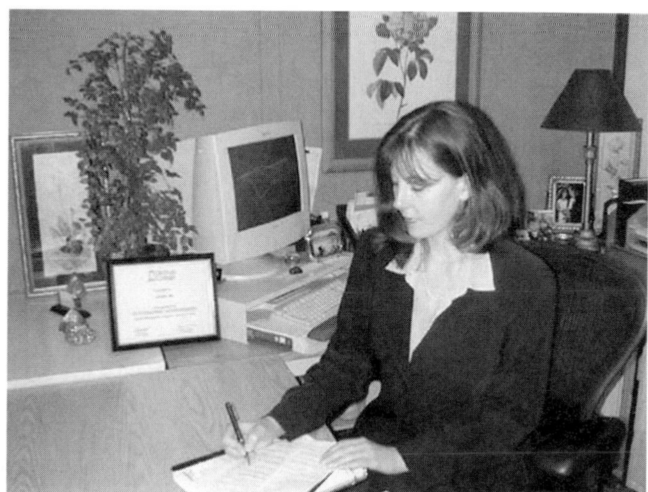

Computers are an essential tool in any law office.

SEC. 18-2 THE MODERN LAW OFFICE

The modern law office is equipped with the latest technology tools. Computer hardware, software, and Internet connection are standard, both in and out of the office. As technology develops, the legal profession will take advantage of it. The following is a list of the technology tools that are standard in law firms.

Computer Hardware

Basic computer—No office is complete without the mainstay of technology, the computer.

Laptop computer—Many attorneys feel the need to carry laptops wherever they go. This allows them to work outside their office. No longer must they waste time at court waiting for a case to be called or for a client to appear. Furthermore, a great deal of information is always available to them.

Scanner—Rekeying lengthy documents can be avoided with the use of a scanner and proper software.

Copy machines—Modern copy machines copy, collate, staple, and more. Most copiers have internal computers that allow the user to keep track of the copies made for each client, so that the client is accurately billed for the cost of copies related to his or her case.

Fax machines—Attorneys frequently communicate quickly with one another and with their clients via fax machine. Many courts accept documents via fax.

PDA (Personal Digital Assistant) —These small handheld computers (such as the PalmPilot) allow attorneys to keep track of court appearances and appointments as well as other important dates. Names and phone numbers can be stored. Newer versions have limited wireless Internet connection, allowing the user to send and receive e-mail. Limited access to legal databases such as Westlaw is also available.

Digital cameras—Trial lawyers can photograph evidence and use the digital photos at trial. Key parts of the photo can be enlarged for a jury.

Projection equipment—State-of-the-art projectors, often connected to laptop computers, are used by trial attorneys to help present evidence to jurors.

Computer Software

Word processing—All offices have one or more word processing packages. The most popular program is Microsoft Word, although some offices use Corel WordPerfect. Both of these word processing programs have special applications for law offices, such as templates for setting up a pleading.

Time and billing—These packages help legal professionals (1) keep track of their billable time and (2) create correct and timely billing statements for clients. Many have calendaring capabilities.

Litigation support—There are numerous litigation support packages available. Some packages enable the user to easily summarize a deposition transcript; others calculate economic damages. Still others allow the user to scan in thousands of documents in order to organize and index them quickly and efficiently.

Forms/specialty software—In areas such as family law, bankruptcy, personal injury, real property, and estate planning, excellent software products are available. These programs provide sample documents, blank forms, and general assistance for the law office working in one or more specialty areas.

Presentation software—Litigation attorneys have found that visual aids can be helpful in making their point before a jury. Software programs such as Microsoft PowerPoint help attorneys create some visual aids.

A POINT TO REMEMBER

Law offices are becoming more and more sophisticated. To be truly prepared to work as a legal professional, you must master the use of the computer. Take your skills as far beyond simple word processing as possible. Read the current literature on legal technology. Do not wait until you are looking for that first position to worry about your computer knowledge and skills. It may be necessary to take continuing education classes to stay current on technology issues and advancements.

SEC. 18-3 THE INTERNET

The Internet revolutionized the way we communicate and the way we acquire information. It has had, and undoubtedly will continue to have, a tremendous impact on many professions and business, including the legal profession. The Internet provides numerous advantages to the legal profession, including a global communication network, an advertising medium, a resource for information, and a forum for special-interest groups.

COMMUNICATION—E-MAIL

With its global network, the Internet allows legal personnel to communicate with one another almost anywhere in the world. The value of the Internet is not only that it allows them to talk to one another, but that it also allows them to exchange lengthy files and records. For example, a large law firm may have several branch offices in different geographical locations. An attorney in a London office might need to see an office file that is isolated in its New York office. The information can be sent instantaneously through the Internet.

ADVERTISING

The Internet also offers an advertising medium for law firms as well as for professional organizations. Legal professionals can have Web pages in which they describe their practice and their services.

INFORMATION RESOURCES

Hooked up to the Internet are thousands of computerized data banks that provide sources of incredible amounts of information. Anyone using the Internet from his or her own computer can access this information. Included in this storehouse of data are numerous public records, U.S. Supreme Court cases, selected state legislation, and a variety of articles on legal topics. Different Internet indexes provide many Internet addresses for legal providers. By using these resources, legal professionals keep abreast of the latest developments in the law.

Discussion Forums

The Internet provides a forum for special-interest groups to carry on discussions in their area of interest. Here legal professionals participate in discussions with others throughout the world or simply read what others have to say.

Legal Research

The Internet is an important legal research tool for lawyers. Many primary sources of law are readily available to anyone on the Internet. Federal and state statutes and cases can be accessed. Sites such as *www.findlaw.com/* provide a gateway to legal authorities on the Internet. Additionally, the major legal research databases, Westlaw and LEXIS, are now accessed through the Internet, although there is a fee to use these services. Several other fee-based legal research databases are also available.

The Internet and the Courts

Today, most courts maintain their own Web sites with important information about the courts, such as calendars, addresses, and telephone numbers, as well as local rules of court. Some courts post their rulings in motions and trials. Additionally, courts are finding that the Internet can provide a means for attorneys to obtain information from the courts. The U.S. courts provide access to certain information in federal court files through the Internet. The PACER (Public Access to Court Electronic Records) system is maintained by the federal judiciary. Using this system, attorneys (or any member of the public) can conduct limited searches of court documents online. Some courts are beginning to allow "e-filing" of documents, that is, documents are sent to court for filing via e-mail.

Document Depository

With cases such as the Micro case, law firms are often faced with the practical problem of where to store thousands of documents and still have them available for discovery and trial. One solution to this problem involves the Internet. Documents are scanned into files and then are maintained in a secure site on the Internet, thus taking no space in the law office or on the law office computers. Any attorney with the proper password can access the document.

Intranets and Extranets

The Internet is a global network, allowing access to anyone, anywhere. It is possible to establish networks that have limited access. These are sometimes referred to as *intranets* and *extranets*. An intranet is a system that is accessible by a very limited group. In the legal community, this might be a single law firm. Such a system allows information and resources to be shared by all members of the firm. It is not necessary that all users of the intranet be located in the same geographical area. Firms that have offices in New York and California can be connected to the same intranet. Extranets are similar in concept to an intranet. The major difference is that individuals outside one office can be connected. For example, a law firm could set up a system accessible not only by members of the firm, but also by clients of the firm.

ETHICAL CHOICES

A fax was forwarded to your law firm, which represents a large tobacco company, a defendant in a lawsuit. The fax is from the plaintiff's counsel in a complex class action involving the tobacco industry. The fax was supposed to be sent to the fifteen plaintiffs. A mistake was made and your office received a copy of an extremely confidential document. What should you do?

SEC. 18-4 GENERAL OFFICE PROCEDURES

The modern law office takes advantage of the latest technology. However, traditional office procedures are still followed in law offices. Technology makes it easier for law offices to follow these procedures. This section describes the general office procedures that occur when a law firm takes a case.

ACCEPTING A NEW CASE

When a law firm accepts a new client, or a new case for an old client, several office procedures take place. The following usually occur:

- A conflict-of-interest check is made.
- A retainer agreement or letter is produced.
- A new file is opened.
- A ledger sheet is created.
- Client information is entered into a firm database.
- Important dates are calendared or entered into a tickler system.

conflict of interest
A situation that arises when a firm has a business or personal relationship with one of the litigants, or when the firm has represented the party the client wishes to sue.

Before accepting a case, a firm must determine that no **conflict of interest** exists. Legal support staff run the client's name, the name of the client's business (if necessary), and the opposing party's name through the office conflict-of-interest software program to be sure that there is no conflict of interest. Recall from previous chapters that a conflict of interest can occur if a law firm currently represents or represented in the past an opposing party. A conflict can also exist if the firm has an interest in the pending litigation.

The retainer agreement, which is easily generated from a word processing template, spells out the fee agreement and sets forth the duties and responsibilities of the attorney.

client intake sheet
A form used to collect information on the client and data on the client's legal matter.

client file
The office file that contains copies of all documents related to the client's case.

The client file contains information and documents related to the case. When a potential client is interviewed, a **client intake sheet** is often completed. Information from this document and from interview notes is then used to start the **client file**. Office files are given a name, a file number, or both. The name on the file usually includes the client's name first and then the opposing party's. In the simplest of office procedures, files are kept in a file drawer in alphabetical or numerical order. In some instances, the files are separated by type of case. Sometimes entire files are kept on a computer for fast reference and easy storage. In any event, basic information about the client, such as name and address, is usually kept in a general database.

ledger sheet
A bookkeeping document that will be used to record all expenditures and income in connection with the case.

At the time an office file is opened, a **ledger sheet** is created. A ledger sheet is a bookkeeping document that is used to record all expenditures and income in connection with the case. Today, this information is often computerized. Most law offices use software that manages billing, calendaring, and other client tracking needs.

Maintaining Client Files

Client files are amended and added to as necessary. The client file contains copies of all documents related to the case unless the case has too many documents to make this practical. Some lawsuits involve hundreds of thousands of documents. In such a case, the documents are usually stored in a separate location. They are also indexed in such a way that a computerized database can be created to make access easier.

Copies of all correspondence as well as any official documents must be included in the office file. As the case grows, additional files may be used. Maintaining neat, organized files in a law firm is a continuing challenge and paralegals are often asked to take a disorganized file and make some sense of it. Usually this is a matter of identifying and understanding the various legal documents within the file, putting them into a logical sequence, and preparing an appropriate index.

Calendaring

statute of limitations
A law that places a time limit on when a lawsuit can be filed.

tickler system
A calendaring system used to keep track of dates or time limits for action that needs to be taken in a case.

When a file is opened, certain initial dates, such as a **statute of limitations**, are calendared. Most offices have special calendaring systems to accomplish this. These are referred to as **tickler systems**. As the case progresses, several other dates may be important. Court appointments, meetings, and filing dates must be recorded. If an attorney is scheduled to appear in court at 9 A.M. Monday to argue a matter in front of a judge, and the attorney fails to appear, the judge might rule against the attorney. When attorneys are supposed to be somewhere at a particular time, especially if they are required to appear in court, they must be there. In a successful law practice, attorneys are required to keep a multitude of appointments and appearances in court. In addition to court appearances, attorneys (and paralegals) meet with clients, insurance adjusters, other attorneys, and witnesses. In a busy office, keeping track of where the attorney is to be at any particular time can be a nightmare. This is compounded in firms with numerous attorneys. A law office must, therefore, have some method of keeping track of this information. Most firms

master calendar
A calendar that details all appointments and appearances of all attorneys in the firm.

maintain a **master calendar**, that is, a calendar that details appointments and appearances of all attorneys. In a modern office, calendaring of appointments, appearances, and due dates for documents are often kept on an automated or computerized calendaring system. As mentioned before, a number of software programs are available. In addition, attorneys often maintain their own individual calendars of appointments and appearances. Handheld computers such as the PalmPilot, which keep track of dates and appointments, are popular and essential tools for busy attorneys and paralegals.

Paralegals or other support staff are often responsible not only for keeping their own calendars but also for maintaining the calendar of the attorneys in the firm. If you work as a paralegal in a law firm you cannot keep an accurate calendar if you do not receive or recognize information about dates. You should be familiar with the various ways that court appearances and other appointments are set in a law office. Sometimes dates are arranged over the telephone. Sometimes attorneys receive formal notice of court appearances by mail. A document entitled "Notice of Motion" or "Notice of Hearing" should always alert the reader that a court date is probably contained in the document. Still other times, attorneys appear in court and are given a date to return for a follow-up hearing. It is important that you know your office's procedure for making certain that all appearances and appointments are recorded.

A POINT TO REMEMBER

Review all correspondence carefully for dates that should be calendared and verify that this has been done. If an attorney has been in court, ask whether any follow-up dates should be calendared.

BILLING

contingent fee
A fee based on a fixed percentage of whatever amount is recovered by the attorney on behalf of the client.

costs
Out-of-pocket expenses in connection with a case.

Law offices are businesses. As such, they must take in fees and pay operating expenses. Attorneys bill for their services in three main ways. They may charge an hourly rate for time spent on a case. (They are also allowed to charge for paralegal time.) Occasionally they charge a *flat rate* (fixed amount) to handle a matter. In some types of cases, they may also charge a **contingent fee**, or a fixed percentage of what is recovered. If a law firm charges an hourly fee, the attorney and the paralegal must keep accurate records of time spent so that it is properly billed. Keeping track of time is done manually or by computer. Again, a number of software programs do this. Regardless of the type of fee charged, the attorney must keep track of all expenses incurred for each case. Usually, the client pays these expenses, sometimes called **costs**, in addition to any fee. The ledger sheet is used to keep accurate records for each case. Any expense and any income (fee) is posted on the ledger sheet. The client's total bill can then be calculated, using computer software.

SEC. 18-5 COMMUNICATION TECHNIQUES

If you work in a law office as a paralegal, you need to develop strong communication skills, both verbal and written. This involves speaking, listening, and writing skills. You are constantly conveying and receiving information from attorneys, legal support staff, clients, and others. Your communication skills must meet law office standards both in form and in substance. You must speak and write in a professional manner that is always grammatically correct. You must always avoid slang. You must be able to convey your ideas or messages to others clearly and be able to understand messages or ideas conveyed to you. Misunderstandings in a law office can cause great harm.

In a law office, the ability to listen and understand is tested in several ways. A paralegal assists an attorney. That attorney constantly asks you to do things. Before undertaking any task, always be certain that you understand all directions. If you are unclear about something, ask. Your listening skills are also tested in your dealing with clients and other parties outside your office. If you are unclear about anything, check. Ask for clarification or repeat your understanding of the matter.

Your speaking ability is as important in a law office as your listening ability. One of the most important aspects of this is knowing and understanding your audience. The way you speak to an attorney or other legal personnel is often different from the way you need to speak to a client. Students in law-related classes often find that understanding the legal vocabulary is very difficult. At some point in time anyone who studies law or works in a law office develops a strong legal vocabulary. Remember when you are dealing with clients that they probably have not had a legal education. Always make certain that clients understand what you tell them.

In a law office, superior writing skills are essential. You use these skills in a number of ways. You write letters to clients and to other legal personnel. You prepare written messages for your co-workers, often in the form of an interoffice memorandum. You draft or write legal documents such as contracts or court pleadings. You may also prepare legal memoranda, as explained in Chapter 5. In all of these cases, certain writing skills are required. All documents must be grammatically correct. They must be clear and concise. Legal documents such as contracts, pleadings, or legal memoranda also have legal requirements that must be followed.

Writing Business Letters

The business letter is probably the most common way in which legal personnel communicate with others. Letters are often sent to other legal personnel, to clients, and to courts, and serve many different purposes. Simple letters are used to confirm conversations; to request information, from either a client or someone else; to convey information; or to accompany and explain documents that are enclosed with the letter. More complex letters are used to explain a legal position to a client or an adversary. The letter may also demand that some action be taken by the person to whom it is directed. All letters must look professional, be grammatically correct, and be clear and understandable.

Legal correspondence follows the standard format for any type of business letter (see Figure 18–1). It includes the name and address of the sender, the date, the inside address, a reference line, the salutation, the body, the closing, the signature, and an indication of copies. The name and address of the sender is normally preprinted on the office stationery. A paralegal's name may or may not be included, depending on the law of the state and the policy of the office. All legal correspondence must be correctly dated. The inside address contains the name, title, and address of the person to whom the correspondence is sent. If you write a letter and are uncertain about the spelling of a name or the person's exact title,

Friedman, Bosckovich & Wong 4 Plaza del Rey Centerville, CA 98765 (520) 234–5678	**Office Stationery**
March 15, 20XX	**Date** All legal correspondence must be dated
Veronica Rhinehart Attorney-at-Law 786 Milton Ave. Centerville, CA 98765	**Inside Address** Name, title, and address of person to whom letter is sent
Re: *Young v. E.G.T. Inc.*	**Reference Line** Describe the subject matter of the correspondence
Dear Ms. Rhinehart:	**Salutation**
Please be advised that this firm has recently been retained by E.G.T. Inc. to represent them in the lawsuit filed by your client Jonathan Young. Our client has advised us that they were served with a copy of a complaint on March 9, 20XX. Our responsive pleadings should be filed soon.	**Body**
Sincerely,	**Closing** This should always be formal
Terry Jacobs Paralegal	**Signature**
cc: E.G.T. Inc.	**Copies**

FIGURE 18–1 Basic letter format.

check and obtain the correct information. A telephone call to the person's place of business will usually provide the necessary information.

reference line
A line in a business letter that describes the subject of the letter.

A **reference line** describing the subject matter is always included in legal correspondence. A reference line serves two purposes. It allows the recipient to know immediately what the letter concerns. If the recipient is another law office, an insurance company, or other business, this allows the person opening the mail to attach the letter to the office file before giving it to the named recipient. Also, should the letter ever be separated from your file (which happens in busy law offices, especially when attorneys remove documents from files), anyone finding it knows where it belongs. The information on the reference line varies. The most obvious is your client's name. However, that may not be very helpful to recipients of the letter, especially if they represent someone else. It is, therefore, preferable to include not only your client's name, but also the name of the client to whom the letter is sent. If legal correspondence is sent in response to other letters that contain client names or file numbers, these should be referenced in your letter. Such a reference line might read as follows:

> Re: *Young v. E.G.T. Inc.*
> Your File No. A12345

The salutation in a letter from the law office should be kept formal. Unless some special relationship exists between you and the recipient, avoid the use of first names and use the terms "Mr." and "Ms." If the communication is sent to an unknown person, such as the clerk of the court, the person's title can be used—for example, "Dear Clerk."

The body of the letter depends on the purpose in sending the letter. Some of the more common purposes are discussed in the following sections. However, regardless of the purpose, always keep the tone professional and businesslike. Avoid slang and never use contractions (such as *didn't* instead of *did not*). Be concise and to the point. Know what you want to say before you begin writing. Start with the end in mind.

The closing is very simple in a business letter. The phrases "Sincerely," "Sincerely yours," and "Very truly yours," are most commonly used. If you work as a paralegal, you might be allowed to sign letters on your own behalf. If so, always indicate your title following your name (such as "Paralegal" or "Legal Assistant"). In many cases, however, you draft letters on behalf of your supervising attorney. In such a case, the attorney's name and signature appear at the end of the letter.

With any legal correspondence, the question of who receives copies is an important one. In addition to the named recipient, copies of legal correspondence are sometimes sent to the client. This lets the client know what is happening on the case and serves as some justification for billing statements. However, before sending copies to the client, always check with the attorney. If legal correspondence is sent in connection with a pending lawsuit and multiple attorneys are involved in the case, copies of correspondence between two of the attorneys are usually sent to all of the attorneys, especially if the matter relates to any time deadlines, court appearances, or other action being undertaken in the case.

COMMON TYPES OF LEGAL CORRESPONDENCE

Confirming Letter

confirming letter
A letter that confirms or puts in writing an oral understanding or agreement of parties.

In order to avoid misunderstandings, **confirming letters** are sent to confirm an oral (usually telephone) conversation. Confirming letters are sent to confirm the following:

1. A substantive agreement reached between two attorneys.
2. An agreement between two attorneys or members of the support staff regarding the due date of any document.

3. A conversation between attorneys or members of the support staff setting or changing any court date.
4. A conversation between an attorney or a member of the support staff and a client or witness in which the client or witness was advised of any court appearance or deposition.

Confirming letters are sent for several reasons. Primarily, of course, the reason is to avoid misunderstandings that sometimes result from oral communications. They are also necessary because of the way that law firms operate. Often, files in offices are reassigned, or attorneys and paralegals may leave one firm and join another. The result is that the new attorney or paralegal has no way of knowing what agreements were reached by their predecessors unless some written memorandum or letter is contained in the file.

Appointment Letter

When a person is represented by an attorney in any lawsuit, all notices from the courts or other attorneys in the case are sent to the attorney and not the client. This is true even when the notice requires that the client appear in court or at some other legal proceeding. The attorneys are obligated to notify their clients of the time, date, and place of any appearance or appointment. While such notice can be given by telephone, an **appointment letter** should also be sent. The letter should clearly set forth the essential information, such as time, date, and place. The place should be completely described; if the client is to appear in court, the letter should give the address of the court, not just a reference to the "district court." Furthermore, always make certain that you have some way of confirming that the client has received the letter and will appear as directed. This is done either by asking the client to call you to confirm his or her appearance or by your calling the client at some future date. The body of an appointment letter might look something like this:

appointment letter
A letter that schedules an appointment.

> A settlement conference in your case has been set by the court on Wednesday, April 13, at 11:00 a.m. in Department 12 of the district court. The court is located at 123 North First Street, Centerville, CA.
>
> At a settlement conference, the judge and the attorneys for both sides discuss the case and try to reach some agreement. Since your consent is necessary for any settlement, the court requires that you attend this hearing.
>
> Attorney Alan Brock will meet you in Department 12 of the court at 10:45 a.m. Please call me prior to April 7 to confirm that you will appear.
>
> If you have any questions, please do not hesitate to call at any time.

A POINT TO REMEMBER

When you send a letter such as this one, be sure that all times have been placed on the appropriate calendar. In this case, Attorney Brock's calendar should indicate that he is meeting the client at court at 10:45 a.m.

Cover Letter

cover letter
A letter that accompanies and explains documents that are enclosed.

A **cover letter** is used when an attorney or paralegal is sending documents to someone for the purpose of explaining the enclosed documents. A cover letter should state exactly what documents are enclosed and what the recipient is to do with the documents. In other words, is the recipient to review the documents, sign the documents, file the documents, or record the documents? The cover letter should also describe any expected response. Do you want the recipient to sign the documents and return them to you? Do you want the court to file the documents and return endorsed or conformed copies to you? An **endorsed copy** shows the date of filing of the original. *Conformed copy* is another term for *endorsed copy*. If you want copies returned to you, enclose a self-addressed stamped envelope. Many courts will not return documents unless you do this. The body of a cover letter to the clerk of the court requesting filing of an answer to a complaint might appear as follows:

endorsed copy
A document that has been conformed to look like the original.

> Enclosed is an original answer to complaint, proof of service by mail, and three copies. I ask that you file the original answer and proof of service, endorse the copies, and return them to me in the enclosed self-addressed stamped envelope. Also enclosed is a check in the amount of $100.00 to cover the cost of filing.

Information Letter

A letter requesting or conveying information may be used to obtain information from a client, a witness, or some other third party. Sometimes the information sought is solely related to a specific case. For example, in an automobile accident case you might need the clients to send you copies of all of their medical bills. Other times, the information is more general. For example, suppose you have a client who wants to obtain a zoning variance for a piece of real estate and you need to know whether the local regulating agency has any specific forms or guidelines to follow. The most difficult part about preparing a letter requesting information is identifying the party who has the information. This may take some preliminary work on your part.

In addition to requesting information, letters are sent conveying information. This might involve advising a client about the status of his or her case or responding to an inquiry from another attorney. In all cases, be sure that you understand the information to be conveyed before writing any letter. If you are in doubt, check your facts.

Opinion Letter

opinion letter
A letter that analyzes a particular factual situation in light of existing law and offers a legal opinion to the reader.

An **opinion letter** analyzes a particular factual situation in light of existing law and offers a legal opinion to the reader. For example, if you were asked to review the legal issues related to the Case File at the beginning of this chapter and then draft a letter to your client explaining that law, this would be an opinion letter. This type of letter requires that you do legal research and analysis, skills that were discussed in Chapters 4 and 5. However, remember that in writing such a letter, you are not writing it for an attorney or other legal professional. Try to avoid legal jargon or citations that would be understood only by legal personnel. Because an opinion letter gives legal advice, it must always be signed by an attorney.

Demand Letter

demand letter
A letter in which the writer is seeking settlement of some matter.

In a **demand letter**, the writer seeks settlement of some matter. These types of letters, and the tone that is used, vary considerably. In some cases, the letter may be as harsh as the name suggests. For example, if your client in a divorce case advises you that the separated spouse (who is not represented by an attorney) has been harassing your client at work, you might send a letter demanding that the behavior stop. Such a letter might read as follows:

> My client advises me that on four separate occasions over the past two weeks, you have come to her place of employment and have interfered with her ability to perform her job. You must stop contacting her at work immediately. Should you fail to do so, we will take appropriate legal action, including requesting the court for a restraining order.

On the other hand, sometimes demand letters are much more conciliatory in their tone, especially where the attorney is attempting to reach a monetary settlement in a case. Demand letters are frequently sent to insurance companies for this purpose. Such a letter would contain a brief statement showing why the client is entitled to some settlement. This is a brief analysis of the facts and the law. The letter would also contain a statement or itemization of the damages that were incurred. Finally, the letter includes a sum of money that the writer is willing to accept as settlement. While these letters are certainly *adversarial* (that is, they argue one side of the issue), they are not necessarily "demanding" in their tone.

File Copy

Regardless of the type of letter that is sent, always maintain a copy of the letter. This should be kept in the client file.

Fax

Most legal correspondence is still sent by mail. However, fax machines do offer speed in communicating and for that reason are sometimes favored by attorneys. There are, however, some concerns when using a fax machine to transmit a letter. First, confidentiality is a concern. Sending information via fax does not assure any degree of confidentiality, as anyone can be on the receiving end. Many lawyers add a paragraph to any information they transmit by fax asserting the confidentiality of the matter. Such a paragraph might read as follows:

> ***Caution—Confidential***
>
> The document being transmitted to you may contain information protected by attorney-client privilege. It is intended *only* for the person to whom it is addressed. If you have received this facsimile in error, please notify us immediately and destroy the document.

However, this serves little purpose if the receiver is not an attorney or is not otherwise bound by an ethical standard of behavior. Faxing is too risky a method to use with highly confidential or sensitive material.

E-Mail

The Internet has made electronic mail a viable means of business communication for anyone. It is quick and it is more confidential than faxing. However, because law offices need to keep copies of correspondence that is sent and received, e-mail cannot be used without making certain that hard copies also are made of any correspondence.

> **A POINT TO REMEMBER**
>
> Always proofread carefully any written correspondence. Spelling and grammatical errors are not tolerated in a law office.

Handling the Telephone

If you work in a law office, you conduct considerable business over the telephone. You talk to clients, to other legal personnel, to courts, and to countless others. Unlike other features in a law office, the telephone is certainly familiar to even the novice. However, remember that when you use the telephone in a law office, you are using it for business purposes. Always remain professional. Remember the following rules:

1. Whether making a call or answering one, always introduce yourself first, explaining your position in the firm.
2. Never talk on the telephone while you are eating, drinking, or chewing gum.
3. Remain polite, even if the other speaker is rude or angry.
4. If you are making a telephone call to a client or to anyone else and you need to obtain extensive information, make a written list of the questions you need to ask before making the call.
5. Do not put a speaker on hold for a lengthy time.
6. Try not to answer telephone calls while you are in conference with a client.
7. If, during the telephone call, you make any agreements or representations (or receive any representations) with other legal personnel, always make sure that a confirming letter is sent either by you or by the other side.
8. Make written notes in the office file of any telephone calls concerning the case reflecting any information you have received or conveyed.
9. Most important, if you receive a telephone call that you are unable to answer immediately, *always return the call promptly*.

Writing Interoffice Memoranda

One of the ways that legal personnel communicate with one another is through an interoffice memorandum. This is a writing sent from one member of a firm to another employee of the firm conveying some information. An interoffice memorandum is used in lieu of oral communication for a variety of reasons. In a busy office, sometimes it is simply too difficult for people to coordinate their schedules to have time to sit down and discuss something. Putting it in writing is just easier. For example, suppose that your attorney wants you research an issue because the attorney is in trial and does not have time. The attorney may be in the office only in the early morning hours or evening hours, times when you do not work. The attorney may prepare an interoffice memorandum, explaining the client's question and asking you to research the issue and draft a letter to the client. When attorneys write interoffice memoranda they often use shorthand symbols that are commonly recognized by legal personnel (see Figure 18–2).

COMMON SYMBOLS AND ABBREVIATIONS

π	plaintiff
Δ	defendant
S.O.L.	statute of limitations
S/L	statute of limitations
D/A	date of accident
C/A	cause of action
K	contract
TX	transcript
S.D.T.	subpoena duces tecum
P & As	memorandum of points and authorities
TRO	temporary restraining order
OEX	order of examination
OSC	order to show cause
INJ.	injunction
§	section
R.T.	reporter's transcript
C.T.	clerk's transcript
pg/ln	page/line
w/	with
∴	therefore
<	less than
>	greater than
(10)k	thousand
P.I.	personal injury
DA	district attorney
PD	public defender
G.J.	grand jury
PX	preliminary examination transcript
DBA	doing business as
Ltd.	limited
Inc.	incorporated
IPO	initial public offering

FIGURE 18–2 Common symbols and abbreviations.

Interoffice memoranda also are used in situations where it may be prudent or necessary for the office file to have a written record of some fact. This is particularly true when the information is significant to the case and may be important at a later date. For example, suppose you have interviewed a witness in a case, and that witness gave you some important facts about your client. You need to prepare some writing, often in the form of an interoffice memorandum, for the file, so that a permanent record of your conversation is made. This allows any attorney working on the case at a future time to know what happened. It also keeps you from forgetting the substance of your interview. When you write an interoffice memorandum, you should prepare two copies; you will send one to the person with whom you are communicating, and place the other in the file. Certain items should always be included in the memorandum: the name of the person preparing the memo, the person to whom it is directed, the date it is prepared, and a reference line stating the subject matter of the memorandum.

Interviewing Clients and Witnesses

Paralegals often interview or question clients and witnesses in a case. Interviewing obviously involves all of your communication skills. You must be thorough and all of your questions should be clear and concise. You must listen attentively to be sure that you understand what is being said and what is *not* being said. You must be able to write summaries of the information you receive in your interview. Here are some guidelines for interviewing a client or witness in a law office.

1. *Always prepare ahead of time.* Know the purpose of your interview and find out what information you can about the case. If there is an office file, review it. If you do not understand the legal issues in the case, do some preliminary research or ask an attorney to explain it to you. Prepare a list of questions or a checklist of information you want to obtain.
2. *Arrange a proper setting.* Make sure you have a private office to use and make arrangements to have any telephone calls answered for you.
3. *Introduce yourself.* Describe your position with the law firm.
4. *Ask general questions, followed by specific ones.* Begin the interview by asking a very general question, such as "Tell me what you saw," or "Explain your problem to me." These questions can then be followed by more specific questions to fill in the details. The specific questions will vary depending on the nature of the case and the nature of the interview, but the traditional questions of who, what, when, and where usually provide a good starting point.
5. *Avoid asking leading questions.* A *leading question* is one that suggests the answer. "You were going about 35 miles per hour when the accident happened, right?" is a leading question. The correct way to phrase such a question would be "How fast were you going when the accident happened?"
6. *Take copious notes during the interview.* It is important to record immediately the information you receive in the interview. If you have to go back and reconstruct what you were told, you will forget details that might prove to be important. At times an interview may be tape-recorded, but this should be done only with express permission.

7. *Review your checklist and your notes before terminating the interview.* Interviews often digress into nonrelated areas. It is important to go back and make sure that nothing was left out of your interview. Also verify the spelling of all names, even names that appear to be common. Even the name John has alternative spellings. Do the same with all addresses and telephone numbers.
8. *Only an attorney may give legal advice to a client during an interview.* During a client interview, the client may ask questions about the case. A paralegal cannot answer questions that call for legal advice. These questions must be answered by an attorney. If you give legal advice, and you are not an attorney, you are engaged in the unauthorized practice of law.
9. *After ending the interview, make certain that your notes are legible.* If not, copy them or, even better, prepare a narrative summary of your interview in the form of a written interoffice memorandum.

Occasionally, you are asked not only to interview a witness in a case, but also to obtain a written statement from that witness. In such a case, it would generally be your responsibility to write the statement based on the information you receive in the interview, and then ask the witness to sign the statement.

ETHICAL CHOICES

The client you have just interviewed asks to take a break and to use a phone. You inadvertently overhear a conversation indicating that the client has been untruthful with you during the interview. What do you do?

SEC. 18-6 FACT INVESTIGATION

The practice of law is not limited to researching legal issues, writing legal documents, and appearing in court. In fact, much of the time, legal issues are not in dispute. Rather, it is the facts that are the subject of disagreement. For example, suppose an attorney is handling an automobile accident case. The client says that she was injured when another motorist ran a red light. The other motorist denies running a red light. The legal issues in this type of case are not a problem. If a motorist drives negligently (for example, runs a red light) and causes an accident, injuring another person, the negligent motorist is responsible for damages. The questions in this type of case are factual ones, such as "Who ran the red light?" or "Was there a problem with the light?" The attorneys handling this case must do some factual investigation. They review police reports, obtain statements from witnesses, and take photographs of the scene. Although paralegals sometimes do this type of investigation, in most law offices this is still done by private investigators. However, many types of factual research or investigation are done by paralegals. Usually this involves finding information that is contained in a public record or researching factual questions. For example, in the preceding example, the attorney might want to know whether any of the parties were involved in prior lawsuits or whether there was any previous problem with those specific lights. This involves checking court records and the maintenance records of the governmental entity responsible for the lights. Additionally, the injured party may claim that as a result of the trauma and stress from the accident, her blood pressure has risen. This would involve researching medical texts or journals to see what can cause increases in blood pressure. It might also involve questioning experts in the field. A paralegal might be asked to research any or all of these questions. Factual research usually involves three steps:

1. Identifying the information you need.
2. Identifying where that information is stored.
3. Determining how to obtain the information from its source.

Researching general factual information is no different in a law firm than it is in any setting. Public libraries and libraries affiliated with colleges and universities are valuable sources. Databases available on the Internet provide incredible sources of information. Researching material in public records is not difficult if you know which public record contains the information you seek. Your state probably publishes a directory of the various agencies in the state with a description of their functions. This is helpful in locating the proper source for your information. If the information is contained in public records, you are probably entitled to it. If the record is a federal record, the Freedom of Information Act provides the method of obtaining the information. To obtain such information you should write to the governmental agency that controls the information.

The following is an example of an interoffice memorandum written by a paralegal who was asked to do factual research. The memorandum is in connection with a criminal case in which a defendant was charged with embezzlement. The defendant asked for leniency, claiming the funds were needed to pay medical bills for a seriously ill child. A paralegal working for the prosecutor's office was asked to verify the defendant's claim. Note how interviews played a large role in the fact-finding process.

Investigation Report[1]

To: Supervising deputy district attorney
From: Senior Paralegal
Subject: Defendant, ______
Date: ______

This investigation was performed in an effort to validate the defendant's statement that she embezzled funds from the victim company because she needed the money to pay to collection agencies which were collecting for hospital treatments performed upon her daughter, who has cancer. The defendant claimed she did not have insurance coverage and was forced to pay all of her daughter's medical bills herself and was being hounded by collection agencies. The defendant provided her attorney, who in turned submitted to our office, copies of billing statements from Grand Receivables, a collection agency.

[1]Reprinted with permission of the auhtor, Delene Waltrip.

On August 4, 1998, I telephoned Reno, Nevada to locate Grand Receivables, as defense attorney Byron Green's letter indicated Grand Receivables was located there. I was informed by Directory Assistance that there was no listing for Grand Receivables in Reno. I then performed an Internet search and obtained information about Grand Receivables, located in Napa, California.

On August 5, 1998, I telephoned Grand Receivables at (800) 555-5500 and spoke with Jonas Polk, a supervisor. I briefly explained the nature of my call, indicating I wanted to verify payments made on the Grand Receivables account for their client, Lucille Packard Children's Hospital, for services rendered to the defendant's daughter. Jonas indicated to me that his records did not show an account for any amount nearing $120,000, and requested that I fax to him a copy of the billing statement to which I was referring.

I faxed to Jonas the first page and last page of the Grand Receivables billing statements provided to us by the defense attorney, Byron Green, showing the original collection balance of $106,424.00 and the total payments, including interest, of $119,621.00.

I then spoke again with Jonas Polk at Grand Receivables. Jonas had received my fax. I asked Jonas if he could verify the payments and source of payments for me. He began by laughing, stating, "It's marvelous what scanners and computers will do." I asked him to explain. He provided the following information, stating that "the whole thing is garbage."

1. Grand Receivables did not obtain Lucille Packard Children's Hospital as a client until approximately February, 1998. These statements show billing dates of January 13, 1996 through August 15, 1997, which is an impossibility.
2. Grand Receivables does provide billing statements which look similar to the billing statements provided to us by Byron Green.
3. On February 17, 1998, Lucille Packard Children's Hospital assigned a collection account to Grand Receivables under the debtor name of ______, the defendant's husband, for services rendered to ______, the defendant's daughter. Grand's account number for this assigned account is 30957 as indicated on the billing statements provided to us. However, the balance assigned to Grand Receivables for collection was $72.00. Grand's records indicate that the original balance on the bill being collected was only $176.00, of which $72.00 was unpaid and sent to them for collection.
4. Jonas verified that Lucille Packard Children's Hospital's Client Debtor # with Grand is: 5886857 as indicated on these billing statements.
5. No payments have been made by anyone to Grand Receivables on the $72.00 balance.
6. Grand purges its records and billing accounts from its computers over time. There is "no way" an account number from the 1996–1997 time period would be used again to open up a new account in February, 1998. This account number is a brand new account number, opened in February, 1998 with the defendant and her husband as the debtors.

(continued)

7. Jonas believes that a Grand Receivables billing statement with the actual debtor name, client name, and correct account and client numbers was used as a basis for creating fake billing statements.
8. There are no other offices for Grand Receivables. The only office is located in Napa, California.
9. Jonas indicated they would require a subpoena in order to provide us with anything in writing on this subject.

Next, I telephoned the Lucille Packard Children's Hospital and asked for the billing department. I spoke with David Jeffers. I briefly explained the nature of my inquiry to Mr. Jeffers. Mr. Jeffers provided the following information.

1. Lucille Packard Children's Hospital (LPCH) hired Grand Receivables to perform collections on their behalf in January, 1998. LPCH never used Grand prior to January, 1998. Prior to January, 1998, LPCH used a company called Nationwide Collections, Inc. for their collections.
2. In January or February of 1998, LPCH did turn over a collection account to Grand Receivables for services rendered to the defendant's daughter, in the amount of $72.00. This account is the only account LPCH has turned over to Grand Receivables with regard to the defendant's daughter.
3. Most of the defendant's daughter's bills have been covered by insurance. Since 1991, the defendant has had the following insurance companies making payments on her daughter's bills at LPCH: Principal Mutual, Aetna, Blue Cross, The Guardian Life, Great Western and Prudential. LPCH records indicate that the defendant's daughter has been covered by insurance continuously throughout all of her treatments.
4. There have been some portions of bills which were to be payable by the defendant. LPCH records indicate "small" amounts have been paid directly to the hospital by the defendant in amounts such as $150.00 twice in 1992, for a total of $300.00. Mr. Jeffers could not find any other payments made directly to the hospital by the defendant, although there may have been some other "small" payments, which he could not identify without a very time-consuming search. However, Mr. Jeffers stated that most of the bills have been paid by insurance, or written off as per managed care agreements. Mr. Jeffers indicated that, although the defendant's daughter's treatments may have reached a very high total, the defendant was not responsible for very much of it, since the defendant's husband's insurance covered nearly all of it and most of the rest of it was "written off."
5. In 1992, LPCH sent an account to collection for services rendered to the defendant's daughter. The amount assigned to collection was: $156.31. Another account was subsequently sent to collection for the amount of $651.21.

6. Mr. Jeffers could not find any other accounts sent to collection regarding the defendant or her daughter. The total balance which Mr. Jeffers could determine was sent to various collection agencies from 1991 to the present is $879.52, including the two above-referenced accounts and the Grand account for $72.00.
7. I asked Mr. Jeffers if there was anything indicating the defendant paid, or was responsible for, any amounts nearing $120,000. Mr. Jeffers indicated there was nothing "near that" and said, "She's obviously lying."

I then telephoned the billing office for Stanford Hospital and its doctors at (800) 555-5850. They have an account for the defendant's daughter, numbered: A56990. Stanford does the billing for its doctors which perform services at Lucille Packard Children's Hospital. Stanford Hospital itself does not have a pediatric ward—all children go to the LPCH, but the Stanford doctors use Stanford Hospital's billing services for their own bills. Although Mrs. Allen, a supervisor, was reluctant to give me any information due to "the patient's rights of privacy," she did answer a few questions.

I asked Mrs. Allen if Stanford used Grand Receivables for collection of their past due accounts. Mrs. Allen said they do not.

I asked Mrs. Allen if there is insurance covering the defendant's daughter. Mrs. Allen said, "Yes, there is insurance on the account."

Mrs. Allen indicated she would require a release from the patient in order to provide any further information to us.

In any event, the billing done by Stanford is just for doctor's services, not for the hospital treatments.

In conclusion, there is no substantiation for the defendant's claim that the embezzled funds were used to pay for medical expenses for her daughter. Additionally, the documentation that the defendant provided to us appears to be fraudulent.

Featured Web Site: www.abanet.org/tech/ltrc/home.html

The Web site for the Technology Resource Center of the American Bar Association has extensive information about technology and the law office. Latest news is reported and lists of vendors and their products appear.

Go Online

1. Summarize one article dealing with recent developments in technology.
2. Review the information on vendors and their products. Describe the various products that are now available.

Chapter Summary

The practice of law requires not only knowledge of the legal system but also a general familiarity with computers and general office procedures. Today's law office is equipped with the latest technology. Computers and related hardware are essential components of the office. Specialized software is also widely used, as is the Internet. Anyone working in a law office must have skills necessary to use these resources. Employees such as paralegals must also understand office procedures such as methods of maintaining client files, calendaring systems, and billing. Working in a law office requires that paralegals develop strong written and verbal communication skills. Paralegals frequently write different types of business letters and interoffice memoranda. They must communicate over the telephone and in person with clients, other legal personnel, and third parties. Investigating factual information is also part of the day-to-day practice of law and is a task that often is assigned to paralegals. General research skills are necessary.

Terms to Remember

conflict of interest
client intake sheet
client file
ledger sheet
statute of limitations
tickler system
master calendar
contingent fee
costs
reference line
confirming letter
appointment letter
cover letter
endorsed copy
opinion letter
demand letter

Questions for Review

1. List the types of computer hardware found in law offices.
2. Describe the types of computer software found in law offices.
3. Explain how a law firm uses the Internet.
4. Explain how client files are kept in a law firm.
5. Describe the different types of things that need to be calendared in a law office.
6. What is a tickler system?
7. What is the difference between costs and fees?
8. Describe different types of business letters that a paralegal might write.
9. Why are strong verbal communication skills needed in a law office?

Questions for Analysis

1. Assume that you are working as a paralegal in the law firm of Smith and Wesson. You have been assigned to work on a case involving a dispute between two neighbors, Sam Nabors and Victor Vice, over the repair of a "good neighbor" fence. In the last big storm, the fence dividing their two properties was destroyed by severe winds. Sam tried to get his neighbor to cooperate in repairing the fence, but the neighbor refused to even talk to Sam about it. Sam hired a contractor to fix the fence and now wants his neighbor to pay one-half of the cost.

   The following statute exists in your jurisdiction:

   "Coterminous owners are mutually bound equally to maintain:

   1. The boundaries and monuments between them;
   2. The fences between them, unless one of them chooses to let his land lie without fencing; in which case, if he afterwards encloses it, he must refund to the other a just proportion of the value, at that time, of any division made by the latter."

The fence repair cost Sam $1,250.00. Sam's address is 497 Oak Canyon Way, Centerville, CA 98765. Victor Vice's address is 496 Cedar Tree Lane, Centerville, CA 98765. Write a demand letter to Sam's neighbor requesting payment of one-half of the repair bill.

2. Also draft a letter to Sam, to be signed by your supervising attorney, advising Sam of his rights under the code section and explaining what action has been taken by the law firm.
3. Review the Ethical Choices boxes in this chapter. Which NALA and/or NFPA rules or guidelines apply to the situations? Review your state's ethical rules. (*Hint*: Go to www.nala.org/ and find a link.) Which of those rules apply?
4. Techology played an important role in the case of *Kyllo v. United States*, found in Appendix VII. Read the case and explain how technology is affecting the law.

Assignments and Projects

1. Watch any television interview program. Take notes and write a narrative summary of the interview.
2. Interview the office manager of a local law firm, in a phone conference or in person. Find out (1) what hardware the firm uses, (2) what software the firm likes best and why, (3) whether there are plans are for upgrading their hardware and software, and (4) how the office handles training the staff on new hardware and software. Finally, ask the office manager to explain how the firm has evolved over the past decade.
3. Review your local legal newspaper, newsletter, bar journal, or any legal periodical. Make a list of the different software products that are advertised and explain the use of each.

APPENDIX I

THE UNITED STATES CONSTITUTION

PREAMBLE

We the People of the United States, in order to form a more perfect Union, establish justice, insure domestic tranquility, provide for the common defense, promote the general welfare, and secure the blessings of liberty to ourselves and our posterity, do ordain and establish this Constitution for the United States of America.

ARTICLE I

SECTION 1. All legislative powers herein granted shall be vested in a Congress of the United States, which shall consist of a Senate and House of Representatives.

SECTION 2. The House of Representatives shall be composed of members chosen every second year by the people of the several States, and the electors in each State shall have the qualifications requisite for electors of the most numerous branch of the State Legislature.

No person shall be a Representative who shall not have attained to the age of twenty-five years, and been seven years a citizen of the United States, and who shall not, when elected, be an inhabitant of that State in which he shall be chosen.

Representatives and direct taxes shall be apportioned among the several States which may be included within this Union, according to their respective numbers, which shall be determined by adding to the whole number of free persons, including those bound to service for a term of years, and excluding Indians not taxed, three-fifths of all other persons. The actual enumeration shall be made within three years after the first meeting of the Congress of the United States, and within every subsequent term of ten years, in such manner as they shall by law direct. The number of representatives shall not exceed one for every thirty thousand, but each State shall have at least one Representative; and until such enumeration shall be made, the State of New Hampshire shall be entitled to choose three, Massachusetts eight, Rhode Island and Providence Plantations one, Connecticut five, New York six, New Jersey four, Pennsylvania eight, Delaware one, Maryland six, Virginia ten, North Carolina five, South Carolina five, and Georgia three.

When vacancies happen in the representation from any State, the executive authority thereof shall issue writs of election to fill such vacancies.

The House of Representatives shall choose their Speaker and other officers; and shall have the sole power of impeachment.

SECTION 3. The Senate of the United States shall be composed of two Senators from each State, chosen by the legislature thereof, for six years and each Senator shall have one vote.

Immediately after they shall be assembled in consequence of the first election, they shall be divided as equally as may be into three classes. The seats of the Senators of the first class shall be vacated at the expiration of the second year, of the second class at the expiration of the fourth year, and of the third class at the expiration of the sixth year, so that one-third may be chosen every second year; and if vacancies happen by resignation, or otherwise, during the recess of the legislature of any State, the executive thereof may make temporary appointments until the next meeting of the legislature, which shall then fill such vacancies.

No person shall be a Senator who shall not have attained to the age of thirty years, and been nine years a citizen of the United States, and who shall not, when elected, be an inhabitant of that State for which he shall be chosen.

The Vice President of the United States shall be President of the Senate, but shall have no vote, unless they be equally divided.

The Senate shall choose their other officers, and also a President pro tempore, in the absence of the Vice President, or when he shall exercise the office of President of the United States.

The Senate shall have the sole power to try all impeachments. When sitting for that purpose, they shall be on oath or affirmation. When the President of the United States is tried, the Chief Justice shall preside: and no person shall be convicted without the concurrence of two thirds of the members present.

Judgment in cases of impeachment shall not extend further than to removal from office, and disqualification to hold and enjoy any office of honor, trust or profit under the United States: but the party convicted shall nevertheless be liable and subject to indictment, trial, judgment and punishment, according to law.

SECTION 4. The times, places and manner of holding elections for Senators and Representatives, shall be prescribed in each State by the legislature thereof; but the Congress may at any time by law make or alter such regulations, except as to the places of choosing Senators.

The Congress shall assemble at least once in every year, and such meeting shall be on the first Monday in December, unless they shall by law appoint a different day.

SECTION 5. Each House shall be the judge of the elections, returns and qualifications of its own members, and a majority of each shall constitute a quorum to do business; but a smaller number may adjourn from day to day, and may be authorized to compel the attendance of absent members, in such manner, and under such penalties as each House may provide.

Each House may determine the rules of its proceedings, punish its members for disorderly behaviour, and, with the concurrence of two-thirds, expel a member.

Each House shall keep a journal of its proceedings, and from time to time publish the same, excepting such parts as may in their judgment require secrecy; and the yeas and the nays of the members of either house on any question shall, at the desire of one-fifth of those present, be entered on the journal.

Neither House, during the session of Congress, shall, without the consent of the other, adjourn for more than three days, nor to any other place than that in which the two Houses shall be sitting.

SECTION 6. The Senators and Representatives shall receive a compensation for their services, to be ascertained by law, and paid out of the Treasury of the United States. They shall in all cases, except treason, felony and breach of the peace, be privileged from arrest during their attendance at the session of their respective Houses, and in going to and returning from the same; and for any speech or debate in either House, they shall not be questioned in any other place.

No Senator or Representative shall, during the time for which he was elected, be appointed to any civil office under the authority of the United States, which shall have been created, or the emoluments whereof shall have been increased during such time; and no person holding any office under the United States, shall be a member of either House during his continuance in office.

SECTION 7. All bills for raising revenue shall originate in the House of Representatives; but the Senate may propose or concur with amendments as on other bills.

Every bill which shall have passed the House of Representatives and the Senate, shall, before it becomes a law, be presented to the President of the United States; if he approves he shall sign it, but if not he shall return it, with his objections to that House in which it shall have originated, who shall enter the objections at large on their journal, and proceed to reconsider it. If after such reconsideration two thirds of that House shall agree to pass the bill, it shall be sent, together with the objections, to the other House, by which it shall likewise be reconsidered, and if approved by two thirds of that House, it shall become a law. But in all such cases the votes of both Houses shall be determined by yeas and nays, and the names of the persons voting for and against the bill shall be entered on the journal of each House respectively. If any bill shall not be returned by the President within ten days (Sundays excepted) after it shall have been presented to him, the same shall be a law, in like manner as if he had signed it, unless the Congress by their adjournment prevent its return, in which case it shall not be a law.

Every order, resolution, or vote to which the concurrence of the Senate and House of Representatives may be necessary (except on a question of adjournment) shall be presented to the President of the United States; and before the same shall take effect, shall be approved by him, or being disapproved by him, shall be repassed by two thirds of the Senate and House of Representatives, according to the rules and limitations prescribed in the case of a bill.

SECTION 8. The Congress shall have power to lay and collect taxes, duties, imposts and excises, to pay the debts and provide for the common defense and general welfare of the United States; but all duties, imposts and excises shall be uniform throughout the United States;

To borrow money on the credit of the United States;

To regulate commerce with foreign nations, and among the several States, and with the Indian tribes;

To establish a uniform rule of naturalization, and uniform laws on the subject of bankruptcies throughout the United States;

To coin money, regulate the value thereof, and of foreign coin, and fix the standard of weights and measures;

To provide for the punishment of counterfeiting the securities and current coin of the United States;

To establish post offices and post roads;

To promote the progress of science and useful arts, by securing for limited times to authors and inventors the exclusive right to their respective writings and discoveries;

To constitute tribunals inferior to the Supreme Court;

To define and punish piracies and felonies committed on the high seas, and offenses against the law of nations;

To declare war, grant letters of marque and reprisal, and make rules concerning captures on land and water;

To raise and support armies, but no appropriation of money to that use shall be for a longer term than two years;

To provide and maintain a navy;

To make rules for the government and regulation of the land and naval forces;

To provide for calling forth the militia to execute the laws of the Union, suppress insurrections and repel invasions;

To provide for organizing, arming, and disciplining the militia, and for governing such part of them as may be employed in the service of the United States, reserving to the States respectively, the appointment of the officers, and the authority of training the militia according to the discipline prescribed by Congress;

To exercise exclusive legislation in all cases whatsoever, over such district (not exceeding ten miles square) as may, by cession of particular States, and the acceptance of Congress, become the seat of the Government of the United States, and to exercise like authority over all places purchased by the consent of the legislature of the State in which the same shall be, for the erection of forts, magazines, arsenals, dock-yards, and other needful buildings;—And

To make all laws which shall be necessary and proper for carrying into execution the foregoing powers, and all other powers vested by this Constitution in the Government of the United States, or in any department or officer thereof.

SECTION 9. The migration or importation of such persons as any of the States now existing shall think proper to admit, shall not be prohibited by the Congress prior to the year one thousand eight hundred and eight, but a tax or duty may be imposed on such importation, not exceeding ten dollars for each person.

The privilege of the writ of habeas corpus shall not be suspended, unless when in cases of rebellion or invasion the public safety may require it.

No bill of attainder or ex post facto law shall be passed.

No capitation, or other direct, tax shall be laid, unless in proportion to the census or enumeration herein before directed to be taken.

No tax or duty shall be laid on articles exported from any State.

No preference shall be given by any regulation of commerce or revenue to the ports of one State over those of another: nor shall vessels bound to, or from, one State, be obliged to enter, clear, or pay duties in another.

No money shall be drawn from the Treasury, but in consequence of appropriations made by law; and a regular statement and account of the receipts and expenditures of all public money shall be published from time to time.

No title of nobility shall be granted by the United States: And no person holding any office of profit or trust under them, shall, without the consent of the Congress, accept of any present, emolument, office, or title, of any kind whatever, from any King, Prince, or foreign State.

SECTION 10. No State shall enter into any treaty, alliance, or confederation; grant letters of marque and reprisal; coin money; emit bills of credit; make any thing but gold and silver coin a tender in payment of debts; pass any bill of attainder, ex post facto law, or law impairing the obligation of contracts, or grant any title of nobility.

No State shall, without the consent of the Congress, lay any imposts or duties on imports or exports, except what may be absolutely necessary for executing its inspection laws: and the net produce of all duties and imposts, laid by any state on imports or exports, shall be for the use of the Treasury of the United States; and all such laws shall be subject to the revision and control of the Congress.

No State shall, without the consent of Congress, lay any duty of tonnage, keep troops, or ships of war in time of peace, enter into any agreement or compact with another State, or with a foreign power, or engage in war, unless actually invaded, or in such imminent danger as will not admit of delay.

ARTICLE II

SECTION 1. The executive power shall be vested in a President of the United States of America. He shall hold his office during the term of four years, and together with the Vice President, chosen for the same term, be elected, as follows:

Each State, shall appoint, in such manner as the legislature thereof may direct, a number of electors, equal to the whole number of Senators and Representatives to which the State may be entitled in the Congress; but no Senator or Representative, or person holding an office of trust or profit under the United States, shall be appointed an elector.

The electors shall meet in their respective States, and vote by ballot for two persons, of whom one at least shall not be an inhabitant of the same State with themselves. And they shall make a list of all the persons voted for, and of the number of votes for each; which list they shall sign and certify, and transmit sealed to the seat of the Government of the United States, directed to the President of the Senate. The President of the Senate shall, in the presence of the Senate and House of Representatives, open all the certificates, and the votes shall then be counted. The person having the greatest number of votes shall be the President, if such number be a majority of the whole number of electors appointed; and if there be more than one who have such majority, and have an equal number of votes, then the House of Representatives shall immediately choose by ballot one of them for President; and if no person have a majority, then from the five highest on the list the said House shall in like manner choose the President. But in choosing the President, the votes shall be taken by States, the representation from each State having one vote; a quorum for this purpose shall consist of a member or members from two thirds of the States, and a majority of all the States shall be necessary to a choice. In every case, after the choice of the President, the person having the greatest number of votes of the electors shall be the Vice President. But if there should remain two or more who have equal votes, the Senate shall choose from them by ballot the Vice President.

The Congress may determine the time of choosing the electors, and the day on which they shall give their votes; which day shall be the same throughout the United States.

No person except a natural born citizen, or a citizen of the United States, at the time of the adoption of this Constitution, shall be eligible to the office of President; neither shall any person be eligible to that office who shall not have attained to the age of thirty-five years, and been fourteen years a resident within the United States.

In case of the removal of the President from office, or of his death, resignation, or inability to discharge the powers and duties of the said office, the same shall devolve on the Vice President, and the Congress may by law provide for the case of removal, death, resignation, or inability, both of the President and Vice President, declaring what officer shall then act as President, and such officer shall act accordingly, until the disability be removed, or a President be elected.

The President shall, at stated times, receive for his services, a compensation, which shall neither be increased nor diminished during the period for which he shall have been elected, and he shall not receive within that period any other emolument from the United States, or any of them.

Before he enter on the execution of his office, he shall take the following oath or affirmation:—"I do solemnly swear (or affirm) that I will faithfully execute the office of President of the United States, and will to the best of my ability, preserve, protect and defend the Constitution of the United States."

SECTION 2. The President shall be Commander in Chief of the Army and Navy of the United States, and of the militia of the several States, when called into the actual service of the United States; he may require the opinion, in writing, of the principal officer in each of the executive departments, upon any subject relating to the duties of their respective offices, and he shall have power to grant reprieves and pardons for offenses against the United States, except in cases of impeachment.

He shall have power, by and with the advice and consent of the Senate, to make treaties, provided two thirds of the Senators present concur; and he shall nominate, and by and with the advice and consent of the Senate, shall appoint ambassadors, other public ministers and consuls, Judges of the Supreme Court, and all other officers of the United States, whose appointments are not herein otherwise provided for, and which shall be established by law: but the Congress may by law vest the appointment of such inferior officers, as they think proper, in the President alone, in the courts of law, or in the heads of departments.

The President shall have power to fill up all vacancies that may happen during the recess of the Senate, by granting commissions which shall expire at the end of their next session.

SECTION 3. He shall from time to time give to the Congress information of the State of the Union, and recommend to their consideration such measures as he shall judge necessary and expedient; he may, on extraordinary occasions, convene both Houses, or either of them, and in case of disagreement between them, with respect to the time of adjournment, he may adjourn them to such time as he shall think proper; he shall receive ambassadors and other public ministers; he shall take care that the laws be faithfully executed, and shall commission all the officers of the United States.

SECTION 4. The President, Vice President and all civil officers of the United States, shall be removed from office on impeachment for, and conviction of, treason, bribery, or other high crimes and misdemeanors.

ARTICLE III

SECTION 1. The judicial power of the United States, shall be vested in one Supreme Court, and in such inferior courts as the Congress may from time to time ordain and establish. The judges, both of the Supreme and inferior Courts, shall hold their offices during good behaviour, and shall, at stated times, receive for their services, a compensation, which shall not be diminished during their continuance in office.

SECTION 2. The judicial power shall extend to all cases, in law and equity, arising under this Constitution, the laws of the United States, and treaties made, or which shall be made, under their authority;—to all cases affecting ambassadors, other public ministers and consuls;—to all cases of admiralty and maritime jurisdiction;—to controversies to which the United States shall be a party;—to controversies between two or more States;—between a State and citizens of another State;—between citizens of different States,—between citizens of the same State claiming lands under grants of different States, and between a State, or the citizens thereof, and foreign States, citizens or subjects.

In all cases affecting ambassadors, other public ministers and consuls, and those in which a State shall be a party, the Supreme Court shall have original jurisdiction. In all the other cases before mentioned, the Supreme Court shall have appellate jurisdiction, both as to law and fact, with such exceptions, and under such regulations as the Congress shall make.

The trial of all crimes, except in cases of impeachment, shall be by jury; and such trial shall be held in the State where the said crimes shall have been committed; but when not committed within any State, the trial shall be at such place or places as the Congress may by law have directed.

SECTION 3. Treason against the United States, shall consist only in levying war against them, or in adhering to their enemies, giving them aid and comfort. No person shall be convicted of treason unless on the testimony of two witnesses to the same overt act, or on confession in open court.

The Congress shall have power to declare the punishment of treason, but no attainder of treason shall work corruption of blood, or forfeiture except during the life of the person attainted.

ARTICLE IV

SECTION 1. Full faith and credit shall be given in each State to the public acts, records, and judicial proceedings of every other State. And the Congress may by general laws prescribe the manner in which such acts, records, and proceedings shall be proved, and the effect thereof.

SECTION 2. The citizens of each State shall be entitled to all privileges and immunities of citizens in the several States.

A person charged in any State with treason, felony, or other crime, who shall flee from justice, and be found in another State, shall on demand of the executive authority of the State from which he fled, be delivered up, to be removed to the State having jurisdiction of the crime.

No person held to service or labour in one State, under the laws thereof, escaping into another, shall, in consequence of any law or regulation therein, be discharged from such service or labour, but shall be delivered up on claim of the party to whom such service or labour may be due.

Section 3. New States may be admitted by the Congress into this Union; but no new State shall be formed or erected within the jurisdiction of any other State; nor any State be formed by the junction of two or more States, or parts of States, without the consent of the legislatures of the States concerned as well as of the Congress.

The Congress shall have power to dispose of and make all needful rules and regulations respecting the Territory or other property belonging to the United States; and nothing in this Constitution shall be so construed as to prejudice any claims of the United States, or of any particular State.

Section 4. The United States shall guarantee to every State in this Union a republican form of Government, and shall protect each of them against invasion; and on application of the legislature, or of the executive (when the legislature cannot be convened) against domestic violence.

Article V

The Congress, whenever two thirds of both Houses shall deem it necessary, shall propose amendments to this Constitution, or on the application of the legislatures of two thirds of the several States, shall call a convention for proposing amendments, which, in either case, shall be valid to all intents and purposes, as part of this Constitution, when ratified by the legislatures of three fourths of the several States, or by conventions in three fourths thereof, as the one or the other mode of ratification may be proposed by the Congress; provided that no amendment which may be made prior to the year one thousand eight hundred and eight shall in any manner affect the first and fourth clauses in the Ninth Section of the First Article; and that no State, without its consent, shall be deprived of its equal suffrage in the Senate.

Article VI

All debts contracted and engagements entered into, before the adoption of this Constitution, shall be as valid against the United States under this Constitution, as under the Confederation.

This Constitution, and the laws of the United States which shall be made in pursuance thereof; and all treaties made, or which shall be made, under the authority of the United States, shall be the supreme law of the land; and the judges in every State shall be bound thereby, any thing in the Constitution or laws of any State to the contrary notwithstanding.

The Senators and Representatives before mentioned, and the members of the several State legislatures, and all executive and judicial officers, both of the United States and of the several States, shall be bound by oath or affirmation, to support this Constitution; but no religious test shall ever be required as a qualification to any office or public trust under the United States.

Article VII

The ratification of the conventions of nine States shall be sufficient for the establishment of this Constitution between the States so ratifying the same.

Done in convention by the unanimous consent of the States present the seventeenth day of September in the year of our Lord one thousand seven hundred and eighty seven and of the independence of the United States of America the twelfth. In witness whereof we have hereunto subscribed our names,

Go. Washington—*Presid't.*
and deputy from Virginia
Attest William Jackson *Secretary*

New Hampshire

John Langdon	Nicholas Gilman

Massachusetts

Nathaniel Gorham	Rufus King

Connecticut

Wm. Saml. Johnson	Roger Sherman

New York

Alexander Hamilton

New Jersey

Wil: Livingston	Wm. Paterson
David Brearley	Jona: Dayton

Pennsylvania

B. Franklin	Thos. FitzSimons
Thomas Mifflin	Jared Ingersoll
Robt Morris	James Wilson
Geo. Clymer	Gouv Morris

Delaware

Geo: Read	Richard Bassett
Gunning Bedford jun	Jaco: Broom
John Dickinson	

Maryland

James McHenry	Danl Carroll
Dan of St. Thos. Jenifer	

Virginia

John Blair—	James Madison Jr.

North Carolina

Wm. Blount	Hu Williamson
Richd. Dobbs Spaight	

South Carolina

J. Rutledge	Charles Pinckney
Charles Cotesworth Pinckney	Pierce Butler

Georgia

William Few	Arb Baldwin

Amendments

(The first ten amendments to the Constitution are called the Bill of Rights and were adopted in 1791.)

Amendment I

Congress shall make no law respecting an establishment of religion, or prohibiting the free exercise thereof; or abridging the freedom of speech, or of the press; or the right of the people peaceably to assemble, and to petition the Government for a redress of grievances.

Amendment II

A well regulated militia, being necessary to the security of a free State, the right of the people to keep and bear arms, shall not be infringed.

Amendment III

No soldier shall, in time of peace be quartered in any house, without the consent of the owner, nor in time of war, but in a manner to be prescribed by law.

Amendment IV

The right of the people to be secure in their persons, houses, papers, and effects, against unreasonable searches and seizures, shall not be violated, and no warrants shall issue, but upon probable cause, supported by oath or affirmation, and particularly describing the place to be searched, and the persons or things to be seized.

Amendment V

No person shall be held to answer for a capital, or otherwise infamous crime, unless on a presentment or indictment of a Grand Jury, except in cases arising in the land or naval forces, or in the militia, when in actual service in time of war or public danger; nor shall any person be subject for the same offense to be twice put in jeopardy of life or limb; nor shall be compelled in any criminal case to be a witness against himself, nor be deprived of life, liberty, or property, without due process of law; nor shall private property be taken for public use, without just compensation.

Amendment VI

In all criminal prosecutions, the accused shall enjoy the right to a speedy and public trial, by an impartial jury of the State and district wherein the crime shall have been committed, which district shall have been previously ascertained by law, and to be informed of the nature and cause of the accusation; to be confronted with the witnesses against him; to have compulsory process for obtaining witnesses in his favor, and to have the assistance of counsel for his defense.

Amendment VII

In suits at common law, where the value in controversy shall exceed twenty dollars, the right of trial by jury shall be preserved, and no fact tried by a jury, shall be otherwise reexamined in any Court of the United States, than according to the rules of the common law.

Amendment VIII

Excessive bail shall not be required, nor excessive fines imposed, nor cruel and unusual punishments inflicted.

Amendment IX

The enumeration in the Constitution, of certain rights, shall not be construed to deny or disparage others retained by the people.

Amendment X

The powers not delegated to the United States by the Constitution, nor prohibited by it to the States, are reserved to the States respectively, or to the people.

Amendment XI

The judicial power of the United States shall not be construed to extend to any suit in law or equity, commenced or prosecuted against one of the United States by citizens of another State, or by citizens or subjects of any foreign State.

Amendment XII

The electors shall meet in their respective States, and vote by ballot for President and Vice President, one of whom, at least, shall not be an inhabitant of the same State with themselves; they shall name in their ballots the person voted for as President, and in distinct ballots the person voted for as Vice President, and they shall make distinct lists of all persons voted for as President, and of all persons voted for as Vice President, and of the number of votes for each, which lists they shall sign and certify, and transmit sealed to the seat of the government of the United States, directed to the President of the Senate;—The President of the Senate shall, in the presence of the Senate and House of Representatives, open all the certificates and the votes shall then be counted;—The person having the greatest number of votes for President, shall be the President, if such number be a majority of the whole number of electors appointed; and if no person have such majority, then from the persons having the highest numbers not exceeding three on the list of those voted for as president, the House of Representatives shall choose immediately, by ballot, the President. But in choosing the President, the votes shall be taken by States, the representation from each State having one vote; a quorum for this purpose shall consist of a member or members from two-thirds of the States, and a majority of all the States shall be necessary to a choice. And if the House of Representatives shall not choose a President whenever the right of choice shall devolve upon them, before the fourth day of March next following, then the Vice President shall act as President, as in the case of the death or other constitutional disability of the President.—The person having the greatest number of votes as Vice President, shall be the Vice President, if such number be a majority of the whole number of electors appointed, and if no person have a majority, then from the two highest numbers on the list, the Senate shall choose the Vice President; a quorum for the purpose shall consist of two-thirds of the whole number of Senators, and a majority of the whole number shall be necessary to a choice. But no person constitutionally ineligible to the office of President shall be eligible to that of Vice President of the United States.

Amendment XIII

SECTION 1. Neither slavery nor involuntary servitude, except as a punishment for crime whereof the party shall have been duly convicted, shall exist within the United States, or any place subject to their jurisdiction.

SECTION 2. Congress shall have power to enforce this article by appropriate legislation.

Amendment XIV

SECTION 1. All persons born or naturalized in the United States, and subject to the jurisdiction thereof, are citizens of the United States and of the State wherein they reside. No State shall make or enforce any law which shall abridge the privileges or immunities of citizens of the United States; nor shall any State deprive any person of life, liberty or property, without due process of law; nor deny to any person within its jurisdiction the equal protection of the laws.

SECTION 2. Representatives shall be appointed among the several States according to their respective numbers, counting the whole number of persons in each State, excluding Indians not taxed. But when the right to vote at any election for the choice of electors for President and Vice President of the United States, Representatives in Congress, the executive and judicial officers of a State, or members of the legislature thereof, is denied to any of the male inhabitants of such State, being twenty-one years of age, and citizens of the United States, or in any way abridged, except for participation in rebellion, or other crime, the basis of representation therein shall be reduced in the proportion which the number of such male citizens shall bear to the whole number of male citizens twenty-one years of age in such State.

SECTION 3. No person shall be a Senator or Representative in Congress, or elector of President and Vice President, or hold any office, civil or military, under the United States, or under any State, who, having previously taken an oath, as a member of Congress, or as an officer of the United States, or as a member of any State legislature, or as an executive or judicial officer of any State, to support the Constitution of the United States, shall have engaged in insurrection or rebellion against the same, or given aid or comfort to the enemies thereof. But Congress may by a vote of two-thirds of each house, remove such disability.

SECTION 4. The validity of the public debt of the United States, authorized by law, including debts incurred for payment of pensions and bounties for services in suppressing insurrection or rebellion, shall not be questioned. But neither the United States nor any State shall assume or pay any debt or obligation incurred in aid of insurrection or rebellion against the United States, or any claim for the loss or emancipation of any slave; but all such debts, obligations and claims shall be held illegal and void.

SECTION 5. The Congress shall have power to enforce, by appropriate legislation, the provisions of this article.

Amendment XV

SECTION 1. The right of citizens of the United States to vote shall not be denied or abridged by the United States or by any State on account of race, color, or previous condition of servitude.

SECTION 2. The Congress shall have power to enforce this article by appropriate legislation.

Amendment XVI

The Congress shall have power to lay and collect taxes on incomes, from whatever source derived, without apportionment among the several States, and without regard to any census of enumeration.

Amendment XVII

SECTION 1. The Senate of the United States shall be composed of two Senators from each State, elected by the people thereof, for six years; and each Senator shall have one vote. The electors in each State shall have the qualifications requisite for electors of the most numerous branch of the State legislatures.

SECTION 2. When vacancies happen in the representation of any State in the Senate, the executive authority of such State shall issue writs of election to fill such vacancies: *Provided*, That the legislature of any State may empower the executive thereof to make temporary appointments until the people fill the vacancies by election as the legislature may direct.

SECTION 3. This amendment shall not be so construed as to affect the election or term of any Senator chosen before it becomes valid as part of the Constitution.

Amendment XVIII

SECTION 1. After one year from the ratification of this article the manufacture, sale, or transportation of intoxicating liquors within, the importation thereof into, or the exportation thereof from the United States and all territory subject to the jurisdiction thereof for beverage purposes is hereby prohibited.

SECTION 2. The Congress and the several States shall have concurrent power to enforce this article by appropriate legislation.

SECTION 3. This article shall be inoperative unless it shall have been ratified as an amendment to the Constitution by the legislatures of the several States, as provided in the Constitution, within seven years from the date of the submission hereof to the States by the Congress.

Amendment XIX

SECTION 1. The right of citizens of the United States to vote shall not be denied or abridged by the United States or by any State on account of sex.

SECTION 2. Congress shall have power to enforce this article by appropriate legislation.

Amendment XX

SECTION 1. The terms of the President and Vice President shall end at noon on the 20th day of January, and the terms of Senators and Representatives at noon on the 3d day of January, of the years in which such terms would have ended if this article had not been ratified; and the terms of their successors shall then begin.

SECTION 2. The Congress shall assemble at least once in every year, and such meeting shall begin at noon on the 3d day of January, unless they shall by law appoint a different day.

SECTION 3. If, at the time fixed for the beginning of the term of the President, the President elect shall have died, the Vice President elect shall become President. If a President shall not have been chosen before the time fixed for the beginning of his term, or if the President elect shall have failed to qualify, then the Vice President elect shall act as President until a President shall have qualified; and the Congress may by law provide for the case wherein neither a President elect nor a Vice President elect shall have qualified, declaring who shall then act as President, or the manner in which one who is to act shall be selected, and such person shall act accordingly until a President or Vice President shall have qualified.

SECTION 4. The Congress may by law provide for the case of the death of any of the persons from whom the House of Representatives may choose a President whenever the right of choice shall have devolved upon them, and for the case of the death of any of the persons from whom the Senate may choose a Vice President whenever the right of choice shall have devolved upon them.

SECTION 5. Sections 1 and 2 shall take effect on the 15th day of October following the ratification of this article.

SECTION 6. This article shall be inoperative unless it shall have been ratified as an amendment to the Constitution by the legislatures of three-fourths of the several States within seven years from the date of its submission.

Amendment XXI

SECTION 1. The eighteenth article of amendment to the Constitution of the United States is hereby repealed.

SECTION 2. The transportation or importation into any State, Territory, or possession of the United States for delivery or use therein of intoxicating liquors, in violation of the laws thereof, is hereby prohibited.

SECTION 3. This article shall be inoperative unless it shall have been ratified as an amendment to the Constitution by conventions in the several States, as provided in the Constitution, within seven years from the date of the submission hereof to the States by the Congress.

Amendment XXII

SECTION 1. No person shall be elected to the office of the President more than twice, and no person who has held the office of President, or acted as President, for more than two years of a term to which some other person was elected President shall be elected to the office of the President more than once. But this article shall not apply to any person holding the office of President when this article was proposed by the Congress, and shall not prevent any person who may be holding the office of President, or acting as President, during the term within which this article becomes operative from holding the office of President or acting as President during the remainder of such term.

SECTION 2. This article shall be inoperative unless it shall have been ratified as an amendment to the Constitution by the legislatures of three-fourths of the several States within seven years from the date of its submission to the States by the Congress.

Amendment XXIII

SECTION 1. The District constituting the seat of Government of the United States shall appoint in such manner as the Congress may direct:

A number of electors of President and Vice President equal to the whole number of Senators and Representatives in Congress to which the District would be entitled if it were a State, but in no event more than the least populous State; they shall be in addition to those appointed by the States, but they shall be considered, for the purposes of the election of President and Vice President, to be electors appointed by a State; and they shall meet in the District and perform such duties as provided by the twelfth article of amendment.

SECTION 2. The Congress shall have power to enforce this article by appropriate legislation.

Amendment XXIV

SECTION 1. The right of citizens of the United States to vote in any primary or other election for President or Vice President, for electors for President or Vice President, or for Senator or Representative in Congress, shall not be denied or abridged by the United States or any State by reason of failure to pay any poll or other tax.

SECTION 2. The Congress shall have power to enforce this article by appropriate legislation.

Amendment XXV

SECTION 1. In case of the removal of the President from office or of his death or resignation, the Vice President shall become President.

SECTION 2. Whenever there is a vacancy in the office of the Vice President, the President shall nominate a Vice President who shall take office upon confirmation by a majority vote of both Houses of Congress.

SECTION 3. Whenever the President transmits to the President pro tempore of the Senate and the Speaker of the House of Representatives his written declaration that he is unable to discharge the powers and duties of his office, and until he transmits to them a written declaration to the contrary, such powers and duties shall be discharged by the Vice President as Acting President.

SECTION 4. Whenever the Vice President and a majority of either the principal officers of the executive departments or of such other body as Congress may by law provide, transmit to the President pro tempore of the Senate and the Speaker of the House of Representatives their written declaration that the President is unable to discharge the powers and duties of his office, the Vice President shall immediately assume the powers and duties of the office as Acting President.

Thereafter, when the President transmits to the President pro tempore of the Senate and the Speaker of the House of Representatives his written declaration that no inability exists, he shall resume the powers and duties of his office unless the Vice President and a majority of either the principal officers of the executive department or of such other body as Congress may by law provide, transmit within four days to the President pro tempore of the Senate and the Speaker of the House of Representatives their written declaration that the President is unable to discharge the powers and duties of his office. Thereupon Congress shall decide the issue, assembling within forty-eight hours for the purpose if not in session. If the Congress, within twenty-one days after receipt of the latter written declaration, or, if Congress is not in session, within twenty-one days after Congress is required to assemble, determines by two-thirds vote of both Houses that the President is unable to discharge the powers and duties of his office, the Vice President shall continue to discharge the same as Acting President; otherwise, the President shall resume the powers and duties of his office.

Amendment XXVI

SECTION 1. The right of citizens of the United States who are 18 years of age or older, to vote shall not be denied or abridged by the United States or by any State on account of age.

SECTION 2. The Congress shall have power to enforce this article by appropriate legislation.

Amendment XXVII

No law, varying the compensation for the services of the Senators and Representatives, shall take effect, until an election of Representatives shall have intervened.

APPENDIX II

PARALEGAL ETHICS

NALA Code of Ethics and Professional Responsibility

NALA Model Standards and Guidelines for Utilization of Legal Assistants (Annotated)

NFPA Model Code of Ethics and Professional Responsibility

THE NATIONAL ASSOCIATION OF LEGAL ASSISTANTS, INC. CODE OF ETHICS AND PROFESSIONAL RESPONSIBILITY[1]

Preamble

A legal assistant must adhere strictly to the accepted standards of legal ethics and to the general principles of proper conduct. The performance of the duties of the legal assistant shall be governed by specific canons as defined herein so that justice will be served and goals of the profession attained. (See Model Standards and Guidelines for Utilization of Legal Assistants, Section II.)

The canons of ethics set forth hereafter are adopted by the National Association of Legal Assistants, Inc., as a general guide intended to aid legal assistants and attorneys. The enumeration of these rules does not mean there are not others of equal importance although not specifically mentioned. Court rules, agency rules and statutes must be taken into consideration when interpreting the canons.

Definition

Legal assistants, also known as paralegals, are a distinguishable group of persons who assist attorneys in the delivery of legal services. Through formal education, training, and experience, legal assistants have knowledge and expertise regarding the legal system and substantive and procedural law which qualify them to do work of a legal nature under the supervision of an attorney.

Canon 1

A legal assistant must not perform any of the duties that attorneys only may perform nor take any actions that attorneys may not take.

[1]Reprinted with permission of the National Association of Legal Assistants. For further information, call 918-587-6828 or visit the NALA Web site at *www.nala.org/*.

Canon 2

A legal assistant may perform any task which is properly delegated and supervised by an attorney, as long as the attorney is ultimately responsible to the client, maintains a direct relationship with the client, and assumes professional responsibility for the work product (See NALA Model Standards and Guidelines, Section IV, Guideline 5.)

Canon 3

A legal assistant must not: (see NALA Model Standards and Guidelines for Utilization of Legal Assistants, Section IV, Guideline 2.)

a. engage in, encourage, or contribute to any act which could constitute the unauthorized practice of law; and
b. establish attorney-client relationships, set fees, give legal opinions or advice or represent a client before a court or agency unless so authorized by that court or agency; and
c. engage in conduct or take any action which would assist or involve the attorney in a violation of professional ethics or give the appearance of professional impropriety.

Canon 4

A legal assistant must use discretion and professional judgment commensurate with knowledge and experience but must not render independent legal judgment in place of an attorney. The services of an attorney are essential in the public interest whenever such legal judgment is required. (See NALA Model Standards and Guidelines, Section IV, Guideline 3.)

Canon 5

A legal assistant must disclose his or her status as a legal assistant at the outset of any professional relationship with a client, attorney, a court or administrative agency or personnel thereof, or a member of the general public. A legal assistant must act prudently in determining the extent to which a client may be assisted without the presence of an attorney. (See NALA Model Standards and Guidelines, Section IV, Guideline 1.)

Canon 6

A legal assistant must strive to maintain integrity and a high degree of competency through education and training with respect to professional responsibility, local rules and practice, and through continuing education in substantive areas of law to better assist the legal profession in fulfilling its duty to provide legal service.

Canon 7

A legal assistant must protect the confidences of a client and must not violate any rule or statute now in effect or hereafter enacted controlling the doctrine of privileged communications between a client and an attorney. (See ANLA Model Standards and Guidelines, Section IV, Guideline 1.)

Canon 8

A legal assistant must do all other things incidental, necessary, or expedient for the attainment of the ethics and responsibilities as defined by statute or rule of court.

Canon 9

A legal assistant's conduct is guided by bar associations' codes of professional responsibility and rules of professional conduct.

Adopted May 1, 1975
Revised 1979, 1988, and 1995

THE NATIONAL ASSOCIATION OF LEGAL ASSISTANTS, INC. MODEL STANDARDS AND GUIDELINES FOR UTILIZATION OF LEGAL ASSISTANTS (ANNOTATED)[2]

Introduction

The purpose of this annotated version of the National Association of Legal Assistants, Inc. (NALA) Model Standards and Guidelines for the Utilization of Legal Assistants is to provide references to the existing case law and other authorities where the underlying issues have been considered. The authorities cited will serve as a basis upon which conduct of a legal assistant may be analyzed as proper or improper.

The Guidelines represent a statement of how the legal assistant may function. The Guidelines are not intended to be a comprehensive or exhaustive list of the proper duties of a legal assistant. Rather, they are designed as guides to what may or may not be proper conduct for the legal assistant. In formulating the Guidelines, the reasoning and rules of law in many reported decisions of disciplinary cases and unauthorized practice of law cases have been analyzed and considered. In addition, the provisions of the American Bar Association's Model Rules of Professional Conduct, as well as the ethical promulgations of various state courts and bar associations, have been considered in development of the Guidelines.

These Guidelines form a sound basis for the legal assistant and the supervising attorney to follow. The Model will serve as a comprehensive resource document as well as a definitive, well-reasoned guide to those considering voluntary standards and guidelines for legal assistants.

I Preamble

Proper utilization of the services of legal assistants contributes to the delivery of cost-effective, high quality legal services. Legal assistants and the legal profession should be assured that measures exist for identifying legal assistants and their role in assisting attorneys in the delivery of legal services. Therefore, the National Association of Legal Assistants, Inc., hereby adopts these Standards and Guidelines as an educational document for the benefit of legal assistants and the legal profession.

Comment The three most frequently raised questions concerning legal assistants are (1) How do you define a legal assistant; (2) Who is qualified to be identified as a legal assistant; and (3) What duties may a legal assistant perform? The definition adopted in 1984 by the National Association of Legal Assistants answers the first question. The Model sets forth minimum education, training, and experience through standards which will assure that an individual utilizing the title "legal assistant" has the qualifications to be held out to the legal community and public in that capacity. The Guidelines identify those acts which the reported cases hold to be proscribed and give examples of services which the legal assistant may perform under the supervision of an attorney.

These Guidelines constitute a statement relating to services performed by legal assistants, as defined herein, as approved by court decisions and other sources of authority. The purpose of the Guidelines is not to place limitations or restrictions on the legal profession. Rather, the Guidelines are intended to outline for the legal profession an acceptable course of conduct. Voluntary recognition and utilization of the Standards and Guidelines will benefit the entire legal profession and the public it serves.

[2]Reprinted with permission of the National Association of Legal Assistants. For further information, call 918-587-6828 or visit the NALA Web site at *www.nala.org/*.

II Definition

The National Association of Legal Assistants adopted the following definition in 1984:

> Legal assistants, also known as paralegals, are a distinguishable group of persons who assist attorneys in the delivery of legal services. Through formal education, training, and experience, legal assistants have knowledge and expertise regarding the legal system and substantive and procedural law which qualify them to do work of a legal nature under the supervision of an attorney.

Comment This definition emphasizes the knowledge and expertise of legal assistants in substantive and procedural law obtained through education and work experience. It further defines the legal assistant or paralegal as a professional working under the supervision of an attorney from a non-lawyer who delivers services directly to the public without any intervention or review of work product by an attorney. Statutes, court rules, case law and bar associations are additional sources for legal assistant or paralegal definitions. In applying the Standards and Guidelines it is important to remember that they were developed to apply to the legal assistant as defined therein.

Lawyers should refrain from labeling those who do not meet the criteria set forth in this definition, such as secretaries and other administrative staff, as legal assistants.

For billing purposes, the services of a legal secretary are considered part of overhead costs and are not recoverable in fee awards. However, the courts have held that fees for paralegal services are recoverable as long as they are not clerical functions, such as organizing files, copying documents, checking docket, updating files, checking court dates and delivering papers. As established in *Missouri v. Jenkins,* 491 U.S. 274, 109 S. Ct. 2463, 2471, n. 10 (1989) tasks performed by legal assistants must be substantive in nature which, absent the legal assistant, the attorney would perform.

There are also case law and Supreme Court Rules addressing the issue of disbarred attorney serving in the capacity of a legal assistant.

III Standards

A legal assistant should meet certain minimum qualifications. The following standards may be used to determine an individual's qualifications as a legal assistant:

1. Successful completion of the certified legal assistant ("CLA") certifying examination of the National Association of Legal Assistants, Inc.;
2. Graduation from an ABA approved program of study for legal assistants;
3. Graduation from a course of study for legal assistants which is institutionally accredited but not ABA approved, and which requires not less than the equivalent of 60 semester hours of classroom study;
4. Graduation from a course of study for legal assistants, other than those set forth in (2) and (3) above, plus not less than six months of in-house training as a legal assistant;
5. A baccalaureate degree in any field, plus not less than six months in-house training as a legal assistant;
6. A minimum of three years of law-related experience under the supervision of an attorney, including at least six months of in-house training as a legal assistant; or
7. Two years of in-house training as a legal assistant.

For the purposes of these Standards, "in-house training as a legal assistant" means attorney education of the employee concerning legal assistant duties and these Guidelines. In addition to review and analysis of assignments the legal assistant should receive a reasonable amount of instruction directly related to the duties and obligations of the legal assistant.

Comment The Standards set forth suggested minimum qualifications for a legal assistant. These minimum qualifications as adopted recognize legal related work backgrounds and formal education backgrounds, both of which should provide the legal assistant with a broad base in exposure to and knowledge of the legal profession. This background is necessary to assure the public and the legal profession that the one being identified as a legal assistant is qualified.

The Certified Legal Assistant ("CLA") examination offered by NALA is a voluntary nationwide certification program for legal assistants. The CLA designation is a statement to the legal profession and the public that the legal assistant has met the high levels of knowledge and professionalism required by NALA's certification program. Continuing education requirements, which all certified legal assistants must meet, assure that high standards are maintained. The CLA designation has been recognized as a means of establishing the qualifications of a legal assistant in supreme court rules, state court and bar association standards and utilization guidelines.

Certification through NALA is available to any legal assistant meeting the educational and experience requirements. Certified Legal Assistants may also pursue advanced specialty certification ("CLAS") in the areas of bankruptcy, civil litigation, probate and estate planning, corporate and business law, criminal law and procedure, real estate, intellectual property, and may also pursue state certification based on state laws and procedures in California, Florida, Louisiana and Texas.*

IV Guidelines

These guidelines relating to standards of performance and professional responsibility are intended to aid legal assistants and attorneys. The ultimate responsibility rests with an attorney who employs legal assistants to educate them with respect to the duties they are assigned and to supervise the manner in which such duties are accomplished.

Comment In general, a legal assistant is allowed to perform any task which is properly delegated and supervised by an attorney, so long as the attorney is ultimately responsible to the client and assumes complete professional responsibility for the work product.

ABA Model Rules of Professional Conduct, Rule 5.3 provides:

> With respect to a non-lawyer employed or retained by or associated with a lawyer:
>
> (a) a partner in a law firm shall make reasonable efforts to ensure that the firm has in effect measures giving reasonable assurance that the person's conduct is compatible with the professional obligations of the lawyer;
>
> (b) a lawyer having direct supervisory authority over the non-lawyer shall make reasonable efforts to ensure that the person's conduct is compatible with the professional obligations of the lawyer; and

*The United States Supreme Court has addressed the issue concerning the utilization of professional credentials awarded by private organizations. In *Peel v. Attorney Registration and Disciplinary Committee of Illinois,* 496 U.S. 91, 110 S.Ct. 2281 (1990), the Court suggested that a claim of certification is truthful and not misleading if:

1. the claim itself is true;
2. the bases on which certification was awarded are factual and verifiable;
3. the certification in question is available to all professionals in the field who meet relevant, objective and consistently applied standards; and
4. the certification claim does not suggest any greater degree of professional qualification than reasonably may be inferred from an evaluation of the certification program's requirements.

Further, the Court advised that there must be a qualified organization to stand behind the certification process. For a detailed discussion of the *Peel* decision and the Certified Legal Assistant program, see "The Certified Legal Assistant Credential and Guidelines of the United States Supreme Court," 1996, National association of Legal Assistants, 1516 S. Boston, #200, Tulsa, OK 74119 or *www.nala.org/.*

> (c) a lawyer shall be responsible for conduct of such a person that would be a violation of the rules of professional conduct if engaged in by a lawyer if:
>
> (1) the lawyer orders or, with the knowledge of the specific conduct ratifies the conduct involved; or
>
> (2) the lawyer is a partner in the law firm in which the person is employed, or has direct supervisory authority over the person, and knows of the conduct at a time when its consequences can be avoided or mitigated but fails to take reasonable remedial actions.

There are many interesting and complex issues involving the use of legal assistants. In any discussion of the proper role of a legal assistant, attention must be directed to what constitutes the practice of law. Proper delegation to legal assistants is further complicated and confused by the lack of an adequate definition of the practice of law.

Kentucky became the first state to adopt a Paralegal Code by Supreme Court Rule. This Code sets forth certain exclusions to the unauthorized practice of law:

> For the purpose of this rule, the unauthorized practice of law shall not include any service rendered involving legal knowledge or advice, whether representation, counsel or advocacy, in or out of court, rendered in respect to the acts, duties, obligations, liabilities or business relations of the one requiring services where:
>
> A. The client understands that the paralegal is not a lawyer;
>
> B. The lawyer supervises the paralegal in the performance of his duties; and
>
> C. The lawyer remains fully responsible for such representation, including all actions taken or not taken in connection therewith by the paralegal to the same extent as if such representation had been furnished entirely by the lawyer and all such actions had been taken or not taken directly by the attorney. Paralegal Code, Ky. S. Ct. R. 3.700, Sub-Rule 2

South Dakota Supreme Court Rule 97-25 Utilization Rule a(4) states:

> The attorney remains responsible for the services performed by the legal assistant to the same extent as though such services had been furnished entirely by the attorney and such actions were those of the attorney.

Guideline 1 Legal assistants should:

1. Disclose their status as legal assistant at the outset of any professional relationship with a client, other attorneys, a court or administrative agency or personnel thereof, or members of the general public;
2. Preserve the confidences and secrets of all clients; and
3. Understand the attorney's Code of Professional Responsibility and these guidelines in order to avoid any action which would involve the attorney in a violation of that Code, or give the appearance of professional impropriety.

Comment Routine early disclosure of the legal assistant's status when dealing with persons outside the attorney's office is necessary to assure that there will be no misunderstanding as to the responsibilities and role of the legal assistant. Disclosure may be made in any way that avoids confusion. If the person dealing with the legal assistant already knows of his/her status, further disclosure is unnecessary. If at any time in written or in oral communication the legal assistant becomes aware that the other person may believe the legal assistant is an attorney, immediate disclosure should be made as to the legal assistant's status.

The attorney should exercise care that the legal assistant preserves and refrains from using any confidence or secrets of a client, and should instruct the legal assistant not to disclose or use any such confidences or secrets.

The legal assistant must take any and all steps necessary to prevent conflicts of interest and fully disclose such conflicts to the supervising attorney. Failure to do so may jeopardize both the attorney's representation of the client and the case itself.

Guidelines for the Utilization of Legal Assistant Services adopted December 3, 1994, by the Washington State Bar Association Board of Governors states:

> Guideline 7: A lawyer shall take reasonable measures to prevent conflicts of interest resulting from a legal assistant's other employment or interest insofar as such other employment or interests would present a conflict of interest if it were that of the lawyer.

In re Complex Asbestos Litigation, 232 Cal. App. 3d 572 (1991), addresses the issue wherein a law firm was disqualified due to possession of attorney-client confidences by a legal assistant employee resulting from previous employment by opposing counsel.

The ultimate responsibility for compliance with approved standards of professional conduct rests with the supervising attorney. The burden rests upon the attorney who employs a legal assistant to educate the latter with respect to the duties which may be assigned and then to supervise the manner in which the legal assistant carries out such duties. However, this does not relieve the legal assistant from an independent obligation to refrain from illegal conduct. Additionally, and notwithstanding that the Rules are not binding upon non-lawyers, the very nature of a legal assistant's employment imposes an obligation not to engage in conduct which would involve the supervising attorney in violation of the Rules.

The attorney must make sufficient background investigation of the prior activities and character and integrity of his or her legal assistants.

Further the attorney must take all measures necessary to avoid and fully disclose conflicts of interest due to other employment or interests. Failure to do so may jeopardize both the attorney's representation of the client and the case itself.

Legal assistant associations strive to maintain the high level of integrity and competence expected of the legal profession and, further, strive to uphold the high standards of ethics.

NALA's Code of Ethics and Professional Responsibility states:

> A legal assistant's conduct is guided by bar associations' codes of professional responsibility and rules of professional conduct.

Guideline 2 Legal assistants should not:

1. Establish attorney-client relationships; set legal fees, give legal opinions or advice; or represent a client before a court unless authorized to do so by said court; nor
2. Engage in, encourage, or contribute to any act which could constitute the unauthorized practice of law.

Comment Case law, court rules, codes of ethics and professional responsibilities, as well as bar ethics opinions now hold which acts can and cannot be performed by a legal assistant. Generally, the determination of what acts constitute the unauthorized practice of law is made by State Supreme Courts.

Numerous cases exist relating to the unauthorized practice of law. Courts have gone so far as to prohibit a legal assistant from preparation of divorce kits and assisting in preparation of bankruptcy forms and, more specifically, from providing basic information about procedures and requirements, deciding where information should be placed on forms and responding to questions from debtors regarding the interpretation or definition of terms.

Cases have identified certain areas in which an attorney has a duty to act, but it is interesting to note that none of these cases state that it is improper for an attorney to have the initial work performed by the legal assistant. This again points out the importance of adequate supervision by the employing attorney.

An attorney can be found to have aided in the unauthorized practice of law when delegating acts which cannot be performed by a legal assistant.

Guideline 3 Legal assistants may perform services for an attorney in the representation of a client, provided:

1. The services performed by the legal assistant do not require the exercise of independent professional legal judgment;
2. The attorney maintains a direct relationship with the client and maintains control of all client matters;
3. The attorney supervises the legal assistant;
4. The attorney remains professionally responsible for all work on behalf of the client; including any actions taken or not taken by the legal assistant in connection therewith; and
5. The services performed supplement, merge with, and become the attorney's work product.

Comment Legal assistants, whether employees or independent contractors, perform services for the attorney in the representation of a client. Attorneys should delegate work to legal assistants commensurate with their knowledge and experience and provide appropriate instruction and supervision concerning the delegated work, as well as ethical acts of their employment. Ultimate responsibility for the work product of a legal assistant rests with the attorney. However, a legal assistant must use discretion and professional judgment and must not render independent legal judgment in place of an attorney.

The work product of a legal assistant is subject to civil rules governing discovery of materials prepared in anticipation of litigation, whether the legal assistant is viewed as an extension of the attorney or as anther representative of the party itself. Fed. R. Civ. P. 26 (b)(2).

Guideline 4 In the supervision of a legal assistant, consideration should be given to:

1. Designating work assignments that correspond to the legal assistant's abilities, knowledge, training and experience;
2. Educating and training the legal assistant with respect to professional responsibility, local rules and practices, and firm policies;
3. Monitoring the work and professional conduct of the legal assistant to ensure that the work is substantively correct and timely performed;
4. Providing continuing education for the legal assistant in substantive matters through courses, institutes, workshops, seminars and in-house training; and
5. Encouraging and supporting membership and active participation in professional organizations.

Comment Attorneys are responsible for the actions of their employees in both malpractice and disciplinary proceedings. In the vast majority of cases, the courts have not censured attorneys for the particular act delegated to the legal assistant, but rather, have been critical of and imposed sanctions against attorneys for failure to adequately supervise the legal assistants. The attorney's responsibility for supervision of legal assistants must be more than a willingness to accept responsibility and liability for the legal assistant's work. Supervision of legal assistants must be offered in both the procedural and substantive legal areas in the law office. The attorney must delegate work based upon the education, knowledge and abilities of the legal assistant and must monitor the work product and conduct of the legal assistant to insure that the work performed is substantively correct and competently performed in a professional manner.

Michigan State Board of Commissioners has adopted Guidelines for the Utilization of Legal Assistants (April 23, 1993). These guidelines, in part, encourage employers to support legal assistant participation in continuing education programs to ensure that the legal assistant remains competent in the fields of practice in which the legal assistant is assigned.

The working relationship between the lawyer and the legal assistant should extend to cooperative efforts on public service activities wherever possible. Participation in pro bono activities is encouraged in ABA Guideline 10.

Guideline 5 Except as otherwise provided by statute, court rule or decision, administrative rule or regulation, or the attorney's rules of professional responsibility, and within the preceding parameters and proscriptions, a legal assistant may perform any function delegated by an attorney, including but not limited to the following:

1. Conduct client interviews and maintain general contact with the client after the establishment of the attorney-client relationship, so long as the client is aware of the status and function of the legal assistant, and the client contact is under the supervision of the attorney.
2. Locate and interview witnesses, so long as the witnesses are aware of the status and function of the legal assistant.
3. Conduct investigations and statistical and documentary research for review by the attorney.
4. Conduct legal research for review by the attorney.
5. Draft legal documents for review by the attorney.
6. Draft correspondence and pleadings for review by and signature of the attorney.
7. Summarize depositions, interrogatories, and testimony for review by the attorney.
8. Attend executions of wills, real estate closings, depositions, court or administrative hearings, and trials with the attorney.
9. Author and sign letters provided the legal assistant's status is clearly indicated and the correspondence does not contain independent legal opinions or legal advice.

Comment The United States Supreme Court has recognized the variety of tasks being performed by legal assistants and has noted that use of legal assistants encourages cost effective delivery of legal services, *Missouri v. Jenkins,* 491 U.S. 274, 109 S. Ct. 2463, 2471, n. 10 (1989). In *Jenkins,* the court further held that legal assistant time should be included in compensation for attorney fee awards at the prevailing practice in the relevant community to bill legal assistant time.

Courts have held that legal assistant fees are not a part of the overall overhead of a law firm. Legal assistant services are billed separately by attorneys, and decrease litigation expenses. Tasks performed by legal assistants must contain substantive legal work under the direction or supervision of an attorney, such that if the legal assistant were not present, the work would be performed by the attorney.

In *Taylor v. Chubb,* 874 P.2d 806 (Okla. 1994), the Court ruled that attorney fees awarded should include fees for services performed by legal assistants and, further, defined tasks which may be performed by the legal assistant under the supervision of an attorney including, among others: interview clients; draft pleadings and other documents; carry on legal research, both conventional and computer aided; research public records; prepare discovery requests and responses; schedule depositions and prepare notices and subpoenas; summarize depositions and other discovery responses; coordinate and manage document production; locate and interview witnesses; organize pleadings, trial exhibits and other documents; prepare witness and exhibit lists; prepare trial notebooks; prepare for the attendance of witnesses at trial; and assist lawyers at trials.

Except for the specific proscription contained in Guideline 1, the reported cases do not limit the duties which may be performed by a legal assistant under the supervision of the attorney.

An attorney may not split legal fees with a legal assistant, nor pay a legal assistant for the referral of legal business. An attorney may compensate a legal assistant based on the quantity and quality of the legal assistant's work and value of that work to a law practice.

Conclusion

The Standards and Guidelines were developed from generally accepted practices. Each supervising attorney must be aware of the specific rules, decisions and statutes applicable to legal assistants within his jurisdiction.

Addendum

For further information, the following cases may be helpful to you:

Duties

Taylor v. Chubb, 874 P.2d 806 (Okla. 1994)
McMackin v. McMackin, 651 A.2d 778 (Del. Fam. Ct. 1993)

Work Product

Fine v. Facet Aerospace Products Co., 133 F.R.D. 439 (S.D.N.Y. 1990)

Unauthorized Practice of Law

Akron Bar Assn. v. Green, 673 N.E.2d 1307 (Ohio 1997)
In re Hessinger & Associates, 192 B.R. 211 (N.D. Calif. 1996)
In the Matter of Bright, 171 B.R. 799 (Bkrtcy. E.D. Mich)
Louisiana State Bar Assn. v. Edwins, 540 So. 2d 294 (La. 1989)

Attorney/Client Privilege

In re Complex Asbestos Litigation, 232 Cal. App. 3d 572 (Calif. 1991)
Makita Corp. v. United States, 819 F. Supp. 1099 (CIT 1993)

Conflicts

In re Complex Asbestos Litigation, 232 Cal. App. 3d 572 (Calif. 1991)
Makita Corp. v. United States, 819 F. Supp. 1099 (CIT 1993)
Smart Industries v. Superior Court, 876 P.2d 1176 (Ariz. App. Div. 1994)

Supervision

Matter of Martinez, 754 P.2d 842 (N.M. 1988)
State v. Barrett, 483 P.2d 1106 (Kan. 1971)

Fee Awards

In re Bicostal Corp., 121 B.R. 653 (Bkrtcy. M.D. Fla. 1990)
Taylor v. Chubb, 874 P.2d 806 (Okla. 1994)
Missouri v. Jenkins, 491 U.S. 274, 109 S. Ct. 2463, 105 L. Ed. 2d 229 (1989), 11 U.S.C.A. Section 330
McMackin v. McMackin, 651 A.2d 778 (Del. Fam. Ct. 1993)
Miller v. Alamo, 983 F.2d 856 (8th Cir. 1993)
Stewart v. Sullivan, 810 F. Supp. 1102 (D. Hawaii 1993)
In re Yankton College, 101 B.R. 151 (Bkrtcy D.S.D. 1989)
Stacey v. Stroud, 845 F. Supp. 1135 (S.D.W.Va. 1993)

Court Appearances

Louisiana State Bar Assn. v. Edwins, 540 So. 2d 294 (La. 1989)

NATIONAL FEDERATION OF PARALEGAL ASSOCIATIONS, INC. MODEL CODE OF ETHICS AND PROFESSIONAL RESPONSIBILITY AND GUIDELINES FOR ENFORCEMENT[3]

PREAMBLE

The National Federation of Paralegal Associations, Inc. ("NFPA") is a professional organization comprised of paralegal associations and individual paralegals throughout the United States and Canada. Members of NFPA have varying backgrounds, experiences, education and job responsibilities that reflect the diversity of the paralegal profession. NFPA promotes the growth, development and recognition of the paralegal profession as an integral partner in the delivery of legal services.

In May 1993 NFPA adopted its Model Code of Ethics and Professional Responsibility ("Model Code") to delineate the principles for ethics and conduct to which every paralegal should aspire.

Many paralegal associations throughout the United States have endorsed the concept and content of NFPA's Model Code through the adoption of their own ethical codes. In doing so, paralegals have confirmed the profession's commitment to increase the quality and efficiency of legal services, as well as recognized its responsibilities to the public, the legal community, and colleagues.

Paralegals have recognized, and will continue to recognize, that the profession must continue to evolve to enhance their roles in the delivery of legal services. With increased levels of responsibility comes the need to define and enforce mandatory rules of professional conduct. Enforcement of codes of paralegal conduct is a logical and necessary step to enhance and ensure the confidence of the legal community and the public in the integrity and professional responsibility of paralegals.

In April 1997 NFPA adopted the Model Disciplinary Rules ("Model Rules") to make possible the enforcement of the Canons and Ethical Considerations contained in the NFPA Model Code. A concurrent determination was made that the Model Code of Ethics and Professional Responsibility, formerly aspirational in nature, should be recognized as setting forth the enforceable obligations of all paralegals.

The Model Code and Model Rules offer a framework for professional discipline, either voluntarily or through formal regulatory programs.

§1. NFPA MODEL DISCIPLINARY RULES AND ETHICAL CONSIDERATIONS

1.1 A PARALEGAL SHALL ACHIEVE AND MAINTAIN A HIGH LEVEL OF COMPETENCE

Ethical Considerations

EC-1.1(a) A paralegal shall achieve competency through education, training, and work experience.

EC-1.1(b) A paralegal shall participate in continuing education in order to keep informed of current legal, technical and general developments.

EC-1.1(c) A paralegal shall perform all assignments promptly and efficiently.

[3]Printed with permission of the National Federal of Paralegal Associations.

1.2 A Paralegal Shall Maintain a High Level of Personal and Professional Integrity

Ethical Considerations

EC-1.2(a) A paralegal shall not engage in any ex parte communications involving the courts or any other adjudicatory body in an attempt to exert undue influence or to obtain advantage or the benefit of only one party.

EC-1.2(b) A paralegal shall not communicate, or cause another to communicate, with a party the paralegal knows to be represented by a lawyer in a pending matter without the prior consent of the lawyer representing such other party.

EC-1.2(c) A paralegal shall ensure that all timekeeping and billing records prepared by the paralegal are thorough, accurate, honest, and complete.

EC-1.2(d) A paralegal shall not knowingly engage in fraudulent billing practices. Such practices may include, but are not limited to: inflation of hours billed to a client or employer; misrepresentation of the nature of tasks performed; and/or submission of fraudulent expense and disbursement documentation.

EC-1.2(e) A paralegal shall be scrupulous, thorough and honest in the identification and maintenance of all funds, securities, and other assets of a client and shall provide accurate accounting as appropriate.

EC-1.2(f) A paralegal shall advise the proper authority of non-confidential knowledge of any dishonest or fraudulent acts by any person pertaining to the handling of the funds, securities or other assets of a client. The authority to whom the report is made shall depend on the nature and circumstances of the possible misconduct, (e.g., ethics committees of law firms, corporations and/or paralegal associations, local or state bar associations, local prosecutors, administrative agencies, etc.). Failure to report such knowledge is in itself misconduct and shall be treated as such under these rules.

1.3 A Paralegal Shall Maintain a High Standard of Professional Conduct

Ethical Considerations

EC-1.3(a) A paralegal shall refrain from engaging in any conduct that offends the dignity and decorum of proceedings before a court or other adjudicatory body and shall be respectful of all rules and procedures.

EC-1.3(b) A paralegal shall avoid impropriety and the appearance of impropriety and shall not engage in any conduct that would adversely affect his/her fitness to practice. Such conduct may include, but is not limited to: violence, dishonesty, interference with the administration of justice, and/or abuse of a professional position or public office.

EC-1.3(c) Should a paralegal's fitness to practice be compromised by physical or mental illness, causing that paralegal to commit an act that is in direct violation of the Model Code/Model Rules and/or the rules and/or laws governing the jurisdiction in which the paralegal practices, that paralegal may be protected from sanction upon review of the nature and circumstances of that illness.

EC-1.3(d) A paralegal shall advise the proper authority of non-confidential knowledge of any action of another legal professional that clearly demonstrates fraud, deceit, dishonesty, or misrepresentation. The authority to whom the report is made shall depend on the nature and circumstances of the possible misconduct, (e.g., ethics committees of law firms, corporations and/or paralegal associations, local or state bar associations, local prosecutors, administrative agencies, etc.). Failure to report such knowledge is in itself misconduct and shall be treated as such under these rules.

EC-1.3(e) A paralegal shall not knowingly assist any individual with the commission of an act that is in direct violation of the Model Code/Model Rules and/or the rules and/or laws governing the jurisdiction in which the paralegal practices.

EC-1.3(f) If a paralegal possesses knowledge of future criminal activity, that knowledge must be reported to the appropriate authority immediately.

1.4 A Paralegal Shall Serve the Public Interest by Contributing to the Improvement of the Legal System and Delivery of Quality Legal Services, Including Pro Bono Publico Services

Ethical Considerations

EC-1.4(a) A paralegal shall be sensitive to the legal needs of the public and shall promote the development and implementation of programs that address those needs.

EC-1.4(b) A paralegal shall support efforts to improve the legal system and access thereto and shall assist in making changes.

EC-1.4(c) A paralegal shall support and participate in the delivery of Pro Bono Publico services directed toward implementing and improving access to justice, the law, the legal system or the paralegal and legal professions.

EC-1.4(d) A paralegal should aspire annually to contribute twenty-four (24) hours of Pro Bono Publico services under the supervision of an attorney or as authorized by administrative, statutory or court authority to:

1. persons of limited means; or
2. charitable, religious, civic, community, governmental and educational organizations in matters that are designed primarily to address the legal needs of persons with limited means; or
3. individuals, groups or organizations seeking to secure or protect civil rights, civil liberties or public rights.

1.5 A Paralegal Shall Preserve all Confidential Information Provided by the Client or Acquired from Other Sources Before, During, and After the Course of the Professional Relationship

Ethical Considerations

EC-1.5(a) A paralegal shall be aware of and abide by all legal authority governing confidential information in the jurisdiction in which the paralegal practices.

EC-1.5(b) A paralegal shall not use confidential information to the disadvantage of the client.

EC-1.5(c) A paralegal shall not use confidential information to the advantage of the paralegal or of a third person.

EC-1.5(d) A paralegal may reveal confidential information only after full disclosure and with the client's written consent; or, when required by law or court order; or, when necessary to prevent the client from committing an act that could result in death or serious bodily harm.

EC-1.5(e) A paralegal shall keep those individuals responsible for the legal representation of a client fully informed of any confidential information the paralegal may have pertaining to that client.

EC-1.5(f) A paralegal shall not engage in any indiscreet communications concerning clients.

1.6 A Paralegal Shall Avoid Conflicts of Interest and Shall Disclose any Possible Conflict to the Employer or Client, as Well as to the Prospective Employers or Clients

Ethical Considerations

EC-1.6(a) A paralegal shall act within the bounds of the law, solely for the benefit of the client, and shall be free of compromising influences and loyalties. Neither the paralegal's personal or business interest, nor those of other clients or third persons, should compromise the paralegal's professional judgment and loyalty to the client.

EC-1.6(b) A paralegal shall avoid conflicts of interest that may arise from previous assignments, whether for a present or past employer or client.

EC-1.6(c) A paralegal shall avoid conflicts of interest that may arise from family relationships and from personal and business interests.

EC-1.6(d) In order to be able to determine whether an actual or potential conflict of interest exists a paralegal shall create and maintain an effective recordkeeping system that identifies clients, matters, and parties with which the paralegal has worked.

EC-1.6(e) A paralegal shall reveal sufficient non-confidential information about a client or former client to reasonably ascertain if an actual or potential conflict of interest exists.

EC-1.6(f) A paralegal shall not participate in or conduct work on any matter where a conflict of interest has been identified.

EC-1.6(g) In matters where a conflict of interest has been identified and the client consents to continued representation, a paralegal shall comply fully with the implementation and maintenance of an Ethical Wall.

1.7 A Paralegal's Title Shall Be Fully Disclosed

Ethical Considerations

EC-1.7(a) A paralegal's title shall clearly indicate the individual's status and shall be disclosed in all business and professional communications to avoid misunderstandings and misconceptions about the paralegal's role and responsibilities.

EC-1.7(b) A paralegal's title shall be included if the paralegal's name appears on business cards, letterhead, brochures, directories, and advertisements.

EC-1.7(c) A paralegal shall not use letterhead, business cards or other promotional materials to create a fraudulent impression of his/her status or ability to practice in the jurisdiction in which the paralegal practices.

EC-1.7(d) A paralegal shall not practice under color of any record, diploma, or certificate that has been illegally or fraudulently obtained or issued or which is misrepresentative in any way.

EC-1.7(e) A paralegal shall not participate in the creation, issuance, or dissemination of fraudulent records, diplomas, or certificates.

1.8 A Paralegal Shall not Engage in the Unauthorized Practice of Law

Ethical Considerations

EC-1.8(a) A paralegal shall comply with the applicable legal authority governing the unauthorized practice of law in the jurisdiction in which the paralegal practices.

§2. NFPA GUIDELINES FOR THE ENFORCEMENT OF THE MODEL CODE OF ETHICS AND PROFESSIONAL RESPONSIBILITY

2.1 Basis for Discipline

2.1(a) Disciplinary investigations and proceedings brought under authority of the Rules shall be conducted in accord with obligations imposed on the paralegal professional by the Model Code of Ethics and Professional Responsibility.

2.2 Structure of Disciplinary Committee

2.2(a) The Disciplinary Committee ("Committee") shall be made up of nine (9) members including the Chair.

2.2(b) Each member of the Committee, including any temporary replacement members, shall have demonstrated working knowledge of ethics/professional responsibility-related issues and activities.

2.2(c) The Committee shall represent a cross-section of practice areas and work experience. The following recommendations are made regarding the members of the Committee.

1) At least one paralegal with one to three years of law-related work experience.
2) At least one paralegal with five to seven years of law-related work experience.
3) At least one paralegal with over ten years of law-related work experience.
4) One paralegal educator with five to seven years of work experience; preferably in the area of ethics/professional responsibility.
5) One paralegal manager.
6) One lawyer with five to seven years of law-related work experience.
7) One lay member.

2.2(d) The Chair of the Committee shall be appointed within thirty (30) days of its members' induction. The Chair shall have no fewer than ten (10) years of law-related work experience.

2.2(e) The terms of all members of the Committee shall be staggered. Of those members initially appointed, a simple majority plus one shall be appointed to a term of one year, and the remaining members shall be appointed to a term of two years. Thereafter, all members of the Committee shall be appointed to terms of two years.

2.2(f) If for any reason the terms of a majority of the Committee will expire at the same time, members may be appointed to terms of one year to maintain continuity of the Committee.

2.2(g) The Committee shall organize from its members a three-tiered structure to investigate, prosecute and/or adjudicate charges of misconduct. The members shall be rotated among the tiers.

2.3 Operation of Committee

2.3(a) The Committee shall meet on an as-needed basis to discuss, investigate, and/or adjudicate alleged violations of the Model Code/Model Rules.

2.3(b) A majority of the members of the Committee present at a meeting shall constitute a quorum.

2.3(c) A Recording Secretary shall be designated to maintain complete and accurate minutes of all Committee meetings. All such minutes shall be kept confidential until a decision has been made that the matter will be set for hearing as set forth in Section 6.1 below.

2.3(d) If any member of the Committee has a conflict of interest with the Charging Party, the Responding Party, or the allegations of misconduct, that member shall not take part in any hearing or deliberations concerning those allegations. If the absence of that member creates a lack of a quorum for the Committee, then a temporary replacement for the member shall be appointed.

2.3(e) Either the Charging Party or the Responding Party may request that, for good cause shown, any member of the Committee not participate in a hearing or deliberation. All such requests shall be honored. If the absence of a Committee member under those circumstances creates a lack of a quorum for the Committee, then a temporary replacement for that member shall be appointed.

2.3(f) All discussions and correspondence of the Committee shall be kept confidential until a decision has been made that the matter will be set for hearing as set forth in Section 6.1 below.

2.3(g) All correspondence from the Committee to the Responding Party regarding any charge of misconduct and any decisions made regarding the charge shall be mailed certified mail, return receipt requested, to the Responding Party's last known address and shall be clearly marked with a "Confidential" designation.

2.4 Procedure for the Reporting of Alleged Violations of the Model Code/Disciplinary Rules

2.4(a) An individual or entity in possession of non-confidential knowledge or information concerning possible instances of misconduct shall make a confidential written report to the Committee within thirty (30) days of obtaining same. This report shall include all details of the alleged misconduct.

2.4(b) The Committee so notified shall inform the Responding Party of the allegation(s) of misconduct no later than ten (10) business days after receiving the confidential written report from the Charging Party.

2.4(c) Notification to the Responding Party shall include the identity of the Charging Party, unless, for good cause shown, the Charging Party requests anonymity.

2.4(d) The Responding Party shall reply to the allegations within ten (10) business days of notification.

2.5 Procedure for the Investigation of a Charge of Misconduct

2.5(a) Upon receipt of a Charge of Misconduct ("Charge"), or on its own initiative, the Committee shall initiate an investigation.

2.5(b) If, upon initial or preliminary review, the Committee makes a determination that the charges are either without basis in fact or, if proven, would not constitute professional misconduct, the Committee shall dismiss the allegations of misconduct. If such determination of dismissal cannot be made, a formal investigation shall be initiated.

2.5(c) Upon the decision to conduct a formal investigation, the Committee shall:

1) mail to the Charging and Responding Parties within three (3) business days of that decision notice of the commencement of a formal investigation. That notification shall be in writing and shall contain a complete explanation of all Charge(s), as well as the reasons for a formal investigation and shall cite the applicable codes and rules;

2) allow the Responding Party thirty (30) days to prepare and submit a confidential response to the Committee, which response shall address each charge specifically and shall be in writing; and

3) upon receipt of the response to the notification, have thirty (30) days to investigate the Charge(s). If an extension of time is deemed necessary, that extension shall not exceed ninety (90) days.

2.5(d) Upon conclusion of the investigation, the Committee may:
1) dismiss the Charge upon the finding that it has no basis in fact;
2) dismiss the Charge upon the finding that, if proven, the Charge would not constitute Misconduct;
3) refer the matter for hearing by the Tribunal; or
4) in the case of criminal activity, refer the Charge(s) and all investigation results to the appropriate authority.

2.6 Procedure for a Misconduct Hearing Before a Tribunal

2.6(a) Upon the decision by the Committee that a matter should be heard, all parties shall be notified and a hearing date shall be set. The hearing shall take place no more than thirty (30) days from the conclusion of the formal investigation.

2.6(b) The Responding Party shall have the right to counsel. The parties and the Tribunal shall have the right to call any witnesses and introduce any documentation that they believe will lead to the fair and reasonable resolution of the matter.

2.6(c) Upon completion of the hearing, the Tribunal shall deliberate and present a written decision to the parties in accordance with procedures as set forth by the Tribunal.

2.6(d) Notice of the decision of the Tribunal shall be appropriately published.

2.7 Sanctions

2.7(a) Upon a finding of the Tribunal that misconduct has occurred, any of the following sanctions, or others as may be deemed appropriate, may be imposed upon the Responding Party, either singularly or in combination:
1) letter of reprimand to the Responding Party; counseling; 2) attendance at an ethics course approved by the Tribunal; probation; 3) suspension of license/authority to practice; revocation of license/authority to practice; 4) imposition of a fine; assessment of costs; or 5) in the instance of criminal activity, referral to the appropriate authority.

2.7(b) Upon the expiration of any period of probation, suspension, or revocation, the Responding Party may make application for reinstatement. With the application for reinstatement, the Responding Party must show proof of having complied with all aspects of the sanctions imposed by the Tribunal.

2.8 Appellate Procedures

2.8(a) The parties shall have the right to appeal the decision of the Tribunal in accordance with the procedure as set forth by the Tribunal.

Definitions

"Appellate Body" means a body established to adjudicate an appeal to any decision made by a Tribunal or other decision-making body with respect to formally-heard Charges of Misconduct.

"Charge of Misconduct" means a written submission by any individual or entity to an ethics committee, paralegal association, bar association, law enforcement agency, judicial body, government agency, or other appropriate body or entity, that sets forth non-confidential information regarding any instance of alleged misconduct by an individual paralegal or paralegal entity.

"Charging Party" means any individual or entity who submits a Charge of Misconduct against an individual paralegal or paralegal entity.

"Competency" means the demonstration of: diligence, education, skill, and mental, emotional, and physical fitness reasonably necessary for the performance of paralegal services.

"Confidential Information" means information relating to a client, whatever its source, that is not public knowledge nor available to the public. ("Non-Confidential Information" would generally include the name of the client and the identity of the matter for which the paralegal provided services.)

"Disciplinary Hearing" means the confidential proceeding conducted by a committee or other designated body or entity concerning any instance of alleged misconduct by an individual paralegal or paralegal entity.

"Disciplinary Committee" means any committee that has been established by an entity such as a paralegal association, bar association, judicial body, or government agency to: (a) identify, define and investigate general ethical considerations and concerns with respect to paralegal practice; (b) administer and enforce the Model Code and Model Rules and; (c) discipline any individual paralegal or paralegal entity found to be in violation of same.

"Disclose" means communication of information reasonably sufficient to permit identification of the significance of the matter in question.

"Ethical Wall" means the screening method implemented in order to protect a client from a conflict of interest. An Ethical Wall generally includes, but is not limited to, the following elements: (1) prohibit the paralegal from having any connection with the matter; (2) ban discussions with or the transfer of documents to or from the paralegal; (3) restrict access to files; and (4) educate all members of the firm, corporation, or entity as to the separation of the paralegal (both organizationally and physically) from the pending matter. For more information regarding the Ethical Wall, see the NFPA publication entitled "The Ethical Wall—Its Application to Paralegals."

"Ex parte" means actions or communications conducted at the instance and for the benefit of one party only, and without notice to, or contestation by, any person adversely interested.

"Investigation" means the investigation of any charge(s) of misconduct filed against an individual paralegal or paralegal entity by a Committee.

"Letter of Reprimand" means a written notice of formal censure or severe reproof administered to an individual paralegal or paralegal entity for unethical or improper conduct.

"Misconduct" means the knowing or unknowing commission of an act that is in direct violation of those Canons and Ethical Considerations of any and all applicable codes and/or rules of conduct.

"Paralegal" is synonymous with "Legal Assistant" and is defined as a person qualified through education, training, or work experience to perform substantive legal work that requires knowledge of legal concepts and is customarily, but not exclusively performed by a lawyer. This person may be retained or employed by a lawyer, law office, governmental agency, or other entity or may be authorized by administrative, statutory, or court authority to perform this work.

"Pro Bono Publico" means providing or assisting to provide quality legal services in order to enhance access to justice for persons of limited means; charitable, religious, civic, community, governmental and educational organizations in matters that are designed primarily to address the legal needs of persons with limited means; or individuals, groups or organizations seeking to secure or protect civil rights, civil liberties or public rights.

"Proper Authority" means the local paralegal association, the local or state bar association, Committee(s) of the local paralegal or bar association(s), local prosecutor, administrative agency, or other tribunal empowered to investigate or act upon an instance of alleged misconduct.

"Responding Party" means an individual paralegal or paralegal entity against whom a Charge of Misconduct has been submitted.

"Revocation" means the recision of the license, certificate or other authority to practice of an individual paralegal or paralegal entity found in violation of those Canons and Ethical Considerations of any and all applicable codes and/or rules of conduct.

"Suspension" means the suspension of the license, certificate or other authority to practice of an individual paralegal or paralegal entity found in violation of those Canons and Ethical Considerations of any and all applicable codes and/or rules of conduct.

"Tribunal" means the body designated to adjudicate allegations of misconduct.

APPENDIX III

MOCK TRIAL

An important part of our legal system is the trial. In this text we have introduced you to that process, including the roles of the various courtroom personnel, the rules of evidence, the burden of proof, and the trial procedure itself. However, there is no better way to appreciate the complexities of the process than to be involved in a trial. The following is a factual situation and directions that can be used to form the basis of a mock trial to be presented by students. This is not a trial transcript to be re-enacted. Students participating in this are expected to prepare the case for trial including drafting questions for voir dire, drafting questions for witnesses, preparing opening statements and closing arguments, and drafting proposed jury instructions. Students might also wish to prepare trial exhibits. Explanation and samples of these are found in the relevant chapters in the text. There is no need to refer to any legal source material other than this text. All of the facts and relevant law are provided. In presenting a mock trial, careful attention must be paid to the time allotted for each step of the process. Suggestions have been made to keep the time under three hours. Of course, participants will spend additional time in preparation.

PEOPLE V. STUART
CHARGE: MURDER

THE FACTS

Background

Mary Stuart, age thirty-four, married Lawrence Stuart fifteen years ago. Everything was fine for the first two years and then problems arose. Mary got pregnant and Lawrence lost his job and began to drink. On one occasion, when Mary was seven months pregnant, Lawrence struck her in the face, blackening one eye. Their fight was so loud that a neighbor, Vicki Townsend, called the police, who arrested Lawrence. He was charged with battery but the charges were dropped because Mary refused to cooperate with the prosecutor. At the time of arrest, the police took pictures of Mary. The pictures were kept in their files.

After this incident, things improved for the Stuarts. Lawrence found another job and Mary was busy with the baby. After five years, however, the situation changed. Lawrence lost his job again and Mary was pregnant with their third child. Lawrence was angry at Mary for getting pregnant again and had started drinking. During one fight he hit Mary with a closed fist. As a result she fell backward. She did not seek any medical attention for this and she never told anyone about it. After the incident, Lawrence was apologetic and swore he would never do anything like this again. Mary thought about leaving Lawrence at this time but did not know how she would manage. The only job she had ever had was as a receptionist for a dentist, and that was before her first child was born. She had no skills, no experience, and no money. Because she stayed at home, her only real friend in the last several years was Vicki Townsend. Although Vicki encouraged her to leave Lawrence, she could not offer any real help.

For the past seven years Mary and Lawrence have led a turbulent life. They have had numerous fights. On several occasions, Vicki has seen Mary with bruises on her face and arms. At first Mary told her that she was clumsy and had fallen or walked into things, but in the last two years Mary has told her that Lawrence beat her. One year ago, Mary finally did leave Lawrence, going to a women's shelter in town. They found a job for Mary as a receptionist at a small company. After two weeks, Lawrence discovered where Mary was working and visited her at work. In front of a co-worker, George Riordin, Lawrence told Mary that he wanted her to come home and that she should know that he would never let her leave him. Mary felt that the situation was hopeless. She was not making enough money to support herself and her children. She could not hide from Lawrence. In any event, she knew he would have rights to see the children. Therefore, she decided to quit her job and go back to him. The head of the shelter, Martha Olsen, tried to discourage her from doing this, telling her that they would help her, but Mary went back to Lawrence anyway.

For a while things were better, but then old habits returned. Mary and Lawrence fought and Lawrence would hit her. Aside from talking to her friend and neighbor, Vicki, Mary kept to herself most of the time. Six months ago, after one especially violent fight, Mary did go to the emergency room of the county hospital. Lawrence had pushed her down and she twisted her ankle so badly she thought it was broken. It turned out to be badly sprained. She told the doctor, Jonathon Jung, that the accident happened when she fell. The doctor's notes also indicated bruises on her arm and face. Vicki also insisted on taking pictures of Mary. She still has those pictures.

The Day of the Alleged Offense

On the evening of January 23 of this year, Lawrence lay down after dinner to take a nap. Two hours later Mary went in to check on him and noticed that he was not breathing. Mary called 911 and police and ambulance arrived shortly. The paramedic tried to resuscitate Lawrence but all attempts failed. He was pronounced dead.

At the time, police asked Mary what happened and she told them she did not know. Lawrence had just eaten dinner, said he was tired, and went to take a nap. An autopsy was performed on Lawrence and the cause of death was listed as respiratory failure due to excessive amounts of alcohol and barbiturates. His blood alcohol was .07. The coroner identified the drug as one that is commonly found in sleeping pills. Because of the quantity of drugs in Lawrence's system, the coroner did not think the death was accidental. After receiving the coroner's report, the police conducted further investigation. They discovered that Lawrence had been arrested twelve years previously for spousal abuse. Their records also reflected that the police had been called two times in the past two years by neighbors who thought a domestic disturbance was taking place. In each of these two instances, the police responded, but were told by Mary that there was no problem. In neither instance did the police see any evidence of physical violence. The investigating police officer, Officer Richard Post, also decided to question Mary further, primarily to determine whether Lawrence had been particularly depressed or despondent. During this questioning, Mary broke down and told the police officer the following.

On the afternoon of his death, she and Lawrence had had a terrible fight and Lawrence had struck her. This was witnessed by their twelve-year-old daughter, who screamed at her father to stop. Lawrence had turned to the daughter and threatened to beat her to a pulp if she ever interfered. Lawrence had never beat the children in the past, but Mary was afraid that he was totally out of control. She remembered the sleeping pills that the doctor had given her the prior week and decided to give Lawrence a few pills at dinner so that he would sleep the rest of the evening. She knew he had a couple of beers before dinner and thought that a few sleeping pills would probably incapacitate him for the rest of the night. Hopefully by morning he would not be so angry at her and their daughter. The police officer then asked Mary for the bottle of pills, which Mary gave to him. The officer noted that the prescription was for 30 pills and had been filled six days prior to the date of death. The directions indicated that Mary was to take one pill at bedtime as needed. Ten pills remained in the bottle. The officer again asked Mary how many pills she had put in Lawrence's food and she said, "A few, I can't remember exactly how many." The officer asked Mary how many sleeping pills she had taken since filling the prescription and she indicated that she had taken one each evening. She also said that Lawrence had taken one the evening before his death. When Mary showed the officers the bottle of sleeping pills, she retrieved the bottle from a medicine cabinet in the bathroom. The officer, who was also the officer who responded to the 911 call, did not remember seeing the pills anywhere at the time he responded to the initial 911 call.

Continuing their investigation, police also talked to the neighbor, Vicki Townsend. Upon questioning, Vicki told the police that she had seen Mary on the day of death at approximately 6:00 P.M. Mary had come over to borrow a can of tomato sauce for dinner. She said Mary seemed normal. She was not upset and said nothing about a fight. Vicki did not notice any bruises. Vicki also said that for the past week, Mary seemed happier than she had in years. In fact Mary had told her that she thought that her problems with Lawrence had finally been resolved. Police also talked to the twelve-year-old daughter, Sally, who confirmed her mother's story about the fight and her father's threat. Also, after the coroner, Dr. Michael Zane, was shown the bottle of sleeping pills, he estimated that Lawrence had probably ingested about ten pills. Based on the evidence, the prosecutors have charged Mary with first-degree murder.

The Law

You will find the definitions of the various degrees of murder and manslaughter in Chapter 12.

The law of self-defense and defense of others is as follows:

1. It is lawful to defend oneself from attack if, as a reasonable person, one has grounds for believing and does believe that bodily injury is about to be inflicted upon him or her. In doing so, such person may use all force and means which he or she believes to be reasonably necessary and which would appear to a reasonable person to be necessary to prevent the injury that appears to be imminent.
2. The right of self-defense exists only as long as real or apparent threatened danger continues to exist. When such danger ceases to appear to exist, the right to use force in self-defense ends.
3. It is lawful for a person who, as a reasonable person, has grounds for believing and does believe that bodily injury is about to be inflicted upon another to protect that individual from attack. In doing so, he or she may use all force and means which he or she believes to be reasonably necessary and which would appear to a reasonable person to be necessary to prevent injury which appears to be imminent.

Potential Witnesses

Richard Post

Dr. Jonathon Jung ✓

Vicki Townsend ✓

Martha Olsen

George Riordin

Sally Stuart

Dr. Michael Zane

Mary Stuart

PARTICIPANTS

Prosecuting team

Defense team

Judge

Court staff

Jury panel

DIRECTIONS

Both the prosecuting team and the defense team will have to do the following:

1. Prepare questions for voir dire
2. Prepare opening statements
3. Determine what witnesses to call
4. Draft questions for witnesses
5. Prepare closing arguments
6. Submit proposed jury instructions

Each team should consist of at least two attorneys and support staff to help with the preparation of the case.

The court staff should review the job of each member of the court staff. The bailiff and the clerk should be responsible for setting up the courtroom for each day of trial. If a record of the trial is desired, a court reporter can maintain a tape-recorded record of the proceedings.

The judge can be either the instructor or a student. The judge will preside over the proceeding. The judge will also be responsible for keeping the participants within their time limits. The judge's rulings are final.

The jury panel should consist of all students not otherwise participating or of any volunteers. Those on the jury panel should develop an assumed persona for the purpose of answering questions on voir dire.

PRETRIAL PROCEEDINGS

Before the start of the trial, each side should exchange witness lists. They should also allow inspection of any physical or documentary evidence they will use.

THE JURY AND JURY SELECTION

The judge will begin by giving a brief synopsis of the case to prospective jurors. The judge will ask each person to state his or her name, address, and occupation. The judge will also ask if any of the jurors know any of the parties or witnesses. (None of the assumed personae on the jury panel will know any parties or witnesses.) The judge will also ask if there is anything about the nature of this case that would make it impossible for any juror to be fair and impartial, or if any juror has any hardship in sitting on the jury. Each side will be allowed to ask three additional questions. In the interest of time, the jury should consist of six people, with each side having one peremptory challenge. The judge will make any rulings on challenges for cause. Jury selection should be limited to thirty minutes. Participants should review the jury questionnaire found in Chapter 17 in developing their questions.

Opening statements are given by each side. Only one attorney from each side may speak. These are limited to five to ten minutes. Participants should review the sample opening statement in Chapter 17 before preparing their opening statements.

The Evidence

Either side may call any of the witnesses. However, the list of witnesses to be called must be exchanged before trial, at a time set by the judge. The trial is limited to the facts that are presented and to any natural and logical inferences that can be drawn from the facts. If any witness testifies to any different facts, the judge will instruct the jury that the witness has given prior statements that contradict the testimony and that they are to disregard the testimony.

Participants may use physical or documentary evidence, but it must be limited to items that are described in the facts. Any side wishing to use physical evidence must make it available for inspection by the other side before trial, at a time set by the judge.

Experts

1. Both sides stipulate that the coroner is a medical expert.
2. Either side may call one expert in the area of spousal abuse. The expert can testify only to material that is supported in published material on the subject. That written material must be turned over to the other side before trial, at a time set by the judge.

The order of presenting evidence shall follow the procedure described in Chapter 17. If questioning of any witness is taking too long and is not relevant, the judge may order the attorney to limit or stop the questioning. The judge's order is final. The judge also rules on all objections regarding evidentiary matters. The rulings are final.

Before drafting questions and deciding on physical evidence, participants should review Chapter 16, "Rules of Evidence." No more than 1½ hours should be allotted for the presentation of evidence.

Closing Arguments

The order of closing arguments shall follow the procedure described in Chapter 17. The prosecutor shall be allowed fifteen minutes, to be divided between the opening and rebuttal. The defense is allowed ten minutes.

Jury Instructions

The judge shall read the jury instructions, which should include some general instructions and the specific law of this case. The law of this case consists of the definitions of the different degrees of homicide (found in Chapter 12) and the defenses previously listed. General instructions should include instructions on the duty of the jury and on the presumptions and burden of proof in a criminal case.

Jury Deliberation

A time limit should be placed on the deliberation process, at the discretion of the instructor or the judge.

APPENDIX IV

BASIC CITATION REFERENCE GUIDE

This citation information is based on *The Bluebook: A Uniform System of Citation* (Harvard 16th ed., 1991).

Note: Many states have their own legal style or citation manual. Check with your instructor for your state guidelines.

CASE LAW

THE U.S. SUPREME COURT

Most case citations follow this basic format:

Name	*Volume*	*Reporter*	*Page*	*Year*
Miranda v. Arizona,	384	U.S.	436	(1966)

Miranda v. Arizona is the name of the case. Case names are underlined or italicized.

The *Miranda* case is located in volume 384 of the *United States Reports*. The *United States Reports* is the official reporter for U.S. Supreme Court cases. It is "official" because it is published by the U.S. government. The proper abbreviation for this reporter is *U.S.*

In Volume 384, the *Miranda* case is located at page 436. The case was decided in 1966. The year is placed in parentheses.

This information allows anyone looking at the citation to locate the actual decision. All U.S. Supreme Court cases are located in three separate reporters, published by three different publishers. The full citation for the *Miranda* case is as follows:

Miranda v. Arizona, 384 U.S. 436, 86 S. Ct. 1602, 16 L. Ed. 2d 694 (1966).

"86 S. Ct. 1602" and "16 L. Ed. 2d 694" are referred to as *parallel citations.*

STATE CASE LAW

State cases are cited much the same as Supreme Court cases. For example, in the state of California, either of the following citations would be correct for a California case.

Long Beach v. Superior Court, 64 Cal. App. 3d 65, 134 Cal. Rptr. 468 (1976).

or

Long Beach v. Superior Court (1976) 64 Cal. App. 3d 65, 134 Cal. Rptr. 468.

In California and other states, there is an unofficial publisher of state case law. In the preceding citation, "Cal. Rptr." is the abbreviation for the *California Reporter,* published by West Publishing. "134 Cal. Rptr. 468" is the parallel citation.

In some instances, you will see references to *regional reporters.* The regional reporter abbreviations are:

Atlantic Reporter	A.2d
Northeastern Reporter	N.E.2d
Northwestern Reporter	N.W.2d
Pacific Reporter	P.2d
Southern Reporter	So. 2d
Southeastern Reporter	S.E.2d
Southwestern Reporter	S.W.2d

The "2d" following the regional reporter abbreviation indicates that each of these reporters is in the second edition.

U.S. CONSTITUTION

The Fourteenth Amendment to the U.S. Constitution should be written as follows:

U.S. Const. amend. XIV

If you wanted to indicate a certain section of the amendment, you would add:

§ 1

The full citation would look like this:

U.S. Const. amend. XIV, § 1

THE UNITED STATES CODE (STATUTES)

The United States Code is cited in the following manner:

Number of Code Title	*Code*	*Section Cited*	*Date*
28	U.S.C.	§ 1291	(1988)

The proper citation is 28 U.S.C. § 1291 (1988).

STATE STATUTES

A statute citation must show

1. the numbers of the statutory topic,
2. the abbreviated name of the publication,

3. the specific statute or section of the statute, and
4. the year of the publication.

Examples:

Ariz. Rev. Stat. Ann. § x (20XX)	Arizona Revised Statutes Annotated
Cal. Educ. Code § x (20XX)	California Education Code
Conn. Gen. Stat. § x (20XX)	Connecticut General Statutes
Ind. Code § x (20XX)	Indiana Code
Kan. Civ. Proc. Code Ann. § x (Vernon 20XX)	Kansas Civil Procedure Code Annotated (Vernon is the publisher of the annotated code)

In some states, more than one publisher produces the annotated codes. In such instances, the name of the publisher should precede the date.

APPENDIX V

THE *MARVIN V. MARVIN* CASES

134 Cal. Rptr. 815
557 P.2d 106
18 Cal. 3d 660
Michelle MARVIN, Plaintiff and Appellant,
v.
Lee MARVIN, Defendant and Respondent.
L.A. 30502.
Supreme Court of California,
In Bank.
Dec. 27, 1976.

Woman who had lived with man for seven years without marriage brought suit to enforce alleged oral contract under which she was entitled to half the property which had been acquired during that period and taken in man's name, and to support payments. The Superior Court, Los Angeles County, William A. Munnell, J., granted the judgment on the pleadings for defendant, and plaintiff appealed. The Supreme Court, Tobriner, J., held that provisions of the Family Law Act do not govern the distribution of property acquired during a nonmarital relationship; that court should enforce express contracts between nonmarital partners except to the extent the contract is explicitly founded on the consideration of meretricious sexual services, despite contention that such contracts violate public policy; that in the absence of express contract, the court should inquire into the conduct of the parties to determine whether that conduct demonstrates implied contract, agreement of partnership of joint venture, or some other tacit understanding between the parties, and may also employ the doctrine of quantum meruit or equitable remedies such as constructive or resulting trust, when warranted by the facts of the case; that in the instant case plaintiff's complaint stated a cause of action for breach of an express contract and furnished suitable basis on which trial court could render declaratory relief; and that the complaint also could be amended to state a cause of action founded on theory of implied contract or equitable relief.

Reversed and remanded.

Clark, J., filed concurring and dissenting opinion.

1. Appeal and Error ⊶916(1)

Where trial court rendered judgment for defendant on the pleadings, Supreme Court had to accept the allegations of the complaint as true, determining whether such allegations stated or could be amended to state a cause of action.

2. Parties ⊶52
Pleading ⊶248(1)

No error was committed in denying plaintiff's motion, made on the opening day set for trial, seeking to file a proposed amendment complaint which would have added two counts and a new defendant to the action.

3. Lewdness ⊶3

Where married man was living with unmarried woman, only the man could have been guilty of violating former statute prohibiting living in a state of cohabitation and adultery, and the unmarried partner could neither be convicted of adulterous cohabitation nor of aiding and abetting other partner's violations. West's Ann. Pen. Code, § 269a.

4. Contracts ⊶112

Contract between nonmarital partners is unenforceable only to the extent that it explicitly rests on the immoral and illicit consideration of meretricious sexual services, despite contention that enforcement of such a contract would violate public policy, and enforceability of such a contract is not precluded when one partner contributes only homemaking services.

5. Contracts ⊶61, 103

A promise to perform homemaking services is a lawful and adequate consideration for a contract.

6. Contracts ⊶112

The fact that a man and woman live together without marriage and engage in a sexual relationship does not in itself invalidate agreements between them relating to their earnings, property or expenses, nor is such an agreement invalid merely because the parties may have contemplated the creation or continuation of a nonmarital relationship when they entered into it; such agreements fail only to the extent that they rest on a consideration of meretricious sexual services, and not on the ground that the agreement is "involved in" or made "in contemplation of" a nonmarital relationship; disapproving *Heaps v. Toy,* 54 Cal. App. 2d 158, 128 P.2d 813. West's Ann. Civ. Code, §§ 1607, 1676.

7. Contracts ⊶112, 137(3)

Court will not enforce a contract for the pooling of property and earnings if it is explicitly and inseparably based upon services as a paramour, but even if sexual services are part of the contractual consideration, any severable portion of the contract supported by independent consideration will be enforced.

8. Husband and Wife ⊶267(7)

An improper transfer of community property is not void ab initio, but merely voidable at the instance of the aggrieved spouse. Civ.Code, § 172, St. 1917, p. 829.

9. Contracts ⚷108(2)

Where wife had opportunity to assert her community property rights in divorce action and her interest was fixed and limited in interlocutory and final decrees in that action, enforcement of alleged contract between the former husband and another woman, with whom he lived during the period which began before the divorce was final, against property awarded to the former husband by the divorce decree would not impair any rights of the former wife, and contract was not on that account violative of public policy. Civ. Code, § 169.2, St. 1959, p. 3767; West's Ann. Civ. Code, §§ 169, 5118.

10. Contracts ⚷111

Where alleged contract between man and woman who lived together did not by its terms require the man to divorce his wife nor reward him for so doing, it was not invalid as an agreement to promote or encourage divorce, and such ground for invalidity of the contract would not apply in any event if the marriage in question was beyond redemption.

11. Frauds, Statute of ⚷4

"Marriage settlement," within statute providing that all contracts for such settlements must be in writing, is an agreement in contemplation of marriage in which each party agrees to release or modify property rights which would otherwise arise from the marriage, and thus alleged oral contract between man and woman who lived together without marriage, to effect that they would combine efforts and earnings and share equally in property accumulated, was not within the compass of that statute and was not unenforceable on the ground that it was oral. West's Ann. Civ. Code, § 5134.

See publication Words and Phrases for other judicial constructions and definitions.

12. Breach of Marriage Promise ⚷2

Alleged oral contract between man and woman who lived together without marriage that they would combine their efforts and earnings and share equally all property accumulated was not unenforceable under statute which provides that no cause of action arises for breach of a promise of marriage. West's Ann. Civ. Code, § 43.5(d).

13. Contracts ⚷108(2), 112

Adults who voluntarily live together and engage in sexual relations are nonetheless as competent as any other persons to contract respecting their earnings and property rights, except that they cannot lawfully contract to pay for the performance of sexual services; such parties may order their economic affairs as they choose, and no policy precludes the courts from enforcing such agreements.

14. Contracts ⚷112

Adults who voluntarily live together and engage in sexual relations may agree to pool their earnings and hold all property acquired during relationship in accord with the law governing community property, or agree that each partner's earnings and property acquired from those earnings remain separate property, or may pool only part of their earnings and property, form a partnership or joint venture, hold property acquired as joint tenants or tenants in common, or agree to any other such arrangement.

15. Declaratory Judgment ⚷316

Complaint alleging that a man and woman entered into an oral agreement providing, inter alia, that while the parties lived together they would combine their efforts and earnings and would share equally any and all property accumulated as result of their efforts, that they would hold themselves out to the general public as husband and wife, that woman would give up career and render her services as companion, homemaker, housekeeper and cook and man would provide for her financial support and needs for life, that substantial property was accumulated in man's name during seven years they lived together, and that man had refused further support, stated a cause of action for breach of an express contract, and furnished a suitable basis on which trial court could render declaratory relief.

16. Husband and Wife ⊶248

Mere fact that a couple have not participated in a valid marriage ceremony does not serve as a basis for a court's inference that the couple intended to keep their earnings and property separate and independent; parties' intention can only be ascertained by a more searching inquiry into the nature of their relationship.

17. Work and Labor ⊶7(1)

Putative spouse need not prove that he rendered services in expectation of monetary reward in order to recover the reasonable value of those services. West's Ann. Civ. Code, §§ 4452, 4800.

18. Marriage ⊶63

Where neither party claimed the status of an actual or putative spouse, action for nullity of marriage could not serve as a device to adjudicate contract and property rights arising from the nonmarital relationship, and woman correctly chose to assert her rights by the means of an ordinary civil action.

19. Husband and Wife ⊶272(5)

The Family Law Act does not require an equal division of property accumulated in a nonmarital "actual family relationship." West's Ann. Civ. Code, §§ 4000 et seq., 4452, 4455.

20. Husband and Wife ⊶272(5)

Provisions of the Family Law Act do not govern distribution of property acquired during a nonmarital relationship; such a relationship remains subject solely to judicial decision. West's Ann. Civ. Code, § 4000 et seq.

21. Equity ⊶65(2)

Concepts of "guilt" cannot justify unequal division of property between two equally "guilty" persons who have lived together without marriage.

22. Gifts ⊶47(1)

There is no more reason to presume that services rendered between nonmarital partners are contributed as a gift than to presume that funds are contributed as a gift; rather it should be presumed that the parties intended to deal fairly with each other.

23. Husband and Wife ⊶272(5)
Marriage ⊶1

Public policy is to foster and promote the institution of marriage, but perpetuation of judicial rules which result in an equitable distribution of property accumulated during a nonmarital relationship is neither a just nor effective way of carrying out that policy.

24. Husband and Wife ⚷272(5)

In the absence of express contract between man and woman living together in a nonmarital relationship, the courts should inquire into the conduct of the parties to determine whether that conduct demonstrates an implied contract, agreement of partnership or joint venture, or some other tacit understanding between the parties, and may employ the doctrine of quantum meruit, or equitable remedies such as constructive or resulting trusts, when warranted by the facts of the case.

25. Marriage ⚷54

Man and woman living together in a nonmarital relationship were not "married" or entitled to rights granted valid or putative spouses, but they had the same rights to enforce contracts and assert equitable interest in property acquired through their own efforts as would any other unmarried person. West's Ann. Civ. Code, §§ 4000 et seq., 4452, 4455.

26. Work and Labor ⚷7(7)

Nonmarital partner may recover in quantum meruit for the reasonable value of household services rendered, less the reasonable value of support received, if such partner can show that he or she rendered services with the expectation of monetary reward.

27. Pleading ⚷248(16)

Complaint alleging oral agreement that, inter alia, while man and woman lived together they would combine their efforts and earnings and share equally in any and all property accumulated could be amended to state a cause of action independent of allegations of express contract, on theories of implied contract or equitable relief.

Marvin M. Mitchelson, Donald N. Woldman, Robert M. Ross, Los Angeles, Fleishman, McDaniel, Brown & Weston and David M. Brown, Hollywood, for plaintiff and appellant.

Jettie Pierce Selvig, San Francisco, Ruth Miller, Foster City, and Suzie S. Thorn, San Francisco, as amici curiae on behalf of plaintiff and appellant.

Goldman & Kagon, Mark A. Goldman and William R. Bishin, Los Angeles, for defendant and respondent.

Herma Hill Kay, Berkeley, John Sutter, Doris Brin Walker and Treuhaft, Walker, Nawi & Hendon, Oakland, as amici curiae on behalf of defendant and respondent.

Isabella H. Grant and Livingston, Grant, Stone & Shenk, San Francisco, as amici curiae.

TOBRINER, Justice.

During the past 15 years, there has been a substantial increase in the number of couples living together without marriage.[1] Such nonmarital relationships lead to legal controversy when one partner dies or the couple separates. Courts of Appeal, faced with the task of determining property rights in such cases, have arrived at conflicting positions: two cases (*In re Marriage of Cary* (1973) 34 Cal. App. 3d 345, 109 Cal. Rptr. 862; *Estate of Atherley* (1975) 44 Cal. App. 3d 758, 119 Cal. Rptr. 41) have held that the Family Law Act (Civ. Code, § 4000 et seq.) requires division of the property according to community property principles, and one decision (*Beckman v. Mayhew* (1975) 49 Cal. App. 3d 529, 122 Cal. Rptr. 604) has rejected that holding. We take this opportunity to resolve that controversy and to declare the principles which should govern distribution of property acquired in a nonmarital relationship.

We conclude: (1) The provisions of the Family Law Act do not govern the distribution of property acquired during a nonmarital relationship; such a relationship remains subject solely to judicial decision. (2) The courts should enforce express contracts between nonmarital partners except to the extent that the contract is explicitly founded on the consideration of meretricious sexual services. (3) In the absence of an express contract, the courts should inquire into the conduct of the parties to determine whether that conduct demonstrates an implied contract, agreement of partnership or joint venture, or some other tacit understanding between the parties. The courts may also employ the doctrine of quantum meruit, or equitable remedies such as constructive or resulting trusts, when warranted by the facts of the case.

In the instant case plaintiff and defendant lived together for seven years without marrying; all property acquired during this period was taken in defendant's name. When plaintiff sued to enforce a contract under which she was entitled to half the property and to support payments, the trial court granted judgment on the pleadings for defendant, thus leaving him with all property accumulated by the couple during their relationship. Since the trial court denied plaintiff a trial on the merits of her claim, its decision conflicts with the principles stated above, and must be reversed.

1. The factual setting of this appeal

[1] Since the trial court rendered judgment for defendant on the pleadings, we must accept the allegations of plaintiff's complaint as true, determining whether such allegations state, or can be amended to state, a cause of action. (See *Sullivan v. County of Los Angeles* (1974) 12 Cal. 3d 710, 714–715, fn. 3, 117 Cal. Rptr. 241, 527 P.2d 865; 4 Witkin, Cal. Procedure [2d ed. 1971] pp. 2817–2818.) We turn therefore to the specific allegations of the complaint.

Plaintiff avers that in October of 1964 she and defendant "entered into an oral agreement" that while "the parties lived together they would combine their efforts and earnings and would share equally any and all property accumulated as a result of their efforts whether individual or combined." Furthermore, they agreed to "hold themselves out to the general public as husband and wife" and that "plaintiff would further render her services as a companion, homemaker, housekeeper and cook to . . . defendant."

Shortly thereafter plaintiff agreed to "give up her lucrative career as an entertainer [and] singer" in order to "devote her full time to defendant . . . as a companion, homemaker, housekeeper and cook"; in return defendant agreed to "provide for all of plaintiff's financial support and needs for the rest of her life."

Plaintiff alleges that she lived with defendant from October of 1964 through May of 1970 and fulfilled her obligations under the agreement. During this period the parties as a result of their efforts and earnings acquired in defendant's name substantial real and personal property, including motion picture rights worth over $1 million. In May of 1970, however, defendant compelled plaintiff to leave his household. He continued to support plaintiff until November of 1971, but thereafter refused to provide further support.

On the basis of these allegations plaintiff asserts two causes of action. The first, for declaratory relief, asks the court to determine her contract and property rights; the second seeks to impose a constructive trust upon one half of the property acquired during the course of the relationship.

[2] Defendant demurred unsuccessfully, and then answered the complaint. Following extensive discovery and pretrial proceedings, the case came to trial.[2] Defendant renewed his attack on the complaint by a motion to dismiss. Since the parties had stipulated that defendant's marriage to Betty Marvin did not terminate until the filing of a final decree of divorce in January 1967, the trial court treated defendant's motion as one for judgment on the pleadings augmented by the stipulation.

After hearing argument the court granted defendant's motion and entered judgment for defendant. Plaintiff moved to set aside the judgment and asked leave to amend her complaint to allege that she and defendant reaffirmed their agreement after defendant's divorce was final. The trial court denied plaintiff's motion, and she appealed from the judgment.

2. Plaintiff's complaint states a cause of action for breach of an express contract

In *Trutalli v. Meraviglia* (1932) 215 Cal. 698, 12 P.2d 430 we established the principle that nonmarital partners may lawfully contract concerning the ownership of property acquired during the relationship. We reaffirmed this principle in *Vallera v. Vallera* (1943) 21 Cal. 2d 681, 685, 134 P.2d 761, 763, stating that "If a man and woman [who are not married] live together as husband and wife under an agreement to pool their earnings and share equally in their joint accumulations, equity will protect the interests of each in such property."

In the case before us plaintiff, basing her cause of action in contract upon these precedents, maintains that the trial court erred in denying her a trial on the merits of her contention. Although that court did not specify the ground for its conclusion that plaintiff's contractual allegations stated no cause of action,[3] defendant offers some four theories to sustain the ruling; we proceed to examine them.

[3, 4] Defendant first and principally relies on the contention that the alleged contract is so closely related to the supposed "immoral" character of the relationship between plaintiff and himself that the enforcement of the contract would violate public policy.[4] He points to cases asserting that a contract between nonmarital partners is unenforceable if it is "involved in" an illicit relationship (see *Shaw v. Shaw* (1964) 227 Cal. App. 2d 159, 164, 38 Cal. Rptr. 520 (dictum); *Garcia v. Venegas* (1951) 106 Cal. App. 2d 364, 368, 235 P.2d 89 (dictum)), or made in "contemplation" of such a relationship (*Hill v. Estate of Westbrook* (1950) 95 Cal. App. 2d 599, 602, 213 P.2d 727; see *Hill v. Estate of Westbrook* (1952) 39 Cal. 2d 458, 460, 247 P.2d 19; *Barlow v. Collins* (1958) 166 Cal. App. 2d 274, 277, 333 P.2d 64 (dictum); *Bridges v. Bridges* (1954) 125 Cal. App. 2d 359, 362, 270 P.2d 69 (dictum)). A review of the numerous California decisions concerning contracts between nonmarital partners, however, reveals that the courts have not employed such broad and uncertain standards to strike down contracts. The decisions instead disclose a narrower and more precise standard: a contract between nonmarital partners is unenforceable only to the extent that it explicitly rests upon the immoral and illicit consideration of meretricious sexual services.

In the first case to address this issue, *Trutalli v. Meraviglia,* supra, 215 Cal. 698, 12 P.2d 430, the parties had lived together without marriage for 11 years and had raised two children. The man sued to quiet title to land he had purchased in his own name during this relationship; the woman defended by asserting an agreement to pool earnings and hold all property jointly. Rejecting the assertion of the illegality of the agreement, the court stated that "The fact that the parties to this action at the time they agreed to invest their earnings in property to be held jointly between them were living together in an unlawful relation did not disqualify them from entering into a lawful agreement with each other, so long as such immoral relation was not made a *consideration* of their agreement." (Emphasis added.) (215 Cal. at pp. 701–702, 12 P.2d 430, 431.)

In *Bridges v. Bridges* (1954) 125 Cal. App. 2d 359, 270 P.2d 69, both parties were in the process of obtaining divorces from their erstwhile respective spouses. The two parties agreed to live together, to share equally in property acquired, and to marry when their divorces became final. The man worked as a salesman and used his savings to purchase properties. The woman kept house, cared for seven children, three from each former marriage and one from the nonmarital relationship, and helped construct improvements on the properties. When they separated, without marrying, the court awarded the woman one-half the value of the property. Rejecting the man's contention that the contract was illegal, the court stated that: "Nowhere is it expressly testified to by anyone that there was anything in the agreement for the pooling of assets and the sharing of accumulations that contemplated meretricious relations as any part of the consideration or as any object of the agreement." (125 Cal. App. 2d at p. 363, 270 P.2d at p. 71.)

Croslin v. Scott (1957) 154 Cal. App. 2d 767, 316 P.2d 755, reiterates the rule established in *Trutalli* and *Bridges.* In *Croslin* the parties separated following a three-year nonmarital relationship. The woman then phoned the man, asked him to return to her, and suggested that he build them a house on a lot she owned. She agreed in return to place the property in joint ownership. The man built the house, and the parties lived there for several more years. When they separated, he sued to establish his interest in the property. Reversing a nonsuit, the Court of Appeal stated that "The mere fact that parties agree to live together in meretricious relationship does not necessarily make an agreement for disposition of property between them invalid. It is only when the property agreement is made in connection with the other agreement, or the illicit relationship is made a consideration of the property agreement, that the latter becomes illegal." (154 Cal. App. 2d at p. 771, 316 P.2d at p. 758.)

[5] Numerous other cases have upheld enforcement of agreements between nonmarital partners in factual settings essentially indistinguishable from the present case. (*In re Marriage of Foster* (1974) 42 Cal. App. 3d 577, 117 Cal. Rptr. 49; *Weak v. Weak, supra,* 202 Cal. App. 2d 632, 639, 21 Cal. Rptr. 9; *Ferguson v. Schuenemann* (1959) 167 Cal. App. 2d 413, 334 P.2d 668; *Barlow v. Collins, supra,* 166 Cal. App. 2d 274, 277–278, 333 P.2d 64; *Ferraro v. Ferraro* (1956) 146 Cal. App. 2d 849, 304 P.2d 168; *Cline v. Festersen* (1954) 128 Cal. App. 2d 380, 275 P.2d 149; *Profit v. Profit* (1953) 117 Cal. App. 2d 126, 255 P.2d 25; *Garcia v. Venegas, supra,* 106 Cal. App. 2d 364, 235 P.2d 89; *Padilla v. Padilla* (1940) 38 Cal. App. 2d 319, 100 P.2d 1093; *Bacon v. Bacon* (1937) 21 Cal. App. 2d 540, 69 P.2d 884.)[5]

[6] Although the past decisions hover over the issue in the somewhat wispy form of the figures of a Chagall painting, we can abstract from those decisions a clear and simple rule. The fact that a man and woman live together without marriage, and engage in a sexual relationship, does not in itself invalidate agreements between them relating to their earnings, property, or expenses. Neither is such an agreement invalid merely because the parties may have contemplated the creation or continuation of a nonmarital relationship when they entered into it. Agreements between nonmarital partners fail only to the extent that they rest upon a consideration of meretricious sexual services. Thus the rule asserted by defendant, that a contract fails if it is "involved in" or made "in contemplation" of a nonmarital relationship, cannot be reconciled with the decisions.

The three cases cited by defendant which have declined to enforce contracts between nonmarital partners involved consideration that was expressly founded upon illicit sexual services. In *Hill v. Estate of Westbrook, supra,* 95 Cal. App. 2d 599, 213 P.2d 727, the woman promised to keep house for the man, to live with him as man and wife, and to bear his children; the man promised to provide for her in his will, but died without doing so. Reversing a judgment for the woman based on the reasonable value of her services, the Court of Appeal stated that "the action is predicated upon a claim which seeks, among other things, the reasonable value of living with decedent in meretricious relationship and bearing him two children. . . . The law does not award compensation for living with a man as a concubine and bearing him children. . . . As the judgment is, at least in part, for the value of the claimed services for which recovery cannot be had, it must be reversed." (95 Cal. App. 2d at p. 603, 213 P.2d at p. 730.) Upon retrial, the trial court found that it could not sever the contract and place an independent value upon the legitimate services performed by claimant. We therefore affirmed a judgment for the estate. (*Hill v. Estate of Westbrook* (1952) 39 Cal. 2d 458, 247 P.2d 19.)

In the only other cited decision refusing to enforce a contract, *Updeck v. Samuel* (1964), 123 Cal. App. 2d 264, 266 P.2d 822, the contract "was based on the consideration that the parties live together as husband and wife." (123 Cal. App. 2d at p. 267, 266 P.2d at p. 824.) Viewing the contract as calling for adultery, the court held it illegal.[6]

[7] The decisions in the *Hill* and *Updeck* cases thus demonstrate that a contract between nonmarital partners, even if expressly made in contemplation of a common living arrangement, is invalid only if sexual acts form an inseparable part of the consideration for the agreement. In sum, a court will not enforce a contract for the pooling of property and earnings if it is explicitly and inseparably based upon services as a paramour. The Court of Appeal opinion in *Hill,* however, indicates that even if sexual services are part of the contractual consideration, any *severable* portion of the contract supported by independent consideration will still be enforced.

The principle that a contract between nonmarital partners will be enforced unless expressly and inseparably based upon an illicit consideration of sexual services not only represents the distillation of the decisional law, but also offers a far more precise and workable standard than that advocated by defendant. Our recent decision in *In re Marriage of Dawley* (1976) 17 Cal. 3d 342, 551 P.2d 323, offers a close analogy. Rejecting the contention that an antenuptial agreement is invalid if the parties contemplated a marriage of short duration, we pointed out in Dawley that a standard based upon the subjective contemplation of the parties is uncertain and unworkable; such a test, we stated, "might invalidate virtually all antenuptial agreements on the ground that the parties contemplated dissolution . . . but it provides no principled basis for determining which antenuptial agreements offend public policy and which do not." (17 Cal. 3d 342, 352, 551 P.2d 323, 329.)

Similarly, in the present case a standard which inquires whether an agreement is "involved" in or "contemplates" a nonmarital relationship is vague and unworkable. Virtually all agreements between nonmarital partners can be said to be "involved" in some sense in the fact of their mutual sexual relationship, or to "contemplate" the existence of that relationship. Thus defendant's proposed standards, if taken literally, might invalidate all agreements between nonmarital partners, a result no one favors. Moreover, those standards offer no basis to distinguish between valid and invalid agreements. By looking not to such uncertain tests, but only to the consideration underlying the agreement, we provide the parties and the courts with a practical guide to determine when an agreement between nonmarital partners should be enforced.

[8] Defendant secondly relies upon the ground suggested by the trial court: that the 1964 contract violated public policy because it impaired the community property rights of Betty Marvin, defendant's lawful wife. Defendant points out that his earnings while living apart from his wife before rendition of the interlocutory decree were community property under 1964 statutory law (former Civ. Code, §§ 169, 169.2)[7] and that defendant's agreement with plaintiff purported to transfer to her a half interest in that community property. But whether or not defendant's contract with plaintiff exceeded his authority as manager of the community property (see former Civ. Code, § 172), defendant's argument fails for the reason that an improper transfer of community property is not void ab initio, but merely voidable at the instance of the aggrieved spouse. (See *Ballinger v. Ballinger* (1937) 9 Cal. 2d 330, 334, 70 P.2d 629; *Trimble v. Trimble* (1933) 219 Cal. 340, 344, 26 P.2d 477.)

[9, 10] In the present case Betty Marvin, the aggrieved spouse, had the opportunity to assert her community property rights in the divorce action. (See *Babbitt v. Babbitt* (1955) 44 Cal. 2d 289, 293, 282 P.2d 1.) The interlocutory and final decrees in that action fix and limit her interest. Enforcement of the contract between plaintiff and defendant against property awarded to defendant by the divorce decree will not impair any right of Betty's, and thus is not on that account violative of public policy.[8]

[11] Defendant's third contention is noteworthy for the lack of authority advanced in its support. He contends that enforcement of the oral agreement between plaintiff and himself is barred by Civil Code section 5134, which provides that "All contracts for marriage settlements must be in writing. . . ." A marriage settlement, however, is an agreement in contemplation of marriage in which each party agrees to release or modify the property rights which would otherwise arise from the marriage. (See *Corker v. Corker* (1891) 87 Cal. 643, 648, 25 P. 922.) The contract at issue here does not conceivably fall within that definition, and thus is beyond the compass of section 5134.[9]

[12] Defendant finally argues that enforcement of the contract is barred by Civil Code section 43.5, subdivision (d), which provides that "No cause of action arises for . . . [b]reach of a promise of marriage." This rather strained contention proceeds from the premise that a promise of marriage impliedly includes a promise to support and to pool property acquired after marriage (see *Boyd v. Boyd* (1964) 228 Cal. App. 2d 374, 39 Cal. Rptr. 400) to the conclusion that pooling and support agreements not part of or accompanied by promise of marriage are barred by the section. We conclude that section 43.5 is not reasonably susceptible to the interpretation advanced by defendant, a conclusion demonstrated by the fact that since section 43.5 was enacted in 1939, numerous cases have enforced pooling agreements between nonmarital partners, and in none did court or counsel refer to section 43.5.

[13, 14] In summary, we base our opinion on the principle that adults who voluntarily live together and engage in sexual relations are nonetheless as competent as any other persons to contract respecting their earnings and property rights. Of course, they cannot lawfully contract to pay for the performance of sexual services, for such a contract is, in essence, an agreement for prostitution and unlawful for that reason. But they may agree to pool their earnings and to hold all property acquired during the relationship in accord with the law governing community property; conversely they may agree that each partner's earnings and the property acquired from those earnings remains the separate property of the earning partner.[10] So long as the agreement does not rest upon illicit meretricious consideration, the parties may order their economic affairs as they choose, and no policy precludes the courts from enforcing such agreements.

[15] In the present instance, plaintiff alleges that the parties agreed to pool their earnings, and they contracted to share equally in all property acquired, and that defendant agreed to support plaintiff. The terms of the contract as alleged do not rest upon any unlawful consideration. We therefore conclude that the complaint furnishes a suitable basis upon which the trial court can render declaratory relief. (See 3 Witkin, Cal. Procedure (2d ed.) pp. 2335–2336.) The trial court consequently erred in granting defendant's motion for judgment on the pleadings.

3. Plaintiff's complaint can be amended to state a cause of action founded upon theories of implied contract or equitable relief

As we have noted, both causes of action in plaintiff's complaint allege an express contract; neither asserts any basis for relief independent from the contract. In *In re Marriage of Cary, supra,* 34 Cal. App. 3d 345, 109 Cal. Rptr. 862, however, the Court of Appeal held that, in view of the policy of the Family Law Act, property accumulated by nonmarital partners in an actual family relationship should be divided equally. Upon examining the *Cary* opinion, the parties to the present case realized that plaintiff's alleged relationship with defendant might arguably support a cause of action independent of any express contract between the parties. The parties have therefore briefed and discussed the issue of the property rights of a nonmarital partner in the absence of an express contract. Although our conclusion that plaintiff's complaint states a cause of action based on an express contract alone compels us to reverse the judgment for defendant, resolution of the Cary issue will serve both to guide the parties upon retrial and to resolve a conflict presently manifest in published Court of Appeal decisions.

[16] Both plaintiff and defendant stand in broad agreement that the law should be fashioned to carry out the reasonable expectations of the parties. Plaintiff, however, presents the following contentions: that the decisions prior to *Cary* rest upon implicit and erroneous notions of punishing a party for his or her guilt in entering into a nonmarital relationship, that such decisions result in an inequitable distribution of property accumulated during the relationship, and that *Cary* correctly held that the enactment of the Family Law Act in 1970 overturned those prior decisions. Defendant in response maintains that the prior decisions merely applied common law principles of contract and property to persons who have deliberately elected to remain outside the bounds of the community property system.[11] *Cary,* defendant contends, erred in holding that the Family Law Act vitiated the force of the prior precedents.

As we shall see from examination of the pre-*Cary* decisions, the truth lies somewhere between the positions of plaintiff and defendant. The classic opinion on this subject is *Vallera v. Vallera, supra,* 21 Cal. 2d 681, 134 P.2d 761. Speaking for a four-member majority, Justice Traynor posed the question: "whether a woman living with a man as his wife but with no genuine belief that she is legally married to him acquires by reason of cohabitation alone the rights of a co-tenant in his earnings and accumulations during the period of their relationship." (21 Cal. 2d at p. 684, 134 P.2d at p. 762.) Citing *Flanagan v. Capital Nat. Bank* (1931) 213 Cal. 664, 3 P.2d 307, which held that a nonmarital "wife" could not claim that her husband's estate was community property, the majority answered that question "in the negative." (21 Cal. 2d pp. 684–685, 134 P.2d 761.) *Vallera* explains that "Equitable considerations arising from the reasonable expectation of the continuation of benefits attending the status of marriage entered into in good faith are not present in such a case." (P. 685, 134 P.2d p. 763.) In the absence of express contract, *Vallera* concluded, the woman is entitled to share in property jointly accumulated only "in the proportion that her funds contributed toward its acquisition." (P. 685, 134 P.2d p. 763.) Justice Curtis, dissenting, argued that the evidence showed an implied contract under which each party owned an equal interest in property acquired during the relationship.

The majority opinion in *Vallera* did not expressly bar recovery based upon an implied contract, nor preclude resort to equitable remedies. But *Vallera's* broad assertion that equitable considerations "are not present' in the case of a nonmarital relationship (21 Cal. 2d at p. 685, 134 P.2d 761) led the Courts of Appeal to interpret the language to preclude recovery based on such theories. (See *Lazzarevich v. Lazzarevich* (1948) 88 Cal. App. 2d 708, 719, 200 P.2d 49; *Oakley v. Oakley* (1947) 82 Cal. App. 2d 188, 191–192, 185 P.2d 848.)[12]

Consequently, when the issue of the rights of a nonmarital partner reached this court in *Keene v. Keene* (1962) 57 Cal. 2d 657, 21 Cal. Rptr. 593, 371 P.2d 329, the claimant forwent reliance upon theories of contract implied in law or fact. Asserting that she had worked on her partner's ranch and that her labor had enhanced its value, she confined her cause of action to the claim that the court should impress a resulting trust on the property derived from the sale of the ranch. The court limited its opinion accordingly, rejecting her argument on the ground that the rendition of services gives rise to a resulting trust only when the services aid in acquisition of the property, not in its subsequent improvement. (57 Cal. 2d at p. 668, 21 Cal. Rptr. 593, 371 P.2d 329.) Justice Peters, dissenting, attacked the majority's distinction between the rendition of services and the contribution of funds or property; he maintained that both property and services furnished valuable consideration, and potentially afforded the ground for a resulting trust.

[17] This failure of the courts to recognize an action by a nonmarital partner based upon implied contract, or to grant an equitable remedy, contrasts with the judicial treatment of the putative spouse. Prior to the enactment of the Family Law Act, no statute granted rights to a putative spouse.[13] The courts accordingly fashioned a variety of remedies by judicial decision. Some cases permitted the putative spouse to recover half the property on a theory that the conduct of the parties implied an agreement of partnership or joint venture. (See *Estate of Vargas* (1974) 36 Cal. App. 3d 714, 717–718, 111 Cal. Rptr. 779; *Sousa v. Freitas* (1970) 10 Cal. App. 3d 660, 666, 89 Cal. Rptr. 485.) Others permitted the spouse to recover the reasonable value of rendered services, less the value of support received. (See *Sanguinetti v. Sanguinetti* (1937) 9 Cal. 2d 95, 100–102, 69 P.2d 845.)[14] Finally, decisions affirmed the power of a court to employ equitable principles to achieve a fair division of property acquired during putative marriage. (*Coats v. Coats* (1911) 160 Cal. 671, 677–678, 118 P. 441; *Caldwell v. Odisio* (1956) 142 Cal. App. 2d 732, 735, 299 P.2d 14.)[15]

Thus in summary, the cases prior to *Cary* exhibited a schizophrenic inconsistency. By enforcing an express contract between nonmarital partners unless it rested upon an unlawful consideration, the courts applied a common law principle as to contracts. Yet the courts disregarded the common law principle that holds that implied contracts can arise from the conduct of the parties.[16] Refusing to enforce such contracts, the courts spoke of leaving the parties "in the position in which they had placed themselves" (*Oakley v. Oakley, supra,* 82 Cal. App. 2d 188, 192, 185 P.2d 848, 850), just as if they were guilty parties "in pari delicto."

Justice Curtis noted this inconsistency in his dissenting opinion in *Vallera,* pointing out that "if an express agreement will be enforced, there is no legal or just reason why an implied agreement to share the property cannot be enforced." (21 Cal. 2d 681, 686, 134 P.2d 761, 764; see Bruch, *Property Rights of De Facto Spouses Including Thoughts on the Value of Homemakers' Services* (1976) 10 Family L.Q. 101, 117–121.) And in *Keene v. Keene, supra,* 57 Cal. 2d 657, 21 Cal. Rptr. 593, 371 P.2d 329, Justice Peters observed that if the man and woman "were not illegally living together . . . it would be a plain business relationship and a contract would be implied." (Diss. opn. at p. 672, 21 Cal. Rptr. at p. 602, 371 P.2d at p. 338.)

Still another inconsistency in the prior cases arises from their treatment of property accumulated through joint effort. To the extent that a partner had contributed funds or property, the cases held that the partner obtains a proportionate share in the acquisition, despite the lack of legal standing of the relationship. (*Vallera v. Vallera, supra,* 21 Cal. 2d at p. 685, 134 P.2d at 761; see *Weak v. Weak, supra,* 202 Cal. App. 2d 632, 639, 21 Cal. Rptr. 9.) Yet courts have refused to recognize just such an interest based upon the contribution of services. As Justice Curtis points out, "Unless it can be argued that a woman's services as cook, housekeeper, and homemaker are valueless, it would seem logical that if, when she contributes money to the purchase of property, her interest will be protected, then when she contributes her services in the home, her interest in property accumulated should be protected." (*Vallera v. Vallera, supra,* 21 Cal. 2d 681, 686–687, 134 P.2d 761, 764 (diss. opn.); see Bruch, *op. cit, supra,* 10 *Family L.Q.* 101, 110–114; Article, *Illicit Cohabitation: The Impact of the* Vallera *and* Keene *Cases on the Rights of the Meretricious Spouse* (1973) 6 U.C. Davis L. Rev. 354, 369–370; Comment (1972) 48 Wash. L. Rev. 635, 641.)

Thus as of 1973, the time of the filing of *In re Marriage of Cary, supra,* 34 Cal. App. 3d 345, 109 Cal. Rptr. 862, the cases apparently held that a nonmarital partner who rendered services in the absence of express contract could assert no right to property acquired during the relationship. The facts of *Cary* demonstrated the unfairness of that rule.

Janet and Paul Cary had lived together, unmarried, for more than eight years. They held themselves out to friends and family as husband and wife, reared four children, purchased a home and other property, obtained credit, filed joint income tax returns, and otherwise conducted themselves as though they were married. Paul worked outside the home, and Janet generally cared for the house and children.

[18] In 1971 Paul petitioned for "nullity of the marriage."[17] Following a hearing on that petition, the trial court awarded Janet half the property acquired during the relationship, although all such property was traceable to Paul's earnings. The Court of Appeal affirmed the award.

Reviewing the prior decisions which had denied relief to the homemaking partner, the Court of Appeal reasoned that those decisions rested upon a policy of punishing persons guilty of cohabitation without marriage. The Family Law Act, the court observed, aimed to eliminate fault or guilt as a basis for dividing marital property. But once fault or guilt is excluded, the court reasoned, nothing distinguishes the property rights of a nonmarital "spouse" from those of a putative spouse. Since the latter is entitled to half the "quasi marital property" (Civ. Code, § 4452), the Court of Appeal concluded that, giving effect to the policy of the Family Law Act, a nonmarital cohabitator should also be entitled to half the property accumulated during an "actual family relationship." (34 Cal. App. 3d at p. 353, 109 Cal. Rptr. 862.)[18]

Cary met with a mixed reception in other appellate districts. In *Estate of Atherley, supra,* 44 Cal. App. 3d 758, 119 Cal. Rptr. 41, the Fourth District agreed with *Cary* that under the Family Law Act a nonmarital partner in an actual family relationship enjoys the same right to an equal division of property as a putative spouse. In *Beckman v. Mayhew, supra,* 49 Cal. App. 3d 529, 122 Cal. Rptr. 604, however, the Third District rejected *Cary* on the ground that the Family Law Act was not intended to change California law dealing with nonmarital relationships.

[19, 20] If *Cary* is interpreted as holding that the Family Law Act requires an equal division of property accumulated in nonmarital "actual family relationships," then we agree with *Beckman v. Mayhew* that *Cary* distends the act. No language in the Family Law Act addresses the property rights of nonmarital partners, and nothing in the legislative history of the act suggests that the Legislature considered that subject.[19] The delineation of the rights of nonmarital partners before 1970 had been fixed entirely by judicial decision; we see no reason to believe that the Legislature, by enacting the Family Law Act, intended to change that state of affairs.

But although we reject the reasoning of *Cary* and *Atherley,* we share the perception of the *Cary* and *Atherley* courts that the application of former precedent in the factual setting of those cases would work an unfair distribution of the property accumulated by the couple. Justice Friedman in *Beckman v. Mayhew, supra,* 40 Cal. App. 3d 529, 535, 122 Cal. Rptr. 604, also questioned the continued viability of our decisions in *Vallera* and *Keene;* commentators have argued the need to reconsider those precedents.[20] We should not, therefore, reject the authority of *Cary* and *Atherley* without also examining the deficiencies in the former law which lead to those decisions.

The principal reason why the pre-*Cary* decisions result in an unfair distribution of property inheres in the court's refusal to permit a nonmarital partner to assert rights based upon accepted principles of implied contract or equity. We have examined the reasons advanced to justify this denial of relief, and find that none have merit.

[21] First, we note that the cases denying relief do not rest their refusal upon any theory of "punishing" a "guilty" partner. Indeed, to the extent that denial of relief "punishes" one partner, it necessarily rewards the other by permitting him to retain a disproportionate amount of the property. Concepts of "guilt" thus cannot justify an unequal division of property between two equally "guilty" persons.[21]

Other reasons advanced in the decisions fare no better. The principal argument seems to be that "[e]quitable considerations arising from the reasonable expectation of . . . benefits attending the status of marriage . . . are not present [in a nonmarital relationship]." (*Vallera v. Vallera, supra,* 21 Cal. 2d at p. 685, 134 P.2d 761, 763.) But, although parties to a nonmarital relationship obviously cannot have based any expectations upon the belief that they were married, other expectations and equitable considerations remain. The parties may well expect that property will be divided in accord with the parties' own tacit understanding and that in the absence of such understanding the courts will fairly apportion property accumulated through mutual effort. We need not treat nonmarital partners as putatively married persons in order to apply principles of implied contract, or extend equitable remedies; we need to treat them only as we do any other unmarried persons.[22]

[22] The remaining arguments advanced from time to time to deny remedies to the nonmarital partners are of less moment. There is no more reason to presume that services are contributed as a gift than to presume that funds are contributed as a gift; in any event the better approach is to presume, as Justice Peters suggested, "that the parties intend to deal fairly with each other." (*Keene v. Keene, supra,* 57 Cal. 2d 657, 674, 21 Cal. Rptr. 593, 603, 371 P.2d 329, 339 (dissenting opn.); see Bruch, *op. cit., supra,* 10 Family L.Q. 101, 113.)

[23] The argument that granting remedies to the nonmarital partners would discourage marriage must fail; as *Cary* pointed out, "with equal or greater force the point might be made that the pre-1970 rule was calculated to cause the income producing partner to avoid marriage and thus retain the benefit of all of his or her accumulated earnings." (34 Cal. App. 3d at p. 353, 109 Cal. Rptr. at p. 866.) Although we recognize the well-established public policy to foster and promote the institution of marriage (see *Deyoe v. Superior Court* (1903) 140 Cal. 476, 482, 74 P. 28), perpetuation of judicial rules which result in an inequitable distribution of property accumulated during a nonmarital relationship is neither a just nor an effective way of carrying out that policy.

In summary, we believe that the prevalence of nonmarital relationships in modern society and the social acceptance of them, marks this as a time when our courts should by no means apply the doctrine of the unlawfulness of the so-called meretricious relationship to the instant case. As we have explained, the nonenforceability of agreements expressly providing for meretricious conduct rested upon the fact that such conduct, as the word suggests, pertained to and encompassed prostitution. To equate the nonmarital relationship of today to such a subject matter is to do violence to an accepted and wholly different practice.

We are aware that many young couples live together without the solemnization of marriage, in order to make sure that they can successfully later undertake marriage. This trial period,[23] preliminary to marriage, serves as some assurance that the marriage will not subsequently end in dissolution to the harm of both parties. We are aware, as we have stated, of the pervasiveness of nonmarital relationships in other situations.

The mores of the society have indeed changed so radically in regard to cohabitation that we cannot impose a standard based on alleged moral considerations that have apparently been so widely abandoned by so many. Lest we be misunderstood, however, we take this occasion to point out that the structure of society itself largely depends upon the institution of marriage, and nothing we have said in this opinion should be taken to derogate from that institution. The joining of the man and woman in marriage is at once the most socially productive and individually fulfilling relationship that one can enjoy in the course of a lifetime.

[24–26] We conclude that the judicial barriers that may stand in the way of a policy based upon the fulfillment of the reasonable expectations of the parties to a nonmarital relationship should be removed. As we have explained, the courts now hold that express agreements will be enforced unless they rest on an unlawful meretricious consideration. We add that in the absence of an express agreement, the courts may look to a variety of other remedies in order to protect the parties' lawful expectations.[24]

The courts may inquire into the conduct of the parties to determine whether that conduct demonstrates an implied contract or implied agreement of partnership or joint venture (see *Estate of Thornton* (1972) 81 Wash. 2d 72, 499 P.2d 864), or some other tacit understanding between the parties. The courts may, when appropriate, employ principles of constructive trust (see *Omer v. Omer* (1974) 11 Wash. App. 386, 523 P.2d 957) or resulting trust (see *Hyman v. Hyman* (Tex. Civ. App.1954) 275 S.W.2d 149). Finally, a nonmarital partner may recover in quantum meruit for the reasonable value of household services rendered less the reasonable value of support received if he can show that he rendered services with the expectation of monetary reward. (See *Hill v. Estate of Westbrook, supra,* 39 Cal. 2d 458, 462, 247 P.2d 19.)[25]

[27] Since we have determined that plaintiff's complaint states a cause of action for breach of an express contract, and, as we have explained, can be amended to state a cause of action independent of allegations of express contract,[26] we must conclude that the trial court erred in granting defendant a judgment on the pleadings.

The judgment is reversed and the cause remanded for further proceedings consistent with the views expressed herein.[27]

WRIGHT, C. J., and McCOMB, MOSK, SULLIVAN and RICHARDSON, JJ., concur.

CLARK, Justice (concurring and dissenting).

The majority opinion properly permits recovery on the basis of either express or implied in fact agreement between the parties. These being the issues presented, their resolution requires reversal of the judgment. Here, the opinion should stop.

This court should not attempt to determine all anticipated rights, duties and remedies within every meretricious relationship—particularly in vague terms. Rather, these complex issues should be determined as each arises in a concrete case.

The majority broadly indicates that a party to a meretricious relationship may recover on the basis of equitable principles and in quantum meruit. However, the majority fails to advise us of the circumstances permitting recovery, limitations on recovery, or whether their numerous remedies are cumulative or exclusive. Conceivably, under the majority opinion a party may recover half of the property acquired during the relationship on the basis of general equitable principles, recover a bonus based on specific equitable considerations, and recover a second bonus in quantum meruit.

The general sweep of the majority opinion raises but fails to answer several questions. First, because the Legislature specifically excluded some parties to a meretricious relationship from the equal division rule of Civil Code section 4452, is this court now free to create an equal division rule? Second, upon termination of the relationship, is it equitable to impose the economic obligations of lawful spouses on meretricious parties when the latter may have rejected matrimony to avoid such obligations? Third, does not application of equitable principles—necessitating examination of the conduct of the parties—violate the spirit of the Family Law Act of 1969, designed to eliminate the bitterness and acrimony resulting from the former fault system in divorce? Fourth, will not application of equitable principles reimpose upon trial courts the unmanageable burden of arbitrating domestic disputes? Fifth, will not a quantum meruit system of compensation for services—discounted by benefits received—place meretricious spouses in a better position than lawful spouses? Sixth, if a quantum meruit system is to be allowed, does fairness not require inclusion of all services and all benefits regardless of how difficult the evaluation?

When the parties to a meretricious relationship show by express or implied in fact agreement they intend to create mutual obligations, the courts should enforce the agreement. However, in the absence of agreement, we should stop and consider the ramifications before creating economic obligations which may violate legislative intent, contravene the intention of the parties, and surely generate undue burdens on our trial courts.

By judicial overreach, the majority perform a nunc pro tunc marriage, dissolve it, and distribute its property on terms never contemplated by the parties, case law or the Legislature.

References

1. "The 1970 census figures indicate that today perhaps eight times as many couples are living together without being married as cohabited ten years ago." (Comment, *In re Cary: A Judicial Recognition of Illicit Cohabitation* (1974) 25 Hastings L. J. 1226.)

2. When the case was called for trial, plaintiff asked leave to file an amended complaint. The proposed complaint added two causes of action for breach of contract against Santa Ana Records, a corporation not a party to the action, asserting that Santa Ana was an alter ego of defendant. The court denied leave to amend, and plaintiff claims that the ruling was an abuse of discretion. We disagree; plaintiff's argument was properly rejected by the Court of Appeal in the portion of its opinion quoted below.

No error was committed in denial of plaintiff's motion, made on the opening day set for trial, seeking leave to file a proposed amended complaint which would have added two counts and a new defendant to the action. As stated by plaintiff's counsel at the hearing, "[T]here is no question about it that we seek to amend the Complaint not on the eve of trial but on the day of trial."

In *Hayutin v. Weintraub,* 207 Cal. App. 2d 497, 24 Cal. Rptr. 761, the court said at pages 508–509, 24 Cal. Rptr. at page 768 in respect to such a motion that had it been granted, it "would have required a long continuance for the purpose of canvassing wholly new factual issues, a redoing of the elaborate discovery procedures previously had, all of which would have imposed upon defendant and his witnesses substantial inconvenience . . . and upon defendant needless and substantial additional expense. . . . The court did not err in denying leave to file the proposed amended complaint." (See also: *Nelson v. Specialty Records, Inc.,* 11 Cal. App. 3d 126, 138–139, 89 Cal. Rptr. 540; *Moss Estate Co. v. Adler,* 41 Cal. 2d 581, 585, 261 P.2d 732; *Bogel v. Thrifty Drug Co.,* 43 Cal. 2d 184, 188, 272 P.2d 1.) "The ruling of the trial judge will not be disturbed upon appeal absent a showing by appellant of a clear abuse of discretion. [Citations.]" (*Nelson v. Specialty Records, Inc., supra,* 11 Cal. App. 3d at p. 139, 89 Cal. Rptr. at p. 548.) No such showing here appears.

3. The colloquy between court and counsel at argument on the motion for judgment on the pleadings suggests that the trial court held the 1964 agreement violated public policy because it derogated the community property rights of Betty Marvin, defendant's lawful wife. Plaintiff, however, offered to amend her complaint to allege that she and defendant reaffirmed their contract after defendant and Betty were divorced. The trial court denied leave to amend, a ruling which suggests that the court's judgment must rest upon some other ground than the assertion that the contract would injure Betty's property rights.

4. Defendant also contends that the contract was illegal because it contemplated a violation of former Penal Code section 269a, which prohibited living "in a state of cohabitation and adultery." (§ 269a was repealed by Stats. 1975, ch. 71, eff. Jan. 1, 1976.) Defendant's standing to raise the issue is questionable because he alone was married and thus guilty of violating section 269a. Plaintiff, being unmarried, could neither be convicted of adulterous cohabitation nor of aiding and abetting defendant's violation. (See *In re Cooper* (1912) 162 Cal. 81, 85–86, 121 P. 318.)

The numerous cases discussing the contractual rights of unmarried couples have drawn no distinction between illegal relationships and lawful nonmarital relationships. (Cf. *Weak v. Weak* (1962) 202 Cal. App. 2d 632, 639, 21 Cal. Rptr. 9 (bigamous marriage).) Moreover, even if we were to draw such a distinction—a largely academic endeavor in view of the repeal of section 269a—defendant probably would not benefit; his relationship with plaintiff continued long after his divorce became final, and plaintiff sought to amend her complaint to assert that the parties reaffirmed their contract after the divorce.

5. Defendant urges that all of the cited cases, with the possible exception of *In re Marriage of Foster, supra,* 42 Cal. App. 3d 577, 117 Cal. Rptr. 49, and *Bridges v. Bridges, supra,* 125 Cal. App. 2d 359, 270 P.2d 69, can be distinguished on the ground that the partner seeking to enforce the contract contributed either property or services additional to ordinary homemaking services. No case, however, suggests that a pooling agreement in which one partner contributes only homemaking services is invalid, and dictum in *Hill v. Estate of Westbrook* (1950) 95 Cal. App. 2d 599, 603, 213 P.2d 727, states the opposite. A promise to perform homemaking services is, of course, a lawful and adequate consideration for a contract (see *Taylor v. Taylor* (1954) 66 Cal. App. 2d 390, 398, 152 P.2d 480)—otherwise those engaged in domestic employment could not sue for their wages—and defendant advances no reason why his proposed distinction would justify denial of enforcement to contracts supported by such consideration. (See *Tyranski v. Piggins* (1973) 44 Mich. App. 570, 205 N.W.2d 595, 597.)

6. Although not cited by defendant, the only California precedent which supports his position is *Heaps v. Toy* (1942) 54 Cal. App. 2d 178, 128 P.2d 813. In that case the woman promised to leave her job, to refrain from marriage, to be a companion to the man, and to make a permanent home for him; he agreed to support the woman and her child for life. The Court of Appeal held the agreement invalid as a contract in restraint of marriage (Civ. Code, § 1676) and, alternatively, as "contrary to good morals" (Civ. Code, § 1607). The opinion does not state that sexual relations formed any part of the consideration for the contract, nor explain how—unless the contract called for sexual relations—the woman's employment as a companion and housekeeper could be contrary to good morals.

The alternative holding in *Heaps v. Toy,* [supra], finding the contract in that case contrary to good morals, is inconsistent with the numerous California decisions upholding contracts between nonmarital partners when such contracts are not founded upon an illicit consideration, and is therefore disapproved.

7. Sections 169 and 169.2 were replaced in 1970 by Civil Code section 5118. In 1972 section 5118 was amended to provide that the earnings and accumulations of *both* spouses "while living separate and apart from the other spouse, are the separate property of the spouse."

8. Defendant also contends that the contract is invalid as an agreement to promote or encourage divorce. (See 1 Witkin, *Summary of Cal. Law* (8th ed.) pp. 390–392 and cases there cited.) The contract between plaintiff and defendant did not, however, by its terms require defendant to divorce Betty, nor reward him for so doing. Moreover, the principle on which defendant relies does not apply when the marriage in question is beyond redemption (*Glickman v. Collins* (1975) 13 Cal. 3d 852, 858–859, 120 Cal. Rptr. 76, 533 P.2d 204); whether or not defendant's marriage to Betty was beyond redemption when defendant contracted with plaintiff is obviously a question of fact which cannot be resolved by judgment on the pleadings.

9. Our review of the many cases enforcing agreements between nonmarital partners reveals that the majority of such agreements were oral. In two cases (*Ferguson v. Schuenemann, supra,* 167 Cal. App. 2d 413, 334 P.2d 668; *Cline v. Festersen, supra,* 128 Cal. App. 2d 380, 275 P.2d 149), the court expressly rejected defenses grounded upon the statute of frauds.

10. A great variety of other arrangements are possible. The parties might keep their earnings and property separate, but agree to compensate one party for services which benefit the other. They may choose to pool only part of their earnings and property, to form a partnership or joint venture, or to hold property acquired as joint tenants or tenants in common, or agree to any other such arrangement. (See generally Weitzman, *Legal Regulation of Marriage: Tradition and Change* (1974) 62 Cal. L. Rev. 1169.)

11. We note that a deliberate decision to avoid the strictures of the community property system is not the only reason that couples live together without marriage. Some couples may wish to avoid the permanent commitment that marriage implies, yet be willing to share equally any property acquired during the relationship; others may fear the loss of pension, welfare, or tax benefits resulting from marriage (see *Beckman v. Mayhew, supra,* 49 Cal. App. 3d 529, 122 Cal. Rptr. 604). Others may engage in the relationship as a possible prelude to marriage. In lower socioeconomic groups the difficulty and expense of dissolving a former marriage often leads couples to choose a nonmarital relationship; many unmarried couples may also incorrectly believe that the doctrine of common law marriage prevails in California, and thus that they are in fact married. Consequently we conclude that the mere fact that a couple have not participated in a valid marriage ceremony cannot serve as a basis for a court's inference that the couple intend to keep their earnings and property separate and independent; the parties' intention can only be ascertained by a more searching inquiry into the nature of their relationship.

12. The cases did not clearly determine whether a nonmarital partner could recover in quantum meruit for the reasonable value of services rendered. But when we affirmed a trial court ruling denying recovery in *Hill v. Estate of Westbrook, supra,* 39 Cal. 2d 458, 247 P.2d 19, we did so in part on the ground that whether the partner "rendered her services because of expectation of monetary reward" (p. 462, 247 P.2d p. 21) was a question of fact resolved against her by the trial court—thus implying that in a proper case the court would allow recovery based on quantum meruit.

13. The Family Law Act, in Civil Code section 4452, classifies property acquired during a putative marriage as "quasi-marital property," and requires that such property be divided upon dissolution of the marriage in accord with Civil Code section 4800.

14. The putative spouse need not prove that he rendered services in expectation of monetary reward in order to recover the reasonable value of those services. (*Sanguinetti v. Sanguinetti, supra,* 9 Cal. 3d 95, 100, 69 P.2d 845.)

15. The contrast between principles governing nonmarital and putative relationships appears most strikingly in *Lazzarevich v. Lazzarevich, supra,* 88 Cal. App. 2d 708, 200 P.2d 49. When Mrs. Lazzarevich sued her husband for divorce in 1945, she discovered to her surprise that she was not lawfully married to him. She nevertheless reconciled with him, and the Lazzareviches lived together for another year before they finally separated. The court awarded her recovery for the reasonable value of services rendered, less the value of support received, until she discovered the invalidity of the marriage, but denied recovery for the same services rendered after that date.

16. "Contracts may be express or implied. These terms, however, do not denote different kinds of contracts, but have reference to the evidence by which the agreement between the parties is shown. If the agreement is shown by the direct words of the parties, spoken or written, the contract is said to be an express one. But if such agreement can only be shown by the acts and conduct of the parties, interpreted in the light of the subject-matter and of the surrounding circumstances, then the contract is an implied one." (*Skelly v. Bristol Sav. Bank* (1893) 63 Conn. 83, 26 A. 474, 475, quoted in 1 Corbin, *Contracts* (1963) p. 41.) Thus, as Justice Schauer observed in *Desny v. Wilder* (1956) 46 Cal. 2d 715, 299 P.2d 257, in a sense all contracts made in fact, as distinguished from quasi-contractual obligations, are express contracts, differing only in the manner in which the assent of the parties is expressed and proved. (See 46 Cal. 2d at pp. 735–736, 299 P.2d 257.)

17. The Court of Appeal opinion in *In re Marriage of Cary, supra,* does not explain why Paul Cary filed his action as a petition for nullity. Briefs filed with this court, however, suggest that Paul may have been seeking to assert rights as a putative spouse. In the present case, on the other hand, neither party claims the status of an actual or putative spouse. Under such circumstances an action to adjudge "the marriage" in the instant case a nullity would be pointless and could not serve as a device to adjudicate contract and property rights arising from the parties' nonmarital relationship. Accordingly, plaintiff here correctly chose to assert her rights by means of an ordinary civil action.

18. The court in *Cary* also based its decision upon an analysis of Civil Code section 4452, which specifies the property rights of a putative spouse. Section 4452 states that if the "court finds that either party or both parties believed in good faith that the marriage was valid, the court should declare such party or parties to have the status of a putative spouse, and shall divide, in accordance with Section 4800, that property acquired during the union. . . ." Since section 4800 requires an equal division of community property, *Cary* interpreted section 4452 to require an equal division of the property of a putative marriage, so long as one spouse believed in good faith that the marriage was valid. Thus under section 4452, *Cary* concluded, the "guilty spouse" (the spouse who knows the marriage is invalid) has the same right to half the property as does the "innocent" spouse.

Cary then reasoned that if the "guilty" spouse to a putative marriage is entitled to one-half the marital property, the "guilty" partner in a nonmarital relationship should also receive one-half of the property. Otherwise, the court stated, "We should be obliged to presume a legislative intent that a person, who by deceit leads another to believe a valid marriage exists between them, shall be legally guaranteed half of the property they acquire even though most, or all, may have resulted from the earnings of the blameless partner. At the same time we must infer an inconsistent legislative intent that two persons who, candidly with each other, enter upon an unmarried family relationship, shall be denied any judicial aid whatever in the assertion of otherwise valid property rights." (34 Cal. App. 3d at p. 352, 109 Cal. Rptr. at p. 866.)

This reasoning in *Cary* has been criticized by commentators. (See Note, *op. cit., supra,* 25 Hastings L. J. 1226, 1234–1235; Comment, *In re Marriage of Carey* [sic]: *The End of the Putative-Meretricious Spouse Distinction in California* (1975) 12 San Diego L. Rev. 436, 444–446.) The Commentators note that Civil Code section 4455 provides that an "innocent" party to a putative marriage can recover spousal support, from which they infer that the Legislature intended to give only the "innocent" spouse a right to one-half of the quasi-marital property under section 4452.

We need not now resolve this dispute concerning the interpretation of section 4452. Even if *Cary* is correct in holding that a "guilty" putative spouse has a right to one-half of the marital property, it does not necessarily follow that a nonmarital partner has an identical right. In a putative marriage the parties will arrange their economic affairs with the expectation that upon dissolution the property will be divided equally. If a "guilty" putative spouse receives one-half of the property under section 4452, no expectation of the "innocent" spouse has been frustrated. In a nonmarital relationship, on the other hand, the parties may expressly or tacitly determine to order their economic relationship in some other manner, and to impose community property principles regardless of such understanding may frustrate the parties' expectations.

19. Despite the extensive material available on the legislative history of the Family Law Act neither *Cary* nor plaintiff cites any reference which suggests that the Legislature ever considered the issue of the property rights of nonmarital partners, and our independent examination has uncovered no such reference.

20. See *Bruch, op. cit., supra,* 10 Family L.Q. 101, 113; Article, *op. cit., supra,* 6 U.C. Davis L. Rev. 354; Comment (1975) 6 Golden Gate L. Rev. 179, 197–201; Comment, *op. cit., supra,* 12 San Diego L. Rev. 4356; Note, *op. cit., supra,* 25 Hastings L. J. 1226, 1246.

21. Justice Finley of the Washington Supreme Court explains: "Under such circumstances [the dissolution of a nonmarital relationship], this court and the courts of other jurisdictions have, in effect, sometimes said, 'We will wash our hands of such disputes. The parties should and must be left to their own devices, just where they find themselves.' To me, such pronouncements seem overly fastidious and a bit fatuous. They are unrealistic and, among other things, ignore the fact that an unannounced (but nevertheless effective and binding) rule of law is inherent in any such terminal statements by a court of law. The unannounced but inherent rule is simply that the party who has title, or in some instances who is in possession, will enjoy the rights of ownership of the property concerned. The rule often operates to the great advantage of the cunning and the shrewd, who wind up with possession of the

property, or title to it in their names, at the end of a so-called meretricious relationship. So, although the courts proclaim that they will have nothing to do with such matters, the proclamation in itself establishes, as to the parties involved, an effective and binding rule of law which tends to operate purely by accident or perhaps by reason of the cunning, anticipatory designs of just one of the parties." (*West v. Knowles* (1957) 50 Wash. 2d 311, 311 P.2d 689, 692 (conc. opn.).)

22. In some instances a confidential relationship may arise between nonmarital partners, and economic transactions between them should be governed by the principles applicable to such relationships.

23. Toffler, *Future Shock* (Bantam Books, 1971) page 253.

24. We do not seek to resurrect the doctrine of common law marriage, which was abolished in California by statute in 1895. (See *Norman v. Thomson* (1898) 121 Cal. 620, 628, 54 P. 143; *Estate of Abate* (1958) 166 Cal. App. 2d 282, 292, 333 P.2d 200.) Thus we do not hold that plaintiff and defendant were "married," nor do we extend to plaintiff the rights which the Family Law Act grants valid or putative spouses; we hold only that she has the same rights to enforce contracts and to assert her equitable interest in property acquired through her effort as does any other unmarried person.

25. Our opinion does not preclude the evolution of additional equitable remedies to protect the expectations of the parties to a nonmarital relationship in cases in which existing remedies prove inadequate; the suitability of such remedies may be determined in later cases in light of the factual setting in which they arise.

26. We do not pass upon the question whether, in the absence of an express or implied contractual obligation, a party to a nonmarital relationship is entitled to support payments from the other party after the relationship terminates.

27. We wish to commend the parties and amici for the exceptional quality of the briefs and argument in this case.

176 Cal. Rptr. 555
122 Cal. App. 3d 871
Michelle MARVIN, aka Michelle Triola,
Plaintiff and Respondent,
v.
Lee MARVIN, Defendant and Appellant.
Civ. 59130.
Court of Appeal, Second District,
Division 3.
Aug. 11, 1981.

Female cohabitant brought suit asking that male cohabitant be ordered to pay to her a reasonable sum per month as and for her support and maintenance. The Superior Court, Los Angeles County, Arthur K. Marshall, J., ordered that defendant pay to plaintiff the sum of $104,000, to be used by her primarily for her economic rehabilitation, and defendant appealed. The Court of Appeal, Cobey, J., held that: (1) challenged rehabilitation award was not within issues framed by pleadings and thus special findings of fact and conclusions of law in support of award would be disregarded, and (2) furthermore, where female cohabitant benefited economically and socially from her relationship with male cohabitant and suffered no damage therefrom, even with respect to its termination, and where male cohabitant never had any obligation to pay female cohabitant a reasonable sum as and for her maintenance and male was not unjustly enriched by reason of relationship or its termination and never acquired anything of value from female cohabitant by any wrongful act, female cohabitant was not entitled to rehabilitative award.

As modified, affirmed.

Klein, P. J., dissented with opinion.

1. Implied and Constructive Contracts ⊶83

Where cohabitants' amended complaint, upon which action went to trial, asked, with respect to support of plaintiff cohabitant by defendant cohabitant, only that defendant be ordered to pay to plaintiff a reasonable sum per month as and for her support and maintenance and did not ask in basic pleading for any limited rehabilitative support, any findings of fact and conclusions of law in support of award would be disregarded as not being within issues framed by pleadings.

2. Implied and Constructive Contracts ⊶1

Equitable remedies should be devised to protect expectations of parties to nonmarital relationship.

3. Implied and Constructive Contracts ⊶3

Where female cohabitant benefited economically and socially from her relationship with male cohabitant and suffered no damage therefrom, even with respect to its termination, and where male cohabitant never had any obligation to pay female cohabitant a reasonable sum for her maintenance and male cohabitant had not been unjustly enriched by reason of relationship or its termination and never acquired anything of value from female cohabitant by any wrongful act, female cohabitant was not entitled to rehabilitative award.

4. Implied and Constructive Contracts ⊶1

Rehabilitative award, being nonconsensual in nature, must be supported by some recognized underlying obligation in law or in equity.

5. Equity ⚷1

A court of equity admittedly has broad powers, but it may not create totally new substantive rights under guise of doing equity.

Goldman & Kagon, A. David Kagon and Charles D. Meyer, Los Angeles, for defendant and appellant.

Marvin M. Mitchelson and Penelope Mercurio, Los Angeles, for plaintiff and respondent.

COBEY, Associate Justice.

Defendant, Lee Marvin, appeals from that portion of a judgment ordering him to pay to plaintiff, Michelle Marvin, the sum of $104,000, to be used by her primarily for her economic rehabilitation.

Defendant contends, among other things, that the challenged award is outside the issues of the case as framed by the pleadings of the parties (see Code Civ. Proc., § 588) and furthermore lacks any basis in equity or in law.[1] We agree and will therefore modify the judgment by deleting therefrom the challenged award.

Facts

This statement of facts is taken wholly from the findings of the trial court, which tried the case without a jury. The parties met in June 1964 and started living together occasionally in October of that year. They lived together almost continuously (except for business absences of his) from the spring of 1965 to May or June of 1970, when their cohabitation was ended at his insistence. This cohabitation was the result of an initial agreement between them to live together as unmarried persons so long as they both enjoyed their mutual companionship and affection.

More specifically, the parties to this lawsuit never agreed during their cohabitation that they would combine their efforts and earnings or would share equally in any property accumulated as a result of their efforts, whether individual or combined. They also never agreed during this period that plaintiff would relinquish her professional career as an entertainer and singer in order to devote her efforts full time to defendant as his companion and homemaker generally. Defendant did not agree during this period of cohabitation that he would provide all of plaintiff's financial needs and support for the rest of her life.

Furthermore, the trial court specifically found that: (1) defendant has never had any obligation to pay plaintiff a reasonable sum as and for her maintenance;[2] (2) plaintiff suffered no damage resulting from her relationship with defendant, including its termination and thus defendant did not become monetarily liable to plaintiff at all; (3) plaintiff actually benefited economically and socially from the cohabitation of the parties, including payment by defendant for goods and services for plaintiff's sole benefit in the approximate amount of $72,900.00, payment by defendant of the living expenses of the two of them of approximately $221,400.00, and other substantial specified gifts;[3] (4) a confidential and fiduciary relationship never existed between the parties with respect to property; (5) defendant was never unjustly enriched as a result of the relationship of the parties or of the services performed by plaintiff for him or for them; (6) defendant never acquired any property or money from plaintiff by any wrongful act.

The trial court specifically found in support of its challenged rehabilitation award that the market value of defendant's property at the time the parties separated exceeded $1 million, that plaintiff at the time of the trial of this case had been recently receiving unemployment insurance benefits, that it was doubtful that plaintiff could return to the career that she had enjoyed before the relationship of the parties commenced, namely, that of singer, that plaintiff was in need of rehabilitation *i.e.*, to learn new employable skills, that she should be able to accomplish such rehabilitation in two years and that the sum of $104,000 was not only necessary primarily for such rehabilitation, but also for her living expenses (including her debts) during this period of rehabilitation, and that defendant had the ability to pay this sum forthwith.

Moreover, the trial court concluded as a matter of law that inasmuch as defendant had terminated the relationship of the parties and plaintiff had no visible means of support, "in equity," she had a right to assistance by defendant until she could become self-supporting. The trial court explained that it fixed the award at the highest salary that the plaintiff had ever earned, namely, $1,000 a week for two years, although plaintiff's salary had been at that level for only two weeks and she ordinarily had earned less than one-half that amount weekly.

DISCUSSION

1. The challenged rehabilitation award is not within the issues framed by the pleadings

This is a judgment roll appeal in the sense that we have no transcript of the evidence taken at the apparently lengthy trial below. The issues in a lawsuit are, aside from those added by a pretrial order, either those framed by the pleadings or as expanded at trial. (See 4 Witkin, *Cal. Procedure* (2d ed. 1971) Trial, § 336, p. 3138.) Here, however, since we do not have before us the evidence taken at trial and there was no pretrial order expanding the issues, we can look only to the pleadings to determine the issues between the parties.

[1] Plaintiff's amended complaint, upon which this action went to trial, asks, with respect to the support of plaintiff by defendant, only that defendant be ordered to pay to plaintiff a reasonable sum per month as and for her support and maintenance. Plaintiff did not ask in this basic pleading for any limited rehabilitative support of the type the trial court apparently on its own initiative subsequently awarded her. Consequently, the special findings of fact and conclusions of law in support of this award must be disregarded as not being within the issues framed by the pleadings. (See *Crescent Lumber Co. v. Larson* (1913) 166 Cal. 168, 171, 135 P. 502; *Gardiana v. Small Claims Court* (1976) 59 Cal. App. 3d 412, 421, 130 Cal. Rptr. 675.) When this is done, the challenged portion of the judgment becomes devoid of any support whatsoever and therefore must be deleted.

2. In any event there is no equitable or legal basis for the challenged rehabilitative award

The trial court apparently based its rehabilitative award upon two footnotes in the opinion of our Supreme Court in this case. (*Marvin v. Marvin* (1976) 18 Cal. 3d 660, 134 Cal. Rptr. 815, 557 P.2d 106.) These are footnotes 25 and 26, which respectively read as follows:

> Our opinion does not preclude the evolution of additional equitable remedies to protect the expectations of the parties to a nonmarital relationship in cases in which existing remedies prove inadequate; the suitability of such remedies may be determined in later cases in light of the factual setting in which they arise. (*Id.* at p. 684, 134 Cal. Rptr. 815, 557 P.2d 106.)
>
> We do not pass upon the question whether, in the absence of an express or implied contractual obligation, a party to a nonmarital relationship is entitled to support payments from the other party after the relationship terminates. (*Id.* at p. 685, 134 Cal. Rptr. 815, 557 P.2d 106.)

[2] There is no doubt that footnote 26 opens the door to a support award in appropriate circumstances. Likewise, under footnote 25, equitable remedies should be devised "to protect the expectations of the parties to a nonmarital relationship." The difficulty in applying either of these footnotes in the manner in which the trial court has done in this case is

that, as already pointed out, the challenged limited rehabilitative award of the trial court is not within the issues of the case as framed by the pleadings and there is nothing in the trial court's findings to suggest that such an award is warranted to protect the expectations of both parties.

[3] Quite to the contrary, as already noted, the trial court expressly found that plaintiff benefited economically and socially from her relationship with defendant and suffered no damage therefrom, even with respect to its termination. Furthermore, the trial court also expressly found that defendant never had any obligation to pay plaintiff a reasonable sum as and for her maintenance and that defendant had not been unjustly enriched by reason of the relationship or its termination and that defendant had never acquired anything of value from plaintiff by any wrongful act.

[4, 5] Furthermore, the special findings in support of the challenged rehabilitative award merely established plaintiff's need therefor and defendant's ability to respond to that need. This is not enough. The award, being nonconsensual in nature, must be supported by some recognized underlying obligation in law or in equity. A court of equity admittedly has broad powers, but it may not create totally new substantive rights under the guise of doing equity. (See *Rosenberg v. Lawrence* (1938) 10 Cal. 2d 590, 594–595, 75 P.2d 1082; *Lande v. Jurisich* (1943) 59 Cal. App. 2d 613, 618, 139 P.2d 657.)

The trial court in its special conclusions of law addressed to this point attempted to state an underlying obligation by saying that plaintiff had a right to assistance from defendant until she became self-supporting. But this special conclusion obviously conflicts with the earlier, more general, finding of the court that defendant has never had and did not then have any obligation to provide plaintiff with a reasonable sum for her support and maintenance and, in view of the already-mentioned findings of no damage (but benefit instead), no unjust enrichment and no wrongful act on the part of defendant with respect to either the relationship or its termination, it is clear that no basis whatsoever, either in equity or in law, exists for the challenged rehabilitative award. It therefore must be deleted from the judgment.[4]

Disposition

The judgment under appeal is modified by deleting therefrom the portion thereof under appeal, namely, the rehabilitative award of $104,000 to plaintiff, Michelle Marvin. As modified it is affirmed. Costs on appeal are awarded to defendant, Lee Marvin.

POTTER, J., concurs.

KLEIN, Presiding Justice, dissenting.

I dissent.

This case was tried by the court sitting without a jury over a three-month period, during which time presumably extensive evidence was taken. The trial court was able to evaluate the parties and witnesses as they appeared and gave testimony. However, since the record on this appeal consists only of the judgment roll rather than a reporter's transcript, we do not know the extent and nature of the evidence presented, or whether the issues as framed by the pleadings were expanded during the trial.

We do know that at the conclusion of the trial, the trial court awarded Michelle $104,000 pursuant to finding number 26 that: "Plaintiff is in need of funds to be used in the course of rehabilitation, so that she may re-educate herself and learn new employable skills. . . . ," and finding number 27 that: "The sum of $104,000.00 is necessary primarily for rehabilitation and also living expenses and debts to be paid during such rehabilitation."

In her first amended complaint, Michelle pled as follows:

> That in order that Plaintiff would be able to devote her full time to Defendant Marvin as a companion, homemaker, housekeeper and cook, it was further agreed that Plaintiff would give up her lucrative career as an entertainer/singer.

> That in return, Defendant Marvin would provide for all of Plaintiff's financial support and needs for the rest of her life.

Michelle prayed for "such other relief as this Court deems just and proper."

We are also made aware of the fact that Marvin was paying Michelle monies on a monthly basis after their separation pursuant to some kind of an "arrangement."

The trial court in its memorandum opinion recognizes that *Marvin v. Marvin* (1976) 18 Cal. 3d 660, 134 Cal. Rptr. 815, 557 P.2d 106, ". . . urges the trial court to employ whatever equitable remedy may be proper under the circumstances."

Marvin v. Marvin, supra, at page 685, footnote 26, 134 Cal. Rptr. 815, 557 P.2d 106, specifically states: "We do not pass upon the question whether, in the absence of an express or implied contractual obligation, a party to a nonmarital relationship is entitled to support payments from the other party after the relationship terminates."

In finding number 3, the trial court herein concludes: "The parties did not enter into any agreement to the following effect: That Plaintiff would give up any career which she might have had, whether as an entertainer/singer, or in any other calling, in order to enable Plaintiff to devote her full time to Defendant as a companion, homemaker, housekeeper and cook of Defendant," the contents of which finding was echoed in finding numbers 6 and 7. In finding number 18(c), the trial court found that the plaintiff did not in fact give up her career at the defendant's request in order to devote her full time and attention to defendant's personal needs.

In view of all the evidence that the trial court had before it, including the plaintiff's sex, age, earning ability and career status, the length of the relationship, and other circumstances of the factual setting, *Marvin v. Marvin, supra,* seems to say that the trial court was authorized by way of remedy to provide support payments from the other party after the relationship terminated, provided it also found some equitable right to such a remedy. Apparently, this is what the trial court herein attempted to do in granting a support-type award for rehabilitation for a two-year period, which seemed to reinstate to some extent the prior "arrangement" the parties had.

However, it is the trial court's responsibility to provide findings of fact and conclusions of law which are consistent with the judgment in order that we may conduct proper appellate review. (*Spaulding v. Cameron* (1952) 38 Cal. 2d 265, 270, 239 P.2d 625; *Kaiser Foundation Hospitals v. Workers' Comp. Appeals Bd.* (Fuchs) (1979) 91 Cal. App. 3d 501, 506, fn. 5, 154 Cal. Rptr. 765; *Machado v. Machado* (1914) 26 Cal. App. 16, 18, 145 P. 738.)

Indeed, " 'it is essential that [the trial court's findings of fact and conclusions of law] be sufficient in form and substance so that by reading them and referring to the record the parties can tell and this court can tell with reasonable certainty not only the theory upon which the [trial court] has arrived at its ultimate finding and conclusion but that the [trial court] has in truth found those facts which as a matter of law are essential to sustain its award.' (*Mercer-Fraser Co. v. Industrial Acc. Com.* [1953] 40 Cal. 2d [102], 124 [251 P.2d 955]." (*Kaiser Foundation Hospitals v. Workers' Comp. Appeals Bd.* (Fuchs), *supra,* 91 Cal. App. 3d at p. 506, fn. 5, 154 Cal. Rptr. 765.)

As "it is impossible to reconcile this judgment with the findings . . . , it is clearly the duty of this court to reverse this judgment and remand the case to the trial court for . . . correction . . . of the [inconsistencies] in its findings [and conclusions] or its judgment or both." (*Machado v. Machado, supra,* 26 Cal. App. at p. 18, 145 P. 738; 6 Witkin, Cal. Procedure (2d ed. 1971) Appeal, § 541, pp. 4482–4483.)

I would reverse the judgment and remand for further proceedings consistent with this dissent.

1. Defendant challenges the constitutionality of the award on various grounds, but we will not reach the issues there raised because it is unnecessary to do so. (See *People v. Green* (1980) 27 Cal. 3d 1, 50, 164 Cal. Rptr. 1, 609 P.2d 468; *People v. Kozden* (1974) 36 Cal. App. 3d 918, 123, 111 Cal. Rptr. 826.)

2. The judgment under appeal tracks this finding in the following language: "Defendant never had, and does not now have, the duty and obligation to pay to plaintiff a reasonable sum as and for her support and maintenance."

3. The trial court also found that "Defendant made a substantial financial effort to launch Plaintiff's career as a recording singer and to continue her career as a nightclub singer."

4. We obviously disagree with our dissenting colleague regarding the clarity and consistency (with the judgment) of the trial court's special findings of fact and conclusions of law in support of the challenged rehabilitative award. There is no need to remand this case to the trial court for correction of these matters since the award itself is without support in either equity or law.

APPENDIX VI

FEDERAL RULES OF EVIDENCE §§ 801–806

Federal Rules of Evidence 801 through 806

Article VIII. Hearsay
Rule 801. Definitions

The following definitions apply under this article:

(a) Statement. A "statement" is (1) an oral or written assertion or (2) nonverbal conduct of a person, if it is intended by the person as an assertion.
(b) Declarant. A "declarant" is a person who makes a statement.
(c) Hearsay. "Hearsay" is a statement, other than one made by the declarant while testifying at the trial or hearing, offered in evidence to prove the truth of the matter asserted.
(d) Statements which are not hearsay. A statement is not hearsay if—
  (1) Prior statement by witness. The declarant testifies at the trial or hearing and is subject to cross-examination concerning the statement, and the statement is (A) inconsistent with the declarant's testimony, and was given under oath subject to the penalty of perjury at a trial, hearing, or other proceeding, or in a deposition, or (B) consistent with the declarant's testimony and is offered to rebut an express or implied charge against the declarant of recent fabrication or improper influence or motive, or (C) one of identification of a person made after perceiving the person; or
  (2) Admission by party-opponent. The statement is offered against a party and is (A) the party's own statement, in either an individual or a representative capacity, or (B) a statement of which the party has manifested an adoption or belief in its truth, or (C) a statement by a person authorized by the party to make a statement concerning the subject, or (D) a statement by the party's agent or servant concerning a matter within the scope of the agency or employment, made during the existence of the relationship, or (E) a statement by a co-conspirator of a party during the course and in furtherance of the conspiracy.

Rule 802 Hearsay Rule

Hearsay is not admissible except as provided by these rules or by other rules prescribed by the Supreme Court pursuant to statutory authority or by Act of Congress.

Rule 803 Hearsay Exceptions; Availability of Declarant Immaterial

The following are not excluded by the hearsay rule, even though the declarant is available as a witness:

(1) **Present sense impression.** A statement describing or explaining an event or condition made while the declarant was perceiving the event or condition, or immediately thereafter.

(2) **Excited utterance.** A statement relating to a startling event or condition made while the declarant was under the stress of excitement caused by the event or condition.

(3) **Then existing mental, emotional, or physical condition.** A statement of the declarant's then existing state of mind, emotions, sensation, or physical condition (such as intent, plan, motive, testing, mental feeling, pain, and bodily health), but not including a statement of memory or belief to prove the fact remembered or believed unless it relates to the execution, revocation, identification, or terms of declarant's will.

(4) **Statements for purposes of medical diagnosis or treatment.** Statements made for purposes of medical diagnosis or treatment and describing medical history, or past or present symptoms, pain, or sensation, or the inception or general character of the cause or external source thereof insofar as reasonably pertinent to diagnosis or treatment.

(5) **Recorded recollection.** A memorandum or record concerning a matter about which a witness once had knowledge but now has insufficient recollection to enable the witness to testify fully and accurately, shown to have been made or adopted by the witness when the matter was fresh in the witness' memory and to reflect that knowledge correctly. If admitted, the memorandum or record may be read into evidence but may not itself be received as an exhibit unless offered by an adverse party.

(6) **Records of regularly conducted activity.** A memorandum, report, record, or data compilation, in any form, of acts, events, conditions, opinions, or diagnoses, made at or near the time by, or from information transmitted by, a person with knowledge, if kept in the course of a regularly conducted business activity, and if it was the regular practice of that business activity to make the memorandum, report, record, or data compilation, all as shown by the testimony of the custodian or other qualified witness, unless the source of information or the method or circumstances of preparation indicate lack of trustworthiness. The term "business" as used in this paragraph includes business, institution, association, profession, occupation, and calling of every kind, whether or not conducted for profit.

(7) **Absence of entry in records kept in accordance with the provisions of paragraph (6).** Evidence that a matter is not included in the memoranda, reports, records, or data compilations, in any form, kept in accordance with the provisions of paragraph (6), to prove the nonoccurrence or nonexistence of the matter, if the matter was of a kind of which a memorandum, report, record, or data compilation was regularly made and preserved, unless the sources of information or other circumstances indicate lack of trustworthiness.

(8) **Public records and reports.** Records, reports, statements, or data compilation, in any form, of public offices or agencies, setting forth (A) the activities of the office or agency, or (B) matters observed pursuant to duty imposed by law as to which matters there was a duty to report, excluding, however, in criminal cases matters observed by police officers and other law enforcement personnel, or (C) in civil actions and proceedings and against the Government in criminal cases, factual findings resulting from an investigation made pursuant to authority granted by law, unless the sources of information or other circumstances indicate lack of truthworthiness.

(9) **Records of vital statistics.** Records or data compilations, in any form, of births, fetal deaths, deaths, or marriages, if the report thereof was made to a public office pursuant to requirements of law.

(10) **Absence of public record or entry.** To prove the absence of a record, report statement, or data compilation, in any form, or the nonoccurrence or nonexistence of a matter of which a record, report, statement, or data compilation, in any form, was regularly made and preserved by a public office or agency, evidence in the form of a certification in accordance with rule 902, or testimony, that diligent search failed to disclose the record, report, statement, or data compilation, or entry.

(11) Records of religious organizations. Statements of births, marriages, divorces, deaths, legitimacy, ancestry, relationship by blood or marriage, or other similar facts of personal or family history, contained in a regularly kept record of a religious organization.

(12) Marriage, baptismal, and similar certificates. Statements of fact contained in a certificate that the maker performed a marriage or other ceremony or administered a sacrament, made by a clergyman, public official, or other person authorized by the rules or practices of a religious organization or by law to perform the act certified, and purporting to have been issued at the time of the act or within a reasonable time thereafter.

(13) Family records. Statements of fact concerning personal or family history contained in family Bibles, genealogies, charts, engravings on rings, inscriptions on family portraits, engravings on urns, crypts, or tombstones, or the like.

(14) Records of documents affecting an interest in property. The record of a document purporting to establish or affect an interest in property, as proof of the content of the original recorded document and its execution and delivery by each person by whom it purports to have been executed, if the record is a record of a public office and an applicable statute authorizes the recording of documents of that kind in that office.

(15) Statements in documents affecting an interest in property. A statement contained in a document purporting to establish or affect an interest in property if the matter stated was relevant to the purpose of the document, unless dealings with the property since the document was made have been inconsistent with the truth of the statement or the purport of the document.

(16) Statements in ancient documents. Statements in a document in existence twenty years or more the authenticity of which is established.

(17) Market reports, commercial publications. Market quotations, tabulations, lists, directories, or other published compilations, generally used and relied upon by the public or by persons in particular occupations.

(18) Learned treatises. To the extent called to the attention of an expert witness upon cross-examination or relied upon by the expert witness in direct examination, statements contained in published treatises, periodicals, or pamphlets on a subject of history, medicine, or other science or art, established as a reliable authority by the testimony or admission of the witness or by other expert testimony or by judicial notice. If admitted, the statements may be read into evidence but may not be received as exhibits.

(19) Reputation concerning personal or family history. Reputation among members of a person's family by blood, adoption, or marriage, or among a person's birth, adoption, marriage, divorce, death, legitimacy, relationship by blood, adoption, or marriage, ancestry, or other similar fact of personal or family history.

(20) Reputation concerning boundaries or general history. Reputation in a community, arising before the controversy, as to boundaries of or customs affecting lands in the community, and reputation as to events of general history important to the community or state or nation in which located.

(21) Reputation as to character. Reputation of a person's character among associates or in the community.

(22) Judgment of previous conviction. Evidence of a final judgment, entered after a trial or upon a plea of guilty (but not upon a plea of nolo contendere), adjudging a person guilty of a crime punishable by death or imprisonment in excess of one year, to prove any fact essential to sustain the judgment, but not including, when offered by the Government in a criminal prosecution for purposes other than impeachment, judgments against persons other than the accused. The pendency of an appeal may be shown but does not affect admissibility.

(23) Judgment as to personal, family, or general history, or boundaries. Judgments as proof of matters of personal, family, or general history, or boundaries, essential to the judgment, if the same would be provable by evidence of reputation.

(24) Other exceptions. A statement not specifically covered by any of the foregoing exceptions but having equivalent circumstantial guarantees of trustworthiness, if the court determines that (A) the statement is offered as evidence of a material fact; (B) the statement is more probative on the point for which it is offered than any other evidence which the proponent can procure through reasonable efforts; and (C) the general purposes of these rules and the interests of justice will best be served by admission of the statement into evidence. However, a statement may not be admitted under this exception unless the proponent of it makes known to the adverse party sufficiently in advance of the trial or hearing to provide the adverse party with a fair opportunity to prepare to meet it, the proponent's intention to offer the statement and the particulars of it, including the name and address of the declarant.

Rule 804 Hearsay Exceptions; Declarant Unavailable

(a) Definition of unavailability. "Unavailability as a witness" includes situations in which the declarant—

- **(1)** is exempted by ruling of the court on the ground of privilege from testifying concerning the subject matter of the declarant's statement; or
- **(2)** persists in refusing to testify concerning the subject matter of the declarant's statement despite an order of the court to do so; or
- **(3)** testifies to a lack of memory of the subject matter of the declarant's statement; or
- **(4)** is unable to be present or to testify at the hearing because of death or then existing physical or mental illness or infirmity; or
- **(5)** is absent from the hearing and the proponent of a statement has been unable to procure the declarant's attendance (or in the case of a hearsay exception under subdivision (b) (2), (3), or (4), the declarant's attendance or testimony) by process or other reasonable means.

A declarant is not unavailable as a witness if exemption, refusal, claim of lack of memory, inability or absence is due to the procurement or wrongdoing of the proponent of a statement for the purpose of preventing the witness from attending or testifying.

(b) Hearsay exceptions. The following are not excluded by the hearsay rule if the declarant is unavailable as a witness:

- **(1) Former testimony.** Testimony given as a witness at another hearing of the same or a different proceeding, or in a deposition taken in compliance with law in the course of the same or another proceeding, if the party against whom the testimony is now offered, or, in a civil action or proceeding, a predecessor in interest, had an opportunity and similar motive to develop the testimony by direct, cross, or redirect examination.
- **(2) Statement under belief of impending death.** In a prosecution for homicide or in a civil action or proceeding, a statement made by a declarant while believing that the declarant's death was imminent, concerning the cause or circumstances of what the declarant believed to be impending death.
- **(3) Statement against interest.** A statement which was at the time of its making so far contrary to the declarant's pecuniary or proprietary interest, or so far tended to subject the declarant to civil or criminal liability, or to render invalid a claim by the declarant against another, that a reasonable person in the declarant's position would not have made the statement unless believing it to be true. A statement tending to expose the declarant to criminal liability and offered to exculpate the accused is not admissible unless corroborating circumstances clearly indicate the trustworthiness of the statement.
- **(4) Statement of personal or family history.** (A) A statement concerning the declarant's own birth, adoption, marriage, divorce, legitimacy, relationship by blood, adoption, or marriage, ancestry, or other similar fact of personal or family history, even though declarant had no means of acquiring personal knowledge of the matter stated; or (B) a statement concerning the foregoing matters, and death also, of another person, if the declarant was related to the

other by blood, adoption, or marriage or was so intimately associated with the other's family as to be likely to have accurate information concerning the matter declared.

(5) **Other exceptions.** A statement not specifically covered by any of the foregoing exceptions but having equivalent circumstantial guarantees of trustworthiness, if the court determines that (A) the statement is offered as evidence of a material fact; (B) the statement is more probative on the point for which it is offered than any other evidence which the proponent can procure through reasonable efforts; and (C) the general purposes of these rules and the interests of justice will best be served by admission of the statement into evidence. However, a statement may not be admitted under this exception unless the proponent of it makes known to the adverse party sufficiently in advance of the trial or hearing to provide the adverse party with a fair opportunity to prepare to meet it, the proponent's intention to offer the statement and the particulars of it, including the name and address of the declarant.

Rule 805 Hearsay within Hearsay

Hearsay included within hearsay is not excluded under the hearsay rule if each part of the combined statements conforms with an exception to the hearsay rule provided in these rules.

Rule 806 Attacking and Supporting Credibility of Declarant

When a hearsay statement, or a statement defined in Rule 801(d) (2), (C), (D), or (E), has been admitted in evidence, the credibility of the declarant may be attacked, and if attacked may be supported, by evidence which would be admissible for those purposes if declarant had testified as a witness. Evidence of a statement or conduct by the declarant at any time, inconsistent with the declarant's hearsay statement, is not subject to any requirement that the declarant may have been afforded an opportunity to deny or explain. If the party against whom a hearsay statement has been admitted called the declarant as a witness, the party is entitled to examine the declarant on the statement as if under cross-examination.

APPENDIX VII

RECENT UNITED STATES SUPREME COURT DECISIONS

The following decisions are not in full case format.

1. *Bush v. Gore*
2. *United States v. Lopez*
3. *United States v. Morrison*
4. *Kyllo v. United States*
5. *Good News Club v. Milford Central School*
6. *United States v. Oakland Cannabis Buyers Cooperative*
7. *United States v. Playboy Entertainment Group, Inc.*
8. *Atwater v. City Of Lago Vista*
9. *New York Times Co., Inc. v. Tasini*
10. *Idaho v. United States*
11. *Texas v. Cobb*
12. *Lorillard Tobacco Co. v. Reilly*

Bush v. Gore

531 U.S. 98, 121 S. Ct. 525, 148 L. Ed. 2d 388 (2000)

PER CURIAM

I

On December 8, 2000, the Supreme Court of Florida ordered that the Circuit Court of Leon County tabulate by hand 9,000 ballots in Miami-Dade County. It also ordered the inclusion in the certified vote totals of 215 votes identified in Palm Beach County and 168 votes identified in Miami-Dade County for Vice President Albert Gore, Jr., and Senator Joseph Lieberman, Democratic Candidates for President and Vice President. The Supreme Court noted that petitioner, Governor George W. Bush asserted that the net gain for Vice President Gore in Palm Beach County was 176 votes, and directed the Circuit Court to resolve that dispute on remand. ___ So. 2d, at ___ (slip op., at 4, n. 6). The court further held that relief would require manual recounts in all Florida counties where so-called "undervotes" had not been subject to manual tabulation. The court ordered all manual recounts to begin at once. Governor Bush and Richard Cheney, Republican Candidates for the Presidency and Vice Presidency, filed an emergency application for a stay of this mandate. On December 9, we granted the application, treated the application as a petition for a writ of certiorari, and granted certiorari. Post, p. ___.

The proceedings leading to the present controversy are discussed in some detail in our opinion in *Bush v. Palm Beach County Canvassing Bd.*, ante, p. ____ (per curiam) (Bush I). On November 8, 2000, the day following the Presidential election, the Florida Division of Elections reported that petitioner, Governor Bush, had received 2,909,135 votes, and respondent, Vice President Gore, had received 2,907,351 votes, a margin of 1,784 for Governor Bush. Because Governor Bush's margin of victory was less than "one-half of a percent . . . of the votes cast," an automatic machine recount was conducted under §102.141(4) of the election code, the results of which showed Governor Bush still winning the race but by a diminished margin. Vice President Gore then sought manual recounts in Volusia, Palm Beach, Broward, and Miami-Dade Counties, pursuant to Florida's election protest provisions. Fla. Stat. §102.166 (2000). A dispute arose concerning the deadline for local county canvassing boards to submit their returns to the Secretary of State (Secretary). The Secretary declined to waive the November 14 deadline imposed by statute. §§102.111, 102.112. The Florida Supreme Court, however, set the deadline at November 26. We granted certiorari and vacated the Florida Supreme Court's decision, finding considerable uncertainty as to the grounds on which it was based. Bush I, ante, at ___-___ (slip. op., at 6–7). On December 11, the Florida Supreme Court issued a decision on remand reinstating that date. ___ So. 2d ___, ___ (slip op. at 30–31).

On November 26, the Florida Elections Canvassing Commission certified the results of the election and declared Governor Bush the winner of Florida's 25 electoral votes. On November 27, Vice President Gore, pursuant to Florida's contest provisions, filed a complaint in Leon County Circuit Court contesting the certification. Fla. Stat. §102.168 (2000). He sought relief pursuant to §102.168(3)(c), which provides that "[r]eceipt of a number of illegal votes or rejection of a number of legal votes sufficient to change or place in doubt the result of the election" shall be grounds for a contest. The Circuit Court denied relief, stating that Vice President Gore failed to meet his burden of proof. He appealed to the First District Court of Appeal, which certified the matter to the Florida Supreme Court.

Accepting jurisdiction, the Florida Supreme Court affirmed in part and reversed in part. *Gore v. Harris,* ___ So. 2d. ____ (2000). The court held that the Circuit Court had been correct to reject Vice President Gore's challenge to the results certified in Nassau County and his challenge to the Palm Beach County Canvassing Board's determination that 3,300 ballots cast in that county were not, in the statutory phrase, "legal votes."

The Supreme Court held that Vice President Gore had satisfied his burden of proof under §102.168(3)(c) with respect to his challenge to Miami-Dade County's failure to tabulate, by manual count, 9,000 ballots on which the machines had failed to detect a vote for President ("undervotes"). ___ So. 2d., at ___ (slip. op., at 22–23). Noting the closeness of the election, the Court explained that "[o]n this record, there can be no question that there are legal votes within the 9,000 uncounted votes sufficient to place the results of this election in doubt." *Id.*, at ___ (slip. op., at 35). A "legal vote," as determined by the Supreme Court, is "one in which there is a 'clear indication of the intent of the voter. '" Id., at ____ (slip op., at 25). The court therefore ordered a hand recount of the 9,000 ballots in Miami-Dade County. Observing that the contest provisions vest broad discretion in the circuit judge to "provide any relief appropriate under such circumstances," Fla. Stat. §102.168(8) (2000), the Supreme Court further held that the Circuit Court could order "the Supervisor of Elections and the Canvassing Boards, as well as the necessary public officials, in all counties that have not conducted a manual recount or tabulation of the undervotes . . . to do so forthwith, said tabulation to take place in the individual counties where the ballots are located." ____ So. 2d, at ____ (slip. op., at 38).

The Supreme Court also determined that both Palm Beach County and Miami-Dade County, in their earlier manual recounts, had identified a net gain of 215 and 168 legal votes for Vice President Gore. *Id.*, at ___ (slip. op., at 33–34). Rejecting the Circuit Court's conclusion that Palm Beach County lacked the authority to include the 215 net votes submitted past the November 26 deadline, the Supreme Court explained that the deadline was not intended to exclude votes identified after that date through ongoing manual recounts. As to Miami-Dade County, the Court concluded that although the 168 votes identified were the result of a partial recount, they were "legal votes [that] could change the outcome of the election." *Id.*, at (slip op., at 34). The Supreme Court therefore directed the Circuit Court to include those totals in the certified results, subject to resolution of the actual vote total from the Miami-Dade partial recount.

The petition presents the following questions: whether the Florida Supreme Court established new standards for resolving Presidential election contests, thereby violating Art. II, §1, cl. 2, of the United States Constitution and failing to comply with 3 U. S. C. §5, and whether the use of standardless manual recounts violates the Equal Protection and Due Process Clauses. With respect to the equal protection question, we find a violation of the Equal Protection Clause.

II

A

The closeness of this election, and the multitude of legal challenges which have followed in its wake, have brought into sharp focus a common, if heretofore unnoticed, phenomenon. Nationwide statistics reveal that an estimated

2% of ballots cast do not register a vote for President for whatever reason, including deliberately choosing no candidate at all or some voter error, such as voting for two candidates or insufficiently marking a ballot. *See* Ho, More Than 2M Ballots Uncounted, AP Online (Nov. 28, 2000); Kelley, Balloting Problems Not Rare But Only In A Very Close Election Do Mistakes And Mismarking Make A Difference, Omaha World-Herald (Nov. 15, 2000). In certifying election results, the votes eligible for inclusion in the certification are the votes meeting the properly established legal requirements.

This case has shown that punch card balloting machines can produce an unfortunate number of ballots which are not punched in a clean, complete way by the voter. After the current counting, it is likely legislative bodies nationwide will examine ways to improve the mechanisms and machinery for voting.

B

The individual citizen has no federal constitutional right to vote for electors for the President of the United States unless and until the state legislature chooses a statewide election as the means to implement its power to appoint members of the Electoral College. U. S. Const., Art. II, §1. This is the source for the statement in *McPherson v. Blacker,* 146 U. S. 1, 35 (1892), that the State legislature's power to select the manner for appointing electors is plenary; it may, if it so chooses, select the electors itself, which indeed was the manner used by State legislatures in several States for many years after the Framing of our Constitution. *Id.,* at 28–33. History has now favored the voter, and in each of the several States the citizens themselves vote for Presidential electors. When the state legislature vests the right to vote for President in its people, the right to vote as the legislature has prescribed is fundamental; and one source of its fundamental nature lies in the equal weight accorded to each vote and the equal dignity owed to each voter. The State, of course, after granting the franchise in the special context of Article II, can take back the power to appoint electors. See *Id.,* at 35 ("[T]here is no doubt of the right of the legislature to resume the power at any time, for it can neither be taken away nor abdicated") (*quoting* S. Rep. No. 395, 43d Cong., 1st Sess.).

The right to vote is protected in more than the initial allocation of the franchise. Equal protection applies as well to the manner of its exercise. Having once granted the right to vote on equal terms, the State may not, by later arbitrary and disparate treatment, value one person's vote over that of another. *See, e.g., Harper v. Virginia Bd. of Elections,* 383 U. S. 663, 665 (1966) ("[O]nce the franchise is granted to the electorate, lines may not be drawn which are inconsistent with the Equal Protection Clause of the Fourteenth Amendment"). It must be remembered that "the right of suffrage can be denied by a debasement or dilution of the weight of a citizen's vote just as effectively as by wholly prohibiting the free exercise of the franchise." *Reynolds v. Sims,* 377 U. S. 533, 555 (1964).

There is no difference between the two sides of the present controversy on these basic propositions. Respondents say that the very purpose of vindicating the right to vote justifies the recount procedures now at issue. The question before us, however, is whether the recount procedures the Florida Supreme Court has adopted are consistent with its obligation to avoid arbitrary and disparate treatment of the members of its electorate.

Much of the controversy seems to revolve around ballot cards designed to be perforated by a stylus but which, either through error or deliberate omission, have not been perforated with sufficient precision for a machine to count them. In some cases a piece of the card—a chad—is hanging, say by two corners. In other cases there is no separation at all, just an indentation.

The Florida Supreme Court has ordered that the intent of the voter be discerned from such ballots. For purposes of resolving the equal protection challenge, it is not necessary to decide whether the Florida Supreme Court had the authority under the legislative scheme for resolving election disputes to define what a legal vote is and to mandate a manual recount implementing that definition. The recount mechanisms implemented in response to the decisions of the Florida Supreme Court do not satisfy the minimum requirement for non-arbitrary treatment of voters necessary to secure the fundamental right. Florida's basic command for the count of legally cast votes is to consider the "intent of the voter." *Gore v. Harris,* ___ So. 2d, at ___ (slip op., at 39). This is unobjectionable as an abstract proposition and a starting principle. The problem inheres in the absence of specific standards to ensure its equal application. The formulation of uniform rules to determine intent based on these recurring circumstances is practicable and, we conclude, necessary.

The law does not refrain from searching for the intent of the actor in a multitude of circumstances; and in some cases the general command to ascertain intent is not susceptible to much further refinement. In this instance, however, the question is not whether to believe a witness but how to interpret the marks or holes or scratches on an inanimate object, a piece of cardboard or paper which, it is said, might not have registered as a vote during the machine count. The factfinder confronts a thing, not a person. The search for intent can be confined by specific rules designed to ensure uniform treatment.

The want of those rules here has led to unequal evaluation of ballots in various respects. *See Gore v. Harris,* ___ So. 2d, at ___ (slip op., at 51) (Wells, J., dissenting) ("Should a county canvassing board count or not count a 'dimpled chad' where the voter is able to successfully dislodge the chad in every other contest on that ballot? Here, the county canvassing boards disagree"). As seems to have been acknowledged at oral argument, the standards for accepting or rejecting contested ballots might vary not only from county to county but indeed within a single county from one recount team to another.

The record provides some examples. A monitor in Miami-Dade County testified at trial that he observed that three members of the county canvassing board applied different standards in defining a legal vote. 3 Tr. 497, 499 (Dec. 3, 2000). And testimony at trial also revealed that at least one county changed its evaluative standards during the counting process. Palm Beach County, for example, began the process with a 1990 guideline which precluded counting completely attached chads, switched to a rule that considered a vote to be legal if any light could be seen through a chad, changed back to the 1990 rule, and then abandoned any pretense of a per se rule, only to have a court order that the county consider dimpled chads legal. This is not a process with sufficient guarantees of equal treatment.

An early case in our one person, one vote jurisprudence arose when a State accorded arbitrary and disparate treatment to voters in its different counties. *Gray v. Sanders,* 372 U. S. 368 (1963). The Court found a constitutional violation. We relied on these principles in the context of the Presidential selection process in *Moore v. Ogilvie,* 394 U. S. 814 (1969), where we invalidated a county-based procedure that diluted the influence of citizens in larger counties in the nominating process. There we observed that "[t]he idea that one group can be granted greater voting strength than another is hostile to the one man, one vote basis of our representative government." *Id.,* at 819.

The State Supreme Court ratified this uneven treatment. It mandated that the recount totals from two counties, Miami-Dade and Palm Beach, be included in the certified total. The court also appeared to hold *sub silentio* that the recount totals from Broward County, which were not completed until after the original November 14 certification by the Secretary of State, were to be considered part of the new certified vote totals even though the county certification was not contested by Vice President Gore. Yet each of the counties used varying standards to determine what was a legal vote. Broward County used a more forgiving standard than Palm Beach County, and uncovered almost three times as many new votes, a result markedly disproportionate to the difference in population between the counties.

In addition, the recounts in these three counties were not limited to so-called undervotes but extended to all of the ballots. The distinction has real consequences. A manual recount of all ballots identifies not only those ballots which show no vote but also those which contain more than one, the so-called overvotes. Neither category will be counted by the machine. This is not a trivial concern. At oral argument, respondents estimated there are as many as 110,000 overvotes statewide. As a result, the citizen whose ballot was not read by a machine because he failed to vote for a candidate in a way readable by a machine may still have his vote counted in a manual recount; on the other hand, the citizen who marks two candidates in a way discernable by the machine will not have the same opportunity to have his vote count, even if a manual examination of the ballot would reveal the requisite indicia of intent. Furthermore, the citizen who marks two candidates, only one of which is discernable by the machine, will have his vote counted even though it should have been read as an invalid ballot. The State Supreme Court's inclusion of vote counts based on these variant standards exemplifies concerns with the remedial processes that were under way.

That brings the analysis to yet a further equal protection problem. The votes certified by the court included a partial total from one county, Miami-Dade. The Florida Supreme Court's decision thus gives no assurance that the recounts included in a final certification must be complete. Indeed, it is respondent's submission that it would be consistent with the rules of the recount procedures to include whatever partial counts are done by the time of final certification, and we interpret the Florida Supreme Court's decision to permit this. *See* ____ So. 2d, at ____, n. 21 (slip op., at 37, n. 21) (noting "practical difficulties" may control outcome of election, but certifying partial Miami-Dade total nonetheless). This accommodation no doubt results from the truncated contest period established by the Florida Supreme Court in Bush I, at respondents' own urging. The press of time does not diminish the constitutional concern. A desire for speed is not a general excuse for ignoring equal protection guarantees.

In addition to these difficulties the actual process by which the votes were to be counted under the Florida Supreme Court's decision raises further concerns. That order did not specify who would recount the ballots. The county canvassing boards were forced to pull together ad hoc teams comprised of judges from various Circuits who had no previous training in handling and interpreting ballots. Furthermore, while others were permitted to observe, they were prohibited from objecting during the recount.

The recount process, in its features here described, is inconsistent with the minimum procedures necessary to protect the fundamental right of each voter in the special instance of a statewide recount under the authority of a single state judicial officer. Our consideration is limited to the present circumstances, for the problem of equal protection in election processes generally presents many complexities.

The question before the Court is not whether local entities, in the exercise of their expertise, may develop different systems for implementing elections. Instead, we are presented with a situation where a state court with the power to assure uniformity has ordered a statewide recount with minimal procedural safeguards. When a court orders a statewide remedy, there must be at least some assurance that the rudimentary requirements of equal treatment and fundamental fairness are satisfied.

Given the Court's assessment that the recount process underway was probably being conducted in an unconstitutional manner, the Court stayed the order directing the recount so it could hear this case and render an expedited decision. The contest provision, as it was mandated by the State Supreme Court, is not well calculated to sustain the confidence that all citizens must have in the outcome of elections. The State has not shown that its procedures include the necessary safeguards. The problem, for instance, of the estimated 110,000 overvotes has not been addressed, although Chief Justice Wells called attention to the concern in his dissenting opinion. *See* ____ So. 2d, at ____, n. 26 (slip op., at 45, n. 26).

Upon due consideration of the difficulties identified to this point, it is obvious that the recount cannot be conducted in compliance with the requirements of equal protection and due process without substantial additional work. It would require not only the adoption (after opportunity for argument) of adequate statewide standards for determining what is a legal vote, and practicable procedures to implement them, but also orderly judicial review of any disputed matters that might arise. In addition, the Secretary of State has advised that the recount of only a portion of the ballots requires that the vote tabulation equipment be used to screen out undervotes, a function for which the machines were not designed. If a recount of overvotes were also required, perhaps even a second screening would be necessary. Use of the equipment for this purpose, and any new software developed for it, would have to be evaluated for accuracy by the Secretary of State, as required by Fla. Stat. §101.015 (2000).

The Supreme Court of Florida has said that the legislature intended the State's electors to "participat[e] fully in the federal electoral process," as provided in 3 U. S. C. §5. ___ So. 2d, at ___ (slip op. at 27); *see also Palm Beach Canvassing Bd. v. Harris,* 2000 WL 1725434, (Fla. 2000). That statute, in turn, requires that any controversy or contest that is designed to lead to a conclusive selection of electors be completed by December 12. That date is upon us, and there is no recount procedure in place under the State Supreme Court's order that comports with minimal constitutional standards. Because it is evident that any recount seeking to meet the December 12 date will be unconstitutional for the reasons we have discussed, we reverse the judgment of the Supreme Court of Florida ordering a recount to proceed.

Seven Justices of the Court agree that there are constitutional problems with the recount ordered by the Florida Supreme Court that demand a remedy. See post, at 6 (SOUTER, J., dissenting); post, at 2, 15 (BREYER, J., dissenting). The only disagreement is as to the remedy. Because the Florida Supreme Court has said that the Florida Legislature intended to obtain the safe-harbor benefits of 3 U. S. C. §5, JUSTICE BREYER's proposed remedy—remanding to the Florida Supreme Court for its ordering of a constitutionally proper contest until December 18-contemplates action in violation of the Florida election code, and hence could not be part of an "appropriate" order authorized by Fla. Stat. §102.168(8) (2000).

None are more conscious of the vital limits on judicial authority than are the members of this Court, and none stand more in admiration of the Constitution's design to leave the selection of the President to the people, through their legislatures, and to the political sphere. When contending parties invoke the process of the courts, however, it becomes our unsought responsibility to resolve the federal and constitutional issues the judicial system has been forced to confront.

The judgment of the Supreme Court of Florida is reversed, and the case is remanded for further proceedings not inconsistent with this opinion.

Pursuant to this Court's Rule 45.2, the Clerk is directed to issue the mandate in this case forthwith.

It is so ordered.

United States v. Lopez
514 U.S. 549 (1995)

After respondent, then a 12th-grade student, carried a concealed handgun into his high school, he was charged with violating the Gun-Free School Zones Act of 1990, which forbids "any individual knowingly to possess a firearm at a place that [he] knows . . . is a school zone," 18 U.S.C. §922(q)(1)(A). The District Court denied his motion to dismiss the indictment, concluding that §922(q) is a constitutional exercise of Congress' power to regulate activities in and affecting commerce. In reversing, the Court of Appeals held that, in light of what it characterized as insufficient congressional findings and legislative history, §922(q) is invalid as beyond Congress' power under the Commerce Clause.

Held:
The Act exceeds Congress' Commerce Clause authority. First, although this Court has upheld a wide variety of congressional Acts regulating intrastate economic activity that substantially affected interstate commerce, the possession of a gun in a local school zone is in no sense an economic activity that might, through repetition elsewhere, have such a substantial effect on interstate commerce. Section §922(q) is a criminal statute that by its terms has nothing to do with "commerce" or any sort of economic enterprise, however broadly those terms are defined. Nor is it an essential part of a larger regulation of economic activity, in which the regulatory scheme could be undercut unless the intrastate activity were regulated. It cannot, therefore, be sustained under the Court's cases upholding regulations of activities that arise out of or are connected with a commercial transaction, which viewed in the aggregate, substantially affects interstate commerce. Second, §922(q) contains no jurisdictional element which would ensure, through case-by-case inquiry, that the firearms possession in question has the requisite Page II nexus with interstate commerce. Respondent was a local student at a local school; there is no indication that he had recently moved in interstate commerce, and there is no requirement that his possession of the firearm have any concrete tie to interstate commerce. To uphold the Government's contention that §922(q) is justified because firearms possession in a local school zone does indeed substantially affect interstate commerce would require this Court to pile inference upon inference in a manner that would bid fair to convert congressional Commerce Clause authority to a general police power of the sort held only by the States. Pp. 2–19.

Affirmed.

United States v. *Morrison*
529 U.S. 598, 120 S. Ct. 1740, 146 L. Ed. 2d 658 (2000)

Petitioner Brzonkala filed suit, alleging, *inter alia*, that she was raped by respondents while the three were students at the Virginia Polytechnic Institute, and that this attack violated 42 U. S. C. §13981, which provides a federal civil remedy for the victims of gender-motivated violence. Respondents moved to dismiss on the grounds that the complaint failed to state a claim and that §13981's civil remedy is unconstitutional. Petitioner United States intervened to defend the section's constitutionality. In dismissing the complaint, the District Court held that it stated a claim against respondents, but that Congress lacked authority to enact §13981 under either §8 of the Commerce Clause or §5 of the Fourteenth Amendment, which Congress had explicitly identified as the sources of federal authority for §13981. The en banc Fourth Circuit affirmed.

Held:
Section 13981 cannot be sustained under the Commerce Clause or §5 of the Fourteenth Amendment. Pp. 7–28.

(a) The Commerce Clause does not provide Congress with authority to enact §13981's federal civil remedy. A congressional enactment will be invalidated only upon a plain showing that Congress has exceeded its constitutional bounds. *See United States v. Lopez,* 514 U.S. 549, 568, 577–578. Petitioners assert that §13981 can be sustained under Congress' commerce power as a regulation of activity that substantially affects interstate commerce. The proper framework for analyzing such a claim is provided by the principles the Court set out in *Lopez.* First, in *Lopez,* the noneconomic, criminal nature of possessing a firearm in a school zone was central to the Court's conclusion that Congress lacks authority to regulate such possession. Similarly, gender-motivated crimes of violence are not, in any sense, economic activity. Second, like the statute at issue in *Lopez,* §13981 contains no jurisdictional element establishing that the federal cause of action is in pursuance of Congress' regulation of interstate commerce. Although *Lopez* makes clear that such a jurisdictional element would lend support to the argument that §13981 is sufficiently tied to interstate commerce to come within Congress' authority, Congress elected to cast §13981's remedy over a wider, and more purely intrastate, body of violent crime. Third, although §13981, unlike the *Lopez* statute, *is* supported by numerous findings regarding the serious impact of gender-motivated violence on victims and their families, these findings are substantially weakened by the fact that they rely on reasoning that this Court has rejected, namely a but-for causal chain from the initial occurrence of violent crime to every attenuated effect upon interstate commerce. If accepted, this reasoning would allow Congress to regulate any crime whose nationwide, aggregated impact has substantial effects on employment, production, transit, or consumption. Moreover, such reasoning will not limit Congress to regulating violence, but may be applied equally as well to family law and other areas of state regulation since the aggregate effect of marriage, divorce, and childrearing on the national economy is undoubtedly significant. The Constitution requires a distinction between what is truly national and what is truly local, and there is no better example of the police power, which the Founders undeniably left reposed in the States and denied the central government, than the suppression of violent crime and vindication of its victims. Congress therefore may not regulate noneconomic, violent criminal conduct based solely on the conduct's aggregate effect on interstate commerce. Pp. 7–19.

(b) Section 5 of the Fourteenth Amendment, which permits Congress to enforce by appropriate legislation the constitutional guarantee that no State shall deprive any person of life, liberty, or property, without due process or deny any person equal protection of the laws, *City of Boerne v. Flores,* 521 U.S. 507, 517 also does not give Congress the authority to enact §13981. Petitioners' assertion that there is pervasive bias in various state justice systems against victims of gender-motivated violence is supported by a voluminous congressional record. However, the Fourteenth Amendment places limitations on the manner in which Congress may attack discriminatory conduct. Foremost among them is the principle that the Amendment prohibits only state action, not private conduct. This was the conclusion reached in *United States v. Harris,* and the *Civil Rights Cases,* 109 U.S. 3 which were both decided shortly after the Amendment's adoption. The force of the doctrine of *stare decisis* behind these decisions stems not only from the length of time they have been on the books, but also from the insight attributable to the Members of the Court at that time, who all had intimate knowledge and familiarity with the events surrounding the Amendment's adoption. Neither *United States v. Guest,* 383 U.S. 745, nor *District of Columbia v. Carter,* 409 U.S. 418, casts any doubt on the enduring vitality of the *Civil Rights Cases* and *Harris.* Assuming that there has been gender-based disparate treatment by state authorities in this case, it would not be enough to save §13981's civil remedy, which is directed not at a State or state actor but at individuals who have committed criminal acts motivated by gender bias. Section 13981 visits no consequence on any Virginia public official involved in investigating or prosecuting Brzonkala's assault, and it is thus unlike any of the §5 remedies this Court has previously upheld. *See e.g., South Carolina v. Katzenbach,* 383 U.S. 381. Section 13981 is also different from previously upheld remedies in that it applies uniformly throughout the Nation, even though Congress' findings indicate that the problem addressed does not exist in all, or even most, States. In contrast, the §5 remedy in *Katzenbach* was directed only to those States in which Congress found that there had been discrimination. Pp. 19–27.

Affirmed.

Kyllo v. United States
No. 998508.

DECIDED JUNE 11, 2001

Suspicious that marijuana was being grown in petitioner Kyllo's home in a triplex, agents used a thermal imaging device to scan the triplex to determine if the amount of heat emanating from it was consistent with the high-intensity lamps typically used for indoor marijuana growth. The scan showed that Kyllo's garage roof and a side wall were relatively hot compared to the rest of his home and substantially warmer than the neighboring units. Based in part on the thermal imaging, a Federal Magistrate Judge issued a warrant to search Kyllo's home, where the agents found marijuana growing. After Kyllo was indicted on a federal drug charge, he unsuccessfully moved to suppress the evidence seized from his home and then entered a conditional guilty plea. The Ninth Circuit ultimately affirmed, upholding the thermal imaging on the ground that Kyllo had shown no subjective expectation of privacy because he had made no attempt to conceal the heat escaping from his home. Even if he had, ruled the court, there was no objectively reasonable expectation of privacy because the thermal imager did not expose any intimate details of Kyllo's life, only amorphous hot spots on his home's exterior.

Held:
Where, as here, the Government uses a device that is not in general public use, to explore details of a private home that would previously have been unknowable without physical intrusion, the surveillance is a Fourth Amendment search, and is presumptively unreasonable without a warrant. Pp. 3–13.

(a) The question whether a warrantless search of a home is reasonable and hence constitutional must be answered no in most instances, but the antecedent question whether a Fourth Amendment search has occurred is not so simple. This Court has approved warrantless visual surveillance of a home, *see California v. Ciraolo,* 476 U.S. 207, 213, ruling that visual observation is no search at all, *see Dow Chemical Co. v. United States,* 476 U.S. 227, 234235, 239. In assessing when a search is not a search, the Court has adapted a principle first enunciated in *Katz v. United States,* 389 U.S. 347, 361: A search does not occur even when its object is a house explicitly protected by the Fourth Amendment unless the individual manifested a subjective expectation of privacy in the searched object, and society is willing to recognize that expectation as reasonable, *see, e.g., California v. Ciraolo, supra,* at 211. Pp. 3–5.

(b) While it may be difficult to refine the *Katz* test in some instances, in the case of the search of a homes interior the prototypical and hence most commonly litigated area of protected privacy there is a ready criterion, with roots deep in the common law, of the minimal expectation of privacy that *exists,* and that is acknowledged to be *reasonable.* To withdraw protection of this minimum expectation would be to permit police technology to erode the privacy guaranteed by the Fourth Amendment. Thus, obtaining by sense-enhancing technology any information regarding the homes interior that could not otherwise have been obtained without physical intrusion into a constitutionally protected area, *Silverman v. United States,* 365 U.S. 505, 512, constitutes a search at least where (as here) the technology in question is not in general public use. This assures preservation of that degree of privacy against government that existed when the Fourth Amendment was adopted. Pp. 6–7.

(c) Based on this criterion, the information obtained by the thermal imager in this case was the product of a search. The Court rejects the Governments argument that the thermal imaging must be upheld because it detected only heat radiating from the homes external surface. Such a mechanical interpretation of the Fourth Amendment was rejected in *Katz,* where the eavesdropping device in question picked up only sound waves that reached the exterior of the phone booth to which it was attached. Reversing that approach would leave the homeowner at the mercy of advancing technology including imaging technology that could discern all human activity in the home. Also rejected is the Governments contention that the thermal imaging was constitutional because it did not detect intimate details. Such an approach would be wrong in principle because, in the sanctity of the home, *all* details are intimate details. *See e.g., United States v. Karo,* 468 U. S. 705; *Dow Chemical, supra,* at 238, distinguished. It would also be impractical in application, failing to provide a workable accommodation between law enforcement needs and Fourth Amendment interests. *See Oliver v. United States,* 466 U. S. 170, 181. Pp. 7–12.

(d) Since the imaging in this case was an unlawful search, it will remain for the District Court to determine whether, without the evidence it provided, the search warrant was supported by probable cause and if not, whether there is any other basis for supporting admission of that evidence. Pp. 12–13.

Reversed and remanded.

Good News Club v. Milford Central School
No. 992036

DECIDED JUNE 11, 2001

Under New York law, respondent Milford Central School (Milford) enacted a policy authorizing district residents to use its building after school for, among other things, (1) instruction in education, learning, or the arts and (2) social, civic, recreational, and entertainment uses pertaining to the community welfare. Stephen and Darleen Fournier, district residents eligible to use the schools facilities upon approval of their proposed use, are sponsors of the Good News Club, a private Christian organization for children ages 6 to 12. Pursuant to Milford's policy, they submitted a request to hold the Club's weekly after-school meetings in the school. Milford denied the request on the ground that the proposed use to sing songs, hear Bible lessons, memorize scripture, and pray was the equivalent of religious worship prohibited by the community use policy. Petitioners (collectively, the Club), filed suit under 42 U.S.C. 1983, alleging, *inter alia*, that the denial of the Club's application violated its free speech rights under the First and Fourteenth Amendments. The District Court ultimately granted Milford summary judgment, finding the Club's subject matter to be religious in nature, not merely a discussion of secular matters from a religious perspective that Milford otherwise permits. Because the school had not allowed other groups providing religious instruction to use its limited public forum, the court held that it could deny the Club access without engaging in unconstitutional viewpoint discrimination. In affirming, the Second Circuit rejected the Club's contention that Milford's restriction was unreasonable, and held that, because the Club's subject matter was quintessentially religious and its activities fell outside the bounds of pure moral and character development, Milford's policy was constitutional subject discrimination, not unconstitutional viewpoint discrimination.

Held:

1. Milford violated the Club's free speech rights when it excluded the Club from meeting after hours at the school. Pp. 5–11.

(a) Because the parties so agree, this Court assumes that Milford operates a limited public forum. A State establishing such a forum is not required to and does not allow persons to engage in every type of speech. It may be justified in reserving its forum for certain groups or the discussion of certain topics. *E.g., Rosenberger v. Rector and Visitors of Univ. of Va.,* 515 U.S. 819, 829. The power to so restrict speech, however, is not without limits. The restriction must not discriminate against speech based on viewpoint, *ibid.,* and must be reasonable in light of the forums purpose, *Cornelius v. NAACP Legal Defense & Ed. Fund, Inc.,* 473 U.S. 788, 806. Pp. 5–6.

(b) By denying the Club access to the schools limited public forum on the ground that the Club was religious in nature, Milford discriminated against the Club because of its religious viewpoint in violation of the Free Speech Clause. That exclusion is indistinguishable from the exclusions held violative of the Clause in *Lambs Chapel v. Center Moriches Union Free School Dist.,* 508 U.S. 384, where a school district precluded a private group from presenting films at the school based solely on the religious perspective of the films, and in *Rosenberger,* where a university refused to fund a student publication because it addressed issues from a religious perspective. The only apparent difference between the activities of Lambs Chapel and the Club is the inconsequential distinction that the Club teaches moral lessons from a Christian perspective through live storytelling and prayer, whereas Lambs Chapel taught lessons through films. *Rosenberger* also is dispositive: Given the obvious religious content of the publication there at issue, it cannot be said that the Clubs activities are any more religious or deserve any less Free Speech Clause protection. This Court disagrees with the Second Circuits view that something that is quintessentially religious or decidedly religious in nature cannot also be characterized properly as the teaching of morals and character development from a particular viewpoint. What matters for Free Speech Clause purposes is that there is no logical difference in kind between the invocation of Christianity by the Club and the invocation of teamwork, loyalty, or patriotism by other associations to provide a foundation for their lessons. Because Milford's restriction is viewpoint discriminatory, the Court need not decide whether it is unreasonable in light of the forums purposes. Pp. 6–11.

2. Permitting the Club to meet on the schools premises would not have violated the Establishment Clause. Establishment Clause defenses similar to Milford's were rejected in *Lambs Chapel, supra,* at 395 where the Court found that, because the films would not have been shown during school hours, would not have been sponsored by the school, and would have been open to the public, not just to church members, there was no realistic danger that the community would think that the district was endorsing religion and in *Widmar v. Vincent,* 454 U.S. 263, 272273, and n.13 where a university's forum was already available to other groups. Because the Club's activities are materially indistinguish-

able from those in *Lambs Chapel* and *Widmar*, Milford's reliance on the Establishment Clause is unavailing. As in *Lambs Chapel*, the Club's meetings were to be held after school hours, not sponsored by the school, and open to any student who obtained parental consent, not just to Club members. As in *Widmar*, Milford made its forum available to other organizations. The Court rejects Milford's attempt to distinguish those cases by emphasizing that its policy involves elementary school children who will perceive that the school is endorsing the Club and will feel coerced to participate because the Club's activities take place on school grounds, even though they occur during non-school hours. That argument is unpersuasive for a number of reasons. (1) Allowing the Club to speak on school grounds would ensure, not threaten, neutrality toward religion. Accordingly, Milford faces an uphill battle in arguing that the Establishment Clause compels it to exclude the Club. *See, e.g., Rosenberger, supra,* at 839. (2) To the extent the Court considers whether the community would feel coercive pressure to engage in the Club's activities, *cf. Lee v. Weisman,* 505 U.S. 577, 592593, the relevant community is the parents who choose whether their children will attend Club meetings, not the children themselves. (3) Whatever significance it may have assigned in the Establishment Clause context to the suggestion that elementary school children are more impressionable than adults, cf., *e.g., Id.,* at 592, the Court has never foreclosed private religious conduct during non-school hours merely because it takes place on school premises where elementary school children may be present. *Lee, supra,* at 592, and *Edwards v. Aguillard,* 482 U.S. 578, 584, distinguished. (4) Even if the Court were to consider the possible misperceptions by schoolchildren in deciding whether there is an Establishment Clause violation, the facts of this case simply do not support Milford's conclusion. Finally, it cannot be said that the danger that children would misperceive the endorsement of religion is any greater than the danger that they would perceive a hostility toward the religious viewpoint if the Club were excluded from the public forum. Because it is not convinced that there is any significance to the possibility that elementary school children may witness the Club's activities on school premises, the Court can find no reason to depart from *Lambs Chapel* and *Widmar*. Pp. 12–20.

3. Because Milford has not raised a valid Establishment Clause claim, this Court does not address whether such a claim could excuse Milford's viewpoint discrimination. Pp. 12–20.

Reversed and remanded.

United States v. Oakland Cannabis Buyers Cooperative 121 S. Ct. 1711

DECIDED MAY 14, 2001

Respondent Oakland Cannabis Buyers Cooperative was organized to distribute marijuana to qualified patients for medical purposes. The United States sued to enjoin the Cooperative and its executive director, also a respondent (together, the Cooperative), under the Controlled Substances Act. The United States argued that the Cooperatives activities violated the Acts prohibitions on distributing, manufacturing, and possessing with the intent to distribute or manufacture a controlled substance. The District Court enjoined the Cooperatives activities, but the Cooperative continued to distribute marijuana. The District Court found the Cooperative in contempt, rejecting its defense that any distributions were medically necessary. The court later rejected the Cooperatives motion to modify the injunction to permit medically necessary distributions. The Cooperative appealed, and the Ninth Circuit reversed and remanded the ruling on the motion to modify the injunction. According to the Ninth Circuit, medical necessity is a legally cognizable defense likely applicable in the circumstances, the District Court mistakenly believed it had no discretion to issue an injunction more limited in scope than the Controlled Substances Act, and the District Court should have weighed the public interest and considered factors such as the serious harm in depriving patients of marijuana in deciding whether to modify the injunction.

Held:

1. There is no medical necessity exception to the Controlled Substances Acts prohibitions on manufacturing and distributing marijuana. Pp. 5–11.

(a) Because that Act classifies marijuana as a schedule I controlled substance, it provides only one express exception to the prohibitions on manufacturing and distributing the drug: Government-approved research projects. The Cooperative's contention that a common-law medical necessity defense should be written into the Act is rejected. There is an open question whether federal courts ever have authority to recognize a necessity defense not provided by statute. But that question need not be answered to resolve the issue presented here, for the terms of the Controlled Substances Act leave no doubt that the medical necessity defense is unavailable. Pp. 5–7.

(b) Under any conception of legal necessity, the defense cannot succeed when the legislature itself has made a determination of values. Here, the Act reflects a determination that marijuana has no medical benefits worthy of an exception (other than Government-approved research). Whereas other drugs can be dispensed and prescribed for medical use, see 21 U. S.C. § 829, the same is not true for marijuana, which has no currently accepted medial use at all, § 811. This conclusion is supported by the structure of the Act, which divides drugs into five schedules, depending in part on whether a drug has a currently accepted medical use, and then imposes restrictions according to the schedule in which it has been placed. The Attorney General is authorized to include a drug in schedule I, the most restrictive schedule, only if the drug has no currently accepted medical use. The Cooperative errs in arguing that, because Congress, instead of the Attorney General, placed marijuana into that schedule, marijuana can be distributed when medically necessary. The statute treats all schedule I drugs alike, and there is no reason why drugs that Congress placed there should be subject to fewer controls than those that the Attorney General placed there. Also rejected is the Cooperatives argument that a drug may be found medically necessary for a particular patient or class even when it has not achieved general acceptance as a medical treatment. It is clear from the text of the Act that Congress determined that marijuana has no medical benefits worthy of an exception granted to other drugs. The statute expressly contemplates that many drugs have a useful medical purpose, *see* § 801(1), but it includes no exception at all for any medical use of marijuana. This Court is unwilling to view that omission as an accident and is unable, in any event, to override a legislative determination manifest in the statute. Finally, the canon of constitutional avoidance has no application here, because there is no statutory ambiguity. Pp. 7–11.

2. The discretion that courts of equity traditionally possess in fashioning relief does not serve as a basis for affirming the Ninth Circuit in this case. To be sure, district courts properly acting as courts of equity have discretion unless a statute clearly provides otherwise. But the mere fact that the District Court had discretion does not suggest that the court, when evaluating the motion, could consider any and all factors that might relate to the public interest or the parties conveniences, including medical needs. Equity courts cannot ignore Congress judgment expressed in legislation. Their choice is whether a particular means of enforcement should be chosen over another permissible means, not whether enforcement is preferable to no enforcement at all. To the extent a district court considers the public interest and parties conveniences, the court is limited to evaluating how those factors are affected by the selection of an injunction over other enforcement mechanisms. Because the Controlled Substances Act covers even those who have what could be termed a medical necessity, it precludes consideration of the evidence that the Ninth Circuit deemed relevant. Pp. 11–15.

Reversed and remanded.

Thomas, J., delivered the opinion of the Court, in which *Rehnquist, C.J.,* and *O'Connor, Scalia,* and *Kennedy, JJ.,* joined. *Stevens, J.,* filed an opinion concurring in the judgment, in which *Souter* and *Ginsburg, JJ.,* joined. *Breyer, J.,* took no part in the consideration or decision of the case.

United States v. Playboy Entertainment Group, Inc. 529 U.S. 803, 120 S. Ct. 1878, 146 L. Ed. 2d 865 (2000)

Section 505 of the Telecommunications Act of 1996 requires cable television operators providing channels "primarily dedicated to sexually-oriented programming" either to "fully scramble or otherwise fully block" those channels or to limit their transmission to hours when children are unlikely to be viewing, set by administrative regulation as between 10 p.m. and 6 a.m. Even before §505's enactment, cable operators used signal scrambling to limit access to certain programs to paying customers. Scrambling could be imprecise, however; and either or both audio and visual portions of the scrambled programs might be heard or seen, a phenomenon known as "signal bleed." The purpose of §505 is to shield children from hearing or seeing images resulting from signal bleed. To comply with §505, the majority of cable operators adopted the "time channeling" approach, so that, for two-thirds of the day, no viewers in their service areas could receive the programming in question. Appellee Playboy Entertainment Group, Inc., filed this suit challenging §505's constitutionality. A three-judge District Court concluded that §505's content-based restriction on speech violates the First Amendment because the Government might further its interests in less restrictive ways. One plausible, less restrictive alternative could be found in §504 of the Act, which requires a cable operator, "[u]pon request by a cable service subscriber . . . without charge, [to] fully scramble or otherwise fully block" any channel the subscriber does not wish to receive. As long as subscribers knew about this opportunity, the court reasoned, §504 would provide as much protection against unwanted programming as would §505.

Held:

Because the Government failed to prove §505 is the least restrictive means for addressing a real problem, the District Court did not err in holding the statute violative of the First Amendment. Pp. 6–23.

(a) Two points should be understood: (1) Many adults would find the material at issue highly offensive, and considering that the material comes unwanted into homes where children might see or hear it against parental wishes or consent, there are legitimate reasons for regulating it; and (2) Playboy's programming has First Amendment protection. Section 505 is a content-based regulation. It also singles out particular programmers for regulation. It is of no moment that the statute does not impose a complete prohibition. Since §505 is content-based, it can stand only if it satisfies strict scrutiny, *e.g., Sable Communications of Cal., Inc. v. FCC,* 492 U. S. 115, 126. It must be narrowly tailored to promote a compelling Government interest, and if a less restrictive alternative would serve the Government's purpose, the legislature must use that alternative. Cable television, like broadcast media, presents unique problems, but even where speech is indecent and enters the home, the objective of shielding children does not suffice to support a blanket ban if the protection can be obtained by a less restrictive alternative. There is, moreover, a key difference between cable television and the broadcasting media: Cable systems have the capacity to block unwanted channels on a household-by-household basis. Targeted blocking is less restrictive than banning, and the Government cannot ban speech if targeted blocking is a feasible and effective means of furthering its compelling interests. Pp. 6–11.

(b) No one disputes that §504 is narrowly tailored to the Government's goal of supporting parents who want sexually explicit channels blocked. The question here is whether §504 can be effective. Despite empirical evidence that §504 generated few requests for household-by-household blocking during a period when it was the sole federal blocking statute in effect, the District Court correctly concluded that §504, if publicized in an adequate manner, could serve as an effective, less restrictive means of reaching the Government's goals. When the Government restricts speech, the Government bears the burden of proving the constitutionality of its actions, *e.g., Greater New Orleans Broadcasting Assn., Inc. v. United States,* 527 U. S. 173, 183. Of three explanations for the lack of individual blocking requests under §504—(1) individual blocking might not be an effective alternative, due to technological or other limitations; (2) although an adequately advertised blocking provision might have been effective, §504 as written does not require sufficient notice to make it so; and (3) the actual signal bleed problem might be far less of a concern than the Government at first had supposed—the Government had to show that the first was the right answer. According to the District Court, however, the first and third possibilities were "equally consistent" with the record before it, and the record was not clear as to whether enough notice had been issued to give §504 a fighting chance. Unless the District Court's findings are clearly erroneous, the tie goes to free expression. With regard to signal bleed itself, the District Court's thorough discussion exposes a central weakness in the Government's proof: There is little hard evidence of how widespread or how serious the problem is. There is no proof as to how likely any child is to view a discernible explicit image, and no proof of the duration of the bleed or the quality of the pictures or sound. Under §505, sanctionable signal bleed can include instances as fleeting as an image appearing on a screen for just a few seconds. The First Amendment requires a more careful assessment and characterization of an evil in order to justify a regulation as sweeping as this. The Government has failed to establish a pervasive, nationwide problem justifying its nationwide daytime speech ban. The Government also failed to prove §504, with adequate notice, would be ineffective. There is no evidence that a well-promoted voluntary blocking provision would not be capable at least of informing parents about signal bleed (if they are not yet aware of it) and about their rights to have the bleed blocked (if they consider it a problem and have not yet controlled it themselves). A court should not assume a plausible, less restrictive alternative would be ineffective; and a court should not presume parents, given full information, will fail to act. The Government also argues society's independent interests will be unserved if parents fail to act on that information. Even upon the assumption that the Government has an interest in substituting itself for informed and empowered parents, its interest is not sufficiently compelling to justify this widespread restriction on speech. The regulatory alternative of a publicized §504, which has the real possibility of promoting more open disclosure and the choice of an effective blocking system, would provide parents the information needed to engage in active supervision. The Government has not shown that this alternative would be insufficient to secure its objective, or that any overriding harm justifies its intervention. Although, under a voluntary blocking regime, even with adequate notice, some children will be exposed to signal bleed, children will also be exposed under time channeling, which does not eliminate signal bleed around the clock. The record is silent as to the comparative effectiveness of the two alternatives. Pp. 11–22.

Atwater v. City Of Lago Vista
121 S. Ct. 1536

DECIDED APRIL 24, 2001

Texas law makes it a misdemeanor, punishable only by a fine, either for a front-seat passenger in a car equipped with safety belts not to wear one or for the driver to fail to secure any small child riding in front. The warrantless arrest of anyone violating these provisions is expressly authorized by statute, but the police may issue citations in lieu of arrest. Petitioner Atwater drove her truck in Lago Vista, Texas, with her small children in the front seat. None of them was wearing a seatbelt. Respondent Turek, then a Lago Vista policeman, observed the seatbelt violations, pulled Atwater over, verbally berated her, handcuffed her, placed her in his squad car, and drove her to the local police station, where she was made to remove her shoes, jewelry, and eyeglasses, and empty her pockets. Officers took her mug shot and placed her, alone, in a jail cell for about an hour, after which she was taken before a magistrate and released on bond. She was charged with, among other things, violating the seatbelt law. She pleaded no contest to the seatbelt misdemeanors and paid a $50 fine. She and her husband (collectively Atwater) filed suit under 42 U.S.C. § 1983, alleging, *inter alia,* that the actions of respondents (collectively City) had violated her Fourth Amendment right to be free from unreasonable seizure. Given her admission that she had violated the law and the absence of any allegation that she was harmed or detained in any way inconsistent with the law, the District Court ruled the Fourth Amendment claim meritless and granted the City summary judgment. Sitting en banc, the Fifth Circuit affirmed. Relying on *Whren v. United States,* 517 U.S. 806, 817, 818 the court observed that, although the Fourth Amendment generally requires a balancing of individual and governmental interests, the result is rarely in doubt where an arrest is based on probable cause. Because no one disputed that Turek had probable cause to arrest Atwater, and there was no evidence the arrest was conducted in an extraordinary manner, unusually harmful to Atwater's privacy interests, the court held the arrest not unreasonable for Fourth Amendment purposes.

Held:

The Fourth Amendment does not forbid a warrantless arrest for a minor criminal offense, such as a misdemeanor seatbelt violation punishable only by a fine.

(a) In reading the Fourth Amendment, the Court is guided by the traditional protections against unreasonable searches and seizures afforded by the common law at the time of the framing. *E.g., Wilson v. Arkansas,* 514 U.S. 927, 931. Atwater contends that founding-era common-law rules forbade officers to make warrantless misdemeanor arrests except in cases of breach of the peace, a category she claims was then understood narrowly as covering only those nonfelony offenses involving or tending toward violence. Although this argument is not insubstantial, it ultimately fails. Pp. 4–24.

(1) Even after making some allowance for variations in the prefounding English common-law usage of breach of the peace, the founding-era common-law rules were not nearly as clear as Atwater claims. Pp. 5–14.

(i) A review of the relevant English decisions, as well as English and colonial American legal treatises, legal dictionaries, and procedure manuals, demonstrates disagreement, not unanimity, with respect to officers warrantless misdemeanor arrest power. On one side, eminent authorities support Atwater's position that the common law confined warrantless misdemeanor arrests to actual breaches of the peace. *See, e.g., Queen v. Tooley, 2 Ld. Raym. 1296, 1301,* 92 Eng. Rep. 349, 352. However, there is also considerable evidence of a broader conception of common-law misdemeanor arrest authority unlimited by any breach-of-the-peace condition. *See, e.g., Holyday v. Oxenbridge,* Cro. Car. 234, 79 Eng. Rep. 805, 805806; 2 M. Hale, The History of the Pleas of the Crown 88. Thus, the Court is not convinced that Atwaters is the correct, or even necessarily the better, reading of the common-law history. Pp. 6–11.

(ii) A second, and equally serious, problem for Atwater's historical argument is posed by various statutes enacted by Parliament well before this Republics founding that authorized peace officers (and even private persons) to make warrantless arrests for all sorts of relatively minor offenses unaccompanied by violence, including, among others, nightwalking, unlawful game-playing, profane cursing, and negligent carriage-driving. Pp. 11–14.

(2) An examination of specifically American evidence is to the same effect. Neither the history of the framing era nor subsequent legal development indicates that the Fourth Amendment was originally understood, or has traditionally been read, to embrace Atwaters position. Pp. 14–24.

(i) Atwater has cited no particular evidence that those who framed and ratified the Fourth Amendment sought to limit peace officers warrantless misdemeanor arrest authority to instances of actual breach of the peace, and the Courts review of framing-era documentary history has likewise failed to reveal any such design. Nor is there in any of the modern historical accounts of the Fourth Amendments adoption any substantial indication that the Framers intended such a restriction. Indeed, to the extent the modern histories address the issue, their conclusions are to the contrary. The evidence of actual practice also counsels against Atwater's position. During the period leading up to and surrounding the framing of the Bill of Rights, colonial and state legislatures, like Parliament before them, regularly authorized local officers to make warrantless misdemeanor arrests without a breach of the peace condition. That the Fourth Amendment did not originally apply to the States does not make state practice irrelevant in unearthing the Amendments original meaning. A number of state constitutional search-and-seizure provisions served as models for the Fourth Amendment, and the fact that many of the original States with such constitutional limitations continued to grant their officers broad warrantless misdemeanor arrest authority undermines Atwaters position. Given the early state practice, it is likewise troublesome for Atwater's view that one year after the Fourth Amendments ratification, Congress gave federal marshals the same powers to execute federal law as sheriffs had to execute state law. Pp. 14–18.

(ii) Nor is Atwaters argument from tradition aided by the historical record as it has unfolded since the framing, there being no indication that her claimed rule has ever become woven into the fabric of American law. *E.g., Wilson, supra,* at 933. The story, in fact, is to the contrary. First, what little this Court has said about warrantless misdemeanor arrest authority tends to cut against Atwaters argument. *See, e.g., United States v. Watson,* 423 U.S. 411, 418. Second, this is not a case in which early American courts embraced an accepted common-law rule with anything approaching unanimity. *See Wilson, supra,* at 933. None of the 19th-century state-court decisions cited by Atwater is ultimately availing. More to the point are the numerous 19th-century state decisions expressly sustaining (often against constitutional challenge) state and local laws authorizing peace officers to make warrantless arrests for misdemeanors not involving any breach of the peace. Finally, legal commentary, for more than a century, has almost uniformly recognized the constitutionality of extending warrantless arrest power to misdemeanors without limitation to breaches of the peace. Small wonder, then, that today statutes in all 50 States and the District of Columbia permit such arrests by at least some (if not all) peace officers, as do a host of congressional enactments. Pp. 18–24.

(b) The Court rejects Atwater's request to mint a new rule of constitutional law forbidding custodial arrest, even upon probable cause, when conviction could not ultimately carry any jail time and the government can show no compelling need for immediate detention. She reasons that, when historical practice fails to speak conclusively to a Fourth Amendment claim, courts must strike a current balance between individual and societal interests by subjecting particular contemporary circumstances to traditional standards of reasonableness. *See, e.g., Wyoming v. Houghton,* 526 U.S. 295, 299, 300. Atwater might well prevail under a rule derived exclusively to address the uncontested facts of her case, since her claim to live free of pointless indignity and confinement clearly outweighs anything the City can raise against it specific to her. However, the Court has traditionally recognized that a responsible Fourth Amendment balance is not well served by standards requiring sensitive, case-by-case determinations of government need, lest every discretionary judgment in the field be converted into an occasion for constitutional review. *See, e.g., United States v. Robinson,* 414 U.S. 218, 234, 235. Complications arise the moment consideration is given the possible applications of the several criteria Atwater proposes for drawing a line between minor crimes with limited arrest authority and others not so restricted. The assertion that these difficulties could be alleviated simply by requiring police in doubt not to arrest is unavailing because, first, such a tie breaker would in practice amount to a constitutionally inappropriate least-restrictive-alternative limitation, *see, e.g., Skinner v. Railway Labor Executives Assn.*, 489 U.S. 602, 629, n.9, and, second, whatever guidance the tie breaker might give would come at the price of a systematic disincentive to arrest in situations where even Atwater concedes arresting would serve an important societal interest. That warrantless misdemeanor arrests do not demand the constitutional attention Atwater seeks is indicated by a number of factors, including that the law has never jelled the way Atwater would have it; that anyone arrested without formal process is entitled to a magistrates review of probable cause within 48 hours, *County of Riverside v. McLaughlin,* 500 U.S. 44, 55–58; that many jurisdictions have chosen to impose more restrictive safeguards through statutes limiting warrantless arrests for minor offenses; that it is in the polices interest to limit such arrests, which carry costs too great to incur without good reason; and that, under current doctrine, the preference for categorical treatment of Fourth Amendment claims gives way to individualized review when a defendant makes a colorable argument that an arrest, with or without a warrant, was conducted in an extraordinary manner, unusually harmful to his privacy or physical interests, *e.g., Whren,* 517 U.S., at 818. The upshot of all these influences, combined with the good sense (and, failing that, the political accountability) of most local lawmakers and peace officers, is a dearth of horribles [sic] demanding redress. Thus, the probable cause standard applies to all arrests, without the need to balance the interests and circumstances involved in particular situations. *Dunaway v. New York,* 442 U.S. 200, 208. An officer may arrest an individual without violating the Fourth Amendment if there is probable cause to believe that the offender has committed even a very minor criminal offense in the officer's presence. Pp. 24–33.

(c) Atwater's arrest satisfied constitutional requirements. It is undisputed that Turek had probable cause to believe that Atwater committed a crime in his presence. Because she admits that neither she nor her children were wearing seat belts, Turek was authorized (though not required) to make a custodial arrest without balancing costs and benefits or determining whether Atwater's arrest was in some sense necessary. Nor was the arrest made in an extraordinary manner, unusually harmful to her privacy or physical interests. *See Whren,* 517 U.S., at 818. Whether a search or seizure is extraordinary turns, above all else, on the manner in which it is executed. *See, e.g., ibid.* Atwater's arrest and subsequent booking, though surely humiliating, were no more harmful to her interests than the normal custodial arrest. Pp. 33–34.

Affirmed.

New York Times Co., Inc. v. Tasini
No. 00201.

Decided June 25, 2001

Respondent freelance authors (Authors) wrote articles (Articles) for newspapers and a magazine published by petitioners New York Times Company (Times), Newsday, Inc. (Newsday), and Time, Inc. (Time). The Times, Newsday, and Time (Print Publishers) engaged the Authors as independent contractors under contracts that in no instance secured an Authors consent to placement of an Article in an electronic database. The Print Publishers each licensed rights to copy and sell articles to petitioner LEXIS/NEXIS, owner and operator of NEXIS. NEXIS is a computerized database containing articles in text-only format from hundreds of periodicals spanning many years. Subscribers access NEXIS through a computer, may search for articles using criteria such as author and subject, and may view, print, or download each article yielded by the search. An article's display identifies its original print publication, date, section, initial page number, title, and author, but each article appears in isolation without visible link to other stories originally published in the same periodical edition. NEXIS does not reproduce the print publications formatting features such as headline size and page placement. The Times also has licensing agreements with petitioner University Microfilms International (UMI), authorizing reproduction of Times materials on two CDROM products. One, the New York Times OnDisc (NYTO), is a text-only database containing Times articles presented in essentially the same way they appear in LEXIS/NEXIS. The other, General Periodicals OnDisc (GPO), is an image-based system that reproduces the Times Sunday Book Review and Magazine exactly as they appeared on the printed pages, complete with photographs, captions, advertisements, and other surrounding materials. The two CDROM products are searchable in much the same way as LEXIS/NEXIS; in both, articles retrieved by users provide no links to other articles appearing in the original print publications.

The Authors filed this suit, alleging that their copyrights were infringed when, as permitted and facilitated by the Print Publishers, LEXIS/NEXIS and UMI (Electronic Publishers) placed the Articles in NEXIS, NYTO, and GPO (Databases). The Authors sought declaratory and injunctive relief, and damages. In response to the Authors complaint, the Print and Electronic Publishers raised the privilege accorded collective work copyright owners by § 201(c) of the Copyright Act. That provision, pivotal in this case, reads: Copyright in each separate contribution to a collective work is distinct from copyright in the collective work as a whole, and vests initially in the author of the contribution. In the absence of an express transfer of the copyright or of any rights under it, the owner of copyright in the collective work is presumed to have acquired only the privilege of reproducing and distributing the contribution as part of that particular collective work, any revision of that collective work, and any later collective work in the same series. The District Court granted the Publishers summary judgment, holding, *inter alia*, that the Databases reproduced and distributed the Authors works, in § 201(c)s words, as part of [a] revision of that collective work to which the Authors had first contributed. The Second Circuit reversed, granting the Authors summary judgment on the ground that the Databases were not among the collective works covered by § 201(c), and specifically, were not revisions of the periodicals in which the Articles first appeared.

Held:

Section § 201(c) does not authorize the copying at issue here. The Publishers are not sheltered by § 201(c) because the Databases reproduce and distribute articles standing alone and not in context, not as part of that particular collective work to which the author contributed, as part of any revision thereof, or as part of any later collective work in the same series. Pp. 8–21.

(a) Where, as here, a freelance author has contributed an article to a collective work, copyright in the contribution vests initially in its author, § 201(c). Copyright in the collective work vests in the collective author (here, the Print Publisher) and extends only to the creative material contributed by that author, not to the preexisting material employed in the work, § 103(b). Congress enacted the provisions of the 1976 revision of the Copyright Act at issue to address the unfair situation under prior law, whereby authors risked losing their rights when they placed an article in a collective work. The 1976 Act recast the copyright as a bundle of discrete exclusive rights, 106, each of which may be transferred and owned separately, § 201(d)(2). The Act also provided, in § 404(a), that a single notice applicable to the collective work as a whole is sufficient to protect the rights of freelance contributors. Together, §§ 404(a) and 201(c) preserve the authors copyright in a contribution to a collective work. Under § 201(c)s terms, a publisher could reprint a contribution from one issue in a later issue of its magazine, and could reprint an article from one edition of an encyclopedia in a later revision of it, but could not revise the contribution itself or include it in a new anthology or an entirely different collective work. Essentially, § 201(c) adjusts a publishers copyright in its collective work to accommodate a freelancers copyright in her contribution. If there is demand for a freelance article standing alone or in a new collection, the Copyright Act allows the freelancer to benefit from that demand; after authorizing initial publication, the freelancer may also sell the article to others. *Cf. Stewart v. Abend,* 495 U.S. 207, 229, 230. It would scarcely preserve the authors copyright in a contribution as contemplated by Congress if a print publisher, without the authors permission, could reproduce or distribute discrete copies of the contribution in isolation or within new collective works. Pp. 812.

(b) The Publishers view that inclusion of the Articles in the Databases lies within the privilege of reproducing and distributing the [Articles] as part of [a] revision of that collective work, § 201(c), is unacceptable. In determining whether the Articles have been reproduced and distributed as part of a revision, the Court focuses on the Articles as presented to, and perceptible by, a Database user. *See* §§ 102, 101. Here, the three Databases present articles to users clear of the context provided either by the original periodical editions or by any revision of those editions. The Databases first prompt users to search the universe of their contents: thousands or millions of files containing individual articles from thousands of collective works (*i.e.,* editions), either in one series (the Times, in NYTO) or in scores of series (the sundry titles in NEXIS and GPO). When the user conducts a search, each article appears as a separate item within the search result. In NEXIS and NYTO, an article appears to a user without the graphics, formatting, or other articles with which it was initially published. In GPO, the article appears with the other materials published on the same page or pages, but without any material published on other pages of the original periodical. In either circumstance, the Database does not reproduce and distribute the article as part of either the original edition or a revision of that edition. The articles may be viewed as parts of a new compendium namely, the entirety of works in the Database. Each edition of each periodical, however, represents only a miniscule fraction of the ever-expanding Database. The massive whole of the Database is not recognizable as a new version of its every small part. Furthermore, the Articles in the Databases may be viewed as part of no larger work at all, but simply as individual articles presented individually. That each article bears marks of its origin in a particular periodical suggests the article was *previously* part of that periodical, not that the article is *currently* reproduced or distributed as part of the periodical. The Databases reproduction and distribution of individual Articles simply as *individual Articles* would invade the core of the Authors exclusive rights. The Publishers analogy between the Databases and microfilm and microfiche is wanting: In the Databases, unlike microfilm, articles appear disconnected from their original context. Unlike the conversion of newsprint to microfilm, the transfer of articles to the Databases does not represent a mere conversion of intact periodicals (or revisions of periodicals) from one medium to another. The Databases offer users individual articles, not intact periodicals. The concept of media-neutrality invoked by the Publishers should therefore protect the Authors rights, not the Publishers. The result is not changed because users can manipulate the Databases to generate search results consisting entirely of articles from a particular periodical edition. Under 201(c), the question is not whether a user can assemble a revision of a collective work from a database, but whether the database itself perceptibly presents the authors contribution as part of a revision of the collective work. That result is not accomplished by these Databases. Pp. 12–19.

(c) The Publishers warning that a ruling for the Authors will have devastating consequences, punching gaping holes in the electronic record of history, is unavailing. It hardly follows from this decision that an injunction against the inclusion of these Articles in the Databases (much less all freelance articles in any databases) must issue. The Authors and Publishers may enter into an agreement allowing continued electronic reproduction of the Authors works; they, and if necessary the courts and Congress, may draw on numerous models for distributing copyrighted works and remunerating authors for their distribution. In any event, speculation about future harms is no basis for this Court to shrink authorial rights created by Congress. The Court leaves remedial issues open for initial airing and decision in the District Court. Pp. 19–21.

Affirmed.

Ginsburg, J., delivered the opinion of the Court, in which *Rehnquist, C.J.,* and *O'Connor, Scalia, Kennedy, Souter,* and *Thomas, JJ.,* joined. *Stevens, J.,* filed a dissenting opinion, in which *Breyer, J.,* joined.

IDAHO v. UNITED STATES
No. 00189

DECIDED JUNE 18, 2001

This suit involves a dispute between the United States and Idaho over the ownership of submerged lands underlying portions of Lake Coeur d'Alene and the St. Joe River. The Coeur d'Alene Tribe once inhabited vast acreage in and about what is now Idaho, and traditionally used Lake Coeur d'Alene and the St. Joe River for food, fiber, transportation, recreation, and cultural activities. In 1873, the Tribe agreed to relinquish for compensation all claims to its aboriginal lands outside the bounds of a specified reservation that included part of the river and virtually all of the lake. The agreement required congressional approval, but President Grant set the land aside in an 1873 Executive Order, which set the reservations northern boundary directly across the lake. An 1883 Government survey indicated that the reservation included submerged lands. When Congress neither ratified the agreement nor compensated the Tribe, the Tribe petitioned the Government to make a proper treaty and Congress authorized negotiations. In 1887, the Tribe agreed to cede its rights to all land except that within the Executive Order reservation, and the Government promised to compensate the Tribe and agreed to hold the land forever as Indian land. Still, Congress did not ratify the agreement. In 1888, the Interior Secretary responded to a Senate enquiry about the reservations boundaries, reporting that the reservation appeared to embrace all but a small fragment of the lakes navigable waters and that the St. Joe River flowed through the reservation. Also in 1888, Congress approved a railroad right-of-way that crossed the reservation's navigable waters, but directed that the Tribe's consent be obtained and that the Tribe be compensated.

Responding to a growing desire to obtain for the public an interest in portions of the reservation, Congress authorized negotiations that produced a new agreement in 1889, in which the Tribe agreed to cede the reservations northern portion, including two-thirds of the lake, for compensation. In 1890, the Senate passed a bill ratifying the 1887 and 1889 agreements, but while the bill was pending in the House, Congress passed the Idaho Statehood Act, admitting Idaho to the Union. In 1891, Congress ratified the 1887 and 1889 agreements. The United States initiated this action against Idaho to quiet title in the United States, in trust for the Tribe, to the submerged lands within the current reservation. The Tribe intervened to assert its interest in those lands, and Idaho counter-claimed to quiet title in its favor. The District Court quieted title in the United States as trustee, and the Tribe as beneficiary, to the bed and banks of the lake and the river within the reservation. The Ninth Circuit affirmed.

Held:

The National Government holds title, in trust for the Tribe, to lands underlying portions of Lake Coeur d'Alene and the St. Joe River. Pp. 9–18.

(a) Armed with the strong presumption against defeat of a States title to land under navigable waters, *United States v. Alaska,* 521 U.S. 1, 34, the Court looks to Congress declarations and intent when resolving conflicts over submerged lands claimed to be reserved or conveyed by the United States before statehood, *e.g., id.,* at 36. The two-step enquiry used in reservation cases asks whether Congress intended to include submerged lands within the federal reservation, and, if so, whether Congress intended to defeat the future States title to those lands. *Ibid.* Where, as here, the Executive Branch initially reserved the land, the two-step test is satisfied when an Executive reservation clearly includes submerged lands, and Congress recognizes that reservation in a way that demonstrates its intent to defeat state title. *Id.,* at 4146, 5561. Here, Idaho has conceded that the Executive Branch intended, or interpreted, the 1873 Executive Order reservation to include submerged lands. Pp. 9–11.

(b) Congress recognized the full extent of the Executive Order reservation and it intended to bar passage to Idaho of title to the submerged lands at issue. Idaho's concession, in the Ninth Circuit, that the Executive Order reservation included submerged lands and that Congress was on notice regarding the scope of the reservation was prudent in light of the District Courts findings of facts. That court concluded that the submerged lands and related water rights had been continuously important to the Tribe throughout the period prior to congressional action confirming the reservation and granting Idaho statehood, and that the Federal Government could only achieve its goals of promoting settlement in the Tribes aboriginal area, avoiding hostilities with the Tribe, and extinguishing aboriginal title by agreeing to a reservation that included the submerged lands. That is the background of the 1873 Executive Orders inclusion of such lands, which in turn were the subject of the Senates 1888 request to the Interior Secretary, whose response was consistent with the 1883 survey results. The manner in which Congress then proceeded to deal with the Tribe shows clearly that preservation of the reservations land, absent contrary agreement with the Tribe, was central to Congress' complementary objectives of dealing with pressures of white settlement and establishing the reservation by permanent legislation. Congress made it expressly plain that its object was to obtain tribal interests only by tribal consent. When it sought to extinguish aboriginal title to lands outside the 1873 reservation and to reduce the reservations size, it did so by authorizing negotiations with the Tribe to cede title for compensation. It also honored the reservations boundaries by requiring that the Tribe be compensated for the railroad right-of-way. The intent was that anything not consensually ceded by the Tribe would remain for the Tribes benefit, an objective flatly at odds with Idaho's view that Congress meant to transfer the balance of submerged lands to the State in what would have amounted to an act of bad faith accomplished by unspoken operation of law. Idaho's position is also at odds with later manifestations of congressional understanding that statehood had not affected the submerged lands. Pp. 11–17.

Affirmed.

Souter, J., delivered the opinion of the Court, in which *Stevens, O'Connor, Ginsburg, and Breyer, JJ.*, joined. *Rehnquist, C.J.*, filed a dissenting opinion, in which *Scalia, Kennedy*, and *Thomas, JJ.*, joined.

TEXAS *v.* COBB
No. 99–1702

DECIDED APRIL 2, 2001

While under arrest for an unrelated offense, respondent confessed to a home burglary, but denied knowledge of a woman and child's disappearance from the home. He was indicted for the burglary, and counsel was appointed to represent him. He later confessed to his father that he had killed the woman and child, and his father then contacted the police. While in custody, respondent waived his rights under *Miranda v. Arizona*, 384 U. S. 436, and confessed to the murders. He was convicted of capital murder and sentenced to death. On appeal to the Texas Court of Criminal Appeals, he argued, *inter alia*, that his confession should have been suppressed because it was obtained in violation of his Sixth Amendment right to counsel, which he claimed attached when counsel was appointed in the burglary case. The court reversed and remanded, holding that once the right to counsel attaches to the offense charged, it also attaches to any other offense that is very closely related factually to the offense charged.

Held:

Because the Sixth Amendment right to counsel is "offense specific,"it does not necessarily extend to offenses that are 'factually related' to those that have actually been charged." Pp. 4–11.

(a) In *McNeil v. Wisconsin*, 501 U. S. 171, 176, this Court held that a defendant's statements regarding offenses for which he has not been charged are admissible notwithstanding the attachment of his Sixth Amendment right to counsel on other charged offenses. Although some lower courts have read into *McNeil's* offense-specific definition an exception for crimes that are "factually related" to a charged offense, and have interpreted *Brewer v. Williams*, 430 U. S. 387, and *Maine v. Moulton*, 474 U. S. 159, to support this view, this Court declines to do so. Brewer did not address the question at issue here. And to the extent *Moulton* spoke to the matter at all, it expressly referred to the offense-specific nature of the Sixth Amendment right to counsel. In predicting that the offense-specific rule will prove disastrous to suspects' constitutional rights and will permit the police almost total license to conduct unwanted and uncounseled interrogations, respondent fails to appreciate two critical considerations. First, there can be no doubt that a suspect must be apprised of his rights against compulsory self-incrimination and to consult with an attorney before authorities may conduct custodial interrogation. *See Miranda, supra,* at 479. Here, police scrupulously followed *Miranda's* dictates when questioning respondent. Second, the Constitution does not negate society's interest in the police's ability to talk to witnesses and suspects, even those who have been charged with other offenses. *See McNeil, supra,* at 181. Pp. 4–9.

(b) Although the Sixth Amendment right to counsel clearly attaches only to charged offenses, this Court has recognized in other contexts that the definition of an "offense" is not necessarily limited to the four corners of a charging document. The test to determine whether there are two different offenses or only one is whether each provision requires proof of a fact which the other does not. *Blockburger v. United States,* 284 U. S. 299, 304. The *Blockburger* test has been applied to delineate the scope of the Fifth Amendment's Double Jeopardy Clause, which prevents multiple or successive prosecutions for the "same offense." *See, e.g., Brown v. Ohio,* 432 U. S. 161, 164–166. There is no constitutional difference between "offense" in the double jeopardy and right-to-counsel contexts. Accordingly, when the Sixth Amendment right to counsel attaches, it encompasses offenses that, even if not formally charged, would be considered the same offense under the *Blockburger* test. Pp. 9–11.

(c) At the time respondent confessed to the murders, he had been indicted for burglary but had not been charged in the murders. As defined by Texas law, these crimes are not the same offense under *Blockburger.* Thus, the Sixth Amendment right to counsel did not bar police from interrogating respondent regarding the murders, and his confession was therefore admissible. P. 11.

Reversed.

Rehnquist, C.J., delivered the opinion of the Court, in which *O'Connor, Scalia, Kennedy,* and *Thomas, JJ.,* joined. *Kennedy, J.,* filed a concurring opinion, in which *Scalia* and *Thomas, JJ.,* joined. *Breyer, J.,* filed a dissenting opinion, in which *Stevens, Souter,* and *Ginsburg, JJ.,* joined.

LORILLARD TOBACCO CO. v. REILLY, ATTORNEY GENERAL OF MASSACHUSETTS
No. 00596

DECIDED JUNE 28, 2001

After the Attorney General of Massachusetts (Attorney General) promulgated comprehensive regulations governing the advertising and sale of cigarettes, smokeless tobacco, and cigars, petitioners, a group of tobacco manufacturers and retailers, filed this suit asserting, among other things, the Supremacy Clause claim that the cigarette advertising regulations are pre-empted by the Federal Cigarette Labeling and Advertising Act (FCLAA), which prescribes mandatory health warnings for cigarette packaging and advertising, 15 U.S.C. § 1333, and pre-empts similar state regulations, § 1334(b); and a claim that the regulations violate the First and Fourteenth Amendments to the Federal Constitution. In large measure, the District Court upheld the regulations. Among its rulings, the court held that restrictions on the location of advertising were not pre-empted by the FCLAA, and that neither the regulations prohibiting outdoor advertising within 1,000 feet of a school or playground nor the sales practices regulations restricting the location and distribution of tobacco products violated the First Amendment. The court ruled, however, that the point-of-sale advertising regulations requiring that indoor advertising be placed no lower than five feet from the floor were invalid because the Attorney General had not provided sufficient justification for that restriction. The First Circuit affirmed the District Court's rulings that the cigarette advertising regulations are not pre-empted by the FCLAA and that the outdoor advertising regulations and the sales practices regulations do not violate the First Amendment under *Central Hudson Gas & Elec. Corp. v. Public Serv. Commn of N. Y.,* 447 U.S. 557, but reversed the lower courts invalidation of the point-of-sale advertising regulations, concluding that the Attorney General is better suited than courts to determine what restrictions are necessary.

Held:

1. The FCLAA pre-empts Massachusetts regulations governing outdoor and point-of-sale cigarette advertising. Pp. 9–23.

(a) The FCLAA's pre-emption provision, § 1334, prohibits (a) requiring cigarette packages to bear any statement relating to smoking and health, other than the statement required by § 1333, and (b) any requirement or prohibition based on smoking and health imposed under state law with respect to the advertising or promotion of any cigarettes the packages of which are labeled in conformity with § 1333. The Courts analysis begins with the statutes language. *Hughes Aircraft Co. v. Jacobson,* 525 U.S. 432, 438. The statutes interpretation is aided by considering the predecessor pre-emption provision and the context in which the current language was adopted. *See, e.g., Medtronic, Inc. v. Lohr,* 518 U.S. 470, 486. The original provision simply prohibited any statement relating to smoking and health in the advertising of any cigarettes the packages of which are labeled in conformity with the [Act's] provisions. Without question, the current pre-emption provisions plain language is much broader. *Cipollone v. Liggett Group, Inc.,* 505 U.S. 504, 520. Rather than preventing only statements, the amended provision reaches all requirement[s] or prohibition[s] imposed under State law. And, although the former statute reached only statements in the advertising, the current provision governs with respect to the advertising or promotion of cigarettes. At the same time that Congress expanded the pre-emption provision with respect to the States, it enacted a provision prohibiting cigarette advertising in electronic media altogether. Pp. 10–15.

(b) Congress pre-empted state cigarette advertising regulations like the Attorney General's because they would upset federal legislative choices to require specific warnings and to impose the ban on cigarette advertising in electronic media in order to address concerns about smoking and health. In holding that the FCLAA does not nullify the Massachusetts regulations, the First Circuit concentrated on whether they are with respect to advertising and promotion, concluding that the FCLAA only pre-empts regulations of the content of cigarette advertising. The court also reasoned that the regulations are a form of zoning, a traditional area of state power, and, therefore, a presumption against preemption applied, *see California Div. of Labor Standards Enforcement v. Dillingham Constr., N. A., Inc.,* 519 U.S. 316, 325. This Court rejects the notion that the regulations are not with respect to cigarette advertising and promotion. There is no question about an indirect relationship between the Massachusetts regulations and cigarette advertising: The regulations expressly target such advertising. *Id.,* at 324, 325. The Attorney General's argument that the regulations are not based on smoking and health since they do not involve health-related content, but instead target youth exposure to cigarette advertising, is unpersuasive because, at bottom, the youth exposure concern is intertwined with the smoking and health concern. Also unavailing is the Attorney General's claim that the regulations are not pre-empted because they govern the location, not the content, of cigarette advertising. The content/location distinction cannot be squared with the pre-emption provisions language, which reaches all requirements and prohibitions imposed under State law. A distinction between advertising content and location in the FCLAA also cannot be reconciled with Congress own location-based restriction, which bans advertising in electronic media, but not elsewhere. The Attorney General's assertion that a complete state ban on cigarette advertising would not be pre-empted because Congress did not intend to preclude local control of zoning finds no support in the FCLAA, whose comprehensive warnings, advertising restrictions, and pre-emption provision would make little sense if a State or locality could simply target and ban all cigarette advertising. Pp. 15–21.

(c) The FCLAA's pre-emption provision does not restrict States and localities ability to enact generally applicable zoning restrictions on the location and size of advertisements that apply to cigarettes on equal terms with other products, *see, e.g., Metromedia, Inc. v. San Diego,* 453 U.S. 490, 507, 508, or to regulate conduct as it relates to the sale or use of cigarettes, as by prohibiting cigarette sales to minors, *see* 42 U.S.C. § 300x26(a)(1), 300x21, as well as common inchoate offenses that attach to criminal conduct, such as solicitation, conspiracy, and attempt, *cf. Central Hudson, supra,* at 563,564. Pp. 21–22.

(d) Because the issue was not decided below, the Court declines to reach the smokeless tobacco petitioners argument that, if the outdoor and point-of-sale advertising regulations for cigarettes are pre-empted, then the same regulations for smokeless tobacco must be invalidated because they cannot be severed from the cigarette provisions. Pp. 22–23.

2. Massachusetts' outdoor and point-of-sale advertising regulations relating to smokeless tobacco and cigars violate the First Amendment, but the sales practices regulations relating to all three tobacco products are constitutional. Pp. 23–41.

(a) Under *Central Hudson's* four-part test for analyzing regulations of commercial speech, the Court must determine (1) whether the expression is protected by the First Amendment, (2) whether the asserted governmental interest is substantial, (3) whether the regulation directly advances the governmental interest asserted, and (4) whether it is not more extensive than is necessary to serve that interest. 447 U.S., at 566. Only the last two steps are at issue here. The Attorney General has assumed for summary judgment purposes that the First Amendment protects the speech of petitioners, none of whom contests the importance of the States interest in preventing the use of tobacco by minors. The third step of *Central Hudson* requires that the government demonstrate that the harms it recites are real and that its restriction will in fact alleviate them to a material degree. *Edenfield v. Fane,* 507 U.S. 761, 770, 771. The fourth step of *Central Hudson* requires a reasonable fit between the legislatures ends and the means chosen to accomplish those ends, a means narrowly tailored to achieve the desired objective. *E.g., Florida Bar v. Went For It, Inc.,* 515 U.S. 618, 632. Pp. 23–26.

(b) The outdoor advertising regulations prohibiting smokeless tobacco or cigar advertising within 1,000 feet of a school or playground violate the First Amendment. Pp. 26–38.

(1) Those regulations satisfy *Central Hudson's* third step by directly advancing the governmental interest asserted to justify them. The Court's detailed review of the record reveals that the Attorney General has provided ample documentation of the problem with underage use of smokeless tobacco and cigars. In addition, the Court disagrees with petitioner's claim that there is no evidence that preventing targeted advertising campaigns and limiting youth exposure to advertising will decrease underage use of those products.

On the record below and in the posture of summary judgment, it cannot be concluded that the Attorney General's decision to regulate smokeless tobacco and cigar advertising in an effort to combat the use of tobacco products by minors was based on mere speculation and conjecture. *Edenfield, supra,* at 770. Pp. 26–31.

(2) Whatever the strength of the Attorney General's evidence to justify the outdoor advertising regulations, however, the regulations do not satisfy *Central Hudson's* fourth step. Their broad sweep indicates that the Attorney General did not carefully calculat[e] the costs and benefits associated with the burden on speech imposed. *Cincinnati v. Discovery Network, Inc.,* 507 U.S. 410, 417. The record indicates that the regulations prohibit advertising in a substantial portion of Massachusetts' major metropolitan areas; in some areas, they would constitute nearly a complete ban on the communication of truthful information. This substantial geographical reach is compounded by other factors. Outdoor advertising includes not only advertising located outside an establishment, but also advertising inside a store if visible from outside. Moreover, the regulations restrict advertisements of any size, and the term advertisement also includes oral statements. The uniformly broad sweep of the geographical limitation and the range of communications restricted demonstrate a lack of tailoring. The governmental interest in preventing underage tobacco use is substantial, and even compelling, but it is no less true that the sale and use of tobacco products by adults is a legal activity. A speech regulation cannot unduly impinge on the speakers ability to propose a commercial transaction and the adult listeners opportunity to obtain information about products. The Attorney General has failed to show that the regulations at issue are not more extensive than necessary. Pp. 31–36.

(c) The regulations prohibiting indoor, point-of-sale advertising of smokeless tobacco and cigars lower than 5 feet from the floor of a retail establishment located within 1,000 feet of a school or playground fail both the third and fourth steps of the *Central Hudson* analysis. The 5-foot rule does not seem to advance the goals of preventing minors from using tobacco products and curbing demand for that activity by limiting youth exposure to advertising. Not all children are less than 5 feet tall, and those who are can look up and take in their surroundings. Nor can the blanket *height e.g., Texas v. Johnson,* 491 U.S. 397-403, but attempts to regulate directly the communicative impact of indoor restriction be construed as a mere regulation of communicative action *under United States v. O'Brien,* 391 U.S. 367, since it is not unrelated to expression advertising. Moreover, the restriction does not constitute a reasonable fit with the goal of targeting tobacco advertising that entices children. Although the First Circuit decided that the restrictions burden on speech is very limited, there is no *de minimis* exception for a speech restriction that lacks sufficient tailoring or justification. Pp. 36–38.

(d) Assuming that petitioners have a cognizable speech interest in a particular means of displaying their products, *cf. Cincinnati v. Discovery Network, Inc.,* 507 U.S. 410, the regulations requiring retailers to place tobacco products behind counters and requiring customers to have contact with a salesperson before they are able to handle such a product withstand First Amendment scrutiny. The State has demonstrated a substantial interest in preventing access to tobacco products by minors and has adopted an appropriately narrow means of advancing that interest. *See e.g., O'Brien, supra,* at 382. Because unattended displays of such products present an opportunity for access without the proper age verification required by law, the State prohibits self-service and other displays that would allow an individual to obtain tobacco without direct contact with a salesperson. It is clear that the regulations leave open ample communication channels. They do not significantly impede adult access to tobacco products, and retailers have other means of exercising any cognizable speech interest in the presentation of their products. The Court presumes that vendors may place empty tobacco packaging on open display, and display actual tobacco products so long as that display is only accessible to sales personnel. As for cigars, there is no indication that a customer is unable to examine a cigar prior to purchase, so long as that examination takes place through a salesperson. Pp. 38–40.

(e) The Court declines to address the petitioner's First Amendment challenge to a regulation prohibiting sampling or promotional giveaways of cigars and little cigars. That claim was not sufficiently briefed and argued before this Court. Pp. 40–41.

Affirmed in part, reversed in part, and remanded.

OConnor, J., delivered the opinion of the Court, Parts I, IIC, and IID of which were unanimous; Parts IIIA, IIIC, and IIID of which were joined by *Rehnquist, C.J.,* and *Scalia, Kennedy, Souter,* and *Thomas, JJ.*; Part IIIB1 of which was joined by *Rehnquist, C.J.,* and *Stevens, Souter, Ginsburg,* and *Breyer, JJ.*; and Parts IIA, IIB, IIIB2, and IV of which were joined by *Rehnquist, C.J.,* and *Scalia, Kennedy,* and *Thomas, JJ. Kennedy, J.,* filed an opinion concurring in part and concurring in the judgment, in which *Scalia, J.,* joined. *Thomas, J.,* filed an opinion concurring in part and concurring in the judgment. *Souter, J.,* filed an opinion concurring in part and dissenting in part. *Stevens, J.,* filed an opinion concurring in part, concurring in the judgment in part, and dissenting in part, in which *Ginsburg* and *Breyer, JJ.,* joined, and in Part I of which *Souter, J.,* joined.

GLOSSARY

acknowledge To affirm that a document is genuine.

acquittal A finding of *not guilty* in a criminal case.

actual authority The power given in fact to an agent by the principal or employer.

actual evidence Also called *real evidence*; tangible evidence that may be admitted during a hearing on a motion or at trial.

actus reus The physical element of a crime; the guilty act or the physical aspect of the crime.

adjudicate To resolve; when the court adjudicates an issue, the issue is resolved. Adjudication is the process of exercising judicial power.

administrative hearing A hearing before an administrative agency regarding a dispute between an individual and the agency.

affidavit A non-oral statement of facts that is confirmed by affirmation or oath of the person making the statement.

affirm To uphold; used in connection with an appeal to uphold the lower court's decision.

affirmative defenses Defenses raised by the defendant in the answer; reasons why the plaintiff should not recover even if all of the allegations of the complaint are true.

agent One who acts on behalf of another.

alternative dispute resolution (ADR) Methods of resolving disputes outside the normal court process.

annotation A brief summary of a statute or a case.

annulment To annul something is to nullify it or make it void; the term is often used in connection with a marriage.

answer The pleading used by the defendant to respond to the plaintiff's complaint.

apparent authority Authority created by conduct that leads a third person to believe that authority exists.

appear As used in a summons, to appear means to file appropriate documents in the action.

appellate brief A written document containing factual and legal contentions; prepared by attorneys dealing with an appeal in a case.

appellate jurisdiction The power of a court to review what happened in a lower court.

appointment letter A letter that schedules an appointment.

arbitration An out-of-court hearing before a neutral party who listens to two or more disputing parties and renders a decision resolving the dispute.

arbitration award The decision of the arbitrator in an arbitration hearing.

arbitrator An individual who presides over an arbitration hearing and renders a decision.

arraignment A hearing where the criminal defendant comes before the court to enter a plea; it is a hearing in open court where the information and/or indictment are read and the defendant is asked to plead.

arrest The physical seizure of a person by the government.

assault The placing of another in apprehension or fear of an imminent battery; it is both a crime and a tort.

assignee The person to whom a transfer or assignment is made.

assignment The transfer of one's rights under a contract.

assignor The person who makes a transfer or assignment of rights under a contract.

assumption of the risk Knowingly and voluntarily assuming a risk; a defense to negligence.

attestation clause A clause at the end of a will wherein all witnesses declare that the document was executed before them.

attorney Another term for *lawyer*.

attractive nuisance A condition on land that appeals to children; a doctrine that requires homeowners to use reasonable care to avoid injury to trespassing children.

bail An amount of money set by the court, payment of which is a condition of pretrial release from police custody.

bailiff An individual who is responsible for the safety of the judge and for order within the courtroom; sometimes known as a *court deputy* or *court attendant*.

bar examination An examination administered by a state that tests an individual's knowledge of the law and is a prerequisite to being allowed to practice law.

battery A reckless or intentional, harmful or offensive touching of another; it is both a crime and a tort.

beneficiary A person named in a will who will benefit from a transfer of specific property.

bequest A gift by will of specific personal property.

beyond a reasonable doubt The amount of proof necessary for a conviction in a criminal case.

bicameral A term that describes a legislature consisting of two houses.

bifurcate To sever from the trial; in family law, it means that the divorce or dissolution may be granted, but the parties will need to come back to court to adjudicate another issue—for example, their property issues.

bilateral contract A contract in which both parties have made promises to perform.

bill Proposed legislation.

bill of particulars A device used to provide a defendant with a statement of the facts enumerating the specific acts charged.

Bill of Rights The first ten amendments to the Constitution.

binding case law Case law that must be followed by lower courts.

blue-sky laws State securities regulations.

booking The process after arrest when the police have entered formal charges against a defendant.

breach of contract The failure of one party to a contract to perform his or her obligations under the contract.

brief A written document that might contain a summary of the facts, issues, rules, and analysis used by a court and a comparison with a client's facts; a *case brief* is a short summary of a published case.

burden of proof The necessity of establishing a particular fact or the necessity of going forward with the evidence.

burglary The unlawful entry of a structure or building for the purpose of committing a felony inside.

business corporation A corporation formed for any business purpose.

bylaws The internal rules and regulations for a corporation.

capital offense A criminal offense that carries a death penalty.

case at law A civil action in which one party is seeking money damages.

case brief A short summary of a published case.

case in chief The part of the trial where the plaintiff presents evidence.

case in equity A civil case in which one party is seeking equitable or specific relief, such as specific performance of a contract or an injunction.

case law A collection of reported cases.

cause of action The basis upon which a lawsuit may be brought to the court.

Certified Legal Assistant (CLA) A paralegal or legal assistant who has passed a special examination given by the National Association of Legal Assistants.

characterize To determine whether an item is separate, community, or quasi-community property.

child custody The immediate control and care of a minor; the court will determine which spouse will have custody of a child.

circumstantial evidence Indirect evidence that provides the jury with information from which inferences may be drawn.

citation A standard abbreviated way of explaining where law is found.

clerk's transcript A record containing copies of documents filed in connection with a court proceeding; prepared by a court clerk.

client file The office file that contains copies of all documents related to the client's case.

client intake sheet A form used to collect information on the client and data on the client's legal matter.

close corporation A small corporation whose shares of stock are not available to the public.

closing argument The argument given just prior to the judge instructing the jury; the attorney's last opportunity to address the court and the jury. It includes a summary of the facts, issues, evidence, and conclusions that may be drawn from the evidence.

code A topical organization of statutes.

codicil An addition or change to a will. A codicil does not contain the entire will; it simply supplements the original document.

commingling Mixing client funds with the attorney's business or personal funds.

common law A body of law developed through the courts.

community property Property owned jointly by married persons; not all states recognize community property.

comparative negligence A doctrine that compares the negligence of the plaintiff and the defendant and allows recovery based on apportionment of fault.

complaint A document filed in a civil or criminal lawsuit that describes the allegations of the plaintiff and the basis for the lawsuit.

compromise and release A settlement agreement that ends a case.

conciliation The settlement of disputes in a nonadversary manner.

concur To act together.

concurrent jurisdiction A term that describes situations where more than one entity has the power to regulate or act.

concurring opinion A separate opinion written by one or more justices in a case; this opinion agrees with the ultimate decision of the majority of the court, but with a reasoning that differs from the reasoning of the majority of the court.

confession A voluntary statement made by a person charged with a crime, acknowledging that he or she is guilty of the charge.

confirming letter A letter that confirms or puts in writing an oral understanding or agreement of parties.

conflict of interest A situation that arises when a firm has a business or personal relationship with one of the litigants, or when the firm has represented the party the client wishes to sue.

consortium Companionship, comfort, and society given by one spouse to another.

constitution A document whose primary purpose is to establish a government and define its powers.

constructive trust A trust created by law; the court may determine that a person has by actual or constructive fraud or duress obtained a legal right to property that he or she should not in good faith possess.

contempt Willful disregard of a court order.

contingent fee A fee based on a fixed percentage of whatever amount is recovered by the attorney on behalf of the client.

contributory negligence Negligence of a plaintiff that contributes to the injury; a doctrine that is a defense to negligence.

corporation A business that is a legal entity unto itself and is formed according to the corporate laws of one state.

corroborate To support the statements of another.

costs Out-of-pocket expenses in connection with a case.

counterclaim A pleading in which the defendant asks for damages or other relief from a plaintiff.

court clerk A court employee who assists the court and the judge by filing documents, marking and safeguarding evidence, reviewing documents that are submitted to the judge, and other similar tasks.

court reporter A person who records (electronically or stenographically) the testimony that takes place during the open court proceedings; the court reporter will produce a transcript.

cover letter A letter that accompanies and explains documents that are enclosed.

credibility A witness's testimony is weighed by the jury; credibility of the witness is established when his or her testimony is found to be worthy of belief.

crime An act in violation of a criminal statute.

cross-claim A pleading in which the defendant asks for damages or other relief from a co-defendant.

cross-examination Questioning that occurs when a witness is questioned by someone other than the direct examiner; in other words, questioning by opposing counsel, after the party who called the witness has completed his or her examination.

debt security A certificate indicating that the holder is owed money by a business.

decedent A person who has died; a deceased person.

deed A document that evidences title to real property; it is also used to convey property.

deed of trust A document that evidences a debt secured by real property.

default Failure to appear.

defense The explanation of why the person complaining should not prevail in his or her action.

delegation The transfer of obligations under a contract.

deliberation The process of analyzing and discussing the evidence heard during the course of the trial by the jury; it takes place in the jury room without the judge or the attorneys present.

delinquent A minor, as defined by law, who violates a criminal law.

demand letter A letter in which the writer is seeking settlement of some matter.

demonstrative evidence A type of actual evidence or exhibits created for use in court; includes diagrams, charts, and photographs.

demonstrative legacy A gift of a specified amount of money in which the testator includes directions as to exactly which fund will be used to fulfill the legacy.

demurrer A pleading used in some states to challenge the legal sufficiency of the complaint.

deponent The person whose testimony is given under oath during a deposition.

depose To give evidence at a deposition.

deposition The testimony of a witness, given under oath, outside the courtroom and taken before a court reporter; the *deponent* (the person whose deposition is being taken) will be asked questions by the attorney who requested the deposition.

deter To stop, discourage, or prevent a person from performing a certain act.

devise A gift by will of specific real property.

digest An index to reported cases, arranged by subject; a short summary of the case is provided.

direct evidence Evidence that proves a point; for example, the testimony of an eyewitness.

directors The individuals who exercise general management and control of a corporation.

disbarment The action of denying an attorney the right to practice law in the state.

discharge To relieve or forgive.

discovery A pretrial process of acquiring information; the most common discovery tools are written interrogatories, depositions, and requests for production of documents and things.

disinheritance clause A clause used to deprive an heir of the right to inherit.

disparagement Another term for the business torts of slander of title and trade libel.

dissenting opinion A separate opinion written by one or more justices in a case; this opinion disagrees with the decision of the majority of the court.

dissolution The dissolving or termination of a marriage; the terms *divorce* and *dissolution* are often interchangeable. Some states, such as California, no longer use the legal term *divorce*, but call the termination of a marriage a *dissolution of marriage*.

diversity of citizenship A basis for federal court jurisdiction where the plaintiff and defendant are residents of different states and the amount in controversy exceeds $75,000.

dividends Profits of a corporation that are distributed to the shareholders.

divorce The total dissolving of a marriage.

docket number The court's numerical designation for a case; used by the court to organize files.

documentary evidence A type of actual evidence including writings such as reports, business records, and correspondence.

domestic relations The area of law that deals with family law issues such as divorce, custody, and support.

due process clause A clause in the Fifth and Fourteenth Amendments to the U.S. Constitution that protects people from state actions which would deprive them of basic rights.

early neutral evaluation A proceeding that takes place early in a civil case in which the disputing parties meet with a neutral person who evaluates the case in an attempt to settle the dispute.

easement The right to a limited use of a portion of another's property.

en banc A term that describes the entire panel of judges on a court hearing a case.

endorsed copy A document that has been conformed to look like the original.

equitable title A trust beneficiary holds equitable title; the person holding equitable title has the right to benefit from the trust property.

equity security An ownership interest in a business; an interest whose value is determined by the net worth of the business.

ex post facto "After the fact"; refers to laws that impose criminal responsibility for acts that were not crimes at the time the acts occurred.

exclusionary rule A rule that excludes evidence when it has been acquired in violation of constitutional protections.

exclusive jurisdiction The sole power or authority to act in a certain situation.

excused for cause Jurors may be excused for cause if it appears that there is bias or other legitimate reasons that a person cannot sit as a juror.

executor/executrix A person chosen by a testator/testatrix to carry out the directions in the will; an *executor* is a man, while an *executrix* is a woman.

exemplary damages Another term for *punitive damages*.

exhibit A physical (tangible) piece of evidence that is offered to the court for consideration; for example, exhibits may be documents, charts, and photographs.

exigent circumstances An emergency that requires immediate action; such situations do not allow time for law enforcement officers to obtain a search or arrest warrant.

exordium clause The introductory part of a document.

expert A person who, through education or experience, has special expertise or knowledge in a particular field.

expert witness A person who, because of special qualifications, testifies about conclusions that may be drawn based on his or her expertise.

false imprisonment The intentional interference with another person's liberty through force or threat without authority.

federal jurisdiction The power of the federal courts to hear a case.

federal question A case that involves a federal law, either in statutes, in the Constitution, or in treaties.

Federal Rules of Evidence The rules of evidence used in the federal courts.

federalism A system of government in which the people are regulated by both federal and state governments.

fee simple Outright ownership of land.

felony A serious crime; includes murder, robbery, burglary and arson; a crime designated as a felony is punishable by death or imprisonment for more than one year.

fiduciary A person whose duties involve trust and good faith.

fiduciary relationship A special relationship of trust and confidence; it forms the basis of the attorney-client relationship.

file To turn a document over to the court clerk, along with any required filing fee.

finding tools The resources used to locate primary and secondary sources; for example, a digest.

first-degree murder A homicide that is premeditated, willful, and deliberate.

foreclosure A legal proceeding involving the sale of encumbered or mortgaged property when the owner fails to pay the debt.

foreign corporation A corporation incorporated in one state and doing business in another.

form book A legal resource filled with sample forms and explanations on how and when to use the forms; many are now available on disk or CD-ROM.

foundation A requirement for the admission of evidence at trial. Preliminary questions are asked to connect the legal issue with the evidence sought to be admitted; in connection with documentary evidence, questions are asked to determine the genuineness of the documents.

general damages Damages not based on a monetary loss; includes items such as pain and suffering.

general denial A responsive pleading that denies each and every allegation contained in the complaint.

general legacy A gift of a specific amount of money.

grand jury A jury that is called upon to receive and review accusations and complaints in criminal matters; this jury will hear evidence and issue indictments.

grant deed A type of deed used in some states that implies certain representations regarding title.

guardian A person who has the duty of taking care of a person and that person's property.

hearsay An out-of-court statement offered in evidence to prove the truth of the matter asserted.

holding The legal principle to be taken from the court's decision.

holographic will A will written entirely by the testator; the handwritten document is not witnessed. Not all states recognize holographic wills.

homicide The taking of the life of a human being by another.

hot pursuit In some instances, law enforcement officers may follow a suspect into an otherwise protected area, such as a residence; when officers are in hot pursuit, they may make warrantless arrests and searches.

hung jury A jury that cannot attain the necessary consensus or majority to reach a verdict.

impeachment A tool used to attack the credibility of a witness.

***in rem* jurisdiction** Jurisdiction conferred on a court that may lack personal jurisdiction because the "thing" that is the subject of the dispute is located within the state.

incapacitation The act of restraining a person from taking certain actions.

incorporation When two documents are incorporated, they become one document.

independent contractor One who does work for another but who is not subject to control of the one who has hired him or her.

indictment A written accusation given by a grand jury to the court in which it is impaneled; a criminal charge against a defendant that must be proved at trial.

indigent Without funds or assets and therefore unable to afford an attorney.

inference A logical conclusion of a fact that is not supported by direct evidence; a deduction made by a judge or a jury, based on common sense and the evidence presented in the trial.

information An accusation made by a prosecutor against a criminal defendant that does not involve a grand jury.

infringement Improper interference in the intellectual property rights of another.

initial appearance The first court appearance of a criminal defendant after the arrest.

initiative An action by citizens to enact legislation through the voter process.

integration clause A clause in a contract that indicates that the contract is meant to embody all of the terms of the parties' agreement.

intellectual property Property rights in the result of one's thoughts, ideas or inventions; includes patents, copyrights, and trademarks.

intentional tort A tort that is willful and meant to cause harm.

interrogation The process used by law enforcement officers to elicit information from a criminal suspect.

interrogatories Written questions sent by one party to another party; must be answered under oath.

intestate succession When a person dies without a will, his or her estate will be disposed of under the laws of intestate succession. The laws of intestate succession will dispose of the property under the state laws of descent and distribution.

investigation The process of asking questions and locating evidence.

issue A question that must be decided by a court.

joint tenancy Co-ownership of property characterized by a right of survivorship.

judge An individual who presides over an American court.

judicial notice An action taken by the court; the recognition by the court of the existence and truth of specific facts that are universally accepted or are public records. For example, judicial notice is used to acknowledge the laws of a state, the Constitution, or geographical statistics.

jurisdiction The power or authority to act in a certain situation; the power of a court to hear cases and render judgments.

jury instructions The directions read to the jury by the judge; they simplify the law applicable to the case.

kidnapping The unlawful taking, confinement, and carrying away of another person, by threat, force, fraud, or deception.

knowing act An act that is performed consciously or with knowledge.

last clear chance A doctrine that prevents the harsh result that follows from the doctrine of contributory negligence; if a negligent defendant had the last opportunity to avoid an accident, the contributory negligence of the plaintiff will not be a bar to recovery.

law clerk A term used to refer to a law student interning or working in a law firm while attending school.

law review A publication containing articles written by judges, professors, and attorneys; it also contains case summaries written by law school students. Most law schools publish one or more periodic law reviews each year.

lawyer An individual who is authorized by a state to practice law.

lay witness A person who gives testimony about a subject of which the witness has personal knowledge.

lease An agreement between an owner of property and another in which the owner of the property gives the other person the right to use the property for a set period of time.

ledger sheet A bookkeeping document that will be used to record all expenditures and income in connection with the case.

legal analysis The process of comparing and contrasting facts and legal issues.

legal assistant Another term for *paralegal.*

legal encyclopedia A collection of legal information; a secondary source of the law.

legal memorandum An informal interoffice document written to communicate the results of legal research and the resulting legal analysis.

legal separation An order granted by the court when a couple wish to live separately but do not wish to dissolve or terminate their marriage.

legal technician A term used to describe a nonattorney who is authorized to engage in a limited practice of law.

legal title Title that is enforceable in a court of law; legal title involves the full ownership of the trust property.

LEXIS A computer-assisted legal research service provided by Reed Elsevier.

liability A finding of responsibility in a civil case.

life estate The right to use real property for the term of someone's life.

limited liability company A type of business organization that provides limited liability to its owners, similar to a corporation, but not taxed as a corporation.

limited liability partnership An organization that provides limited liability to the partners without the restrictions imposed by a limited partnership; may be limited to certain types of professions.

limited partnership A partnership meeting certain legal formalities and including at least one *general partner* and at least one *limited partner*; the limited partner's liability is limited to the extent of his or her capital contribution.

living trust A trust that is operative during the lifetime of the settlor.

local rules of court Procedural rules adopted by an individual court for practice in that specific court.

long-arm statutes State laws that describe the circumstances in which the state may exercise jurisdiction over nonresident defendants.

magistrate A judicial officer; federal magistrates are appointed by judges of federal district courts; magistrates have some of the powers of a judge.

malpractice Professional negligence.

manslaughter A lesser crime than murder.

master calendar A calendar that details all appointments and appearances of all attorneys in the firm.

mediation An informal, out-of-court dispute resolution process; a *mediator*, or neutral person, assists the parties in reaching an agreement.

mens rea The mental element of a crime; sometimes called the "guilty mind."

mini-trial A type of informal nonbinding trial in which disputing parties, usually businesses, present their side of the dispute to a jury of executives from the businesses.

Model Penal Code A collection of criminal statutes; it was created for the states to adopt in whole or in part, and has helped create uniformity in criminal law.

mortgage An encumbrance against real property.

motion A request made to a court; for example, a motion could request temporary support or a change in custody.

negligence A tort; failure to act as a reasonably prudent person would act under the same or similar circumstances.

negligence per se Negligence that is presumed because the tortfeasor has violated a statute.

negligent act An act in which a person acts with a substantial and unjustifiable risk.

negotiation The process of discussing contested issues in an attempt to resolve disputes.

nolo contendere A criminal plea that means "I will not contest it." This plea means that the defendant does not deny or admit the charge.

nonbinding arbitration A form of arbitration in which the parties are not obligated to accept the arbitrator's decision.

nonprofit corporation A corporation formed for a charitable, religious, educational, or like purpose; it uses all income for the stated purpose.

nullity An action seeking a nullity of marriage requests the court to find that the "marriage" is null and void.

nuncupative will An oral will; not all states recognize nuncupative wills.

officers The individuals who are responsible for the day-to-day management of a corporation.

opening statement An attorney's first opportunity to address the jury with a summary of the case; it might include a summary of the facts and an outline of the evidence that the attorney plans to present.

opinion letter A letter that analyzes a particular factual situation in light of existing law and offers a legal opinion to the reader.

original jurisdiction The power to first hear a case; court of original jurisdiction is where trial takes place.

paralegal An individual whose training and education enables him or her to assist lawyers by performing certain legal tasks that have traditionally been done by lawyers.

parol evidence rule A rule of contract law stating that when parties have put their agreement in writing, evidence of prior or contemporaneous statements regarding the agreement are not admissible if a dispute arises and the parties go to trial.

partnership A business operated by two or more individuals for profit.

peculiar risk doctrine A doctrine that makes an employer liable for the acts of an independent contractor when the independent contractor has been engaged to perform a nondelegable duty.

pendent jurisdiction The power of the federal court to hear an issue which would normally belong in state court, if that issue is incident to the adjudication of a federal question.

peremptory challenge The right of an attorney to challenge a prospective juror without stating a reason for the challenge.

personal jurisdiction Authority over the person of the defendant in a case.

personal property Goods and money; in general, property is either real or personal.

petition In a family law matter, the initial pleading filed by the petitioner; a family law petition will request a divorce/dissolution, nullity of marriage, or legal separation.

petition for writ of certiorari A document filed with the Supreme Court requesting a hearing.

petitioner The person who files a petition with the court.

plain-view doctrine Items are said to be in plain view if an officer has the legal right to be in sight of the evidence; such items are subject to warrantless seizure.

plea The criminal defendant's response to the charge against him or her.

pleadings The formal written allegations filed with the court by both sides to a lawsuit; claims and defenses are clearly set out so that both parties are placed on notice of the position of the opposing party.

pocket part A removable supplement to a volume of statutory law; includes all changes or additions to the material contained in the hardbound volume.

precedent The example set by the decision of an earlier court for similar cases or similar legal questions which arise in later cases.

preemption A doctrine referring to the right of the federal government to be the exclusive lawmaker in certain areas.

preliminary hearing A defendant's second appearance before the court; the purpose is to establish that probable cause exists.

premarital agreement An agreement entered into before a couple marries; it often explains how the property belonging to each prospective spouse is to be characterized or distributed upon death or dissolution/divorce. This term is often used interchangeably with the term *prenuptial agreement.*

prenuptial agreement Another term for *premarital agreement.*

preponderance of the evidence The amount of proof necessary for most civil cases; more likely than not.

presumption An inference in support of a specific fact.

pretrial conference A meeting between the attorneys and the judge that takes place before trial.

primary sources The resources that provide the actual law; laws are found in statutes, case law, and the Constitution.

private judge An individual hired by the parties to preside over a trial; often a retired judge.

probable cause Probable cause exists when an officer has a reasonable basis for the belief that a person should be searched or arrested.

probate The judicial procedure by which a will is proved valid or invalid; includes distributing property to the heirs and paying debts and taxes.

probate court A court that has jurisdiction over the probate of a will and the administration of a decedent's estate.

procedural laws Laws that dictate how we enforce our rights and obligations.

product liability Liability of manufacturers and distributors for defective products that cause injury.

professional corporation A corporation formed for the purpose of engaging in certain professions, such as medicine or law.

proof of service The document that details when and how the papers were served; it is signed under penalty of perjury by the person serving the papers.

propound To propose or offer.

public corporation A corporation whose shares of stock can be purchased by anyone.

publish To make something known to people.

punitive damages Damages meant to punish.

purposeful act An act that is performed willfully or voluntarily.

quasi contract A contract imposed by law; a transaction that will be treated as a valid contract even though one or more elements may be missing, because it is the equitable thing to do.

quasi-community property Property that would be considered community property if it had been acquired while the married couple were living in a community property state.

***quasi in rem* jurisdiction** Jurisdiction based on personal property located within the state; any judgment is limited to an amount equal to the value of the property.

quasi-judicial officers Individuals who are not judges but who fulfill limited judicial functions; they include magistrates, commissioners, and referees.

question presented A statement of the legal issue presented to the court for resolution.

quitclaim deed A deed that implies no representations or warranties regarding title.

real property Land, including anything affixed to the land or growing upon the land.

rebuttable presumption An inference that may be rebutted or challenged.

rebuttal Presentation of evidence and additional witnesses in response to evidence and issues raised in the defendant's case in chief.

reckless act An act in which a person is careless or indifferent to the consequences of the action.

recross-examination Examination of a witness that occurs when the cross-examiner questions the witness after the redirect examination.

redirect examination Examination of a witness that occurs when the direct examiner questions the witness after the cross-examination.

referee An individual hired by the parties to decide disputed pretrial matters in civil actions.

reference line A line in a business letter that describes the subject of the letter.

referendum Approval of legislative action by the voters.

regional reporter A set of published volumes of cases by courts in specific regions of the United States; for example, the *Pacific Reporter* or the *Northeastern Reporter*.

rehabilitation The process of helping a person attain or regain his or her potential as a citizen; may take the form of counseling or therapy.

relevancy The standard by which testimony or physical evidence is evaluated; relates directly to the fact in question and proves, or has a tendency to prove, a particular legal theory.

relevant Relevant evidence relates directly to the issue; a relevant fact is a fact that is tied directly to the client's legal question.

remand To send back.

reporter A set of published volumes of cases by courts.

reporter's transcript A verbatim record of the oral proceedings in court; prepared by the court reporter.

request for admissions A written request by one party to another to admit or deny the truth of a statement or the genuineness of a document.

request to produce or inspect A written request by one party to another to allow one side to see and copy documents or to physically inspect real or personal property that is relevant to the lawsuit.

res ipsa loquitur "The thing speaks for itself"; negligence is implied from the fact that the incident happened.

rescind To undo a contract, usually when the contract is voidable.

respondeat superior The responsibility of an employer for torts of employees that are committed in the course and scope of employment.

respondent The person who answers the petition.

rest An attorney rests his or her client's case by telling the court that his or her presentation of evidence is complete.

restitution To make restitution is to return consideration that was given.

retain To employ or engage the services of a person.

retribution Punishment for a crime.

reverse To change.

revoke To take back or to make void.

rules of court Procedural rules adopted by all courts regulating practice in the court.

rules of evidence Statutes that govern the admissibility of evidence.

rules of law Legal principles that are applied to the facts; generally derived from statutes, case law, and the Constitution.

secondary sources Tools used to understand the law; one such tool is a legal encyclopedia, which explains the law.

second-degree murder A homicide that involves an impulsive act, rather than a premeditated act.

security A financial interest in a business.

self-incrimination The Fifth Amendment to the Constitution prohibits the government from making a person become a witness against himself or herself.

separate property Property that belongs solely to one party; includes property acquired by gift or inheritance.

sequester To isolate; a jury may be isolated from contact with the media and the public during a trial.

serve To deliver documents to another party in accordance with legal requirements.

service of process The actual process of giving the defendant a copy of the plaintiff's pleading.

settlement A settlement occurs when the parties reach an agreement on some or all of the issues without actually going to trial; if settlement is on some issues, the remaining issues are litigated or tried.

settlor The person who creates a trust.

shareholders The owners of a corporation.

shopkeeper's privilege The right of a merchant to make reasonable detention of a patron where there is probable cause to believe that shoplifting has occurred.

slander per se A statement that on its face is defamatory.

sole proprietorship A business owned and operated by one person.

sources of law Places where laws are found: constitutions, cases, statutes, and administrative regulations.

special damages Out-of-pocket losses.

special master An individual hired by the parties to decide disputed pretrial matters in civil actions.

specific denial A detailed or specific responsive pleading; it addresses each allegation by number.

specific performance A court order requiring one party to fulfill his or her obligations under a contract.

spousal support The court, in a family law matter, may award spousal support. Such support awards are designed to ensure that housing, food, and clothing—the necessities of daily living—are available for a spouse who is unable to earn an adequate living. All states have statutes explaining support guidelines and rules.

stare decisis "It stands decided"; another term for *precedent.*

statute A legislatively created law; a written enactment.

Statute of Frauds A law based on English common law requiring certain types of contracts to be evidenced by a writing.

statute of limitations A law that places a time limit on when a lawsuit can be filed.

Statutes at Large A chronological compilation of statutes.

statutory law Law enacted by a legislature.

stay To delay or stop a proceeding.

stipulation An agreement; when opposing counsel agree on an issue, the agreement is usually written or placed onto the record in the presence of the court reporter and binds all parties.

strict liability Liability without fault.

subject matter jurisdiction The power of a court to resolve the kind of dispute in question.

subscribe To sign one's name at the end of a document.

substantive laws Laws that define our rights and obligations.

summary trial An informal nonbinding trial in which disputing parties present their case to a judge or jury in a way that circumvents the numerous rules of evidence.

summons One of the documents used to begin a legal action; it is served on the defendant and tells the defendant to appear in court and respond to the charge or risk a default.

support The court, in a family law matter, may award child or spousal support. Such awards are designed to ensure that housing, food, and clothing—the necessities of daily living—are available for children or a spouse who is unable to earn an adequate living. All states have statutes explaining support guidelines and rules.

supremacy clause The clause in the U.S. Constitution making the Constitution and the laws of the United States the supreme law of the land.

tangible Possessing physical form; tangible items can be seen and touched.

temporary restraining order (TRO) An emergency remedy of short duration granted after the judge is assured that immediate and irreparable damage will be incurred by the party applying for the order. At the earliest possible date, both parties appear before the court for a full hearing on the matter.

tenancy The right to use another's property for a limited time.

tenants in common A term that describes co-ownership of property carrying no right of survivorship.

testamentary trust A trust created by a will.

testator/testatrix A person who has made a will; a *testator* is a man, while a *testatrix* is a woman.

testimonium clause A clause that includes the date on which the document was executed and who signed the document.

testimony Evidence delivered under oath, either orally or through affirmation (by affidavit), by a competent witness.

third-party action A pleading in which the defendant asks for damages or other relief from a new party to the action.

tickler system A calendaring system used to keep track of dates or time limits for action that needs to be taken in a case.

tort A noncontractual civil wrong.

tortfeasor One who commits a tort.

transcript The document produced by the court reporter; the official record of the proceedings.

treatise A book that reviews a special field of law; a summary of the law on a particular subject; often called a *hornbook*.

trial The open-court process where all parties present evidence, question witnesses, and generally put their case before the court.

trier of fact In a trial, the one who determines the true facts; either a jury or, if a case is tried without a jury, the judge.

trust account A special bank account maintained by an attorney into which funds belonging to clients are kept.

trustee A person who holds property in trust; a *trust* is created by a grantor for the benefit of specific beneficiaries.

ultrahazardous activity A dangerous activity; one who engages in an ultrahazardous activity is strictly liable to those who may be injured as a result.

uniform act A set of laws proposed by a group of legal scholars and submitted to the legislatures of the various states for adoption.

Uniform Commercial Code A uniform set of laws dealing with contracts for the sale of goods; adopted by most states.

unlawful detainer A lawsuit to evict a tenant.

venue The proper geographical court in which to file an action.

verdict The formal decision of a jury.

vicarious liability Liability for the acts of another.

void Having no binding effect or legal force, such as a marriage or a contract.

voidable Having a defect that can be cured; often said of a marriage or a contract. If the defect is not cured, the marriage or contract can be nullified.

voir dire The process of questioning the jury to determine their suitability to serve on a jury panel; the prospective jurors may be questioned by the court (the judge) and the attorneys for both parties.

voluntary act An unconstrained act.

warrant A written order of a court allowing law enforcement officers to search a certain place, or search or arrest a certain person.

warranty deed A type of deed used in some states that implies certain representations regarding title.

Westlaw A computer-assisted legal research service provided by West Publishing Company.

witness A person who testifies about something he or she observed.

witnessed A document is witnessed when the witness signs his or her name attesting that he or she observed the execution of a particular document or instrument.

workers' compensation Laws that apply to those who are injured at work.

INDEX